**LOWER AUSTRIA
AND BURGENLAND**
Pages 128–155

VIENNA
Pages 48–123

• Krems

Klosterneuburg

• Linz

• St. Pölten

• Wels

• Wien

Steyr •

**LOWER AUSTRIA
AND BURGENLAND**

**UPPER
AUSTRIA**

Wiener Neustadt •

• Fisenstadt

• Leoben

STYRIA

• Graz

• St. Veit an der Glan

• Klagenfurt

0 km   50

0 miles

D0280360

EYEWITNESS TRAVEL GUIDES

AUSTRIA

Main contributors: TERESA CZERNIEWICZ-UMER,
JOANNA EGERT-ROMANOWSKA
AND JANINA KUMANIECKA

LONDON, NEW YORK,
MELBOURNE, MUNICH AND DELHI
www.dk.com

Produced by Wydawnictwo Wiedza i Życie S.A., Warsaw

ART EDITOR Paweł Pasternak
CONTRIBUTORS Janina Kumianiecka, Ewa Dan, Marianna Dudek,
Konrad Gruda, Małgorzata Omilanowska, Marek Pernal, Jakub Sito,
Barbara Sudnik-Wójcikowska, Roman Taborski, Zuzanna Umer

CONSULTANT Małgorzata Omilanowska

CARTOGRAPHERS Magdalena Polak, Olaf Rodowald,
Dariusz Romanowski

PHOTOGRAPHERS Wojciech and Katarzyna Mędrzakowie

ILLUSTRATORS Michał Burkiewicz, Paweł Marczak,
Bohdan Wróblewski

DTP DESIGNER Paweł Pasternak
EDITORS Teresa Czerniewicz-Umer, Joanna Egert-Romanowska
DESIGNERS Elżbieta Dudzińska, Ewa Roguska, Piotr Kiedrowski

Dorling Kindersley Limited
EDITOR Sylvia Goulding / Silva Editions Ltd.
TRANSLATOR Magda Hannay
DTP DESIGNERS Jason Little, Conrad van Dyk
PRODUCTION CONTROLLER Bethan Blase

Printed and bound in China by Toppan Printing Co., (Shenzen Ltd)

First published in Great Britain in 2003 by
Dorling Kindersley Limited
80 Strand, London WC2R 0RL

Reprinted with revisions in 2006
Copyright 2003, 2006 © Dorling Kindersley Limited, London

**The information in every
DK Eyewitness Travel Guide is checked regularly.**
Every effort has been made to ensure that this book is as
up-to-date as possible at the time of going to press. Some details,
however, such as telephone numbers, opening hours, prices,
gallery hanging arrangements and travel information are
liable to change. The publishers cannot accept responsibility
for any consequences arising from the use of this book,
nor for any material on third party websites, and cannot
guarantee that any website address in this book will
be a suitable source of travel information.

We value the views and suggestions of our readers very highly.
Please write to: Publisher, DK Eyewitness Travel Guides,
Dorling Kindersley, 80 Strand, London WC2R 0RL.

◁ Beautiful winter scenery in Seefeld, Tyrol

CONTENTS

INTRODUCING AUSTRIA

Detail of the façade of a pharmacy
in Obernberg in Upper Austria

12th-century Burg Clam in Upper
Austria, seen from the Danube

Grundlsee and Totes Gebirge (Dead Mountains) in Styria

Memorial on a tombstone in the
church in Maria Saal in Carinthia

Stained-glass window of a church
in Bürserlberg, in Vorarlberg

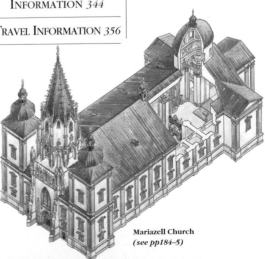

Mariazell Church
(see pp184–5)

HOW TO USE THIS GUIDE

THIS GUIDE will help you to get the most out of a visit to Austria. The first section, *Introducing Austria*, locates the country geographically, and provides an invaluable historical and cultural context. Subsequent sections describe the main sights and attractions of the capital, Vienna, and the different regions. Information on accommodation and restaurants can be found in the *Travellers' Needs* section, while the *Survival Guide* provides many useful tips on everything you need to know during a visit to Austria.

VIENNA

This section is divided into three parts: Inner City, North of Mariahilfer Straße and South of the Ring. Sights outside the centre are described in the *Further Afield* section. All sights are numbered and plotted on the area map. Detailed information for each sight is given in numerical order.

Sights at a Glance lists the sights in an area by category: Historic Streets and Buildings, Museums and Galleries, Churches, Parks and Gardens.

Pages referring to Vienna are marked with a red thumb tab.

A locator map shows where you are in relation to other areas of the city.

1 Area Map
For easy reference the sights are numbered and located on the area map as well as on the map of Vienna, on pp117–21.

2 Street-by-Street Map
This gives a bird's-eye view of each sightseeing area described in the section.

A suggested route for sightseeing is indicated with a dotted red line.

Stars indicate the sights no visitor should miss.

3 Detailed Information
All the sights of Vienna are described individually. The practical information includes addresses, telephone numbers, opening hours, admission charges, transport links and disabled access. The key to the symbols used is on the back flap.

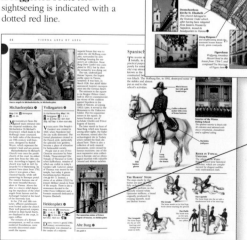

1 Introduction
The landscape, history and character of each region are described, showing how the area has changed through the ages, and the sights on offer for the visitor today.

AUSTRIA REGION BY REGION
In this guide Austria is divided into six regions, each of which is explored in a separate section. The most interesting cities, towns, villages and sights are shown on each Pictorial Map.

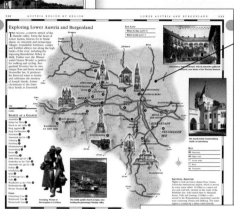

2 Pictorial Map
The pictorial maps show the main roads and the topography. All the important sights are numbered and details on how to get there are given.

Boxes highlight interesting aspects connected with a sight.

Colour coding on each page makes it easy to find a region; the colours are explained on the inside front cover.

3 Detailed Information
Major towns, villages and other tourist sights are listed in order and numbered as on the Pictorial Maps. Each entry contains detailed information on the main places of interest.

A Visitors' Checklist for each of the main sights provides practical information to help you plan your visit.

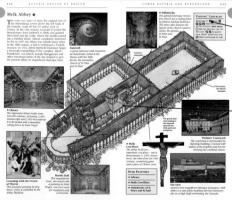

4 Major Sights
At least two pages are devoted to each major sight. Historic buildings are dissected to reveal their interiors. For interesting towns or town centres, street maps are provided, with the main sights marked and described.

INTRODUCING
AUSTRIA

Putting Austria on the Map

LOCATED in the southeastern part of Central Europe, Austria covers an area of 83,858 sq km (32,378 sq miles), and spans five major geological formations: the Eastern Alps, the Alpine and Carpathian Foreland, the Pannonian Basin, the Vienna Valley and the Czech Massif. Its longest river is the Danube, which flows from west to east. Landlocked, Austria borders Germany, the Czech Republic, Slovakia, Hungary, Slovenia, Italy, Switzerland, and Liechtenstein. It has over 8 million inhabitants, 1.5 million of whom live in Vienna.

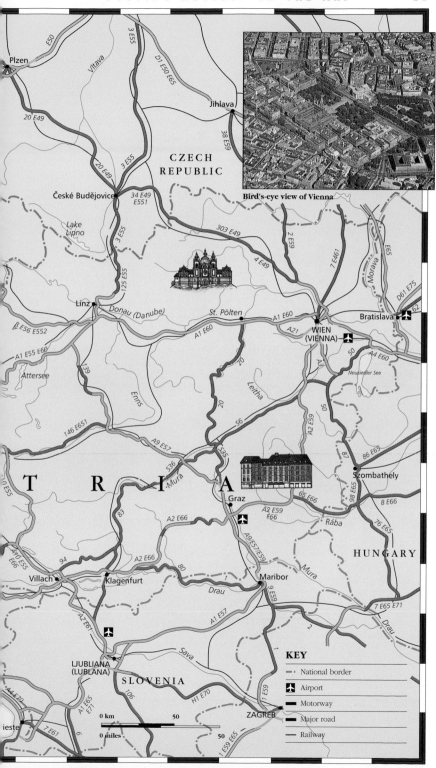

Plzen

E50

Vltava

3 E55

D1 E50 E65

20 E49

Jihlava

38 E59

**CZECH
REPUBLIC**

20 E49

3 E55

České Budějovice

34 E49
E551

Lake
Lipno

3 E55

125 E55

303 E49

4 E49

2 E59

7 E461

E65

Morava

D61 E75

62

Linz

Donau (Danube)

St. Pölten

A1 E60

A1 E60

A21

**WIEN
(VIENNA)**

Bratislava

8 E56 E552

A1 E55 E60

Attersee

139

Enns

20

S6

Leitha

A3

50

A4 E60

Neusiedler See

146 E651

A9 E57

S35

S36

Mura

83

T R I A

50

A2 E59

98 E65

86 E65

Szombathely

8 E66

Graz

A2 E66

A2 E59
E66

Rába

66 E66

76 E65

HUNGARY

0 E55

A10 E55
E66

94

Villach

Klagenfurt

A2 E66

80

A9 E57 E59

Drau

Maribor

Mura

9 E59

Drau

7 E65 E71

A2 E61

A1 E57

2

LJUBLIANA
(LUBLANA)

Sava

SLOVENIA

H1 E70

1 E59

ZAGREB

A4 E70

A1 E65
E71

0 km   50

0 miles   50

1 E59 E65

50 E65

ieste

7 E61

6

Bird's-eye view of Vienna

KEY

- National border
- ✈ Airport
- Motorway
- Major road
- Railway

A PORTRAIT OF AUSTRIA

MAGNIFICENT MOUNTAINS *span two-thirds of present-day Austria, gathering in a massif at the centre of the country. The breathtaking scenery of alpine peaks, lakes and enchanting valleys, together with excellent year-round facilities for a variety of sports, attracts many visitors. Innumerable cultural events and fascinating historical sights make every visit unforgettable.*

Austria grew at a crossroads, when the main routes between northern Europe and Italy, and from western to eastern Europe, met at Vienna. The Habsburg kings and emperors, who ruled the country for almost seven centuries, pursued expansion via matrimonial alliances rather than sending troops into battle. Although not entirely without bloodshed, they managed to incorporate several provinces into Central Austria through a series of arranged marriages, beginning with the duchy of Tyrol, followed by the powerful Czech kingdom, the equally strong Hungary and a sizeable chunk of Italy. Austrian culture, while traditionally

Austrian eagle

linked with that of Germany, also absorbed many Roman, Slav and Hungarian influences, thus creating its own unique combinations. As well as producing many outstanding artists and composers, such as Mozart, it also offered foreign artists the opportunity to further their talents.

Present-day Austria is a federal state, consisting of nine provinces *(Bundesländer)*. The head of state is the president, elected for a term of six years; the most important political figure is the head of the federal government, or Chancellor (as in Germany). Austria's legislative power rests with a two-chamber parliament. Parliamentary elections

View over the Hohe Tauern mountain range, from Heiligenblut in Carinthia

◁ The annual hot-air balloon festival held in Stubenberg, Styria, in mid-September

Europabrücke, connecting northern and southern Europe

AT THE HEART OF EUROPE

Roads once trodden by foreign armies are today packed with sun-seeking tourists from the north. Travelling through Vienna and the Semmering Pass, they cross the Alps at the Brenner Pass, where the huge Europabrücke (European Bridge), a vast viaduct, connects northern Europe with the warm south. The heavy transit traffic constitutes a major problem for Austria, where great emphasis is placed on protecting the natural environment. Protest action by local ecology groups stopped the building of a nuclear power station in Zwentendorf and later prevented the destruction of the unique flora around Hainburg, the intended site for a hydroelectric power plant. The ecology movement gave rise to the Green Federation, which is winning ever more seats in Parliament. It is perhaps thanks to its activities that Austria remains a natural paradise for its many visitors.

are held every four years, when votes are cast for the candidates put up by the political parties. The present Austrian parliament includes representatives of four political parties: the Social Democratic Party of Austria (SPÖ), the Christian-Democratic Austrian People's Party (ÖVP), the Freedom Party of Austria (FPÖ) and a political alliance of various groups known as the Greens (die Grünen).

For modern-day Austrians, the might of their former empire is only a distant memory, yet their country continues to play an important role in international politics. Since 1955, when the Austrian State Treaty was signed and the country found itself at the centre between two worlds – Western capitalism and Soviet communism – it has often acted as an intermediary. Vienna has served as the venue for important summits, and is home to many UN agencies and international organizations, including the United Nations Industrial Development Organization (UNIDO), the International Atomic Energy Agency (IAEA) and the Organization of Petroleum Exporting Countries (OPEC) Central Office. A member of the European Union, Austria does not belong to NATO. The 1955 Treaty pledges neutrality for all time, and despite external and internal pressures, Austria retains this.

TOURISM

Tourism revenue accounts for nearly half of Austria's GDP. The country has much to offer: winter sports on snow-covered slopes, or year-round on the glaciers, and beautiful mountains and lakes in summer all

Thermal pool in Lutzmannsburg

The Alpincenter ski station below Kitzsteinhorn Mountain in the Salzburger Land

attract large numbers of visitors. The impressive infrastructure offers superb conditions for rest and recreation. Nearly every resort boasts funicular railways and cable cars, chair and drag lifts, magnificent pistes and tobog-gan runs, outdoor and indoor swimming pools, well maintained river banks and lakes. There are plenty of places for eating, and overnight accommodation ranges from small pensions and private homes to luxury hotels, all guaranteeing a very pleasant visit.

A traditional horse-drawn carriage

The regional authorities take care to ensure that entertainments are not limited to large resorts, and organize sports events and art exhibitions, theatre and music festivals, as well as festivities devoted to individual towns, streets or even squares. Visitors may enjoy the traditional religious festivities, and the Giant Chocolate Festi-val in Bludenz and the Dumpling Festival in St Johann will prove memorable. Many restaurants organize special weeks when regional cooking or

local game dishes feature on the menu. Although events are often local, Austria is also a venue for acclaimed international festivals, such as the famous music and theatre festivals in Salzburg and Bregenz, the Wiener Festwochen and the Viennale.

LANGUAGE AND RELIGION

Modern Austria is vir-tually a one-nation state, but there are some Slovenians in Carinthia, Croatians in Burgenland, and Czech and Hungarian minorities in Vienna. Austria became a haven for refugees fleeing from the former Yugoslavia in the 1990s, as well as for people from other regions of the Balkan peninsula, and for Turks coming in search of work. Around 95 per cent of the country's population speaks German,

A typical alpine pension in Kartitsch, East Tyrol

The annual church festival in Villach in Carinthia, a weekend of folk music and parades

Habsburg monarchy. The Austrian film directors Ernst Lubitsch, Billy Wilder and Fred Zinneman played an important role in the creation of Hollywood shortly before and immediately after World War II. Today, the best-known Austrian is probably Arnold Schwarzenegger, star of action movies, governor of California and, by marriage, a member of the Kennedy clan. His fame is unmatched even by winter sports champions, who are so popular in Austria. Another prominent Austrian actor is Klaus-Maria Brandauer, who played Mephistopheles in Isztvan Szabo's film of the same name. The late Romy Schneider, revered star of French cinema, was also Austrian and won fame as the unhappy Empress Elisabeth, in the Austrian film *Sissi.*

Austria has also produced many Nobel Prize winners. Perhaps the most famous among them is Konrad Lorenz, a researcher into animal and human behaviour, who was awarded the Nobel Prize for Medicine in 1973. The work of Sigmund Freud, the Viennese psychiatrist who became the founding father of psychoanalysis, has heavily influenced modern psychology, as well as other domains of science and culture.

although not every German speaker will find it easy to communicate with every Austrian. While the Vienna Burgtheater is regarded as one of the foremost German-language theatres in the world, many Austrians speak a pronounced local dialect. When travelling, the visitor needs to remember that many things have different names here than in Germany. A bread roll, for instance, is called a *Semmel* instead of a *Brötchen,* a tomato is a *Paradeiser* and not a *Tomate,* and the hospital is the *Spital,* rather than a *Krankenhaus.*

Austria is traditionally a Roman Catholic country, and some 80 per cent of its inhabitants today belong to the Roman Catholic church.

CULTURE

Austrian culture has reached acclaim and importance far beyond its borders. *The Good Soldier Schweik,* by the Czech writer Jaroslav Hašek, is a bawdy satire about the

The hyper-modern Millennium Tower in Vienna

TRADITIONS

Austria is one of the most modern and efficiently run countries in Europe. However, while admiring the stunning landscapes or strolling along the streets of the impeccably tidy towns and villages, visitors may get the impression that time has stood still here, feeling immersed in the past, a bygone age of the Habsburg empire when the

The traditional parade of Tyrolean hunters in Götzens

benevolent Franz Joseph I was the guardian of stability and justice, and his unhappy wife Sissi fulfilled the public craving for romance.

The Austrians are very fond of their traditions. The most popular newspaper is the arch-conservative *Neue Kronen Zeitung*, which has offices in almost every federal province, while the highly respectable Viennese daily *Die Presse* represents the solid opinions of the Austrian centre. *Der Standard* is the leading liberal newspaper.

In Austria, as perhaps nowhere else in Europe, the *Tracht,* or traditional folk costume, is accepted as formal wear. The costumes, made of high-quality wool and natural linen, can be worn anywhere, even to an elegant ball at the Viennese Opera. An entire branch of the textile industry is devoted to their design and manufacture. Men wear green loden jackets and *Lederhosen* (leather breeches), the women *Dirndl* dresses.

Another Austrian speciality is the *Heurige,* wine taverns serving the year's new-vintage wines. Mostly found in and around Vienna, these taverns

Child in folk costume

were originally attached to vineyards whose owners had a licence to sell beverages but not food. Secretly, though, they also offered home-produced meats, especially when a pig had been slaughtered. Today, they serve grilled pork knuckles – delicious, but very filling – as well as roast hams, grilled ribs and other specialities. As of old, the wine is brought to the tables by waiters who also take payment; the food is available from self-service buffet counters. The *Heurige* are characterized by a uniquely sociable ambience, with all the guests joining in the merriment. Many a dedicated beer-drinker has become a devotee of young wine at a *Heuriger* evening.

One of the many wine taverns (*Heurige*) around Vienna

The Formation of the Alps

About 70 million years ago, during the Cretaceous period, the African plate and the Adriatic microplate both began to move north. The Alpine range was thrown up when the latter collided with the European plate. The Tethys Sea that lay between them was almost entirely obliterated, and sediment deposited at its bottom over millions of years was carried far to the north, and tossed as vast nappes over the rigid block of indigenous rocks of the Central Alps. The formation of the present Alps ended in the Miocene period, some two million years ago, and subsequent erosion gave them their final shape.

The Krimmler Falls *in the Hohe Tauern National Park are the highest waterfalls in the Alps and the fifth highest in the world, dropping almost 400 m (1,312 ft).*

The Northern Limestone Alps *are formed of soft carbonate rock. The mountains, such as the Dachstein Group (2,995 m/9,826 ft), have characteristically steep slopes, yet their summits are rounded domes rather than sharp peaks.*

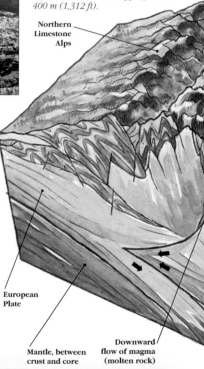

Northern Limestone Alps

European Plate

Mantle, between crust and core

Downward flow of magma (molten rock)

The central part of the Austrian Alps *consists of hard crystalline rock (gneiss, shale). The oldest and the hardest among them form the steep fells of the Hohe Tauern.*

The Alps *possess the right conditions for the formation of glaciers. Largest in the Eastern Alps is the Pasterze; together with 40 others it forms a thick mantle on the Großglockner massif, covering 40 sq km (15 sq miles).*

The end of the Ice Age marked the beginning of a new type of erosion. The Northern Limestone Alps have Europe's largest cave systems and underground streams, typical features in limestone regions.

MOUNTAIN SCENERY

The current shape of the Alps was created during the Ice Age (between 600,000 and 10,000 years ago). It is characterized by distinctive post-glacial cirques, suspended valleys, moraines, thaw lakes and vast U-shaped valleys filled with material carried down the mountains.

THE AUSTRIAN ALPS

The Austrian Alps lie in the European Alpides range, which rose between 70 million and two million years ago. In geological terms they form an entity known as the Eastern Alps. They occupy an area about 500 km (310 miles) long and 150 km (95 miles) wide. One of Europe's most fascinating regions, the Austrian Alps enchant visitors with their beautiful high peaks and the unique idyllic atmosphere in the mountain villages and small towns that nestle in vast, cultivated valleys. The most valuable ecological areas have been made into National Parks, including the Hohe Tauern – the largest in the Alps and one of the largest in Europe, featuring Austria's highest mountain range with some 300 peaks of over 3,000 m (9,800 ft) in height. In summer, the Alps are a magnificent area to explore on foot or bike, while in winter they provide an excellent base for winter sports.

Central Alps

Southern Limestone Alps

Plate movement

Adriatic Plate

Mantle

KEY

☐	Northern Limestone Alps
☐	Central Alps
☐	Hohe Tauern
☐	Southern Limestone Alps
☐	Alpine Foreland

The majority of alpine lakes have been created by retreating glaciers. Some of the most beautiful can be found in the Salzkammergut region, in the Northern Limestone Alps.

The Landscape of Austria

AUSTRIA HAS A HIGHLY DIVERSE landscape because of its location at the junction of four regions. The north of the country is part of the Central European natural region, originally dominated by deciduous and mixed forests, while the southern part belongs to the Alpine region. The southeast lies in the Illyrian region, which benefits from a Mediterranean climate, resulting in a rich flora and fauna including edible chestnuts and rare species of lizards and snakes. The northeastern part of the country belongs to the Pontian-Pannonian region, with surviving species of steppe flora and characteristic fauna including the suslik (a ground squirrel), hamster and great bustard.

The alpine belt stretches from the zone of the mountain pine up to the ice and snow fields. At altitudes of 2,500–3,200 m (8,200–10,500 ft), snow is present all year (this snow-line is called the "nival belt").

The transition zone between forests and alpine grassland is covered in scrub (dwarf mountain pine, rhodo-dendron and alder). Here, the growing season lasts only 70–100 days.

Alpine high mountain grasslands and low meadows include a wide variety of species and plant communities. Mountain arnica (in the foreground) avoids limestone soils; it is a highly regarded medicinal plant.

In gulleys and hollows, in valleys and along the banks of the streams, Austrian flora is at its most magnificent.

Traditional grazing in the forest belt has preserved the natural fauna and flora of the alpine meadows and pastures.

MOUNTAINSCAPES

Climate and flora change with altitude, as is typical of mountain environments. The lower regions are covered with mixed forests (including beech). The upper parts have coniferous trees (Arolla pine, spruce and larch) up to about 1,800 m (5,900 ft) – above which are brush thickets and colourful alpine meadows.

Humid, cool valleys are the perfect habitat to encourage the growth of herbaceous plants.

Lakes situated at higher altitudes are poor in nutrients and hence their surrounding flora and fauna are extremely sparse.

Upper forest region, mainly spruce

AUSTRIAN FAUNA

Austrian fauna is typical of Central Europe. Along with invertebrates (primarily insects: beetles and butterflies), it features a rich avifauna, small numbers of amphibians (newts, salamanders, fire-bellied toads and frogs) and reptiles (Aesculapian snake, grass snake, lizards), and mammals, including rodents, marten, fox, weasel and hoofed animals. Mountain animals – insects, rodents (marmots) and deer (red deer, chamois) – are particularly fascinating.

The marmot, a rodent, burrows deep into mountain meadows and alpine pastures. When disturbed, it emits a high-pitched whistle.

Chamois are ideally adapted for moving over steep rocks.

Red deer (above) live in the deciduous and mixed forests in the high mountains. They have a fawn-coloured coat. The male sheds its antlers in spring.

The Alpine ibex (right, a female) came close to extinction towards the end of the 20th century, but is now being successfully reintroduced.

AUSTRIAN FLORA

Some 60 per cent of Austria's territory is mountainous, which determines the country's key flora. Forests occupy as much as 39 per cent of the country's entire area, occurring mainly in the Alps and in the Czech Massif. Many areas of special environmental interest enjoy some form of legal protection as nature reserves, nature monuments and national parks. One of the first was the Hohe Tauern National Park.

The Arolla pine (Pinus cembra), along with the larch, forms large tree populations in the upper forest regions.

Swiss Rock Jasmin (Androsace helvetica) and its rounded clusters are typical on limestone soil.

Bitterwort (Gentiana lutea) is common in meadows, clusters of herbaceous plants and forest verges. Bitterwort liqueur has long been used in folk medicine.

The Music of Austria

Austria was – and remains to this day – a world-renowned centre for music. Musical life in present-day Austria has typically been closely linked with that of Germany, as well as the Habsburg Empire. Composers belonging to the old Viennese school contributed to the emergence of the Viennese Classical style, with Joseph Haydn, Wolfgang Amadeus Mozart and the German composer, Ludwig van Beethoven, its main proponents. Their work guided 19th-century composers such as Franz Schubert, Johann Strauss, Anton Bruckner, Hugo Wolf and Gustav Mahler.

Franz Schubert, *one of the earliest exponents of the Romantic style, is best-known for his Lieder, or songs. He also composed piano music, chamber music and symphonies.*

Wolfgang Amadeus Mozart

Arnold Schönberg, *together with his students, Alban Berg and Anton von Webern, developed the Viennese dode-caphonic school after 1918. His best-known work is the sextet* Verklärte Nacht.

Mozart's sister, Maria Anna, known as Nannerl

Joseph Haydn, *one of the Viennese Classicists, was a court composer to Count Esterházy. In 1790, he moved to Vienna. His works include over 100 symphonies, 83 string quartets, 52 piano sonatas, 14 masses and many other compositions.*

WOLFGANG AMADEUS MOZART, a child prodigy, had the gift of perfect pitch and an unrivalled memory. He achieved musical perfection with his symphonies, operas (*The Marriage of Figaro, Don Giovanni, The Magic Flute*), and his masses including the unfinished *Requiem*, which is shrouded in mystery.

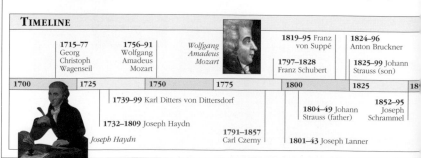

TIMELINE

1700	1725	1750	1775	1800	1825	18
	1715–77 Georg Christoph Wagenseil	**1756–91** Wolfgang Amadeus Mozart	*Wolfgang Amadeus Mozart*	**1819–95** Franz von Suppé	**1824–96** Anton Bruckner	
				1797–1828 Franz Schubert	**1825–99** Johann Strauss (son)	
		1739–99 Karl Ditters von Dittersdorf			**1852–95** Joseph Schrammel	
				1804–49 Johann Strauss (father)		
		1732–1809 Joseph Haydn				
			1791–1857 Carl Czerny			
	Joseph Haydn			**1801–43** Joseph Lanner		

Johann Strauss (son) *has been proclaimed the king of the waltz, thanks to his compositions including* The Blue Danube *and* Tales from the Vienna Woods.

FOREIGN MUSICIANS IN AUSTRIA

Vienna, an important cultural centre on the European map, has always attracted musicians and composers from other countries. The Renaissance brought Flemish artists, the Baroque period attracted Italians. Vienna was home to Christoph Gluck, Ludwig van Beethoven, Johannes Brahms and others. The main exponent of the New Viennese operetta was the Hungarian, Franz Lehár.

Portrait of
Anna Maria,
Mozart's mother

Leopold,
Mozart's father

Johannes Brahms
(1833–97), German composer, outstanding creator of traditional symphonies, piano and chamber music, was unsympathetic towards progressive trends.

Anton Bruckner
is probably best known for his nine symphonies but he also wrote church music, in particular choral works.

Ludwig van Beethoven
(1770–1827), German composer and one of the Viennese Classicists, battled from 1798 with his progressive deafness. His best-known work is perhaps the Ninth Symphony, *with the* Ode to Joy *in its finale.*

Gustav Mahler *started his career as a conductor and only in later years devoted himself to composing music. His most important work is the cycle of ten monumental symphonies.*

1860–1911 Gustav Mahler	**1900–1991** Ernst Křenek	**1935** b. Kurt Schwertsik	**1941** b. Dieter Kaufmann		**1971** b. Michael Huber
1874–1951 Arnold Schönberg	**1927** b. Friedrich Cerha		**1956** b. Herbert Willi		
1875	**1900**	**1925**	**1950**	**1975**	**2000**
1874–1949 Edmund Eysler	**1883–1945** Anton von Webern		**1960** b. Karlheinz Essl		
1885–1935 Alban Berg					
1860–1903 Hugo Wolf	*Edmund Eysler*		**1943** b. Heinz Karl Gruber	**1971** b. Bernhard Gál	

The Architecture of Austria

S INCE the Middle Ages, Austria has been at the fore-front in the development of architecture. Particularly typical of the Austrian architectural landscape are the vast abbeys built in medieval times and modernized during the late Baroque period, as well as the multi-storey town palaces and large country residences built for the aristocracy in the 17th and 18th centuries. The late 1800s and early 1900s marked the birth of modern town architecture, with public buildings such as theatres, banks and government offices. These and other buildings displayed typical Habsburg-era features – monumentality and a distinctly ornamental character.

Cupolas crowned with openwork lanterns, inspired by Renaissance domes in Italy.

Pediment with an early-Renaissance statue of Christ blessing the people.

Heiligenkreuz Abbey (see p136) *was built in the 12th to 13th centuries, but only the Romanesque church remains from that period. The abbey itself is a magnificent Baroque structure erected in the 17th century. The courtyard has an imposing St Mary's column.*

Schwaz church, *dating from the 15th century* (see p245), *with its opulent star vaulting resting on slender columns, and its interior illuminated by vast windows, typifies the lightness of Baroque architecture.*

Windows with grab-frames, typical of the early Baroque period.

Statues of saints by Michael Bernhard Mandel

The decorative railings *of the famous staircase at Mirabell Palace in Salzburg* (see p215) *are the masterpiece of architect Johann Lukas von Hildebrandt and sculptor Georg Raphael Donner.*

The octagonal layout of the top storey of the tower is a typical feature of the Lombardy style.

Statues of Moses and Elijah

Oval tower windows serve to amplify the sound of the bells.

Vast clock faces

The Vienna State Opera House (see p92), conceived by August von Siccardsburg and Eduard van der Nüll, was completed in 1869. Its façade and interior, particularly the auditorium, the foyer and the grand staircase, are examples of the opulence, ornamentation and pomposity typical of 19th-century Austrian architecture.

Melk is one of the most famous Benedictine abbeys and the largest surviving abbey complex in Europe. The spectacular Baroque abbey was designed by J. Prandtauer (see pp142–3).

SALZBURG DOMKIRCHE

The cathedral, begun in 1614 to a design by Santino Solari and finished in 1657, is one of the earliest twin-towered churches of the modern era found anywhere north of the Alps. It is also the earliest and most magnificent example of the Early Baroque style in the entire Danube region *(see p220).*

FRIEDENSREICH HUNDERTWASSER

A painter, graphic designer and architect with the real name of Friedrich Stowasser, Hundertwasser (1928–2000) was an organizer of provocative "happenings". His decorative style of painting was close to that of abstract artists, with subject matter often associated with the natural environment. His buildings *(see pp104–5)* are distinguished by their highly experimental, extravagant shapes, combining colourful new architectural ideas with the artist's vision of structures that blend with the natural environment. Irregular in shape, they employ a variety of unusual materials, including ceramics.

The Rogner Bad Blumau resort complex *(see p170)*

Austrian Art

AUSTRIAN painting, like the country's literature, cannot be considered in isolation from artistic movements in neighbouring countries. Art in Austria developed in close relationship with German art, but it was also influenced by the Italian, Hungarian and Czech cultures. Over many centuries, the imperial court in Vienna acted as a strong magnet for artists from all over Europe. In the 19th century, the artists of the Viennese Secession produced outstanding works of art. Some of Austria's painters have gained international acclaim, but it is well worth becoming acquainted with its lesser artists, too.

The Entombment, Albrecht Altdorfer

MEDIEVAL

THE EARLIEST EXAMPLES of pictorial art in Austria include illuminations and wall paintings. The late 8th-century *Codex Millenarius Maior*, kept in Kremsmünster Abbey, is regarded as the oldest illuminated manuscript. The Austrian art of illumination flourished during the 11th and 12th centuries, particularly thanks to the Salzburg monastery scriptoria, which, among other works, produced the famous Admont Bible (c1130–40).

The oldest wall paintings in Austria, dating from the first half of the 11th century, are found in the Church of St Ulrich in Wieselburg. The Benedictine Abbey church in Lambach has original wall paintings of Old Testament scenes, created in the last quarter of the 11th century. Paintings dating from the 12th century can be seen in

St John's Chapel in Pürgg, the Benedictine abbey church in Nonnberg and in the castle chapel of Burg Ottenstein, near Zwettl.

From the 14th century, panel painting flourished, particularly in Vienna under Rudolph IV. The 15th century is notable for the works of Jakob Kaschauer and Thomas Artula von Villach. At the turn of the 16th century, Austrian painting was influenced by Italian *Quattrocento* art, especially the works of Michael Pacher and his students. The Danube School, influential in the early 1500s, was represented by Wolf Huber and Albrecht Altdorfer of Regensburg, who painted the altar in the abbey of St Florian, near Linz.

RENAISSANCE

THE RENAISSANCE style entered Austrian painting around 1530. Interesting wall paintings, created soon after that date, include the secular decoration of the Knights' Room in Goldegg Castle near St Johann (1536), and the paintings devoted to Reformation themes in Pölling Church, near Wolfsberg. Hans Bocksberger, one of the most outstanding Renaissance artists, decorated Freisal Castle and the castle chapel in Burg Strechau. Until the 16th century, Austrian painting was strongly influenced by

Italian artists such as Giulio Licinio, Teodoro Ghisi and Martino Rota, who worked at the court in Graz, and Donato Arsenio Mascagni in Salzburg. Local artists, such as Anton Blumenthal, whose paintings adorn the presbytery of Gurk Cathedral, and Jakob Seisenegger, a portrait-painter, were also influenced by Italian art.

BAROQUE

IN THE 17TH CENTURY, Italian art continued to influence Austrian painting. One of the most important painters of the Baroque period was Pietro de Pomis.

The Austrian victory in the Battle of Vienna in 1683 was a historic event that proved very influential in the development of art. It brought about political and economic stability and with it many new artistic initiatives. The capital, Vienna, began to attract foreign artists, such as Andrea Pozzo, the Italian master of illusionistic painting. Vast interior compositions were created to complement the magnificent architectural works by Johann Bernhard Fischer von Erlach and Johann Lukas von Hildebrandt. This particular style of fresco painting flourished thanks to artists such as Johann Michael Rottmayr, Martino Altomonte and, in

The Holy Family with St Joachim and St Anna, F.A. Maulbertsch

the following generation, Paul Troger, Daniel Gran and Bartolomeo Altomonte. Great portrait-painters of the 18th-century included Johann Kupetzky, Martin van Meytens and Johann B. Lampi.

A prominent representative of late Baroque painting, Franz Anton Maulbertsch created frescoes as well as numerous works on religious and secular themes. The last great artist of the Baroque era was Martin Johann Schmidt, who produced magnificent wall paintings, for example for Melk Abbey.

***Portrait of Hanna Klinkosch,* Hans Makart**

19TH-CENTURY

THE MOST IMPORTANT Neo-Classical painters in Austria were Heinrich Friedrich Füger and Joseph Anton Koch. In 1809, the Brotherhood of St Luke was formed at the Vienna Academy of Fine Arts. Its members, the Nazarenes, mostly German painters, including Julius Schnorr von Carolsfeld, and only a few Austrians, set out to revise religious art.

An important figure during the Biedermeier and Realism periods in Austria was Ferdinand Georg Waldmüller, creator of small-scale genre paintings. The most outstanding academic painter was undoubtedly Hans Makart, who created vast compositions on allegorical or historic themes, as well as

brilliant portraits. In the town of Szolnok, in today's Hungary, an artists' colony was established by a group of landscape painters inspired by the French Barbizon School.

Probably the best-known of all Austrian painters was Gustav Klimt, the founding member and main representative of the Vienna Secession. He used gold in his paintings and embellished them with striking "mosaics". The subject matter was often allegorical, infused with a subtle eroticism.

***Time of the Rose Blossom,* F.G. Waldmüller**

MODERN

EXPRESSIONISM played a major role in early 20th-century Austrian art. The foremost artists associated with this movement included Egon Schiele, Richard Gerstl and Oskar Kokoschka, and, in Upper Austria, Alfred Kubin. An important figure of the 1930s and the period following World War II was Herbert Boeckl. A versatile artist – he also produced wall paintings – Boeckl drew his inspiration from fantasy realism, popular in post-war

Vienna. Ernst Fuchs, Anton Lehmden and Wolfgang Hutter were members of the Vienna School of Fantastic Realism, which was inspired by surrealism. Abstract art was represented by Max Weiler and Josef Mikl. An unusual late 20th-century figure who escapes easy classification was Friedensreich Hundertwasser, who became famous with his architectural project of unusual buildings erected in and around Vienna.

The artists of Viennese Actionism achieved considerable notoriety in the 1960s. "Happenings" organized by the group revolved around the use of the body as a sculptural medium. Their fascination with self-mutilation and sado-masochism culminated in the death of one of the group's members, Rudolf Schwarzkogler.

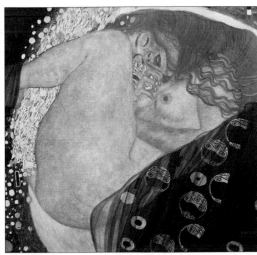

Gustav Klimt's *Danae* (1907/08), one of his famous erotic paintings

Austrian Literature

THERE HAS BEEN a long-standing argument between historians and critics as to whether Austrian literature deserves to be studied as an independent genre or should be considered merely an extension of German culture. The two have always been closely linked, but Austrian writing also displays Hungarian, Slav and Romance language influences. A deeper study of Austrian literature quickly reveals its varied, rich and independent character and unique qualities. Much modern Austrian literature is characterized by its fictional explorations of the individual psyche and analysis of Austria's political past – most notably by writers such as Peter Handke and Thomas Bernhard.

EARLY LITERATURE

THE FIRST significant literary works from Austria date from the 12th–13th centuries, when poetry of courtly love flourished, with chivalrous knights as its heroes; its foremost exponent was Walther von der Vogelweide. The epic *Song of the Nibelungs,* dating from this time, was written in what are now Austria and Bavaria. But it was not until the early 19th century that Austria started to feature more prominently in European literature.

THE 19TH CENTURY

THE FIRST widely acclaimed Austrian writer was Franz Grillparzer (1791–1872), poet, novelist and playwright who drew heavily on themes from antiquity. His works include the trilogy *Das Goldene Vlies* (The Golden Fleece), the tragedy *Des Meeres und der*

F. Raimund on stage, immortalized by Andreas Geiger, 1834

Liebe Wellen (Waves of Sea and Love), and his only comedy, *Weh dem, der lügt!* (Woe to Him Who Lies!). Other classic writers of Austrian literature and drama include Ferdinand Raimund (1790–1836) and Johann Nepomuk Nestroy (1801–62), masters of farce and comedy who are still enjoying great popularity today. Among their celebrated contem-

poraries were the poet Nikolaus Lenau (1802–50) and the prose writer Adalbert Stifter (1805–68).

Prominent figures of the late 19th century were prose writer and playwright Ludwig Anzengruber (1839–89), who wrote about peasant life, and Marie von Ebner-Eschenbach (1830–1916), who in 1898 received Austria's highest literary award for her novels and short stories on social issues.

JUNG-WIEN

AN IMPORTANT phenomenon unique to the Austrian literary scene that exerted great influence on other European countries was the Jung-Wien (Young-Vienna) group, active during the Modernist period at the turn of the 19th century. Its best-known exponent was the poet and playwright Hugo von Hofmannsthal (1874–1929), whose works included adaptations of classical tragedies and of the medieval morality play *Jedermann* (Everyman), which in its Max Reinhardt production won international acclaim at the Salzburg Festival.

The cream of the Jung-Wien movement included one of the principal exponents of naturalism in contemporary European drama and novels – Arthur Schnitzler (1862–1931). His works are still widely read, performed and adapted today. In 1999 Schnitzler's novel *Traumnovelle* (Dream Novella) was famously adapted for screen as "Eyes Wide Shut" by American director Stanley Kubrick.

Other members of the Jung-Wien movement included the essayist and playwright Hermann Bahr (1863–1934), who penned the group's most important philosophical statements and wrote short, romantic portraits of everyday life in contemporary Vienna; Peter Altenberg (1859–1919), master of aphorisms; and the satirist Karl Kraus (1874–1936). Through the

19th-century café, favourite meeting place of Viennese writers

works of the poet Georg Trakl (1887–1914), Austrian literature also played an important role in the international development of Expressionism. His poetic works are characterized by a melancholic disposition and a melodiously rhythmical language. The works of the playwright and poet Franz Theodor Csokor (1885–1969) and of the poet, playwright and prose writer Franz Werfel (1890–1945) were similarly influential in Expressionist literary circles.

THE 20TH CENTURY

A USTRIAN LITERATURE played a particularly important part in paving the way for innovations in 20th-century European novels. Robert Musil (1880–1942) wrote the great unfinished novel *Der Mann ohne Eigenschaften* (The Man Without Qualities), which combines narrative prose with essays and is ranked by critics as one of the most fascinating literary works of the 20th century. Hermann Broch (1886–1951), in his structurally innovative novel *Der Tod des Vergil* (The Death of Virgil), touched upon the subjects of life and death. Joseph Roth (1894–1939) constructed his great novel *Radetzkymarsch* (Radetzky March) around the fall of the Habsburg empire. Heimito von Doderer (1896–1966), in his novels *Die Strudlhofstiege* (The Strudlhof Stairs) and *Die Dämonen* (The Demons), portrayed life in Vienna in the 1920s and 1930s. Stefan Zweig (1881–1942), biographer, essayist and short-story writer, was a highly prolific writer whose work has been translated into over 50 languages.

Two giants of German-language writing are counted as Austrian writers although they lived in Prague: Franz Kafka (1883–1924) and Rainer Maria Rilke (1875–1926).

The multi-ethnic character of the Habsburg monarchy gave access to a variety of cultures. A classic example was the "Polish Viennese" playwright and prose writer Tadeusz Rittner (1873–1921).

MODERN LITERATURE

A MONG the best-known Austrian writers today are Ingeborg Bachmann (1926–73), award-winning writer of poetry, narratives and radio plays, and the drama and prose writers Thomas Bernhard (1931–89) and Peter Handke (b. 1942). Ingeborg Bachmann won the Austrian National Medal for Literature in 1968, and after her death a literary prize was named after her. It has since become one of the most prestigious accolades in Austria. Both Thomas Bernhard and Peter Handke positioned themselves at the forefront in the search for new theatrical forms in Europe. In his plays, Bernhard often dealt with his country's past under National Socialism, and his fascinating play *Heldenplatz* caused great controversy and scandal in Austria. Peter Handke is famous for the language experiments he introduced into his plays, employing "happenings" and conspicuously destroying existing theatrical conventions.

Other important literary figures in present-day Austria are Wolfgang Bauer (b. 1941), Peter Turrini (b. 1944), Elfriede Jelinek (b. 1946: 2004 Nobel Prize for Literature), Robert Menasse (b. 1954), Josef Haslinger (b. 1955), Werner Schwab (1958–94) and Franzobel (b. 1967).

Peter Handke, well-known Austrian writer of drama and prose

AUSTRIAN THEATRE

One Austrian critic described the Burgtheater as "a nursery, a university, a salon, a place of prayer, a temple of the muses and a hall of laughter". The Viennese stage played an important role in shaping the German language and influenced the development of artistic and moral ideals. In addition, many provincial playhouses specialized in Viennese popular comedy.

Max Reinhardt, the outstanding theatrical reformer, established his own troupe at the Theater in der Josefstadt in the 1920s. He also founded the Salzburg Festival *(see p221)*, where the principal works of Austrian and world literature and drama were staged.

The Burgtheater, Austria's most important stage

Sport in Austria

AUSTRIA is one of the most sports-loving nations in Europe, a fact reflected in the great popularity of recreational sports as well as in the country's success in international competitions – relative to its small population, the number of European and world champions, as well as Olympic medallists, in Austria is very high.

Some three million people – members of 27,500 sports clubs – participate actively in various sports and sports contests. The most popular and widely pursued sport is downhill skiing, followed by soccer, nordic (or cross-country) skiing, tennis, swimming, golf, cycling and windsurfing. New sports, such as snowboarding, are also becoming more popular.

ALPINE SKIING

ALPINE or downhill skiing has been the number one national sport in Austria for over 100 years. Matthias Zdarsky (1856–1940) wrote the first handbook of skiing in 1897, invented the first ski bindings worthy of mention, and organized, in 1905, the first slalom race.

The Winter Olympics have twice been held in Innsbruck (1964 and 1976), and European and world championships are hosted by other resorts. The best-known venues for downhill skiing contests are Arlberg in Tyrol, St. Anton (which hosts the Alpine World Championships), Kitzbühel and St. Christoph, with its Ski Academy, the training centre for ski instructors. The international Hahnenkamm races in Kitzbühel are famous the world over. In January, the spectacular World Cup Men's Downhill and Slalom race takes place here; past Austrian champions have included Toni Sailer, Franz Klammer and Hermann Maier.

Austria's eight glacial regions permit year-round skiing. Most popular are the glaciers situated above Kaprun and Stubai.

Up-to-date information on snow cover and the running of some 3,500 ski lifts and cable cars is available from the Alpine Association's website at www.alpenverein.at (in German only).

NORDIC SKIING

IT IS NO coincidence that, in 1999, the World Championships in nordic or cross-country skiing events were held in Styria, in the beautiful town of Ramsau. The local glacier, Dachstein, is a popular year-round training ground for cross-country runners from around the world. Even the national teams of Finland and Norway practise here in summer, polishing up their techniques and developing stamina dressed only in their swimwear – or less: famously, nude cross-country skiing is permitted in this resort.

Two of the prestigious Four Hills ski jump tournaments take place in Innsbruck and Bischofshofen. The event, straddling the last week of December and the first week in January, sees the final event in Bischofshofen.

Record-breaking ski jumper Andreas Goldberg

TOBOGGANING

TOBOGGANING is another winter sport at which Austria excels on the international stage; worldwide, only Germany and Italy achieve comparable results. Over the last decades, Austrian competitors have won several medals in this discipline at the Olympic Games, as well as various World Championships and World Cup events in all age categories.

The reason for this great Olympic and international success is the widespread popularity of the sport in Austria. Competitors train in some 310 tobogganing clubs and associations, represented in all provinces, with the exception of Burgenland.

Hermann Maier on his final slalom run, in Hinterstoder

Johann Wolfmayr and team in the World Championship in pair driving

SOCCER

THE DAYS when Austria ranked as one of the world's great soccer nations, in the 1920s and 1930s, are now buried deep in the past, along with the names of its former stars, including Matthias Sindelar, Toni Polster and Hans Krankl. Yet, although the national team did not qualify for the World Cup 2002 in Korea and Japan, soccer remains the second most popular spectator and participation sport in Austria after skiing.

The present star of the national squad is the mid-fielder Andreas Herzog, who plays for Rapid Wien. As in other countries, many football players are "bought" in from other countries to play in Austrian football clubs, while the best Austrian players join clubs in other countries. Many play in the German Bundesliga, with just a few going to Italy or Spain.

As the Austrian clubs have little success in international competitions, most of the spectators prefer to watch the matches of the Austrian league. The most famous football stadiums are the Ernst-Happel-Stadion and the Hanappi-Stadion, both in Vienna. The First Division consists of ten soccer teams, including two from Vienna and two from Graz, but other teams are ready to take on the challenge.

Roman Mählich of Sturm Graz, playing against Bayer Leverkusen

HORSE RIDING

THE FIRST SPORTS riding club in Austria, the Campagne-reiter-Gesellschaft, founded in 1872, had the Emperor Franz Joseph I, himself a keen rider, as a patron. It consisted mainly of military personnel, and is now considered to be the predecessor of the Bundesfachverband für Reiten und Fahren (Federal League for Riding and Driving), established as recently as 1962.

Austrian riders have achieved many international successes. One of its legends is the pre-war master of horse dressage, Alois Podhajsk. The greatest character among Austrian riders in the 1980s and 1990s was showjumping champion, Hugo Simon. In the 1980s, Austrian competitors began to achieve considerable success in harness racing, involving one- and two-horse carts.

In recent years, rodeos introduced from America – known as *Westernreiten* (wild west riding) – have also gained in popularity.

CANOEING AND MOUNTAIN BIKING

WITH ITS MANY rivers and lakes and its superb mountain scenery, Austria boasts the perfect natural conditions, as well as a well-developed infrastructure, for both these disciplines (though this does not always translate into international medals). The huge popularity of summer mountain sports among Austrians and visitors is nevertheless very noticeable. Mountain canoeing is practised on turbulent mountain streams.

Cycling is also popular throughout Austria: the most recent World Championships were held in Kaprun.

Helmut Oblinger competing in the individual slalom in Sydney

AUSTRIA THROUGH THE YEAR

AUSTRIA is a conservative country and Austrians value their traditions highly. In many regions the population maintains such ancient customs as the rites of spring and ritual re-enactments of death and resurrection, as well as various festivals associated with the grape harvest. Carnival festivities and parades are also big crowd-pullers, and many festivals are associated with the main religious holidays, such as Easter, Corpus

A Tyrolean in regional costume

Christi and Christmas. Labour Day (1 May) is the traditional day for workers' processions. These national festivities, plus scores of regional and local cultural events catering for the arts, fill the Austrian events calendar almost every day of the year. Many festivals enjoy an international reputation, including the Salzburg Festival, the Bregenz Festival and the Vienna Viennale. Information on all events is available from tourist offices or the internet.

SPRING

SPRING sees the re-opening of regional museums that were closed for the winter. The Viennese Prater funfair starts up at full steam. Traditionally, Lent is a period of abstinence and anticipation, but the shops are already full of Easter specialities, their shelves laden with chocolate bunnies, giant Easter eggs and other sweet delicacies.

Narzissenfest on Altausseer See

MARCH

Palmprozessionen Palm Sunday processions, such as the one in Thaur, in Tyrol, based on ancient traditions, yet highly imaginative.
Passionsspiele During Holy Week and in the run up to Easter, many towns and villages stage Passion plays. Some of the most famous plays can be seen in Pongau (Salzburger Land), Tressdorf (Carinthia) and Traunkirchen (Upper Austria).
Frühlingsfestival Vienna. Classical music festival.

Palm Sunday procession, in Thaur

Osterfestspiele *(Holy Week and Easter)* Salzburg. Easter Festival with opera and classical music concerts.

APRIL

Easter On Easter night, many mountain slopes are lit with Easter bonfires called **Oster-feuer**. Easter Sunday begins with the traditional chocolate Easter egg hunt, **Eiersuchen**.
Donaufestival *(mid-April–mid-May)* Krems, Korneuburg. Festival of contemporary theatre and music.

MAY

Wiener Festwochen *(early May–early June)* Vienna. The biggest arts festival.
Labour Day *(1 May)*. Day of workers' marches and demonstrations; also of numerous shows and sporting events.

Passionsspiele Erl in Vorarlberg. Passion plays organized every six years (most recently in 2002). Following the May première, the plays are then performed every Saturday and Sunday until early October.
Musikwochen Millstadt *(mid-May–early October)* Millstadt, in Carinthia. International music festival.
Gauderfest *(1st weekend in May)* Zell am Ziller, in Tyrol. Festival of strong beer, with animal fights and wrestling.
Kufenstechen *(Whit Sunday/ Monday)* Gailtal, in Carinthia. Jousting tournament.
Internationale Barocktage *(Whit Friday–Monday)* Melk Abbey. Baroque music days.
Narzissenfest *(late May–early June)* on the banks of the Altausseer See in Salzkammergut. Narcissus flower festival, music and processions.
St Pauler Kultursommer *(Pentecost–15 August)* St Paul's Abbey, in Carinthia. Festival of classical music.

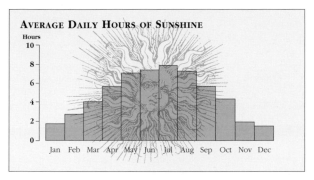

AVERAGE DAILY HOURS OF SUNSHINE

Hours

| | | | | | | | | | | | |
|Jan|Feb|Mar|Apr|May|Jun|Jul|Aug|Sep|Oct|Nov|Dec|

Sunshine Chart

The largest number of sunny days occurs in July, but May, June and August are also sunny. The cloudiest month is December.

SUMMER

SUMMER IS the height of the tourist season. Theatres close for the summer, but the most important arts festivals, including the Salzburg and Bregenz Festivals, take place during this season. There are also numerous popular entertainment events and traditional village feastivals.

Corpus Christi procession in Hallstatt, Salzkammergut

JUNE

Corpus Christi Processions throughout Austria; the best take place in Salzkammergut, Gmunden, Hallstatt and Traunkirchen. In Deutsch-landsberg, Styria, flowering carpets are on show.
Schubertiade *(June, August, September)*, Schwarzenberg, in Vorarlberg. Festival of Schubert's music.
Styriarte *(end June–end August)*, Graz. Festival of early and contemporary music.
Klangbogen Wien *(early July–late August)*, Vienna. Music festival, with a wide variety of events taking place throughout the city.
Donauinselfest *(late June)* Danube Island, Vienna. A three-day pop music event with youth groups.

Orgelfest Stift Zwettl *(late June–late July)* Zwettl, in Lower Austria. Festival of organ music.
Operettenfestival Baden *(late July–early September)* Baden, near Vienna. Festival of operetta.

JULY

Jazzfestival *(mid-July)* Wiesen, Burgenland. Jazz festival.
Salzburger Festspiele *(July–late August)* Salzburg. Festival of music, opera and theatre; most important event of the summer.
Seefestspiele *(end July–late Aug)* Bregenz. Performances of theatre, opera and music on the stage in Bodensee.
Karajan Festival *(July–August)* Vienna. Opera and music films, shown on a big screen in front of the town hall.
Kammermusikfest Lockenhaus Schloss Lockenhaus, in Burgenland. Chamber music.
Samsonumzug *(late July)* Tamsweg, Salzburger Land. Samson's procession; saints' statues are paraded in town.
Operettenfestspiele Mörbisch, on Neusiedler See. Festival of operetta.

Carinthischer Sommer Ossiach, Villach, in Carinthia. Carinthian summer festival.
Operettenfestival *(July–August)*, Bad Ischl, Salzkammergut. Festival of operetta.
Innsbrucker Festwochen der Alten Musik *(July–August)* In and around Innsbruck. One of the world's foremost festivals of early music and Baroque opera.

AUGUST

Jazzfestival Saalfelden. Jazz concerts, performed by several hundred artists.
Internationales Chopin Festival *(mid-August)* Gaming Abbey. International Chopin Festival.
Piratenschlacht *(early August)* Oberndorf near Salzburg. Pirates fight it out on the Salzach River.
Assumption of the Virgin Mary *(15 August)*. Colourful processions all over Austria. The most interesting is the **Schiffsprozession** (procession of ships) on Wörther See.
Internationaler Brahms Wettbewerb Velden and Pörtschach on Wörther See. International Brahms Contest.

Fire dance during the Salzburg Festival

AVERAGE MONTHLY RAINFALL

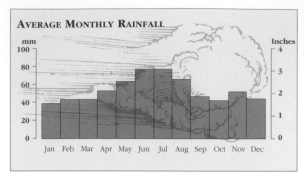

| mm | | | | | | | | | | | | Inches |

(Bar chart showing average monthly rainfall from Jan to Dec, mm scale 0–100 on left, Inches scale 0–4 on right)

Jan Feb Mar Apr May Jun Jul Aug Sep Oct Nov Dec

Rainfall Chart
*The summer months
are not only the hottest
but also the wettest
time of the year.
Western regions tend to
be wetter than central
areas of Austria.*

AUTUMN

IN THE TOWNS, autumn marks the start of the theatre and opera season. In the mountains, the sheep and cows are rounded up and brought back down from their summer pastures, accompanied by various festivities. Grape harvest festivals are held in the wine-producing areas, mainly in Lower Austria and Burgenland. The lightly fizzing *Sturm* appears on the tables, quickly followed by new-vintage wines. Numerous music events attract music lovers throughout the country.

SEPTEMBER

Ars Electronica *(early September)* Linz. Technology exhibition accompanied by concerts of electronic music.
Haydn Tage *(early September)* Eisenstadt. Festival of Music by Haydn.
Festlicher Almabtrieb *(mid-September–mid-October)*

Start of Bruckner Festival, Linz

Flocks return from the mountains. Various festivities, and the mountains echo to the sound of cows' bells.
Brucknerfest Linz *(September)* Linz. The Bruckner festival starts with **Klangwolken** (sound clouds), a series of concerts on the banks of the Danube with laser light shows.
Badener Beethoventage *(September–October)* Baden. Festival of Beethoven music.
Internationale Woche der Alten Musik *(early September)* Krieglach, in Styria. International Week of Early Music.
Internationales Musikfest Brahms *(mid-September)* Mürzuschlag. International Brahms festival.

OCTOBER

Winzerumzüge *(mid-October)* Weinviertel and Wachau Valley, Lower Austria; wine-producing regions of Burgenland. Grape harvest festivals.
Niederösterreichischer Weinherbst Lower Austria. The "Wine Autumn" is a time of increased eating and drinking in the old inns of ancient wine-producing villages, often regarded as historic architectural treasures.
Steirischer Herbst Graz. The Styrian Autumn is an avant-garde arts festival, one of the most prestigious events of the season, taking place over four weeks. Festival-goers are mainly young people, and the events include theatre and opera

productions, performance arts, films, music concerts, talks and art exhibitions.
National Day *(26 October)*. Celebration of the Declaration of Neutrality in 1955.
Viennale *(late October)* Vienna. Two-week International Film Festival.
Wien Modern *(end October– end November)* Vienna. Contemporary Music Festival, initiated by Claudio Abbado.

Krampus Devil and St Nicholas at Christmas fairs

NOVEMBER

Salzburger Jazz-Herbst *(early November)* Salzburg. Ten days of traditional jazz concerts and films.
St Martin's Day *(11 November)*. This is the day when all Austria feasts on *Martinigans* – roast St Martin's goose.
Voicemania *(November– December)* Vienna. A capella festival in unusual venues.
Weihnachtsmärkte *(late November–December)*. Start of the Christmas market season. On offer: tree decorations, gifts, food and drink; best in Vienna, Salzburg, Klagenfurt, Spittal an der Drau and Villach.

AVERAGE MONTHLY TEMPERATURE

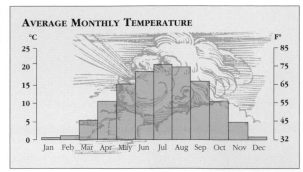

°C | °F

25 — — 85
20 — — 75
15 — — 65
10 — — 55
5 — — 45
0 — — 32

Jan Feb Mar Apr May Jun Jul Aug Sep Oct Nov Dec

Temperature Chart
The hottest month is July, with August and June being only slightly cooler. Winters are cold, particularly in January when temperatures often drop below zero.

WINTER

WINTER begins with the pre-Christmas shopping rush. Christmas figures and decorations adorn every shop window. The main shopping streets in the towns and villages sparkle with lights. As soon as Christmas is over, fresh festivities get under way: New Year's Eve marks the beginning of the carnival season, celebrated in Austria with numerous balls.

The famous Vienna Opera Ball, in February

DECEMBER

St Nicholas parties *(early December)* Tyrol. The most interesting of these include **Klaubaufgehen**, a masquerade in Matrei, **Teufelstag** (Day of the Devil) in Badgastein, and **Nikolospiel** in Bad Mittendorf. In Thaur (Tyrol), people traditionally display cribs in their homes.
Adventsingen Advent concerts held in Salzburg.
Steyrer Kripperl and **Krippenspiel** One of the last stick-puppet theatres. The crib display in Bad Ischl is also worth seeing. Nativity plays are staged throughout the country.

Christmas lights in Getreidegasse, Salzburg

St Stephen's Day (Stefani-tag) *(26 December)*. Colourful festival in the Lavanttal Valley (**Stefaniritt**) in Carinthia.

JANUARY

New Year's Day *(1 January)*. Austria welcomes the New Year with champagne and fireworks; people dance in the streets and squares, regardless of the weather.
Neujahrskonzert *(1 January)*. Traditional New Year's concert of the Vienna Philharmonic Orchestra transmitted throughout the world from the Golden Hall of the Wiener Musikverein.
Epiphany *(6 January)*. Dreikönigssingen (singing for the Three Kings) – Austria bursts into song on the Day of the Three Magi.
Perchtenlauf Carnival procession marking the start of the party season, held in four towns of the Pongau region in turn: St Johann, Altenmarkt, Bischofshofen and Badgastein.
Salzburger Mozart-woche *(late January)* Salzburg. Mozart Week.

FEBRUARY

February is the main carnival season. Masquerades and magnificent balls are held throughout the country.
Opernball *(last Thursday of Carnival)* Vienna Opera Ball.
Villacher Fasching *(end of Carnival)* Villach.
Maschkerertanz *(end of Carnival)* Steinfeld, Carinthia. Colourful festivities mark the end of the carnival season.

PUBLIC HOLIDAYS

Neujahr *New Year* (1 Jan)
Dreikönigsfest *Epiphany* (6 Jan)
Ostern *Easter*
Tag der Arbeit *Labour Day* (1 May)
Fronleichnam *Corpus Christi*
Pfingsten *Pentecost*
Mariä Himmelfahrt *Assumption of the Virgin Mary* (15 Aug)
Nationalfeiertag (26 Oct)
Allerheiligen *All Saints* (1 Nov)
Mariä Empfängnis (8 Dec) *Immaculate Conception*
Weihnachten/Stefanitag *Christmas* (25/26 Dec)

THE HISTORY OF AUSTRIA

DURING THE MIDDLE AGES, *Austria was only one of several small duchies within the Holy Roman Empire, but during 600 years of Habsburg rule it rose to the ranks of a world power and was a determining factor in Europe's fate. The Austro-Hungarian Empire ended with World War I. Since the end of World War II, Austria has been a central element in European democracy.*

PREHISTORY AND EARLY MIDDLE AGES

The geographic nature of Austria's territory, opening up towards the Bohemian-Moravian Valley and the Hungarian Plains, meant that, from the 7th century BC, this area was regularly raided and populated by belligerent Scythians, Celts and Germanic tribes. At the end of the 1st century BC, the land south of the Danube was occupied by the Romans, who in the middle of the 1st century AD, during the reign of the Emperor Claudius, founded the Province of Noricum here, with its main centres in Carnuntum (near Hainburg) and Vindobona (Vienna).

Stone-age Venus, discovered in Willendorf

The influence of the dominant Roman culture and civilization over the entire region began to wane in the 2nd century AD, during a period of increased German raids. In AD 180, Emperor Marcus Aurelius died in Vindobona, in the war against the Marcomanni and Quadi tribes.

From the 4th century onwards, during the Great Migration of Nations, the territories of present-day Austria saw successive waves of invading Huns, Goths and Avars. Later arrivals included Slav and Bavarian settlers. The Bavarian tribal state, established and consolidated during the 7th and 8th centuries, was crushed in 787 when Charlemagne deposed his vassal Tassilo III, the last Prince of Bavaria, and annexed his territories. In 803, Charlemagne also defeated the Avars and established a margravate (territory) on the banks of the Danube, between Enns River and Vienna Woods, which became the nucleus of the Austrian state. Its existence was cut short by Magyars, who raided it in the early 10th century.

BABENBERG AUSTRIA

Following the defeat of the Magyars in 995, on the banks of the Lech River near Augsburg, the German King Otto I restored the margravate; his successor, Otto II, handed it as a fief to Leopold I of the Babenberg dynasty (976–94). The centre of the margravate was Melk, on the Danube river. Having defeated the Magyars, Leopold extended the frontiers of his province up to the

TIMELINE

170 Raid by the Germanic tribes of Marcomanni and Quadi	**493** Raid by Theodoric, King of the Ostrogoths		**803** Charlemagne founds the eastern margravate
		739 Founding of the bishopric of Salzburg	*The "Ostarrichi Urkunde" document of 996*

0	500	650	800	950	1100

4th–7th century AD The Great Migration of Nations. Raids by Huns, Goths, Avars, Slavs and Bavarians		**787** Charlemagne deposes the last independent Bavarian prince, Tassilo III	
45 Foundation of the Roman province, Noricum	*Tassilo's chalice of 777*		**976** Leopold I Babenberg becomes the first Margrave of the margravate

◁ **Emperor Franz Joseph I, who ruled 1848–1916**

Vienna Woods. In 1156, Henry II Jasomirgott was given the title of Duke, and Austria became a hereditary fief of the Empire. Vienna began to assume its role as capital.

BOHEMIAN AUSTRIA

In 1246, the Babenberg line died out and Austria fell into the hands of the Bohemian kings, Vaclav I and Ottokar II. The latter, having annexed Carinthia and Carniola (1269), became the most powerful duke in the Empire. He had his eyes on the German crown, but in the 1273 election a more modest feudal lord rose to the German throne, the landgrave (count) of Upper Alsace, Rudolf von Habsburg (1273–91). He defeated his opponent, Ottokar II, in 1278, took the Austrian territories and handed them to his sons as hereditary fiefs. From then on, for the next 640 years, the fate of Austria became tied to that of the Habsburg dynasty.

Death of Frederick II Babenberg

Stone ducal throne in Maria Saal

THE HABSBURG RISE TO POWER

Rudolf I and his successors pursued a very successful policy of acquiring new territories. During the 14th century, in addition to Austria, Styria, Carinthia and Carniola, the Habsburgs gained control of Tyrol (1363) and Trieste (1382).

An important contribution to the strengthening of the dynasty was made by Rudolf IV, called the Founder (1358–65), who founded Vienna University and laid the foundation stone for St Stephen's Cathedral, the church that to this day remains one of the symbols of the Austrian capital. Rudolf signed a treaty with the Emperor Charles IV – Bohemian king of the Luxemburg dynasty – stating that in the event of one of the dynasties (Habsburgs or Luxemburgs) dying out, the other would reign over both territories. This situation arose in 1438, when, following the death of Emperor Sigismund of Luxemburg, both the imperial crown of Germany and the throne of Hungary and Bohemia passed to the Austrian Duke Albrecht II of Habsburg, and on his death to his cousin Frederick III (1440–93), who was regarded as the last emperor of the Middle Ages. His motto was written as the five vowels – AEIOU – which were variously interpreted, for example as "Austriae Est Imperare Orbi Universo" (The Entire World is Austria's Empire).

THE EMPIRE OF CHARLES V

This maxim appeared close to becoming true during the reign of Maximilian I (1486–1519), who by his marriage to Maria of Burgundy in

TIMELINE

1156 Thanks to privileges granted by Frederick Barbarossa, Austria is elevated to the status of a Duchy of the Reich. Margrave Henry II Jasomirgott becomes its first duke		**1358** Rudolph IV, the Founder, ascends to the throne
	1251 Austria ruled by Ottokar II	

1100	1150	1200	1250	1300	1350

1246 End of the Babenberg line. Vienna occupied by the Bohemian King Vaclav I

Fragment of a medieval altar from Verdun, 1185

1278 Rudolf von Habsburg defeats Ottokar II in the Battle of Dürnkrut. Austria becomes a hereditary fief of the Habsburgs

Gothic altar in Zwettl Abbey

the younger line of Habsburgs, taking control of Austria, Styria, Carniola, Carinthia and Tyrol and the Jagiellon inheritance, Bohemia, Moravia, Silesia and western Hungary.

REFORMATION AND TURKISH THREAT

During the Reformation, the state, now with a population of seven million, became the scene of fierce religious conflicts. Ferdinand and his successor, Maximilian II (1564–76), pursued a policy of tolerance towards the Protestants, but Rudolf II (1576–1612), brought up in the staunchly Catholic Spanish court, declared himself in favour of the Counter-Reformation. The growing religious conflict led to the Thirty-Years' War (1618–48), which ravaged large areas (51 castles, 23 towns and 313 villages in Austrian-ruled countries alone).

Turkish banner, captured in 1683

1477 gained control of Alsace, Lorraine and the Netherlands, one of the richest countries in Europe. He also entered into a treaty with the Jagiellons – thus reviving his claims to the Bohemian and Hungarian crowns – and, by arranging the betrothal of his son Philip to the Spanish Infanta Joan, extended Habsburg rule over the Iberian Peninsula and the South American dominions. In 1519, Maximilian's successor, his grandson Charles V (1519–56), heir to the Spanish and Austrian territories, succeeded to the throne of an empire over which, it could be said, "the sun never set". Following the abdication of King Charles in 1556, the imperial crown passed to his brother Ferdinand (1556–64); he represented

Panel inscribed "AEIOU", Frederick III's motto

Even greater destruction was caused by the wars fought during the 16th and 17th centuries against the Turks, who twice tried to conquer Vienna (1529, 1683). The crushing defeat suffered by the Sultan's army during the second siege of Vienna allowed the Habsburgs to take control of the whole of Hungary, Transylvania and Croatia.

1438 Albrecht II becomes the first Habsburg emperor

1469 Founding of the bishopric of Vienna

1493 Coronation of Maximilian I

1519–1556 Reign of Charles V. Height of Habsburg territorial power

1556 Abdication of Charles V and ascension to the throne of his brother, Ferdinand I

1618–48 Thirty Years' War

1683 Outbreak of Great Turkish-Austrian war

1697 Prince Eugene of Savoy becomes the chief commander of the imperial army

)0	1450	1500	1550	1600	1650	1700

Maximilian I

The First Habsburg Monarchy

THE HABSBURGS rose to the ranks of the most influential German feudal families during the first half of the 1300s, and in the following centuries they became the rulers of one of Europe's most powerful countries. This advancement was due mainly to their far-sighted dynastic policy and expedient marriages. Strategic matches brought under their control territories far beyond their native Austria and Styria, to include Tyrol, Flanders, the Netherlands, Bohemia, Hungary and the possessions of the Spanish crown in both Europe and South America. The Habsburgs' marriage policy was later summed up in the motto "Let others fight wars, you, lucky Austria, get married".

AUSTRIA OF RUDOLF I

▨ *Austria in 1278*

Gravy Boat of Rudolf II
The gravy-boat from the famous collection of objets d'art from the Mannerist period, collected by Rudolf II, can be seen in Vienna's Kunsthistorisches Museum (see pp84-7).

Regalia of Rudolf II
The intricate sceptre, orb and crown became the insignia of the Austrian Empire.

Ferdinand I, grandson of Maximilian I, ruled Bohemia, Austria and Hungary.

Maximilian I

Relief of the Siege of Vienna in 1683
The 70,000-strong Christian army, led by the Polish King Jan III Sobieski, broke through the ring around Vienna and forced the 110–115,000 Turkish troops of the Grand Vizier Kara Mustapha to flee.

Rudolf II
During his reign, Rudolf II attracted scholars such as Kepler, as well as famous sorcerers, alchemists and seers to the imperial court.

Philip I, son of Maximilian I, gained control of Spain as the result of his marriage to Joanna the Mad.

Mary of Burgundy, wife of Maximilian I

Rudolf I
The first Habsburg king of Germany, having defeated Bohemian King Ottokar II in 1276, seized Austria, Carinthia and Styria.

Karl V, grandson of Maximilian I, inherited Spain from his mother.

FAMILY OF MAXIMILIAN I
This painting by Bernhard Strigel (c.1520) depicts Maximilian I with his family, a dynasty that turned Austria into a powerful empire.

Rudolf IV the Founder
Rudolf IV died very young (only 26 years old) and was buried in St Stephen's Cathedral – the church he had founded in Vienna.

WHERE TO SEE GOTHIC AUSTRIA

The most interesting early-Gothic remains to be found in Austria, dating back to the 13th–14th centuries, are the cloisters of the Cistercian abbeys in Heiligenkreuz *(see p136)* in the Wiener-wald, as well as Lilienfeld and Zwettl, both in Lower Austria. Among the best examples of Gothic archi-tecture are the impressive Stephansdom (St Stephen's Cathedral) in Vienna, the Franciscan church in Salz-burg *(see p220),* and the four-nave parish church in Schwaz *(see pp244–5),* in Tyrol. The most famous late-Gothic (1481) wing altar, an outstanding work by the Tyrolean artist Michael Pacher, is found in St Wolfgang *(see p205),* in the Salzkammergut. Many churches feature original Gothic sculptures.

Stephansdom *(St Stephen's Cathedral) in Vienna (see pp58–9) is Austria's best-known Gothic building.*

Goldenes Dachl *The "Golden Roof" in Innsbruck (see p240) is an attractive example of secular Gothic architecture.*

THE STRUGGLE FOR SPANISH AND AUSTRIAN SUCCESSION

The expiration of the Spanish line of Habsburgs led to the Spanish War of Succession (1701–14), which brought further territorial gains for Austria, including Belgium, Milan, Naples and Sardinia. Soon the problem of succession also arose in Austria, where Emperor Charles VI (1711–40) had died without a male heir. The so-called Pragmatic Sanction, established by Charles in 1713, stipulated that the Habsburg Austrian territories remain an integral, indivisible whole, with female members of the house also eligible for succession. The Emperor's only daughter, Maria Theresa (1740–80), however, was forced to defend her rights by fighting Prussia, France, Spain and a number of German states in the War of Austrian Succession (1740–48), during which she lost Silesia to Prussia. In 1772 and 1775, Austria participated in the first and third Partitions of Poland, annexing that country's southern territories.

Apotheosis of Eugene of Saxony

ENLIGHTENED ABSOLUTISM

Maria Theresa and her son Joseph II (1780–90), embarked on an extensive course of reforms, in the spirit of enlightened absolutism. They curtailed the rights of the Church, abolished serfdom, created a new administrative structure of the state and declared German the official language for all institutions. Their aim was to obliterate the differences between the individual countries of the Empire, to unify the multi-ethnic state and to centralize power.

REVOLUTION AND RESTORATION

During the revolutionary changes that took place in Europe at the turn of the 18th century, the Habsburgs joined the anti-French coalition forces. Initially they suffered major territorial losses (Belgium, Lombardy, southern Poland). Franz II, Maria Theresa's grandson, relinquished his title of Holy Roman Emperor and in 1806 declared himself Emperor Franz I of Austria. Following the defeat of Napoleon and the Congress of Vienna where proceedings were dominated by the Austrian Foreign Minister, Klemens Metternich, the Habsburg Empire became once again a European superpower. Metternich, who from 1821 held the office of Chancellor, and in fact ruled Austria, became the main exponent of absolutism and the policy of ethnic oppression; hence his nickname, "Europe's coachman".

Emperor Franz I of Austria and Maria Theresa surrounded by their children

TIMELINE

1701–14 War of Spanish Succession. Austria acquires Belgium, Milan, Naples, Parma and Sardinia

1740–48 War of Austrian Succession. Prussian-French-Spanish Coalition opposes Maria Theresa's right to the imperial throne

1700   1720   1740   1760   1780

1756 Birth of Wolfgang Amadeus Mozart

1795 Austria participates in Third Partition of Poland

Maria Theresa

Wolfgang Amadeus Mozart

1772 Austria participates in First Partition of Poland

The Congress of Vienna in 1815

THE 1848 REVOLUTION

In 1848–9, a wave of revolutions swept across Europe and the Austrian Empire. Uprisings against absolute government broke out in Vienna, Milan, Venice, Budapest, Cracow and Prague; the Hungarian revolution was suppressed only with the help of the Russian army. Emperor Ferdinand I saw himself forced to grant several concessions, including giving Austria a constitution (1848). Badly affected by the revolutionary events, the Emperor abdicated in 1848 and the Austrian throne passed to his 18-year old nephew, Franz Joseph I (1848–1916), who quickly reintroduced absolute rule, thus inviting increased resistance, particularly in the Hungarian part of the empire.

THE AUSTRO-HUNGARIAN EMPIRE

Defeat suffered in the wars with Sardinia and France (1859), and with Prussia and Italy (1866), testified to the weakening position of Austria, particularly when confronted with the growing power of the unifying

Germany. Defeat in the international arena also brought about changes in internal policy. In 1867, the emperor signed a treaty with Hungary and transformed the Austro-Hungarian Empire into a state consisting of two parts, united under one common ruler as well as a common army, finances and foreign policy. The adopted model of government eased the tensions in Austro-Hungarian relations, but did not contribute to the solution of other conflicts, including those with the Czechs, who revolted afresh, led by nationalist feelings.

Internationally, the Empire's attention was focused on the Balkans where, with Russian approval, it occupied Bosnia and Herzegovina (1878). Key to Vienna's political strategy was the political-military treaty signed in 1882 with Germany and Italy, the Triple Alliance.

In the late 1800s, Vienna developed as a centre of fashion and became the birthplace of the avant-garde Viennese Secession style.

Vienna during the revolution of 1848

1806 Franz II relinquishes title of Holy Roman Emperor

Johann Strauss (son)

1867 Austria becomes Austro-Hungarian state

1815 Congress of Vienna

1848 Revolution in Vienna

1898 Assassination of Empress Elisabeth, by an Italian anarchist

| 00 | 1820 | 1840 | 1860 | 1880 | 1900 |

1825 Birth of Johann Strauss (son)

1889 Death of the Crown Prince, Archduke Rudolf

1848 Ferdinand I abdicates and Franz Joseph I ascends the throne

1805 Napoleon defeats the Austrian and Russian armies in the Battle of Austerlitz

1866 Defeated by Prussia, Austria loses its status as the main German power

The Monarchy of Franz I

A‍T THE TURN of the 19th century, Austria had to face social and political changes brought about by the French Revolution. Franz II ascended the Austrian throne as Holy Roman Emperor in 1792, and Austria entered a 22-year period of war with France. Franz II declared his opposition to all reformist ideas and, in response to Napoleon's self-coronation, he established the Austrian Empire in 1804. As Emperor Franz I, and with his all-powerful chancellor Klemens Metternich, his main concern in the field of domestic policy, was the preservation of the monarch's absolute power.

AFTER THE VIENNA CONGRESS

☐ *Austria in 1815*

The coffin contains the body of Franz I, which was later laid in a sarcophagus in the crypt of the Capuchin Church in Vienna.

Franz I Crosses the Vosges Mountains
Following Napoleon's defeat at Waterloo in 1815, Franz I marched into France at the head of troops belonging to the coalition's occupying forces.

An officer in Austrian uniform

The Imperial crown of Austria – once the crown of Emperor Rudolf II. Alongside lie other regalia.

Radetzky Statue
Johann Radetzky was one of the most outstanding commanders in Austrian history. After the victory over Italy in the Battle of Custozza (1848), the 82-year old became famous as the main-stay of the Habsburg monarchy.

Emblem of the Empire
In 1836 Austria's national emblem combined Lorraine's two-headed eagle, with imperial crown, sword, sceptre and a shield with the Habsburg family crest.

Technological Progress
The first railway line on the European continent was built in Austria, in 1832. It linked Linz with České Budejovice.

An officer in Hungarian uniform

WHERE TO SEE BIEDERMEIER STYLE IN AUSTRIA

The Biedermeier style of furniture, interior design and painting, popular during the early 19th century, reflected the virtues and aspirations of the middle classes. Draped curtains, patterned carpets, bureaus and glazed cabinets became standard features. Domestic architecture flourished. Typical interiors can be seen in Vienna, in the Geymüller Schlössl (home to the Biedermeier Museum), the Museum of Applied Arts (MAK – *see p60*) and the Dreimäderlhaus. Works of prominent artists such as Ferdinand Waldmüller, Josef Danhauser and Moritz M. Daffinger can be found in Wien Museum Karlsplatz (*see pp84–7*), the Historisches Museum der Stadt Wien (*see p97*), and in the Schlossmuseum in Linz (*see p190*), among others.

Biedermeier-style furniture was highly valued by the prosperous middle classes, particularly in the first half of the 19th century.

FUNERAL CEREMONY OF FRANZ I
When Napoleon declared himself Emperor of France in 1804, Franz II countered by proclaiming himself Franz I, Emperor of Austria. He was the last ruler of the Holy Roman Empire of the German Nation. He died in 1835.

Franz I in his Coronation Robes
In 1804, Franz I took on the newly created role of Emperor of Austria and King of Hungary. Two months later, he added the title King of Bohemia.

The Dreimäderlhaus, at No. 10 Schreyvogelgasse, is one of the most beautiful examples of Viennese Biedermeier.

Depiction of the assassination of Archduke Ferdinand

WORLD WAR I

In 1908, Austro-Hungary decided on a formal annexation of Bosnia-Herzegovina, leading to increased tensions with Russia, which had begun to strengthen its position in the Balkans, and with Serbia, which pursued its own expansionist aims. On 28 June 1914, in Sarajevo, the Serbian student Gavrilo Princip shot dead the heir to the Austrian throne, Franz Ferdinand. His assassination resulted in the outbreak of World War I. Germany, Austria's old ally from the Triple Alliance, declared itself on the side of Austria (Italy remained neutral for a while), while the Entente countries – Russia, France and England – sided with Serbia. The war exposed the weakness of the Habsburg

monarchy and brought about its collapse. Charles I, Austria's last emperor, was exiled to Madeira in 1921.

THE FIRST REPUBLIC

On 12 November 1918, the Provisional National Assembly proclaimed the birth of the Austro-German Republic. Its first elected chancellor was the socialist Karl Renner. The peace treaty, signed in St-Germain-en-Laye (1919), imposed war compensations on Austria and forbade unification with Germany. During the 1920s, Austria's economic situation steadily worsened, giving rise to radical sentiments. The worsening internal problems were exploited by nationalist circles calling for Austria to join with Germany. Chancellor Engelbert Dollfuss, elected to office in 1932, tried to counteract such dangers by introducing "strong-arm government", repressing the Social-Democratic opposition and dissolving Communist and National-Socialist parties. These steps led to bloody riots in Vienna and Linz, in February 1934. In July of that year, the National Socialists unsuccessfully attempted a coup, and murdered Dollfuss in the process. The new chancellor, Kurt Schuschnigg, under

German troops marching into Austria during the annexation

TIMELINE

1914 Assassination of Archduke Ferdinand, in Sarajevo. Outbreak of WWI	**1916** Death of Franz Joseph I. Emperor Charles I ascends the throne		**1938** *Anschluss* – Austria's integration into the Third Reich
		1934 Workers riot in Vienna and Linz; bloody suppression by the police	**1943** Moscow Conference

1900	1910	1920	1930	1940	1950

1908 Annexation of Bosnia and Herzegovina

Archduke Ferdinand's jacket

1918 End of WWI. Collapse of Austro-Hungary. Creation of the Republic of Austria

1934 Unsuccessful Nazi coup. Murder of Engelbert Dollfuss

Engelbert Dollfuss

Soldiers of the occupying forces in Vienna in 1951

pressure from Adolf Hitler, agreed in February 1937 to admit National Socialist politicians into his government, but resigned in the face of demands for Austria to be incorporated into Germany. His successor, the National Socialist activist Arthur Seyss-Inquart, proclaimed Austria's integration into the Third Reich *(Anschluss)* on 13 March 1938, which met with the approval of the majority of the Austrian population. German troops marched into the country.

WORLD WAR II AND THE SECOND REPUBLIC

Following the *Anschluss*, Austria became a part of Greater Germany until the end of World War II. Opposition against the National Socialist administration was negligible. Before the end of the war, at the Moscow Conference in 1943, the Allied forces decided to restore an independent Austrian state. In April 1945, Karl Renner formed the first provisional

government of the restored Second Republic, and in December he was elected president. In July 1945, Austria was divided into four occupation zones by the Allied powers.

The first parliamentary elections, in November 1945, were won by the Christian-Democratic Party (ÖVP), with the Socialist Party (SPÖ) coming second. Both parties were to control the political life of the country for the next 50 years. De-Nazification continued until 1948. In 1955, after years of negotiations between the superpowers, the Austrian State Treaty was signed, restoring Austria to full sovereignty. Foreign troops were withdrawn from its territory and Parliament proclaimed permanent neutrality. In December 1955 Austria became a member of UNO, and in 1995 joined the European Union.

In the 1990s, the nationalist and anti-immigration Austrian Freedom Party (FPÖ) gained in popular support. It formed a coalition government with the Christian-Democratic ÖVP in 2000, arousing international fears of a resurgence of National Socialism in Austria. However, the coalition soon collapsed, and in the 2002 elections the nationalist vote had plummeted to only around 10 per cent of the vote.

Simon Wiesenthal and Ariel Musicant, Austrian investigators into Nazi crimes, at the Jewish memorial

1961 Vienna Summit of John F. Kennedy and Nikita Khrushchev	**1973** Konrad Lorenz receives Nobel Prize in Physiology and Medicine		**1995** Austria joins the EU	**2004** Elfriede Jelinek receives Nobel Prize for Literature
1960	1970	1980	1990	2000	2010
55 Treaty of State toring full sovereignty Austria. Parliament :lares Austria to be utral for all time	**1972–1981** Austrian diplomat Kurt Waldheim holds office of UN Secretary General *Austrian anti-globalization protest*			**2000** Nationalist Austrian Freedom Party enters government coalition

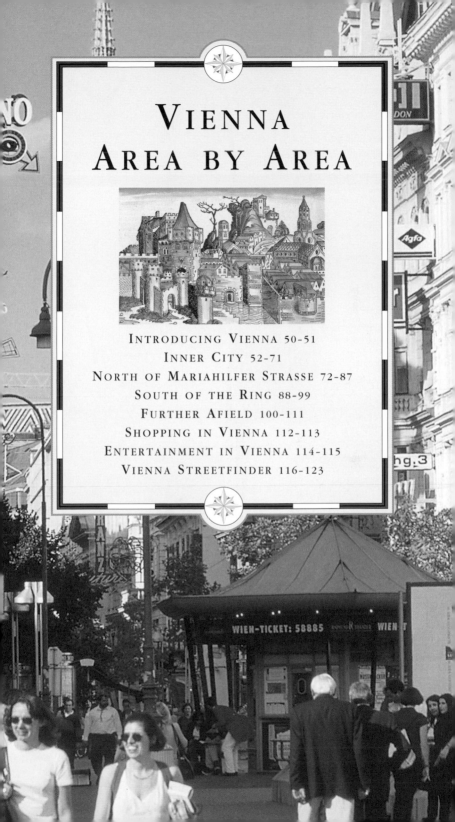

VIENNA
AREA BY AREA

Introducing Vienna

CENTRAL VIENNA incudes the Inner City demarcated by Ringstraße (often shortened to Ring) and Franz-Josefs-Kai, plus the area between Ring and Gürtel. Gürtel is Vienna's second ring road, running almost parallel with the Ring. In this guide, central Vienna is divided into three districts, in line with its administrative sectors. The most interesting sights outside the centre are also featured.

Majolikahaus Façade
The façade of Majolikahaus, at No. 40 Linke Wienzeile, was designed in 1899 by Otto Wagner, one of the foremost representatives of Viennese Secession style.

Freyung
Freyung Square is dominated by the Austria Fountain; in the background is the Schottenkirche, the church of Vienna's Benedictine monks.

KEY

	Major sight
	Tourist information office
	Police
	Church
	Synagogue
P	Parking
	U-Bahn station
	Post office
	Railway station

◁ **Graben Street in Vienna**

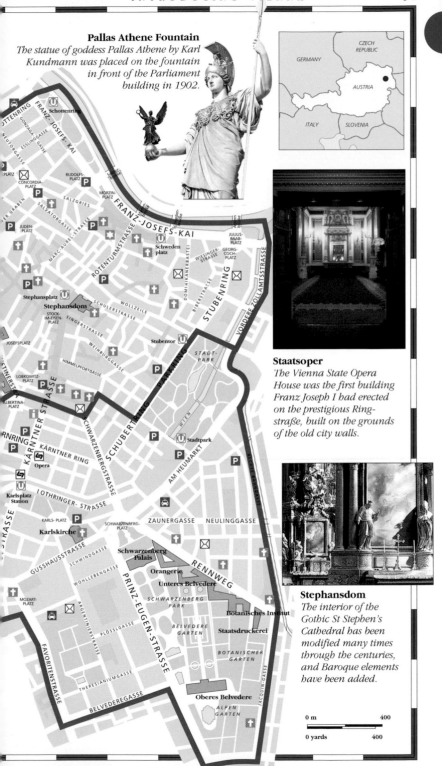

Pallas Athene Fountain
The statue of goddess Pallas Athene by Karl Kundmann was placed on the fountain in front of the Parliament building in 1902.

Staatsoper
The Vienna State Opera House was the first building Franz Joseph I had erected on the prestigious Ring-straße, built on the grounds of the old city walls.

Stephansdom
The interior of the Gothic St Stephen's Cathedral has been modified many times through the centuries, and Baroque elements have been added.

0 m   400

0 yards   400

INNER CITY

Vienna's old town, the Innere Stadt or "inner city", developed in the area enclosed on one side by the present-day Danube canal, and on the other three sides by fortifications. In the 19th century, these were replaced by the town's elegant artery – the Ringstraße. The Ring encircles many splendid historic remains, bearing

Statues on a portal in Josefsplatz

witness to Vienna's turbulent history from Roman times until the present day, while numerous museum collections convey Austria's rich heritage. It is also one of Vienna's liveliest areas, where the smartest cafés and restaurants and most expensive shops await the visitor, and where bars and clubs stay open until the early hours.

SIGHTS AT A GLANCE

Streets and Squares
Am Hof **20**
Dr.-Ignaz-Seipel-Platz **8**
Freyung **21**
Graben **2**
Heldenplatz **26**
Herrengasse **22**
Hoher Markt **17**
Jewish Quarter **14**
Josefsplatz **29**
Kärntner Straße **34**
Michaelerplatz **24**
Minoritenplatz **23**
Schulhof **19**
Schwedenplatz **12**

Historic Buildings
Alte Burg pp68–9 **27**
Altes Rathaus **16**
Böhmische
   Hofkanzlei **18**
Figarohaus **5**
*Spanische Reitschule
p67* **28**

Urania **11**
Winterpalais des Prinzen Eugen **33**

Churches
Augustinerkirche **30**
Deutschordenskirche
   St. Elisabeth **6**
Dominikanerkirche **9**
Franziskanerkirche **7**
Kapuzinerkirche, Kaisergruft **32**
Maria am Gestade **15**
Peterskirche **1**

Ruprechtskirche **13**
Stephansdom pp58–9 **3**

Museums
Albertina **31**
Dom- und Diözesanmuseum **4**
Österreichisches Museum
   für Angewandte Kunst **10**

Parks and Gardens
Volksgarten **25**

KEY

▨	Street-by-Street map *see pp54–5*
▨	Street-by-Street map *see pp64–5*
Ⓤ	U-Bahn station
P	Parking

0 m   250
0 yards   250

GETTING THERE

Stephansplatz can be reached by the U1 or U3 metro lines. Ringstraße is served by the U2, U3 and U4 lines, as well as by trams 1 and 2, and lines D and J. You can also use buses 1A, 2A and 3A.

◁ **Sculpture in the Peterskirche by Lorenzo Mattielli (1729), of St John Nepomuk's martyrdom**

Street-by-Street: Around Stephansdom

THE origins of this district date back to the 13th century, but much of it was changed in the 17th and 18th centuries, when many churches and public buildings were refashioned in the spirit of the increasingly powerful Habsburg monarchy. Narrow, medieval alleys adjoin monumental Baroque structures and bourgeois town houses, whose ground floors are often occupied by shops, cafés and restaurants. In the evenings, when the churches and museums close for the night, the area is still lively with people.

★ Dom- und Diözesanmuseum
This crucifix, containing the relics of St Andrew, is one of the many treasures of medieval sacred art kept in the Cathedral Museum **4**

Haas & Haas Grocery Shop offers the best selection of teas and coffees in Vienna, as well as delicious snacks. The tea house is set in a courtyard filled with lush greenery.

★ Stephansdom
St Stephen's Cathedral has a Baroque main altar, the work of Tobias Pock, showing the martyrdom of its patron saint **3**

STEPHANS-PLATZ

BLUTGASSE

Deutschordens-kirche St. Elisabeth
This church belonged to the Teutonic Order which, after having been relegated from Eastern Prussia by Napoleon, moved its headquarters to Vienna **6**

Along Blutgasse
and neighbouring streets the tenement houses feature lovely, green courtyards.

Figarohaus
Wolfgang Amadeus Mozart lived in this house from 1784–7, and composed The Marriage of Figaro *here* **5**

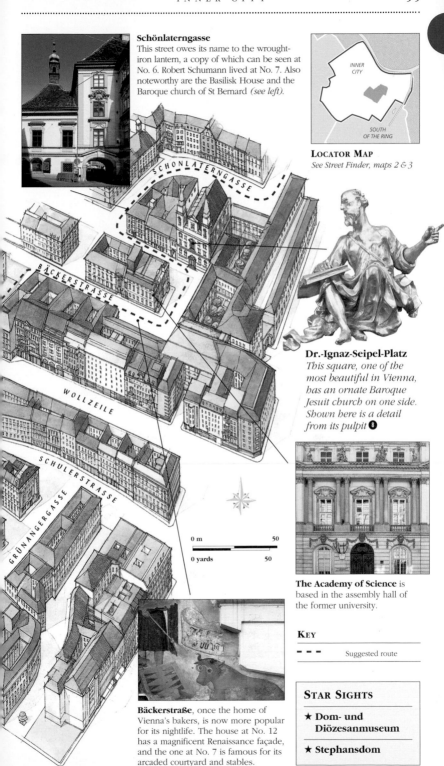

Schönlaterngasse
This street owes its name to the wrought-iron lantern, a copy of which can be seen at No. 6. Robert Schumann lived at No. 7. Also noteworthy are the Basilisk House and the Baroque church of St Bernard *(see left)*.

LOCATOR MAP
See Street Finder, maps 2 & 3

Dr.-Ignaz-Seipel-Platz
This square, one of the most beautiful in Vienna, has an ornate Baroque Jesuit church on one side. Shown here is a detail from its pulpit ❽

The Academy of Science is based in the assembly hall of the former university.

0 m   50
0 yards   50

KEY

– – – Suggested route

STAR SIGHTS

★ **Dom- und Diözesanmuseum**

★ **Stephansdom**

Bäckerstraße, once the home of Vienna's bakers, is now more popular for its nightlife. The house at No. 12 has a magnificent Renaissance façade, and the one at No. 7 is famous for its arcaded courtyard and stables.

Peterskirche ❶

Petersplatz 6. **Map** 2 B4.
📞 *53 36 443.* Ⓤ *Stephansplatz.*
🚌 *1A, 2A, 3A.* 🕐 *6:30am–7pm Mon–Fri, 8am–7pm Sat, Sun* 📷

ST PETER'S CHURCH, one of Vienna's oldest, was, according to legend, founded in 792 by Charlemagne, as commemorated in a marble relief on the church's façade, *The Placing of the Cross by Charlemagne*, by Rudolf Weyr (1906).

The site was occupied by a Roman basilica as early as the 12th century. The present Baroque church was built in the 18th century to designs by Gabriele Montani. It received its final form from Johann Lukas von Hildebrandt, who also gave the church its magnificent green patina-covered dome, which towers over the whole district. The frescoes inside the dome, depicting the Assumption of the Virgin Mary, were created by J.M. Rottmayr.

The Chapel of St Michael, the first on the right, holds a glass coffin containing the relics of St Benedict.

The striking patina-covered copper dome of Peterskirche

Graben ❷

Map 2 B4, C4. Ⓤ *Stephansplatz.*
🚌 *1A, 2A, 3A.* **Jewish Museum** 📞 *53 50 431.* 🕐 *10am–6pm Mon–Wed, Fri, Sun, 10am–8pm Thu.* 📷 🎫 🆆 *www.jmw.at*

THIS FULLY pedestrianized street, running through a bustling part of the city centre, is one of the most

The Baroque plague column in Graben

fashionable shopping areas in Vienna, full to bursting with lively restaurants and cafés. There are two identical fountains in the square, St Joseph Fountain on the northwestern side and St Leopold Fountain on the southeastern side.

In the centre of the square stands the Baroque Pestsäule (Plague Column), also known as the Dreifaltigkeitssäule (Trinity Column), which the Emperor Leopold had erected after the end of the plague that decimated the town in 1687–93. It depicts the Holy Trinity, with a statue of the praying emperor at the top. A carved group, entitled *Faith Conquers the Plague*, adorns the southern side of the column. A short distance from here, towards Stephansplatz, stands a modest statue of St John Nepomuk, which is a favourite spot with buskers.

The modern Haas Haus on Graben, at Stephansplatz, was built in 1985–90 on the site of older buildings destroyed during a bombing raid. Made from glass and aluminium, it is the most controversial building at the heart of the city. Its windows beautifully reflect the cathedral towers. The top floor

Gothic Madonna and Child, Cathedral Museum

is a café-restaurant, from where you get a great view over Vienna.

One of the original Baroque structures is the Bartolotti Palace, at the corner of Dorotheergasse. Next to it is a popular Trzesniewski Sandwich Buffet. Further along Dorotheergasse, at No. 11, is the **Jewish Museum** (Jüdisches Museum), which moved into the former Eskeles Palace from the old synagogue. The museum chronicles the history of Jews in Vienna.

Otto Wagner, an outstanding architect of the Viennese Secession, had his studio at Graben No.10; in the 1980s, the house belonged to the eccentric Austrian artist Friedensreich Hundertwasser.

Stephansdom ❸

See pp58–9.

Dom- und Diözesanmuseum ❹

Stephansplatz 6. **Map** 2 C4.
📞 *51 552-35 60.* Ⓤ *Stephansplatz.*
🚌 *1A, 2A, 3A.* 🕐 *10am–5pm Tue–Sat.* 📷 🆆 *www.dommuseum.at*

THE CATHEDRAL museum contains a large collection of sacral paintings and sculptures, as well as fascinating examples of folk art. Many pieces were donated to the cathedral by Duke Rudolf IV. Star exhibits include the famous portrait of the duke (c.1360), and the *Erlacher Madonna*, a life-size statue of the Madonna and Child, a Gothic masterpiece (c.1330) from Lower Austria. The Cathedral Museum also holds sacral vessels and reliquaries from St Stephen's Cathedral, valuable masterpieces of the Gothic, Baroque and Romantic eras, and the Otto Mauer collection of 20th-century Austrian art.

Figarohaus ❺

Domgasse 5. **Map** 2 C4.
【 51 36 294. ⓤ *Stephansplatz.*
▥ *1A.* ◯ *9am–6pm Tue–Sun.*
● *1 Jan, 1 May, 25 Dec.* 🈚 🄾

DOMGASSE 5 is the most famous of Mozart's various homes in Vienna. He lived here with his family in 1784–7, and composed many of his masterpieces here, including *The Marriage of Figaro*, which gave the house its name. The first-floor apartment – where Mozart actually resided – has been turned into a museum, commemorating his life and work.

Deutschordenskirche St. Elisabeth ❻

Singerstraße 7. **Map** 2 C4.
【 51 21 065. ⓤ *Stephansplatz.*
▥ *1A.* **Church** ◯ *7am–6pm daily.*
Treasury ◯ *10am–noon Mon, Thu, Sat, 3–5pm Wed, Fri, Sat* 🈚

THE KNIGHTS of the Teutonic Order arrived in Vienna in the 13th century. They established their quarters near the Stephansdom, but only the tower still stands today. In the 15th century, they built the present Gothic **church** of St Elizabeth. Its Baroque façade, added between 1725 and 1735, hides the original Gothic features.

In 1807, when Napoleon abolished the Order of Teutonic Knights in Eastern Prussia, the knights moved their headquarters to Vienna and

brought the Order Treasury here. The four rooms of the **Treasury** hold collections of objects associated with the history of the Order: insignia of the Grand Masters, coins, medals, seals, sacral vessels and tableware, as well as masterpieces of European art collected by the knights.

The walls of the church are hung with the coats of arms of the Teutonic knights. The beautiful winged altar (1520) is made from elaborate carved and painted panels depicting scenes from the Passion, surrounded by intricate tracery.

Within the complex of buildings belonging to the Order is the apartment where Mozart first lived in Vienna, later occupied by Johannes Brahms (1863–5).

Franziskanerkirche ❼

Franziskanerplatz 4. **Map** 2 C4.
【 51 24 578. ⓤ *Stephansplatz.* ◯
7:30–11:30am, 2:30–5:30pm daily.

IN THE 14TH CENTURY, the Franciscans took over this church, originally built by wealthy citizens as a "house of the soul" for prostitutes wishing to reform. The present church, designed in the South German Renaissance style by Bonaventura Daum, was built in 1601–11. Its façade is topped by a scrolled gable with obelisks and carvings. The interior was decorated by Austrian and Italian masters of the Baroque, including Andrea Pozzo and Johann Georg Schmidt. An axe has been stuck in

the wooden statue of Madonna and Child above the tabernacle, known as *Madonna and Axe*, ever since an attack during the religious wars. The Moses Fountain in front of the church dates from 1798.

A charming 18th-century wall fountain, Academy of Science

Dr.-Ignaz-Seipel-Platz ❽

Map 3 D4. ⓤ *Schwedenplatz.* ▥ *1A.*

DR. IGNAZ SEIPEL, a conservative politician, was twice Chancellor of Austria in the 1920s. The square bearing his name is one of the most attractive in Vienna. At its centre (at No. 2) stands a Rococo structure designed by Jean Nicolas Jadot de Ville-Issey, originally intended as part of the Old University. Since 1857 it has served as the headquarters of the Österreichische Akademie der Wissenschaften (Austrian Academy of Sciences). The frescoes on the ceiling of the Rococo assembly hall, painted by Gregorio Guglielmi, show an allegory of the four academic faculties. Damaged by fire in 1961, they have been meticulously restored, together with the rest of the hall.

Opposite the Academy of Sciences stands the impressive High Baroque Jesuitenkirche. The Jesuits took over the university in the 1620s and, from 1703–5, rebuilt the church next to it, with a new façade and interior, the works of the Italian painter Andrea Pozzo.

The impressive winged altarpiece in Deutschordenskirche

Stephansdom  ❸

SITUATED IN THE centre of Vienna, the cathedral, dedicated to the first Christian martyr, St Stephen, is the very soul of the city. Although built on this site some 800 years ago, the present building is mainly late-Gothic in style – the only fragments remaining of the original 13th-century Romanesque church are the Giants' Doorway and the Towers of the Heathens. Largely destroyed during World War II, the cathedral was restored to its former glory by the efforts of the entire nation. In a vault beneath its main altar are urns containing the internal organs of some of the Habsburgs – other body parts were kept elsewhere in Vienna.

Rudolf IV the Founder

★ Giants' Doorway
This masterpiece of late-Romanesque art, with its richly carved portal and the twin Towers of the Heathens, stands on the site of an earlier heathen shrine.

The North Tower, housing the Pummerin Bell

Entrance to the catacombs

★ Cathedral's Pulpit
The pulpit in the main nave is decorated with portraits of the Four Fathers of the Church. The sculptor himself looks on from a "window" below, under the stairs.

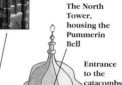

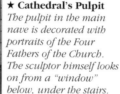

Singer Gate
At one time, this was the entrance for male visitors. The superb sculptures depict scenes from the life of St Paul, and Duke Rudolf IV the Founder.

Main entrance

Lifts to the bell

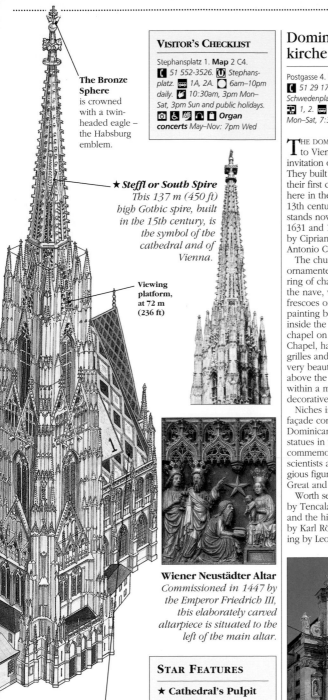

The Bronze Sphere is crowned with a twin-headed eagle – the Habsburg emblem.

★ **Steffl or South Spire**
This 137 m (450 ft) high Gothic spire, built in the 15th century, is the symbol of the cathedral and of Vienna.

Viewing platform, at 72 m (236 ft)

The mosaic roof is covered with almost 250,000 glazed tiles.

VISITOR'S CHECKLIST

Stephansplatz 1. **Map** 2 C4.
📞 51 552-3526. Ⓤ *Stephansplatz.* 🚌 *1A, 2A.* 🕐 *6am–10pm daily.* 📷 *10:30am, 3pm Mon–Sat, 3pm Sun and public holidays.*
📷 ♿ 🎧 📷 📷 **Organ concerts** *May–Nov: 7pm Wed*

Wiener Neustädter Altar
Commissioned in 1447 by the Emperor Friedrich III, this elaborately carved altarpiece is situated to the left of the main altar.

STAR FEATURES

★ **Cathedral's Pulpit**

★ **Giants' Doorway**

★ **Steffl** – the South Spire

Dominikaner-kirche ❾

Postgasse 4. **Map** 3 D4.
📞 51 29 174. Ⓤ *Stephansplatz, Schwedenplatz, Stubentor.*
🚋 *1, 2.* 🚌 *1A.* 🕐 *7am–7pm Mon–Sat, 7:30am–9pm Sun.*

THE DOMINICAN monks came to Vienna in 1226, at the invitation of Duke Leopold VI. They built and consecrated their first church and convent here in the second half of the 13th century. The church that stands now, built between 1631 and 1674, was designed by Ciprian Biasino and Antonio Canevale.

The church has a richly ornamented interior, with a ring of chapels surrounding the nave, with early-Baroque frescoes on the ceiling and a painting by Franz Geyling inside the dome. The second chapel on the right, St Vincent Chapel, has swirling Rococo grilles and candelabra, and a very beautiful gilt organ above the west door, set within a mid-18th century decorative enclosure.

Niches in the majestic façade contain statues of Dominican saints. The two statues in the corner recesses commemorate two great scientists and medieval religious figures, St Albert the Great and St Thomas Aquinas.

Worth seeing are the frescoes by Tencala and Rauchmiller, and the high altar (1839–40) by Karl Rösner, with a painting by Leopold Kuppelwieser.

The majestic Baroque façade of Dominikanerkirche

Österreichisches Museum für Angewandte Kunst ⑩

Stubenring 5. **Map** 3 D4.
📞 71 136-0. 🚋 1, 2. 🚌 74A. Ⓤ Stubentor, Landstraße. Ⓢ Landstraße.
🕐 10am–midnight Tue, 10am–6pm Wed–Sun. 🎟️ Admission free Sat.
🅦 www.mak.at

THE AUSTRIAN Museum of Applied Arts (MAK), founded in 1864, the first of its kind in Europe, exercised a strong influence on the development of the applied arts for some time. It houses the archives and collections of the Wiener Werkstätte – workshops famous for their promotion of good design.

The building was designed by one of the Ring architects, Heinrich von Ferstel, in Florentine Renaissance style. A new wing was added in 1909, and the museum was completely refurbished in 1993. Each room is unique, designed by a different artist, thus creating a fine setting for the items on display.

The permanent collection includes glass, pottery, porcelain, jewellery, metalwork, furniture, textiles, Eastern carpets and decorative items from the Far East. Separate rooms are devoted to the Secession period.

Biedermeier-style sofa, in MAK

Urania ⑪

Uraniastraße 1. **Map** 3 E3.
📞 71 26 191–15. 🚋 1, 2, 21, N.
Ⓤ Schwedenplatz. **Planetarium**
🕐 Apr–Sep: 9pm Tue, Fri, Sat; Oct–Mar: 8pm Tue, Fri, Sat.
🅦 www.urania-sternwarte.at

ON THE SOUTH side of Julius-Raab-Platz, on the banks of the Danube Canal, stands a round building with a distinctive dome that is visible from afar. Urania, named after the Greek muse, was built in 1910 to designs by Max Fabian. It is the home of Vienna's oldest educational establishment that is not a school. Inside the building are lecture halls and a theatre for visiting theatre performances as well as the resident puppet theatre; it is also home to a cinema and a **planetarium**. Every year, Urania holds a symposium devoted to the outstanding Austrian writer and Nobel prize winner, Elias Canetti.

Schwedenplatz ⑫

Map 3 D3. Ⓤ Schwedenplatz.

SCHWEDENPLATZ, the Swedish Square, is one of Vienna's busiest spots. Here, on the banks of the Danube Canal, under Schwedenbrücke, is a landing stage with riverboats inviting visitors on to a variety of pleasure cruises.

Another attraction awaits at No. 13: an Italian ice-cream parlour, reputed to sell the best ice cream in Vienna.

In Laurenzberg, on one side of Schwedenplatz, remains of the old town wall can be seen, with a metal ring that was used to tie up horses and an old sign with traffic regulations. Steep, narrow steps lead down to Griechenbeisl, a small cosy Greek bar. Visitors are welcomed by a board showing the *Lieber Augustin*; from the entrance hall you can see down to a small, illuminated cellar where his statue is on display. The story of Augustin, a piper, goes back to the times of the Great Plague in Vienna. In a drunken stupor, he slumped into the gutter. When undertakers mistook him for dead and threw him into a plague pit, he woke up and terrified them by singing: *O du lieber Augustin…* (Oh, dear Augustin). Miraculously, he survived, and today, tourists wishing to return to Vienna throw a coin into the cellar.

Ivy-clad façade of Ruprechtskirche

Ruprechtskirche ⑬

Ruprechtsplatz. **Map** 2 C3.
📞 53 56 003. Ⓤ Schwedenplatz.
🚋 2A, 3A. 🕐 Sep–Jun: 10am–1pm Mon–Fri, during mass: 5pm Sat, 10:30am Sun; Jul–Aug: 10am–1pm Mon–Fri, during mass: 6pm Sat, 10:30am Sun.

THE CHURCH OF St Ruprecht, rising on an escarpment overlooking Ruprechtsplatz, is Vienna's oldest church. At one time, an arm of the Danube flowed nearby with a landing stage for salt transported from Salzburg. According to legend, the church was founded in 740 by disciples of the Salzburg bishop, St Ruprecht, patron saint of salt merchants. The Romanesque nave and three lower floors of the tower date from the 11th century. In the choir is a 12th-century stained-glass window, Vienna's oldest, depicting the Crucifixion and the Virgin Mary on the throne.

Jewish Quarter ⑭

Map 2 C2, 3. Ⓤ Schwedenplatz, Herrengasse. 🚌 1A, 2A, 3A. **Jewish Museum of the Town of Vienna** Palais Eskeles, Dorotheergasse 11.
📞 535 04 31. Ⓤ Stephansplatz. 🕐 10am–6pm Sun–Fri, 10am–8pm Thu.
🎟️ **Museum Judenplatz** Misrachi-Haus, Judenplatz 8. Ⓤ Schwedenplatz, Herrengasse. 🕐 guided tours 11:30am, 3:30pm Sun, 5pm Tue, Thu. 🎟️

A TANGLE OF narrow streets west of Rotenturmstraße makes up the earliest Jewish quarter in Vienna. Today, the

Jewish quarter is a busy area of discothèques, bars and kosher restaurants, but during the Middle Ages, Judenplatz was the site of the Jewish ghetto, with a synagogue, the remains of which can be seen under the square. There was also a Jewish hospital, rabbi's house, bathhouse and school.

Stadttempel, the beautiful present synagogue, is hidden on Seitenstettengasse and guarded by armed police after an attack in 1983.

In 1895, the first **Jewish Museum** in the world was founded here. It was closed down by the Nazis, but a new museum opened in 1993 in Palais Eskeles in Dorotheergasse *(see p56)*. In 2000, the **Museum Judenplatz**, devoted to medieval Jewish life, was opened in Misrachi House. A modern monument by Rachel Whiteread at the centre of the square commemorates the victims of the holocaust.

The Gothic interior of the church Maria am Gestade

Maria am Gestade ⓯

Salvatorgasse 12. **Map** 2 C3. 533 95 94. Ⓤ Schwedenplatz, Stephansplatz. 1A, 3A. 7am–6pm daily.

THE CHURCH OF St Mary's on the Riverbank was once flooded by the waters of an old Danube canal, but today it rises on a steep escarpment, its lofty, 56-m (180-ft) high Gothic steeple dominating the town. The stone helmet at the top of the steeple is a masterpiece of Viennese Gothic art.

First mentioned in the 12th century, the present building dates from the late 1300s. It was used as an arsenal during Napoleon's occupation of the city in 1809, but later restored.

Inside, the stained-glass panes behind the main altar are mostly original medieval features. The pillars are adorned with six Gothic statues, plus some from the 17th and 19th centuries. To the left of the main altar is a chapel with a Renaissance stone altar, adorned with colourful painted carvings. The church also holds the tomb of Clemens Maria Hofbauer, the city's patron saint.

Altes Rathaus ⓰

Wipplingerstraße 8. **Map** 2 B3. Ⓤ Schwedenplatz, Stephansplatz. 1, 2. 1A, 3A. **Archives and Museum of the Austrian Resistance** 53 436–90319. 9am–5pm Mon–Thu (by appointment only).

VIENNA'S OLDEST town hall probably first stood at neighbouring Tuchlaubenstraße. The building at Wipplingerstraße was once owned by the rich and influential brothers Otto and Heymo Neuburg, who headed a burghers' rebellion against the Habsburgs. In 1309, Prince Friedrich the Fair confiscated

Ironwork at the entrance to Altes Rathaus, in Wipplingerstraße

the building and gave it to the town. It served as the town's main administrative centre until 1883.

The entrance of Altes Rathaus is festooned with beautiful Baroque ironwork. In the courtyard stands the Andromeda Fountain (1741), the last work of the sculptor Georg Raphael Donner. A door leads from the courtyard to Salvatorkapelle (St Saviour's chapel), the former Neuburg family chapel, which has a Renaissance portal (1520–30), facing Salvatorgasse, a rare example in Vienna of the Italian Renaissance style.

Today, the Old Town Hall houses the **Archives and Museum of the Austrian Resistance**, devoted to the memory of those who risked their lives by opposing National Socialism in Austria, in the years 1934–45.

VIENNA'S JEWS – PAST AND PRESENT

A Jewish merchant community thrived in Vienna from the 12th century, with the original Jewish quarter centred around Judenplatz. During the 1421 persecutions many Jews were murdered, while others were forced to convert to the Christian faith or to leave the town. The 1781 Edict of Tolerance, issued by Joseph II, lifted legal constraints on Jews, and the centre of Jewish life gradually moved to the opposite bank of the Danube Canal, around the Prater. In 1938, some 200,000 Jews lived in Vienna, contributing to its cultural and intellectual life. After Nazi persecution, only 7,000 remained. Now Eastern European immigrants are again adding to their total number.

The lavish interior of Stadttempel

Anker Clock in Hoher Markt, with cut-out historical figures

Hoher Markt ⑰

Map 2 C3. Ⓤ *Stephansplatz, Schwedenplatz.* 🚌 *1A, 3A.*

H OHER MARKT is the oldest square in Vienna. After World War II, the foundations of the Roman military camp of Vindobona, where Emperor Marcus Aurelius died in AD 180, were discovered under the square. The ruins are now a popular tourist attraction.

In medieval times, fish and cloth markets as well as executions were held in the square. Since the early 18th century, it has been a venue for town court trials.

The Ankeruhr (Anker Clock), above the way to Bauernmarkt, is a copper and bronze sculptural clock designed in 1911 by Franz von Matsch. It features 12 historical figures who contributed to Vienna's development and reputation. Every hour one of these emerges, and at noon the entire set parades past. The procession is headed by Marcus Aurelius, followed by Rudolf IV, and closes with the composer Joseph Haydn.

In the centre of the square stands the Baroque Josephs-brunnen (Joseph's fountain) or Vermählungsbrunnen (nuptial fountain), commissioned by Leopold I and designed by Johann Bernhard Fischer von Erlach, depicting Joseph and Mary's betrothal.

Böhmische Hofkanzlei ⑱

Judenplatz 11. **Map** 2 B3.
🏛 *53 122.* Ⓤ *Stephansplatz.*
🚌 *1A, 3A.* 🕐 *7:30am–3:30pm Mon–Fri.* Ⓦ *www.vfgh.gv.at*

T HE HABSBURG rulers were also kings of Bohemia, which was initially governed from Prague; in 1627, however, Emperor Ferdinand II transferred the administration to Vienna. In 1714, the Bohemian Court Chancery moved into this grand palace, designed by Johann Bernhard Fischer von Erlach, and henceforth the Austrian emperors ruled Bohemia from here.

The vast original Baroque portals, with sculptures added later by Lorenzo Mattielli, create a harmonious exterior, which is subtle yet powerful. Also noteworthy are the beautiful carved and elegantly curved window frames.

Schulhof ⑲

Map 2 B3. Ⓤ *Stephansplatz, Herrengasse.* 🚌 *1A, 2A, 3A.*
🚊 *1, 2, 37, 38, 40, 41, 42, 43.*
Clock Museum 🏛 *53 32 265.*
🕐 *9am–4:30pm Tue–Sun.*
⬤ *1 Jan, 1 May, 25 Dec.* 🎟 *Free admission – 9am–12pm Fri.*
Doll and Toy Museum
🏛 *53 56 860.* 🕐 *10am–6pm Tue–Sun and public holidays.*

S CHULHOF IS a small alley connecting the imperial Am Hof square with the

Musical doll from the Doll and Toy Museum in Schulhof

elegant residential area of Kurrentgasse.

The building at No. 2, the former Obizzi Palace (1690), now houses a fascinating **Clock Museum**. Its collection includes some 3,000 exhibits, ranging from 16th-century tower clock mechanisms to the latest inventions and astronomical clocks.

The Baroque building at No. 4 houses the **Doll and Toy Museum**. A private collection opened to the public in 1989, it comprises dolls and toys from the past two centuries, mainly of French and German origin. It also exhibits doll houses, theatres, model trains, mechanical toys and teddy bears. Particularly intriguing are the early 20th-century examples of "exotic" dolls: African, Polynesian and Oriental. Historical dolls are on sale in the museum shop.

A short distance from here, at No 10 Kurrentgasse, is the bakery Grimm, one of the most famous in Vienna.

Am Hof ⑳

Map 2 B3. Ⓤ *Stephansplatz, Schottentor.* 🚌 *1A.*

T HE NAME of the square (meaning "by the Court") refers to the medieval princes' residence nearby. It later housed the mint, and then the royal military chancery. Today it is a bank.

The main architectural gem of present-day Am Hof is the chapel of the Nine Angel Choirs, built in the late 14th century by the Carmelite Friars and rebuilt after the fire of 1607. It was adorned with a Baroque façade crowned with a triangular pediment featuring Our Lady, the queen of the nine angel choirs. The dissolution of the Holy Roman Empire was proclaimed from the chapel's terrace on 6 August 1806.

There are a number of other interesting houses in the square. The building at No. 10 with a magnificent façade incorporating sculptures by Mattielli, is the former citizens' armoury, today housing the headquarters of façade and a magnificent Baroque interior, which still bears features of its former Romanesque decor. Above the tabernacle stands the 13th-century statue of Our Lady, the oldest Romanesque sculpture in Vienna.

The adjacent abbey buildings house a picture gallery with an interesting collection of medieval art.

Other interesting buildings in Freyung include the Baroque Harrach Palace at No. 3, designed by Domenic Martinelli (1690) and, at No. 4, the Kinsky Palace, designed by Johann Lukas von Hildebrandt, who became the court architect in 1700.

Nearby is one of the few remaining, largely unaltered Renaissance buildings, the Porcia Palace of 1546, one of the oldest in Vienna.

At the centre of the square, in a glass-roofed, hexagonal atrium, stands the Austria Fountain. Erected in 1846, it shows an allegorical figure of Austria surrounded by four mermaids representing the major rivers (Danube, Elbe, Po, Vistula) in the Habsburg Empire at the time.

In the courtyard, a tablet from 1571 warns visitors not to carry weapons or fight here. The injunction was famously ignored when the 1848 Revolution was ignited on this very spot. In 1918 the Republic was proclaimed from the Landhaus.

Statue on top of No. 10 Am Hof, the former citizens' armoury

the city's fire services. No. 14 is the Collalto Palace, where, in 1762, the six-year-old Mozart gave his first performance.

In front of the church stands the Mariensäule (Column of Our Lady), a monument commissioned by Ferdinand III to commemorate the end of the threat of the Swedish invasion, at the conclusion of the Thirty Years' War.

Austria Fountain in a courtyard in Freyung Passage

Freyung ㉑

Map 2 B3. Ⓤ Herrengasse. 🚌 1A. 🚋 1, 2, D.

THE SQUARE derives its name from the right of sanctuary (frey is an old word for "free") granted to any fugitive seeking refuge in the Schottenkirche (Scottish church), now at No. 6. The priory church was founded by Irish Benedictine friars, who came to Vienna in 1177. Although much altered, the church has a Neo-Classical

Herrengasse ㉒

Map 2 A3, B4. Ⓤ Herrengasse. 🚌 2A, 3A.

HERRENGASSE was once one of the smartest addresses in Vienna, where the nobility had their palaces. Nowadays, most buildings are occupied by government offices. Herrengasse's name, meaning gentlemen's alleyway, dates from the 16th century, when the Landhaus at No. 13 was the seat of the Provincial Government of Lower Austria, the province surrounding Vienna. It fulfilled this function until 1986, when the small town of St Pölten became the new capital of the province. Some very old parts of the Landhaus still remain; the chapel is believed to have been built by Anton Pilgram, one of the architects of Stephansdom. The present building was rebuilt in 1837–48, under the supervision of Ludwig Pichl.

Liechtenstein Palace, seen from Minoritenplatz

Minoritenplatz ㉓

Map 2 B4. Ⓤ Herrengasse. 🚌 2A, 3A.

THE DOMINANT feature of the square is Minoritenkirche. Built originally by Minor Friars in 1224, the present structure is a Franciscan church from the 14th century. It was rebuilt during the Baroque period, and restored to its original Gothic form in the 19th century. The church retains a fine west portal (1340). The tower acquired its unusual pyramid shape during the Turkish siege of Vienna in 1529, when a shell sliced the top off the steeple. Inside the church is a mosaic copy of Leonardo da Vinci's Last Supper.

Between Minoritenplatz and Bankgasse is the town palace of the Liechtenstein family.

On the south side of the square, at No. 3, is the former palace of the Dietrichstein family. This palace, an early work in 1755 by Franz Hillebrand, now houses the Austrian Chancellor's Office and the Foreign Office. Its rooms have witnessed many historic events.

Street-by-Street: The Hofburg Complex

THE HOFBURG COMPLEX, the former Emperor's residence, is a permanent reminder of the glory of the Habsburg Empire, with its majestic palace – particularly impressive when seen from Heldenplatz – and the harmony of the squares and palaces in Augustiner-straße. This part of Vienna is one of the capital's most fashionable and lively areas, both during the daytime and at night, when the former palace rooms serve as theatre and concert halls.

Michaelerplatz
The Michaelertrakt, on the site of the former court theatre on the south side of the square, was commissioned by Franz Joseph as a passageway and built to designs by Ferdinand Kirschner **24**

MICHAELER
PLATZ

Heldenplatz
The square between Ring and Hofburg is used for large public gatherings **26**

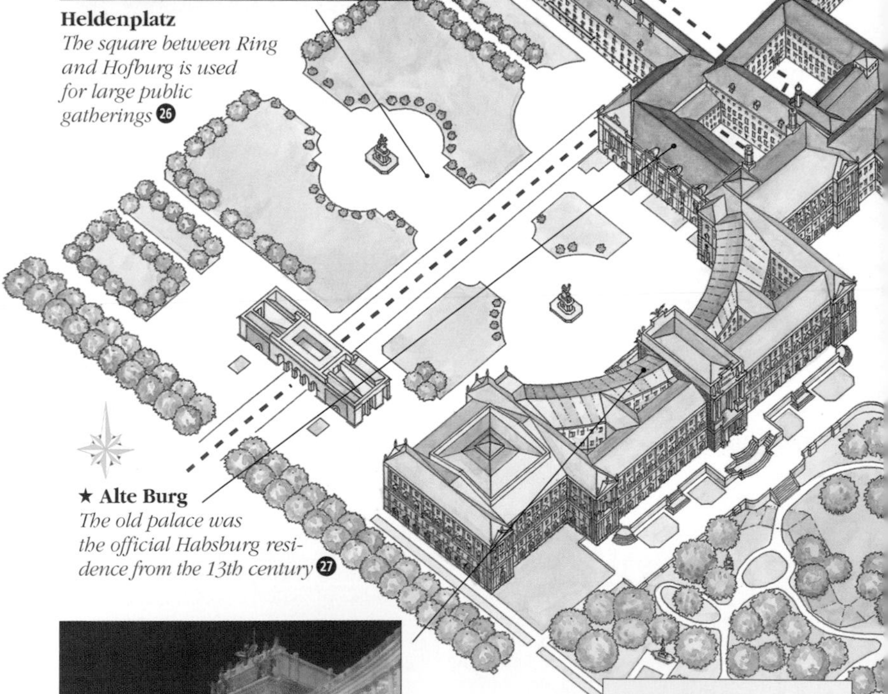

★ **Alte Burg**
The old palace was the official Habsburg resi-dence from the 13th century **27**

Neue Burg, the last wing of Hofburg, was built just before the outbreak of World War I, during the final days of the monarchy.

STAR SIGHTS

★ **Albertina**

★ **Alte Burg**

★ **Josefsplatz**

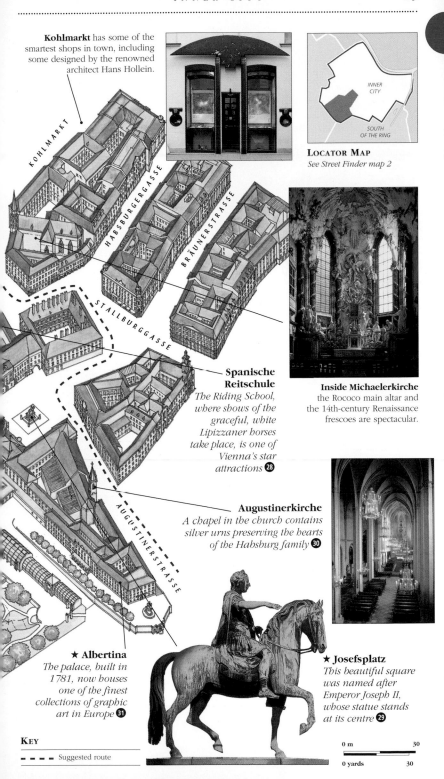

Kohlmarkt has some of the smartest shops in town, including some designed by the renowned architect Hans Hollein.

KOHLMARKT

HABSBURGERGASSE

BRÄUNERSTRASSE

STALLBURGGASSE

AUGUSTINERSTRASSE

LOCATOR MAP
See Street Finder map 2

INNER
CITY

SOUTH
OF THE RING

Spanische Reitschule
The Riding School, where shows of the graceful, white Lipizzaner horses take place, is one of Vienna's star attractions ㉘

Inside Michaelerkirche
the Rococo main altar and the 14th-century Renaissance frescoes are spectacular.

Augustinerkirche
A chapel in the church contains silver urns preserving the hearts of the Habsburg family ㉚

★ **Albertina**
The palace, built in 1781, now houses one of the finest collections of graphic art in Europe ㉛

★ **Josefsplatz**
This beautiful square was named after Emperor Joseph II, whose statue stands at its centre ㉙

KEY

- - - Suggested route

0 m   30

0 yards   30

Stucco angels in Michaelerkirche, in Michaelerplatz

Michaelerplatz ㉔

Map 2 B4. **Ⓤ** *Herrengasse.*
🚌 *2A, 3A.*

Michaelerplatz faces the grand main entrance into the imperial residence, the Michaelertor (St Michael's Doorway), which leads to the Hofburg's inner courtyard. On both sides of the doorway are 19th-century wall fountains, designed by Rudolf Weyer, which represent the empire's land and sea power.

Michaelerkirche (St Michael's Church) was once the parish church of the court. Its oldest parts date from the 13th century. According to legend, the church was built in 1221 by Leopold VI of Babenberg. Its present form dates from 1792, when it was given a Neo-Classical façade, while still preserving its Baroque portal. The interior features one of the most beautiful Rococo altars in Vienna. Above the altar is a stucco relief depicting the expulsion of the rebel angels from heaven and the Archangel Gabriel at the head of the heavenly host.

In the 17th and 18th centuries, affluent parishioners were buried under the church. Their well-preserved corpses, clothed in their burial finery, are displayed in the crypt, in open coffins.

The remains of a Roman encampment, as well as some medieval foundations, were recently discovered underneath the square.

Volksgarten ㉕

Dr.-Karl-Renner-Ring. **Map** 2 A4.
Ⓤ *Herrengasse.* 🚋 *1, 2, D, J.*
🚌 *2A.* ◯ *Apr–Nov: 6am–10pm daily; Dec–Mar: 6:30am–10pm daily.*

Volksgarten (the People's Garden) was created in 1820, when Napoleon had the city walls destroyed. The formal plantations created in the French style, particularly the splendid rose gardens, became a place of relaxation for fashionable society.

People met at one of two Classicist structures by Peter Nobile, Theseustempel (the Temple of Theseus) or Cortisches Kaffeehaus, remains of which are visible in today's Garden Café. Canova's statue of Theseus was meant for the temple, but today it graces Kunsthistorisches Museum *(see pp 84–7)*. Instead, a statue of an athlete (1921) by Joseph Möllner stands in front of the temple. There is also a monument devoted to the writer Franz Grillparzer and a fountain memorial dedicated to Empress Elisabeth.

Heldenplatz ㉖

Map 2 A4, A5. **Ⓤ** *Volkstheater.*
🚋 *1, 2, 46, D, J.* 🚌 *2A.* **Neue Burg** 🗲 *52 524-484.* ◯ *10am–6pm Mon, Wed–Sun.* 📷 🔲

During vienna's grand 19th-century reconstruction, Heldenplatz was planned as the centre of a majestic imperial forum that was to adjoin the old Hofburg complex, surrounded by new buildings housing the emperor's art collection. Neue Burg (New Castle) was completed in 1913, but by then the monarchy was dying out.

The vast, undeveloped Heroes' Square, the largest public space in Vienna, remained. It was here, in March 1938, that Adolf Hitler announced Austria's incorporation into the German Reich.

The entrance to the square is via Burgtor (Palace Gate), built in 1824 to commemorate the victory of the coalition against Napoleon at the Battle of Nations, at Leipzig (1813). Later, it served as the Monument to the Unknown Soldier. The two equestrian statues in the square, by Anton Fernkorn, are of Archduke Charles and Prince Eugene of Saxony.

The latter stands in front of Neue Burg, which now houses, among other sights, the Ephesos Museum, named after the archaeological site in Turkey which yielded the finds displayed here. There is also a collection of early musical instruments, some owned by famous musicians; one of the most impressive arms collections in Europe; and an ethnological museum with valuable Oriental and African exhibits.

The equestrian statue of Prince Eugene of Saxony, on Heldenplatz

Alte Burg ㉗

See pp68–9.

Spanische Reitschule 🄯

THE SPANISH RIDING SCHOOL was founded in 1572. Initially, its circus-style training of horses served a practical purpose, but today performances are staged purely for entertainment, and have become one of the city's top attractions. Shows are held in the building known as the Winterreitschule (Winter Riding School), constructed between 1729 and 1735 by Joseph E. Fischer von Erlach. The Hofburg fire, in 1992, destroyed some of the stables and almost put an end to the school's activities.

VISITORS' CHECKLIST

Michaelerplatz 1. **Map** 2 B4.
📞 53 39 031. Ⓤ Herrengasse, Stephansplatz. 🚌 2A, 3A.
🕐 9am–5:30pm Tue–Sat. 🈂
🌐 www.srs.at

Black bicorn hat with gold braid stripe

Coffee-coloured jacket with rows of brass buttons

Buckskin jodhpurs

Long boots covering the knees

Pale leather gloves

Interior of the Winter Riding School
The opulent interior is lined with 46 columns and adorned with stucco ornaments, chandeliers and a coffered ceiling.

RIDER IN TYPICAL UNIFORM

The riders of the Winter Riding School wear historical uniforms, which are complemented by elegant saddles with embroidered cloth.

THE HORSES' STEPS

The steps made by the horses are part of a carefully orchestrated ballet. The riders perform on the specially trained white Lipizzaner stallions, a breed originally produced by crossing Spanish, Arab and Berber horses.

The Levade
The horse stands on its hind legs, hocks almost touching the ground.

The Capriole
The horse leaps into the air with a simultaneous kick of the hind legs.

The Croupade
The horse leaps into the air with hind legs and forelegs bent under its belly.

The Piaffe
The horse trots on the spot, often between two pillars.

Alte Burg ㉗

THE IMPERIAL PALACE is a vast complex. Its construction was started by the Babenbergs, but the Neue Burg (New Castle) was not completed until 1913. Apart from housing several museums, including in the royal apartments a museum dedicated to Empress Elisabeth, the Alte Burg is today also a conference centre. Different architectural styles are represented in individual parts of the complex: the Gothic Schweizerhof, the Renaissance Stallburg courtyard and the Baroque Josefsplatz.

In der Burg
This large inner courtyard, called "inside the fortress", has a large statue of Franz I, built by Pompeo Marchesi, in 1842–46.

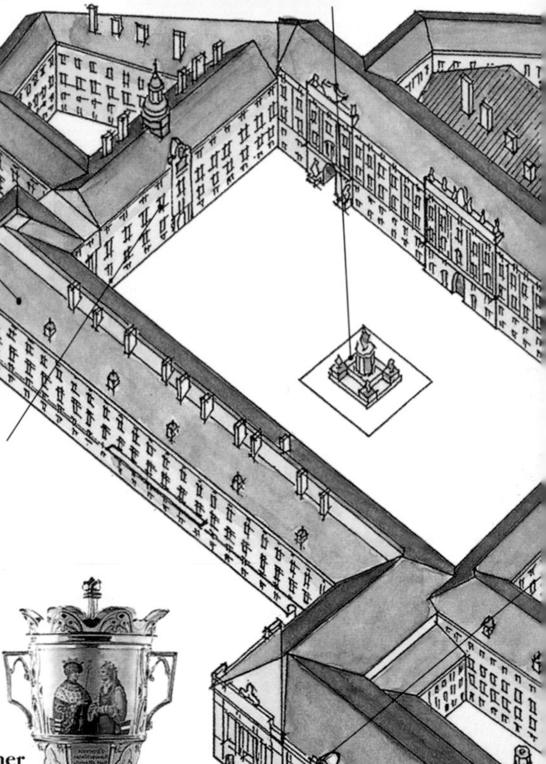

The Leopoldinischer Trakt, dating from 1660–70 and built by Leopold I, today houses the offices of the President of Austria.

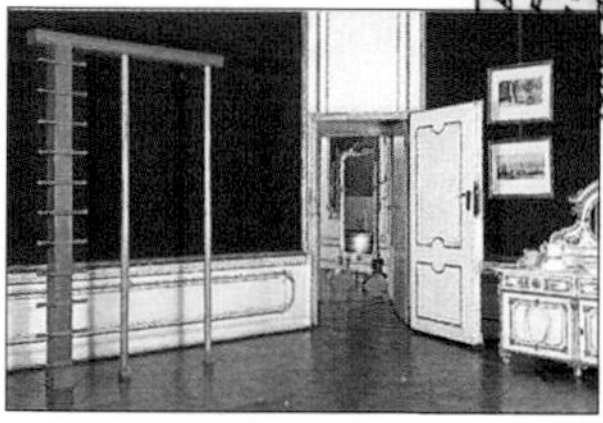

Amalienburg
In the 19th century, this Renaissance palace, built for Rudolf II in 1575, was the home of Empress Elisabeth. Shown above is her dressing room with gymnastic equipment.

The Silberkammer
The Silver Chamber displays stunning silver, gold and porcelain tableware, and vessels used at official receptions, such as this 1821 goblet.

STAR FEATURES

★ **Reichskanzleitrakt**

★ **Schatzkammer**

★ **Schweizertor**

★ **Schweizertor**
The 16th-century Baroque Swiss Gate leads to the oldest parts of the castle, originally a four-tower stronghold.

★ **Reichskanzleitrakt**
Franz Joseph's apartments in the Imperial Chancery Wing, built in 1726–30, are open to visitors. This portrait of Empress Elisabeth (1865) hangs in the Sissi Museum.

VISITORS' CHECKLIST

Michaelerplatz 1. **Map** 2 B4.
Ⓤ *Stephansplatz, Herrengasse.*
🚊 *1, 2, D, J.* 🚌 *57A.*
Imperial Apartments
📞 *533 75 70.*
🕐 *9am–5pm daily.* 📷
Treasury 📞 *52 52 40.*
🕐 *10am–6pm Wed–Mon.* 📷

★ **Schatzkammer**
The collection of sacred and secular treasures, including this 10th-century crown, is regarded as the most magnificent of its kind in the world.

Michaelertor, leading to Hofburg

The Spanische Reitschule stages its world-famous horse riding performances at the Winterreitschule (Winter Riding School).

Stallburg, a Renaissance palace, houses the stables.

Redouten-säle, the former ballrooms

The Burgkapelle
The Gothic Royal Chapel was completed in 1449. The Wiener Sängerknaben (the Vienna Boys' Choir) sings here on Sundays.

Nationalbibliothek
The showpiece of the Austrian National Library (1722–35) is the opulent Prunksaal, or Hall of Honour, panelled in wood.

The magnificent Prunksaal in the National Library, on Josefsplatz

Josefsplatz ㉙

Map 2 B4. **Ⓤ** *Stephansplatz, Herrengasse.* 🚌 *2A, 3A.*

IN THE CENTRE of Josefsplatz stands an equestrian statue (1807) of Joseph II portrayed as a Roman emperor, by Franz Anton Zauner.

Behind the statue, to the right, is the entrance to the National Library building designed by Johann Bernhard Fischer von Erlach. Its Prunksaal (Hall of Honour) is regarded as the most beautiful library in Europe. Frescoes by the Baroque painter Daniel Gran adorn its vault. The walls of the historic reading room are graced by Johann Bergel's frescoes.

Perhaps the grandest items in the library's rich collection are the cartographic treasures exhibited just behind the Prunksaal.

The Redoutensäle, in the wing adjacent to the library and once the Court Ballrooms, now serve as the head office of the Vienna Congress Centre.

On the opposite side of Josefsplatz are two interesting palaces: at No. 5 is the 18th-century Pallavicini Palace by Ferdinand von Hohenberg,

and at No. 6 the 16th-century Palffy Palace by Nikolaus Pacassi. They now serve as cultural venues for the city.

Augustiner-kirche ㉚

Augustinerstraße 3. **Map** 2 B5. **【** *53 37 099.* **Ⓤ** *Stephansplatz, Karlsplatz, Oper.* 🚌 *3A.* ☐ *7am–6pm Mon–Sat, 9am–7pm Sun.*

THE 14TH-CENTURY Gothic Augustinian church was refurbished in the Baroque style, but some 100 years later was restored again to its original character. Inside is one of the most powerful works by Antonio Canova (1805), the tomb of Maria Christina, Maria Theresa's favourite daughter. It is shaped like a pyramid, approached by a funeral procession. St George's Chapel, on the right, contains the tomb of Emperor Leopold II and, further along, is a small crypt with silver urns containing the hearts of the Habsburg family as well as the heart of Napoleon's son, the King of Rome, who died when young.

The church was once the Court Chapel and, as such,

Tomb of Maria Christina in Augustinerkirche

the scene of many historic events including the wedding of Marie Louise (1812) to Napoleon, and that of Elisabeth of Bavaria (Sissi) to Franz Joseph (1854).

Albertina ㉛

Albertinaplatz 1. **Map** 2 B5. **【** *53 483.* **Ⓤ** *Stephansplatz, Karlsplatz.* 🚊 *1, 2, D, J, 62, 65.* 🚌 *2A, 3A.* ☐ *10am–6pm daily, 10am–9pm Wed.*

THE ALBERTINA was once the Habsburg palace of Duke Albert of Sachsen-Teschen and his wife Archduchess Marie-Christina, the favourite daughter of Maria Theresa.

The beautiful Neo-Classical Historic State Rooms in the palace are among the most valuable examples of Classical architecture. They have been opened up to visitors.

The Albertina houses one of the world's finest collection of graphics, including works by Leonardo da Vinci, Michelangelo, Dürer, Rubens, Manet and Cezanne, as well as by Schiele, Klimt and Picasso. It has a million prints, over 65,000 watercolours and drawings and some 70,000 photographs. There is no permanent exhibition, but three halls are available for a programme of around ten temporary exhibitions per year.

Kapuzinerkirche and Kaisergruft ㉜

Neuer Markt. **Map** 2 C5. 🎫 *51 26 853.* Ⓤ *Stephansplatz, Karlsplatz.* 🚌 *3A.* 🕐 *9:30am–4pm, daily.* 🅰

THE CAPUCHIN church stands at the southwestern corner of Neuer Markt, formerly a cereal and flour market. In 1617, Anna of Tyrol, wife of Emperor Matthias, founded a crypt in its vaults in which the Habsburg family members were laid to rest. Today, the Kaisergruft (imperial crypt) contains the earthly remains of 138 family members. The only Habsburg monarchs not present are Ferdinand II, whose vast tomb-mausoleum is in Graz, and Charles I, the last Austrian emperor who died in exile and is buried on Madeira. The only non-Habsburg buried here is Maria Theresa's governess, Countess Caroline Fuchs.

The double sarcophagus of Maria Theresa and her husband Franz Stephan I, the work of Balthasar Ferdinand Moll, is worth looking at. It bears the statues of the imperial couple and four figures with the crowns of Austria, Hungary, Bohemia and Jerusalem (the Habsburgs were also the titular Kings of Jerusalem).

The most poignant tomb is the crypt of Franz Joseph I, where the long-lived monarch rests flanked by separate tombs containing the remains of his wife Elisabeth, assassinated by an Italian anarchist, and their only son Crown Prince Rudolf, who committed suicide in 1889.

Tomb of Karl VI, by Balthasar Moll

The last person to be buried in the imperial crypt was the Empress Zita, wife of Charles I, last Emperor of Austria, who was interred in 1989.

It is worth noting that, on their death, the Habsburgs were dismembered; their hearts are kept in silver urns in Augustinerkirche *(see p70),* their entrails are held in the catacombs of Stephansdom *(see pp58–9),* and only what remained is in the Kaisergruft.

Grand stairway in the Winterpalais des Prinzen Eugen

Winterpalais des Prinzen Eugen ㉝

Himmelpfortgasse 1A. **Map** 2 C5. 🎫 *51 433.* Ⓤ *Stephansplatz.* 🚌 *I8.*

THE PALACE was commissioned in 1694, by Prince Eugene of Savoy, one of the most brilliant military commanders of his day, who entrusted the task to Johann Bernhard Fischer von Erlach. It was subsequently extended by Johann Lukas von Hildebrandt. Its central part includes the original magnificent staircase, adorned with sculptures by Giovanni Giuliani. The central portal reliefs depict the figure of Aeneas carrying his father out of the burning city of Troy, and the hero Hercules who is slaying a monster.

Since 1848, the palace has been home to the Ministry of Finance. It is not open to the public, but visitors may view the famous staircase and glance into the courtyard with its Rococo fountain.

Nearby, at Seilerstätte No. 30, is the Haus der Musik (House of Music). This is a museum dedicated to the Wiener Philharmoniker (Vienna Philharmonic), it also houses a high-tech exhibition on the nature of sound, which allows visitors to see and feel as well as hear music.

Kärntner Straße ㉞

Map 2 B5, C4, C5. Ⓤ *Stephansplatz, Karlsplatz.* 🚋 *1A, 2A, 3A.* 🚆 *1, 2, 62, 65, D, J.*

KÄRNTNER STRASSE was once the main road running south across town to Kärnten (Carinthia), hence its name.

Today, the view down the street is blocked at its Ring end by the silhouette of the opera house, and at the Stock-im-Eisen-Platz end by the modern Haas-Haus, which reflects the spires of the Stephansdom. At Stock-im-Eisen-Platz there is a wooden block into which every passing apprentice ironworker used to drive a nail, in the hope that this would ensure his safe return.

In the mid-section, at No. 37, stands the Malteserkirche (Church of the Knights of Malta). The Maltese Knights came to Vienna in the early 13th century, and the church remains under their jurisdiction to this day. The church walls display the coats of arms of the Grand Masters of the Maltese Order.

Malteserkirche is one of the few older buildings in the street. When Kärntner Straße was widened during the 19th century, to transform it into the old town's main artery, most of the buildings were demolished.

Today, the pedestrianized street is one of Vienna's most fashionable and expensive shopping streets. Here, you can shop at one of many exclusive boutiques, eat and drink in busy restaurants, bars and outdoor cafés, and listen to street musicians or just watch others stroll by.

Frauenhuber, a café near Kärntner Straße

NORTH OF MARIAHILFER STRASSE

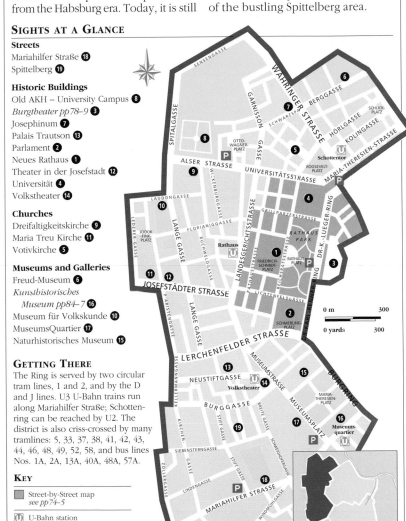

THIS DISTRICT, to the north of Mariahilfer Straße and along the Ring, includes some of the most magnificent and monumental buildings in Vienna. The semicircular Ring or Ringstraße, developed during the 1870s and 1880s, is a grand boulevard divided into nine sections, each named after architectural landmarks or prominent politicians from the Habsburg era. Today, it is still

Figure of a saint in Sankt-Ulrichs-Platz

Vienna's most prestigious street. In this district visitors will find many of the city's cultural institutions, including the biggest concentration of museums in Austria. Mariahilfer Straße is also a very busy shopping street, with large department stores and many cafés and bars, concentrated especially in the cobbled, pedestrianized streets of the bustling Spittelberg area.

SIGHTS AT A GLANCE

Streets
Mariahilfer Straße ⑱
Spittelberg ⑲

Historic Buildings
Old AKH – University Campus ⑧
Burgtheater pp78–9 ③
Josephinum ⑦
Palais Trautson ⑬
Parlament ②
Neues Rathaus ①
Theater in der Josefstadt ⑫
Universität ④
Volkstheater ⑭

Churches
Dreifaltigkeitskirche ⑨
Maria Treu Kirche ⑪
Votivkirche ⑤

Museums and Galleries
Freud-Museum ⑥
Kunsthistorisches Museum pp84–7 ⑯
Museum für Volkskunde ⑩
MuseumsQuartier ⑰
Naturhistorisches Museum ⑮

GETTING THERE

The Ring is served by two circular tram lines, 1 and 2, and by the D and J lines. U3 U-Bahn trains run along Mariahilfer Straße; Schottenring can be reached by U2. The district is also criss-crossed by many tramlines: 5, 33, 37, 38, 41, 42, 43, 44, 46, 48, 49, 52, 58, and bus lines Nos. 1A, 2A, 13A, 40A, 48A, 57A.

KEY

- ▢ Street-by-Street map see pp74–5
- Ⓤ U-Bahn station
- Ⓟ Parking
- ⓘ Tourist information

◁ **The opulent façade of Neues Rathaus by night, in the pre-Christmas period**

Street-by-Street: Around the Town Hall

THE most prestigious buildings in Vienna were
erected in the second half of the 19th century,
in Ringstraße, at the command of Emperor Franz
Joseph I. These include Neues Rathaus (the new
town hall, seat of the town administration), the
immense Parliament (the seat of Austria's Upper
and Lower Houses), the magnificent buildings of
the University, and the Burgtheater.

The square in front of the town hall, with its
adjacent park, is Vienna's largest open-air arena,
serving as a stage for theatre and concert performances, and in the summer for vast film screenings.

**The Town Hall
forecourt** turns into a
vast Christmas market
in December, selling
gifts and Christmas
decorations.

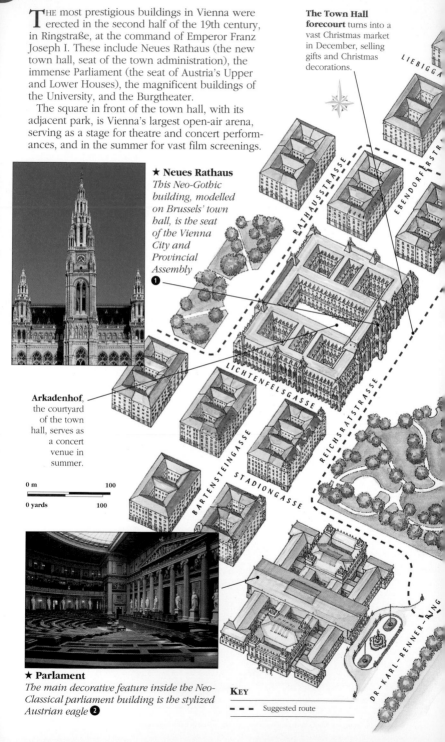

★ Neues Rathaus
*This Neo-Gothic
building, modelled
on Brussels' town
hall, is the seat
of the Vienna
City and
Provincial
Assembly* ❶

Arkadenhof,
the courtyard
of the town
hall, serves as
a concert
venue in
summer.

0 m   100

0 yards   100

★ Parlament
*The main decorative feature inside the Neo-
Classical parliament building is the stylized
Austrian eagle* ❷

KEY

– – – Suggested route

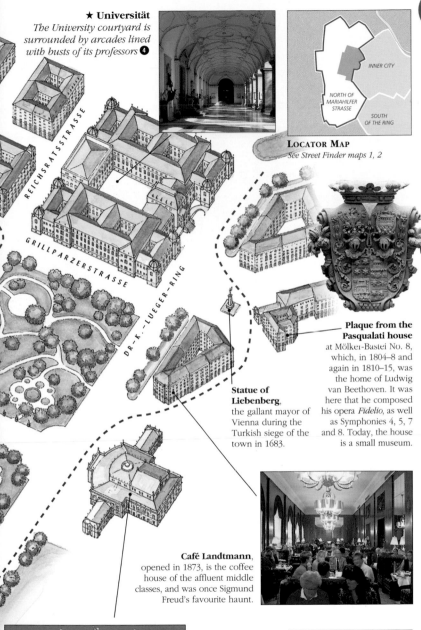

★ Universität
The University courtyard is surrounded by arcades lined with busts of its professors ❹

LOCATOR MAP
See Street Finder maps 1, 2

INNER CITY

NORTH OF MARIAHILFER STRASSE

SOUTH OF THE RING

Plaque from the Pasqualati house
at Mölker-Bastei No. 8, which, in 1804–8 and again in 1810–15, was the home of Ludwig van Beethoven. It was here that he composed his opera *Fidelio*, as well as Symphonies 4, 5, 7 and 8. Today, the house is a small museum.

Statue of Liebenberg,
the gallant mayor of Vienna during the Turkish siege of the town in 1683.

Café Landtmann,
opened in 1873, is the coffee house of the affluent middle classes, and was once Sigmund Freud's favourite haunt.

REICHSRATSSTRASSE

GRILLPARZERSTRASSE

DR.-K.-LUEGER-RING

★ Burgtheater
The high attic above the centre of the building is decorated with a frieze depicting a Bacchanalian procession ❸

STAR SIGHTS

★ Burgtheater

★ Neues Rathaus

★ Parlament

★ Universität

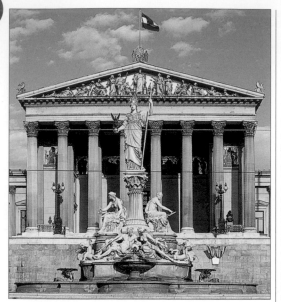

Pallas Athena monument in front of the parliament building

Neues Rathaus ❶

Friedrich-Schmidt-Platz 1. **Map** 1 C3.
(52 550. **Ⓤ** Rathaus. **🚊** 1, 2, D.
◯ **✉** 1pm Mon, Wed, Fri. Telephone
reservations for group visits. **◼**
during meetings and public holidays.

THE NEW TOWN HALL, built in
1872–83 by Friedrich
Schmidt, lies in an attractive
park. The symmetrical, triple
façade of the Neo-Gothic
building faces Ringstraße.
Its huge central tower, 98 m
(321 ft) high, is topped by the
statue of a knight-in-armour,
one of Vienna's symbols. The
main tower is flanked by two
smaller towers, 60 m (197 ft)
high. The town hall cellar is a
restaurant. The whole length
of the first floor is taken up
by a reception hall. The forecourt is used for many events,
including the Christmas fair.

Parlament ❷

Dr.-Karl-Renner-Ring 3. **Map** 1 C4.
(40 11 00-25 70. **Ⓤ** Volkstheater.
🚊 1, 2, D, J. **✉** 11am, 3pm Mon–
Thu; 11am, 1pm, 2pm, 3pm Fri.
Ⓦ www.parlament.gv.at

TODAY'S ASSEMBLY HALL of
Austria's two-chamber
parliament originally served as

the location of the highest
legislative body of the Austrian
part of the Austro-Hungarian
Empire. An imposing Neo-
Classical building, the Parlament was completed in 1883
to designs by the Dutch architect, Theophil Hansen.
The entrance is raised
above street level. A gently
sloping ramp leads to the
main portico, which is modelled on a Greek temple. Both
the ramp and the attic are
adorned with carved marble
figures of Greek and Roman
historians, scholars and states-
men. The relief depicts
the Emperor Franz Joseph I
handing the constitution to

the representatives of the
17 peoples of the Empire.
The magnificently decorated
state apartments and conference rooms can be visited in
a guided tour. The lower
vestibule contains busts of
prominent members of the
Austrian National Assembly.
The side wings have four
bronze chariot groups, each
driven by Nike, the Greek
goddess of victory. Another,
smaller statue of Nike is held
aloft by her fellow goddess, of
wisdom, Pallas Athena, whose
5-m (16-ft) statue is the main
feature of the monumental
fountain in front of the
central portico, designed by
Karl Kundmann and placed
here in 1902. It is flanked by
allegorical figures representing Law Enforcement (left)
and Legislation (right), as well
as figures symbolizing the
major rivers of the empire.

Burgtheater ❸

See pp78–9.

Universität ❹

Dr.-Karl-Lueger-Ring 1. **Map** 2 A3.
(42 77 0. **Ⓤ** Schottentor. **🚊**
1, 41, 42, 43, 44. **🚌** 1A.

VIENNA UNIVERSITY is the
oldest university in the
German-speaking world and
the third oldest in Central
Europe, after Prague and
Cracow. It was founded in
1365, by Rudolf IV, and
flourished and grew in the
late 15th century. Its present

The main building of Vienna University

home, designed by Heinrich Ferstel in the style of the Italian Renaissance, was completed in 1883.

The university complex has its buildings arranged around one large and eight smaller courtyards. The courtyard arcades, modelled on the Palazzo Farnese in Rome, are adorned with statues of famous scholars associated with Vienna University, including one of Freud.

Neo-Gothic stone figures from the façade of Votivkirche

Votivkirche ❺

Rooseveltplatz 8. **Map** 2 A2.
C 40 61 192. **U** Schottentor.
🚊 1, 2, 37, 38, 43, 44, D. ☐ 9am–1pm, 4–6:30pm Tue–Sat, 9am–1pm Sun

OPPOSITE THE spot where a deranged man tried to assassinate Franz Joseph I in 1853, stands this Neo-Gothic church with its two 99-m (325-ft) high, lacy steeples completed 26 years later as a grateful offering for sparing the Emperor's life. The architect was Heinrich von Ferstel.

The most beautiful historic relic in the Votivkirche is its late 15th-century Antwerpian altar, a masterpiece of Flemish woodcarving, representing scenes from the Passion. The main portal sculptures depict the four Evangelists and figures from the Old Testament, along with four patrons of the Empire's regions.

Many of the chapels inside the church are dedicated to the Austrian regiments and to military heroes.

Sigmund Freud's waiting room in the Freud-Museum

Freud-Museum ❻

Berggasse 19. **Map** 2 A1.
C 31 91 596. **U** Schottentor.
🚊 37, 38, 40, 41, 42, D. 🚌 40A.
☐ Jul–Oct: 9am–6pm daily; Oct–Jun: 9am–5pm daily. 🖼
W www.freud-museum.at

BERGGASSE NO. 19, a typical 20th-century Viennese town house, was the home of Sigmund Freud, the famous doctor and father of psychoanalysis, from 1891–1938. Here he created his most acclaimed works and treated patients before he was forced to flee Austria at the arrival of the National Socialists.

The room in which Freud received patients is on the mezzanine floor. In the small, dark lobby hangs Freud's frayed hat; in a corner stands his travel trunk. A cabinet contains some archaeological objects collected by Freud. The world-famous couch, however, now stands in the Freud museum in London.

A Foundation for the Arts was initiated in 1989 in order to confront a scientific institution with contemporary art.

Josephinum ❼

Wahringerstraße 25. **Map** 1 C2.
C 42 77-63 401. **U** Schottentor.
🚊 37, 38, 40, 41, 42. ☐ 9am–3pm Mon–Fri, 10am–2pm 1st Sat of the month. 🔴 public holidays. 🖼

DESIGNED BY Isidor Canevale and built in 1783–85, this building once housed the Military Surgical Institute. Life-sized anatomical wax models, commissioned by Joseph II to teach human anatomy to his army surgeons, are now the main attraction of the medical museum based here today.

Old AKH – University Campus ❽

Alsergasse 4. **Map** 1 A1, B1.
U Schottentor. **Federal Museum of Pathological Anatomy** **C** 40 68 672. ☐ 3–6pm Wed, 8–11am Thu, 10am–1pm 1st Sat of the month. 🔴 Public holidays. **W** www.univie.ac.at/universiätscampus

VIENNA 's Old General Hospital (AKH), built in 1784, was donated to the Unversity of Vienna in 1988 and adapted to house the 15 academic faculties of the university. It was inaugurated in 1998 as university campus. The complex consists of several buildings around one vast and 12 smaller courtyards. The Narrenturm (Madman's Tower) of the former lunatic asylum, designed by Canevale, now houses the **Federal Museum for Pathological Anatomy**.

FREUD'S THEORIES

With his theory of psychoanalysis, Sigmund Freud (1856–1939) has exerted a lasting influence not only on medicine but also on our culture generally. According to Freud, the unconscious psyche, driven by certain instincts and impulses, in particular the sexual instinct (libido), is the main engine behind all our conscious and unconscious actions. An imbalance in the psychological system, so posited Freud, could lead to very serious emotional disorders and might result in severe mental disturbance.

Various objects used by Sigmund Freud

Burgtheater ❸

T HE BURGTHEATER IS one of the most prestigious stages in the German-speaking world. The original theatre, built in Maria Theresa's reign, was replaced in 1888 by today's Italian Renaissance-style building by Karl von Hasenauer and Gottfried Semper. In 1897, after the discovery that the auditorium had several seats with no view of the stage, it closed for refurbishment. A bomb devastated the building in 1945, leaving only the side wings and Grand Staircases intact, but subsequent restoration was so successful that today the damage is hard to see.

JOHANN
NESTROY
1801 – 1862

Statue of the muse, Melpomene

Ceiling frescoes
by the Klimt brothers, Gustav and Ernst, and Franz Matsch cover the north and south wings.

Busts of Playwrights
Lining the walls of the Grand Staircases are busts of playwrights whose works are still performed here, including this one of Johann Nepomuk Nestroy (left) by Hans Knesl.

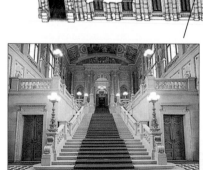

★ Grand Staircases
The two majestic gala staircases in the side wings are the only original parts of the building that escaped destruction in World War II.

Main entrance on Dr.-Karl-Lueger-Ring

STAR FEATURES
★ **Der Thespiskarren**
★ **Front Façade**
★ **Grand Staircases**

Foyer
The walls of the curving first-floor foyer are lined with the portraits of famous actors and actresses.

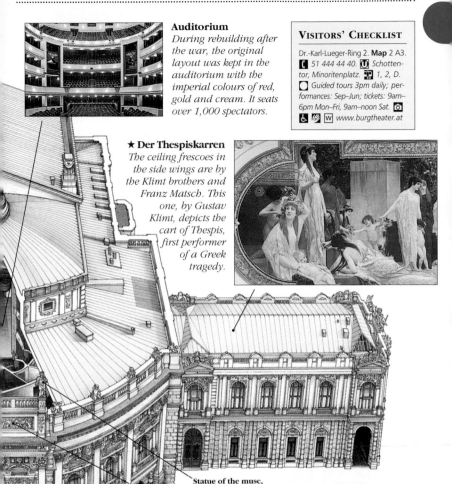

Auditorium
During rebuilding after the war, the original layout was kept in the auditorium with the imperial colours of red, gold and cream. It seats over 1,000 spectators.

★ Der Thespiskarren
The ceiling frescoes in the side wings are by the Klimt brothers and Franz Matsch. This one, by Gustav Klimt, depicts the cart of Thespis, first performer of a Greek tragedy.

Statue of the musc, Thalia

★ Front Façade
The façade is crowned by a frieze of Bacchus and Ariadne, by Rudolf Weyr. Above the frieze towers the statue of Apollo.

TIMELINE

1741 Maria Theresa founds the Burgheater in an empty ballroom at the Hofburg, to stage mainly Italian operas

1874 Work on the present building begins

1955 After its destruction in World War II, the theatre reopens with Grillparzer's *King Ottokar*

1750	1850	1900	1950

1776 Joseph II reorganizes the theatre and promotes it to the status of a national theatre

The Old Burgtheater in the Michaelaplatz in Hofburg, in the mid-18th century

14 Oct 1888 The Burgtheater opens in the presence of the Emperor Franz Joseph I and family

Dreifaltigkeitskirche der Minoriten ❾

Alserstraße 17. **Map** 1 B2.
📞 *40 57 225.* ⓤ *Rathaus.* 🚋 *5, 33, 43.* ⏰ *7:30am–noon Mon–Fri, Sun, 7:30–8:30am Sat.*

BUILT BETWEEN 1685 and 1727, the church of the Holy Trinity is a typical Baroque structure, with a twin-tower façade. It contains an altarpiece (1708) in the north aisle by the painter Martino Altomonte, and a beautiful crucifix in the south aisle from the workshop of Veit Stoß.

In 1827, the body of the composer Ludwig van Beethoven was brought to this church, from Schwarzspanierhaus in neighbouring Garnisonsgasse, where he had died. Following the funeral service, attended by his contemporaries (including Schubert and the playwright Franz Grillparzer), the cortège conveyed his coffin to its final resting place, the cemetery in Währing, on the city outskirts.

16th-century crucifix in the Dreifaltigkeitskirche

Museum für Volkskunde ❿

Laudongasse 15–19. **Map** 1 B3.
📞 *40 68 905.* ⓤ *Rathaus.* 🚋 *5, 33, 43, 44.* 🚌 *13A.* ⏰ *10am–5pm Tue–Sun.* 📷 ♿ ⓦ *www.volkskundemuseum.at*

NEAR A QUIET park stands the charming Austrian Folklore Museum. Founded in

Entrance to the Museum für Volkskunde, in Schönborn Palace

1895, it moved in 1917 to its present premises, the former Schönborn Palace, built in 1706–11 to designs by Lukas von Hildebrandt as a homely two-storey mansion, and altered in 1760 by Isidor Canevale. The building has a rather imposing façade with statuary running along its top.

In the museum you will find artifacts reflecting popular culture in Austria and neighbouring countries that were once part of the Habsburg Empire. The collection includes furniture, textiles and ceramics, household and work tools, religious objects and two complete living rooms that illustrate the lifestyle, customs and rituals in the various regions. The core of the collection consists of objects from the 17th to 19th centuries.

On Lange Gasse, a couple of blocks along towards Josefstädter Straße, you will pass the **Alte Backstube**, at No. 34. This old bakery is one of the loveliest town houses in Vienna. It was built in 1697 by the jeweller Hans Bernhard Leopold and was in continuous use until 1963. The rooms have been lovingly restored, retaining the old baking ovens, and now house a traditional restaurant and café, and a small baking museum where 300-year-old baking equipment is to be seen.

Maria Treu Kirche ⓫

Jodok-Fink-Platz. **Map** 1 B3.
📞 *40 50 425.* ⓤ *Rathaus.* 🚋 *I.* 🚌 *13A.* ⏰ *during mass or by appointment.*

ORIGINALLY DESIGNED by Johann Lukas von Hildebrandt in 1716, Maria Treu Kirche (church of Mary the Faithful) acquired its present form in the mid-19th century, when twin towers were added.

The church, as well as the adjacent monastic buildings, was founded by fathers of the Piarist Order, one of whose main aims is education; they also founded a primary and a secondary school next door. The homely cellar of the former monastery is today a pleasant restaurant.

The interior of the church is one of the best preserved in Vienna. Its Baroque ceiling frescoes, the work of the great Austrian painter Franz Anton Maulbertsch, are very lovely. They depict scenes from the life of the Virgin Mary and events from the Old and New Testaments. In one of the chapels, to the left of the presbytery, you can see an altarpiece of the crucifixion, also painted by Franz Anton Maulbertsch.

The Chapel of Our Lady of Sorrows contains the *pietà* known as Our Lady from Malta, which was brought here by the Knights of Malta.

In front of the church is a Baroque pillar, topped with a statue of the Madonna (1713), one of many such plague columns erected in Vienna as thanksgiving at the end of the plague era. In this case the column commemorates the epidemic of 1713.

Baroque frescoes in Maria Treu Kirche

The opulent auditorium of Theater in der Josefstadt

Theater in der Josefstadt ⑫

Josefstädter Straße 26. **Map** 1 B4.
█ 42 700. Ⓤ Rathaus. ▓ J.
▭ 13A. Ⓦ www.josefstadt.org

Tʜɪꜱ ɪɴᴛɪᴍᴀᴛᴇ theatre, one of the oldest still standing in Vienna, has enjoyed a glorious history. First established in 1788, the theatre was later much altered. After renovation by Joseph Kornhäusel, for its reopening in 1822, Ludwig van Beethoven composed his overture *The Consecration of the House,* conducting it himself at the reopening gala.

In 1924, the directorship of the theatre was given to Max Reinhardt, one of the most outstanding theatre directors and reformers, who supervised its further restoration and introduced an ambitious modern repertoire as well as magnificent productions of classic drama. He transformed what was once a middle-of-the-road provincial theatre into the most exciting stage in the German-speaking world.

The theatre is worth a visit for viewing its interior alone. As the lights slowly dim, the crystal chandeliers float gently to the ceiling. It offers excellent productions of Austrian plays, with an emphasis on comedy, classics and the occasional musical.

Palais Trautson ⑬

Museumstraße 7. **Map** 1 C4.
Ⓤ Volkstheater. ▓ 48. ▭ 48A. ◐

Tʜᴇ ʙᴀʀᴏQᴜᴇ Trautson Palace, built between 1710 and 1712 for Prince Johann Leopold Donat Trautson, to a design by Johann Bernhard Fischer von Erlach, was acquired by Maria Theresa in 1760. She then donated it to the Royal Hungarian Bodyguard, which she had founded.

The Neo-Classical façade, with double rows of Doric columns, is heavily ornamented. Its finest sculptures, including that of Apollo playing the lyre, tower above the first-floor windows. The palace has an immense, beautiful staircase, decorated with carvings of the sphinx, and columns of male figures who support the ceiling, by the sculptor Giovanni Giuliani. Since 1961 the palace has housed the Ministry of Justice, so there is no public access.

Volkstheater ⑭

Neustiftgasse 1. **Map** 1 C5.
█ 52 47 263. Ⓤ Volkstheater, Lerchenfelderstraße. ▓ 49. ▭ 48.
Ⓦ www.volkstheater.at

Fᴀᴍᴇᴅ ᴀꜱ ᴀ venue able to combine classic and modern drama with popular Viennese plays, the Volkstheater (People's Theatre) was, for many years, a staging post for directors and actors on their way from the provincial theatres to the estimable Burgtheater. Today, classic and modern, or even experimental drama dominate the repertoire. The Volkstheater presents many plays for the first time, or for the first time in the German language.

The Volkstheater was built in 1889 by the Austrian architects Ferdinand Fellner and Hermann Helmer. They employed the latest in theatre technology, including electric lighting throughout, and many theatre designers later copied their work. The auditorium, with more than 1,000 seats, is one of the largest in a theatre devoted to German-language drama, and is a great example of Viennese *fin-de-siècle* architecture. In front of the theatre stands a statue (1898) of the dramatist Ferdinand Raimund.

The majestic entrance to the 19th-century Volkstheater

The dinosaur room in the Naturhistorisches Museum

Naturhistorisches Museum ⑮

Burgring 7. **Map** 2 A5. 📞 *52 177.* 🚇 *Volkstheater.* 🚊 *2, 46, 49, D, J.* 🚌 *2A, 48A.* ○ *9am–6:30pm Thu–Mon, 9am–9pm Wed.* ● *Tue, 1 Jan, 1 May, 1 Nov, 25 Dec.* ♿ 🅆 *www.nhm-wien.ac.at*

O N TWO SIDES of Maria-Theresien-Platz are two identical buildings, designed by Gottfried Semper and Karl von Hasenauer. They were both built as museums at the time of Franz Joseph I, as part of the Ringstraße development. Today, one is an art museum (Kunsthistorisches Museum, *see pp84–7*), the other the Natural History Museum, home to one of the richest and most wide-ranging collections in the world.

Many exhibits originally belonged to Maria Theresa's husband, Francis Stephen of Lorraine. The present permanent exhibition occupies two floors and consists of archaeological and anthropological displays, reconstructed specimens of extinct animals and one of the best gem collections in the world.

Among the most famous exhibits are the Hallstatt archaeological finds, dating from the early Iron Age, and the famous Venus of Willendorf – a 24,000-year-old stone statuette of a woman.

The Natural History Museum plays a very important role within the education system and its temporary exhibitions are organized mainly with schools in mind. The once famous exhibition showing the imaginary life of dinosaurs toured much of the world in the wake of Steven Spielberg's film *Jurassic Park*. The museum holds several casts of dinosaur skeletons in its palaeontology department.

In the square between the buildings stands an imposing monument of Maria Theresa (1888) by Kaspar von Zumbusch. It shows the empress clasping the Pragmatic Section of 1713, enabling women to ascend to the throne. Below her are her generals and her principal nobles and advisors.

Kunsthistorisches Museum ⑯

See pp84–7.

MuseumsQuartier ⑰

Museumsplatz 1. **Map** 1 C5. 📞 *52 35 881.* 🚇 *MuseumsQuartier, Volkstheater.* 🚊 *1, 2, 49, D, J.* 🚌 *2A, 48A.* **Information** ○ *10am–7pm daily.* 🅆 *www.mqw.at.* **Museum of Modern Art** ○ *10am–6pm Tue, Wed, Fri–Sun, 10am–9pm Thu.* ● *Mon, 24–25 Dec.* 🎟 *Admission free 26 Oct.* **Leopold Museum** ○ *10am–7pm Mon, Wed, Thu, Sat, Sun. 10am–9pm Fri.* ● *Tue, public holidays.* 🎟 **Kunsthalle Wien** ○ *10am–7pm Fri–Wed, 10am–10pm Thu.* 🎟 ♿

J OHANN BERNHARD Fischer von Erlach was commissioned by Emperor Karl VI to build the imperial stables on the escarpment behind the old town

fortifications. In 1921, these Baroque buildings became a venue for fairs, and in the 1980s they were converted into a museum complex to designs by Laurids and Manfred Ortner. They changed the furnishings of the existing structures and added new ones, resulting in one of the world's largest cultural centres.

The new MuseumsQuartier (Museum District) includes the **Kunsthalle Wien** (Vienna Art Hall) opposite the main entrance, behind the former premises of the Winter Riding School. Vienna's main showcase for international contemporary art, the Kunsthalle is one of the city's most important art spaces, focusing on transdisciplinary work including photography, video, film and new media, as well as modern-art retrospectives.

To the left of the Kunsthalle is the white limestone façade of the **Leopold Museum**, which houses the art collection of Rudolph Leopold. This encompasses over 5,000 works of art, including major pieces by Gustav Klimt, together with the world's largest Egon Schiele collection.

The **Museum of Modern Art Ludwig Foundation Vienna**, or **MUMOK**, to the right of the Kunsthalle, is clad in contrasting dark basalt. It contains one of the largest European collections of modern art, from American Pop to Cubism, Expressionism and Viennese Actionism, as well as contemporary art from Central and Eastern Europe.

Elsewhere on the site the **Tabakmuseum**, traces the development of tobacco from its discovery in 1492 to its economic significance today.

The **Architektur Zentrum Wien** is a venue for temporary exhibitions of modern architecture and architectural history. Its permanent exhibition features 20th-century Austrian architecture.

The **Tanzquartier Wien** is dedicated to dance, providing facilities and training to performers and choreographers, and presenting various types of dance and other performances to the public.

Rossbändiger (1892), the tamer of horses, near the MuseumsQuartier

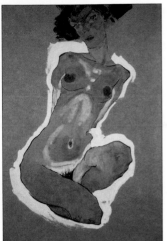

Schiele's *Kneeling Female Nude* (1910), in Museum of Modern Art, MuseumsQuartier

The MuseumsQuartier also has archives and facilities for lectures, workshops and seminars, as well as Austria's first centre for museum and exhibition studies. Children can play, explore and learn about a variety of subjects in the **ZOOM Kindermuseum**, an unconventional centre.

Amid this extraordinary cultural setting, numerous cafés, bars, green spaces, shops and bookstores invite visitors to relax.

Mariahilfer Straße ⑱

Map 4 A1, B1. Ⓤ *Westbahnhof, Zieglergasse, Neubaugasse, MuseumsQuartier*. 🚌 *2A, 13A.*

MARIAHILFER STRASSE is one of the longest streets in Vienna, a main artery running west from the town centre to the area around Schönbrunn.

The part between Getreidemarkt (Grain Market) and Westbahnhof (the Western Railway Station) is also the busiest shopping street in this part of the city. Here you will find Vienna's largest department stores and its best window displays. Shopping tends to be better value here than in Kärntner Straße, but is still more costly than in Meidling or Favoriten, for instance. Mariahilfer Straße took its

name from the church of St Mary, Our Lady of Perpetual Succour, built in the late 17th century on the site of an older church, but was not consecrated until 1730. Its façade is an austere pyramidal structure, rising to a bulbous steeple, and there are lively Rococo reliefs set in its walls. In front of the church stands a monument to the composer Joseph Haydn *(see p108)*, who lived at this address for 12 years.

Mariahilfer Straße No. 45 is the longest and most famous double-exit house in Vienna, the birthplace in 1790 of the popular Austrian playwright Ferdinand Raimund *(see p28)*.

Spittelberg ⑲

Map 1 C5. Ⓤ *Volkstheater.* 🚋 *49.* 🚌 *2A, 48A.* **Amerlinghaus** Stiftgasse 8. ☎ *52 36 475.* 🕐 *2–10pm Mon–Fri.* 🖃 🌐 *www.amerlinghaus.at*

SPITTELBERG is the oldest and most colourful part of the elegant 7th District. In the 17th century, the cluster of streets between Siebensterngasse and Burggasse, around Spittelberggasse, was Vienna's first immigrant worker district. Its inhabitants were mainly craftsmen, merchants and servants from Croatia and Hungary, brought here to work at the court. Today, the

district's crafts heritage lives on in the street market, held on the first weekend of each month and prior to Christmas. Among the stalls with wood carvings, tie-dyed fabrics and silver jewellery, waiters from the local bars negotiate the busy crowds; there are some 58 bars in this small area, which contains just 138 houses. The number of bars may change from one week to the next, but the bustling, festive party atmosphere can be experienced almost every evening. The Spittelberg area also comprises small art galleries, and artists display their work in the restaurants.

At one time, attractive bar maids offered "additional services", and legend has it that Emperor Joseph II once decided to explore the Spittelberg district for himself. However, when, in disguise, he entered the Witwe Bolte (Widow Bolte) restaurant, still open today, he was unceremoniously thrown out.

Nos. 18 and 20 Spittelberggasse are fine Baroque houses.

The beautifully restored **Amerlinghaus**, in which the painter Friedrich Amerling (1803–87) was born, is now a cultural and community centre, and a restaurant.

A little further along, between Siebensterngasse and Mariahilfer Straße, is an enclosed area around former barracks now housing the Military Academy, and the Stiftkirche, topped with an onion-shaped cupola, which serves as a garrison church. Its walls are lined with very expressive Rococo reliefs.

Community centre in Amerlinghaus, in Spittelberg

Kunsthistorisches Museum ⑯

THE WORLD'S FOURTH largest gallery, the Museum of Art History houses a collection based on works amassed over the centuries by generations of Habsburg monarchs. The public was given access to these art treasures when two museums were built in Ringstraße to designs by Karl Hasenauer and Gottfried Semper. One was to house the art collection, a second, identical building the Natural History Museum *(see p82)*. Both opened in 1891. The art museum's lavish interior complements its exhibits, today seen by more than one and a half million people each year.

Second floor

★ **Hunters in the Snow** *(1565)*
The last in a cycle of seasonal paintings by Pieter Bruegel the Elder, this winter scene graces a gallery room containing the world's largest collection of this artist's work.

First floor

★ **The Artist's Studio** *(1665)*
This painting, one of the most famous by Vermeer, is believed by some to be a self-portrait of the artist at work.

Ground floor

MUSEUM GUIDE

The ground floor area to the right of the main entrance displays artifacts from the ancient civilizations of Egypt, Greece, Rome and the Near East. The area to the left is closed to the public until 2007. The entire first floor is given over to the picture gallery, while the second floor houses the impressive coin collection as well as temporary exhibitions.

KEY

  Egyptian and Near Eastern collection

Collection of Greek and Roman Antiquities

Sculpture and Decorative Arts

Picture gallery

Coin cabinets

Non-exhibition space

Salt Cellar
Benvenuto Cellini made this sumptuous Saliera of the sea god Neptune and an earth goddess for the French King François I. It was stolen in 2003.

★ Velázquez's Infanta
The Spanish artist Diego Velázquez immortalized the eight-year-old Margarita Teresa (1659), the future wife of Emperor Leopold I.

★ Gemma Augustea
The famous Roman cameo, carved in great precision from onyx, shows the goddess Roma and Emperor Augustus welcoming his son Tiberius after his heroic victory over the barbarians in Pannonia.

Rooms K1-K7

King Thutmosis III
This king from the 18th Dynasty (c.1500 BC) was one of the foremost warriors of ancient Egypt. He is depicted in the style typical of the Late Kingdom period.

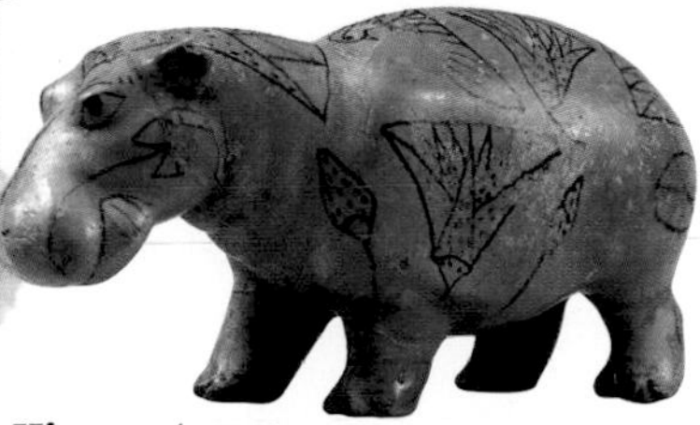

Hippopotamus
This blue ceramic figure from Middle-Kingdom Egypt (around 2000 BC) was placed in the tombs of important persons, to mark their status in society.

DECORATION OF THE MUSEUM

The museums built in Ringstraße in the 1890s were among the first to be designed with particular collections in mind. Many prominent artists were employed to decorate the interiors. Their great masterpiece is the main staircase in the Museum of Art History. Hans Makart created the symbolic scenes above the windows, while Gustav and Ernst Klimt painted frescoes depicting stages in the development of art. The *Apotheosis of the Renaissance* (1890) is the fabulous *trompe l'oeil* ceiling fresco by Michael Munkácsy.

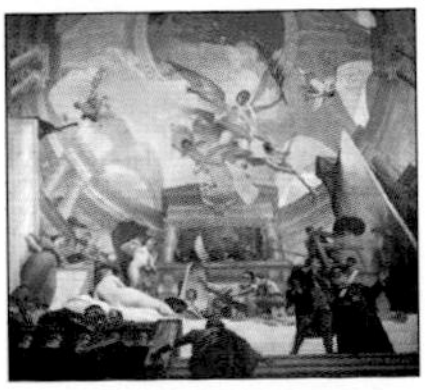

Apotheosis of the Renaissance

STAR EXHIBITS

★ *The Artist's Studio*

★ **Gemma Augustea**

★ *Hunters in the Snow*

★ Velázquez's *Infanta*

Exploring the Kunsthistorisches Museum

THE MUSEUM OF ART HISTORY has a fine collection of Egyptian, Greek and Roman objects, which provide an intriguing record of the world's earliest civilizations. Most European sculpture and decorative art dates from the 15th to the 18th centuries, which is also the focus of the picture gallery, largely reflecting the personal tastes of its Habsburg founders. Venetian and 17th-century Flemish paintings are well represented, and there is an excellent display of works by earlier Dutch and German artists. There is also a vast coin collection.

ORIENTAL AND EGYPTIAN ANTIQUITIES

THE CORE OF THIS collection are the objects unearthed by Austrian archaeologists in Giza. Particularly fascinating are the well-preserved relics from the tomb of Ka-Ni-Nisut, dating from the Early Kingdom era, including a meticulously reconstructed burial chamber. The blue ceramic figure of a hippopotamus dates from the Middle Kingdom era. Such animal figures were placed in the tombs to mark the social status of the deceased – the hippopotamus was regarded as a royal beast and could be hunted only with the pharaoh's permission.

The exhibits from the Late Kingdom, mainly associated with the mortuary cult, include a papyrus book of the dead, the mummified corpses of people and animals, sarcophagi and Canopic jars used to preserve the entrails of mummified corpses.

Near-Eastern antiquities are represented in the museum collections by the Babylonian reliefs, a lion made of red ceramic brick and various exhibits from Arabia.

GREEK AND ROMAN ANTIQUITIES

ONLY PART OF the museum's Greek and Roman collection is housed in the main building; the finds from Ephesus and on Samothrace are on display in the Ephesus Museum in Neue Burg *(see p66)*. The main building in Burgring has a beautiful collection of early Greek urns, in a variety of shapes, including vessels presented to winners at the Panathenaean Games. The sculpture rooms house many examples of early Greek and Roman art. Some are of outstanding quality: for example, the *Youth from Magdalensburg*, a cast of a lost Roman statue found buried in an Austrian field; the huge *Head of Athena*, probably from the school of Phidias; and fragments of a frieze with a dying Amazon. The Hellenic era is represented by the magnificent *Head of a Philosopher*, likely to have been that of Aristotle. One of the most precious items in the entire collection of antiquities is *Gemma Augustea*, a Roman cameo depicting Emperor Augustus welcoming his son

Tiberius on his return from war, together with Roma, the goddess of Rome.

The antiquities section also contains some Etruscan ceramics and statuettes from Tanagra. Early Coptic, Byzantine and German items are shown in the other rooms, but the true jewel among the antiquities is the Treasure of Nagyszentmiklós, a collection of 9th-century golden vessels with stunning reliefs, showing Far-Eastern influences, found in Romania in 1799.

SCULPTURE AND DECORATIVE ARTS

THIS COLLECTION (closed until 2007) consists of magnificent works of art bought or commissioned by successive Habsburg rulers, scientific instruments and clocks regarded as masterpieces of applied art, as well as curiosities and artifacts from the rulers' *Kunstkammern* (chambers of art). Some of the royals worked in the studio; exhibits include, for example, glass blown by Archduke Ferdinand II and embroidery by Maria Theresa. Some of the most intriguing items, however, are splendid examples of craftsmanship,

Virgin with Child (c1495) by Tilman Riemenschneider

including pieces of jewellery and items made from gold. Until it was stolen in 2003, the showpiece of the collection was the golden *Saliera* or Salt Cellar *(see p84)*, made by the Italian goldsmith and sculptor Benvenuto Cellini for the French King, François I.

Other gems in these rooms include the magnificent chalice from the collegiate church in Wilten and the precious Burgundy cup of Friedrich III.

A separate section is devoted to wood and stone sculptures from the Middle Ages, mainly of religious subjects, among them the amazing *Madonna from Krumlowa* (c.1400), the poignant *Virgin with Child* by Tilman Riemenschneider

Room I of the Egyptian galleries

Susanna and the Elders (1555) by Tintoretto

(c.1495) and stone statues from the cathedral churches of Bamberg and Naumburg.

Highlights of the Italian Renaissance and Baroque rooms are the marble bust of a laughing boy, by Desiderio da Settignano, a marble relief of Bacchus and Ariadne, and a fine bronze and gilt figurine known as *Venus Felix*, after an antique marble statue.

The collection of decorative arts also includes fine pieces of furniture and tapestries, gilded table ornaments and vases, a number of statuettes and figurines, miniature clocks and jewellery.

PICTURE COLLECTION

EXHIBITS IN THE painting galleries are mostly hung according to regional schools or styles of painting, and arranged chronologically.

Summer (1563) by
Giuseppe Arcimboldo

Paintings go back as far as the 16th century, and include several works by early Flemish masters, such as Rogier van der Weyden, Hans Memling and Jan van Eyck. The highlight is the collection of Pieter Bruegel the Elder's surviving works, the largest collection of his work and the museum's greatest treasure.

Two rooms are devoted to Rubens, with large-scale religious works and an intimate portrait of his wife. Antony van Dyck is represented by some outstanding works, and there are paintings by Dutch genre painters. All the Rembrandts on show are portraits. The only painting by Johannes Vermeer is *The Artist's Studio*, an enigmatic work.

The Italian collection of 16th-century paintings from Venice and the Veneto include works by Titian, from his early *Gypsy Madonna* (1510) to the late *Nymph and Shepherd* (1570–75). Other highlights are Giovanni Bellini's graceful *Young Woman at her Toilette* (1515) and Tintoretto's *Susanna and the Elders*, one of the major works of Venetian Mannerism. There is a series of allegorical portrait heads representing the elements and the seasons by Giuseppe Arcimboldo. Italian Baroque painting includes works by Annibale

Carracci and Michelangelo Merisi da Caravaggio, including the huge *Madonna of the Rosary* (1606–7).

French treasures include the formal court portrait of the youthful Charles IX of France (1569) by François Clouet, and *The Destruction of the Temple in Jerusalem* (1638) by Nicolas Poussin.

Among the few British works are the *Landscape of Suffolk* (around 1750) by Thomas Gainsborough and paintings by Reynolds. The German collection contains several works by Albrecht Dürer, including his *Madonna with the Pear* (1512), and by Lucas Cranach the Elder and Hans Holbein the Younger.

There are several fine portraits of the Spanish royal family by Diego Velázquez, including his *Portrait of the Infanta* (1659).

COIN CABINETS

THE COIN AND MEDAL collection of the Museum of Art History comprises 500,000 individual items, making it one of the most extensive numismatic collections in the world. Its first inventory was compiled in 1547. The nucleus of the collection derives from the former possessions of the Habsburgs, but has been added to by modern curators. The exhibits illustrate the history of money, with coins from ancient Egypt, Greece and Rome, examples of Celtic, Byzantine, medieval and Renaissance money, right up to present-day Austrian currency.

**Medal of Ulrich II
Molitor** (1581)

Also on display is a collection of 19th- and 20th-century medals, with portraits that are often outstanding miniature works of art. Particularly noteworthy are the silver and gilt medals of Ulrich II Molitor, the Abbot of Heiligenkreuz, and the silver medallion engraved by Bertrand Andrieu and minted to commemorate the baptism of Napoleon's son, showing the emperor as proud father.

SOUTH OF THE RING

T HIS PART of town is an area of great diversity, ranging from the stateliness of the Opera House to the raucous modernity of bustling Karlsplatz, from the magnificence of Karlskirche, one of Johann Bernhard Fischer von Erlach's greatest churches, to the secular attractions of the Belvedere. Once

Relief on the façade of the Secession Building

Prince Eugene of Savoy's palace, the Belvedere is now the home of the Gallery of Austrian Art, with an extensive collection of works by Gustav Klimt. The district also has beautiful buildings with façades decorated in the Vienna Secession style. The stalls of the bustling Naschmarkt are also a popular attraction.

SIGHTS AT A GLANCE

Streets and Squares
Schwarzenbergplatz ⑬

Historic Buildings
Hotel Sacher ①
Karlsplatz Pavilions ⑨
Musikverein ⑪
Staatsoper ②
Technische Universität ⑦
Theater an der Wien ⑤

Museums and Galleries
Academy of Fine Arts ③
Belvedere see pp98–9 ⑮

Künstlerhaus ⑩
Secession Building ④
Wien Museum Karlsplatz ⑫

Markets
Naschmarkt ⑥

Churches
Karlskirche see pp94–5 ⑧

Parks
Stadtpark ⑭

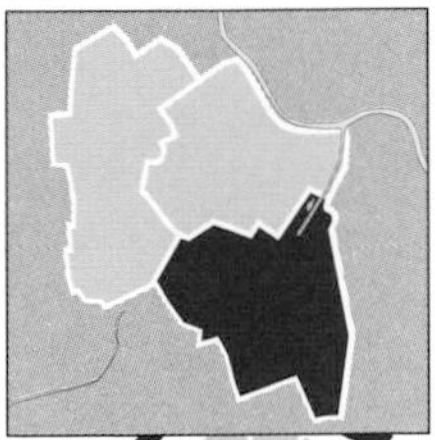

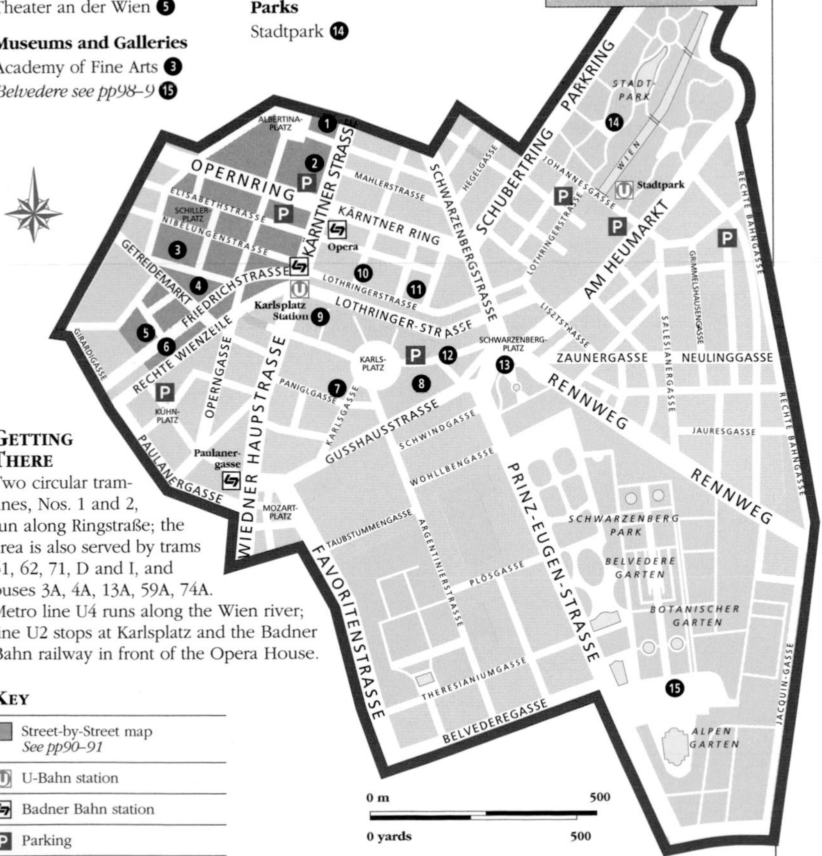

GETTING THERE

Two circular tramlines, Nos. 1 and 2, run along Ringstraße; the area is also served by trams 61, 62, 71, D and I, and buses 3A, 4A, 13A, 59A, 74A. Metro line U4 runs along the Wien river; line U2 stops at Karlsplatz and the Badner Bahn railway in front of the Opera House.

KEY

▦	Street-by-Street map *See pp90–91*
Ⓤ	U-Bahn station
🚈	Badner Bahn station
P	Parking

0 m   500
0 yards   500

◁ **The opulent central hall of the Opera House, seen from the main staircase**

Street-by-Street: Around the Opera

Between two of Vienna's key landmarks, the Opera House and Karlskirche, lies an area that typifies the varied cultural vitality of the city as a whole. Here, you will find cultural monuments such as an 18th-century theatre, a 19th-century art academy and the superb Secession Building, mixed in with emblems of the Viennese devotion to good living: the Hotel Sacher and the Café Museum, both as popular today as ever, and the colourful Naschmarkt, Vienna's best market for vegetables and exotic fruits.

Academy of Fine Arts
This Italianate building is home to one of the best collections of old masters in Vienna ❸

The Goethe Statue

The Schiller Statue dominates the park in front of the Academy of Fine Arts.

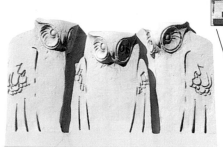

★ Secession Building
This delightful structure, built in 1898 as a showroom for the Secession artists, houses Gustav Klimt's Beethoven Frieze, *created for an exhibition in honour of the great composer* ❹

Theater an der Wien
The 18th-century theatre on the banks of the Wien river now stages only opera, but for ten years it hosted the musical Elisabeth, *about Sissi, Franz Joseph I's unhappy wife* ❺

SCHILLERPLATZ

ELISA

NIBELUNGE

MAKARTGASSE

GETREIDEMARKT

LINKE WIENZELLE

★ Naschmarkt
This market sells fresh produce on weekdays and antiques or bric-a-brac on Saturday mornings ❻

Hotel Sacher
This hotel is the home of the famous Sachertorte, which you can eat in its café ❶

LOCATOR MAP
See Street Finder, maps 2 & 4

INNER CITY

SOUTH OF THE RING

0 m		50
0 yards		50

★ **Staatsoper**
The majestic state opera, erected on this site in 1869, is still the hub of Vienna's glorious cultural life ❷

The Café Museum had been remodelled in the 1930s but it has been restored to its original late 19th-century appearance in accordance with Adolf Loos's forward-looking design.

The Mark Anthony Statue (1899), alongside the Secession Building, is a gloriously decadent bronze statue by Arthur Strasser. It depicts the Roman leader sitting in a chariot drawn by lions.

KEY

--- ■ ■ ■ Suggested route

STAR SIGHTS

★ **Naschmarkt**

★ **Secession Building**

★ **Staatsoper**

The imposing building of the Vienna State Opera House

Hotel Sacher **❶**

Philharmonikerstraße 4. **Map** 2 B5.
(51 45 60. **Ⓤ** Karlsplatz.
Ⓣ 1, 2, D, J. **Ⓦ** www.sacher.com

THE HOTEL SACHER is one of the "must-see" places in Vienna. It was founded by the son of Franz Sacher, who was said to have created the famous *Sachertorte* in 1832. Although this cake can now be bought in any café, the genuine article is still the best.

The hotel came into its own under Anna Sacher, the founder's cigar-smoking daughter-in-law, who ran the hotel from 1892 until her death in 1930. She collected autographs, and, to this day, a vast white tablecloth signed by Emperor Franz Joseph I is on display. During her time, the Sacher became a venue for the extra-marital affairs of the rich and noble. It is still a discreetly sumptuous hotel with red velvet sofas, draped curtains and stylish furniture.

Staatsoper **❷**

Opernring 2. **Map** 2 B5. **(** 51 444-0. **Ⓤ** Karlsplatz. **Ⓣ** 1, 2, D, J.
Ⓦ www.wiener-staatsoper.at

IN MAY 1869, WHEN Vienna's State Opera House opened to the strains of Mozart's *Don Giovanni*, music lovers rejoiced that it would no longer be necessary to travel to Paris in order to hear good opera. Built in Neo-Renaissance style, the Opera House initially failed to impress the Viennese. The distressed interior designer, Eduard van der Nüll, committed suicide, and two months later, the architect, August Sicard von Sicardsburg, also died. Yet, when the opera was hit by an allied bomb in 1945, the event was seen as a symbolic blow to the city. With a new state-of-the-art auditorium and stage, the Opera House eventually reopened on 5 November 1955 with a performance of Beethoven's

Fidelio. Its illustrious directors have included Gustav Mahler, Richard Strauss and Herbert von Karajan.

Each year, on the last Thursday of Carnival, the stage is extended to create a vast dance floor for the Vienna Opera Ball. This prestigious high-society event opens when Vienna's youth – well-to-do girls clad in white and their smartly dressed escorts – take to the floor.

Academy of Fine Arts **❸**

Schillerplatz 3. **Map** 4 C1.
(588 16-225. **Ⓤ** Karlsplatz.
Ⓣ 1, 2, D, J. **🚌** 57A, 59A.
◯ 10am–4pm Tue–Sun and public holidays. **●** 1 Jan, 1 May, 1 Nov, 24, 25, 31 Dec.

THE ACADEMY of Fine Arts is not only an educational establishment, but also one of the finest galleries of Old Masters. It was built in 1872–6, by Theophil Hansen, as a school and museum. In 1907, Adolf Hitler applied to be admitted but was refused a place on the grounds that he lacked talent.

Today, the gallery shows changing exhibitions. Its pride is late-Gothic and early-Renaissance works, including some pieces by Rubens, a winged altarpiece by Hieronymus Bosch depicting the Last Judgement and works by Titian, Cranach and Botticelli. It also has some 17th-century Dutch and Flemish landscapes and an Austrian collection.

Secession Building **❹**

Friedrichstraße 12. **Map** 4 C1.
(58 75 307. **Ⓤ** Karlsplatz.
🚋 59A. **◯** 10am–6pm Tue, Wed, Fri– Sun; 10am–8pm Thu. **📷**

THE UNUSUAL Secession Building was designed in *Jugendstil* style by Joseph Maria Olbrich, as a showcase for the Secessionist artists, including Gustav Klimt, Kolo Moser and Otto Wagner, who broke away from Vienna's traditional art scene.

OTTO WAGNER (1841–1918)

The most prominent architect at the turn of the 20th century, Wagner studied in Vienna and Berlin. Initially, he was associated with the historicist style, but in time he became the foremost representative of the Austrian Secession. He prepared plans for the re-routing of the Wien river and the modernization of the town's transport system. His most outstanding works include the **Majolikahaus** *(see Naschmarkt, opposite)*, train stations *(see p96)*, the Post Office Savings Bank building, a hospital and the Kirche am Steinhof *(see p108)*.

Detail of Otto Wagner's design

Façade of the Secession Building, with its golden filigree dome

The almost windowless building, with its filigree globe of entwined laurel leaves on the roof, is a squat cube with four towers. Gustav Klimt's *Beethoven Frieze* (1902) is its best known exhibit. Designed as a decorative painting running along three walls, it shows interrelated groups of figures thought to be a commentary on Beethoven's *Ninth Symphony*.

The Secession Building is Vienna's oldest independent exhibition space dedicated to showing contemporary and experimental Austrian and international art.

Theater an der Wien 5

Linke Wienzeile 6. **Map** 4 C1.
58 83 00.
Kettenbrückengasse. 59A.

THE "THEATRE on the Wien river", one of the oldest theatres in Vienna, was founded by Emanuel Schikaneder. A statue above the entrance shows him playing Papageno in the premiere of Mozart's *Magic Flute*. Schikaneder, who had written the libretto for this same opera, was the theatre's first director. The premiere of Beethoven's *Fidelio* was staged here in 1805, and for a while the composer lived in the theatre. Many plays by prominent playwrights such as Kleist, Grillparzer and Nestroy, and many Viennese operettas were premiered here, too, including works by Johann Strauss (son), Zeller, Lehár and Kalman. After many years as a venue for musicals, the Theater an der Wien now stages only opera.

The Neo-Classical entrance to the Theater an der Wien

Naschmarkt 6

Map 4 C1. Kettenbrückengasse, Pilgramgasse. 59A. 6am–6:30pm Mon–Fri, 6am–2pm Sat.
Schubert Memorial Apartment 58 16 730. 1:30–4:30pm Tue–Sun.

THE NASCHMARKT is Vienna's liveliest market, selling all types of market goods as well as delicatessen food. The Saturday flea market is particularly popular.

Nearby, at Kettenbrückengasse No. 6, is the simple apartment where the composer Franz Schubert died in 1828. It displays facsimiles, prints and a piano.

Overlooking Naschmarkt, at Linke Wienzeile Nos. 38 and 40, are two remarkable apartment blocks. Designed by Otto Wagner in 1899 and known as the Wagner Apartments, they represent the peak of *Jugendstil* style. No. 38 has sparkling gilt ornament, mostly by Kolo Moser. No. 40 is known as **Majolikahaus**, after the glazed pottery used to weather-proof the walls. Its façade has subtle flower patterns in pink, blue and green, and even the sills are moulded and decorated.

Technische Universität 7

Karlsplatz 13. **Map** 5 D1.
588 01–0. Karlsplatz.
1, 2, D, J. 4A, 59A.

VIENNA's Technical University has a Neo-Classical façade, beautiful colonnades and attic statues by Joseph Klieber. It was built in 1816 by Joseph Schemerl von Leytenbach, to the designs of the Imperial Office of Public Works. Klieber also created the eight stone heads flanking the main entrance, featuring some of the university's famous professors.

Inside, the most beautiful room is the Assembly Hall, with carved wall panelling.

The University fronts on to Resselpark, which contains many busts and statues of Austria's most important scientists and engineers.

Karlskirche ❽

DURING VIENNA's plague epidemic of 1713, Emperor Karl VI vowed that as soon as the city was delivered from its plight he would build a church dedicated to St Charles Borromeo (1538–84), the patron saint of the plague. Johann Bernhard Fischer von Erlach created a richly eclectic building, later completed by his son. At 72 m (236 ft), it is the tallest Baroque church in Vienna. The Neo-Classical giant dome and portico are flanked by two minaret-like towers and the Oriental-style gatehouses. The most striking features inside are the beautiful cupola frescoes, high altar and side altarpieces painted by the foremost artists of the day, Martino Altomonte, Daniel Gran and Sebastian Ricci.

An angel representing the New Testament

The Pulpit
Two putti crown the canopy of the richly gilded pulpit, adorned with rocailles and flower garlands.

★ High Altar
A stucco relief by Albert Camesina shows St Charles Borromeo being assumed into heaven on a cloud laden with angels and putti.

Stairway (closed to the public)

The two gatehouses leading into the side entrances of the church seem to combine the architecture of Roman triumphal arches with that of Chinese pavilions.

Pediment reliefs by Giovanni Stanetti show the suffering of the Viennese population during the 1713 plague.

Main entrance

STAR FEATURES

★ Cupola Frescoes

★ High Altar

★ The Two Columns

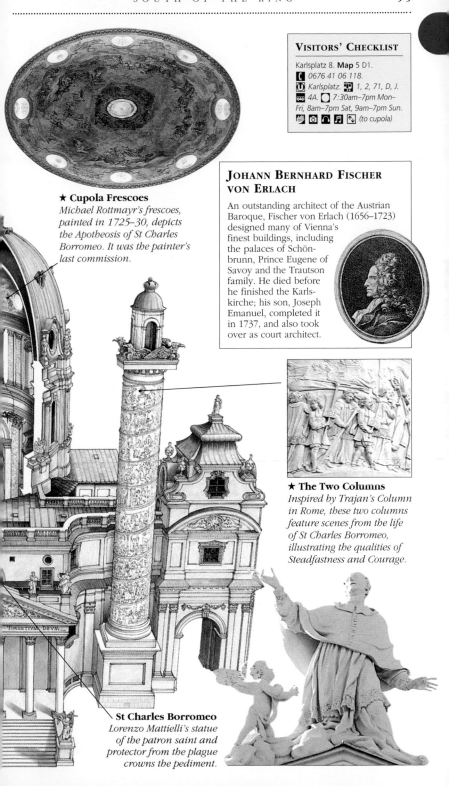

VISITORS' CHECKLIST

Karlsplatz 8. **Map** 5 D1.
0676 41 06 118.
Karlsplatz. 1, 2, 71, D, J.
4A. 7:30am–7pm Mon–
Fri, 8am–7pm Sat, 9am–7pm Sun.
(to cupola)

★ **Cupola Frescoes**
*Michael Rottmayr's frescoes,
painted in 1725–30, depicts
the Apotheosis of St Charles
Borromeo. It was the painter's
last commission.*

JOHANN BERNHARD FISCHER VON ERLACH

An outstanding architect of the Austrian
Baroque, Fischer von Erlach (1656–1723)
designed many of Vienna's
finest buildings, including
the palaces of Schön-
brunn, Prince Eugene of
Savoy and the Trautson
family. He died before
he finished the Karls-
kirche; his son, Joseph
Emanuel, completed it
in 1737, and also took
over as court architect.

★ **The Two Columns**
*Inspired by Trajan's Column
in Rome, these two columns
feature scenes from the life
of St Charles Borromeo,
illustrating the qualities of
Steadfastness and Courage.*

St Charles Borromeo
*Lorenzo Mattielli's statue
of the patron saint and
protector from the plague
crowns the pediment.*

Sunflower motif on the façade of the Karlsplatz pavilions

Karlsplatz Pavilions ⑨

Karlsplatz. **Map** 5 D1. 🚇 *Karlsplatz.* 🚆 *1, 2, 62, D, J.* 🚌 *3A, 4A, 59A.* 🚋 *Kärntner Ring.* 📞 *50 58 747-84 059.* ☐ *1:30–4:30pm Tue–Sun.*

OTTO WAGNER *(see p92)* was responsible for designing and engineering many aspects of Vienna's early underground system in the late 19th century. His plans, however, did not materialize until the 1960s, when work on the metro started. One of the underground lines, the U4, runs almost exactly along his train route linking the city centre with Schönbrunn *(see p110).*

A few of Wagner's stations remain to this day – it is worth looking at the stations in Stadtpark, Kettenbrückengasse and Schönbrunn, for example – but none can match his stylish pair of underground railway exit pavilions (1898–9) alongside Karlsplatz. The patina-green copper roofs and the ornamentation complement the Karlskirche beyond. Gilt patterns are stamped onto the white marble cladding and eaves, with repetitions of Wagner's beloved sunflower motif. The greatest impact is made by the buildings' elegantly curving rooflines. The two pavilions face each other; one is now a café, the other is used for exhibitions.

Künstlerhaus ⑩

Karlsplatz 5. **Map** 5 D1. 📞 *58 79 663.* 🚇 *Karlsplatz.* 🚆 *1, 2, 62, 65, D, J.* 🚌 *3A, 4A, 59A.* ☐ *10am–6pm Fri–Wed, 10am–9pm Thu.* 🌐 W *www.kuenstlerhaus.at*

COMMISSIONED BY the Vienna Artists' Society as an exhibition hall for its members, the Künstlerhaus (Artists' House) was built in 1868. The society favoured grandiose, academic styles of painting in tune with the historicist Ringstraße architecture which was also being developed around that time. The Artists' House itself is typical of this style. Designed by August Weber (1836–1903) to look like a Renaissance *palazzo*, it is decorated with marble statues of the masters of art, including Albrecht

Dürer, Michelangelo, Raphael, Peter Paul Rubens, Leonardo da Vinci, Diego Velázquez and Titian, symbolizing the timeless value of art.

Today, the Künstlerhaus still serves as an exhibition space, focusing on architecture, interdisciplinary themes and international cooperation. There is also a space for live performances, a cinema, theatre and restaurant.

Musikverein ⑪

Bösendorferstraße 12. **Map** 5 D1. 📞 *50 58 190.* 🚇 *Karlsplatz.* 🚆 *1, 2, 62, 71, D, J.* 🚌 *3A, 4A, 59A.* ☐ *guided tours: 1:30pm Mon, Wed, Fri–Sun, box office: 9am–6:30pm Mon–Fri, 9am–5pm Sat.*

NEXT TO THE Künstlerhaus is the Musikverein, headquarters of the Society of the Friends of Music. It was designed by Theophil Hansen in 1867–9 and features terracotta statues and balustrades.

The Musikverein is the home of the famous Vienna Philharmonic Orchestra, which performs both here and in the Opera House. The concert hall, seating almost 2,000, has excellent acoustics and superb decor. The balcony is supported by vast columns; the gilded ceiling shows nine muses and Apollo; along the walls are the statues of various famous musicians.

The most famous annual event here is the New Year's Day concert, which is broadcast live around the world.

The monumental, historicist façade of the Musikverein

Wien Museum Karlsplatz ⑫

Karlsplatz. **Map** 5 D1.
(50 58 747-84 021.
Ⓤ Karlsplatz. **🚊** 1, 2, 62, 71, D,
J. **🚌** 3A, 4A, 59A. **◯** 9am–6pm
Tue–Sun. **📷** Admission free –
9am–noon Fri.

Visitors to the Historical Museum of the City of Vienna are greeted by a vast model of the city from the era when the Ringstraße was developed. The exhibition covers nearly 3,000 years of urban history. It illustrates the lives of its first settlers and life in the Roman camp of Vindobona, and it chronicles the threat from Turkish invaders and the subsequent rise of Vienna to the magnificent capital of a great empire.

The museum has collections of memorabilia of many of Vienna's famous citizens. Perhaps the most interesting of these are the reconstructed apartments of the writer Franz Grillparzer (1791–1872) and the architect Adolf Loos (1870–1933).

Schwarzenberg-platz ⑬

Map 5 E1. **Ⓤ** Karlsplatz. **🚊** 71.
🚌 4A.

The elongated Schwarzenberg square, one of the city's grandest spaces, is best seen from the Ringstraße, from where several important structures come into view together. In the foreground is the equestrian statue of Prince Karl Schwarzenberg, who commanded the Austrian and allied armies in the Battle of Leipzig in 1813 against the French army under Napoleon.

The Hochstrahlbrunnen (high jet fountain) was built in 1873 to mark the connection of Vienna's first Alpine water supply. The fountain is floodlit in summer. It partly obscures the heroic-style Soviet monument to the Red Army that commemorates the Russian liberation of Vienna. Beyond the Russian monument, the beautiful Schwarzenberg Palace can be

Fountain and Soviet Monument at Schwarzenbergplatz

seen. It was built in 1697 by Johann Lukas von Hildebrandt and altered by the Fischer von Erlachs, Johann Bernhard and Joseph Emanuel. Part of it has now been converted into a luxurious hotel and restaurant, and one wing houses the Swiss Embassy.

Stadtpark ⑭

Map 3 D5. **Ⓤ** Stadtpark, Stubentor.
Ⓢ Wien Mitte. **🚊** 1, 2. **🚌** 74A.

On the Weihburggasse side of the municipal park stands one of the most photographed sights in Vienna, the gilded statue of the King of Waltz, Johann Strauss the Younger. It was designed by Edmund Hellmer in the Neo-Romantic style of the 1920s. The park, opened in 1862, also contains the statues of the composers Franz Schubert and Franz Lehár, the painter Hans Makart and portraitist Friedrich von Amerling.

Parallel to the Ringstraße, along the Wien River, runs an attractive promenade designed in Secession style by Friedrich Ohmann. It includes several magnificent portals, part of a project to regulate the flow of the Wien river, as well as several pavilions, bridges and stone playgrounds.

A Secession-style portal in the Stadtpark, built in 1903–04

Belvedere ⑮

T HE BELVEDERE WAS BUILT as the summer residence of Prince Eugene of Savoy by Johann Lucas von Hildebrandt. A brilliant military commander whose strategies helped vanquish the Turks in 1683, the Prince became a favourite at the Austrian court and with the people. Situated on a gently sloping hill, the Belvedere consists of two palaces linked by a formal garden designed in the French style by Dominique Girard. The garden is laid out on three levels, each conveying a complicated series of Classical allusions: the lower part represents the domain of the Four Elements, the centre is Parnassus and the upper section Mount Olympus.

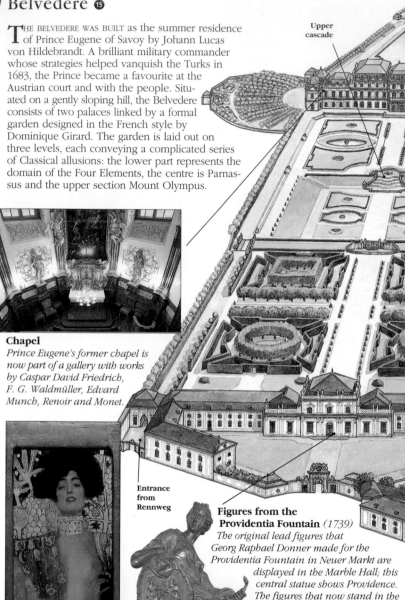

Upper cascade

Chapel
Prince Eugene's former chapel is now part of a gallery with works by Caspar David Friedrich, F. G. Waldmüller, Edvard Munch, Renoir and Monet.

Entrance from Rennweg

Figures from the Providentia Fountain *(1739)*
The original lead figures that Georg Raphael Donner made for the Providentia Fountain in Neuer Markt are displayed in the Marble Hall; this central statue shows Providence. The figures that now stand in the market are copies.

★ Gustav Klimt Collection
Klimt's portrait of the Old-Testament figure of Judith I *(1901, above) and his famous* The Kiss *(1907–08) hang in this superb collection.*

STAR FEATURES

★ **Gustav Klimt Collection**

★ **Hall of Mirrors**

★ **Sala Terrena**

Main Gate leading to the Upper Belvedere

Entrance to the Upper Belvedere from Prinz-Eugen-Straße

Upper Belvedere: Gallery of 19th- and 20th-Century Austrian Art

Lower Belvedere: Baroque Museum

★ **Sala Terrena**
One of the finest rooms of the Upper Belvedere, this hall has beautiful stucco work by Santino Bussi and statues by Lorenzo Mattielli.

Statues of Sphinxes
With their lion bodies and human heads, the imposing Sphinx statues adorning the Belvedere gardens represent strength and intelligence.

Head of a Jester (c.1770)
Franz Xaver Messerschmidt's character heads with their exaggerated expressions – far from idealized portraits – are one of the museum's gems.

★ **Hall of Mirrors**
A statue of Prince Eugene by Balthasar Permoser stands in this richly ornamented Baroque room, whose walls are covered with huge gilt-framed mirrors.

The Orangerie
now houses the Museum of Austrian Medieval Art.

FURTHER AFIELD

OR A CITY OF 1.6 million inhabitants, Vienna is surprisingly compact. Nonetheless, some of the most interesting sights are a fair distance from the historic city centre. At Schönbrunn sprawls the vast Neo-Classical palace of the same name, with its Rococo state rooms and superb gardens. The Habsburgs' summer residence, it was greatly beloved by Maria Theresa. It is also worth

Detail in Karl-Marx-Hof

going to Kahlenberg, which offers the most splendid panoramic views of Vienna. You should spend at least one evening tasting the new-vintage wines in one of the *Heurigen* in Grinzing. Many parks and gardens, including the Prater, featured in the film *The Third Man* and one of Europe's best funfairs, as well as the Lainzer Tiergarten, are former Habsburg domains now open to the public.

SIGHTS AT A GLANCE

Historic Buildings
Amalienbad ⑪
Augarten ⑤
Hundertwasser-Haus ⑨
Karl-Marx-Hof ③
Liechtenstein Museum ④
Schönbrunn
   see pp110–11 ⑮
Wagner Villas ⑰

Museums and Galleries
Haydn-Museum ⑬
Heeresgeschichtliches
   Museum ⑩
Museum of Technology ⑭

Parks and Gardens
Donauinsel ⑥
Lainzer Tiergarten ⑱
Prater ⑧

Interesting Districts
Grinzing ②
Kahlenberg ①
UNO-City ⑦

Churches
Kirche am Steinhof ⑯
Wotruba-Kirche ⑲

Cemeteries
Zentralfriedhof see pp106–7 ⑫

KEY
▩	Central Vienna
▢	Greater Vienna
⚡	Railway station
🚌	Coach and bus station
═	Motorway
⋯	Motorway tunnel
▬	Major road
═	Other road

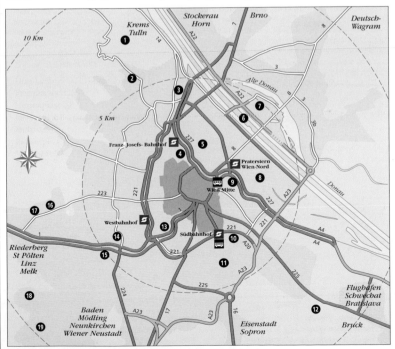

Part of the façade of the eccentric Hundertwasser Haus, built in 1985

Cobenzlgasse, one of the charming streets in Grinzing

Kahlenberg ❶

🚌 38A.

NORTH OF THE city, on the edge of the Vienna Woods, rise two almost identical peaks. The lower of the two, with ruins visible on top, is Leopoldsberg, the former seat of Margrave Leopold who ruled Austria in the 12th century. The second, with a television mast and the outline of a white church at the top, is Kahlenberg, the highest peak in Vienna.

It was from here, on the 12 September 1683, that the Polish King Jan III Sobieski led his troops to relieve the besieged city. Pope Innocent III's papal legate celebrated a thanksgiving mass in the ruins of the church that had been destroyed by the Turks.

The restored church of St Joseph on Kahlenberg is now maintained by Polish monks. Two tablets beside the church door commemorate the battle and the visit by Pope John Paul II, in 1983. Inside the church is a chapel with frescoes by the Polish artist, Henryk Rosen, and a display of the coats of arms of families whose members took part in the battle.

A short distance behind the church is an observation terrace and a restaurant. The views over the vineyards below and the city beyond are fabulous, with the Danube bridges to the left and the Vienna Woods to the right. No wonder then that Kahlenberg is a popular weekend destination.

Grinzing ❷

🚉 38. 🚌 38A.

THE QUIET VILLAGES scattered among the vineyards on the slopes of the Vienna Woods usually come to life during the wine-making season, when large groups of tourists descend on them to sample the new-vintage *Heuriger*. Originally, the vintners were licensed to sell their own wine, while snacks were offered for free. This tradition developed into today's *Heurigen* – new-vintage wine taverns, typical of Vienna.

Today, of course, such hospitality is no longer offered for free. At *Heurigen* inns, wine and other drinks are served at the table and food is available from self-service buffets. Guests sit on benches around wide wooden tables, where they can drink and enjoy themselves until the early hours.

A plaque on No. 31 Himmelstraße in Grinzing

There are many such villages in the area around Vienna, but undoubtedly the most famous of all is Grinzing. Although it may have lost some of its original charm, this is still a nice place to spend an evening.

On the way to Grinzing, it is worth taking the time to visit the Heiligenstädter Testament-Haus at No. 6 in the narrow Probusgasse, Ludwig van Beethoven's most famous home in Vienna. It was here that the great composer tried to find a cure for his worsening deafness; when he failed, he wrote a dramatic letter to his brothers, known as *The Testament*.

Karl Marx-Hof ❸

Heiligenstädterstraße 82–92.
🚇 Heiligenstadt. 🚉 D. 🚌 10A, 11A, 38A, 39A.

IN THE 1920s, VIENNA was governed by a social-democratic town council, elected mainly thanks to the votes of first-time women voters, a period known as Red Vienna. The council formed the ambitious plan to build houses for its entire working population. As a result, between 1923 and 1933 more than 60,000 new apartments, well-appointed for the time, were built. The programme was financed by a luxury tax imposed on wealthy citizens. Its execution was so strict that the municipal finance director, Hugo Breitner, earned himself the

The peach- and salmon-coloured façade of the Karl Marx-Hof

The Baroque building of the Wiener Porzellanmanufaktur

nickname the "financial vampire". Karl Marx-Hof is an immense complex of 1,382 council apartments and recreational facilities, and is the most celebrated of the municipal housing developments of that period. The project's architect, Karl Ehn, was a pupil of Otto Wagner.

The delightful ceiling frescoes in the Liechtenstein Museum

Liechtenstein Museum ❹

Fürstengasse 1. **Map** 2 A1.
📞 31 95 767. 🚇 Friedensbrücke.
🚌 40A. 🚊 D.

COMPLETED IN 1692 to designs by Domenico Martinelli in the Rococo style, this was the Liechtenstein family's summer palace. It has a monumental façade, with tall pilasters and typically Baroque windows.

Inside, the colourful ceiling paintings in the vast ground-floor room are the work of Michael Rottmayr. Vault paintings by Antonio Belucci can be seen on both sides of

the stairway. The grand hall is decorated with frescoes by Andrea Pozzo, a masterpiece of Baroque interior design.

The museum houses the art collection of Prince Hans-Adam II von und zu Liechtenstein – one of the richest private collections in the world. The collection is centred on the Baroque with special focus on Rubens, and ranges from the Renaissance (for example, Raphael and the Breugels) through to the early 19th century (Waldmüller and Füger). The Liechtenstein family also acquired many masterpieces of modern art, dating from the early 20th century. The palace stands in an extensive garden, which was remodelled in the 19th century in the English style.

Augarten ❺

Obere Augartenstraße 1. **Map** 3 D1.
📞 21 12 418. 🚊 21, 31, N.
Wiener Porzellanmanufaktur
🕙 guided tours 9:30am Mon–Fri.
🔴 public holidays, summer holidays.

THERE HAS BEEN a palace on this site since the days of Leopold I, but it was destroyed by the Turks in 1683 and then rebuilt around 1700 to designs attributed to Johann Bernhard Fischer von Erlach. Since 1948 it has been the home of the world-famous Vienna Boys' Choir and is consequently closed to the public.

The surrounding park is one of the oldest in Vienna; it was first planted in 1650 by Emperor Ferdinand III, later renewed and opened to the public in 1775. Topiary lines long paths; the handsome gates were designed by Isidor Canevale. Mozart, Beethoven and Johann Strauss (father) all

gave concerts in the park pavilion, which was once the imperial porcelain factory.

The **Wiener Porzellan-manufaktur**, established in 1718, is today run by the municipal authorities, but its products are still stamped with the imperial crest. The factory is open to the public, and there are displays on the history of Augarten porcelain.

Donauinsel ❻

🚇 Donauinsel, Handelskai.

THE NUMEROUS side-arms and rivulets of the Danube river regularly flooded the town until it was first canalized between 1870 and 1875. The second period of canalization in the Vienna region began in 1972 and was completed in 1987. The New Danube, a 5-km (3-mile) canal that acts as an "over-flow", dates from this period.

The wooded island created between the Danube and its canals by the first stage of canalization is known as Donauinsel, or Danube Island. It is Vienna's largest recreation area and a favour-ite with the local population, who come here to swim and sunbathe in the summer. The vast park is criss-crossed by dozens of avenues, walking and cycling paths, picnic areas with built-in barbecues as well as nudist areas. Even water-skiing and surfing are possible. Once the weather warms up, the Copa Cabana entertainment centre attracts visitors with its array of bars, restaurants, discos and the popular *Heurigen*.

The island hosts an annual festival, with open-air pop concerts and other events.

The vast, modern complex of UNO-City on the Danube

UNO-City ❼

🔲 Alte Donau, Vienna International Center. 🚌 20B. **UNO** 📷 11am, 2pm Mon–Fri. **Donauturm** 📞 263 35 72. 🔲 www.unvienna.org

ON THE LEFT bank of the Danube is UNO-City, one of only three United Nations headquarters. The complex stands on international, non-Austrian territory; its post office uses its own special postage stamps and UN postmarks. UNO-City consists of four vast semicircular buildings and a large congress hall, one of the most strikingly modern in Europe, designed by the architect Johann Staber and opened in 1979. Today, visitors can join one of the regular guided tours of UNO-City. The entire area is being redeveloped.

UNO-City is surrounded by a green park, covering an area of over 600,000 sq m (700,000 sq yds), with excellent recreational facilities. One of the main attractions is the Donauturm, a TV tower rising to 252 m (827 ft), with two revolving restaurants and an observation platform.

Prater ❽

📞 Praterverband 728 05 16. Ferris Wheel 72 95 430. 🔲 Praterstern. 🚋 5, 21, O. Ⓢ Wien Nord. 🕐 15 Mar–15 Oct: 10am–midnight daily. 🔲 www.wiener-prater.at

ORIGINALLY an imperial hunting ground, the woods and meadows between the Danube and its canal were opened to the public by Joseph II in 1766. The Hauptallee (central avenue) was for a long time the preserve of the nobility and their footmen. During the 19th century, the western end of Prater became a massive funfair with booths, sideshows, shooting galleries, merry-go-rounds and beer gardens. Today, it is one of Europe's best-equipped amusement parks, with high-tech rides. Its most famous attraction is the giant Riesenrad (ferris wheel) built in 1896 by the English engineer Walter Basset. The setting for the tense final scene in Carol Reed's film *The Third Man* (1949), it is now one of the city's symbols.

The Prater is also a vast sports park, home to a soccer and a trotting stadium, the Freudenau Racetrack, swimming pools, tennis courts, a golf course and cycling trails, as well as a planetarium and open-air restaurants and bars.

Nearby are the pavilions and vast grounds of the annual Vienna Fair for numerous temporary exhibitions.

The Prater funfair at night

Hundertwasser-Haus ❾

Löwengasse/Kegelgasse. 🔲 Landstraße. 🚋 N, O. 🔲 www.hundertwasserhaus.at. ⚫ no admission to the public. **Kunsthaus Wien** 📞 71 20 495-12.

HUNDERTWASSER-Haus is a municipal apartment block created in 1985 by the artist Friedensreich Hundertwasser. An eclectic-style building, combining the elements of a Moorish mosque with features of Spanish villages and Venetian palaces, it has become one of Vienna's main attractions. The shopping centre opposite was designed by the artist, whose work is on show at the Kunsthaus Wien, Untere Weißgerberstraße 13.

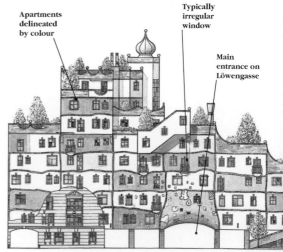

Apartments delineated by colour

Typically irregular window

Main entrance on Löwengasse

Heeresgeschicht-liches Museum ⑩

Ghegastraße Arsenal, Objekt 18.
■ 79 56 10. Ⓤ Südtiroler Platz,
Schlachthausgasse. Ⓢ Südbahnhof.
▥ 13A, 69A. ▦ 18, O & D.
○ 9am–5pm Mon–Thu, Sat, Sun.
Guided tours: 11am, 2:15pm Sun
and public holidays. ● 1 Jan, 1 May,
All Saints, 4, 25, 31 Dec. ▨

Decorative tiling from the 1920s in Amalienbad

THE IMPRESSIVE Museum of Army History is housed in the military complex known as the Arsenal, built as a fortress in 1856. The museum, which chronicles Austria's military prowess from the 16th century, was designed by Theophil Hansen and Ludwig Förster.

Exhibits relate to the Turkish Siege of Vienna in 1683, the French Revolution and the Napoleonic wars. There are documents relating to the battles fought by the Habsburgs, a collection of arms, banners, uniforms and military vehicles. Among the most fascinating exhibits are memorabilia relating to Prince Eugene of Savoy, as well as a collection of model ships that illustrates the past glories of imperial power at sea – since it is landlocked, it is easy to forget that Austria was once a formidable naval power. A separate section is devoted to

the events in Sarajevo on 28 June 1914, when Archduke Ferdinand and his wife Sophie von Hohenberg were assassinated by a Serbian nationalist, provoking a crisis that led to the outbreak of World War I.

Amalienbad ⑪

Reumannplatz 23. ■ 60 74 747.
Ⓤ Reumannplatz. ▥ 67, 68A.
○ 12:30–3pm Mon, 9am–6pm Tue,
9am–9:30pm Wed, Fri, 7am–9:30pm
Thu, 7am–8pm Sat, 7am–6pm Sun.

PUBLIC BATHS may not seem like an obvious tourist attraction, but the *Jugendstil*-style Amalienbad (1923–6) is a fine example of a far-sighted municipal authority providing

essential public facilities for the local working population, and doing so with style and panache. Named after one of the councillors, Amalie Pölzer, the baths were designed by Otto Nadel and Karl Schmalhofer, employees of the city's architectural department.

The magnificent main pool, overlooked by galleries, is covered by a glass roof that can be opened in minutes. There are saunas, smaller baths and therapeutic pools. When first opened, the baths were one of the largest of their kind in Europe. The interior is enlivened by fabulous Secession tile decorations. The baths were damaged in World War II but have been impeccably restored.

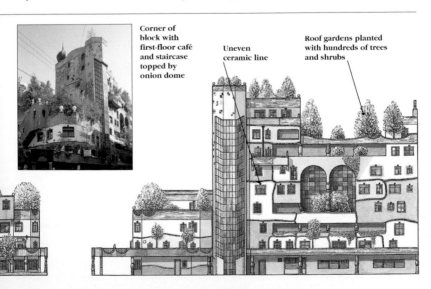

Corner of block with first-floor café and staircase topped by onion dome

Uneven ceramic line

Roof gardens planted with hundreds of trees and shrubs

Zentralfriedhof ⑫

Headstone on Johannes Brahms' grave

Aᴜꜱᴛʀɪᴀ'ꜱ ʟᴀʀɢᴇꜱᴛ burial ground, containing two and a half million graves and covering over 2.5 sq km (1 sq mile), was opened in 1874. The central section includes the graves of artists, composers, architects, writers and local politicians. Funerals in Vienna are often quite lavish affairs, and the cemetery contains a vast array of funerary monuments, from the humble to the ostentatious, paying tribute to the city's enduring obsession with death.

★ Dr.-Karl-Lueger-Kirche
This church and mausoleum is dedicated to Vienna's much-esteemed mayor of 1907–10.

Arcades around the cemetery's Secession church

Presidential Vault
This contains the remains of Dr Karl Renner, the first President of the Austrian Republic after World War II.

CᴇᴍᴇᴛᴇʀY Lᴀʏᴏᴜᴛ

The cemetery is divided into numbered sections: apart from the central garden of honour (reached via gate II), where VIPs are buried, there are old (gate I) and new (gate IV) Jewish cemeteries, a Protestant cemetery (gate III), a Russian Orthodox section, and various war graves and memorials. It is easiest to explore the cemetery on board the circulating minibus.

The Monument to the Dead of World War II is a powerful representation of a grieving mother by Anton Hanak.

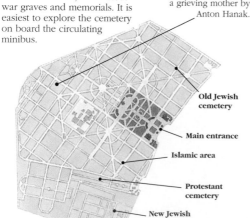

Old Jewish cemetery

Main entrance

Islamic area

Protestant cemetery

New Jewish cemetery

Arnold Schönberg's Cube
The grave of the modernist composer Arnold Schönberg, creator of dodecaphonic music, is marked with this bold cube by Fritz Wotruba.

Sᴛᴀʀ Fᴇᴀᴛᴜʀᴇꜱ

★ Dr.-Karl-Lueger-Kirche

★ Musicians' Graves

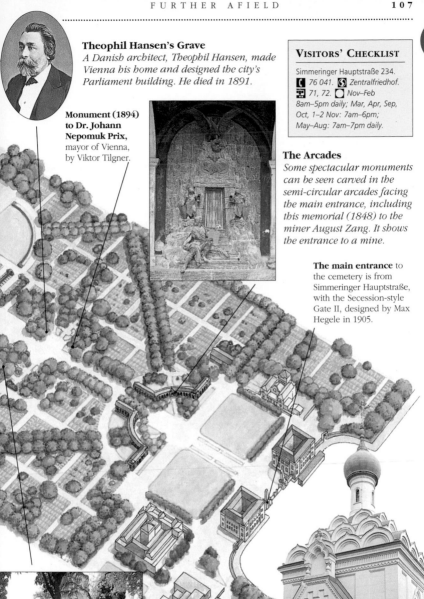

Theophil Hansen's Grave
A Danish architect, Theophil Hansen, made Vienna his home and designed the city's Parliament building. He died in 1891.

Monument (1894) to Dr. Johann Nepomuk Prix, mayor of Vienna, by Viktor Tilgner.

VISITORS' CHECKLIST

Simmeringer Hauptstraße 234.
76 041. Zentralfriedhof.
71, 72. Nov–Feb
8am–5pm daily; Mar, Apr, Sep,
Oct, 1–2 Nov: 7am–6pm;
May–Aug: 7am–7pm daily.

The Arcades
Some spectacular monuments can be seen carved in the semi-circular arcades facing the main entrance, including this memorial (1848) to the miner August Zang. It shows the entrance to a mine.

The main entrance to the cemetery is from Simmeringer Hauptstraße, with the Secession-style Gate II, designed by Max Hegele in 1905.

★ Graves of the Musicians
The musicians buried here include Johann Strauss father and son (shown left), Brahms, Beethoven and Schubert. There is also a monument to Mozart.

Russian Orthodox Chapel
This small chapel, built in traditional Russian Orthodox style in 1894, is used by Vienna's Russian community.

Brahms' Room in the Haydn-Museum

Haydn-Museum ⑬

Haydngasse 19. 📞 59 61 307.
🚇 Zieglergasse. 🕐 9am–12:15pm,
1–4:30pm Tue–Sun. ● 1 Jan, 1 May,
25 Dec. 🎫 Admission free – Fri am.

HAYDN built this house in what was then a new suburb with money that he had earned on his successful trips to London between 1791 and 1795. He lived in the house from 1797 until his death in 1809, and composed many major works here, including *The Seasons* and *The Creation*.

The museum is not very comprehensive but it has a few portraits, autographs, documents and original scores on display. A separate room is devoted to another great composer, Johannes Brahms. Here, you can see some furniture and a few mementoes as well as the clavichord, originally Haydn's, that was bought by Brahms.

Museum of Technology ⑭

Mariahilfer Straße 212. 📞 89 998 6000. 🚇 Schönbrunn, Johnstraße. 🚋 52, 58. 🚌 10A, 57A. 🕐 9am–6pm Mon–Fri, 10am–6pm Sat, Sun and holidays. 🌐 www.tmw.at

FOLLOWING complete reconstruction over several years, Vienna's Museum of Technology, originally founded by Franz Joseph I in 1908, was reopened in 1999.

The museum documents technical progress over the past centuries, from domestic appliances to heavy industry, with a particular emphasis on Austrian engineers and scientists. Exhibits include the world's first sewing machine

(Madersperger, 1830), the oldest typewriter (Mitterhofer, 1860), the ship's propeller, designed by Ressel in 1875, and the first petrol-driven car built in the same year by Siegfried Marcus. A major new section features displays on computer technology and oil and gas refining, as well as a reconstructed coal mine.

The Railway Museum, which is an integral part of the museum, houses a large collection of imperial railway carriages and engines. Its prize exhibit is the carriage used by Franz Joseph I's wife, the Empress Elisabeth. The Post Office Museum displays the world's first postcard – an Austrian invention.

A huge lighthouse at the entrance recalls the Habsburg Empire's once formidable extent, from the Tatra Mountains to the Atlantic Ocean.

Schönbrunn ⑮

See pp110–11.

Kirche am Steinhof ⑯

Baumgartner Höhe 1.
📞 91 060-11 204. 🚌 47A, 48A.
🎫 3pm Sat.

AT THE EDGE of the Vienna Woods rises the conspicuous copper dome of the astonishing Church at Steinhof. Built in 1902–7 by Otto Wagner, the church is considered to be one of the most important works of the Secession. It is an integral part of the large mental hospital complex, also designed by Wagner, who laid out the church to facilitate access for disabled churchgoers.

The church, dedicated to St Leonard, is clad in marble with copper nailhead ornament, and has spindly screw-shaped pillars topped by wreaths supporting the porch, and four stone columns. The light and airy interior is a single space with shallow side chapels. Its main decoration consists of gold and white friezes as well as gilt nailhead and beautiful blue stained-glass windows by Kolo Moser. The altar mosaics are by Rudolf Jettmar.

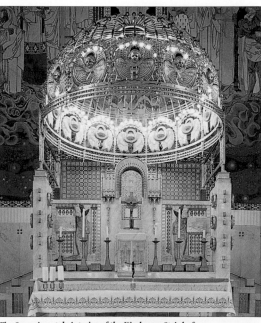

The Secession-style interior of the Kirche am Steinhof

Hermes Villa in Lainzer Tiergarten, retreat of the imperial family

Wagner Villas ⓱

Hüttelbergstraße 26 & 28. **℡** 914 85 75. **Ⓤ** Hütteldorf. **🚌** 148, 152. **Fuchs Villa ◯** 10am–5pm Mon–Fri. 🎟 ✔

HIDDEN behind dense, leafy greenery, at the start of a road to Kahlenberg, stand two villas built by the architect Otto Wagner. The oldest, built for himself, still has some Classical elements such as Ionic columns, once favoured by Wagner. It was meticulously restored by the present owner, the painter Ernst Fuchs, who added his own colours and established a museum. The villa is now a famous meeting place for Vienna's artistic community as well as a venue for fund-raising auctions. The second villa, built some 20 years later, was completed in pure Secession style. Privately owned, it can be viewed only from outside.

Lainzer Tiergarten ⓲

Hermesstraße. **🚌** 60B. **Hermes Villa ℡** 80 41 324. **◯** Special exhibitions: Apr–Sep: 10am–6pm Tue–Sun and public holidays; Oct–Mar: 9am–4:30pm Tue–Sun and public holidays. **◐** Closed for long periods between exhibitions. 🎟 Admission free – Fri am.

THE LAINZER TIERGARTEN in the Vienna Woods, once an imperial hunting ground, was enclosed within a 25-km (16-mile) long wall on the orders of Maria Theresa. The wall still stands today and

successfully stops herds of deer and wild boar escaping as well as building development encroaching.

The Tiergarten was opened to the public in 1923, and in 1941 the entire area was declared a nature reserve. Walks in the woods and meadows of this large park will transport the visitor into another world. It is forbidden to disturb the animals; bikes and dogs are banned, turning the reserve into a true haven for wildlife.

There are now also bars and cafés here. From the observation platform on top of Karlbründl, there are great views over Vienna and the Vienna Woods.

Detail on the stables in Hermes Villa

A 15-minute walk along paths brings you to the **Hermes Villa**. In 1885, the Emperor Franz Joseph I ordered a hunting lodge to be built here and presented it to his wife Elisabeth, in the hope that this would keep her close to the court and stop her from perpetually seeking to escape the clamour of the city. He did not succeed, but the beautiful Hermes Villa was built by Karl von Hasenauer as a retreat for the imperial family. The couple's rooms were on the first floor; Elisabeth's quarters were designed with

flourish and elegance; Franz Joseph's were much more spartan. The villa, named after a marble statue of Hermes, was fully equipped with electricity, and was served by one of the first lit-up streets. Bathtubs and toilets were added by the Empress in the 1890s. Attractive murals show scenes from *A Midsummer Night's Dream*, designed by Hans Makart and painted by the young Gustav Klimt.

Today, Hermes Villa holds exhibitions, while the stables act as summer quarters for the Lipizzaner horses from the Winter Riding School.

Wotruba-Kirche ⓳

Georgsgasse/Rysergasse. **℡** 88 85 003. **🚌** 60A. **◯** 2–8pm Sat, 9am–5pm Sun and public holidays. ✔ by appointment.

STANDING ON hillside close to the Vienna Woods, this church was designed in uncompromisingly modern style in 1965 by the Austrian sculptor Fritz Wotruba (1907–75), after whom it is named.

It was built in 1974–6 by Fritz Mayer. The church is made up of a pile of uneven concrete slabs and glass panels that provide its principal lighting and views for the congregation out onto the hills.

The building is raw in style, but powerful and compact. The church looks different from every angle and has a strong sculptural quality. The central section, consisting of 152 concrete blocks, can accommodate a congregation of up to 250.

The sculptural Wotruba-Kirche

Schönbrunn ⑮

IN 1695, EMPEROR LEOPOLD I asked Johann Bernhard Fischer von Erlach to rebuild the former summer residence of the imperial family. However, it was not until the reign of Maria Theresa that the project was completed by Nikolaus Pacassi (1744–9). It is to him that the palace owes the magnificent Rococo decorations of its state rooms. Schönbrunn has been the scene of many important historic events.

Round Chinese Cabinet
Maria Theresa used this room for private discussions with her State Chancellor, Prince Kaunitz. The walls of the white-and-gold room are adorned with lacquered panels.

★ Great Gallery
Used for imperial banquets, this room has a lovely ceiling fresco by Georgio Gugliemi.

A hidden staircase leads to the apartment of the State Chancellor, above which he had secret conferences with the Empress.

Blue Chinese Salon
The last Austrian emperor, Karl I, signed his abdication in 1918 in this Rococo room with Chinese scenes.

Napoleon Room

Millionen-Zimmer (Millions Room), with superb Rococo decor, was Maria Theresa's conference room.

★ Vieux-Lacque Room
During her widowhood Maria Theresa lived in this room, which is decorated with exquisite oriental lacquered panels.

Main entrance

Miniatures Cabinet
*The paintings on the wall of
Maria Theresa's breakfast room
are copies of Dutch and German
paintings by Franz Stephan
and his daughters Maria Anna,
Maria Christine and Maria
Antonia.*

VISITORS' CHECKLIST

Schönbrunner Schlossstraße 147.
📞 81 11 32 39. Ⓤ Schönbrunn,
Hietzing. 🚋 10, 58, 60. 🚌 10A.
Palace 🕐 1 Apr–30 Jun, Sep–Oct:
8:30am–5pm; Jul–Aug: 8:30am–
6pm; Nov–Mar: 8:30am–4:30pm
daily. 🖼 **Gardens** 🕐 morning
till dusk. 🌐 www.schoenbrunn.at

Large Rosa Room
*This is one of three rooms
decorated with monu-
mental Swiss and Italian
landscape paintings by
Josef Rosa, after whom the
room is named.*

PALACE GUIDE
*On the first floor, the suite of rooms
to the right of the Blue Staircase was
occupied by Emperor Franz Joseph I
and his wife Elisabeth. The rooms in
the east wing include Maria Theresa's
bedroom and rooms used by Grand
Duke Karl.*

STAR FEATURES

★ **Great Gallery**

★ **Vieux-Lacque Room**

The Blue Staircase
leads to the entrance for all
tours of the state rooms.

THE COACH MUSEUM

One wing of Schönbrunn Palace, formerly housing the
Winter Riding School, now contains a marvellous
collection of coaches – one of the most interesting in the
world. It includes over 60 carriages dating back to the
17th century, as well as riding uniforms, horse tackle,
saddles, coachman liveries, and paintings and drawings
of horses and carriages. The pride of the collection is the
coronation coach of Emperor
Karl VI. Other exhibits
include sleighs and sedan
chairs belonging
to Maria Theresa,
among others.

**Coronation
coach of Karl VI**

KEY

☐ Franz Joseph I's apartments

☐ Empress Elisabeth's apartments

☐ Ceremonial and reception rooms

☐ Maria Theresa's rooms

☐ Grand Duke Karl's rooms

☐ Closed to visitors

SHOPPING IN VIENNA

SINCE VIENNA is a compact city, it is a pleasant place to shop. The main shopping area is pedestrianized and you can browse around at a leisurely pace. Austrian glassware, food and traditional crafts are all good buys. However, the shops tend to cater for fairly mature tastes and full purses. Vienna has a

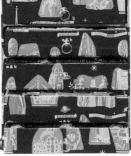

Augarten porcelain Lipizzaner

number of markets selling anything from produce to trinkets. The pedestrian shopping areas of Kärntner Straße, Graben and Kohlmarkt have more expensive shops. The largest shopping centre is SCS (Shopping Centre Süd), in the suburbs. It can be reached on the southern motorway or the Baden train.

WHERE TO SHOP

THE MOST elegant shops are found within the Ring, and the most attractive window displays can be seen in Kärntner Straße, Graben, Kohlmarkt and the central shopping passage connecting Kärntner Straße with Weihburggasse. The shops here are also the more expensive ones; there are no big department stores in this area. Instead, you will find smaller shops, tastefully decorated, offering goods of guaranteed quality and which are often truly unique. This applies to clothes, glass and porcelain, as well as to confectionery and decorative items. There are also some excellent bookshops here.

The shops along Mariahilfer Straße are more middle-of-the-range; this is where you will find many of the multinational chains (C&A, H&M, Mango and many others), as well as large shoe shops, stationery and book shops, and a variety of food shops. A similar range of goods, but at lower prices, can be found in

Meidlinger Hauptstraße, and even less costly ones are on sale in Favoritenstraße.

All of Vienna's shopping areas can easily be explored by public transport.

OPENING HOURS

SHOPS GENERALLY open at 8:30 or 9am and close at 6 or 7pm. Traditionally, shops closed at noon on Saturdays, but nowadays many stay open till 5pm. Shops stay closed on Sundays and public holidays.

You can buy some items at petrol stations, the major railway stations and at the airports, but you will be charged for the privilege.

HOW TO PAY

VIENNA IS more credit-card orientated than before, and most of the large stores accept all major credit cards, including Visa, MasterCard and American Express. It is still wise to carry some cash. Visitors normally resident outside the EU are entitled to claim back the VAT (Mehrwertsteuer – MwSt) if the

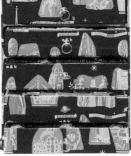

A chest of drawers with chocolates from Altman & Kühne

total value of goods purchased in any one shop exceeds 73 euros. Take your passport when shopping and ask the shopkeeper to complete the appropriate form; keep the receipts. The VAT rate is 20 per cent and the goods listed in the form must be unused and available for inspection by Customs officers.

RIGHTS AND SERVICES

IF YOU HAVE purchased goods that turn out to be defective, you are usually entitled to a refund, provided you have kept the receipt. This is not always the case with goods bought in the sales – inspect them carefully before you buy. Many shops in Vienna will pack goods for you – and often gift-wrap them at no extra charge – and send them anywhere in the world.

ANTIQUES AND ART

A PAWNSHOP established by Emperor Joseph I in 1703 has been transformed into Austria's largest auction house,

Opulent glassware in a shop on Kärntner Straße

Dorotheum, one of the best known in the world. Items auctioned here include mainly antique furniture and objects of decorative value. Its vast store at Dorotheergasse No. 17 is open to the public and also conducts a non-auction sale. Dorotheum has several branches all over the city.

Lovely second-hand and antique items can also be bought at the flea markets that take place regularly in one part of town or other; the largest of them, but also the most expensive, is the **Naschmarkt** *(see p93)*.

FOOD AND DRINK

VIENNA IS JUSTLY famous for its cakes, pastries and *Torten*, and any good *Café-Konditorei* (cake shop and café) will post cakes back home for you. In the pre-Christmas period, try the buttery Advent *Stollen* from **Meinl am Graben**, or the original *Sachertorte*, directly from the **Hotel Sacher**, at any time of year. The specialist chocolate shops are also worth a visit if you have a sweet tooth. And look out for *Eiswein,* a delicious dessert wine made from grapes left on the vine after the first frosts.

Kohlmarkt, one of Vienna's most fashionable shopping streets

SOUVENIRS

THERE ARE MANY things you can buy to remind you of Austria, from the kitsch, such as the giant Ferris Wheel in a snowstorm or drinking glasses playing *O du lieber Augustin*, to the classy, such as Biedermeier-style flower posies, handbags embroidered with folkloric designs or figurines and tableware from the

Augarten porcelain manufactury. There are also cups with the profile of Romy Schneider in her role as Sissi, or pictures of the young Franz Joseph I. Traditional Austrian clothes or *Trachten* are sold by **Witzky** and others, including *Loden*, a felt-like fabric used to make warm coats, jackets and capes, and *Dirndls* (dresses). Zauberklingl is the place for practical jokers, with great party jokes.

DIRECTORY

ANTIQUES & ART

Dorotheum
Dorotheergasse 17.
Map 2 B4. 51 560.

Galerie Rauhenstein
Rauhensteingasse 3.
Map 2 C4.
513 30 09.

Kunst- und Antikmarkt
Donaukanal-Promenade.
Map 3 D3.
May–Sep: 2–6pm Sat, 10am–8pm Sun.

Naschmarkt
Map 4 C1.
6am–6:30pm Mon–Fri, 6am–3pm Sat, Flea market: 6am–2pm Sat.

FOOD & DRINK

Altmann & Kühne
Graben 30.
Map 2 B4.
533 09 27.

Hotel Sacher
Philharmonikerstraße 4.
Map 2 B5.
514 56 0–0.

Meinl am Graben
Graben 19.
Map 2 B4.
532 33 34.

Vinotek St. Stephan
Stephansplatz 6.
Map 2 C4.
512 68 58.

Delikatessen Böhle
Wollzeile 30. **Map** 2 B4.
512 31 55.

Zum Schwarzen Kameel
Bognergasse 5.
Map 2 B3.
533 81 25.

SOUVENIRS

Augarten
Stock-im-Eisen-Platz 3–4.
Map 2 C4.
512 14 94.

J. & J. Lobmeyr
Kärntner Straße 26.
Map 2 C5.
512 05 08.

Kalke Village
Kegelgasse 37–39.
Map 2 C4.
710 46 16.

Maria Stransky
Hofburg Passage 2.
Map 2 B4.
533 60 98.

Metzger
Stephansplatz 7.
Map 2 C4.
512 34 33.

Österreichische Werkstätten
Kärntner Straße 6.
Map 2 C4.
512 24 18.

Petit Point
Kärntner Straße 16.
Map 2 C4.
512 48 86.

Witzky Landhausmode
Stephansplatz 7.
Map 2 C4.
512 48 43.

Zauberklingl
Führichgasse 4.
Map 2 C4.
512 68 68.

ENTERTAINMENT IN VIENNA

VIENNA OFFERS a wide range of entertainment of every kind, from street theatre in the famous Prater funfair to classical drama in one of the opulent theatres. But most of all, Vienna is a musical town. There is grand opera at the Staatsoper, or the latest musical at the Theater an der Wien; dignified orchestral music and elegant waltzes; relaxed dances in the Stadtpark and free open-air concerts. Even the famous Lipizzaner horses perform to Viennese music. The city also takes pride in its Burgtheater, one of the most

Papageno puppet

foremost stages in the German-speaking world, as well as its many smaller dramatic theatres. There are two excellent theatres performing in English and several cinemas which specialize in classic films. Restaurants tend to close early but you can still be entertained around the clock at one of the many nightspots: jazz clubs, discos, casinos and bars with live music all beckon within the Ringstraße. Or you can end your day sipping coffee and indulging in the gorgeous pastries at one of the late-night cafés.

The giant Ferris wheel in the Prater funfair

PRACTICAL INFORMATION

LISTINGS OF CURRENT events and theatre, concert and cinema programmes can be found in most daily newspapers; check *Neue Kronen Zeitung, Die Presse, Standard* or *Kurier*. The weekly guide *Der Falter* (www.falter.at) is entirely devoted to the arts. The Vienna Tourist Office (Wiener Tourismusverband) publishes a monthly guide with listings of art and sports events taking place that month, and every hotel has a range of free leaflets with details of concerts, theatre performances and other artistic events. You can also check the fat round billboard columns all over the city, which have posters advertising the latest events.

Most theatres, concert halls and public buildings have been specially adapted to accommodate disabled spectators (ramps, lifts), and many museums also offer wheelchairs for hire. All have at least one disabled toilet.

BOOKING TICKETS

YOU CAN BUY TICKETS directly from the appropriate box office, or reserve them by telephone or via the Internet. Hotel receptions can often help. Theatres offer various concessions and the opera house sells cheap tickets for standing-only places. Tickets bought in advance tend to be up to 10 per cent cheaper than those bought just before the start of a performance.

MUSIC

THE PRINCIPAL VENUES for classical concerts, including the ever-popular waltzes, are the **Staatsoper** (State Opera), the concert halls of the **Musikverein**, where the Wiener Philharmoniker perform, and the **Konzerthaus**. Here you can hear the world's greatest performers. Classical music concerts are also held in many churches. Open-air concerts are very popular during the summer season. Another Viennese favourite is the **Kursalon Hübner**, where you can enjoy old and new tunes while overlooking the Stadtpark.

The **Donauinselfestival**, staged in the summer on the Danube island, is a great way to hear free pop concerts by some of the world's most popular performers. During local festivals, in wine bars

A young street musician entertaining with his cello

and cafés you can often hear Viennese folk music called *Schrammelmusik* after the music by the Schrammel Brothers. Kärntner Straße is another kind of music venue – many street performers and buskers here hope for hand-outs from the generally well-to-do passers-by.

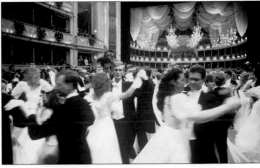

The famous Vienna State Opera Ball

THEATRES

VIENNA'S **Staatsoper** enjoys an excellent international reputation. Opera is also shown at the **Wiener Volksoper** (Vienna People's Opera) and the **Wiener Kammeroper** (Vienna Chamber Opera). The **Raimund Theater** is one of the best places for musicals. The **Theater an der Wien** specializes in opera productions. The **Burgtheater** is still regarded by many as one of the most interesting theatres; a smaller and more intimate stage is called **Akademietheater**. The **Volkstheater** stages modern plays and the occasional classic drama, while the **Theater in der Josefstadt** specializes in subtle takes on comedy, both old and new, as well as performances of past and contemporary Austrian drama.

CINEMAS

MOST FILMS are dubbed and shown in German; those that can be watched in their original language are always advertised as such in the programme. Some cinemas specialize in foreign films. The **Österreichisches Filmmuseum,** based in the Albertina building, screens classics of the silver screen, while the **Votivkino** and the **Filmhaus Stöbergasse** cinemas often put on a season of films devoted to one artist or subject; it is usually these art-house and repertory cinemas that show the most interesting films in the city.

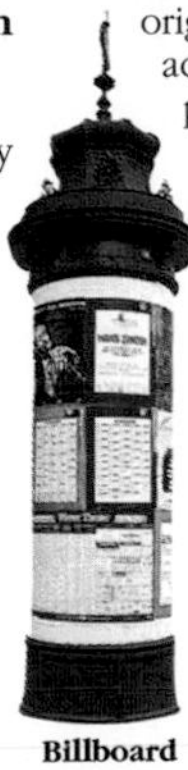

Billboard column

CASINOS

CASINO WIEN is set in the fabulous Baroque Esterházy Palace, where you can play French or American roulette, baccarat and poker.

AFTER A NIGHT OUT

AT NIGHT, public transport is provided by a network of hourly buses, departing from the central points at Schwedenplatz or Franz-Josef-Kai and travelling in various directions. It is worth buying a ticket in advance from the kiosk, as these are cheaper than the ones sold on the bus. Buses, trams and trains open doors only on request. Taxis can be found outside all the major venues and at taxi ranks.

DIRECTORY

BOOKINGS

Bundestheaterkassen
Opernring 2.
Map 2 B5.
513 15 13.
8am–6pm Mon–Fri, 9am–noon Sat, Sun and public holidays.

CONCERT HALLS

Konzerthaus
Lothringerstraße 20.
Map 5 D1. *24 20 02.*
www.konzerthaus.at.

Kursalon Hübner
Johannesgasse 33.
Map 3 D5. *512 57 90.*

Staatsoper
Opernring 2.
Map 2 B5. *51444 2250.* *www.wiener-staatsoper.at.*

Musikverein
Bösendorferstraße 12.
Map 5 D1. *50 58 190.*
www.musikverein.at.

THEATRES

Akademietheater
Lisztstraße 1. **Map** 5 E1.
Tickets: Opernring 2.
51444–4140.

Burgtheater
Dr.-Karl-Lueger-Ring 2.
Map 2 A3. *51444–4400.*

Raimund Theater
Wallgasse 18–20.
59 9770.

Theater an der Wien
Linke Wienzeile 6.
Map 4 C1.
58 885.

Theater in der Josefstadt
Josefstädter Straße 26.
Map 1 B4. *42 700.*

Volkstheater
Neustiftgasse 1.
Map 1 C5. *52 47 263.*

Wiener Kammeroper
Fleischmarkt 24. **Map** 3 D3.
51 201–0077.

Wiener Volksoper
Währingerstraße 78.
Map 1 C1.
51 444–3670.

CINEMAS

Österreichisches Filmmuseum
Augustinerstraße 1.
Members only.
Map 2 B5. *53 37 054.*

Filmhaus Stöbergasse
Stöbergasse 11–15.
Map 4 A 4/5.
54666–30.

Votivkino
Währingerstraße 12.
Map 2 A2. *31 73 571.*

CASINO

Casino Wien
Kärntner Straße 41.
Map 2 B5.
51 24 836.

MAP OF VIENNA

THE MAP REFERENCES given for all the sights, hotels, restaurants, bars, shops and entertainment venues described in this book refer to the maps in this section. Most of the city's famous sights, historic buildings, tram, bus, U-Bahn and railway stations, and river landing-stages have been marked on the map. Others are indicated by symbols, which are explained in the key below. The names of the streets and squares on the map are given in German. The word *Straße* (Str.) translates as street, while *Gasse* is a smaller street, *Platz* means square, *Hof* means a courtyard, *Brücke* translates as bridge and a *Bahnhof* is a railway station.

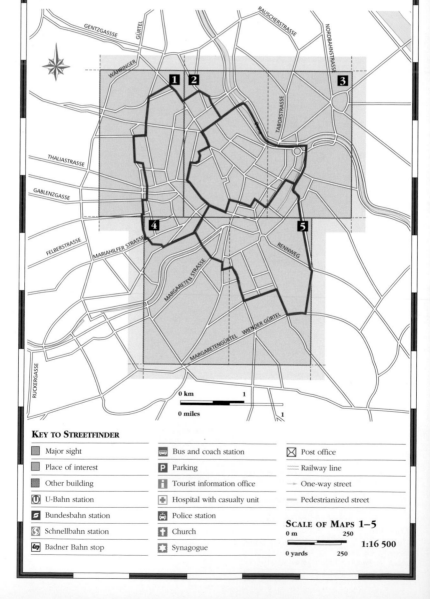

KEY TO STREETFINDER

▦ Major sight	🚌 Bus and coach station	⊠ Post office
▦ Place of interest	🅿 Parking	══ Railway line
▦ Other building	🛈 Tourist information office	→ One-way street
Ⓤ U-Bahn station	✚ Hospital with casualty unit	— Pedestrianized street
🚆 Bundesbahn station	👮 Police station	
Ⓢ Schnellbahn station	✝ Church	**SCALE OF MAPS 1–5**
🚋 Badner Bahn stop	✡ Synagogue	0 m 250
		0 yards 250 **1:16 500**

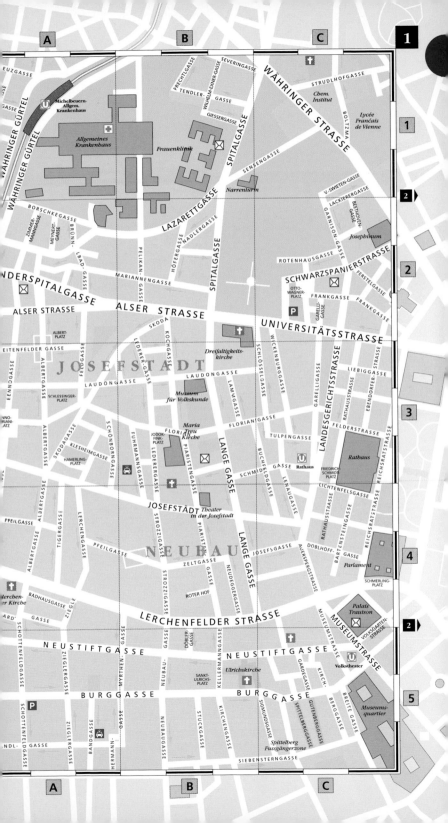

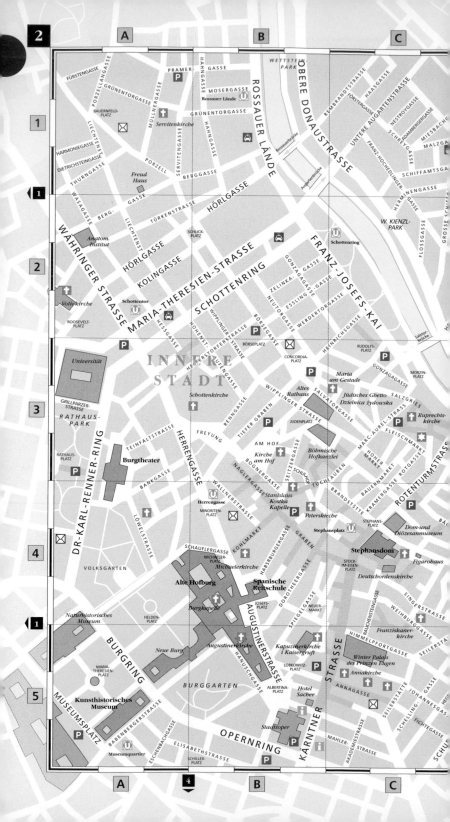

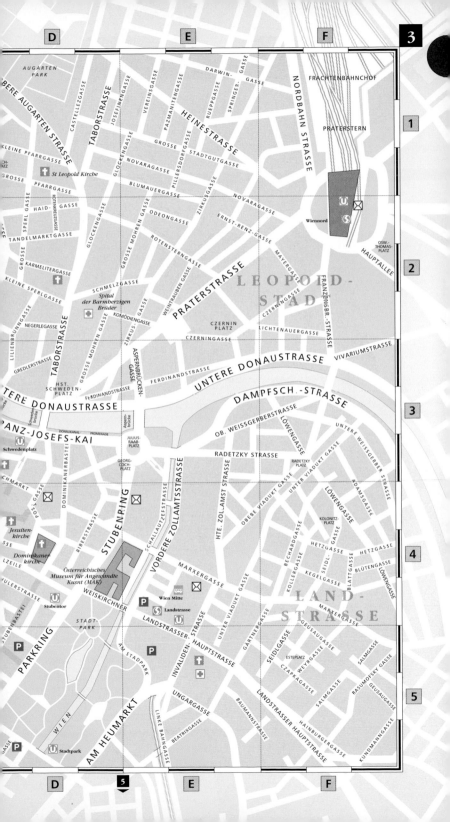

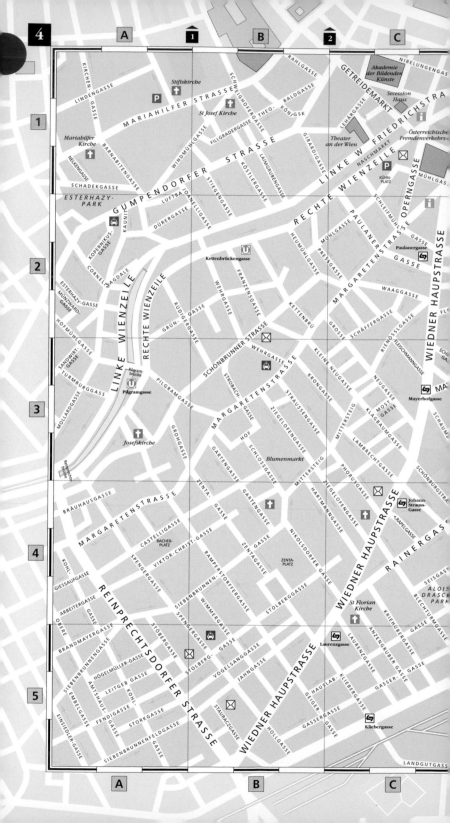

Streetfinder Index

AUSTRIA
REGION
BY REGION

Austria at a Glance

THIS MODEST-SIZED country situated at the heart of Europe is a true paradise for visitors. There is its beautiful countryside – from Neusiedler Lake in the east, surrounded by vast, flat steppes, to the fertile plains of the Danube Valley; the scenic Vienna Woods; and three majestic alpine ranges that cut across the country from west to east. These glorious settings provide stunning backdrops for the historic sites and art treasures that form Austria's cultural highlights, and the names of great artists and Habsburg rulers will follow you wherever you go. There are also grand Baroque abbeys, and everywhere you can enjoy the work of Austria's outstanding musicians – Mozart, Strauss, Haydn and Beethoven, an adopted citizen of Vienna.

The Mirabell Palace in Salzburg was built in the 17th century for Salome Alt, the mistress of Archbishop Wolf Dietrich. The magnificent stairway is adorned with sculptures by Raphael Donner.

Innsbruck, with its picturesque Old Town and church spires rising against the majestic backdrop of the snow-covered Alps, is the capital of the Tyrol, the picture-postcard province most popular with visitors.

UPPER AUSTRIA
(see pp186–209)

SALZBURGER LAND
(see pp210–233)

TYROL & VORARLBERG
(see pp234–263)

CARINTHIA & EAST TYROL
(see pp264–281)

Houses in Bregenz, capital of the Vorarlberg province, are decorated with early heraldic paintings and the figures of saints.

Bruck Castle in Lienz, in East Tyrol, was built in 1252–77 for the Görz family. Today, it is the home of the Heimatmuseum, with a fine collection of 19th- and 20th-century popular Austrian art and folklore items.

◁ **Maria Himmelfahrtskirche and ruins of Künringerburg above Durnstein**

Hauptplatz in Linz, *capital of Upper Austria, is one of the most beautiful architectural sights in Central Europe. In the centre of the square stands the marble column of the Holy Trinity (1723).*

LOWER AUSTRIA
& BURGENLAND
(see pp128–155)

VIENNA
(see pp50–123)

A Monument to Strauss and Lanner *was erected in the spa park of Baden, a sleepy town close to Vienna, famous for its sulphuric baths and casino, one of the oldest in Austria.*

STYRIA
(see pp156–185)

The Landhaus in Klagenfurt, *seat of the Carinthian provincial government, was built in the 16th century in an Italianate style, and is one of Klagenfurt's most attractive buildings. Its glorious galleried inner courtyard remains intact to this day.*

The Zeughaus in Graz, *capital of Styria province, is an impressive display of the city's armoury and former power.*

0 km   50

0 miles   50

LOWER AUSTRIA & BURGENLAND

L OWER AUSTRIA *is the largest province in Austria, both in terms of area and population. It surrounds the Austrian capital, Vienna, which for many years doubled as capital of the province. Following a plebiscite in 1986, the provincial capital was moved to St Pölten. At the edge of Lower Austria, bordering Hungary along one side, is the low-lying province of Burgenland, with its capital Eisenstadt.*

Lower Austria, together with Upper Austria, covers the area that was once the cradle of the country. The low-lying and gently undulating terrain make this region easily accessible. During Roman times, its southern reaches belonged to the provinces of Noricum and Pannonia, while the areas north of the Danube frequently changed hands as Slav and German tribes fought over them. From AD 791, Lower Austria belonged to the Franks and, in AD 970, it was given the name Ostmark (Eastern Margravate). Today, it occupies an area of 19,163 sq km (6,930 sq miles) and stretches along the Danube valley, from the German border in the west, to Hungary in the east. In the south it reaches the slopes of the limestone Rax Mountains, with their highest peak, Schneeberg, and the popular winter resort of Semmering.

Lower Austria's most important towns, beside St Pölten, are Krems, Mödling, Wiener Neustadt, Klosterneuburg and Baden bei Wien. In the north of the province, adjoining the Czech Republic and Slovakia, lies the vine-growing region of Weinviertel. Further west is the wooded Waldviertel.

To the southeast of Lower Austria, from Neusiedler See downwards, is the long province of Burgenland, covering an area of 3,965 sq km (1,530 sq miles), with a population of 278,000. Historically, it was a part of Hungary, but after the Turkish wars (1529–1791) it was settled by Germans and Croats, and finally included in Austria in 1921.

The main town in Burgenland is Eisenstadt, where the mighty Esterházy family established their seat; to this day they continue to play an important role in the region's development.

The ornate 19th-century casino in the spa town of Baden bei Wien

◁ The 19th-century mock-Gothic Franzensburg Castle in Laxenburg

Exploring Lower Austria and Burgenland

THE WACHAU, a narrow stretch of the Danube valley, forms the heart of Lower Austria, famous for its fertile plains, its vineyards and picturesque villages. Formidable fortresses, castles and fortified abbeys rise along the high banks of the river, including the imposing Benedictine Abbey in Melk. Further east, the *Wienerwald* (Vienna Woods) is perfect for walking and cycling. Burgenland Province has its own unique flora and fauna around Neusiedler See. It produces the finest red wines in Austria and celebrates the memory of Joseph Haydn, former choirmaster to the Esterházy family in Eisenstadt.

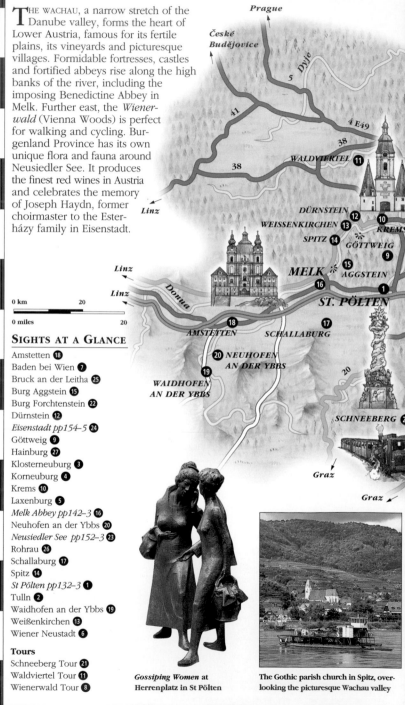

Prague

České Budějovice

Linz

Dyje

WALDVIERTEL 11

DÜRNSTEIN 12

WEISSENKIRCHEN 13   KREMS 10

SPITZ 14   GÖTTWEIG 9

MELK 15   AGGSTEIN

16   ST. PÖLTEN 1

Linz

Linz

Linz

Donau

18   17
AMSTETTEN   SCHALLABURG

20   NEUHOFEN AN DER YBBS

19
WAIDHOFEN AN DER YBBS

SCHNEEBERG 21

Graz

Graz

0 km   20

0 miles   20

Gossiping Women at Herrenplatz in St Pölten

The Gothic parish church in Spitz, overlooking the picturesque Wachau valley

SEE ALSO

• *Where to Stay* pp290–94

• *Where to Eat* pp321–5

16th-century Teisenhoferhof, with its attractive galleried
courtyard, now home of the Wachau Museum

The mock-Gothic Franzensburg
Castle, in Laxenburg

KEY

▬	Motorway
▬	Major road
▬	Scenic route
▬	River
✳	Viewpoint

GETTING AROUND

Flights to both provinces depart from Vienna-
Schwechat International Airport, which is served
by every major airline. St Pölten is a major railway and road hub, situated on the route of the
Westbahn line, with branch lines to Mariazell,
Krems, Tulln and Gaming. St Pölten is also
served by the Westautobahn (motorway) and the
road connecting Vienna and Salzburg. The entire
region is covered by a dense road network.

St. Pölten ●

THE CAPITAL of Lower Austria since 1986, St. Pölten was the first Austrian city to be granted municipal rights, in 1159. Its history dates back to Roman times, and it achieved considerable status under the Augustinian orders in the 8th century. St. Pölten's fastest period of growth, however, was during the Baroque period, when outstanding masters of that era, such as the architect Jakob Prandtauer and the painters Daniel Gran, Paul Troger and Bartolomeo Altomonte, made their home here. Economically, St. Pölten became the most important city in Lower Austria when trade switched from the Danube waterways to overland roads.

Rathausplatz in St. Pölten, with the Holy Trinity column

Exploring St. Pölten

The beautiful Baroque centre, with several older buildings, lies to the south of the railway station between Domplatz, Riemerplatz and Rathausplatz. The town centre is compact and easy to explore on foot, being largely pedestrianized. Apart from fascinating Baroque buildings and those associated with the town's administrative role, St. Pölten also has more recent architecture of interest.

A detail on the cathedral door

⋔ Domkirche
Mariä Himmelfahrt
Domplatz 1. 【 (02742) 353 402.
Diocesan Museum 【 (02742) 324 331. ◻ May–Oct: 10am–noon, 2–5pm Tue–Fri, 10am–1pm Sat, Sun. ◪
In the 12th century, a church dedicated to St Hippolytus stood on this site. After a devastating fire in 1278, the church was renovated and practically rebuilt in Baroque style to designs by Jakob Prandtauer. Deceptively plain on the outside, the cathedral's interior is a typical example of exuberant Baroque ornamentation. Daniel Gran and Bartolomeo Altomonte created the large wall and ceiling paintings, depicting scenes from the life of Jesus.

Adjoining the cathedral is the Bishops' Palace, once an abbey, with a lovely staircase, also by Prandtauer, and a magnificent library decorated by Paul Troger.

The **Diocesan Museum** houses a collection of sculptures, paintings and decorative art objects dating from the Gothic and Baroque periods. Behind the palace, at No. 1 Klostergasse, is the apartment of Jakob Prandtauer.

⋔ Franziskanerkirche
Rathausplatz.
The Franciscan church of the Holy Trinity, together with its friary, occupies the narrow, northern end of the square. A Rococo church with a delightful pink façade, it is unusual because it has no tower. The church interior, also decorated in Rococo style, features an altarpiece by Andreas Gruber. There are four wing paintings by another well-known Austrian Baroque artist, Martin Johann Schmidt, known as Kremser Schmidt.

⋔ Rathaus
Rathausplatz. 【 (02742) 35 33 54.
The present town hall was built in the 16th century by combining two Gothic buildings in a mishmash of incongruous styles. The niches of the Gothic entrance gate abut a Renaissance portal, the Gothic tower has a Baroque onion dome on top, and the entire structure has been concealed behind a Baroque façade. Inside, however, it is worth seeing the ceiling stuccowork in the Mayor's Chamber and sculptures by Christoph Kirschner.

The town hall occupies the southern side of Rathausplatz, once considered the most beautiful square in Austria. Today, it is lined with modern buildings, and has lost some of its Baroque charm. Next to the town hall you can see the house where Franz Schubert once lived, and at No. 5 is the Montecuccoli Palace. The façades of both buildings were created by Prandtauer's nephew, Joseph Munggenast. At the centre of the square stands the marble column of the Holy Trinity, with a fountain and statues of saints.

The Mayor's Chamber in the Rathaus

✠ Institut der Englischen Fräulein

Linzer Straße 9–11. █ *(02742) 3521 88–0.* ◯ **Church:** *10am–5pm daily.*

The Institute of the English Ladies, founded by the English Catholic nun Mary Ward, established several schools in St. Pölten to educate the girls of aristocratic families. The institute, one of the most beautiful Baroque buildings in Lower Austria, was begun in 1715 and enlarged some 50 years later. Prandtauer created the beautiful white and pink façade, punctuated by black wrought-iron grills on the windows, with three groups of sculptures on two floors.

St Mary column, in the centre of the Baroque Herrenplatz

✠ Riemerplatz

Riemerplatz is another beautiful Baroque square, lined with exquisite buildings such as the striking Herbertstein Palace, at the wider end of Wiener Straße. In Kremser Gasse, which runs north from the square, at No. 41, stands the delightful Stöhr Haus with its breathtakingly beautiful Art Nouveau façade. It is the work of the architect Joseph Maria Olbrich, who also designed the superb Secession Building in Vienna.

✠ Herrenplatz

This is yet another attractive Baroque square in the city; its most outstanding features are the Baroque façades of the buildings around the square.

VISITORS' CHECKLIST

Road map F3. 🏘 *50,000.*
🚌 🚉 ℹ *Rathaus (02742-353354).* **FAX** *3332819.*
🌐 *www.st-poelten.gv.at*
@ *tourismus@st-poelten.gv.at*

Mostly attributed to Jakob Prandtauer, these façades often hide much earlier medieval niches and arcaded courtyards. On top of the house at No. 2 is a lovely sculpture by Georg Raphael Donner, called *Dispersing of Darkness by Light*. At the centre of the square stands St Mary's Column (1718).

✠ Wiener Straße

Wiener Straße, adjacent to Herrenplatz, has been a main thoroughfare since Roman times, as is still obvious today from its many inns. There are a number of interesting historical buildings in this road, including St Pölten's oldest pharmacy, at No. 1, dating back to 1595. Its façade, built in 1727 by Joseph Munggenast, still displays the pharmacist's original coat of arms from 1607 and the 19th-century sign "Zum Goldenen Löwen" (To the Golden Lion).

A statue on the façade of the Institut der Englischen Fräulein

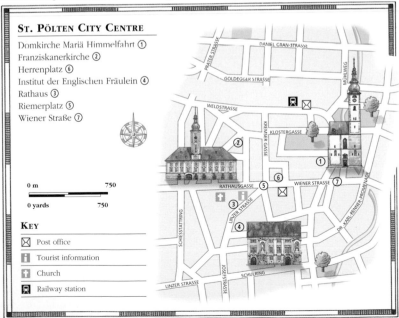

ST. PÖLTEN CITY CENTRE

Domkirche Mariä Himmelfahrt ①
Franziskanerkirche ②
Herrenplatz ⑥
Institut der Englischen Fräulein ④
Rathaus ③
Riemerplatz ⑤
Wiener Straße ⑦

0 m — 750
0 yards — 750

KEY

⊠ Post office
ℹ Tourist information
✝ Church
🚉 Railway station

The 13th-century funerary chapel of the Three Wise Men in Tulln

Tulln ②

Road map F3. 🏛 *12,300.*
🚆 🚌 🚉 ℹ *Tourismusverband
Tullner Donauraum, Minoritenplatz 2
(02272) 65 836.* 📠 *02272/65 838.*
🌐 *www.tulln.at*

TULLN, ON THE right bank of
the Danube river, was the
site of the Roman camp of
Comagena. Two structures
remain from that period: the
3rd-century Roman Tower,
probably the oldest structure
in Austria, and a milestone.

Tulln is famous as the birthplace of Egon Schiele, one of
the foremost painters of the
turn of the 20th century, best
known for his provocative
nudes. The **Egon-Schiele-
Museum**, housed in an old
prison on the banks of the
Danube, shows 90 original
works by the artists and the
permanent exhibition *Egon
Schiele and his Times*.

In Minoritenkloster is a new
museum complex, the **Tullner
Museen**, devoted to the small
town's history.

The Romanesque **Pfarrkirche St Stephan**, the parish
church of St Stephen, was
built in the 12th century, but
subsequently altered, first in
Gothic, then in Baroque style.
It has an interesting Romanesque portal with 12 reliefs,
probably representing the
apostles. Next to the church
is the 13th-century mortuary,
one of the more interesting
historic sites in town. It holds
the cemetery chapel of the
Three Wise Men, the largest
and most famous in Austria,
combining elements of late-

Romanesque style with early
Gothic, and featuring a
beautifully decorated portal
and well-preserved murals.

The remains of the old city
walls are also still preserved.

🏛 **Egon-Schiele-Museum**
Donaulände 28. 📞 *(02272) 645 70.*
⭕ *Mar–Nov: 10am–6pm Tue–Sun;
guided tours on request.* 🌐
www.egonschiele.museum.com. 📷
🏛 **Tullner Museen
im Minoritenkloster**
Minoritenplatz 1. 📞 *(02272) 61
915.* ⭕ *only by prior arrangement.* 📷

Klosterneuburg ③

Road map G3. 🏛 *30,500.* 🚆 🚌
🚉 ℹ *Niedermarkt 4 (02243) 343 96.*
🌐 *www.klosterneuburg.at.*

THIS SMALL TOWN, just outside
Vienna, was once the main
seat of the Babenberg rulers.
In the early 12th century,
Margrave Leopold III built his
castle here, and later the
collegiate church, the
magnificent **Stift
Klosterneuburg**,
supposedly in
atonement for an
act of treason he
committed against
Heinrich V.

The Romanesque
church of the Augus-
tinian Abbey was
altered many times
until the 17th and
18th centuries, when it
acquired its present Baroque
interior, designed by Joseph
Fischer von Erlach and Felice
Donato d'Allio, among others.
Original features include the
early-Gothic cloister
and burial chapel of
Leopold III; the latter
contains the town's
greatest treasure, an
altarpiece by Nicolas of
Verdun, a goldsmith
and master of enamel
from Lorraine. In 1181,
the church acquired its
altar, with 45 gilded
and enamelled tiles
depicting Bible scenes.
The chapel also has fine
stained-glass windows.

The museum in the
former imperial resi-
dence holds a valuable
collection of paintings

**A wine barrel in
Klosterneuburg**

and Gothic and Baroque sculptures. A new highlight is the
Essl Collection, an important
museum specializing in
Austrian art since 1945.

A small museum in nearby
Kierling is devoted to the
writer Franz Kafka, based in
the former Hofmann Sanatorium where he died.

🔒 **Stift Klosterneuburg**
📞 *(02243) 411-212.* ⭕ *10am–5pm
daily.* ● *25, 26 Dec.* 📷
🏛 **Essl Collection of
Contemporary Art**
An der Donau-Au 1. 📞 *(0800) 232 800.*
⭕ *10am–7pm Tue–Sun, 10am–9pm
Wed.* 📷 🌐 *www.sammlung-essl.at*

Korneuburg ④

Road map G3. 🏛 *8,500.*
🌐 *www.korneuburg.gv.at*

KORNEUBURG ONCE formed a
single town with Kloster-
neuburg. In 1298 it became
independent, and grew into an
important trading and
administrative centre.
Hauptplatz, the
main square, is
surrounded by
houses with late-
Gothic, Renais-
sance and Baroque
façades. Other inter-
esting sights include
the late-Gothic Ägid-
kirche (church of St
Giles) and the Roco-
co Augustinerkirche (church
of St Augustine), whose main
altarpiece shows the sky resting on four columns, with
God the Father sitting on his
throne, holding the Earth in

The main altarpiece in Korneuburg

Franzensburg Castle, a mock-Gothic folly in Laxenburg

his hand. The altar painting of the *Last Supper* is the work of Franz Anton Maulbertsch.

Burg Kreuzenstein, on the road to Stockerau, is a fascinating folly of a Gothic castle. Built in the 19th century by Count Hans von Wilczek, on the site of a former fortress (1140) that was almost entirely destroyed by Swedish forces during the Thirty Years' War, it holds the count's extensive collection of late-Gothic art and handicrafts.

Laxenburg ❺

Road map G3. 🚌 **H** Gemeinde-
amt (02236) 71101. **FAX** 73150.

THIS SMALL TOWN, situated 15 km (9 miles) outside Vienna, is a favourite place for day-trips from the capital. It began as a hunting lodge, Lachsenburg, around which a settlement grew. Destroyed during the last Turkish wars, but restored and enlarged in the 17th century, it became a favourite retreat for Maria Theresa, other members of the imperial family and the aristocracy. Laxenburg was chosen as a venue for the signing of many important state treaties, including the Pragmatic Sanction which made it possible for a woman, Maria Theresa, to accede to the throne. Today, the former imperial palace is the seat of the International Institute of

System Analysis (IISA), and it also houses the Austrian Film Archives. The palace is surrounded by a landscaped, English-style **Schlosspark**, one of the grandest such palace parks in Europe at the time of Emperor Joseph II.

The park is dotted with many follies, and one particularly worth visiting is the early 19th-century **Franzensburg**, a mock-Gothic castle, built on an island in an artificial lake within the palace grounds at the height of the fashion for all things historic. It was furnished with original objects collected and pillaged from all over the empire, such as the 12th-century columns with capitals in the chapel, from Klosterneuburg, or the ceiling in the Hungarian Coronation Room from the Hungarian town of Eger. In the summer, open-air theatre performances take place on the castle island.

Wiener Neustadt ❻

Road map G3. 🚶 37,600.
🚌 🚉 **H** Hauptplatz 1–3 (02622) 373-468. **W** www.wiener-neustadt.at

THIS LARGE town, some 40 km (25 miles) south of Vienna, is an industrial city and an important road and rail transport hub, and also the largest shopping city of Lower Austria.

In the centre of the town is the attractive Hauptplatz, with a part-Gothic **Rathaus** (town hall) rebuilt in Baroque style. Gothic houses line the northern side of the square, and the St Mary's Column (1678) stands in the centre. The **Dom** (Cathedral Church of the Ascension of Our Lady) was built in the 13th century. Its outstanding features include 12 wooden statues of the apostles by the columns of the central nave, and the Baroque main altar. The Brautportal (Portal of the Betrothed) dates from 1230.

In **Stift Neukloster** (Holy Trinity church) you can see a beautifully carved stone on the tomb of Eleanor of Portugal, wife of Emperor Friedrich III, by Niklas Gerhaert of Leyden, dating from 1467.

The former castle now houses the prestigious Military Academy, once commanded by General Rommel. In its west wing is the 15th-century **St. Georgs-Kathedrale** (St George's cathedral), with the tomb of Maximilian I under the main altar. A corner tower, a remnant of the old fortified city walls, now houses a criminology museum and a gruesome exhibition of instruments of torture.

The town hall in Hauptplatz, Wiener Neustadt

One of many attractive villas in
Baden bei Wien

Baden bei Wien ⑦

Road map G3. 🏛 28,000. ⑤ 🚌
🅿 ℹ Brusattiplatz 3 (02252)
22 600–600. W www.baden.at.
🎭 Operetta Festival (Jul); Festival of
Roses (Jun).

T HE SPA TOWN of Baden, on
the eastern slopes of the
Vienna Woods, was already
known in Roman times, when
it was called *Aquae Panno-
niae*, and Emperor Marcus
Aurelius praised its sulphuric
springs. Today, its 15 hot
springs make Baden a popular
destination with older patients,
but taking a hot sulphur bath
is a relaxing experience for
younger visitors too. In summer, you can swimm in the
open-air Art-Deco baths.

The small town was com-
pletely rebuilt after a fire in
1812, and many of its attractive Neo-Classical town houses
and Biedermeier-style villas
hail from this period. The
main architect at the time,
Joseph Kornhäusel (1786–
1860), largely shaped the
look of the town.

At one time, the list of
Baden visitors read like a
Who's Who of the rich and
famous, and included such
luminaries as Wolfgang Amadeus Mozart, who composed
his *Ave Verum* here; Franz
Schubert; and, most importantly, Ludwig van Beethoven.
It was here that he composed
his *Ninth Symphony*. Baden
was frequented by the maes-
tros of Viennese operetta as
well: Strauss (father and son),
Lanner and Zille. Napoleon
also holidayed here with his
wife Marie Louise.

Wienerwald Tour ⑧

T HE VIENNA WOODS (Wienerwald), to the west of
the capital, are a favourite weekend destination
for the Viennese. Crossed by numerous walking and
cycling tracks, the wooded hills covering an area of
1,250 sq km (480 sq miles) are a perfect place for
recreation. The main towns in the area are
Klosterneuburg, former capital of the Babenbergs,
Tulln *(see p134)* and Baden, one of Europe's most
famous spa towns. There are also some interesting
works of art and unique scenery worth seeing.

Heiligenkreuz ②
The Cistercian Abbey (1133) at
Heiligenkreuz, founded by
Leopold III of Babenberg, has
retained its fine Romanesque-
Gothic character and some
Baroque furnishings to this day.

• Alland

KEY

▬	Suggested route
▬	Scenic road
═	Other road
≈	River, lake

Mayerling ③
After the suspected
double suicide of Rudolf
and Mary von Vetsera,
Franz Joseph had the
famous hunting lodge
converted into a Carme-
lite chapel of atonement.

THE MAYERLING MYSTERY

Rudolf, the only son of Franz
Joseph I and Elisabeth, was a rest-
less man, unable to adjust to the
rigours of court. After a fierce
quarrel with his father, he went
to Mayerling with his mistress,
Mary von Vetsera. On 30 January,
the two lovers' bodies were
found in the lodge. They had
seemingly committed suicide:
Mary had drunk poison and
Rudolf had then shot himself.
The reason for the tragedy remains
a mystery to this day.

**The tombstone of Mary
von Vetsera**

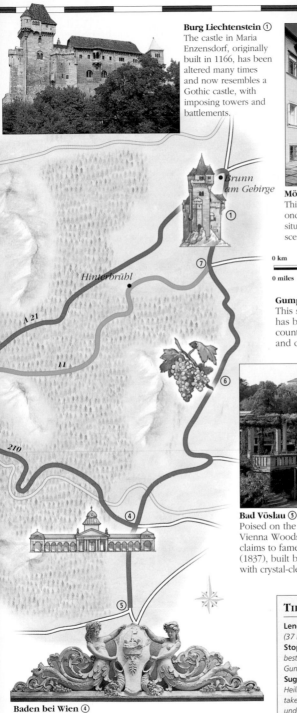

Burg Liechtenstein ①
The castle in Maria Enzensdorf, originally built in 1166, has been altered many times and now resembles a Gothic castle, with imposing towers and battlements.

Mödling ⑦
This small, picturesque town, once a retreat for artists, is situated in beautiful natural scenery of limestone rocks.

```
0 km                    3
0 miles                 3
```

Gumpoldskirchen ⑥
This small wine-making town has become famous for its countless *Heurigen* wine bars and cheerful restaurants.

Bad Vöslau ⑤
Poised on the southern slopes of the Vienna Woods, this village has two claims to fame: its wines and its baths (1837), built by Count Moritz Fries, with crystal-clear natural mineral water.

Baden bei Wien ④
Frauenbad, one of the original 19th-century baths, is today no longer in use but makes an interesting historic sight.

TIPS FOR VISITORS

Length of the route: *60 km (37 miles).*

Stopping places: *most of the best restaurants can be found in Gumpoldskirchen and Baden.*

Suggestions: *visit the abbey in Heiligenkreuz.* ☎ *(02258) 8720; take a boat excursion on the underground lake in Seegrotte Hinterbrühl* ☎ *(02236) 26364.*

The magnificent organ in Göttweig Abbey

Göttweig ⑨

Road map F3. 🚌 🚊 🛈 *Furth (02732) 5582.* ◯ *May–Oct: 9:30am–noon, 1:30–5:30pm Tue, Fri, Sat, Sun and public holidays.*

STIFT GÖTTWEIG, a Benedictine Abbey, crowns a hilltop on the south bank of the Danube, near Krems. Founded in 1083, it was inhabited by Benedictine monks from St Blasien in the Black Forest in 1094. **Stift Göttweig** is sometimes referred to as the Austrian Monte Cassino because, superficially, it resembles the Benedictine mother abbey. The abbey was rebuilt after a fire in 1718, according to plans by Johann Lukas von Hildebrandt. The project was never completed, however, and the present abbey has an interesting but somewhat asymmetrical outline, with a Neo-Classical façade. In 1739, a magnificent flight of stairs, known as Kaiserstiege (imperial staircase) was added to the western section of the abbey. The stairs are lined with statues representing the four seasons and the twelve months of the year. Inside, the abbey is adorned with a fresco by Paul Troger, depicting the apotheosis of Karl VI. The abbey has an interesting collection of sculptures, paintings and graphic art. The

Exhibit from the Wine Museum in Krems

abbey restaurant affords great views of the surroundings.

🛈 **Stift Göttweig**
📞 *(02732) 85581-231.* ◯ *21 Mar–15 Nov: 8am–6pm daily.* 📷

Krems ⑩

Road map F3. 🏠 *23,000.* 🚌
🛈 *Undstraße 6 (02732) 82676.* 🚊
🎭 *Folklore Festival (Jul), Niederöster-reichische Landesmesse (Aug).*

DURING THE 11th and 12th centuries, Krems, then known as *Chremis*, was a serious rival to Vienna. Today, this attractive town on the left bank of the Danube, together with neighbouring Stein, is a popular destination. Visitors are enchanted by the beautiful architecture of its town houses and courtyards, which give Krems a southern, Italian feel. There are remains of the old town walls, but the greatest attraction is the late-Gothic **Piaristenkirche**, an imposing Piarist church built on the foundations of an older church. It boasts a beautiful Baroque altarpiece by the local artist Johann Martin Schmidt, known as Kremser Schmidt. The **Veitskirche**, the parish church of St Veit, is the earliest Baroque church in Austria, the work of the Ciprian Biasin. The former Dominican abbey has

a lovely early-Gothic cloister; it is now the History Museum. Krems also has a Renaissance town hall and the vast, 13th-century **Gozzoburg**, a palace built by Judge Gozzo.

The Minoritenkirche, the Church of the Minorite Monks in Stein dates from the same period. It is adorned with 14th-century paintings of the Virgin Mary on a throne. The parish church of St Nicholas has beautiful ceiling frescoes and an altarpiece painted by Kremser Schmidt.

Waldviertel Tour ⑪

See pp140–41.

Dürnstein ⑫

Road map F3. 🏠 *1,000.* 🚌
🛈 *Rathaus (02711) 219.* ◯
8am–noon, 1–4pm Mon–Fri. 🚊

MUCH OF THE popularity of the idyllically situated town of Dürnstein is due to the adventures of the English King, Richard the Lionheart. On the Third Crusade, undertaken with the French King Philip August and the Austrian Margrave Leopold V, Richard fell out with his fellow crusaders. On his journey home through Babenberg territories, in 1192, he was imprisoned in the Künringerburg fortress above Dürnstein, whose ruins can still be seen today. As legend has it, the King's faithful French minstrel, Jean Blondel, discovered him with a song known only to the two of them. A ransom of 35,000 kg (77,100 lbs) silver was paid and Richard released. The Babenbergs used the money to fortify Enns, Hainburg, Wiener Neustadt and Vienna, while the name of the faithful servant lives on in many of Dürnstein's establishments.

The Baroque silhouette of the **Stiftskirche** (Collegiate Church of the Assumption of the Virgin Mary) towering above the town was created by the masters of the day. The courtyard is probably the work of Jakob Prandtauer;

the entrance is embellished with lovely, decorated portals.

The former convent of St Claire is now an inn; the Renaissance castle a hotel.

The Baroque tower of the Pfarr-kirche in Dürnstein

Weißenkirchen

Road map F3. 1,060.
(02715) 2600.

THE SMALL village in the heart of the Wachau Valley has attracted artists since 1900, who come to paint the magnificent scenery of the Danube gorge and to enjoy the cosy inns. Today, their works can be seen in the **Wachaumuseum**, in the Teisenhoferhof, a Renaissance mansion. Another attraction is the Wehrkirche Maria Himmelfahrt (Church of the Assumption of the Virgin Mary), on a hilltop, fortified against Turkish raiders. The well-preserved defence towers are remains of those fortifications. The main entrance to the church is through the western portal, which has fine mouldings. Inside, on the rainbow arch, is a beautiful painting (1520) of the Madonna, from the Danube School.

Wachaumuseum
(02715) 2268. Apr–Oct: 10am–5pm Tue–Sun. Mon.

ENVIRONS: Situated between Weißenkirchen and Spitz is the small village of **St Michael**, with another example of a fortified church. A few miles

beyond Spitz is **Willendorf**, where the famous statuette of the *Venus of Willendorf* was found. This representation of female fertility is believed to be over 25,000 years old. The figure itself is now kept in Vienna's Natural History Museum *(see p82)*, while an over-life-sized copy stands in a field near Willendorf.

Spitz

Road map F3. 1,930.
(02713) 23 63. 2–4pm Mon–Fri.

ON THE BANKS of the River Danube at the foot of the Tausendeimerberg (thousand bucket hill, so called because of the amount of wine it was said to produce), nestles the enchanting town of Spitz an der Donau. The river was once important to the town's economic life, and the **Schifffahrtsmuseum** tells the story of the Danube navigation.

Another famous sight is the **Pfarrkirche**, the early-Gothic parish church of St Maurice, furnished in late-Gothic style. The church has a presbytery (1508), criss-cross vaulting and elaborate window lace-work. The altar painting is by Kremser Schmidt. Lovely wooden statues from around 1380, showing Christ and the apostles, are set in niches along the Gothic gallery.

High above the town looms the ruin of Hinterhaus Castle, with its Gothic bulwark and Renaissance fortifications.

Schifffahrtsmuseum
Auf der Wehr 21. (02713) 2246.
Apr–Oct: 10am–noon, 2–4pm Mon–Sat, 10am–noon, 1–5pm Sun.

Ruins of the formidable 12th-century Burg Aggstein

Burg Aggstein

Road map F3.

THE IMPRESSIVE ruins of Burg Aggstein, built into the rock, are poised high above the banks of the river. Today the castle lies in ruin, but once it measured some 100 m (330 ft) in length, with tall stairs leading to the Upper Castle. Built by the notorious Künringers, a band of robber barons, it served to repel attacks by Turks and Swedes during the 16th and 17th centuries, thus cementing its rank as one of the most important fortresses in the region.

Many gruesome stories are told about the castle's early days. Its owner, an unmitigated thief, was said to have laid in wait for passing barges and demanded a hefty toll to allow them passage. Those who refused to pay were imprisoned in the Rosengärtlein, a rose garden set on a rocky shelf, where they would either die of hunger or jump to their death.

Today, the picturesque Burg Aggstein and its café are popular destinations for a day trip from Vienna.

The romantic ruins of Hinterhaus Castle in Spitz

Waldviertel Tour ⓫

BITTERLY FOUGHT over by Germans and Slavs, who both wanted to settle here and exploit the area's natural resources, Austria's northwest boasts numerous historic sights, from abbeys built as defensive structures to the magnificent residences of the nobility built during times of peace. The wooded region became known as an idyllic spot for hunting trips and excursions, and today it is still its natural beauty and recreational facilities which draw most visitors; the traditional crafts practised in the area's numerous villages are another attraction.

Gmünd ①
This town, on the Czech border, has a fascinating glass and stone museum. To the north is the Naturpark Blockheide-Eibenstein, with its vast granite rock formations and an unusual open-air exhibition of minerals.

Rosenau ②
First built in 1590 as a Renaissance palace, Rosenau was remodelled some 150 years later in Baroque style. Its owner, Leopold Schallenberg, set aside some rooms for use as a Masonic lodge; today, it is a Masonic museum.

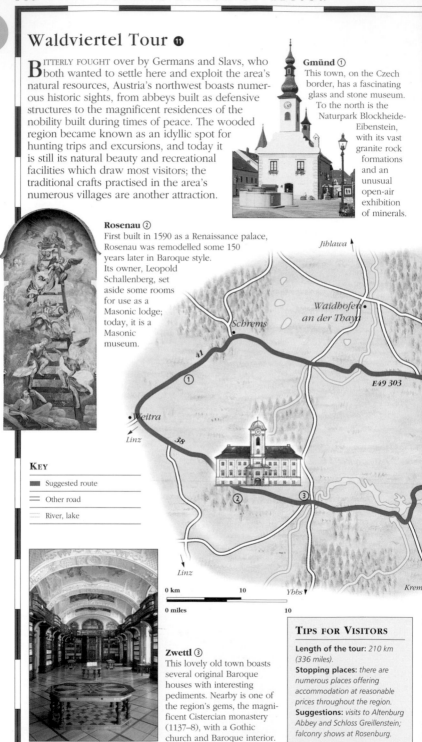

Jihlawa

Waidhofen an der Thaya

Schrems

41

①

E49 303

•Weitra

Linz

38

②

③

KEY

▬ Suggested route

= Other road

≈ River, lake

Linz

0 km — 10

0 miles — 10

Ybbs

Krems

Zwettl ③
This lovely old town boasts several original Baroque houses with interesting pediments. Nearby is one of the region's gems, the magnificent Cistercian monastery (1137–8), with a Gothic church and Baroque interior.

TIPS FOR VISITORS

Length of the tour: *210 km (336 miles).*
Stopping places: *there are numerous places offering accommodation at reasonable prices throughout the region.*
Suggestions: *visits to Altenburg Abbey and Schloss Greillenstein; falconry shows at Rosenburg.*

Greillenstein ⑦
Set in woodland in the Kamp river valley, this Renaissance castle features a beautiful arcaded courtyard and several tall chimneys.

Eggenburg ⑥
A small, medieval town, Eggenburg has two attractions: 1,900 m (6200 ft) of original town walls and towers, and the Museum of Motorcycles & Technology.

Stockerau

Horn

Stockerau

Stockerau

Krems

Rosenburg ⑤
One of Austria's most famous castles, Schloss Rosenburg was rebuilt in Neo-Classical style after a fire. The former state rooms house a splendid museum of old furniture, paintings and arms.

Altenburg ④
This gorgeous Benedictine Abbey (1144) has a great library, a treasury and, above all, a crypt entirely covered in stunning ceiling paintings depicting the dance of death.

FREEMASONRY IN AUSTRIA

Francis Stephen, future husband of Maria Theresa, introduced freemasonry to Austria from Holland. In the late 18th and early 19th centuries, it played a very important role in the Austro-Hungarian empire, with many prominent politicians and artists being counted among its members. An increasing desire for national self-determination and liberal thought slowly removed the masons from power. In 1945, the Grand Masonic Lodge of Austria renewed its activities. Today, it has some 2,400 members in 52 lodges, including many public figures, financiers and artists.

Masonic Lodge in Rosenau

Melk Abbey ⑯

THE TOWN AND ABBEY OF MELK, the original seat of the Babenbergs, tower above the left bank of the Danube, some 60 km (37 miles) west of Vienna. In the 11th century, Leopold II invited the Benedictines from Lambach to Melk and granted them land and the castle, which the monks turned into a fortified abbey. Almost completely destroyed by fire in 1297, the abbey was rebuilt many times. In the 16th century, it had to withstand a Turkish invasion. In 1702, Abbot Berthold Dietmayr began a thorough remodelling of the complex. Jakob Prandtauer, von Erlach, Joseph Munggenast and other renowned artists of the day helped to give the present abbey its magnificent Baroque form.

Stairwell
A spiral staircase with ornamental balustrade connects the library with the Stiftskirche, the monastery church of St Peter and St Paul.

★ Library
The impressive library holds some 100,000 volumes, including 2,000 manuscripts and 1,600 incunabula. It is decorated with a beautiful ceiling fresco by Paul Troger.

Crowning with the Crown of Thorns
This powerful painting by Jörg Breu (1502) is exhibited in the Abbey Museum.

Marble Hall
This magnificent room, decorated with a painting by Paul Troger, was once used for receptions and ceremonies.

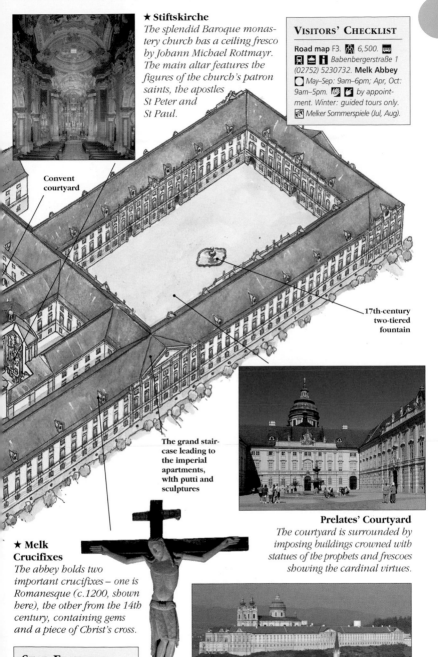

★ Stiftskirche
The splendid Baroque monastery church has a ceiling fresco by Johann Michael Rottmayr. The main altar features the figures of the church's patron saints, the apostles St Peter and St Paul.

Convent courtyard

17th-century two-tiered fountain

The grand staircase leading to the imperial apartments, with putti and sculptures

Prelates' Courtyard
The courtyard is surrounded by imposing buildings crowned with statues of the prophets and frescoes showing the cardinal virtues.

★ Melk Crucifixes
The abbey holds two important crucifixes – one is Romanesque (c.1200, shown here), the other from the 14th century, containing gems and a piece of Christ's cross.

STAR FEATURES

★ Library

★ Melk Crucifixes

★ Stiftskirche of St Peter and St Paul

The view
Austria's most magnificent Baroque monastery, Melk Abbey is a vast yellow building perched dramatically on a high bluff overlooking the Danube.

A figure decorating an elevation of Schallaburg Castle

Schallaburg ⑰

Road map F3. 🚌 📱 *(02754) 6317.*
⭕ *late Apr–Nov: 9am–5pm Mon–Fri,
9am–6pm Sat, Sun, public holidays.* 🅿

SCHALLABURG CASTLE counts as one of the most beautiful Renaissance castles in Lower Austria. It has some early remains of medieval Romanesque and Gothic architecture, but these are overshadowed by later additions. Particularly impressive are the Renaissance courtyard and the two-storey red and white terracotta arcades, the work of Jakob Bernecker. Carved terracotta atlantes support the second-storey arcades; sculptures and terracotta masks decorate the lower niches and walls of the castle. One of the best of these is the mask of a court jester holding a wand. Wilhelm von Losenstein, who owned the castle when the arcades were created, was a Protestant and a Humanist, a fact that is reflected in the works commissioned by him.

At the end of World War II, Schallaburg Castle was totally destroyed by the Russians, and it was not until 1970, when it came into state administration, that work began in order to return the castle to its former splendour.

Today, the Schallaburg houses Lower Austria's Cultural and Educational Centre, and serves as a venue for excellent exhibitions and lectures.

Amstetten ⑱

Road map E3. 🏃 *21,989.* 📱 🚌
🅘 *(07472) 601 456.*

A MAJOR TRANSPORT hub, the town of Amstetten is situated on the Ybbs River near the border with Upper Austria. Originally known as Amistein, the town witnessed the arrival of Illyrian, Celts and Roman settlers over time. It is the largest town in the Mostviertel region, and its regional museum tells the story of local country life in the days prior to the industrial revolution. Also worth seeing in Amstetten are the attractive town hall, the 15th-century parish church of St Stephen with frescoes depicting the Last Judgement, and the Gothic Church of St Agatha.

ENVIRONS: Some 6 km (4 miles) southwest of the town is the medieval **Burg Ulmerfeld**, first recorded in the 10th century. From the 14th century until 1803, the castle belonged to the bishops of Freising. Later transformed into a paper-mill, it is now an important cultural centre and has a collection of arms.

Waidhofen an der Ybbs ⑲

Road map E3. 🏃 *11,744.* 📱 🚌
🅘 *(07442) 511255.*

IN THE 16TH CENTURY, this charming little town in the Ybbs valley was an important centre of iron processing and arms production. Its medieval old town is dominated by church spires and two towers, remains of the medieval fortifications: the 13th-century Ybbsturm and the Stadtturm, which was raised by 50 m (164 ft) in 1534 to celebrate the town's victory over the Turks. Since then, the clock on its north side has shown 11.45am, the hour of victory. The former Capuchin church has an interesting painting by Kremser Schmidt from 1762. Another great attraction is the **Museum**

Regionale, one of the most modern in Lower Austria.

🏛 **Museum Regionale**
Oberer Stadtplatz 32. 📞 *(07442) 511 247.* ⭕ *Easter–26 Oct: 10am–5pm Tue–Sat.* 🅿

Attractive houses and onion-dome spires in Waidhofen an der Ybbs

ENVIRONS: The Carthusian Marienthron Monastery in **Gaming**, the most important structure of its kind in Central Europe, was founded in 1332 by Prince Albrecht II. The monks' cells and the fortified walls with round turrets remain to this day. Its Baroque library has frescoes by the Prague painter Wenzel Lorenz Reiner, his only work on display outside his Czech homeland. Today, the Carthusian monastery is used as a venue for cultural events. One of the best Austrian concert halls, it is much-liked by pianists, and the annual International Chopin Festival is held at Marienthron in late summer.

The town also has an interesting Baroque church, several early buildings, St Mary's column and a pillory.

The Marienthron Monastery in Gaming, seen from the Prelates' Courtyard

Benedictine Abbeys

BENEDICTINE MONASTICISM was established in the 6th century, in Italy, by St Benedict of Nursia, and its mother abbey was Monte Cassino. The first Benedictine abbey in Austria was instituted in the 8th century, in Salzburg, but it was not until the 11th century that the order became a major force. Its growth was linked to the increased importance given to the Austrian state under the rule of the Babenbergs, whose history was chronicled by the Benedictines. Fortified abbeys were built on unassailable hilltops, and rural settlements grew up in the shadow, and under the protection of, the abbeys. The beautiful silhouettes of the abbeys tower over their surroundings. Stunningly decorated inside, they boast marvellous libraries that house outstanding records of the past.

Altenburg Abbey, (see p141) *from the 12th century, was altered in Baroque style in the 18th century. Its façade is adorned with statues and paintings.*

Kremsmünster Abbey (see p200) *houses a tombstone with the figure of Knight Gunther. The inscription tells the legend of how his father founded the abbey in 777, following his son's death.*

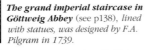

St. Paul im Lavanttal Abbey (see p268) *houses one of the most extensive Benedictine libraries with over 40,000 volumes and manuscripts.*

The grand imperial staircase in Göttweig Abbey (see p138), *lined with statues, was designed by F.A. Pilgram in 1739.*

The family tree of the Babenberg dynasty, who brought the Benedictine monks to their seat in the stunning monastery of Melk, can be studied in Klosterneuburg Abbey (see p134), *just outside Vienna.*

In front of the Stiftskirche in Melk (see pp142–3), *one of the most magnificent abbeys in Austria, extends a terrace affording fabulous views far across the Danube and the surrounding countryside.*

Neuhofen an der Ybbs ⑳

Road map E3. 🏔 *2,550.* 🚌
🏢 *(07475) 52700.* @ *gemeinde
@neuhofen-ybbs.at*

NEUHOFEN is a small town on the Ybbs River, in the foothills of the Alps. Its centre is occupied by a Gothic church with a tall spire. The town was once a stopping place for pilgrims travelling to nearby Sonntagsberg, whose basilica is the central place of worship for followers of the cult of the Virgin Mary.

Today, the **Ostarrichi Kulturhof**, a museum of Austrian history on the outskirts of the village, is the town's top attraction. The modern building was erected in 1980 to designs by Ernst Beneder, who also landscaped the surroundings in an attempt to make new and old blend in a single composition. The museum was built in record time, at a cost of 28.8 million shillings, and in 1996 it became the focus of Austria's 1,000th anniversary celebrations.

The most important exhibit, from which the centre has taken its name, is the facsimile of a document which first mentions the term *Ostarrichi* (the original document is kept in archives in Munich). In this document, dated 1 November 996, Emperor Otto III, ruler of the German Roman Empire, presented the land around

Facsimile of the 996 document, Ostarrichi Kulturhof in Neuhofen an der Ybbs

Niuvanhof (present-day Neuhofen), known as *Ostarrichi* in the local language, to Gottschalk, Bishop of Freising in Bavaria. It was the first time that this name was used to describe the land that was controlled by the Babenbergs and which eventually, in the 11th–12th centuries, would become Austria. The Bishops of Freising had owned estates in this district from as early as the 9th century, and they regularly toured their territories. The names "Osterriche" and "Osterland", which appeared later, referred to the land east of the Enns River. It is fairly likely that originally the name referred to the entire country of Eastern Franconia. With time, Niuvanhof became Neuhofen, and if etymologists are to be believed, the present name of Austria (Österreich) derives from *Ostarrichi*. According to the most widely believed interpretation, it meant "eastern territories",

but an alternative view also exists: at the time when the name *Ostarrichi* first appeared, the area in this part of the Danube valley was still populated by Slav tribes, and the names of many surrounding towns and villages reveal a Slav origin. *Ostarrichi*, as it was then, could come from the Slav word "ostrik", meaning a hill.

Whichever interpretation is accurate, the year 996 is recognized here as the beginning of Austrian history, and the Neuhofen Museum informatively presents the story of the remarkable rise of a small German duchy to the heights of European power as the multi-ethnic Habsburg empire, and the tangled web of history that eventually, in 1918, led to the creation of the Austrian Republic. It also documents the effects of such changes on the population, and demonstrates how the Austrians succeeded in preserving their national identity in the face of the strength of their German neighbours, a culture in many ways akin to their own.

The permanent exhibition in the Kulturhof consists of three parts. The first shows a facsimile of the *Ostarrichi* document in the original Latin version and in its German translation, together with photographs. The second is devoted to the etymological changes that the term has undergone, its geographical, linguistic and political transformations. The third part of the exhibition is devoted to present-day Austria and its provinces. It illustrates how the distinct areas grew together into the Austrian Republic of today, and how each provinces has managed to preserve its own regional identity, customs, traditions, arts and culture.

🏛 **Ostarrichi Kulturhof**
🅒 *(07475) 59065.* 📠 *590652-20.*
🕙 *10am–noon, 1–3pm Tue–Fri,
10am–noon, 1–4pm Sat, Sun, public
holidays.* 🅦 *www.ostarrichi-kulturhof.at*

The Gothic church in the centre of Neuhofen an der Ybbs

Schneeberg Tour ㉑

BOTH THE SCHNEEBERG and Raxalpen mountain ranges are popular with the Viennese for short winter breaks. Situated some 100 km (60 miles) from the capital, they offer excellent and well-developed skiing areas as well as many attractive walking trails for summer outings. The world's first high-mountain railway line was laid here, through the town of Semmering. To this day a ride on the railway is a thrilling experience.

TIPS FOR VISITORS

Length of the route: *130 km (80 miles).*
Stopping places: *hotels and restaurants can be found in Puchberg, Semmering, and at the upper station on Schneeberg.*
Suggestions: *ride on the railway from Puchberg to Schneeberg (late April–early November).*
i *Puchberg (02636) 2256.*

Schneeberg ④
The highest peak in the range and in Lower Austria, whose distinctive silhouette is clearly visible from the motorway between Vienna and Graz, rises to 2,076 m (6,811 ft). The summit affords magnificent views of the Raxalpe range.

Höllental – Hell Valley ⑤
The ravine along the Schwarza River starts from the slopes of Hirschwang, where the first-ever cable car in the world was built in 1926.

Puchberg am Schneeberg ①
A rack-railway links Schneeberg with Puchberg, a popular resort which also boasts an old castle.

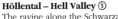

Kernhof

Schwarzau im Gebirge

21

27

Wiener Neustadt

Wiener Neustadt

③

Mariazell

Terz

HÖLLENTAL

⑤

④

26

SCHNEEBERG

①

RAXALPEN

März

Schwarza

②

Glognnitz

Mürzsteg

Kapellen

23

⑥

S6

Mürzzuschlag

Neunkirchen ②
One of the oldest towns in Lower Austria, Neunkirchen has original Renaissance buildings and a church with late-Romanesque details.

Ternitz ③
This small town, in the Sierningbach valley, is a resort as well as a nature reserve. It has a modern church with a large mosaic.

Semmering ⑥
A popular health resort since the early 19th century, this town is known for its long sunshine hours, great views and interesting architecture.

KEY

▬▬ Suggested route

▭▭ Scenic road

═══ Other road

⁓⁓ River, lake

☀ Viewpoint

0 km	5
0 miles	5

Burg Forchtenstein ㉒

Road map G3. 🚉 *Mattersburg.* 🚌
ℹ️ *Hauptstraße 54 (02626) 63125.*
Palace 📞 *(02626) 81212.*
⭘ *Apr–Oct: 9am–4pm, other times by appointment.* ✔️

PERCHED UNASSAILABLY on the rocky slopes of Rosaliengebirge, in a romantic setting, stands Forchtenstein Castle, built in the 14th century by the Mattersdorfer family. Bought and extended by the Esterházys, it now houses a private collection of arms, one of the most magnificent and most extensive in Austria. The castle armoury exhibits arms and war trophies dating from the 16th to 19th centuries as well as memorabilia and pictures from the wars with Turkey, France and Prussia. Forchtenstein Castle was one of the fortresses that defended the Habsburg state during the Turkish raids of 1529 and 1683. Other trophies from that period include a captured Turkish tent, one of the major attractions, as well as vast paintings of battle scenes and a tank, dug 142 m (466 ft) deep into the castle courtyard by the captive Turks. Having played its part in repelling the Turkish threat, the heavily fortified castle, which clings to a near-vertical rock face with walls and turrets encircling a round tower, became

The birthplace of Franz Liszt in Raiding near Forchtenstein

a museum in 1815. Today, a counterpoint to the medieval tower is set by the Baroque onion dome which crowns the Baroque residential parts.

The equestrian statue in the courtyard is of Paul, the first Prince of the Esterházy family, which still owns the castle today. In summer the castle hosts a popular festival.

ENVIRONS: In the village of **Raiding**, 24 km (15 miles) to the south of Forchtenstein, is a lovely cottage, the birthplace of the composer Franz Liszt (the **Liszt Geburtshaus**). The house, which once belonged to the Esterházys, has been turned into a small museum.

🏛 Liszt Geburtshaus
Lisztstraße 46. 📞 *(02619) 7220.* ⭘ *Easter–late Oct: 9am–noon, 1–5pm daily. Other times by appointment.*

Neusiedler See ㉓

See pp152–3.

Eisenstadt ㉔

See pp154–5.

Bruck an der Leitha ㉕

Road map G3. 🚶 *7,000.* 🚉 🚌
ℹ️ *Höfleinerstraße 16 (02162) 6221.*

THIS SMALL town, situated 30 km (19 miles) east of Vienna, was established as a Babenberg fortress in 1230, and formed the main border point between Austria and Hungary. Its present form dates mainly from the turn of the 17th century, but the remains of the medieval fortifications

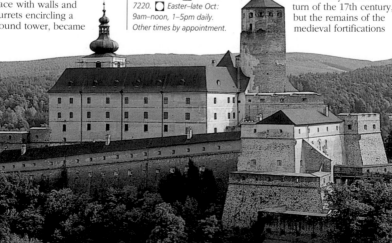

The mighty Burg Forchtenstein, home of the Esterházy arms collection

◁ The tranquil waters of Neusiedler See, jewel of Burgenland from the 13th century, as well as several old houses, remain in the main square today, with some traces of their original Gothic interiors still visible. In the 14th century, Bruck an der Leitha had a thriving Jewish community.

In Hauptplatz, the main square, stands an attractive town hall with a Rococo balcony and an arcaded courtyard. Also here is the Baroque Pfarrkirche (parish church of the Holy Trinity), built by Heinrich Hoffmann. In Friedrich-Schiller-Gasse you stands the Kapuzinerkloster, the Capuchin Friary with its church dating from 1629.

The town's greatest architectural attraction, however, is the **Prugg**, a 13th-century castle with an original early-Gothic turret. In 1707, Lukas von Hildebrandt altered the castle in the Baroque style. The chapel dates from this period, with a 1721 altar painting by Kremser Schmidt.

At No. 1 Johannstraße is an interesting **Heimatmuseum**, devoted to the history and folk art of the region.

Rohrau ㉖

Road map G3. 🏠 *1,260.* 🚌 *Bad Deutsch Altenburg, Petronell.*

EAST OF VIENNA lies the small town of Rohrau, with two attractions: Haydn's birthplace and the Harrach family **castle**. The pretty house in which the composer was born in 1732, and his brother Michael in 1737, is now a small **museum** devoted to both composers.

The nearby Harrach castle is one of the most beautiful private art galleries in Austria. The Harrachs, who occupied important state offices at home and abroad, amassed a splendid collection of 17th- and 18th-century paintings, mainly from Spain and Naples, but also including some from the Netherlands. There are also interesting porcelain pieces. The castle dates from the 16th century but was rebuilt in the 18th century.

The Pagan Gate in the Carnuntum Archaeological Park near Hainburg

🏛 **Geburtshaus Joseph Haydns (Museum)**
📞 *(02164) 2268.* 🕐 *10am–4pm Tue–Sun.* ⚫ *Mon, 24, 25, 26, 31 Dec, 1 Jan.* 📷

🏛 **Harrach'sche Gemälde-galerie (Harrach Castle)**
📞 *(02164) 22538.* 🕐 *Easter–Oct: 10am–5pm Tue–Sun.* ⚫ *Mon.* 📷

Hainburg ㉗

Road map G3. 🏠 *5,700.* 🚌
🅘 *Bad Deutsch Altenburg, Badgasse 17 (02165) 62900-11.*

HAINBURG on the Danube was once a fortified border town of the Eastern Margravate, and it is still a gateway into Austria from the east. The ruins of an 11th-century castle and three substantial town gates remain from this period. The small town has many historic sights, such as the Romanesque cemetery chapel and the Rococo Marian column in Hauptplatz. The best way to

Bust of the composer Joseph Haydn, Rohrau

travel to Hainburg is along the Danube. The marshy area around the town is a nature reserve, and home to rare bird species no longer seen elsewhere. At one time, there were plans to build a dam, drain the marshes and erect a vast hydro-electric power station, but environmental protests stopped the scheme going ahead, and today the area west of Hainburg is preserved as a unique nature reserve.

ENVIRONS: 38 km (24 miles) east of Vienna is the village of **Petronell**, where archaeologists unearthed a Roman town, **Carnuntum**, and the remains of a military camp. The sights open to visitors include a Roman triumphal arch known as Heidentor (pagan gate) and two huge amphitheatres. The ruins of ancient Carnuntum, the former capital of the Roman province of Pannonia, extend to nearby Bad Deutsch-Altenburg, where many of the unearthed objects are on display in the Museum Carnuntinum.

🏛 **Archaeological Park Carnuntum**
🅘 *Petronell Carnuntum, Hauptstraße 296 (02163) 3370.* 🕐 *Apr–Oct: 9am–5pm daily.* @ *md-online@ netway.at* 📷

🏛 **Museum Carnuntinum**
Bad Deutsch Altenburg, Badgasse 42. 📞 *(02165) 62480.* 🕐 *10am–5pm Tue–Sun, Fri till 7pm.* ⚫ *Mon., 1 May, 1 Nov, 24 Dec–6 Jan.* 📷

The enchanting nature reserve around Hainburg

Neusiedler See **㉓**

THE JEWEL OF Burgenland, Neusiedler See is the largest steppe lake in Central Europe. On the border between Austria and Hungary (a small section – around one-fifth of its total area – at the southern end belongs to Hungary) it covers an area of 320 sq km (124 sq miles) and has no natural in- or outlets apart from the Wulka River. The water is slightly saline and never more than 2 m (6½ ft) deep, so it warms up quickly in summer. The banks are densely overgrown with reeds which make ideal nesting grounds for birds, while the lakeside beaches are popular with visitors. In 2001, the lake and the surrounding countryside were declared a World Heritage Site by UNESCO.

Neusiedler See
Neusiedler See, Vienna's "seaside", attracts visitors with its wide range of water sports facilities and enchanting, melancholy landscapes.

★ Rust
This attractive town on the western lakeshore has a perfectly preserved old town with many Renaissance and Baroque buildings. Star sights include the town hall and Fischerkirche.

| 0 km | | 5 |
| 0 miles | | 5 |

Purbach

EISENSTADT

Rust

WIEN (VIENNA)

Klingenbach

Mörbisch am See

Neusiedler See

Sopron

KESZTHELY

Mörbisch am See
Situated on the border with Hungary, this village produces an excellent white wine. Its charming, whitewashed houses, laden with flowers, create a truly unique atmosphere.

Neusiedl am See

A well-known resort and agricultural centre, Neusiedl is situated at the northern end of Neusiedler See. It has a museum devoted to local fauna and flora, and a small ruin.

VISITORS' CHECKLIST

Road map G3. 🚗 🚌 🚤 🛈
Rust (02685) 502; Neusiedl am See (02167) 2229; Illmitz, National-parkhaus (02175) 34420; Neu-siedler Tourismus (02167) 8600.
Ⓦ *www.neusiedlersee.com.*

★ Podersdorf

With its access to the water unencumbered by the wide band of reeds that separates other villages from the lake, and with swimming, boating and wind-surfing facilities, Podersdorf is the most popular resort on the lake's eastern shores.

Neusiedl am See

Podersdorf

Frauenkirchen

Illmitz

Illmitz

Situated amid the marshes of the Seewinkel national park, this is a good base for exploring the surrounding grass- and wetlands.

KEY

▬	Motorway
▬	Major road
▬	Minor road
- -	Walking route
▬ ▪	National border
▭	River

STAR SIGHTS

★ Podersdorf

★ Rust

Seewinkel

This national park, a naturalist's paradise of reedbeds, small lakes and marshes, is home to over 250 different bird species.

Eisenstadt ㉔

THIS SMALL town in Burgenland lies on the southern slopes of the Leitha Hills, 50 km (31 miles) south of Vienna. It became the capital of Burgenland province in 1925, when the larger and more notable Ödenburg – today the Hungarian town of Sopron – ended up on the other side of the border. From this date the town underwent a remarkable growth, and today it is an important transport hub, and wine-making centre. Eisenstadt is mainly associated with the Hungarian Esterházy family and their famous choirmaster, Joseph Haydn. Another great musician, Franz Liszt, was born on the Esterházys' estate, in the village of Raiding *(see p150)*.

Ornamental grille on Joseph Haydn's tomb in the Bergkirche

Exploring Eisenstadt

Above all, Eisenstadt is the town of Haydn, and the main tourist trails retrace his footsteps. Most of the town's historic sights are clustered around the inner town centre, south of Schlosspark. Only the Bergkirche, with its calvary, and the Jewish quarter of Unterberg are situated further to the west.

🔒 Bergkirche

Kalvarienbergplatz.
Haydnmausoleum ◻ Apr–Oct: 9am–noon, 1–5pm daily.
In 1715, Prince Paul Esterházy ordered a hill to be created to the west of the Schloss and of Eisenstadt's centre. He then had a church built on top of that hill, dedicated to the Visitation of the Virgin Mary, with a Way of the Cross made up of 24 stations. The Passion figures are life-size and each tableau stands in a specially laid out room. The rather theatrical, Baroque-style figures are carved from wood or

stone. The north tower of the church contains the most-visited attraction of the church: the tomb of Joseph Haydn. In 1932, on the 200th anniversary of the composer's death, a small mausoleum was built here by the Esterházys for the marble sarcophagus containing Haydn's remains.

🏛 Jüdischer Friedhof

Unterbergstraße.
Jewish Museum Unterbergstraße 6. 🅲 *(02682)* 65145. ◻ May–Oct: 10am–5pm Tue–Sun; winter: groups by arrangement.
Until 1938, the Unterberg district of Eisenstadt was the base of the Jewish population, established in the 17th century by the Esterházys. It remained under their protection and played an important role in the life of the town. Inhabitants of the district included the Chief Rabbi of the Hungarian Jewry, banker Samson Wertheimer, and Sandor Wolf, a famous art collector. Eisenstadt was one of a handful of towns where old traditions were still observed, such as the closing of the district for

Sabbath, and the chains that were once used for that purpose are preserved to this day. The two Jewish cemeteries in Eisenstadt are among the best-preserved in Austria. The adjacent house, which once belonged to Samson Wertheimer, now houses the **Jewish Museum**.

🏛 Burgenländisches Landesmuseum

Museumgasse 1–5. 🅲 *(02682)* 62652-0. ◻ 9am–5pm Tue–Sat, 10am–5pm Sun.
This museum houses a large collection of objects associated with the history and art of the Burgenland province. Its geological collection comprises minerals and exhibits on the local Ice Age fauna. Archaeological findings include the Drassburg Venus, items from burial mounds in Siegendorf and objects which represent the Hallstatt and Roman cultures.

Jug from Burgenländische Landesmuseum

♣ Schloss Esterházy

Esterházyplatz. 🅲 *(02682)* 7193112. ◻ Apr–Oct: 9am–6pm daily; Nov–Mar: 10am–5pm daily.
The Esterházy Castle was built around 1390, on the site of earlier fortifications, remains of which were discovered in the course of excavations. In 1663–72, Carlo Martino Carlone transformed the castle into a magnificent Baroque palace. The main attraction inside is the Haydnsaal, a concert hall beautifully decorated with

Tombstones in one of the Jewish cemeteries in Unterberg

Prince's apartments in Esterházy Castle

frescoes and boasting truly amazing acoustics. Joseph Haydn once used to conduct the castle orchestra here.

Today, the larger part of the castle is leased to the Burgenland provincial authorities. The castle is surrounded by a beautiful English-style park.

🏛 Domkirche
Pfarrgasse.
This late-Gothic church was built in the 15th century on the site of an earlier medieval structure. As with many other churches in this part of Austria, its builders were conscious of the permanent threat of Turkish invasion, and its lofty steeple is therefore full of loopholes which leave no doubt as to their purpose. The eclectic-style

interior features some medieval tombstones and a relief in the church's vestibule depicting the Mount of Olives. The pulpit and the beautiful organ are Baroque, as are the two altar paintings by Stephan Dorfmeister. The large bronze sculpture of the Pietà is the work of Anton Hanak. The Domkirche was given cathedral status in 1960.

🏛 Franziskanerkirche
Joseph-Haydn-Gasse.
The Franciscan church of St Michael was built between 1625 and 1630, but its interior hails from a later period. The magnificent reliefs in the altarpiece date from 1630. Beneath the church you will find the crypt of the powerful local dynasty, the Esterházy family.

🏛 Haydn-Museum
Joseph-Haydn-Gasse 21.
📞 (02682) 719 3900.
🕐 Easter–Oct: 9am–5pm daily.
The house where Joseph Haydn lived 1766–78 is now a small museum displaying a number of the composer's possessions. From 1761,

VISITORS' CHECKLIST

Road map G3. 🏠 *12,400.* 🚌
🚍 ℹ️ *Schloss Esterházy, Esterházyplatz (02682) 67390.* 🎵 *Fest der 1000 Weine (Wine Festival, late August), Internationale Haydntage (Haydn Festival, Sept).* 🌐 *www.eisenstadt.at*

Haydn was employed by the Esterházy family as their Kapellmeister (music director), and in the evening he conducted the court orchestra for performances of his own music. Many of his beautiful compositions were first heard in Eisenstadt.

Haydn's home for 12 years, now a museum devoted to the composer

---

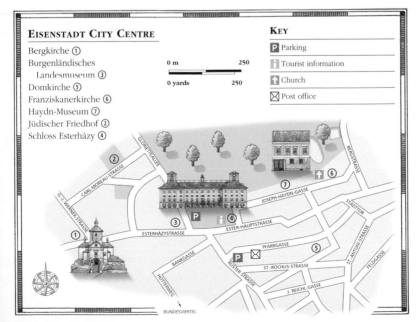

EISENSTADT CITY CENTRE

Bergkirche ①
Burgenländisches
  Landesmuseum ③
Domkirche ⑤
Franziskanerkirche ⑥
Haydn-Museum ⑦
Jüdischer Friedhof ②
Schloss Esterházy ④

KEY

🅿 Parking
ℹ️ Tourist information
🛐 Church
🖂 Post office

0 m — 250
0 yards — 250

BUNDESVIERTEL

STYRIA

AUSTRIA'S SECOND-LARGEST *province, in the country's southeast, Styria has a population of 1.2 million. It is dominated by forests, meadows and vineyards covering some three-quarters of its total area of 16,387 sq km (6,327 sq miles). It is also an area of iron ore extraction and processing, and Erzberg (Iron Ore Mountain), glittering in every hue of red and brown, is a major tourist attraction.*

Iron ore was already extracted by the Romans, who had named this part of Austria the Roman province of Noricum. The mineral shaped the history of this province through the centuries, and its traces survive to this day. Following the highs and lows of the early Middle Ages, Styria fell into the hands of the Habsburg dynasty in the 13th century and shared in its fate and fortunes. The province was repeatedly ravaged by Hungarians and Turks, and, after having staved off the Turkish threat, also became susceptible to attacks by the French. A legacy of these times are its numerous hilltop castle strongholds and imposing fortified abbeys. Some have survived intact, others have been meticulously restored to their former splendour to capture the imagination of visitors to the region.

Styria's great attractions include the south-facing slopes of Raxalpen, its gentle climate and its rural idylls – it is known as "the green heart" of Austria. In the west, along its border with the Salzburger Land, the area is dominated by the lofty peaks of the Salzburg Alps and Lower Tauern. Here you will find excellent winter sport centres around Schladming, and at the foot of Dachstein, the highest peak in the region, with the best cross-country–skiing trails. The Salzkammergut in the north is a stunningly beautiful lake district. The province's main rivers are the Mur, which flows through Graz, its tributary the Mürz, and the Salza.

Bad Blumau, an architectural complex based on Franz Hundertwasser's designs

◁ Rothenfels Castle near Oberwölz

Exploring Styria

Styria, or Steiermark, is rich in attractions and its capital, Graz, is Austria's second largest city. The west of the province offers excellent winter sports facilities; in the north lie the beautiful Mur and Mürz valleys, and many lakes. The quiet, agricultural southeast is covered with vineyards. Special sights are the National Austrian Open-Air Museum in Stübing, the Lipizzaner stud Piber, and the Mariazell Basilica, the country's largest Marian sanctuary.

SEE ALSO

- *Where to Stay* pp294–7
- *Where to Eat* pp325–8

0 km   20

0 miles   20

Enns

Linz

Salzburg

BAD AUSSEE ㉓

SALZATA ②

145

146

ADMONT ㉔

㉖ **EISENERZER ALPEN**

A9 E57 LEOBEN

㉒ **RAMSAU**

HOHENTAUERN ㉕

Salzburg

㉑ **SCHLADMINGER TAUERN**

SECKAU

㉗

S36 *Mur*

OBERWÖLZ ⑳

96

㉙

MURAU

⑯ **JUDEN-BURG**

PIBER

Salzburg

⑰

ST. LAMBRECHT

Klagenfurt

Klagenfurt

TURRACHER HÖHE

⑱

Klagenfurt

VILLA ALBRECHT

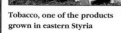

Tobacco, one of the products grown in eastern Styria

One of the grand villas in the spa town of Bad Gleichenberg

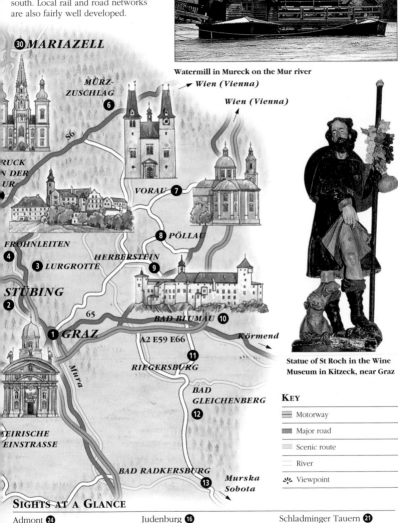

GETTING THERE

Graz has a passenger airport, though most international flights go to Vienna. The Province of Styria extends either side of the main road and rail connections crossing Austria from north to south. Local rail and road networks are also fairly well developed.

Watermill in Mureck on the Mur river

Wien (Vienna)

Wien (Vienna)

Statue of St Roch in the Wine Museum in Kitzeck, near Graz

30 *MARIAZELL*

MÜRZ-ZUSCHLAG
6

RUCK N DER UR

VORAU **7**

8 *PÖLLAU*

FROHNLEITEN
4

HERBERSTEIN
9

3 *LURGROTTE*

STÜBING
2

65

BAD BLUMAU **10**

1 *GRAZ*

A2 E59 E66

Körmend

11

RIEGERSBURG

BAD GLEICHENBERG
12

EIRISCHE EINSTRASSE

BAD RADKERSBURG

Murska Sobota
13

KEY

▭▭	Motorway
▭▭	Major road
▭▭	Scenic route
—	River
☆	Viewpoint

SIGHTS AT A GLANCE

Graz: Street-by-Street ●

GRAZ, THE CAPITAL of Styria, is the second largest city in Austria. During the Middle Ages it was the seat of a junior branch of the Habsburg family, and later of Emperor Friedrich III. The legacy of the Habsburgs is Graz's lovely Altstadt (old town), one of the best preserved in Central Europe and a UNESCO World Heritage Site. Graz was also a stronghold against Turkish attack.

The modern city extends from the foot of Castle Mountain, on both sides of the Mur river. Famed for its universities, architecture and cultural attractions, Graz is the European Cultural Capital in 2003. It hosts two classical music festivals each year, one in the summer at the Music College and the "Styriarte", as well as the avant-garde "Styrian Autumn".

Haus am Luegg
This town house at Nos 11 & 12 Hauptplatz (c.1690) has a striking façade, with Renaissance frescoes and early Baroque stucco work.

Rathaus
The new town hall, built in the late 19th century on the southern side of Rathausplatz, replaced the smaller Renaissance palace that previously stood on the same site.

★ Landhaus
The courtyard in this government building has three magnificent storeys of arcaded Renaissance galleries.

★ Landeszeughaus
The jewel of this old armoury, the largest in the world that has been preserved intact, is the collection of weapons from Austria's 16th- and 17th-century Turkish wars (see pp164–5).

FÄRBERGASSE

HERRENGASSE

ALBRECHTGASSE

LANDHAUSGASSE

SCHMIEDGASSE

KEY

- - - Suggested route

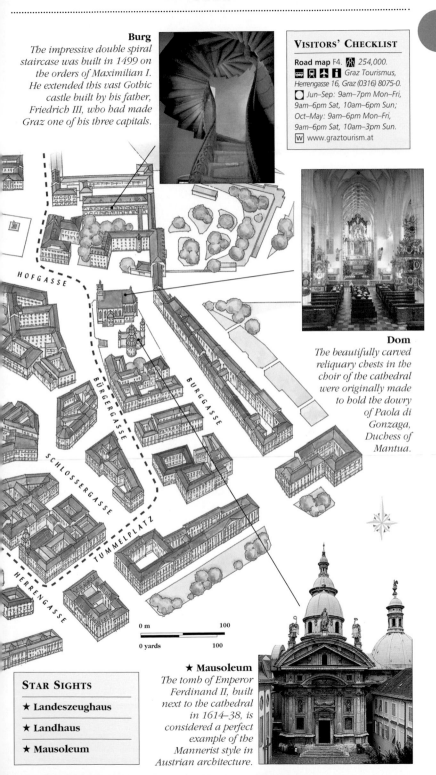

Burg
The impressive double spiral staircase was built in 1499 on the orders of Maximilian I. He extended this vast Gothic castle built by his father, Friedrich III, who had made Graz one of his three capitals.

VISITORS' CHECKLIST

Road map F4. 🚶 *254,000.*
🚌 🚊 ✈ 🛈 *Graz Tourismus, Herrengasse 16, Graz (0316) 8075-0.*
◐ *Jun–Sep: 9am–7pm Mon–Fri, 9am–6pm Sat, 10am–6pm Sun; Oct–May: 9am–6pm Mon–Fri, 9am–6pm Sat, 10am–3pm Sun.*
W̅ *www.graztourism.at*

HOFGASSE

BÜRGERGASSE

BURGGASSE

SCHLOSSERGASSE

TUMMELPLATZ

HERRENGASSE

Dom
The beautifully carved reliquary chests in the choir of the cathedral were originally made to hold the dowry of Paola di Gonzaga, Duchess of Mantua.

0 m   100

0 yards   100

STAR SIGHTS

★ **Landeszeughaus**

★ **Landhaus**

★ **Mausoleum**

★ **Mausoleum**
The tomb of Emperor Ferdinand II, built next to the cathedral in 1614–38, is considered a perfect example of the Mannerist style in Austrian architecture.

View of the city of Graz and Mur river from the Clock Tower

Exploring Graz

The town is built on both banks of the Mur river; the Altstadt, with most of the tourist sights, is on the left bank. It can be reached by tram from the railway and bus stations. The Island in the Mur is Graz's newest attraction.

⌂ Schlossberg

Hofgasse.

At the north of the Altstadt rises the 473-m (1552-ft) high Schlossberg. The top can be reached by a funicular or by a 20-minute walk. The 28-m (92-ft) high Clock Tower (1561), one of the symbols of Graz, offers splendid views over the city. It houses a museum.

⌂ Dom

Hofgasse.

The cathedral is a former castle church, built between 1439 and 1464 for Emperor Friedrich III. Its west portal bears the Emperor's coat of arms and his famous motto, AEIOU *(see p38)*. Originally, the cathedral was built as a defensive church on the outskirts of town. It has survived almost intact to this day and the interior still features some original elements, including Gothic frescoes showing life during the plague, although most of the decorations stem from the Baroque period.

⌂ Franziskanerkirche

Franziskanerplatz.

The church once belonged to the Minorite Friars, but in 1515 it was handed over to

the Franciscans. Inside, the St James's chapel dates from 1320–30, and there are also Gothic cloisters with beautiful tombstones. The interior was redesigned after World War II, and the combination of the restored vault and modern stained-glass windows with earlier details creates a very striking effect. Next to the church is a monastery with a distinctive tower. Both the church and monastery are in an unusually shaped square, surrounded by many interesting buildings with Baroque façades.

⌂ Hauptplatz

The triangular square at the heart of the Old Town is an excellent starting point for exploring the city of Graz. It

is surrounded by many original town houses from different periods, including the famous Haus am Luegg with its Renaissance and Baroque façade decorations. At No. 4 stands Graz's oldest pharmacy, in a house dating from 1534 with some earlier features. The north side of the square is occupied by the neo-Renaissance town hall, built in the 1880s. In the middle of the square stands the fountain of Archduke Johann, who contributed much to the city's development. The four female figures around it symbolize Styria's four main rivers: the Mur, the Enns, the Drau and the Sann.

🏛 Landesmuseum Joanneum

Old Gallery Neutorgasse 45.
🖪 *(0316) 8017-9770.* ◯ 10am–6pm Tue–Sun, 10am–8pm Thu.
New Gallery Sackstraße 16.
🖪 *(0316) 829155.* ◯ 10am–6pm Tue–Sun, 10am–8pm Thu.
Ⓦ *www.neuegalerie.at*

Schloss Eggenberg
Eggenberger Allee 90.
🖪 *(0316) 583264-0.* ◯ Apr–Oct: 10am–5pm Tue–Sat.
The memory of Archduke Johann remains alive in Graz to this day. The grandson of Maria Theresa, he played an important role in the political life of the country and participated in military campaigns, until he finally settled in Graz to devote time to his favourite pursuit of scientific research.

Ducal coronet from the Joanneum collection

Hauptplatz, the distinctive triangular main square in Graz's centre

The Italianate galleried courtyard in the Landhaus

He founded the Technical University as well as the Joanneum, Austria's first public museum, which is named after him. Today the Joanneum has 17 departments, based in ten buildings, and holds several exhibitions, some bequeathed by the Archduke.

The Old Gallery, the most interesting display, is housed in Admont Palace and contains some magnificent medieval paintings by Cranach, Brueghel, and Styrian 17th- and 18th-century artists. The Rococo Herberstein Palace is home to the New Gallery, with 19th- and 20th-century paintings, drawings and sculptures. Another department, holding a collection of coins and medals and various interesting historic objects is based in the lovely Baroque Eggenberg Palace, 3 km (2 miles) west of Graz. The most valuable exhibit in the museum is the Strettweg chariot, which dates from the 7th century BC.

🏛 Landhaus
Herrengasse 16.

The Landhaus, one of the most beautiful Renaissance buildings in Styria, was once the seat of the Styrian diet which under Habsburg rule also covered areas that are now part of Slovenia and Italy. Today it houses the provincial parliament.

The building was altered in the 16th century by the Italian military architect Domenico dell'Allio. The stairs on the northwestern side of the courtyard are the work of another Italian, Bartolomeo di Bosio. The front, with its loggia and

vast arched windows, is kept in the Venetian style. Well worth seeing is the beautiful courtyard with its three storeys of balustraded galleries linked by a raised walkway, and a fountain topped with a forged bronze cupola. In summer months it serves as a venue for festival events. Inside the Landhaus is the Baroque Landtag conference room, which has beautifully carved doors crowned by allegorical scenes, and ceiling stucco work by Johann Fromentini, depicting scenes from Styrian history. Also worth seeing is the Knight's Hall, which was decorated by the same artist.

🏛 Mausoleum
Hofgasse.

This small building, commissioned by Emperor Ferdinand II (1578–1637) as a tomb for himself and his family, is one of the most unusual and magnificent in Graz. A devout Catholic, the Emperor became especially notorious for the extremely harsh measures he took to introduce the Counter-Reformation in his territories, as well as for provoking the outbreak of the Thirty Years' War.

The mausoleum is one of the foremost examples of Austrian Mannerism, successfully blending various different styles. It was designed by an Italian architect, Pietro de Pomis, and completed by another Italian, Pietro Valnegro, who also built the belfry by the eastern apse. Its narrow façade,

exuberantly decorated with sculptures, consists of several architectural planes that create an exceptionally harmonious composition. The interior design is the work of Johann Bernhard Fischer von Erlach, who was born in Graz and began his life and career here.

🏛 Palais Attems
Sackstraße 17.

Palais Attems is the city's most attractive Baroque palace. Built in 1702–16, it was probably designed by Johann Georg Stengg. The palace's main features are its monumental staircase with frescoes and stucco ornaments, and its richly ornamented façades (inside and out, beyond the drive). The uniform furnishing of the rooms, with ceiling stuccos and lovely fireplaces and tiled stoves, is considered to be testimony to the Austrian aristocracy's standard of living during the Baroque period.

🏛 Grazer Congress
Schmiedgasse 2. ☎ (0316) 8049-0.

Next to the town hall stands an old palace which, in 1980, was transformed into a modern congress centre with multiple facilities for arts performances. The building has two magnificent conference suites as well as contemporary entertainment venues furnished with state-of-the-art technology. It also houses the city's largest concert hall, the Stefaniensaal.

The opulent main hall and stairs of the Grazer Congress

Landeszeughaus

THE LANDESZEUGHAUS, or armoury, was built between 1642 and 1645 as a stock of arms to be handed to the local population in the fight against the Turks. Graz was in the vanguard of defending and guarding access to the threatened Austrian provinces of Styria, Carinthia and Carniola, which gave its armoury great importance. With a collection of over 32,000 objects, the Graz armoury today ranks as the world's best-preserved early arsenal. The museum's beautiful Renaissance façade was designed by the Italian Antonio Solari.

Minerva Statue
The Minerva statue in a niche to the right of the entrance, like the Mars statue on the left, is the work of Giovanni Mamola.

★ Horse Armour
Dating from 1505, this armour hails from the workshop of Seusenhofer, master armourer of Innsbruck.

MUSEUM GUIDE

The first floor is devoted to heavy guns, flintlock pistols and rifles. The second floor holds the store of armour used by infantry and cavalry units, and pistols. The third floor displays the armour used by nobles and in tournaments. The fourth floor is devoted to side arms; also shown are musical instruments used by military bands. The cloakroom, toilets and museum shop are located on the ground floor.

Cannons
The first-floor exhibition includes field guns and old naval deck guns.

Wheel-lock Pistol *This type of pistol, with a spherical barrel-end, was introduced to the German and Austrian cavalry in the 17th century, and replaced the spear.*

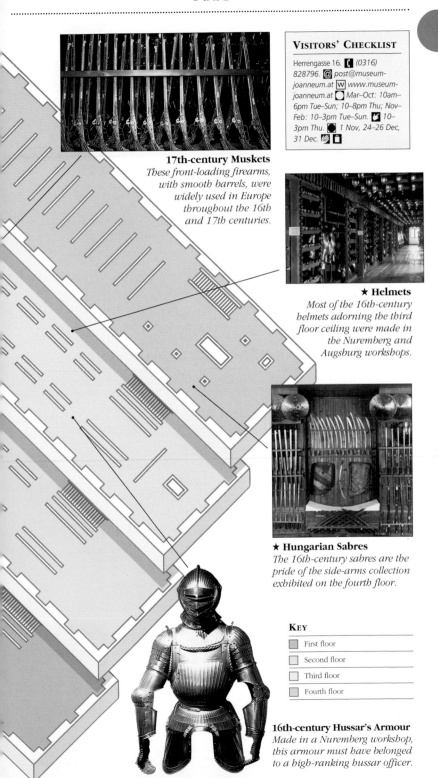

17th-century Muskets
These front-loading firearms, with smooth barrels, were widely used in Europe throughout the 16th and 17th centuries.

VISITORS' CHECKLIST

Herrengasse 16. ☎ *(0316) 828796.* @ *post@museum-joanneum.at* W *www.museum-joanneum.at* ○ *Mar–Oct: 10am–6pm Tue–Sun; 10–8pm Thu; Nov–Feb: 10–3pm Tue–Sun.* ⚑ *10–3pm Thu.* ● *1 Nov, 24–26 Dec, 31 Dec.* ⚑ ▯

★ Helmets
Most of the 16th-century helmets adorning the third floor ceiling were made in the Nuremberg and Augsburg workshops.

★ Hungarian Sabres
The 16th-century sabres are the pride of the side-arms collection exhibited on the fourth floor.

KEY

▢ First floor

▢ Second floor

▢ Third floor

▢ Fourth floor

16th-century Hussar's Armour
Made in a Nuremberg workshop, this armour must have belonged to a high-ranking hussar officer.

Stübing ②

AFTER SEVERAL earlier attempts, the Österreichische Freilichtmuseum (Austrian
Open-Air Museum) was started in 1962, when
work was begun in the Styrian village of
Stübing by the renowned scholar Professor
Viktor Herbert Pöttler. It now occupies an
area of 66 ha (24 acres), only 15 km (10 miles)
north of Graz. The museum displays are
buildings that have been moved here from
other parts of Austria. This journey across the
country, from east to west, from Burgenland
to Vorarlberg, reveals remarkable regional
differences in architecture, furnishings and
workrooms, and document the everyday life
of the houses' former inhabitants.

Farmstead from Alpbach
*This Tyrolean farm is called Hanslerhof
and dates from 1660. It unites all the
essential areas of a farmstead under
one single roof.*

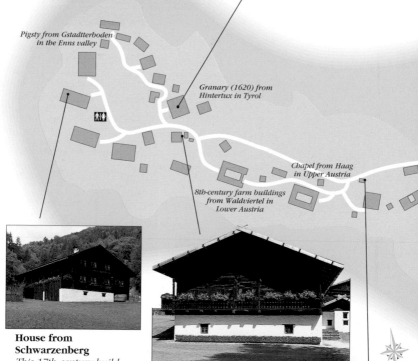

*Pigsty from Gstadtterboden
in the Enns valley*

*Granary (1620) from
Hintertux in Tyrol*

*Chapel from Haag
in Upper Austria*

*8th-century farm buildings
from Waldviertel in
Lower Austria*

**House from
Schwarzenberg**
*This 17th-century build-
ing is typical of the rural
architecture in Bregen-
zer Wald (the Bregenz
Forest) in Vorarlberg.*

Residential House
*St. Walburg in southern Tyrol is the
original location of this house. It
was reconstructed in its present
form following a fire in 1811.*

Brenner Kreuz
*A brick shrine from Ebene
Reichenau in Carinthia, this
little chapel houses a statue of
St. Florian, the patron saint of fire
fighters, who is invoked against fire.*

MUSEUM ACTIVITIES

Every day, the Open-Air Museum offers activities associated with traditional customs and crafts, in which visitors are invited to participate. You can try your hand at lace-making, or on special days sing folk songs or listen with children to classic fairy tales. *Erlebnistag*, or adventure day, held every year on the last Sunday in September, combines a picnic with instruction into the secrets of traditional craft skills, customs and entertainments.

Traditional needlework display in Stübing

VISITORS' CHECKLIST

Road map F4. 🚗 🚌 📞 *(03124) 53700.* ◯ *Apr–Oct: 9am–5pm Tue–Sun; Jun–Aug: 9am–6:30pm Tue–Sun.* 🎫 🍴 *Guided tours on request.* 🆆 *www.freilichtmuseum.at*

0 m   50

0 yards   50

Crucifix
This cross was taken from a granary in Oberzeiring, which was used as the main food store.

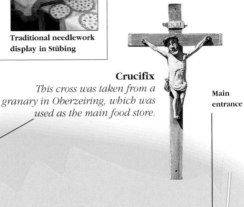

Main entrance

Single-class village school from Styria

...ngs ...Eastern

Apiary from the Enns valley

Belfry from Schallendorf in Burgenland

Sawmill from Festritz near Birkfeld

Barn from St Nikolaus in Burgenland

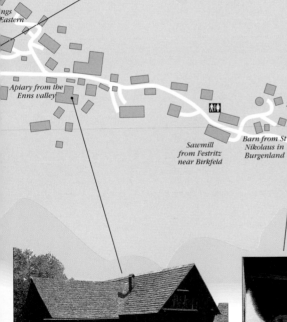

★ Farmstead from Western Styria
The main room in the 16th-century part of this house is the large "black room", where the entire family used to gather around the hearth and stove to cook, eat and socialize.

★ Kitchen
This typical kitchen from a house in the Burgenland province, is whitewashed and chimneyless, with an open hearth and traditional bread oven.

The astonishing Lurgrotte caves close to Peggau

Lurgrotte ❸

Road map F4. 🚗 🛈 (03127) 2580.
🌐 www.lurgrotte. com. 🕐 Apr–Oct:
9am–4pm daily, Nov–Mar: guided tours
on request from Semriach entrance. 🅿️

THE LURGROTTE is the largest
and most interesting cave
in Austria, with superb stalac-
tites and stalagmites. A well-
lit and clearly sign-posted
route leads you through this
world of icy wonders, along
an underground stream. The
largest dripstone, 13 m (43 ft)
tall, is nicknamed the "Giant"
(der Riese). A railway takes
you there from Semriach.

Frohnleiten ❹

Road map F4. 🚶 7,350. 🚗 🚌
🛈 (03126) 2374.
🌐 www.frohnleiten.or.at

SET AMONG gentle hills on
the Mur river, the town of
Frohnleiten is surrounded by
a network of clearly marked
rambling trails which invite
visitors to take long walks.
At one time Frohnleiten was
an important transhipment
post on the Mur. In 1763, the
town almost burned to the
ground in a fire. Sights worth
visiting include the Servite
monastery and the parish
church with Rococo figures in
the altarpiece by Veit Königer
and ceiling frescoes by Josef
Adam von Mölk.
Frohnleiten has won several
awards for its impressive
flower displays, and it has a

splendid alpine garden on
90,000 sq m (107,000 sq ft) of
land, stocked with some 10,000
species from around the world.

ENVIRONS: A short way to the
west, in Adriach, is the **St.
Georgskirche**, church of St
George, with an altarpiece of
the martyrdom of St George
and four frescoes in the main
nave by Josef Adam von Mölk.

Bruck an der Mur ❺

Road map F4. 🚶 14,000. 🚗 🚌
🛈 Koloman-Wallisch-Platz 1
(03862) 890-121. 🎭 Murenschalk
(2nd Thu and Fri in Aug).

THIS MAJOR industrial centre
lies at the mouth of the
Mürz river, where it flows into
the Mur. Bruck flourished
during the 14th and 15th
centuries, thanks to its trade
with Venice, when it had the
right to store grain and salt.
The small but attractive old
town in the fork of the Mürz
and Mur rivers dates from this
period. Bruck was once a
town of blacksmiths and their
works are now its chief
historical attractions. On the
main square stands an iron
well (1626) by the local
master, Hans Prasser, sporting
an intricate wrought-iron
canopy. The **parish church
of Mariä Geburt** features an
interesting door (1500) to the
vestry, a beautiful example of
Styrian metalwork. This
Gothic church was later altered
in the Baroque style. The
former Minorite church has
several important 14th-century
frescoes. In the main square,
Koloman-Wallisch Platz,
stands the town hall with an

attractive arcaded courtyard,
in a former ducal residence.
The town's loveliest building
is the late-Gothic **Kornmes-
serhaus**, built for the iron-
monger Kornmess. It has
open arcades on the ground
floor and a first-floor loggia.
A small distance away, on
the other side of the Mur,
stands St Rupert's church,
with a superb *Last Judgement*
fresco (1420), uncovered in
the 1930s. Above the town
rise the ruins of **Landskron**
fortress, whose only remaining feature is the bell tower.

**Poster from the Winter Sports
Museum in Mürzzuschlag**

Mürzzuschlag ❻

Road map F4. 🚶 10,700. 🚗
🛈 Wiener Straße 9 (03852) 3399.

THIS TOWN on the Mürz at
the foot of Semmering
Mountain is Austria's oldest
winter sports resort. In 1893,
Mürzzuschlag hosted the first
skiing competitions in the
Alps, and in 1934 it was the
venue for the Nordic
Games that later became
the Winter Olympics.
The town's first

Ruins of Landskron Castle rising above Bruck an der Mur

The richly ornamented library in the 12th-century Augustinian Vorau Abbey

historic records date from 1469, when Emperor Friedrich III ordered it to be burned to the ground, following a rebellion led by Count Andreas Baumkircher. Today its main sights of interest are the parish church with a lovely Renaissance altarpiece and its picturesque old houses, including **the house of Johannes Brahms** at No. 4 Wiener Straße. Also worth visiting is the **Winter Sports Museum** which has the world's largest collection of objects and memorabilia relating to all aspects of winter sports.

🏛 Winter Sports Museum
Wiener Straße 13.
◯ 10am–6pm, Tue–Sun.
● 1 Jan, Shrove Tuesday, 1 Nov, 24–25 Dec, 31 Dec. ⬚

Vorau ❼

Road map F4. 🏠 1,500. 🚌
🅸 Stift Vorau (03337) 2351.

ON A REMOTE hill stands the 12th-century Augustinian **Vorau Abbey**. In the 15th century, the abbey was turned into a fortress; its present form is the result of alterations made throughout the 17th and 18th centuries. The main entrance has symmetrical

Bust of Johannes Brahms, who lived in Mürzzuschlag

wings on both sides, adjoining two identical towers. One wing contains the cloister; in the other wing are the prelacy and the magnificent fresco- and stucco-adorned library with its low barrel-vault ceiling. On the floor above is the cabinet of manuscripts, decorated with ceiling paintings of the Gods, the Virtues and The Immaculate. It contains some 415 valuable manuscripts, including the oldest annals of poetry in the German language – the Vorauer and the famous Kaiserchronik. The abbey church, dedicated to St Thomas, acquired its sumptuous decor in 1700–1705. It has a main altarpiece by Matthias Steinl, who also created the beautifully ornamented pulpit.

The small nearby town of Vorau also has a fascinating **Open-air Museum** (Freilichtmuseum) with a collection of typical homes and public buildings (school, pharmacy, smithy) from the neighbouring villages, complete with their distinctive furnishings.

🏛 Open-air Museum
🅲 (03337) 3466.
◯ Easter–Oct: 10am–5pm daily.
● Nov–Easter. ⬚

Pöllau ❽

Road map F4. 🏠 2,200.
🅸 (0335) 4210.
🅆 www.naturpark-poellauertal.at

PÖLLAU LIES at the centre of a national park, surrounded by woodland, vineyards and walking trails. The town's main attraction is the former **Augustinian Abbey** and, above all, the lovely **St Veit's church**. Built between 1701 and 1712 by Joachim Carlone of the famous family of architects from Graz, this is a splendid example of Styrian Baroque. The building is vast: the main nave and presbytery measures 62 m (203 ft), the transept 37 m (121 ft) and the dome is 42 m (138 ft) high. The vaults and the inside of the dome are decorated with *trompe l'oeil* frescoes by Matthias von Görz, depicting the four fathers of the church, two Augustinian saints and the 12 apostles. The main altarpiece has a monumental painting by Josef A. Mölk showing the martyrdom of the patron saint St. Veit.

ENVIRONS: About 6 km (4 miles) northeast of Pöllau, high up on Pöllauberg Hill, stands the 14th-century Gothic pilgrimage church of **Maria-Lebing**, with vault frescoes by Mölk and two statues of the Virgin Mary – from the 15th and 17th centuries.

Herberstein ❾

Road map F4. 🏰 *300.* 🚌
📞 *(03176) 88250.* ⏱ *Mar–Oct:*
10am–5pm daily. ♿

SCHLOSS HERBERSTEIN, perched
on a steep rock amid wild
countryside, has remained in
the hands of the same family
since 1290. Since the Herber-
steins still live in the castle, a
visit feels a bit like peeping
through a keyhole at history.

The medieval fortress,
rebuilt numerous times,
achieved its present form
in the late 16th century. Its
most magnificent part is the
Florence Courtyard, a lovely
arcaded enclosure more
reminiscent of Renaissance
Italian palaces than of northern European fortresses. Once
the castle was a venue for
knightly tournaments.

The rooms that are open to
visitors today display many
exhibits relating to the Herberstein family, paintings and
early porcelain. An exhibition
gives a unique insight into
aristocratic life in the 18th
and 19th centuries. There is
even an original kitchen from
the 16th century. Interesting
temporary exhibitions are
organized during the summer.

The most interesting places
within the castle grounds
include an impressive nature
reserve with wild plants and
animals. Its origins can be
traced back to the 16th century, when the castle was
inhabited by Count Sigmund
von Herberstein, the author
of pioneering works on the
agriculture and geography of
Eastern Europe.

The Bad Blumau resort, designed by Friedensreich Hundertwasser

♣ **Tierpark Herberstein**
🔲 *Apr–Oct: 8am–6pm, Nov–Mar:*
10am–4pm. ♿

Bad Blumau ❿

Road map F4. 🏰 *1,500.* 🚌 🚉
ℹ *Rogner–Bad Blumau (03383)*
51000. 🆆 *www.blumau.com*

IN EASTERN STYRIA, in an area
that has long been famed
for its crystal-clear mineral
waters, is a spa resort that is
certainly worth a detour or
even a few days' visit. The
entire resort of Bad Blumau
was designed by the painter
and architect Friedensreich
Hundertwasser, in a style
similar to his famous building
in Vienna *(see pp104–5).* You
will see rounded façades,
rippling roofs, colourful walls
and irregularly shaped terraces
and balconies which transport
you into a strange and surreal
fairyland. The outside of the
complex can

be seen with a guided tour.
As you stroll along an avenue
lined with trees and shrubs
that represent the Chinese
horoscope, you suddenly
realize that the grass you are
walking on grows on the roof
of a building below.

The main reason for a visit
to the spa is, of course,
taking the waters. Admission
to the complex is available
for half and full days, and
will prove both an artistic
experience and a pleasant way
to while away some time.

Schloss Riegersburg ⓫

Road map F5. 🏰 *2,500.* 🚌 🅖
(03153) 8670. 🆆 *www.riegersburg.com*

ON A STEEP basaltic rock
high above the Grazbach
stream stands Schloss Riegersburg, a mighty medieval fortress, once Styria's most easterly
outpost against raiders from
Hungary, and then Turkey,
and, more recently, a German
stronghold during World War
II. The present castle
dates from the 17th
century. The

The medieval fortress of Schloss Riegersburg, rebuilt in the 17th century

fortress is surrounded and defended by a 3-km (2-mile) long wall with eleven bastions, seven gates and two moats, and can only be approached by a long steep climb. The castle buildings begin beyond the sixth gate. The first building is the former armoury with a collection of arms and war machines used in the defence of the fortress during a siege. In the courtyard stands a monument to soldiers killed during World War II. Beyond the second moat are the buildings of the castle proper, which houses a museum dedicated to the Liechtenstein family, now owners of the castle and who played an important role in the turbulent history of Austria and Europe.

In the inner courtyard you will find a well surrounded by an intricate wrought-iron enclosure featuring a horseshoe. Is it said that those who succeed in tracing the horseshoe among the intricate decorations may count on good luck. The twelve castle rooms housing the Witches' Museum are devoted to those horrendous times in medieval European history when many women (and some men) were tortured, burned at the stake and otherwise persecuted. The museum has many fascinating exhibits recounting the most gruesome of tales.

♟ **Schloss Riegersburg**
🎫 *(02916) 400.* ⬜ *Easter–15 Nov: 10am–5pm daily, Jul–Aug: 10am–7pm.* 📷 ✔

Bad Gleichenberg ⑫

Road map F5. 🏛 *2,100.* 🚌
🛈 *(03159) 2203.*

ONCE THE MOST popular health resort in Styria, Bad Gleichenberg was developed in 1834 by Count von Wickenburg. When the therapeutic properties of the local spring waters – already known to the Romans – were brought to his attention, he set about developing them. A shrewd businessman, he soon turned this quiet corner of southeastern Styria into a modern resort that attracted visitors with its promise of painless treatments for heart disease, circulatory and respiratory ailments, problems of the digestive tract and rheumatic conditions. Consequently, Bad Gleichenberg became one of the most popular destinations for the health-conscious Austrian aristocracy, who also congregated on the local promenade, and in the magnificent park, which now displays statues of its former visitors hidden among the shrubbery. The town has many surviving villas and Secession-style palaces; one of the most beautiful is the old theatre, now housing a cinema.

Statue of Constantine Wickenburg, in Bad Gleichenberg

ENVIRONS: A short way north of the spa town, in Gleichenberg village, stands the medieval **Schloss Kornberg**. Built as a fortress in the 13th century, it was transformed into a residential palace in the 17th century. Today it is a two-storey castle complex with four towers, and a magnificent Renaissance courtyard.

Bad Radkersburg ⑬

Road map F5. 🏛 *1,600.* 🚌 🚉
🛈 *(03476) 2545.*

BAD RADKERSBURG, on the Slovenian border, was founded as a town in 1265 by the Bohemian King Ottokar. Once a fortified border post as well as an important trade centre and transhipment harbour on the Mur river, today it is a peaceful small town, which still bears many

The octagonal tower of the late-Gothic town hall in Bad Radkersburg

signs of its former glory. In the main square stands the late-Gothic town hall with its octagonal clock tower topped by a belfry. The Marian or Plague Column in the square dates from 1681, and the surrounding houses with their patios and shaded galleries are the former homes of noblemen and rich citizens. The house at No. 9 once belonged to the von Eggenbergs, one of Styria's most powerful families.

Like many of its neighbours, Bad Radkersburg is also a spa town and health resort whose health-giving mineral waters attract numerous visitors.

The Plague Column on Hauptplatz in Bad Radkersburg

Steirische Weinstraße ⓮

MUCH OF SOUTHERN Styria is given over to vineyards, with vines planted on steep, south-facing slopes. The roads along the foot of the hills run through fields of maize, the region's second crop. The third crop is pumpkins, and pumpkin seeds are used to make *Kürbiskernöl*, a popular salad oil. Visitors following the Styrian wine routes will find many pleasant places to stop for a meal, but more importantly, a chance to sample the local wine and learn about the grape varieties that cloak the gardens of the restaurants.

Klagenfurt

Graz

Gundersdorf ①
At the entrance to the village stands a high pole with four vanes clattering in the wind. This is the *Klapotetz*, a scarecrow that guards the vineyards against birds. There are many such devices throughout the region, but the one in Gundersdorf is the largest.

Stainz ②
This town owes its former wealth to the wine trade. The former Augustinian Abbey was converted into a palace by Archduke Johann and now houses a department of the Graz Joanneum musuem presenting local and regional traditions.

Eibiswald

Schwarze Suln

Bad Gams ③
A health resort with iron-rich mineral waters, Bag Gams owes its fame mainly to its superb pottery products.

```
0 km        5

0 miles      5
```

KEY

 Suggested route
═ Other road
░ River, lake
☆ Viewpoint

Deutschlandsberg ④
This village is the centre of production for Schilcher rosé wine. It is dominated by the ruins of a former castle, whose remaining 12th-century turret affords spectacular views over the valley.

Kitzeck ⑤
In the centre of town, in an old inn between the church and the pub, is a fascinating wine museum. Kitzeck also boasts the highest vineyards in Europe, growing on steep slopes, at an altitude of 564 m (1,850 ft).

AUSTRIAN WINES

Austria can boast some truly excellent wines, in particular its white wines can take their place among the best in the world, and production meets almost the entire domestic demand. The largest wine-producing area is Lower Austria, particularly the Weinviertel and the Wachau Valley. Burgenland, southern Styria and the environs of Vienna are also key regions. The most popular white wines are Grüner Veltliner, Welschriesling and Weißburgunder. The land around Neusiedler See produces white wines, but is famous for its reds: Zweigelt and the full-bodied Blau-fränkisch. The light Schilcher comes from Deutschlandsberg in Styria. Eiswein, an Austrian speciality, is a sweet dessert wine from grapes picked after the first frosts.

Label for Austrian red wine from Gumpoldskirchen

Leibnitz ⑥
Several traces reveal earlier Roman settlements in the town of Leibnitz. The archaeological finds are now on display in nearby Seggau Castle.

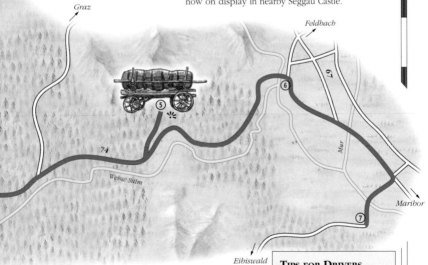

Ehrenhausen ⑦
This historic town makes a good starting point for exploring much of the Styrian wine route. Its greatest attraction is the mausoleum of Rupert von Eggenberg (died 1611), a hero of the Turkish wars, with an interior designed by Johann Bernhard Fischer von Erlach.

TIPS FOR DRIVERS

Length of route: 66 km (41 miles).
Stopping places: restaurants, inns and rooms for rent are dotted along the route.
Suggestions: a visit to the Steirisches Weinmuseum (wine museum) Kitzeck, Steinriegel 16. (03456) 3500. Apr–Nov: 10am–noon, 2–5pm Sat, Sun, public holidays; tours on request.

Piber ⑮

Road map F4. 🚉 *Köflach*. 🚌
🏠 *500*. 🚍 *(03144) 2519-760*.
Stud 🚍 *(03144) 3323*. ⬜ *Easter–Oct: 9–10:15am, 2–3:15pm*. 🚲

PIBER HOUSES the stud farm
for the Spanish Riding
School horses. When the town
of Lipizza was incorporated
into Slovenia after World War I,
it was in a former castle in
Piber, a small Styrian village,
that the famous Lippizaner
horses found a new home.
The horses are a complex
mixture of six different breeds.
Born dark-chestnut or black,
they acquire their famous
white colour between the
ages of four and ten. In Piber
the initial selection of five out
of 40 stallions takes place:
they are assessed for their
suitability and stage talents
before five years of training
at the Spanish Riding School
in Vienna. You can visit the
stables here, and watch a film
on the history of the stud.

Judenburg ⑯

Road map E4. 🏠 *10,500*. 🚌 🚍
🚍 *(03572) 47127*.

THIS TOWN at the fork of a
road is an old mercantile
centre that took its name
from the *Juden*, or Jews, who
once lived and traded here.
When Emperor Maximilian
expelled the Jews in 1496, the
town went into decline. Not
much remains of the medieval
Jewish quarters, but it is worth
visiting **Nikolauskirche**, the
church of St Nicholas. The
only original feature is the

presbytery. Rebuilt in 1673 in
the Baroque style, the church
was subsequently given a
Neo-Renaissance facelift
during the Neo-Classicist
period. Inside are statues of
the 12 apostles by the local
artist Balthasar Brandstätter.
One of the side altars contains a small wooden statue
of the Madonna and Child,
dating from 1500. The Magda-
lenenkirche, church of St Mary
Magdalene, features lovingly
restored Gothic stained-glass
windows. Judenburg also has
a town museum devoted
mainly to the region's
history and art.

ENVIRONS: East
of the town, on
the ledge of a
rock, stand the
ruins of an old
Liechtenstein **castle**
that was once
accessible only
by step ladder. In
the environs of
Judenburg are
some of the most
interesting archae-
ological sites dating
from prehistoric times. The
famous chariot that is now
displayed in the Joanneum
museum in Eggenberg castle
in Graz was unearthed in
nearby **Strettweg**.

St. Lambrecht ⑰

Road map E4. 🏠 *2,000*. 🚌 🚍
🚍 *(03585) 2344-0*.

ST. LAMBRECHT, a Benedictine
Abbey, was founded in the
12th century by Henry III,
Duke of Carinthia. The

monastery complex was built
in 1640 to designs by Domenico Sciassi. The church dates
from the 14th century, but it
was rebuilt in the Baroque
style and today it is a triple-
nave basilica with medieval
frescoes on the walls and
presbytery ceiling, and statues
of the church's fathers in the
organ enclosure. The main
altar (1632) by Valentine
Khautt is 16 m (52 ft) high.

North of the church, by the
cemetery, stands a 12th-
century Romanesque chapel.
The abbey also has a magnificent library and an
interesting museum
with a collection of
the old furnishings
of church and
abbey, including
Romanesque
sculptures, a 15th-
century votive
painting, *The
Mount of Olives*,
by Hans von
Tübingen, and
15th- and 16th-
century stained-
glass panels. The
gem of the
museum, however, is its
collection of birds. Some
1,500 species were assembled
in the 19th century by the
amateur collector Blasius Hanf.

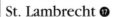

**Image of the patron saint
of St. Lambrecht Abbey**

🏛 **St. Lambrecht Abbey
Museum**
Hauptstraße 1–2. 🚍 *(03585) 2345*.
⬜ *15 May–15 Oct: 10:45am,
2:30pm Mon–Sat, 2:30pm Sun*.

Turracher
Höhe ⑱

Road map E5. 🏠 *60*. 🚌
🚍 *(04275) 8392*.

THIS SMALL SKI resort nestles
at an altitude of 1,700 m
(5,575 ft) high in the Nocky
Mountains, one of Austria's
most scenic Alpine ranges on
the border between Styria
and Carinthia. The town
makes a great base for year-
round walks in the woods
and mountain meadows.
Nearby are the remains of an
old iron-smelting plant. The
blast furnace ended its oper-
ation in the early 20th century, but the remains of heavy

The world-famous Lipizzaner horses in a paddock near Piber

Splendid autumn colours in the woods around Turracher Höhe

industry create a very striking feature set against the backdrop of the pistes and the beautiful snow-covered hills of the ski resort.

Murau ⑲

Road map E4. 👥 2,100. 🚌 🚉
📋 (03532) 2720.

MURAU SPRANG up in the 13th century at a crossroads of trading routes on the scenic Mur river and became a local centre for commerce and industry. The historic town centre of Murau lies on the left bank of the Mur river. Its Renaissance houses are dominated by the Gothic **Matthäuskirche**, the church of St Matthew, consecrated in the 13th century and later altered in the Baroque style. The church contains some

interesting epitaphs of the Liechtenstein family but its star attraction is the main altar (1655), a magnificent work by local Baroque masters, incorporating a Gothic painting of the Crucifixion (c.1500). Also worth seeing are the medieval frescoes of St Anthony in the transept, and the Entombment of Christ and Annunciation in the main nave.

The castle behind the church, **Schloss Murau**, was founded by the Liechtenstein family and later passed into the hands of the Schwarzenbergs. It has an interesting museum of metallurgy. In **Elisabethkirche**, the church of St Elisabeth, at No. 4 Marktgasse, is a Diocesan Protestant Museum that holds documents relating to the events around the Reformation and Counter-Reformation in these parts of Austria.

Oberwölz ⑳

Road map E4. 👥 1,000.
📋 (03581) 8420.

THIS SMALL town, which grew rich through its trade in salt and the smelting of silver excavated in the surrounding hills, has preserved some of its former glory. In the surrounding area many archaeological finds from the Hallstatt period have been unearthed, revealing a long history. Oberwölz once belonged to the bishopric of Freising and up to the time of the Napoleonic wars its envoy resided in the neighbouring **Schloss Rothenfels**.

The town has some wellpreserved remains of medieval fortifications, including three turrets and two town gates. Its pride is the Gothic **Stadtpfarrkirche St Martin**, the parish church of St Martin, a triple-nave basilica with an early-Gothic chapel and a 15th-century Gothic vestibule. In 1777, J. A. von Mölk painted the ceiling frescoes in the chapel vault. On the external south wall is a relief from 1500, showing the Last Judgement. Next to the church stands the 14thcentury chapel of St Sigismund, with the Way of the Cross by Johann Lederwasch from the turn of the 18th century. In the Cultural Centre is a regional museum with a collection of archaeological finds from the area, and a museum of wind instruments.

Historic buildings in the old town of Murau on the Mur River

Schladminger Tauern ㉑

THE SMALL TOWN of Schladming lies at the foot of the Niedere (Lower) Tauern that extend along the Enns Valley. Rising to 2,800 m (9,200 ft), their gentle slopes provide excellent conditions for downhill skiers, from the beginner to the professional. The scenery is superb, excellent for walking in summer, with an efficient bus network, cable cars and ski lifts in winter. If you are looking for more of a challenge, you can find this in the Dachstein massif close by. But for a relaxing break it is still worth going down to Schladming, with its tempting restaurants and cosy cafés lining the broad promenade.

★ **Schladming**
The little town of Schladming has a rich history. Once a centre of peasant revolts, it remains to this day the centre of Austrian Protestantism.

★ **Ennstal – the Enns Valley**
One of Austria's major rivers, the Enns, separates the Niedere Tauern from the Dachstein massif.

The ascent by cable car from the small village of Ramsau am Dachstein *(see p180)* takes visitors to the tops of Dachstein and Hunerkogel. Climbing instructors also give advice to rock climbers.

0 km   5

0 miles   5

KLAGENFURT

Hunerkogel

Filzmoos

Ramsau am Dachstein

ENNSTAL

Schladm

146 E651

Rohrmoos

Radstadt

Hochwurzen

Forstaubach

99

STAR SIGHTS

★ **Dachstein Massif**

★ **Ennstal – the Enns Valley**

★ **Schladming**

◁ **Mountain lake in Styria in autumn**

Rohrmoos
This resort, just outside Schladming, is a good base for climbing the neighbouring Hochwurzen and Planai summits.

★ Dachstein Massif

The highest, most impressive peak is Dachstein itself, which rises to 2,995 m (9,826 ft). A glacier, it is perfect for year-round skiing.

VISITORS' CHECKLIST

Road map D4, E4.
🚌 🚏 ℹ️ *Schladming, Erzherzog-Johann-Straße 213 (03687) 22268.*

Gröbming has an attractive late-medieval church of the Assumption of the Virgin Mary, with a winged altar (1520).

DACHSTEIN-MASSIF

Gröbming

Enns

Haus

○ Bodensee

○ Hüttensee

○ Obersee

Untertalbach

Riesachsee

SCHLADMINGER TAUERN

Hochgolling ▲

Haus

A resort and winter sports centre, Haus has a beautiful Baroque church. It is a good starting point for mountain walks to the nearby scenic lakes, including Bodensee, Hüttensee and Obersee.

Hochgolling, rising to 2,863 m (9,393 ft), is the highest peak in the Schladminger Tauern. The long, arduous climb rewards with stunning views of the mountains from the top.

KEY

═══ Major road

══ Minor road

- - Mountain railway

▭▭▭ River

🏔️ Viewpoint

Riesachsee

One of many mountain lakes set amid beautiful scenery, the Riesachsee lies at an altitude of 1,333 m (4,373 ft). It is a perfect spot for trout fishing.

The resort of Ramsau, famed for cross-country skiing

Ramsau ㉒

Road map D4. 👥 *2,700.*
🚌 🛈 *(03687) 81833.*

AT AN ALTITUDE of 1,000 m (3,280 ft) lies the small town of Ramsau am Dachstein, renowned for its superb cross-country ski runs, extending over some 230 km (143 miles). Snow is almost guaranteed from November until March and the efficient interconnecting system of lifts, cable cars, trains and buses also puts more difficult runs within easy reach. The peaks opposite the Dachstein massif have slopes that are perfectly suited to moderately skilled downhill skiers. In the summer the *Loipen* or cross-country ski runs turn into excellent long-distance walking routes.

From the Ramsau side visitors can ascend the famous Dachstein south face by cable car. A cable car also takes you up the nearby Hunerkogel (2,694 m/8,836 ft), from where a lovely panoramic view of the area unfolds. The descent takes you to nearby Filzmoos, a resort with views of the spectacular Bischofsmütze (Bishop's Mitre).

Ramsau has two museums. **Heimatmuseum Grahhof** is dedicated to local folklore, handicraft and the history of the Reformation, which was very active in this area. The **Alpinmuseum** illustrates the history of mountaineering in the region. There are many other attractions on offer,

such as feeding mountain animals in their nurseries and night toboggan runs.

🏛 **Heimatmuseum Grahhof**
🛈 *(03687) 81812.*
🏛 **Alpinmuseum**
🛈 *(03687) 81522.*
🕐 *Guided tours on request.*

Bad Aussee ㉓

Road map D4. 👥 *5,000.*
🚌 🚆 🛈 *(03622) 54040.*

BAD AUSSEE, the main town in the Styrian part of the Salzkammergut, lies at the fork of the Traun river, which cuts a scenic gorge between the Dachstein massif and the Tote Gebirge (Dead Mountains). The region's original wealth was founded on its salt deposits. Later, Bad Aussee achieved renewed fame when, in 1827, Archduke Johann married Anna Plochl,

daughter of the local postmaster. The Archduke, who made many important contributions to the life of Styria, was a grandson of Maria Theresa, the 13th child of future Emperor Leopold II.

The former seat of the Salt Office, in Chlumeckyplatz, is a lovely 14th-century building which now houses the city's regional museum with its exhibition on salt mining. The 13th-century, Romanesque St Paul's church has a notable stone statue of the Madonna.

ENVIRONS: A scenic road northwest of Bad Aussee will take you to **Altausseer See** and the Loser peak. On the road is an old salt mine, open to the public. During World War II it was reputedly used to hide works of art.

Admont ㉔

Road map E4. 👥 *2,800.*
🚌 🚆 🛈 *(03613) 2164.*

AT THE CENTRE of the village of Admont stands a Benedictine Abbey whose importance once reached far beyond the region. Built in the 11th century and often rebuilt, it burned down in 1865, but the fire spared its priceless collection: with nearly 160,000 volumes, it is said to hold the world's largest monastic library. The present Rococo interior of the library was designed by Gotthard Heyberger in 1774, the work carried out by Josef Hueber. The large hall holding two-storey cabinets is 72 m (236 ft)

A picturesque street in Bad Aussee

Richly ornamented interior of Admont library

long. The ceiling frescoes by Bartolomeo Altomonte show vast allegorical scenes of the arts, the natural sciences and religion. The abbey's south wing has been converted into a museum showcasing both historic treasures and modern art.

⊞ Benedictine Abbey
☎ (03613) 2312-601.
◯ Apr–Oct: 10am–5pm Thu–Tue; Nov–Mar: 10am–noon Thu, Fri; guided tours for groups on request.
W www.stiftadmont.at

ENVIRONS: 5 km (3 miles) beyond Admont, high above the Enns river, stands the 15th-century pilgrimage church **Frauenberg**, rebuilt in the Baroque style. It has a beautiful altarpiece by Josef Stammel.

Hohentauern ㉕

Road map E4. 🏔 550. 🚌
⚐ (03618) 335.

Hohentauern (1,274 m/ 4,180 ft) is the highest village in the Rottenmanner Tauern, surrounded by more than 20 peaks higher than 2,000 m (6,560 ft). This

mountain range is part of the Niedere (Lower) Tauern, which extend also to Salzburger Land. Other ranges in the Niedere Tauern include Radstätter (see p228), Schladminger (see pp178–9) and Wölzer Tauern.

Hohentauern was founded by the Celts. From the 12th century it became important as a commercial centre along Hohentauernpass, the mountain pass connecting the Enns and Mur valleys. St. Bartolomäus Church has magnificent carvings by Josef Stammel.

The Hohentauernpass crosses the range at 1,260 m (4,134 ft) height. A drive along Hohentauern-passstraße is one of the best ways to enjoy the superb mountain scenery. From the north, you pass through **Rottenmann** with its old city walls; **Möderbrugg**, a former centre of the metal industry; **Oberzeiring** and its disused salt mine; and **Halfelden**, with its large ruined castle. Nearby is the ruined **Schloss Reifenstein**.

Eisenerzer Alpen ㉖

Road map E4. 🚌
⚐ (03848) 3700.

You can reach the Eisenerzer Alpen (iron-ore alps) by following the steep, narrow valley of the Enns river. This gorge, called Gesäuse, begins a short distance from Admont, near Hieflau. The entrance to the gorge presents great views of the river and the Hochtor massif, rising 2,369 m (7,772 ft) above. The surrounding area is used as a training ground for advanced mountaineering and as a base for expeditions to the neighbouring peaks. Easily the most famous mountain in the Eisenerzer Alpen is **Erzberg**, which has has been exploited for its large iron ore deposits since ancient times. It looks like a stepped pyramid, the red pigment contrasting with the green forests and meadows.

The area around Erzberg is the largest iron ore basin in this part of Europe. In the summer, visitors can explore one of the mines. **Eisenerz**, an old mining town at the foot of Erzberg, has a mining museum where visitors can take an underground "adventure trip" with Hauly, a vast truck. The village also has a lovely old town and the fine fortified 16th-century church of St Oswald.

⊞ Stadtmuseum
Eisenerz, Schulstraße 1. **☎** (03848) 3615. **◯** May–Oct: 9am–noon, 2–5pm Mon–Sat. **●** Sun. 🈲

The shimmering Erzberg – the red iron-ore mountain in the Eisenerzer Alpen

Salzatal Tour ㉙

THE SMALL Salza river, a tributary of the upper Enns, cuts its way across the eastern end of the High Limestone Alps. A journey along the Salza Valley is an expedition through a thinly populated area of entrancing beauty. The trail leads along the foothills of the Hochschwab massif, beside wild mountain streams, small barrier lakes and through dense woodlands. The river flows through virgin mountain terrains and its waters are so crystal clear that you can see every detail reflected in its stream.

Brunnsee ②
Beyond the village of Wild-alpen, a magnificent view opens onto the valley and the lake at the very heart of the Hochschwab massif. The northern slopes of the mountains present themselves in their full glory.

Prescenyklause ③
Beyond a rock gate is an old dam that once held back the waters of the Salza river so rafts could carry timber to the valleys.

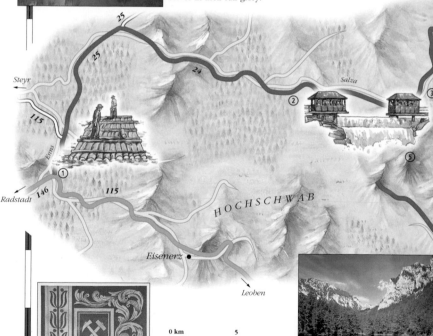

Steyr
25
25
115
Enns
Radstadt
146
115
①
24
Salza
②
HOCHSCHWAB
③
⑤
Eisenerz
Leoben

0 km 5
0 miles 5

Hieflau ①
This former centre of the metal industry is hidden amid dense forests. The local village museum displays objects associated with the region's history.

KEY

 Suggested route

Scenic road

Other road

 River, lake

Hochschwab ⑤
The highest summit in this vast mountain range is the 2,277-m (7,470-ft) high Hochschwab, the destination of both summer and winter excursions.

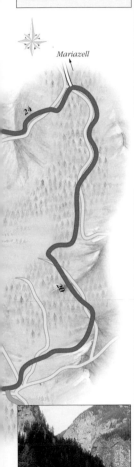

Mariazell

**The main nave of the abbey
church in Seckau Abbey**

Seckau ㉗

Road map E4. **🏃** *1,400.* 🚌 🚉
ℹ *(03514) 5234-0.*

THE SMALL TOWN of Seckau,
established in the 13th
century, has some interesting
houses and the late-Gothic
chapel of St Lucia in the town
square. But the main claim to
fame lies with **Seckau Abbey**,
originally Augustinian and
taken over by the Benedictines in the 19th century. Its
present shape, dating from
the 17th century, is the work
of P.F. Carloni, but the abbey's
basilica of the Assumption
of the Virgin Mary has maintained its original late-Gothic
character. Among its treasures
is the Crucifixion group in the
presbytery, highly expressive
figures from the 12th and
13th centuries. The lion
figures in the portal and the
Madonna and Child in the
church vestibule are Romanesque or early Gothic, and on
the south wall, 13th-century
frescoes were discovered.

Leoben ㉘

Road map F4. **🏃** *29,000.* 🚌 🚉
ℹ *Hauptplatz 12 (03842) 406 20.*
w *www.leoben.at*

LEOBEN, Styria's second
largest town, is an industrial and academic centre.
Beautiful mansion houses line
Hauptplatz (main square), and
the adjacent streets bear witness to the town's early wealth
derived from the local iron
deposits. There is a lovely old
town hall with coats of arms,
and the Hacklhaus has a
glittering red façade.

Also worth seeing in the
old town is the **Pfarrkirche
St. Xaver**, the church of St.
Xaver, built in the 17th century by the Jesuits, with its
beautiful Baroque main altar
and a Romanesque crucifix
on the south wall. On the
other side of the bridge
across the Mur river stands
the Gothic church of **Maria
am Waasen**, with original
stained-glass windows in the
presbytery. On the southern
outskirts, in the district of
Göss, stands Styria's first Benedictine **abbey**, built around
1000 by Archbishop Aribo.
It is mainly 16th-century with
some earlier elements. The
church's main nave is a monument to Styria's late-Gothic
architecture. Other original
features include 14th-century
frescoes in the presbytery and
an 11th-century, early-Roman-
esque crypt.

Austria's most famous
brewery, Gösser, a short way
from the abbey, is also open
to the public. In the city
centre, at No. 6 Kirchgasse, is
a museum of fine arts.

Weichselboden ④
It is worth stopping off in
this small village, one of very
few along this route, to visit
its lime-tree–shaded church.
A very small old hotel invites
visitors to stay.

The elegant Baroque façade of the Hacklhaus in Leoben

Mariazell ㉚

Virgin and child

T HE EARLIEST records of the church devoted to the Birth of the Virgin Mary date from 1266, but it is believed to have been established in 1157 and its 850th anniversary will be celebrated in 2007. Mariazell is the main pilgrimage centre for the Roman Catholic population in this part of Europe. Pilgrims arrive all year, but highpoints are Assumption (15 Aug) and the Birth of the Virgin (8 Sep). Mariazell became famous in the 14th century, when King Louis of Hungary founded Gnadenkapelle (chapel of mercy) to thank for victory over the Turks.

Church Interior
The basilica was originally a Gothic hall church, which is still apparent despite the Baroque-style alterations carried out in the late 17th century by Domenico Sciassi.

View of the Church
In the 17th century, the church was extended to accommodate the growing number of pilgrims, and the central tower was supplemented by two Baroque side towers.

STAR FEATURES

★ **Gnadenkapelle**

★ **Main Altar**

★ **Treasury**

14th-century Gothic tower

Main entrance

★ **Treasury**
The treasury is home to various precious objects, including liturgical vessels, a wooden statuette of the Madonna and Child and an ivory relief – both from the 14th century.

Madonna and Child
Magna Mater Austriae – *the Great Mother of Austria, a late-Romanesque statue of the Madonna and Child – is the main object of veneration by pilgrims to Mariazell.*

VISITORS' CHECKLIST

Road map F4. 🏘 *1,750.*
ℹ *Hauptplatz 13.*
📞 *(03882) 2366.*
Basilica *Kardinal-Tisserant-Platz 1.*
📞 *(03882) 2595.*
Treasury ⬜ *May–Oct: 10am–3pm Tue–Sat, 11am–4pm Sun.*

Vault frescoes by Giovanni Rocco Bertoletti

★ Main Altar
The monumental altar showing the Crucifixion is the work of Johann Bernhard Fischer von Erlach. The silver figures on the altar were created by Lorenzo Mattielli.

CARDINAL JOSEPH MINDSZENTY (1892–1975)

The Hungarian Primate, imprisoned for his opposition to the communist regime, was released in the 1956 uprising. When this was crushed, he took refuge in the US Embassy in Budapest for 15 years. He later lived in Austria and was buried in Mariazell. His body is now in Hungary.

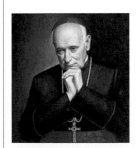

★ Gnadenkapelle
The chapel, with a statue of the Virgin Mary, was probably founded by King Louis of Hungary and was decorated in Baroque style by Fischer von Erlach the Younger and Lorenzo Mattielli.

UPPER AUSTRIA

UPPER AUSTRIA, *so called because of its location in the upper reaches of the Austrian Danube, occupies an area of about 12,000 sq km (4,600 sq miles) and has 1.4 million inhabitants. Its borders are marked by the rivers Enns to the east and Inn to the west. To the north, the Czech Republic is its neighbour, to the south there are Styria and the Salzburger Land, to the west is Germany.*

Upper Austria is, after Vienna, the most industrialized Austrian province and has remained the richest area of the country since the time when Austria was part of the Roman province of Noricum. In later years, Upper Austria joined Bavaria. Then, under Babenberg rule in the 13th century, it became the cradle of the great future empire, in conjunction with neighbouring Lower Austria.

Historically, the province of Upper Austria is divided into five districts: Mühlviertel, which stretches south to the Danube and occupies the Czech Massif, with Freistadt its largest town; the westernmost district of Innviertel, which lies in the foothills of the Alps, and includes the towns of Ried and Braunau; the Hausruckviertel is named after the Hausruck Massif and Vöcklabruck is its largest town; Traunviertel, which includes the Salzkammergut, one of the most picturesque and popular natural areas in Austria. The Danube Valley is generally considered to be a separate region, with scores of small towns, lofty fortresses and magnificent abbeys, including the most glorious of them all, St. Florian, a jewel of Austrian Baroque architecture.

The province's capital, Linz, is Austria's third largest city, comprising an important industrial centre, the largest Austrian Danube port, and a major transport hub. It is beautifully situated in an extensive valley, surrounded by gently rolling hills, and has a charming old town district.

View from the Krippenstein peak across to the imposing Dachstein massif

◁ Houses rising up from the banks of the glorious deep blue Hallstätter See

Exploring Upper Austria

UPPER AUSTRIA is an exceptionally diverse province, with something to interest everyone. Linz, the capital city, has both the oldest church in Austria and a state-of-the-art virtual technology museum. On the banks of the rivers Danube and Enns rise the magnificent abbeys in Kremsmünster, Steyr and St. Florian. The caves in the Dachstein range are fascinating natural monuments. However, Upper Austria's greatest attraction are its glorious lakes set amid limestone peaks in the beautiful Salzkammergut. The mild climate and therapeutic facilities attract visitors to small resorts, and Bad Ischl was once the Emperor's summer home.

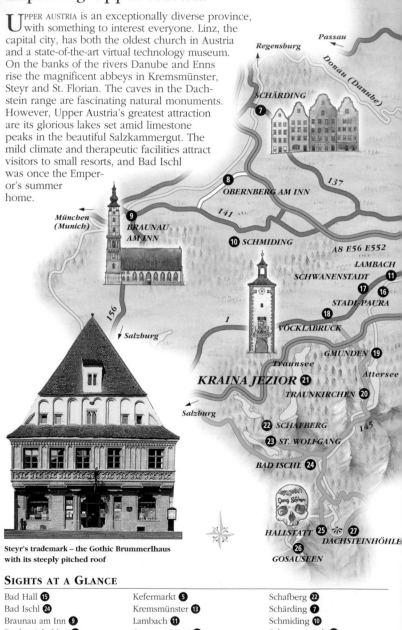

Passau

Regensburg

Donau (Danube)

SCHÄRDING **7**

OBERNBERG AM INN **8**

137

München (Munich)

BRAUNAU AM INN **9**

SCHMIDING **10**

141

A8 E56 E552

LAMBACH **11**

SCHWANENSTADT **17** **16**

STADL-PAURA **18**

156

Salzburg

1

VÖCKLABRUCK

GMUNDEN **19**

Traunsee

Attersee

KRAINA JEZIOR **21**

TRAUNKIRCHEN **20**

Salzburg

145

SCHAFBERG **22**

ST. WOLFGANG **23**

BAD ISCHL **24**

HALLSTATT **25** **27**

DACHSTEINHÖHLE

GOSAUSEEN **26**

Steyr's trademark – the Gothic Brummerlhaus with its steeply pitched roof

SIGHTS AT A GLANCE

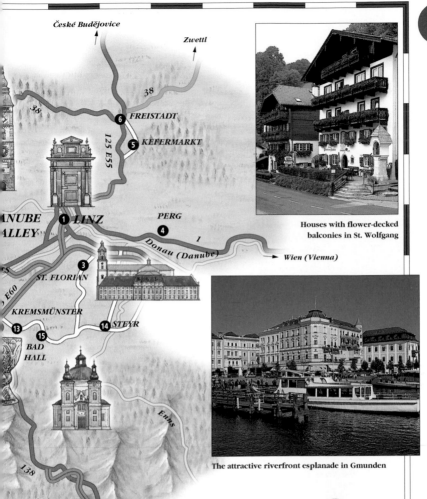

Houses with flower-decked
balconies in St. Wolfgang

The attractive riverfront esplanade in Gmunden

GETTING THERE

Although Linz-Hörsching Airport is served by some international flights, most visitors
fly to Vienna. Linz lies on the
Vienna–Salzburg railway line
and the A1 motorway, which
traverses the province, east to
west, and also connects with
the southern A9 motorway.
There is a dense network of
roads and bus routes throughout. From spring until autumn,
boats on the Danube River
connect Passau with Linz and
Linz with the Wachau Valley.

SEE ALSO

• **Where to Stay** pp297–9

• **Where to Eat** pp328–9

Statue in front of the
Kaiservilla, in Bad Ischl

KEY

▬	Motorway
▬	Major road
▬	Scenic route
▭	River
❧	Viewpoint

0 km   15

0 miles   15

Linz ❶

STRADDLING THE Danube in a scenic spot, Linz owes its former importance and wealth to its location at an intersection of waterways – salt and iron ore were transported along the rivers Traun and Enns, and further along raw materials and finished products travelled down the Danube to Vienna or Passau. This strategic position led the Romans to found a substantial settlement called Lentia on the site. Since the 15th century, Linz has been the capital of Upper Austria. A major industrial centre, it is also a hub of culture with numerous galleries, museums, and the futurist Ars Electronica Center. The composer Anton Bruckner was also associated with Linz in his early career.

A birds-eye view of the town on the banks of the Danube

Exploring Linz

The town sprawls across both banks of the Danube, with the historic old town on the right (south) bank, in the bend of the river. The vast Hauptplatz is regarded as one of Austria's most beautiful architectural complexes. It is also worth taking a trip to a nearby hill, the Pöstlingberg, from where there are splendid views over the town and river. The Ars Electronica Center is situated on the left (north) bank of the Danube.

🛉 Martinskirche

Römerstraße/Martinsgasse.
[(070) 777454.
A modest façade hides Austria's oldest surviving church, dedicated to St Martin. It was first mentioned in the 8th century, during the times of Charlemagne, as part of the Carolingians' former royal residence. The Gothic windows and portals date from the 8th century. There was an older Roman wall on the same site, and ten Roman tombstones, together with other ancient stones, were used as building material to erect the church. The interior also dates from the Carolingian period, the only later addition being the Neo-Gothic presbytery. The rainbow arch that separates the nave from the presbytery and the north wall of the church are adorned with 15th-century frescoes of the Virgin Mary on a throne. Much of the interior can only be seen with a guide.

The tiny Martinskirche, Austria's oldest church

🏛 Schloss

Tummelplatz 10. [(070) 774419.
🕐 9am–6pm Tue–Fri, 10am–5pm Sat, Sun, public holidays. 🖼
In the 15th century, Emperor Friedrich III built his residence on the Römerberg (Roman Mountain), on the foundations of an earlier structure. The castle acquired its present shape between 1600 and 1607, during the times of Rudolf II, and since that time its distinctive silhouette has become one of the most famous sights in Linz. Since 1966, this former imperial residence has housed a museum, a branch of the Oberösterreichisches Landesmuseum. Exhibits include paintings and sculptures from early medieval times to the 19th century and the Secession, 12th–18th-century arms, 16th–19th-century musical instruments, furniture and handicrafts, golden, ceramic and glass objects, and a permanent archaeological exhibition. Part of the museum is devoted to folk traditions; there's a reconstructed physics laboratory from the Jesuit school in Linz and the Schloss Weinberg pharmacy (c.1700). From the castle, there are superb views over Linz.

🏛 Landhaus

Klosterstraße 7. [(070) 7720-11130.
The regional government is based in a Renaissance palace built on the site of a former Minorite monastery. Its north portal, from Klosterstraße, is a beautiful marble work by Renaissance artists. The inner courtyard is surrounded by a colonnade. Here you will find Planetenbrunnen (Fountain of the Planets), built to commemorate the outstanding astronomer and mathematician Johannes Kepler who stayed in Linz and lectured at the college, then based in the Landhaus, for 14 years (1612–26). The seven figures on the fountain's bronze plinth show the planets known at the time.
Close by is the Minoritenkirche, a former Minorite Church, the earliest documented record of which is in the town chronicles of

The Planet Fountain in the inner courtyard of the Landhaus

1288. Altered in the Baroque style in 1751–8, the church has an unusual façade with oval telescopes between the storeys. The lovely Rococo interior is decorated with charming stuccowork and beautiful paintings by Martin Johann Schmidt and Bartolomeo Altomonte.

🚩 Hauptplatz
Hauptplatz, in Linz's Old Town, is one of Austria's finest squares and considered to be one of the foremost achievements of town planning. It is 220 m (720 ft) long

and 60 m (200 ft) wide, and overall it creates a much stronger impression than its component parts would suggest, although many of its buildings are worth a closer look. The Gothic Altes Rathaus (Old Town Hall) at No. 1 was built around 1513, and still has the original octagonal tower with an astronomical clock. In the 17th century, the town hall was given a new façade supported by columns. Other interesting buildings are the Gothic and Baroque houses, including Feichtinger-haus, a former mail inn (No. 21), a Gothic building with an

VISITORS' CHECKLIST

Road map E3. 🏙 186,000.
🚌 🚋 🚆 ✈ 🛈 Hauptplatz 1
(070) 7070-1777.
W www.linz.at 🎭 Pflaster-
spektakel (end Jul); Brucknerfest
(Sep); Ars electronica (Sept).

early-Baroque façade. The Plague Column (1723) in the centre of the square was funded jointly by the local council and all citizens, in thanksgiving for sparing Linz and the Linzers from three deadly disasters: war, fire and the Black Death plague.

Hauptplatz with its Baroque Plague Column

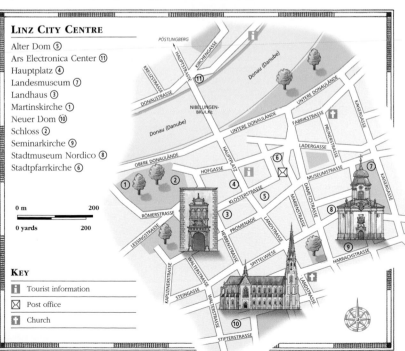

LINZ CITY CENTRE

Alter Dom ⑤
Ars Electronica Center ⑪
Hauptplatz ④
Landesmuseum ⑦
Landhaus ③
Martinskirche ①
Neuer Dom ⑩
Schloss ②
Seminarkirche ⑨
Stadtmuseum Nordico ⑧
Stadtpfarrkirche ⑥

0 m   200
0 yards   200

KEY

🛈 Tourist information
⊠ Post office
✝ Church

The towers of Alter Dom in Domgasse

🏛 Alter Dom

Domgasse 3. **☎** *(070) 770866-0.*
⏰ *7am–noon, 3–7pm daily.*
Thanks to reforms, the capital of the archbishopric of Upper Austria was established at Linz, and in 1785 the former Jesuit church was chosen as the cathedral. Ignatiuskirche, the church of St Ignatius, was built in the second half of the 17th century to designs by Pietro Francesco Carlone, and today its green façade and onion-dome–topped twin towers are distinctive features in the town panorama. The simple, modest elevation of the church conceals a beguiling Baroque interior. The wide main nave has three side chapels on each side. Particularly fascinating are the beautifully engraved stalls in the presbytery, where local artists carved the figures of dwarfs and monsters peeping out from behind the backrests and armrests.

From 1856 until 1868 the composer Anton Bruckner was the cathedral's organist. The present organ, by the famous master Krismann, was altered according to Bruckner's own instructions.

🏛 Stadtpfarrkirche

Pfarrplatz 4. **☎** *(070) 776120-0.*
The parish church of the Assumption of the Virgin Mary (Mariä Himmelfahrt) was built in the 13th century as a triple-nave basilica with Gothic presbytery, and altered in the 17th century, when it

received a new interior and further chapels. The presbytery includes the tombstone of Emperor Friedrich III, who resided in Linz for a while. The urn containing his heart is concealed behind a marble slab in the church wall to the right of the altar. In the eastern end of the south nave is the chapel of St John of Nepomuk. Its lovely Baroque interior is decorated with frescoes and an altar by Bartolomeo Altomonte. St John of Nepomuk was one of the most revered saints in the Austrian empire. Many towns erected statues to him, and the Stadtpfarrkirche in Linz houses two of these. In the external chapel by the presbytery is a figure, probably created by Georg Raphael Donner. The chapel's architecture and dome shape are the work of another Austrian master of the Baroque, Johann Lukas von Hildebrandt.

🏛 Landesmuseum

Museumstraße 14. **☎** *(070) 774482-0.* ⏰ *9am–6pm Tue–Fri, 10am–5pm Sat, Sun.* 🌐
The Landesmuseum building is reminiscent of the Viennese houses along Ringstraße, which is hardly surprising since they were built at the same time and designed in the same spirit of historicism. The museum's architect was a German from Düsseldorf, Bruno Schmitz. The museum

Illumination in a Psalter, Landesmuseum

was named Francisco-Carolinum Museum in honour of Archduke Francis Karl. Originally it was meant to house the collection of the Museum Society of Upper Austria, established in 1833 by Anton Ritter von Spaun. Today, the museum shows mainly modern Austrian art, with a particular emphasis on artists from Upper Austria. It also holds a collection of works by the renowned Bohemian illustrator, Alfred Kubin, and presents exhibitions of its natural history treasures or relating to the province's past.

🏛 Stadtmuseum Nordico

Dametzstraße 23. **☎** *(070) 7070-1900.* ⏰ *9am–6pm Mon–Fri, 2–5pm Sat, Sun.* 🌐
In 1675, this 17th-century Baroque complex was the home of the college known as "Nordisches Stift", which had as its aim the education of young boys from nordic countries – hence the name – and their transformation into good Catholics. Today, this imposing building, now owned by the council, houses the Nordico Town Museum, with its collection of objects relating to the history of Linz from ancient times onwards, including a model of the town from 1740. The top floor is given over to temporary exhibitions, mainly of modern art.

🏛 Seminarkirche

Harrachstraße 7. **☎** *(070) 771205.*
⏰ *7am–5pm daily.*
The former Deutsch-ordenkirche (church of the Teutonic Order) is now a seminary church. Artistically, this is the most valuable historic church building in Linz. It was built in the early 18th century, to a design by Johann Lukas Hildebrandt. Its beautiful Baroque façade is topped with the decorative coats of arms of the Harrach family. The tower, crowned with a distinctive flattened dome, is surrounded by sandstone statues

The impressive Neuer Dom, Austria's largest cathedral

depicting the virtues expected of a Knight of the Order. The interior is in the shape of an ellipse and is covered with an oval dome. The Crucifixion in the main altar is the work of Martin Altomonte. To the right of the entrance stands a statue of St John of Nepomuk, facing which is a painting of the death of St Joseph. The beautiful ceiling relief shows God the Father reigning among a host of angels on a sky adorned with filigree leaf ornaments.

🏛 Neuer Dom
Herrenstraße 26. **(** (070) 777885. **◯** 7:30am–5:30pm Mon–Sat, 1–5:30pm Sun.
Construction of the New Cathedral started in 1862, but it was not completed until 1924. Its architect was Vinzenz Statz, the builder of Cologne cathedral. The Neo-Gothic Neuer Dom is Austria's largest sacred structure, with a capacity of 20,000 faithful. It is said that only one condition was stipulated by the local council, and that was that the steeple must not be taller than that of the Stephansdom

in Vienna *(see p59)*. Statz complied with the request and the tower in Linz is 134 m (440 ft) high – 3 m (10 ft) lower than its counterpart. The interior was designed by Josef Gasser. The most interesting feature of the cathedral are its modern, colourful stained-glass windows, which depict often complex scenes, such as the history of the city.

🏛 Ars Electronica Center
Hauptstraße 2. **(** (070) 7272-0. **◯** 10am–6pm Wed–Sun. **W** www.aec.at
At the entrance to the Nibelungenbrücke (Bridge of the Nibelungs), on the north bank of the Danube, stands one of Austria's most unusual museums, or rather exhibition centres. The Ars Electronica Center is a highly original museum of virtual worlds, created with the help of modern computer technology. It demonstrates the latest computer wizardry and virtual-reality simulations of space and time travel. Visitors can, for example, journey inside various parts of the universe, visit imaginary

Sebastian, mascot of Pöstlingberg's train

Renaissance towns or see a flying saucer disappear into space. There is also a 3D virtual space in the basement where you can explore other worlds with special headsets.

🏛 Lentos Kunstmuseum
Ernst-Koref-Promenade 11. **(** (070) 70703600. **◯** 10am–6pm Wed, Fri–Mon, 10am–10pm Thu. **●** Tue, 1 Jan, 24–25 Dec. **🗺 W** www.lentos.at
This brand-new museum on the south bank of the Danube houses a major collection of paintings, sculptures and prints, concentrating on international and Austrian art from the early 20th century to the present day, featuring Expressionism (Kokoschka, Klimt), Op and Pop Art (Warhol), Pluralism and Austrian photography.

Pöstlingberg
A short distance from the centre of Linz, on the extensive plateau of Urfahr on the north bank of the Danube, rises the 537-m (1,762-ft) Pöstlingberg. The electric mountain train, built in 1898, that climbs almost to the top, was once acclaimed as a wonder of technology. The route is 2.9 km (2 miles) long, and the incline reaches a staggering 10.6 per cent.

On the mountain's summit stands the Wallfahrtskirche zu den Sieben Schmerzen Mariens, the pilgrimage church of Our Lady of Seven Sorrows, which is regarded as one of the main symbols of Linz.

Pilgrimage church built between 1738–47 on Pöstlingberg

The Danube Valley ❷

THE BEAUTIFUL BLUE Danube, extolled by writers and composers, is an extraordinary river. It passes through eight countries, and four capital cities have been built on its banks. The Danube enters Austria as a mountain river right after Passau at Achleiten and leaves 360 km (240 miles) further along, beyond the Hainburg marshes, heading for Bratislava. In Upper Austria, many magnificent towns have been built along its routes; historically, scores of fortresses, abbeys and churches arose on its steep banks (Clam, Melk). The majestic river is an important transport route, and to visitors it offers an excellent network of bicycle routes, with special hotels for cyclists alongside.

Burg Clam
The romantic silhouette of Clam Castle rising above a deep ravine has remained virtually unchanged since the 12th century.

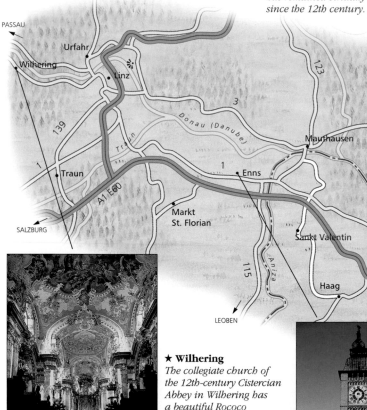

★ **Wilhering**
The collegiate church of the 12th-century Cistercian Abbey in Wilhering has a beautiful Rococo interior with frescoes by Bartolomeo Altomonte.

★ **Enns**
The Renaissance municipal tower of Enns was built in 1565–8. It stands on Hauptplatz, on the left bank of the Enns River, just before it joins the Danube.

STAR SIGHTS
★ Enns
★ Wilhering

Grein
In the town hall is an original Rococo theatre, but Grein's most popular sight is its late-Gothic castle, extended in the 17th century.

VISITORS' CHECKLIST

Road map E3.
Hopfengasse 3, 4020 Linz.
(070) 772545. For full details of
hotels, restaurants and cycling
tours W *www.danube.at*

St. Nikola an der Donau
The Danube ends its journey through Upper Austria near St. Nikola, an area of outstanding natural beauty.

KEY

▤	Motorway
═	Major road
═	Minor road
⋯	River
– –	Bundesland (province) border
☀	Viewpoint

CONCENTRATION CAMPS

During the Third Reich, more than 50 concentration camps were built on Austrian territory. Most were destroyed immediately after the war, but some commemorative plaques and symbolic sites have been preserved: there is a memorial crematorium at Gusen, and in Ebensee the cemetery and underground mine tunnels where prisoners once worked can be seen. The most important memorial, however, is the former camp at Mauthausen, where the quarry, original buildings and the "ash dump" have been preserved. Just outside the camp, a new museum has been opened by the Austrian Government. Each year the liberation is celebrated on the Sunday nearest 8 May.

Mauthausen Todesstiege (Stairway of Death) between quarry and camp

One of the magnificent emperor's rooms in St. Florian Abbey

St. Florian ❸

Road map E3. 🏛 *3,000.* 🚌
🛈 *(07224) 5690.* ⭕ **Stift:** *Guided tours: 10, 11am, 2, 3, 4pm.*
Bruckner organ: *11 May–12 Oct: 2:30pm Wed-Fri, Sun, Mon.* 📷

FLORIAN, the prefect of the Roman Noricum Province, converted to Christianity and was tortured and thrown into the Enns river as a result in 304. His body was retrieved and, in the 11th century, a magnificent abbey and a church were built on the site of his burial place by Augustinian monks; they remain the keepers of St. Florian to this day. The present appearance of the abbey and church is the work of two outstanding Baroque architects: Carlo Carlone and Jakob Prandtauer.

St. Florian is an impressive complex of buildings, with monks' quarters, reception rooms and a church with an adjoining chapel of the Virgin Mary. The main feature in the large courtyard is the Adlerbrunnen (Eagle Well), built in 1603. The east wing houses the library with its vast collection of over 140,000 volumes,

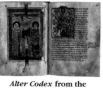

Alter Codex from the library of St. Florian

incunabula and manuscripts. The ceiling painting by Altomonte shows the marriage of Virtue with Knowledge. Next to the library is the Marble Hall with its vast columns, designed by Jakob Prandtauer. The grand staircase in the west wing, also by Prandtauer, leads to the emperor's apartments where important guests stayed. Adjacent is the room of Anton Bruckner, who was associated with St. Florian for many years.

Carlo Carlone remodelled the abbey church – his great masterpiece. Worth seeing inside are the stained-glass windows, the lovely pulpit and the main altar with a painting of the Assumption of the Virgin Mary flanked by columns of pink Salzburg marble. The abbey also has an art gallery.

Perg ❹

Road map E3. 🏛 *7,000.* 🚌 🛈
🛈 *(07262) 52255-0.*

PERG, a small town with a long history situated 30 km (19 miles) east of Linz, was once owned by the

mighty von Perg family, whose last member died in the 12th century, during the Third Crusade. Until the 19th century Perg was the largest centre of millstone production; it is also the home of Manner, the largest manufacturer of sweet wafers in the world. Worth seeing today are some attractive houses on Herrengasse, a 1683 Baroque pillory in the main square and St Jacob's church (1416), which has retained its Gothic interior.

In Perg's environs, graves and numerous remains of the Hallstatt civilization have been unearthed. The Heimathaus at No. 1 Stifterstraße exhibits finds from that period. It also documents the production of millstones and has an interesting collection of 16th–17th-century ceramics, decorated using a special local technique.

Kefermarkt ❺

Road map E3. 🏛 *2,200.* 🚌
🛈 *(07947) 6255-0.*

THE MAIN ATTRACTION in this little town is its 15th-century Wallfahrtskirche (pilgrimage church), built by Christoph von Zelking, the master of Kefermarkt's castle, Schloss Weinberg. He also commissioned its altar dedicated to his favourite saint, St Wolfgang (died 994), Bishop of Regensburg and Henry II's tutor. We do not know who created the altar, but the result is a masterpiece of medieval art. Entirely carved from limewood, it was probably once painted, but now the original texture and colour of the wood are revealed. Its centre is made up of the figures of Saints Peter, Wolfgang and Christopher. On the wings of the altar the unknown artist has placed scenes of the Annunciation, the Birth of Christ, the Adoration of the Magi and the Death of Mary. The altar was once riddled with woodworm and only narrowly escaped total destruction. It was carefully restored in 1852–5, under the supervision of Adalbert Stifter, a writer and school inspector for Upper Austria.

It is to his dedication and appreciation of great art that we owe the altar's survival. There is also an interesting permanent exhibition in the church called "Jesus on the road".

A statue on the splendid wooden altar in Kefermarkt church

Freistadt **6**

Road map E3. 7,400. (07942) 72506.

FREISTADT, THE largest town in the Mühlviertel region, was once the last border fortress on the route leading from the alpine countries to Bohemia. Much of the medieval **town wall** has survived to this day, including several bastions and two impressive gateways; one of these, the late-Gothic Linzer Tor, is the symbol of the town. The focal point of the old town centre, the rectangular Hauptplatz, is lined

JAKOB PRANDTAUER (1660–1726)

Austria's outstanding architect of the Baroque, Prandtauer specialized in sacred buildings and shaped the present look of several medieval abbeys. His greatest masterpiece is generally agreed to be the Benedictine Abbey in Melk. He also created the church of the Carmelite nuns in St. Pölten, and gave a Baroque face to the Augustinian abbey in St. Florian and the Benedictine abbey in Kremsmünster. Distinctive features of his work are the variety of forms he used, and the vigorous way in which he blended architecture with the surrounding countryside.

with historic houses. On its east side stands the town hall, with a carved fountain.

The 15th-century **Katharinenmünster**, the church of St Catherine, on the southwest side of the square, was altered in the Baroque style by Johann Michael Prunner. The altar paintings are the work of Carlo Carlone. The castle, not far from the main square, was built in 1397 for the widow of Prince Albert III. It was devastated by a fire in 1888 and subsequently turned into a military barracks. After restoration in 1995, it now houses the **Schlossmuseum**, a regional museum holding Austria's largest collection of glass paintings.

🏛 **Schlossmuseum**
Schlosshof 2.
(07942)72274.
9am–noon, 2–5pm Mon–Fri, 2–5pm Sat, Sun, public holidays.

Schärding **7**

Road map D3. 5,050. (07712) 4300.

THIS TOWN on the banks of the Inn River was, until 1779, owned by the Bavarian family of Wittelsbach, whose influence can be seen in the local architecture. Schärding's most beautiful feature is its **Stadtplatz**, the central square cut in half by buildings. At the north end of the upper square, **Silberzeile** is a row of beautiful houses with gabled roofs. It is overshadowed by the vast Church of St George's with a grand steeple. Little apart from the gateway and moat remains of the old castle here. The gateway now houses a regional museum with a late-Gothic Madonna, a beautiful crucifix and sculptures by Johann Peter Schwanthaler (1720–95).

Silberzeile, a row of pretty and colourful gabled houses in the Stadtplatz in Schärding

Baroque house façades in Obernberg

Obernberg am Inn ⑧

Road map D3. 🏛 *1,800.* 🚌
🚍 *(05274) 3600.*

UNTIL THE LATE 18th century, Obernberg belonged to Bavaria and was ruled by the bishops of Passau. In 1779, it transferred to Austria. The old market town has preserved its lovely **Marktplatz**, the central town square, lined with pretty houses with exceptionally beautiful, richly ornamented stucco façades. Particularly interesting are the façades of the houses at Nos 37, 38 and 57, with decorations attributed to the prominent Bavarian artist, Johann Baptist Modler. A fountain in the centre of the square is surrounded by sculptures. When visiting the Annakapelle, the parish church of Obernberg, it is worth taking a closer look at the 16th-century wood-carving of the Holy Family.

A castle, once owned by the bishops of Passau, has stood in Obernberg since the 12th century, but little remains of it.

ENVIRONS: Near Obernberg, 15 km (9 miles) to the southwest, is the largest town of the province, **Ried im Innkreis**, an agricultural centre and the home town of the Schwanthaler family of sculptors. Many members of the family were outstanding artists, active in

the region from 1632 to 1838. The local museum, at No. 13 Kirchenplatz, exhibits some of their works.

Braunau am Inn ⑨

Road map D3. 🏛 *16,500.* 🚌 🚍
ℹ️ *Stadtplatz 12 (07722) 62644.*

BRAUNAU is a substantial border town on the Inn River and one of the prettiest spots in the entire region. It was built by the Dukes of Lower Bavaria, who ruled it for a long time. Originally intended as a bridgehead in their battles with the East, the town remained one of the best-fortified towns in this part of Europe until the 17th century. In 1779 it passed to Austria, together with the rest of the province. The Baroque fortifications were dismantled by Napoleon, but some sections survived, including the remains of several medieval buildings. The centre of this Gothic town is occupied by the unusually elongated **Stadtplatz**, surrounded by historic houses. At No. 18 Johann-Fischer-Gasse, built in 1385, an old bell-foundry has survived almost intact. Together with the former ducal castle at No. 10 Altstadt next door, it is now the home of the regional museum, showing art, handicrafts and traditions of the Inn region. The town's

Figure from fountain in Obernberg town square

symbol is the stone tower of the **Stephanskirche** (parish church of St Stephen) which is nearly 100 m (330 ft) tall. Construction began in 1492, but the Baroque cupola dates from a later period. Inside the church is a lovely stone pulpit. The only surviving parts of the original altarpiece by Michael Zürn are figures of the Madonna with Child and Saints Stephen and Laurence. The altar itself dates from 1906; it is a Neo-Gothic copy of Michael Pacher's altar in St. Wolfgang *(see p205).* Among the tombs outside the church is one of Hans Staininger, who is shown with a curly beard that reaches to his toes – and was said to have been the cause of his untimely death.

Braunau was also the birth-place of Adolf Hitler, who lived at No. 15 Salzburger Vorstadt until he was two.

The birthplace of Adolf Hitler in Braunau am Inn

Schmiding ⑩

Road map D3. 🚌 🚍 *Haiding.*

UPPER AUSTRIA'S largest zoo, covering an area of some 120,000 sq m (30 acres), is based at Schmiding, 7 km (4 miles) north of Wels. This modern zoo, with giraffes, monkeys, crocodiles, exotic birds and 1,500 other animal species, is famous for its walk-in aviary with birds of prey – the world's largest. A huge tropical house, an African savannah and Austria's biggest colony of flamingos are further highlights of the zoo. Children love the 5-m (16-ft) high platform which

Flamingoes in the zoo at Schmiding

allows them to come face to face with the giraffes.

The park lies at the foot of a castle dating from 1405. After World War II the castle served as a military hospital; it has since been restored and converted into apartments.

🦜 **Schmiding Zoo**
📞 (07249) 46272. ⬤ Mar–Nov: 9am–7pm daily.

Lambach ⓫

Road map D3. 🚶 3,500. 🚌 🚉
🏛 (07245) 28995-0.

L AMBACH, conveniently located on the left bank of the Traun River, grew rich in the Middle Ages thanks to the flourishing salt trade. Around 1040 Count Arnold II Wels-Lambach and his wife Regilinda transformed the family

seat into a monastery. Their son, Bishop Adalberto, who was later canonized, invited Benedictine monks here in 1089. In the same year, the Lambach monks established a second monastery at Melk which, eventually, was to surpass the mother abbey in terms of status and beauty. The abbey church was mostly rebuilt in the 17th century; rebuilding of the abbey itself was completed 50 years later.

The Baroque interior of the church is very beautiful, but Lambach owes its fame primarily to the Romanesque frescoes, probably dating from the 11th century. Unique in Austria, they are considered to be one of Europe's most resplendent examples of Romanesque art. At their centre is the Madonna with Child, to the left the Adoration of the Magi, who present gifts to the Holy Infant. The south vault depicts Jerusalem and Herod's palace. The abbey treasury also holds the Romanesque chalice of Bishop Adalbert and precious monstrances and chasubles. Also on view are ceiling paintings by Martino Altomonte and Martin Johann Schmidt. The musical archives hold a copy of Mozart's *Lambacher Symphonie*, which the composer reputedly created while staying here. Lambach also has a beautifully preserved Rococo theatre.

Romanesque frescoes in Lambach Abbey

Wels ⓬

Road map E3. 🚶 56,700. 🚌 🚉
🏛 Stadtplatz 55 (07242) 43495.
ⓦ www.wels.at

T HE HISTORY OF Wels dates back to Roman days, as testified by numerous excavations. Some of the objects discovered are on display in the former Minorites' Abbey, including the famous Wels Venus, a bronze statuette from the 1st–2nd century AD and the oldest early-Christian epitaph in Austria, from the first half of the 4th century.

Today Wels is a centre of agriculture and industry, and the venue of an annual agricultural fair of international importance. Many historic features have also been preserved. **Stadtplatz**, the main square in the old town, is entered through a Baroque gate, the **Ledererturm**. Many houses in Stadtplatz have attractive façades, such as the Rococo **Kremsmünstererhof** with its arcaded courtyard, which for 400 years belonged to Kremsmünster Abbey. Adjacent to it stands a water tower (1577) and a two-house complex forming the late-Baroque town hall. Also in Stadtplatz is the Stadtpfarrkirche, the parish church of St John the Evangelist, with an original Romanesque portal and magnificent 14th-century stained-glass windows in the presbytery. **Burg Wels**, the imperial palace first documented in 776, is now a lively cultural centre and home of the regional museum.

The galleried courtyard of Kremsmünsterhof in Stadtplatz, Wels

Kremsmünster ⑬

Road map E3. 🏛 6000. 🚌 🚉
🅸 Rathausplatz 1 (07583) 7212.

Perched high above the Krems river stands the 8th-century Benedictine Abbey of Kremsmünster, its present appearance dating mostly from the 17th century. The abbey was completed by Jakob Prandtauer, to designs by Carlo Carlone. Two of its most remarkable features are the 17th-century fish ponds, surrounded by columns, corridors and sculptural fountains, and the unusual **Sternwarte**, a 50-m (165-ft) high observation tower, which holds collections of palaeontology, physics, anthropology, astronomy and zoology. The **Stiftskirche** (abbey church) has rich stucco decorations and angel statues. The abbey museum comprises works by Austrian and Dutch masters from the Baroque and Renaissance periods, wood carvings and gold objects. The pride of Kremsmünster are its earliest exhibits; these include the gilded-copper chalice and candelabras of Duke Tassilo, the legendary founder of the abbey, and the *Codex millenarius* (c.800), an illuminated gospel manuscript.

The Tassilo Chalice in Kremsmünster

🏛 **Kremsmünster**
☎ (07583) 5275-0. 🅆 www.stift-kremsmuenster.at ◻ Easter–Oct: guided tours 10, 11:15am, 2, 3:30pm Mon–Fri, 10, 11:30am, 1, 2, 3, 4:15pm Sat, Sun; Nov–Easter: 11am, 2, 3pm Tue–Sun; **Sternwarte:** closed; guided tours on request. 🖼

Steyr ⑭

Road map E3. 🏛 40,000. 🚌 🚉
🅸 Stadtplatz 27 (07252) 53229.

Steyr, one of Austria's largest industrial centres, is also a very attractive town which has managed to preserve its old town almost intact. The townscape is punctuated in the north by the turrets of the castle and in the south by the towers of the Stadtpfarrkirche, the parish church at Brucknerplatz. The centre of town is the elongated Stadtplatz (town square) with most of the historic sights. The **Brummerlhaus** (1497) at No. 32, is a well preserved medieval house with a high-pitched roof and three arcaded courtyards, that is now a bank. The Rococo **Rathaus** (town hall), with its slender steeple, was designed by Johann Gottfried Hayberger. The inner courtyards of houses around the square are also worth seeing.

The **Stadtpfarrkirche**, built in 1443, was remodelled in the Neo-Gothic style, but it has preserved some elements of its original 15th-century decor, the work of Hans Puchsbaum, builder of the Stephansdom in Vienna, as well as some lovely wrought-iron grilles. The south wall has magnificent 15th-century stained-glass windows; the sculptures in the north portal and the former cemetery chapel of St Margaret (1430), also by Hans Puchsbaum, date from the same period.

The **Schloss** (castle), first mentioned in 10th-century annals, stands in the oldest part of the town. Today it has a Baroque façade and a mostly Rococo interior. The house at No. 26 Grünmarkt, formerly a granary, is now a museum.

Environs: In **Gleink**, a northern suburb of Steyr, stands a worthy Benedictine Abbey. Some 3 km (2 miles) west of the town centre, in the suburb of **Christkindl**, is the church of the same name (meaning "Infant Christ"), the joint work of Giovanni Battista Carlone and Jakob Prandtauer. In 1695, a devout person placed a wax figure of the Infant Jesus in the hollow of a tree and prayed there every day for a cure. His prayers were answered and soon the crowds of pilgrims drawn to the site of the

Steyr town panorama as seen from the river

miracle were so large that in 1702 the abbot from nearby Garsten decided to build a church. The main object of adoration is the wax figurine of Jesus, kept in a beautifully decorated glass cabinet. The cabinet itself is part of a composition symbolizing the Holy Trinity. Christkindl has its own post office, using the coveted "Christkindl" postmark showing the Infant Jesus. It operates only in the pre-Christmas period, and millions of letters, supposedly from the Infant Jesus, are sent around the world from here.

⛪ Christkindl Church

Christkindlweg 69. ☎ (07252) 54622.

The façade of the Christkindl church, on the outskirts of Steyr

Bad Hall ⓯

Road map E3. 👥 4,300. 🚌
ℹ Kurpromenade 1 (07258) 7200.

Bad Hall, a health resort between Steyr and Kremsmünster, lies on the so-called "Romantic Route", but the idyllic scenery is just one of its attractions: it also boasts the richest iodine springs in Central Europe. A highly modern resort surrounds the springs, which are used to treat eye, circulatory and heart diseases. The lovely Kurpark (spa park), with its excellent sports facilities, makes convalescence a real treat. There is also a Rococo church which belongs to the abbey at Kremsmünster.

The lovely scenery around the resort of Bad Hall

Another sight worth visiting is the fascinating **Forum Hall Museum**, which holds a superb collection devoted to the development of traditional folk handicrafts in Upper Austria, as well as to the history of the local springs.

🏛 Forum Hall Museum

Eduard-Bach-Straße 4.
☎ (07258) 4888. ◯ Apr–Nov: 2–6pm Thu–Sun. 📷

Stadl-Paura ⓰

Road map D3. 👥 5,080. 🚌 🚊
ℹ Marktplatz 1 (07245) 28011-0

Stadl-Paura, a small town on the right bank of the Traun River 2 km (1 mile) south of Lambach, has an imposing **Dreifaltigkeitskirche** (church of the Holy Trinity). Construction of the church was started in 1714 in thanksgiving for the sparing of the town from the plague. In its design, the church represents the Holy Trinity – everything is in triplicate. There are three

The Dreifaltigkeitskirche, pilgrimage church of the Holy Trinity in Stadl-Paura

façades, three portals, three towers and three altars. The church was built by the Linz architect, J. M. Prunner. In the design of the interior decorations some clever false architectural perspectives have been incorporated, creating unusual effects. The paintings in the altarpieces are by Carlo Carlone, Martino Altomonte and Domenico Parodi.

The house at No. 13 Fabrikstraße, once an orphanage for the children of sailors who lost their lives in the waters of the Traun river, is now a museum of shipping.

Schwanenstadt ⓱

Road map D3. 👥 4,400. 🚌 🚊
ℹ Stadtplatz 54 (07673) 2255-22.

This small town, situated between Lambach and Vöcklabruck, is today an important economic centre. In the centre of town stands a Neo-Gothic parish church with a 78-m (256-ft) spire, built in 1900 on the site of an earlier Gothic church. Worth seeing inside are a late-Gothic statue of the Virgin Mary, a 15th-century relief of the Mourning for Christ and 18th-century Baroque statues of the 12 apostles.

The town hall houses a regional museum which exhibits, among other things, Roman and Bavarian archaeological finds.

In front of the town hall is a 13th-century well; the square is lined with attractive houses with Renaissance and Baroque façades.

The riverside townscape of the health resort of Gmunden, on the banks of the Traun river

Vöcklabruck ⑱

Road map D3. 🏛 *12,000.* 🚍 🚉
ℹ *Hinterstadt 14 (07672) 26644.*

IN 1134, WEZELO von Schöndorf built a bridge over the Vöckla River, and next to it a church and a hospital. Soon a trading settlement sprang up which later became a large town. The only original structures that have survived are two medieval towers.

At the centre of town stands the small, 15th-century, late-Gothic **St. Ulrichkirche** (church of St Ulrich), which has a Baroque interior. The site of the 12th-century hospital and chapel is now occupied by the magnificent Baroque **St. Ägiduskirche**, designed by Carlo Carlone, with sculptures by Giovanni Battista Carlone. The ceiling frescoes depict scenes from the lives of Christ and the Virgin Mary.

The former parish house, at No. 10 Hinterstadt, now houses a regional museum with a room devoted to Anton Bruckner.

The south of the town is dominated by the unusual silhouette of **Mariä Himmelfahrtskirche** (church of the Assumption of the Virgin Mary). It has a Neo-Gothic altarpiece with a beautiful 15th-century statue of the Virgin, and stained-glass windows behind the main altar from the same period.

ENVIRONS: West of Vöcklabruck, about 12 km (7 miles)

A detail from Gmunden town hall

away, is the small town of **Gampern**. Its Remigiuskirche (church of St Remigius) has an attractive late-Gothic polyptych (1507) carved in wood.

Gmunden ⑲

Road map D3. 🏛 *15,000.* 🚍 🚉
ℹ *Am Graben 2 (07612) 64305.*

THIS LAKESIDE TOWN, on the northern end of Traunsee, established itself as a trading post in the salt trade. Today, it is a popular and well-run health resort, and it is also known for its fine ceramics. Gmunden's old town centre is situated between the lake and the left (western) bank of the Traun river. Its Hauptplatz boasts a Renaissance town hall with a small, arcaded tower and a carillon that plays a regular tune. The **Stadtpfarrkirche** (parish church) has a two-fold dedication: the Virgin Mary and the Three Kings. The Magi are also depicted in the main altarpiece, one of the most beautiful works by Thomas Schwanthaler. The figures of Saints Elizabeth and Zacharias were carved by Michael Zürn. Each year on Epiphany Eve (5 Jan), a barge travels along the Traun river, bringing the Three Kings to town, who solemnly proceed to "their" church. A ceramic fountain decorated with a figure of a salt miner stands adjacent to the church. The local **museum**, based at No. 8 Kammerhofgasse in the

Renaissance building of the former Salt Mines Authorities, has exhibits on the history of the town and its salt production, a collection of local ceramics as well as displays relating to the composer Johannes Brahms and the German playwright Friedrich Hebbel. At No. 4 Traungasse is the **Sanitärmuseum**, with its amusing displays of locally made sanitaryware, toilet bowls and chamber pots.

In Traunsee stands the water fortress of **Lake Castle Ort**, built in the 15th and 16th centuries and rebuilt inn 1634. It has an enchanting triangular, arcaded courtyard and remnants of Renaissance frescoes. A popular TV series is set in the castle.

Traunkirchen ⑳

Road map D3. 🏛 *1,800.* 🚍
ℹ *Ortsplatz 1 (07617) 2234.*

PRECARIOUSLY perched on a rocky promontory, the small village of Traunkirchen is one of the most popular tourist destinations in Salzkammergut

Picturesque Johannesbergkapelle above Traunsee in Traunkirchen

◁ **The picturesque town of Hallstatt and Christuskirche rising above the Hallstatter See**

(see p209). It creates a lovely picture, clinging to the west shore of Traunsee, Austria's deepest lake, with views of the lake's wild southern shore and the Traunstein peak on the eastern shore, the highest mountain of the region rising to 1,691 m (5,548 ft). Above the village towers the pretty Johannesbergkapelle. On the northern end of the headland stands the Jesuit **Pfarrkirche**, rebuilt after a fire in 1632. It has an unusual fishermen's pulpit shaped like a fishing boat, with the apostles drawing nets filled with fish. Since 1632 Traunkirchen has also hosted the annual Corpus Christi boat procession.

Salzkammergut Lakes ㉑

See pp206–7.

The steam mountain railway leading to the top of Schafberg

Schafberg ㉒

Road map D4.

ONE OF THE most pictur-esque peaks in the area, Schafberg (Sheep Mountain) rises to 1,783 m (5,850 ft) between Attersee and Wolf-gangsee. A mountain railway with steam locomotives takes visitors to the summit, although you have to walk the last bit.

The views from the top are truly unforgettable, embracing the most beautiful lakes of the Salzkammergut: Mondsee, Attersee and Wolfgangsee. Visible in the background are the towering mountain ranges running up to the Dachstein massif in the south, and, beyond Salzburg, you can see the Bavarian Alps on the German-Austrian border.

St. Wolfgang ㉓

Road map D4. 🏔 *2,800.* 🚌
🈯 *(06138) 8003.*

ON THE NORTHERN shore of Wolfgangsee lies the pop-ular town of St. Wolfgang. According to legend it arose around a chapel built by Wolf-gang (died 994), Bishop of Regensburg in Germany and teacher of Emperor Henry II. Although he died a hermit, Wolfgang was an extremely popular figure in his day, and was later canonized. His chapel became a much-visited place of pilgrimage. In the 15th century it was replaced by a church with room for a much larger number of pilgrims. It was around that time that the Abbot of Mond-see commissioned the famed South Tyrolean artist, Michael Pacher, to create an altar for the **pilgrimage church**.

Pacher's high altar, combin-ing sculpture, painting and architecture, is acclaimed as one of the most beautiful works of the late-Gothic era. The four scenes visible on the wings of the altarpiece when they are closed (on week-days) depict events from the life of St. Wolfgang, patron saint of the church. The saint is shown holding a model of the church and is flanked by the figures of the Saints George and Florian. On Sundays, the wings of the altar are opened to reveal eight painted scenes from the life of Christ. They are striking in their color-ation, the dynamics of their life-like figures and, above all, in the architectural per-spective employed by the artist. The brightly gilded, sculpted centrepiece depicts the Coronation of the Virgin Mary attended by Christ, St Benedict and St. Wolfgang.

The church of St. Wolfgang also has a lovely Baroque altarpiece by Thomas Schwan-thaler, depicting the Holy Family on their journey to Jerusalem. The three side altarpieces on the north wall and the magnificently ornate pulpit are the works of a Mondsee master, Meinrad Guggenbichler.

St. Wolfgang is also popular with tourists who come to see the hotel "Weißes Rössl" which inspired an operetta of the same name, *White Horse Inn*, by Ralph Benatzky.

Bad Ischl ㉔

Road map D4. 🏔 *13,900.* 🚌 🚉
🈯 *Bahnhofstraße 6 (06132) 27757.*

UNUSUALLY potent saltwater springs were discovered in this region as early as the 16th century, but Bad Ischl did not become a popular health resort until the early 1800s, when the court doctor ordered saline treatments for the infertile Archduchess Sophie. Soon, she started producing babies. The most famous of these was Franz Joseph I, the future emperor, who spent all his summer holidays with his wife Eliz abeth at the **Kaiservilla**. It was also here that he signed the declaration of war with Serbia, on 1 August 1914, sig-nalling the start of World War I.

Many aristocrats and artists have been attracted to the spa, among them the com-poser Franz Lehár, who lived at No. 8 Lehárkai, which is now a museum devoted to him.

The imposing Spa House in the popular resort of Bad Ischl

Salzkammergut Lakes ㉑

Tʜɪs ᴄᴏʀɴᴇʀ of Austria, which belongs to the Salzkammergut region, is worth visiting at any time of the year. With more than 70 lakes surrounded by mountains, it boasts breathtaking scenery as well as a unique climate, and offers excellent facilities for winter and summer holidays. This is also one of the few areas in Europe to preserve many original folk customs, including the tradition of placing a crib in front of the house at Christmas.

Mondsee
The warmest of the Salzkammergut lakes, at the foot of craggy mountains, is famous for its windsurfing. The little town of the same name arose around a Benedictine abbey, which dominates it to this day.

★ **St. Wolfgang**
The main attraction in this charming small town and holiday resort is the parish church with its beautiful altarpiece by Michael Pacher (see p205).

BRAUNAU

St. Georgen

A1 E55 E60

Mondsee

SALZBURG

154

Mondsee

151

Unterach

Burggrabenklam

St. Wolfgangsee

St. Wolfg

POLITICIANS AND ARTISTS ON HOLIDAY

The shores of the Salzkammergut lakes have seen many famous visitors. The house that witnessed the engagement of Emperor Franz Joseph I to Elizabeth of Bavaria in 1853 is now a museum with memorabilia of famous guests in Bad Ischl. There were scores of them: crowned heads and high-ranking aristocrats were joined by artists. Franz Lehár, composer of operettas such as *The Merry Widow* and *The Land of Smiles*, had his villa here; so did the actor Alexander Girardi and the actress Katharina Schratt, the long-term mistress of Franz Joseph I. Other regular visitors included the writer and actor Johannes Nepomuk Nestroy, the painter Rudolf von Alt, and musicians Johannes Brahms, Anton Bruckner, Johann Strauss and Imre Kálmán. In the late 20th century many politicians spent their holidays in St. Wolfgang, including both the former Austrian and German Chancellors.

Franz Joseph I and his hunting party

KEY

▓▓▓	Motorway
══	Major road
──	Minor road
⠿	River
▪ ▪	Bundesland (province) border
�	Viewpoint

★ **Attersee**
The largest of the Salzkammergut lakes, Attersee is dominated by the Höllengebirge (Mountains of Hell). This popular lake is a great base for boating holidays.

VISITORS' CHECKLIST

Road map D3, D4.
🛈 *Salzkammergut Tourismus Marketing GmbH, Wirerstraße 10, 4820 Bad Ischl.*
📞 *(06132) 26909-0.*
@ *info@salzkammergut.at*
🅦 *www.salzkammergut.at*
🎫 *"Glöcklerlauf" (Bell walk) Night Procession, Traunsee Jan 5*

LINZ

A1 E55 E60

145

Buchberg

see

Gmunden

Altmünster

152

Traunsee

Steinbach

Ebensee

153

145

158

Bad Ischl

GRAZ

Seeschloss Ort
The pretty lakeside castle, built on an island, has a quadrangular tower topped by an onion dome. One of its last owners was Franz Joseph's nephew, Johann Salvator, a colourful character whose political life displeased the court.

0 km   5

0 miles   5

Ebensee
This town, a centre of the salt industry scenically located at the southern end of Traunsee at the bottom of Höllengebirge, is famous for its carnival festivities.

STAR SIGHTS

★ **Attersee**

★ **St. Wolfgang**

Bronze-age finds in Hallstatt's World Heritage Museum

Hallstatt ㉕

Road map D4. 🏔 *1,000.* 🚌 🚠
🚢 ℹ *Seestraße 169 (06134) 8208.*

THE SMALL TOWN of Hallstatt is one of the loveliest tourist destinations in the Salzkammergut. The steep drop of the Dachstein massif provides a scenic backdrop for the town and adjacent Hallstätter See. The houses are clustered together so tightly that many are accessible only from the lakeside, while the old street runs above the rooftops. Even the local Corpus Christi procession is held on the lake, in festive, decorated boats. Rising above the town on a rocky headland is the pagoda-like roof of the **Pfarrkirche**. Its stepped dome dates from a later period, but the church was built in the 15th century and to this day contains many original features, including the carved wooden altarpiece of the Virgin Mary, sometimes compared to Pacher's altar in St. Wolfgang *(see p205)*. The figure of the Madonna at its

Painted skulls in the Beinhaus chapel of Hallstatt's Pfarrkirche

centre is flanked by the Saints Barbara, patron of miners, and Catherine, revered by woodcutters. Depicted on the inner wings are scenes from the lives of Mary and Jesus. The altar is guarded by the statues of two knightly saints, George and Florian.

In the cemetery surrounding the church stands the **Beinhaus**, a chapel that serves as a storehouse for some very bizarre objects. This former mortuary now holds some 1,200 human skulls, painted with floral designs and in many cases inscribed with the name, date and cause of death of the deceased. Shortage of space in the graveyard had meant that some ten years after a funeral, when a body had decomposed, the remains were moved to the chapel to make room for the next coffin to be buried, resulting in this unusual depository.

A short distance below the Catholic Pfarrkirche stands a Neo-Gothic Protestant church, with a slender steeple.

Vertically above the town, about 500 m (1,640 ft) higher, is **Salzwelten**, probably the oldest salt mine in the world, which can be reached by cable car. Salt was mined here as early as 3,000 BC and then transported to the Baltic Sea and the Mediterranean.

In 1846, a large cemetery yielding some 2,000 graves was uncovered in Hallstatt. Rich burial objects dated mainly from the Iron Age but some dated even further back in time, to the Bronze Age. The Hallstatt finds proved so important archaeologically that the Celtic culture of that period (800–400 BC) was

named the **Hallstatt civilization**. Its influence reached far into France, the Slav countries and Hungary. Today, Hallstatt treasures can be seen in many Austrian museums, with the bulk of them held at Schloss Eggenberg, near Graz *(see p162).* The few finds that stayed in Hallstatt are kept in the **World Heritage Museum**. The entire Hallstatt region has been declared a World Heritage Site by UNESCO.

🏛 **Salzwelten Hallstatt**
Lahnstraße 21. 【 *(06132) 200 2400.* ◯ *end Apr–last week Sep: 9:30am–4:30pm daily; last week Sep– end Oct: 9:30am–3pm.* 🍴 🅿 💻
ⓦ *www.salzwelten.at*
🏛 **World Heritage Museum**
Seestraße 56. 【 *(06134) 828015.* ◯ *Jan–Mar: 11am–3pm Mon, Wed– Sun; Apr, Oct: 10am–4pm daily; May–Sep: 9am–6pm daily; Nov–Dec: 11am–3pm daily.* 🍴 🅿
ⓦ *www.museum-hallstatt.at*

Gosauseen ㉖

Road map D4. 🚌
ℹ *Gosau (06136) 8295.*

YOU CANNOT truly appreciate the unique charms of the Salzkammergut without visiting this outstandingly beautiful alpine area. The Gosauseen are two small mountain lakes – Vorderer Gosausee and Hinterer Gosausee – both are beautifully situated in limestone rocks intercut with deep gorges. Vorderer Gosausee lies at an altitude of 933 m (3,061 ft). An undemanding walk around the lake will reward you with superb views of the surrounding mountains and over the Dachstein range with its many glaciers.

The most picturesque mountain, with zigzag peaks and a sheer drop, is Gosaukamm (2,459 m/8,068 ft high). This is the easternmost part of the Alps where the snow stays on the ground all year round. The road to Hinterer Gosausee climbs steeply among thick forest. From this lake, 1,154 m (3,786 ft) high, you can climb some of the adjacent peaks.

A mountain stream racing through a gorge in the Dachstein range

Dachsteinhöhlen ⑳

Road map D4. 🚌 Salzbergstraße 21. ☎ (06134) 8400.
ⓦ *www.dachstein.at.*

THE CAVES in the slopes of the Dachstein range are among Austria's most beautiful and fascinating natural monuments. The vast caves, one of the largest systems on Earth and millions of years old, are covered by 500-year-old permafrost. After the last Ice Age, underground waters created strange ice mountains, glaciers and frozen waterfalls. The most interesting of these is the **Rieseneishöhle** (Giant Ice Cave). The caverns in this surreal underground ice-world are named after King Arthur and the Celtic heroes, Parsifal and Tristan. The most arresting cavern formation is the so-called Ice Chapel.

A little further along, also in a limestone wall of Dachstein,

THE SALZKAMMERGUT

For centuries, the name Salzkammergut applied only to the area around the Hallstätter See and Traunsee lakes, and to the towns of Bad Ischl, Hallstatt and Gmunden. Salt has been excavated here since prehistoric times, ensuring the long-term wealth and development of the entire region. Salt mines exist in the area to this day. In the second half of the 19th century the area became famous for its therapeutic springs, and with time the term Salzkammergut came to refer to the entire land of lakes and mountains that is now Austria's most popular tourist destination. It includes the eastern part of the Salzburg Alps, with the picturesque mountain ranges of Dachstein (eastern part), Totes Gebirge (Dead Mountains) and Höllengebirge (Mountains of Hell). Between the mountains lie 76 lakes, the largest and most famous of which are Traunsee, Mondsee, Attersee, Hallstätter See and Wolfgangsee. For historical reasons, the "land of salt" straddles three Austrian provinces. The largest part is in Upper Austria, a small area in the south belongs to Styria, whilst almost all of Wolfgangsee and the St. Gilgen resort are part of the Salzburger Land.

The much-loved Salzkammergut, land of lakes and mountains

is the entrance to a second system of caves, known as **Mammuthöhle** (Mammoth Caves), so named because of their size rather than after the prehistoric mammal. These caves do not have ice

Dachstein ice caves in Obertraun

formations, but there is a spectacular light show.

Both networks of caves can be reached via paths starting from the first cable-car station. The sightseeing route leads through a labyrinthine network of tunnels, gorges and chambers that stretch over 44 km (27 miles), with a 1,200 m (4,000 ft) change in altitude. Individual caverns have been given evocative names such as the Realm of Shadows or Midnight Cathedral. Also worth seeing is a third cave, **Koppenbrüllerhöhle**, which has a giant water source and is considered to be the largest water cave in the Dachstein massif.

All caves are open to the public only during the spring and summer seasons (May to Oct; Koppenbrüllerhöhle May to Sep). When visiting the caves, especially the ice caves, make sure you take plenty of warm clothing.

SALZBURGER LAND

THE PROVINCE OF *Salzburg, a region of high mountains, covers an area of 7,154 sq km (2,762 sq miles) and has 450,000 inhabitants. Its neighbours are Germany and the Austrian provinces of Tyrol, Upper Austria, Styria and Carinthia. A narrow wedge of land along the peaks of the Hohe Tauern mountains reaches as far as the Italian border in the south.*

Salzburger Land is divided into five regions: Flachgau, Tennengebirge, Pongau, Pinzgau and Lungau. History has made them different in character and traditions; all are great for sports.

Colonization of the Salzach Valley goes back to prehistoric times. The mineral deposits – copper, precious metals and, above all, salt (*Salz* in German) from which both the town and province take their names – were being exploited as early as 1000 BC. It was salt which created the basis for the development of the so-called Hallstatt civilization that spread from here. The Celtic town of Noricum established in the alpine region ultimately became a Roman province of the same name. Christianity arrived here early, and its turbulent progress was halted only by the great Migration of Nations in 5th-century Europe. It was not until the 7th century that monks settled in Mönchsburg, the future Salzburg, which became first a bishopric and then an archbishopric. The entire province was an independent principality for many centuries, governed by an ecclesiastical ruler acting as sovereign prince and, depending on political circumstance and personal preference, associating himself with the Holy Roman Empire, the Austrian Habsburgs or Rome. Following the Congress of Vienna, in 1815, Salzburg became part of Austria. Today, the beauty of Salzburg, inextricably linked with Mozart, makes this province a visitor magnet second only to Vienna.

The Hochkönig alpine meadows in Salzburger Land

◁ Splendid church domes towering above the beautiful Baroque buildings in Salzburg

Passau

Exploring Salzburger Land

MOST OF THE province lies in the Salzach river basin, at a relatively high altitude, offering excellent conditions for both winter sports and summer mountain walks. Austria's most scenic mountain road, the Großglockner Hochalpenstraße *(see pp280–81)*, crosses the southern part of the province. The region abounds in mineral springs and waterfalls, and boasts the world's largest caves. Salzburg, an administrative centre, is also the cultural and artistic capital of the province, the city of Mozart and home of the annual Salzburg Festival.

SALZBU

München (Munich)

HELLBRUN

Alpine meadows near Lungötz, typical of Salzburger Land

SEE ALSO

• *Where to Stay* pp299–301

• *Where to Eat* pp329–31

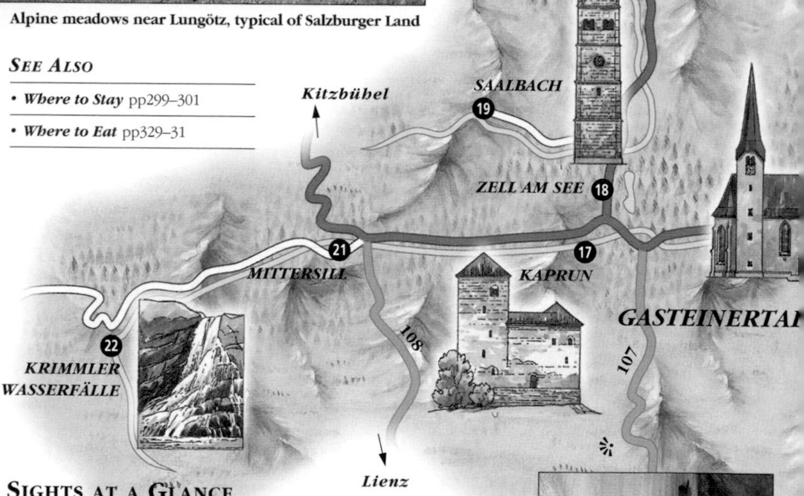

Kitzbühel

LOFER 20

SAALBACH 19

ZELL AM SEE 18

21 **MITTERSILL**

17 **KAPRUN**

GASTEINERTA

22 **KRIMMLER WASSERFÄLLE**

Lienz

SIGHTS AT A GLANCE

Eisriesenwelt near Werfen, the largest ice caves on earth

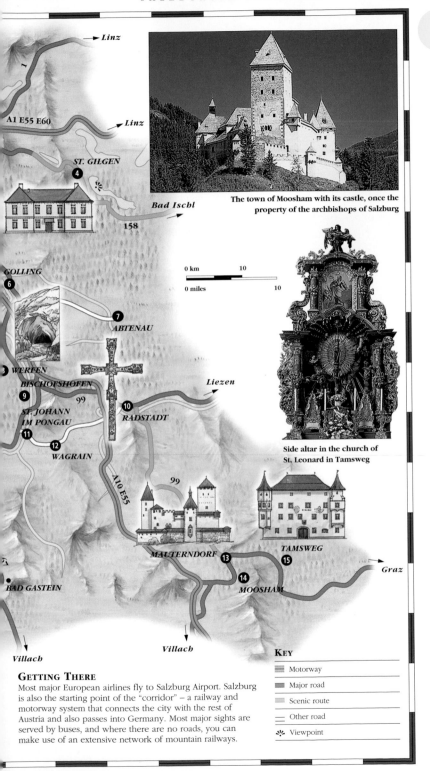

→ *Linz*

A1 E55 E60 → *Linz*

ST. GILGEN ④

Bad Ischl →

158

The town of Moosham with its castle, once the property of the archbishops of Salzburg

GOLLING ⑥

| 0 km | 10 |
| 0 miles | 10 |

⑦ **ABTENAU**

WERFEN

BISCHOFSHOFEN ⑨

Liezen →

99

ST. JOHANN IM PONGAU ⑪

⑩ **RADSTADT**

⑫ **WAGRAIN**

Side altar in the church of St. Leonard in Tamsweg

A10 E55

99

BAD GASTEIN

MAUTERNDORF ⑬

⑭ **MOOSHAM**

TAMSWEG ⑮

Graz →

↓ *Villach*

Villach →

Villach

GETTING THERE

Most major European airlines fly to Salzburg Airport. Salzburg is also the starting point of the "corridor" – a railway and motorway system that connects the city with the rest of Austria and also passes into Germany. Most major sights are served by buses, and where there are no roads, you can make use of an extensive network of mountain railways.

KEY

▬	Motorway
▬	Major road
▬	Scenic route
—	Other road
☀	Viewpoint

Salzburg ●

ACCORDING TO LEGEND, Salzburg was founded by Bishop Rupert, who arrived with Benedictine monks, and by the Irish Bishop Virgil, who built the town's first cathedral. Salzburg, however, owes its glory and its present appearance to the three archbishops who ruled here after them, between 1587 and 1653: Wolf Dietrich, Marcus Sitticus and Paris Lodron. The most famous creator of the Austrian Baroque, Johann Bernhard Fischer von Erlach, began his career as an architect in Salzburg. It is also the town of Mozart, who was born here in 1756. Today, the prestigious Salzburg Festival attracts participants from around the world.

Tanzmeisterhaus, once the home of Wolfgang Amadeus Mozart

View over the churches of Salzburg and Hohensalzburg fortress

Exploring Salzburg

Salzburg is divided into three distinct areas of interest. The first, including the finest churches, the archbishop's residence and Mozart's birthplace, is on the left bank of the Salzach river. The second area, on the right bank of the Salzach, is the New Town. Its most interesting sights are the Mirabell Palace, the Mozart Conservatoire and Kapuzinerberg. The third area is the mighty former fortress of Hohensalzburg.

♨ Makartplatz

Mozart-Wohnhaus
Makartplatz 8. **C** (0662) 874227. ○ Sep–Jun: 9am–6pm; Jul–Aug: 9am–7pm. 🎫
This square was given its current name in memory of the Salzburg-born painter, Hans Makart, whose work greatly influenced contemporary fashion, architecture and interior design in the mid-19th century.

The Tanzmeisterhaus at No. 8 was Wolfgang Amadeus Mozart's home in 1773–87. The original house, destroyed in World War II, was rebuilt,

and is now a small museum dedicated to the composer.

The Dreifaltigkeitskirche (church of the Holy Trinity), in the northeast corner of the square, dates from 1694 and is one of the earliest works of Johann Bernhard Fischer von Erlach. Built shortly after his return from Italy, it shows signs of Roman influence. Its façade is crowned with sculptures of Faith, Love, Hope and the Church by Michael Bernhard Mandel. The frescoes in the dome vault are by Johann Michael Rottmayr.

⛪ Friedhof St. Sebastian

Linzergasse. ○ 7am–7pm daily.
The St. Sebastian cemetery lies just below the church of the same name. All that remains of the old church is a Rococo portal with the bust of its patron saint, and the wrought-iron grille by Philipp Hinterseer. The present, much more modest building, dates from the early 19th century. The cemetery is older, dating from the 15th century. It was designed

along the lines of the Italian *campo santo*, with burial sites surrounded by columns, and has magnificent sculptures and tombstones. Next to the entrance, beside the church, is the tomb of the philosopher, physician and father of pharmacology, Paracelsus, who died in Salzburg in 1541.

At the centre of the cemetery stands the chapel of the Archangel St Gabriel that doubles as Archbishop Wolf Dietrich's mausoleum. Nearby are the graves of Mozart's father Leopold and his wife Constanze.

Kapuzinerberg

Kapuzinerberg, a hill on the right bank of the Salzach river opposite the historic Old Town, drops almost down to the river. Steep stairs with 250 steps, known as the Imbertstiege, lead up to the top from Linzergasse – it's well worth the climb. At the halfway point stands the church of St. Johann am Imberg, built in 1681. Its main altarpiece

A gilded figure from the church of St. Sebastian

has a painting of the Baptism of Christ. Another interesting feature is the carved pulpit by Johann Georg Hitzl.

A small castle once stood on top of the hill and formed part of the medieval fortifications; later it was partly incorporated into the Capuchin monastery complex whose church was completed in 1602. The monastery has a carved oak door made from the medieval stalls of the earlier cathedral. A short distance away stands a villa that was once the home of the Austrian writer, Stefan Zweig. Below the church, from the top of an old tower, the Hettwä Bastei, you can enjoy superb views over the many domes and spires of Salzburg and its immediate environs.

⚜ Schloss Mirabell

Mirabellplatz. 📞 *(0662) 8072-2337.* ◻ *9am–noon, 2–5pm Tue–Sat, 9am–noon Sun.*
The site of the present Mirabell Palace was originally used by Archbishop Wolf Dietrich in 1606 to erect a much more modest mansion, which he intended as a home for his mistress Salome Alt. The daughter of a Jewish merchant, she is said to have borne the archbishop 15 children. Dietrich referred to her as his wife and loved her to the end of his life.

In 1727, Johann Lukas von Hildebrandt rebuilt the palace for Archbishop Franz Anton Harrach as a truly royal Baroque home. A fire in 1818 destroyed part of the building, but fortunately the superb Angels Staircase, with sculptures by Georg Raphael Donner, and the Marble Hall, with rich gilt

Putti on the Angels Staircase in Mirabell

VISITORS' CHECKLIST

Road map D3. 👥 *150,000* 🛫 *Innsbrucker Bundesstraße 95 (0662) 8580251.* 🚉 *Hauptbahnhof, Südtirolerplatz (0800) 660 600.* ℹ *Mozartplatz 5 (0662) 843264, 88987330.* Ⓦ *www.salzburg.info.at.* 🎭 *Salzburger Festspiele (late Jul– late Aug).*

---

stucco ornaments, were spared. The palace is now a civic administration building. It is surrounded by attractive gardens designed by Johann Bernhard Fischer von Erlach, with groups of sculptures and fountains. The south wing of the orangery today houses a Baroque Museum.

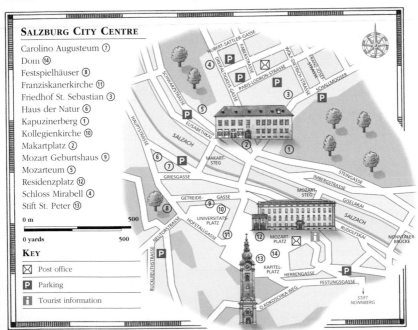

The beautiful gardens of Schloss Mirabell

SALZBURG CITY CENTRE

Carolino Augusteum ⑦
Dom ⑭
Festspielhäuser ⑧
Franziskanerkirche ⑪
Friedhof St. Sebastian ③
Haus der Natur ⑥
Kapuzinerberg ①
Kollegienkirche ⑩
Makartplatz ②
Mozart Geburtshaus ⑨
Mozarteum ⑤
Residenzplatz ⑫
Schloss Mirabell ④
Stift St. Peter ⑬

0 m   500
0 yards   500

KEY

⊠ Post office
🅿 Parking
ℹ Tourist information

Street-by Street: Old Town

SALZBURG'S BEAUTIFUL Old Town occupies the area between Mönchsberg (Monks' Mountain) and the Salzach river. It has been designated a World Cultural Heritage Site by UNESCO. The town that grew up on the left bank of the Salzach was built almost entirely in the Baroque style and is unusually uniform in appearance. Its ubiquitous Baroque period designs have been faultlessly and seamlessly blended with both earlier and modern architecture.

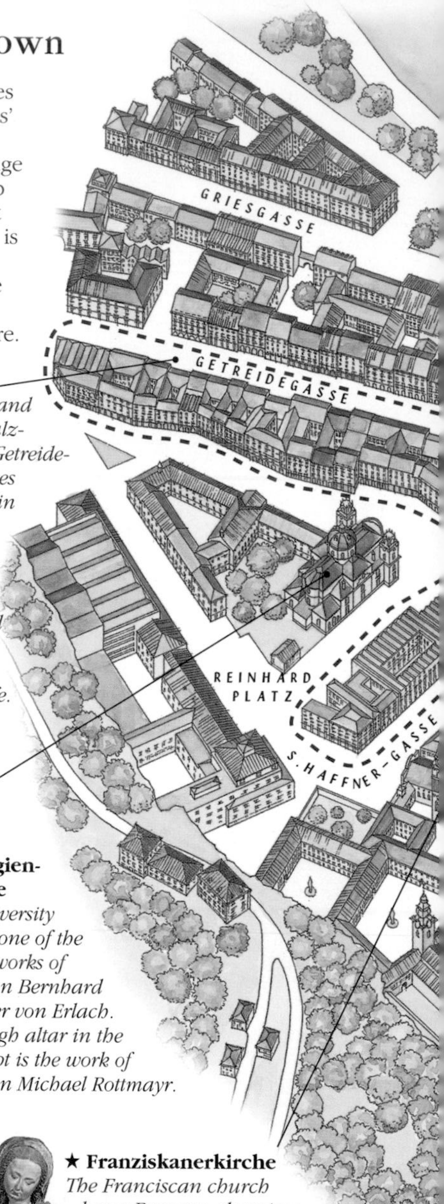

★ Getreidegasse

One of the longest and busiest streets in Salzburg's Old Town, Getreidegasse accommodates present commerce in medieval settings. No. 9 is the house where Wolfgang Amadeus Mozart was born and lived until he was 17; it is now a museum of the composer's life.

Kollegienkirche

The university church is one of the earliest works of Johann Bernhard Fischer von Erlach. The high altar in the transept is the work of Johann Michael Rottmayr.

★ Franziskanerkirche

The Franciscan church has a Baroque altarpiece by Johann Bernhard Fischer von Erlach, which has as its centre an exquisite figure of the Madonna and Child.

0 m   50

0 yards   50

STAR SIGHTS

★ Franziskanerkirche

★ Getreidegasse

★ Residenz

KEY

– – – – Suggested route

Altes Rathaus
The angular tower of the 15th-century Old Town Hall comes into view at the end of a narrow medieval alleyway.

★ **Residenz**
The most opulent building in town, this former home of the Archbishop clearly reveals his wealth and power.

Kapitelplatz
The bustling market square has one of Salzburg's most attractive fountains, and offers outdoor games and fun for everyone.

Dom
The cathedral church of St Rupert & St Virgil was first built in 774, and subsequently altered many times.

Stift St. Peter
This 12th-century Benedictine church is dedicated to St. Peter, whose statue adorns the fountain (1673) in front of the church.

Hohensalzburg
The Fortress (see pp222–3), on top of the rocky Mönchsberg, is best reached by the funicular from Festungsgasse.

The Mozarteum building, Salzburg's Conservatoire

🏛 Mozarteum

Schwarzstraße 26. 📞 *(0662) 88940.*
In 1842 Mozart's home town erected a monument to the composer and, in 1870, the International Foundation of Mozarteum was established here to promote his music. Today, the Mozarteum holds a collection of his letters, and it is also one of the foremost music schools in Europe. In the grounds of the conservatoire stands the cottage in which Mozart wrote the opera *The Magic Flute*, brought here from Vienna. The main building of the Mozarteum was designed by the architect Richard Berndl, and built in 1910–14. Some departments are housed in the completely rebuilt former palace of Archbishop Lodron next to the Foundation gardens.

🏛 Haus der Natur

Museumsplatz 5. 📞 *(0662) 842653-0.*
⏰ *9am–5pm daily.* 🌐
The quarters that were once occupied by the Ursuline Sisters are now the home of the Natural History Museum, one of the most interesting and fun places to visit in Salzburg. The vast complex, consisting of more than 90 rooms arranged on five floors, houses a great variety of fauna. Individual sections of the museum are arranged thematically. In "Sea World", a gigantic aquarium recreates the conditions that closely resemble the natural habitat of various water creatures. The "Reptile Zoo's" 33 terraria house some of the most exciting snakes from around the world. There are also

huge rooms simulating the natural habitat of Mississippi alligators and the lost worlds of Jurassic creatures, including ever-popular dinosaurs. Other themes include "men and animals in myths and fairy tales", "the cosmos" and "forest animals". Finally, the treasury room displays equipment needed for gold-panning, as well as crystalline forms of precious gems and stones.

🏛 Carolino Augusteum

Museumsplatz 1. 📞 *(0662) 620808.*
⏰ *9am–5pm Mon–Sun,*
9am–8pm Thu. 🌐
This History Museum was founded in 1834 by the amateur collector and treasury official, Maria Vinzenz Süß, who donated his collections to the town. It was named after the Bavarian Princess Caroline Augusta, who, in 1850, took over the stewardship of the museum's collections.

The most exciting items on display date back to Celtic times and include a Celtic pitcher from the Dürnberg area and a Bronze-age helmet from the Lueg Pass. The exhibits from Roman Salzburg, or *Juvavum*, are also interesting; there are fragments of mosaics, including one depicting the abduction of Europa, and numerous architectural features and statues. Also worth seeing are paintings by the Baroque masters, Paul Troger and Johann Michael Rottmayr, as well as those by Hans Makart, who was born in Salzburg in 1840. Separate departments are devoted to handicrafts, coins and musical instruments.

🏛 Festspielhäuser

Hofstallgasse 1. 📞 *(0662) 849097.*
⏰ *Jan–Mar, Oct–20 Dec: 2pm; Jun,*
Sep: 2pm & 3:30pm; Jul–Aug:
9:30am, 2pm, 3:30pm. 📞
Guided tours only.
In 1606, Archbishop Wolf Dietrich von Raitenau

Façade of the Festspielhaus, the Grand Festival Theatre

started building the palace stables on the site of the former barracks. The north façade was designed by Johann Bernhard Fischer von Erlach. The marble fountain, or Pferdeschwemme (horses' trough), in the stable yard, was built in 1695.

In 1917, it was decided that Salzburg should host a theatre and opera festival, and the stables were converted into the Small and Grand Festival Theatres. One of Austria's most outstanding architects, Clemens Holzmeister, supervised rebuilding, carried out during the 1920s, and the greatest artists of that time, Oskar Kokoschka, Anton Kolig, Wolfgang Hutter and Rudolf Hoflechner, designed the interior of the theatres. The Grand Theatre was completed in 1960. Its vast stage is carved deep into the rockface of Mönchsberg; the auditorium can easily accommodate up to 2,400 spectators.

🏛 Mozarts Geburtshaus
Getreidegasse 9. 📞 (0662) 844313.
🖼 📷
Hagenauerhaus, at No. 9 of the narrow Getreidegasse, is the house where Wolfgang Amadeus Mozart was born on 27 January 1756. The composer's family occupied only one floor of the house.

In 1880, the Mozarteum (International Mozart Foundation) helped to establish a museum here, featuring a collection of the great composer's memorabilia, including family portraits and the first instruments used by the young Mozart. Recently, a new department has been added which illustrates the history of the theatrical staging of Mozart's operas.

🏛 Kollegienkirche
Universitätsplatz. 📞 (0662) 841327.
🕐 9am–7pm Mon–Sat, Sun, winter: 10am–dusk.
The Collegiate Church, consecrated in 1707, is one of Salzburg's finest Baroque structures. It was designed by Johann Bernhard Fischer von Erlach, who achieved fantastic and unusual effects by letting natural light shine through windows of various shapes.

The paintings on two side altars of the church are by Johann Michael Rottmayr. Italian artisans produced the beautiful stucco work, which decorates the church walls, to a design by Johann Bernhard Fischer von Erlach. The very ornate main altarpiece shows the university as a temple of art and science. It features winged figures symbolizing music, poetry, painting, architecture, theology, philosophy, law and medicine.

The Romanesque south portal of Franziskanerkirche

🏛 Franziskanerkirche
Franziskanergasse 5. 📞 (0662) 843629.
🕐 6am–8pm daily.
The Franciscan Church seems somewhat out of place in Baroque Salzburg. Repeated attempts at refashioning it in the Baroque style have failed to disguise its Romanesque origins, mixed with Gothic. The 13th-century Romanesque portal leading to the presbytery is particularly fine, with a figure of Christ on the throne flanked by St Rupert and St Peter. The presbytery, with its tall tower and magnificent star-vault, is Gothic. In the 16th century, when the Franciscan Church was temporarily used as a cathedral, it gained an additional Baroque portal, a ring of chapels and many rich interior

furnishings. The creator of the new altar, Johann Bernhard Fischer von Erlach, preserved the central statue of the Madonna from the earlier Gothic altar made by Michael Pacher, the outstanding artist of the late-Gothic. The St Francis Chapel has frescoes by Rottmayr, with scenes from the life of its patron saint. On the opposite side of the street are the monastery buildings, which are connected with the church by a bridge.

🏛 Residenzplatz
Residenz. Residenzplatz 1.
📞 (0662) 8042-2690. 🕐 10am–5pm daily; state rooms not open to the public. ● 2 weeks before and 1 week after Easter. 🖼 📷 ♿
Residenzgalerie. 📞 (0662) 840451. 🕐 10am–5pm Tue–Sun.
● Nov, 24 Dec. 🖼 📷
The Residenz, seat of the Prince-Archbishop, the religious and secular ruler of the entire province, was built for Archbishop Wolf Dietrich von Raitenau. His successors further extended the building. Following secularization, the building became the seat of the administration. Now one part of the building houses central government agencies and university offices, while the upper storeys are occupied by a gallery. Not much remains of its erstwhile decor, but the interior decorations, completed under Lukas von Hildebrandt and carried out by the most prominent artists of the Baroque era, including Johann Michael Rottmayr and Martino Altomonte, still charm visitors to this day. On the forecourt of the palace is the Baroque Residence Fountain, with Tritons and horses spouting water. On the opposite side of the square stands the Residenz-Neubau (New Residence), used as a temporary abode while the bishop's seat was being rebuilt. It has a carillon – the bells can be heard at 7am, 11am and 6pm from Mozartplatz, where a statue of the great composer stands.

Statue of Mozart in Mozartplatz

Sculptures decorating the façade of the Dom

🔒 Stift St. Peter

St. Peter Bezirk. **☎** *(0662) 844576-0.*
☐ *8am–noon, 4:30–6:30pm.* 🖼️
Salzburg's Benedictine Abbey
was founded in the 7th century by St Rupert, who is said
to have resurrected the town
after the Great Migration of
Nations. It is the only abbey
in this part of Europe that has
survived intact since then.
The present church and
monastery complexes were
built in the 12th and 13th centuries, but remodelled during
the Baroque era, in the 17th
and 18th centuries. However,
some of the old sculptures
have survived, including the
early 15th-century *Beautiful
Madonna*. The majority of
Baroque altar paintings are by
Kremser Schmidt. The abbey
interior is an impressive
display of Baroque opulence.

In the cemetery, Salzburg's
oldest, are the final resting
places of Mozart's sister Nannerl and of Johann Michael
Haydn, brother of Joseph.

⚜ Dom

Cathedral Domplatz 7.
☎ *(0662) 80477950.* **Cathedral
Museum ☎** *(0662) 844189.* **☐**
*May–Oct: 10am–5pm Mon–Sat,
1–6pm Sun, public holidays.* 🖼️
The first cathedral church in
Salzburg, the Dom was built
in the 8th century. Following
several remodellings and a
fire in 1598, the archbishops
set out to build an almost
entirely new church, designed
by the Italian architect, Santino
Solari, on the site of the earlier
one. The new cathedral, consecrated in 1628, became a
model of Baroque church
architecture north of the Alps.
The façade is decorated with
the vast sculpted figures of

the cathedral's patron saints,
Rupert and Virgil, and Saints
Peter and Paul. The cathedral
was designed to accom-
modate 10,000 worship-
pers, more than the
entire population of
Salzburg. Its monu-
mental interior is still
impressive today.
Stairs lead from the
transept to the crypt
where several prince-
archbishops have
been laid to rest.
Mozart himself
played the Baroque
organ (1703) here. Today, the
great Mozarteum choir often
holds concerts of his music in
the cathedral. The church's
treasures are on show in the
Cathedral Museum.

🔒 Stift Nonnberg

Nonnberggasse 2. **☎** *(0662) 8416070.*
☐ *Summer: 6am–6pm daily; winter:
6am–dusk.*
The Benedictine nunnery on
the slope of Mönchsberg,
now known as Nonnberg
(Nuns' Hill), was founded in
714 by St Rupert, who estab-
lished his
niece, St
Erentrude, as
Mother
Superior.
Her tomb

**The pilgrimage church Maria
Plain on Plainberg**

lies in the crypt of the
church. Emperor Henry II
and his wife Kunegunde had
the convent and the church
extended in the 11th century.
A fire in 1423 destroyed most
of the buildings and, in the
15th century, a new convent
was built on the same site,
with a church devoted to the
Assumption of the Virgin
Mary and to St Erentrude. The
Roman tympanum above the
main door shows the Virgin
Mary accompanied by John
the Baptist and St Erentrude.

A true jewel of Nonnberg is
its late-Gothic main altarpiece,
brought from Scheffau and
reputedly produced to
sketches by Albrecht
Dürer. Behind the main
altar, in the central
window of the apsis, is
an interesting stained-
glass panel by Peter
Hemmel, one of the
most renowned
stained-glass artists
in the late-Gothic
style. Original 12th-
century Roman-
esque frescoes are
preserved in the niches. The
adjacent chapel of St John has
a Gothic altarpiece taken
from the earlier cathedral; its
creator was visibly influenced
by the school of Veit Stoß.

**Fresco (1150)
in Stift Nonnberg**

ENVIRONS: On top of Plainberg, a hill north of Salzburg,
stands the pilgrimage church
of **Maria Plain**, built by
Giovanni Antonio Dario and
consecrated in 1674. In 1779,
Mozart composed the *Coronation Mass* in celebration of
the miraculous picture of the
Madonna and Child. The
interiro was designed by
famous Austrian Baroque
artists, including Kremser
Schmidt and Thomas and
Franz Schwanthaler.

Further north, in the village
of **Oberndorf**, the carol
Silent Night was first performed in 1818. Franz Xaver
Gruber, a local teacher and
organist, wrote the music,
and Joseph Mohr the words.

On the southwestern out-
skirts of Salzburg is **Schloss
Leopoldskron**, since 1918
the home of Max Reinhardt,
theatrical innovator and founder of the Salzburg Festival.

The Salzburg Festival

THE SALZBURGER Festspiele, the largest and most important opera and theatre festival in Europe, was initiated by three people. The eminent writer, Hugo von Hofmannsthal, the composer and conductor Richard Strauss, and the greatest theatrical innovator of the 20th century, the director Max Reinhardt, decided to honour the memory of Mozart by organizing a festival devoted to his work. It was to be held in his home town and be a celebration of theatre and opera. The first festival was held in Salzburg in 1920. Today, it is the most all-embracing event of its type in Europe. The festival programme has become increasingly rich, and the former court stables were converted to create two festival theatres. Performances are also held in the Makartplatz theatre, in Schloss Mirabell and in many open-air venues around town. Theatre troops from all over the world come to Salzburg, often with original performances prepared specifically for the festival. Tickets tend to be sold out several months in advance.

Herbert von Karajan (1908–89), born in Salzburg and one of the most outstanding 20th-century conductors of symphonies and operas, was the musical director of the Salzburg Festivals for almost thirty years.

The stage in front of the cathedral in Salzburg is where the Salzburger Festspiele performances begin each July. Max Reinhardt pioneered the idea of open-air performances at the festival, and theatre troops now play to large audiences.

The Großes Festspielhaus is adorned with a Baroque portal by Johann Bernhard Fischer von Erlach. The modern building of the Grand Festival Theatre was completed in 1960 by Clemens Holzmeister (see pp218–19).

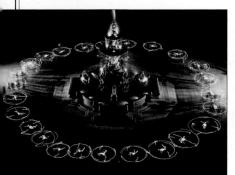

The Fire Dance is one of the most beautiful performances staged regularly during the Salzburg Festival. As soon as night falls, the whole town comes alive with the lights of the spectacle.

Since its very first staging the festival has opened with a performance of Hugo von Hofmannsthal's morality play Jedermann ("Everyman").

Hohensalzburg Fortress

HOHENSALZBURG, the fortress perched on the rocky peak of Festungsberg, was built in the 11th century, during the wars between the Holy Roman Empire and the Papacy, and was gradually extended. The castle served as a refuge for Salzburg's archbishops whenever they felt threatened. Archbishop Leonhard von Keutschach gave it its present look in the 16th century; Archbishop Paris Lodron introduced further architectural changes. A military barracks in the late 19th century, it is today a major tourist attraction.

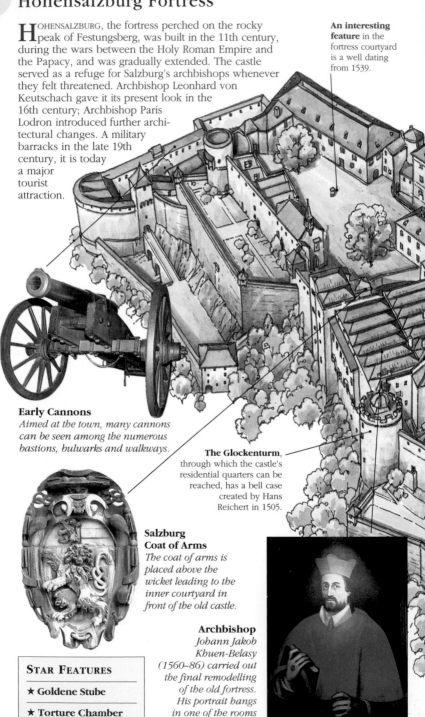

An interesting feature in the fortress courtyard is a well dating from 1539.

Early Cannons
Aimed at the town, many cannons can be seen among the numerous bastions, bulwarks and walkways.

The Glockenturm, through which the castle's residential quarters can be reached, has a bell case created by Hans Reichert in 1505.

Salzburg Coat of Arms
The coat of arms is placed above the wicket leading to the inner courtyard in front of the old castle.

Archbishop
Johann Jakob Khuen-Belasy (1560–86) carried out the final remodelling of the old fortress. His portrait hangs in one of the rooms of the old castle.

STAR FEATURES

★ **Goldene Stube**

★ **Torture Chamber**

Schulhaus and Kuchelturm

Schoolhouse and Kitchen Tower are the remains of fortifications built outside the castle in the 16th century during a revolt against the archbishops.

★ Goldene Stube

The richly ornamented Golden Chamber, with its large tiled stove in Gothic style, is one of the loveliest rooms in the castle.

Small Courtyard

In a small square on the castle ramparts stand an old salt warehouse (former stables), and two towers, Hasenturm (Hares' Tower) and Schwefelturm (Sulphur Tower).

★ Torture Chamber

Reckturm, the corner tower, was once a prison and torture chamber. Prisoners were tortured at Hohensalzburg as recently as 1893.

Portrait of Archbishop Marcus Sitticus in Schloss Hellbrunn

Hellbrunn ❷

Road map D4. 🚌 🚊 🚻 *(0662) 820372-0.* ⚪ *Apr–Oct: 9am–4:30pm; May, Jun, Sep: 9am–5:30pm; Jul–Aug: 9am–10pm daily.* 🅿 🆆 *www.hellbrunn.at*

SCHLOSS HELLBRUNN, once a summer residence of Salzburg's Archbishop Marcus Sitticus, stands about 4 km (2 miles) south of Salzburg. Sitticus was a nephew of Wolf Dietrich von Raitenau, with an Italian mother. He spent most of his life in Italy, and so it is hardly surprising that his small, suburban castle resembles a Venetian villa. It has an interesting state room with architectural paintings and a tall, octagonal music room. However, the most interesting and popular feature is its garden with ornamental fountains and scenic grottoes, including a mechanical theatre, with trick fountains and moving figures powered by water.

Anif ❸

Road map D4. 🚶 *4,200.* 🚌 🚊 🚻 *(06246) 72365.*

ANOTHER 2 km (1 mile) beyond Hellbrunn, also south of Salzburg, stands the small Neo-Gothic castle of Anif. Once a suburban residence, it now lies virtually within the limits of the town Anif. Its earliest historic records date from the 15th century, but it bears signs of an earlier, late-Gothic structure. Once the summer estate of the Salzburg rulers, it belonged to the Chiemsee bishops from 1693 to 1803. After the secularization of the province, it was put up for sale and passed to Count Alois Arco-Stepperg. This new owner had the summer residence converted into a romantic English-style Neo-Gothic castle that has survived unchanged to this day. Its rectangular turret is proudly mirrored in the waters of the lake; the interior is furnished in the English fashion of the day. At the end of World War I, on 13 November 1918, the last king of Bavaria, Ludwig III, signed his abdication in Anif. As the castle is privately owned, visitors can only see its high outside walls.

St. Gilgen ❹

Road map D4. 🚶 *3,400.* 🚌 🚻 *Mondsee, Bundesstraße 1A 1 (06227) 2348.* 🆆 *www.wolfgangsee.at*

ST. GILGEN is the largest resort in the Salzburg area of the Salzkammergut. Set on the western shores of the warm Wolfgangsee, amid mountain scenery, this is one of the most attractive health resorts in Austria. St. Gilgen was the birthplace of Mozart's mother, Anna-Maria Pertl. Later, the composer's sister, Nannerl, lived here with her husband, a local office worker. These Mozart-related facts are commemorated by a plaque on the court building. In 1927, the Mozart Fountain was erected in the town square.

The local church of St Giles (St. Ägyd) shows hints of an earlier structure. It was extended in the 18th century and given three Rococo altars with paintings by Peter Lorenzoni.

St. Gilgen is a major water sports centre and harbour, with cruises on Wolfgangsee aboard the steamer *Emperor Franz Joseph* that has been in continuous service since 1873. Not far from St. Gilgen, on the shores of the neighbouring Fuschlsee, stands **Fuschl**, a small hunting lodge that now houses a luxury hotel.

Hallein ❺

Road map D4. 🚶 *18,300.* 🚌 🚊 🚻 *(06245) 85394.*

THE TOWN of Hallein was founded in the 13th century, but salt was mined here way back in prehistoric times. The long association with the salt trade is apparent from the town's name: *hall* is the Celtic word for "salt". The "white gold", as it was called, brought wealth to the entire region for many centuries, until the 18th-century Counter-Reformation led to the emigration of the predominantly Protestant salt miners.

Hallein's Old Town, on the left bank of the Salzach river, is mainly 18th-century in appearance, following much remodelling. The church of St Antonius has a Gothic presbytery, but the rest is much newer. The painting of the Birth of Christ in the main altarpiece is by the last court painter of the Salzburg rulers, the Neo-Classical Andreas Nesselthaler. Hallein was the home of Franz Xaver Gruber who wrote *Silent Night*, and he is buried here. His house at No. 1 Gruberplatz is now a small museum. The most interesting sight in

Poster of the fascinating Keltenmuseum in Hallein

Hallein, however, is the **Keltenmuseum** with its unique collection of Celtic objects which relate to the history of salt-mining in the area.

🏛 **Keltenmuseum**
Pflegerplatz 5. 📞 (06245) 80783.
⭕ 9am–5pm daily. ♿

ENVIRONS: From the southern end of Hallein you can drive to the top of Dürrnberg, which has some of the most interesting prehistoric finds in Austria. The remains of the settlements that grew up around the rich local salt deposits can be seen to this day. The spa of **Bad Dürrnberg** has a show-mine open specifically for tourists, who are offered rides on an underground salt lake. In the village stands a 14th-century Marian church, now a Baroque structure. The altarpiece contains a miraculous picture of the Madonna, once visited by pilgrims.

go of salt mine
in Dürrnberg

Golling 6

Road map D4. 🏠 4000. 🚌 🚆
📞 (06244) 4356.

SOUTH OF Hallein lies the small town of Golling. At its centre stands the Church of St John the Baptist and St John the Evangelist, with a Gothic main nave and remodelled Baroque side naves. A small medieval castle, devoid of any ornaments and adjoined by a chapel with a Rococo altar, now houses a regional museum.

ENVIRONS: There are many natural features of interest near Golling, including the **Lueg Pass** with the spectacular, 100-m (328-ft) deep Salzach river gorge, and the Schwarzbacher Wasserfall, better known as **Gollinger Wasserfall** (100 m/328 ft), much beloved by romantic painters of natural scenes. Also worth a detour is a visit

The Gollinger Wasserfall, a favourite theme for painters

to two interesting churches in the vicinty – St Ulrich's in **Scheffau** and the late-Gothic St Nicholas's Church near **Torren**, which stands high up on a rocky shelf.

Abtenau 7

Road map D4. 🏠 5,600. 🚌 🚆
📞 (06243) 4040.

ABTENAU, A SUMMER resort situated in the Salzburg Dolomites, is surrounded by the mighty peaks of the Tennengebirge. The church in the valley was built around 1500. Its main nave is guarded by figures of St George and St Florian. On the north wall, an original late-Gothic fresco can be seen, but the new main altar and side altars are built in the Baroque style.

It is worth taking a walk upstream along the Lammer river, which cuts a scenic valley between the Tennengebirge and the craggy wall of the Dachstein.

Werfen 8

Road map D4. 🏠 3,200. 🚌 🚆
📞 (06468) 5388.

THE LITTLE town of Werfen has several interesting churches. St James's Church is mentioned in 14th-century records, but its present style dates from a 17th-century Baroque conversion. The Marian Church was built in the early 18th century.

ENVIRONS: There are two fascinating sights near Werfen. **Hohenwerfen** fortress, built on a rocky outcrop, dates back to the 11th century. Today, it is an interactive museum with many interesting displays, including late-Romanesque frescoes and an exhibition of weapons. It also includes Austria's first museum of falconry.

Eisriesenwelt (giant ice world), one of the world's largest cave systems, is a true wonder of nature. It has dramatic ice formations and superb ice galleries. Some 42 km (26 miles) have been explored so far. A scenic walk or bus or cable car journey will take you from Werfen to the entrance in the western wall of the Hochkögel peak. Inside it is very cold (so take warm clothes).

The enchanting winter landscape of Abtenau

Bischofshofen ❾

Road map D4. 🏛 *10,000.* 🚌 🚉
🛈 *(06462) 2471.*

THE CELTIC settlement that
stood on the site of the
present Bischofshofen was
once a centre of the copper
mining trade; the area was
also rich in salt mines.
Colonization of the region
started well before recorded
history and traces of
ancient cultures can be
found everywhere.

The town is
dominated by the
spire of St Maxi-
milian's Church,
reputedly built on the site
of an older church estab-
lished by St Rupert, founder
of Salzburg. The walls are
decorated with 15th-century
frescoes, and next to the
Neo-Gothic side altar-
pieces stand the orig-
inal Gothic figures of
St Rupert and St Virgil.
In the south arm of
the transept stands a Baroque
altar with a picture of St Anna
attributed to Lienhart Astel
(c.1520) and a relief on the
predella of Christ and the 12
apostles dating from the same
period. The most valuable
historic relic in the church is
St Rupert's crucifix. This
simple, gilded cross, encrusted
with precious stones, was
given to Bischofshofen in the
12th century by the Arch-
bishop of Salzburg.

Bischofshofen is renowned
for its excellent ski-jumping
hills. Every year, on 6th January, the final event of the
world-famous Four Hills Ski-
Jumping event takes place on
the largest of the slopes.

**St Rupert's
Crucifix,
Bischofshofen**

Radstadt ❿

Road map D4. 🏛 *4,800.* 🚌 🚉
🛈 *(06452) 7472.*

THE SMALL TOWN of Radstadt
grew up around a 13th-
century fortress on the banks
of the Enns river. Its wealth
hailed from its propitious
location on the road to
Venice, and its monopoly
position in the wine trade.
Radstadt also had a licence to

stock iron and salt. Its medieval fortifications, built by the
archbishops of Salzburg, have
remained intact.

The surrounding area
boasts many small, beguiling
castles, including Renaissance
Schloss Tandalier, southwest of the town. **Schloss
Lärchen**, in the centre of
town, shows some traces of
original, 13th-century architecture; today it houses a
regional museum.

ENVIRONS: East of Bischofshofen runs **Rad-
städter Tauern-
straße**, one of
the most scenic roads in the
Alps. A vast skiing area
extends on both sides. The
Rossbrand (1,770 m/5,807
ft), rising north of Radstadt
and accessible by car via the
Rossbrand Panorama Street,
offers astonishing
views of more than
150 alpine summits
on a clear day.

St. Johann im Pongau ⓫

Road map D4. 🏛 *10,200.* 🚌
🛈 *(06412) 6036–0.*

THE LARGEST town in the
region, St. Johann im
Pongau is a popular resort,
visited for its excellent skiing
conditions in winter and its
plentiful facilities for swimming and walking in summer.

Little remains of its original
buildings due to a series of
fires in the 19th century; the
present town was almost

entirely rebuilt. The Neo-
Gothic **Domkirche**, the
cathedral of St John the
Baptist (1861), is acclaimed as
the most outstanding work of
Neo-Classicism in the Salzburg area. Its architects were
Georg Schneider and Josef
Wessiken. The charming
carved altarpiece (1530) in
adjacent St Anna's Chapel has
late-Gothic wooden figures of
saints. Some 5 km (3 miles)
south of the town run the tor-
rential waters of **Großarler
Ache**, a rapid mountain
stream that winds through the
scenic **Liechtensteinklamm**.

Wagrain ⓬

Road map D4. 🏛 *3,000.* 🚌 🚉
🛈 *(06413) 8448.*

WAGRAIN, SITUATED at an
altitude of 800 m (2,625
ft), is the centre of a highly
developed winter sports area
known as **Ski Alliance**. This
vast terrain extends between
the Tennengebirge and Radstädter Tauern mountain
ranges, and includes several
villages connected by good
public transport links, funi-
culars and buses. One ski
pass is valid throughout the
entire area, giving the holder
access to some 260 ski lifts
and 860 km (534 miles) of
pistes, suitable for intermed-
iates and beginners.

Year-round fun in the water
is guaranteed by the Amadé
Water World's all-weather
pool. The most interesting
place is **Zauchensee**, the
highest village in the region

View of the town and cathedral in St Johann im Pongau

◁ **The snowy Alpine peaks from Kitzsteinhorn, near Kaprun**

Rushing stream in the Liechten-steinklamm, near Wagrain

(1,361 m/4,465 ft). It is also worth going inside the Gothic church in Altenmarkt im Pongau. Wagrain itself has a museum devoted to Joseph Mohr, who wrote the words for *Silent Night*, and to the popular 20th-century Austrian writer and humorist Karl Heinrich Waggerl.

The views from the tops of Schwarzkopf, Rosskopf and Mooskopf are stunning and worth a detour.

Mauterndorf ⓭

Road map D4. 🏚 *1,600*. 🚌
🚉 *(06472) 7949*.

STRATEGICALLY positioned on the road connecting Salzburg with the Hohe Tauern passes, this little town owed its former wealth to the road tolls it was able to collect. Mauterndorf's greatest attraction is its **Schloss**, built in the 13th century and extended in the 16th century, under Archbishop Leonhard von Keutschach. Scenically located and well proportioned, it is an attractive medieval structure. The rooms are richly decorated with stuccowork and provide interesting interiors. The castle's best feature, however, is the lovely chapel devoted to St Henry (Emperor Henry II), with superb 14th-century frescoes of the

Coronation of the Virgin Mary on the rainbow arch, and a 15th-century carved altar-piece. The castle was well restored in the 20th century, and is now a museum and cultural centre. Mauterndorf also has excellent summer and winter sports facilities.

Moosham ⓮

Road map D4. 🏚 Schloss
Moosham 12. 🚉 *(06476) 305*.
◻ Apr–Oct: 10, 11am, 1, 2, 3, 4pm;
Dec–Mar: 11am, 1, 2:30pm. ⬤ Nov.

NEAR THE southern end of Radstädter Tauernstraße, high above the Mur river, towers Schloss Moosham, which also belonged to the Archbishops of Salzburg. The structure probably dates from the 13th century and consists of an upper and a lower castle. Following the secularization of the archbishop's principality, the castle fell into ruin. But in 1886 it passed to Count Hans Wilczek, who fully renovated it. Among the remaining original features are the Baroque roadway, Gothic stained-glass windows in the presbytery of the castle chapel and a large collection of items relating to the local arts, which are kept in the castle museum. Of interest are also the coach house and the armoury. Some chambers are open to the public, such as a torture chamber, and a Gothic bedchamber with a

Bedchamber in Schloss Moosham

lovely original tiled stove and a panel listing the supposed characteristic traits of various European nationalities.

Below the castle is the popular resort of St Michael, with an interesting Gothic church.

A stained-glass window in the church of St Leonard in Tamsweg

Tamsweg ⓯

Road map E4. 🏚 *5,600*. 🚌 🚉
🚉 *(06474) 2145*. 🎭 Samson
Procession (late Jun, Jul, Aug).

THE LARGEST town in the isolated Lungau region, Tamsweg is famous for its curious Samson Processions, when an effigy of Samson and other figures are paraded around town. Tamsweg owes its past wealth to the iron and salt trade. Fine town houses, such as the 15th-century Mesnerhaus and the 16th-century turreted town hall, line the market square. The 18th-century Post House has frescoes by Gregor Lederwasch, who also painted the pictures in Heiliger Jakobus (St James's Church) built in 1741, to a design by Fidelis Hainzl. The original Rococo interior has been preserved. The 15th-century Church of St Leonard, towering above the town, is one of Austria's foremost pilgrimage churches. It has beautiful stained-glass windows, such as the famous Golden Window (1430–50). The interior furnishings are almost entirely late medieval.

Gasteinertal ⑯

THE THERAPEUTIC properties of the radon-rich mineral springs in and around Badgastein were known to the Celts and Romans, and this was when the first settlements grew in the valley of the Gasteiner Ache stream. The valley flourished in late medieval times and more recently it has become a popular spa, with a long list of clients including royalty, politicians and artists. A cure is sought by those suffering from cardiac and gastric ailments, rheumatism and allergies. At the same time, the valley has developed into a fabulous winter sports centre, with skiing for all levels and snowboarding.

Gasteinertal
This well-developed valley, surrounded by modest mountains, is a popular skiing, snowboarding and summer walking area.

Bad Hofgastein
The late-Gothic parish church was built in the 15th and 16th centuries. The carved tombstones found in its niches show the skills of gold- and silversmiths using locally excavated metals.

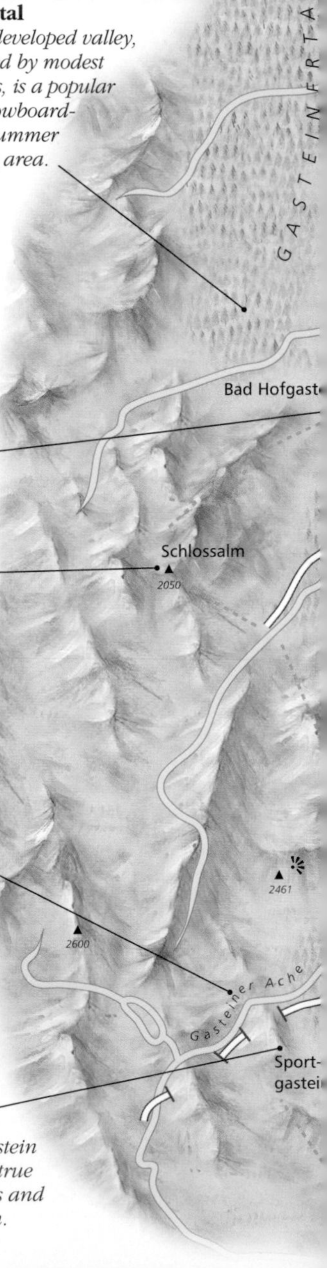

The summit of Schlossalm
has a viewing platform at 2,050 m (6,726 ft), providing panoramic views of the neighbouring peaks. It can be reached by funicular.

The Gasteiner Ache
The stream runs along a scenic valley, down from the Hohe Tauern mountains, finishing as a tributary of the Salzach, the principal river of Salzburger Land.

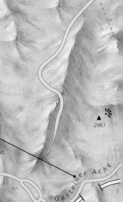

Bad Hofgast

Schlossalm
▲
2050

▲ ☼
2461

▲
2600

Sport-
gastei

Gasteiner Ache

★ **Sportgastein** ——
The wide valley near Sportgastein has been transformed into a true mountain gorge, with bridges and viaducts spanning the stream.

Dorfgastein
The village of Dorfgastein has preserved many traditional, rural customs.

VISITORS' CHECKLIST

Road map D4.
Bad Hofgastein,
Gasteinertal Tourismus GmbH,
Tauernplatz 1.
(06432) 3393-0.
W www.gastein.com

0 km   2

0 miles   2

★ **Badgastein**
The most popular resort in Gasteinertal is crossed by the Gasteiner Ache, which runs right through its centre in a series of attractive waterfalls.

KEY

Major road

Minor road

- - Funicular

River

☀ Viewpoint

★ **Böckstein**
The altar in the Neo-Classical Church of Our Lady of Good Counsel is the work of Johann Baptist Hagenauer. The medieval mine where gold was once excavated now houses a sanatorium.

STAR SIGHTS

★ **Badgastein**

★ **Böckstein**

★ **Sportgastein**

Kaprun ⑰

Road map D4. 🏔 *3,100*. 🚌
ℹ *(06547) 8643-0.*

KAPRUN is a popular winter sports resort. It is also famous for its sophisticated hydroelectric power station, which is acclaimed as a wonder of technology and one of the greatest achievements of human ingenuity. Work on the construction of the Kapruner Ache power station began in 1938, and was completed in 1951. Its highest reservoir is Mooserboden, a lake situated at an altitude of 2,036 m (6,680 ft) and fed by the melting ice of the Pasterze glacier.

Kaprun power station is not only a technological marvel; it is also a tourist attraction. Artificial lakes, weirs and dams, set amid the rocky limestone peaks of the Hohe Tauern mountain range, create a unique natural environment, with numerous trails and attractive scenery for walkers. Following the building of the power station, Kaprun became one of Austria's foremost sports resorts, especially as the nearby glaciers makes year-round skiing possible.

The town of Kaprun itself lies in a valley accessible by road and public transport. It has some of the most modern facilities in Austria, serving the **Kitzsteinhorn** (3,203 m/ 10,509 ft) to the north, an outpost of Austria's highest mountain range. This summit has year-round pistes and excellent snow. In the year 2000, a fire on the Kitzsteinhornbahn, the funicular railway taking visitors to the slopes, caused a major mountain tragedy. The railway has since been re-routed to run outside the tunnel, providing magnificent views of Austria's highest mountains.

On the western edge of Kaprun stands a 15th-century castle destroyed in the 18th century, but recently restored. Today it is a cultural centre.

Kaprun and neighbouring ski resorts have joined forces to attract visitors to this so-called "Europa Sportregion".

Inside St Hippolytus Church in Zell am See

Zell am See ⑱

Road map C4. 🏔 *9,000*. 🚉 🚌
ℹ *(06542) 770-0.*

THIS PICTURE-postcard town on the western shores of Zeller See has a long history. First recorded as the Roman settlement of Bisontio, in medieval times Zell was a mining centre. Among its more interesting historic sights are the 13th-century Vogtturm, and the Church of St. Hippolytus (St Hippolyte) that once belonged to the Augustinian Order. There are some recently discovered medieval frescoes: the figures of Saints George and Florian in the western gallery are by an artist from the Danube School. Zell am See is now considered one of the best developed sports resorts in Austria, with excellent facilities for skiing and water sports, as well as a convenient base for long walks.

ENVIRONS: South of Zell am See is the **Hohe Tauern** mountain range and national park *(see pp278–81)*, to the north the rugged scenery of the Steinernes Meer (Stone Sea) and to the west the Schmittenhöhe, divided into the Sonnkogel and Hirschkogel regions, with its highest peak rising to over 2,000 m (6,562 ft). The **Pinzgauer Spaziergang** is one of the most beautiful walking trails in the Austrian Alps, running at an altitude of about 1,000 m (3,280 ft) above the valley floor, from Zell am See to Saalbach, via Schmittenhöhe (a seven-hour walk).

Saalbach ⑲

Road map C4. 🏔 *2,900*. 🚉 🚌
ℹ *(06541) 6800-0.*

AT THE HEART of the Glemmtal lies this small town, marking the border between Salzburger Land and Tyrol. A charming winter resort with guaranteed snow, it provides access to 200 km (120 miles) of pistes, with beginner and more challenging runs right to the village centres. There is a wide range of entertainments on offer including extra-wide carving pistes, ungroomed moguls, a GS-race course, facilities for tobogganing and tubing as well as snow bars, huts and flood-lit slope dances.

To the north of Saalbach the Spielberghorn comes into view, while to the south the Schattberg marks the end of the Pinzgauer Spaziergang. This trail, leading across several passes, affords breathtaking views over the neighbouring mountain range. The view extending from Rohrertörl Pass (1,918 m/6,293 ft) embraces the town of Saalbach and the entire valley.

Charming, flower-bedecked houses in Saalbach

Lofer ⑳

Road map C4. 👥 *2,000.* 🚌 🚋
🔲 *(06588) 8321-0.*

THE TOWN OF Lofer, in the green Salzach Valley, has retained much of the charm of an old mountain village. It is surrounded by the snow-covered rocky summits of the Loferer Steinberge (Stone Mountains). These limestone mountains hide many caves still waiting to be explored. The Lamprechtsofenloch is said to be the deepest aquiferous cave in the world.

ENVIRONS: A short distance south of Lofer is the small town of **Kirchenthal** with its pilgrimage church of St Mary, built between 1693 and 1701 by Johann Bernhard Fischer von Erlach. It is one of the greatest works by this out-standing architect, in which he employed some of the ideas that he had developed earlier in Salzburg. The build-ing is blended into the rocky mountain scenery of the Saal ach Valley, and two small towers are prominent against the distant snowy mountains. The Neo-Baroque altarpiece includes the 15th-century miraculous picture of the Madonna that was once the destination of pilgrims. On one of the two altars, created by Jakob Zanussi from reddish-pink Salzburg marble, the parents of the Virgin Mary, St Jacob and St Anne, are depicted.

Mittersill ㉑

Road map C4.
👥 *5,500.* 🚌 🚋
🔲 *(06562) 4292.*

THIS SUMMER resort at the main cross-roads of the Upper Salzach Valley sprang up around a castle. The castle was built in the 12th century and since then has been rebuilt many times, following its destruction during the Peasant Wars and numerous fires. Today it is the seat of the International Protestant Youth Community, a cultural centre and a hotel.

The chapel (1533) features an interesting late-Gothic polyptych attributed to an Aussee Master. The Heiliger Leonhardkirche (Church of St Leonard), originally Gothic, was remodelled in the 18th century to a design by Johann Kleber. It contains a heavily ornamented Rococo pulpit and some remains of the old decorations, including an early 15th-century stone statue of Leonard.

Mittersill lies at the Salzburg end of a beautiful mountain trail leading from East Tyrol, among the wild scenery of the Hohe Tauern National Park. The road known as Felberntauernstraße affords lovely views of the rugged slopes of Großvenediger.

The scenic Krimmler Wasserfälle

Krimmler Wasserfälle ㉒

Road map C4. 🚋
🔲 *(06564) 7239.*

IN THE NORTHWESTERN part of the Hohe Tauern National Park *(see pp278-81)*, on the border between the provinces of Salzburger Land and Tyrol, are the famous Krimmler Wasserfälle, the waterfalls of the Krimmler Ache, the stream flowing from the glacier of the same name at an altitude of around 3,000 m (9,850 ft). The water falls in three steps, with a total drop of 380 m (1,247 ft). In winter, the falls freeze over. The journey to the waterfalls can be made by car, but a walk along the Wasserfallweg (waterfall path) will prove a truly unforgettable experi-ence. The best starting points for the walk are the Gerlos Pass or Krimmel village.

View of the Hohe Tauern mountains, near Mittersill

TYROL AND VORARLBERG

B OTH TYROL AND VORARLBERG *lie on a narrow stretch of land west of Salzburg. Their main attractions are the Alps – few areas are below 500 m (1,640 ft) – and tourism is their primary source of income. The Tyrol is famous for its magnificent scenery and world-renowned resorts such as Kitzbühel, Seefeld and St. Anton, while Vorarlberg draws visitors seeking a more relaxed, rural environment.*

The Tyrol occupies an area of 12,648 sq km (4,883 sq miles) and has a population of 675,000. Its neighbours are Bavaria in the north, Italy in the south, Vorarlberg in the west and Salzburger Land in the east. The Enns is the province's main river, winding its way through the Alpine massifs.

In ancient times Tyrol was inhabited by Rhaetian and Illyrian tribes; it came under Roman rule in the 1st century BC, and later fell to the Bavarians and the Longobards. In the 13th century, it became an independent principality of the Reich. Until 1363 it remained a bone of contention between the Habsburgs and the Bavarians, when it was bequeathed to the Habsburgs. Tyrol was a domain of the family's junior line and as such enjoyed a degree of independence. To this day it has maintained its unique character, music, dialect and even fashion, which has shaped cultural life in the rest of Austria.

The province of Vorarlberg, in contrast, has for many years been culturally fairly separate, largely orientating itself towards its neighbours Germany, Liechtenstein and Switzerland. After Vienna, it is the smallest Austrian province, covering an area of just 2,601 sq km (1,000 sq miles), with 347,000 inhabitants. It was once inhabited by Aleman tribes. From the 15th century the area of present-day Vorarlberg passed gradually into the hands of the Habsburgs, and in 1919 it finally became an independent Austrian province.

The beautiful Lünersee in the province of Vorarlberg, hidden between snow-covered alpine peaks

◁ **A typical Tyrolean scene, with the picture-postcard church of Orenberg in Tyrol**

Exploring Tyrol and Vorarlberg

BOTH PROVINCES, in the far west of Austria, are predominantly winter sports regions, although they also offer excellent facilities for summer activities. Among the popular and world-famous tourist centres of Tyrol are Kitzbühel, the area around the Arlberg Pass, and the hinterland of Innsbruck. The latter has twice played host to the Winter Olympic Games, in 1964 and 1976. The capital of the smaller Vorarlberg province is Bregenz, a somewhat sleepy resort located in a romantic spot on the eastern shores of Lake Constance (Bodensee).

Chairlift and ski runs near Zürs

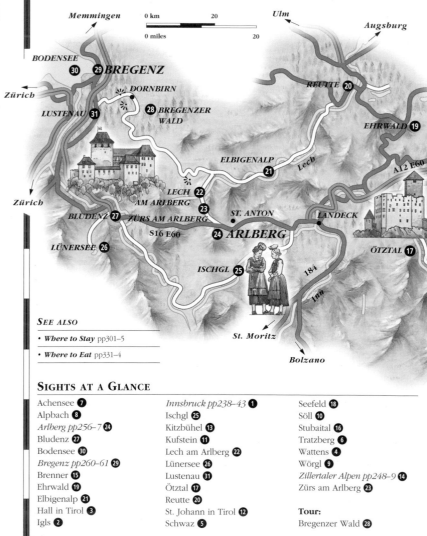

GETTING THERE

From Innsbruck-Kranebitten Airport flights depart to Salzburg, Vienna and most major European cities. Both Tyrol and Vorarlberg are served by the main railway line from Vienna to Bregenz, and the western motorway reaches Bregenz. Austria's first toll road tunnel passes through the Arlberg massif. Both provinces have a good network of bus routes, although many roads may become impassable in winter. From autumn until spring motorists planning excursions to the mountains need to remember to take winter tyres and snow chains.

The Ballunspitze peak, seen from Paznauntal

München (Munich)

München (Munich) ▲

Garmisch-Partenkirchen

Salzburg →

181

KUFSTEIN
11

312

12 **ST. JOHANN IN TIROL**

WÖRGL 9   10
SÖLL

13 **KITZBÜHEL**

ACHENSEE 7

171

8 **ALPBACH**

TRATZBERG 6

HALL IN TIROL 5 **SCHWAZ**

EEFELD

3   4 **WATTENS**

NSBRUCK

Badgastein →

2 **IGLS**

Lienz

'BAITAL
16

ZILLERTALER ALPEN
14

KEY

▬	Motorway
▬	Major road
▬	Scenic route
═	Other road
☆	Viewpoint

15 **BRENNER**

▼ *Bolzano*

A coat of arms on the 15th-century town hall in Hall in Tyrol

Chapel in the snow-covered valley of Stubai

Innsbruck: Street-by-Street ❶

INNSBRUCK was built at the confluence of the Sill and Inn rivers and became an important trading post in the Middle Ages. The present district of Wilten was once the site of the Roman camp of Veldidena, but the founders of the city itself are the counts of Andechs, who built a settlement here in 1187. Today Innsbruck is the capital of the province of Tyrol, Austria's most important tourist region. In 1964 and again in 1976 Innsbruck was the host city for the Winter Olympics; many competitions took place in Axamer Lizum, 20 km (14 miles) southwest of the city.

★ Goldenes Dachl
The symbol of Innsbruck, the Golden Roof is an oriel window added in 1500 by Maximilian I to Friedrich IV's former residence. It is covered with 2,657 gilded copper rooftiles.

Herzog-Friedrich-Straße
The main street of the old town is lined with the attractive façades of numerous Baroque buildings.

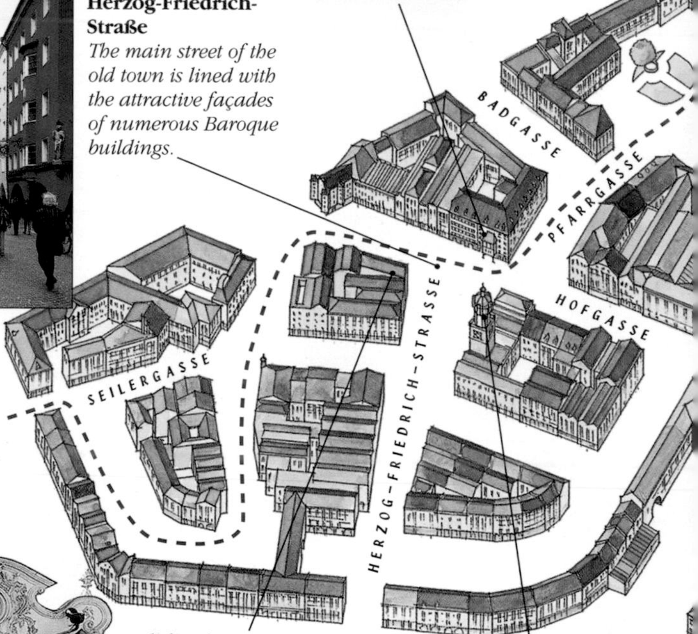

BADGASSE

PFARRGASSE

HOFGASSE

HERZOG–FRIEDRICH–STRASSE

SEILERGASSE

Helblinghaus
The building with an elegant Regency façade at No. 10 Herzog-Friedrich-Straße was originally a medieval corner house in the Gothic style. In 1725 it was decorated with opulent Rococo stuccowork.

Stadtturm
The 14th-century city tower next to the old town hall acquired its present Renaissance look in 1560. At 56 m (184 ft) high it affords great views.

KEY

– – – Suggested route

★ Dom St. Jakob
The Baroque cathedral has enchanting vault frescoes by Cosmas Damian Asam and a picture of the Madonna and Child by Lucas Cranach the Elder.

VISITORS' CHECKLIST

Road map B4. 🚌 124,000.
🛈 Burggraben 3 (0512) 59850.
W www.innsbruck-tourismus.
com. 🎭 Tanzsommer Innsbruck
(Jun, Jul), Innsbrucker Festwochen
der Alten Musik (Festival of Early
Music, Jul, Aug).

0 m	75
0 yards	75

★ Hofburg
The interior of the imperial palace was extensively rebuilt in Rococo style during the reign of Maria Theresa, to designs by Johann Martin Gumpp and Konstantin Johann Walter.

RRENGASSE

BURGGRABEN

UNIVERSITÄTS-STRASSE

ANGERZELLGASSE

PROF. F. MAIR-GASSE

Jesuitenkirche

Landesmuseum

Hofkirche
The court church, built in 1553–63 as a mausoleum for Maximilian I and guarded by large statues (right), was remodelled in the Baroque style by Georg Anton Gumpp (see pp 242–3).

STAR SIGHTS

★ **Dom St. Jakob**

★ **Goldenes Dachl**

★ **Hofburg**

Exploring Innsbruck

Innsbruck straddles the Inn river. Its Old Town is situated on the right bank, close to the river. Leading up to it is the broad Maria-Theresien-Straße with the tall column of St Anna (1706). The most impressive historic buildings are found on Herzog-Friedrich-Straße, Stadtplatz, Hofgasse and Rennweg. Other important sights are Schloss Ambras, on the southern outskirts of the city, and the Panorama of the Battle of Bergisel.

⛪ Dom St. Jakob

Domplatz. 📞 *(0512) 583902.*
St James' Cathedral was built in Baroque style in the early 18th century by Johann Jakob Herkomer. Severely damaged during World War II, it was rebuilt in the 1950s, when the church finally acquired the figures for the niches, as well as the equestrian statue of St. Jakob on top of the building, as envisaged in the original designs; the sculptor was Hans André. The fine Baroque interior is the work of Munich artists, the two brothers Cosman Damian (painter) and Egid Quirin (sculptor) Asam. The vault paintings depict scenes from the life of St James (St. Jakob). The picture of *Madonna and Child* in the high altar, which miracles are attributed to, is by Lucas Cranach the Elder.

The old town houses with their rich stucco ornaments, reliefs and frescoes provide an enchanting backdrop to the cathedral, which is regarded as the most magnificent Baroque church building in North Tyrol.

⛪ Hofburg

Rennweg 1. 📞 *(0512) 587186.*
⏰ *9am–5pm daily.* 🎫
In 1453, Archduke Sigismund embarked on a project to build a princely residence in Innsbruck. His Gothic castle, extended by Maximilian I, survived for several centuries, and to this day the castle dungeons feature the original late-Gothic vaults. A major remodelling took place in 1755, under Maria Theresa, when the

plans for the Baroque south wing were prepared by Johann Martin Gumpp, who also remodelled the front of the building and the grand staircase. His work was continued by Konstantin Johann Walter, who is responsible for the palace's uniform, Classicist shape.

The interior of the Hofburg is furnished in Rococo style. The state-rooms on the second floor were completed in 1773. The most beautiful of these is the Riesenhalle (the Giants' Hall), embellished with white and gold stucco and a ceiling painting by Franz Anton Maulbertsch, depicting the triumph of the House of Habsburg–Lothringen. The walls are hung with vast portraits of Maria Theresa, her 16 children and other members of the imperial family. The remaining rooms of the south wing also have original Rococo decorations and furnishings.

Riesenhalle, a stateroom in Hofburg

⛲ Goldenes Dachl

Herzog-Friedrich-Straße 15.
📞 *(0512) 581111.* ⏰ *May–Oct: 10am–6pm daily; Oct–Apr: 10am–5pm, Tue–Sun.* 🎫
In about 1500 the tall oriel window, with its numerous gilded copper tiles, was added above the balcony of this former residence of the Tyrolean rulers. It created a viewing box from which Emperor Maximilian I could observe street life on the main square of Innsbruck. The two-storey oriel rests on two slender columns. There are six coats of arms under the first-floor windows and the second-floor balustrade is decorated with reliefs; one of these depicts Maximilian I and his two wives: Maria of Burgundy and Bianca Maria Sforza; the second shows the emperor surrounded by court jesters. The building behind the Goldenes Dachl houses the small Maximilianeum, a museum of the emperor's life.

⛲ Herzog-Friedrich-Straße

Herzog-Friedrich-Straße is one of Innsbruck's loveliest streets. Its main historic sights include the Rococo Helblinghaus (No. 10), the Gothic Old Town Hall, dating from the 14th–15th centuries (No. 21), and its adjacent Stadtturm (city tower), with a viewing terrace.

Many of the other houses along the street also warrant a close look. The four-storey Ottoburg at No. 1, close to the Inn river, has four oriels stacked on top of each other and late-Gothic interior vaults. The Baroque façade of Altes

The richly ornamented pulpit in Dom St. Jakob

Regierungsgebäude (old governmental building) at No. 3 hides some beautiful rooms including the Claudia-Saal, the Hall of Claudia de Medici, with a late-Renaissance coffered ceiling. At No. 6 is an old inn, *Der Goldene Adler* (Golden Eagle Inn), and the Katzunghaus (at No. 16) has interesting 16th-century reliefs on the oriels.

⚜ Altes Landhaus
Maria-Theresien-Straße 43.
📞 (0512) 508-0.

This 18th-century house, built in 1725–8 by Georg Anton Gumpp and today the seat of Tyrol's provincial government, is regarded as one of Austria's most beautiful secular structures. It has an attractive inner courtyard and its colourful elevations were embellished by Alessandro Callegari. The niches lining the walls of the monumental internal staircase are filled with marble statues and busts of Greek and Roman gods. Ceiling frescoes depict the Tyrolean eagle with an open map of the country. The most opulent room in the building is the Rococo conference hall. Along the same street the Annasäule (1706) rises in front of the Neues Rathaus.

The impressive, two-tiered 16th-century Schloss Ambras

Georg Anton Gumpp's imposing stairwell in Altes Landhaus

🏛 Ferdinandeum
Museumstraße 15. 📞 (0512) 59489.
◯ Jun–Sep: 10am–6pm daily, 10am–9pm Thu; Oct–May: 10am–6pm Tue–Sun.

Together with the former armoury of Maximilian I at No. 1 Zeughausgasse, this 19th-century building houses the collection of the Tiroler Landesmuseum (the Tyrol Regional Museum), named after Archduke Ferdinand II (1529–95), a Tyrolean ruler and a passionate collector. The museum has individual departments devoted to the natural environment, history, art and handicrafts, and it is also home to a library. Among its most precious exhibits are Gothic panel paintings, sculptures by Michael Pacher, and works by old German and Dutch masters – Lucas Cranach the Elder, Rembrandt, Brueghel and others. The museum also exhibits more recent Austrian art, including works by Klimt, Schiele and Kokoschka.

⚓ Schloss Ambras
Schlossstraße 20. 📞 (0512) 348446.
◯ 10am–5pm daily; 1 Aug–31 Aug: 10am–7pm. ● Nov, 25 Dec. 📷

The castle, on the southeastern city limits, was once the symbol of Tyrol's power and glory. In the 12th century it was the seat of local rulers. The present 16th-century building consists of a lower castle with entrance gate and spacious courtyard, and an upper castle built on the site of an earlier structure. The two parts are connected by the early-Renaissance Spanish Hall, built by Giovanni Luchese in 1571, with original coffered ceiling and inlaid doors.

Archduke Ferdinand II established his own museum at Ambras, but the exhibits ended up in various Viennese museums. Nonetheless, there is still plenty to see, including the Rüstkammer (arsenal), the Kunst- und Wunderkammer (chamber of arts and marvels), and the gallery with portraits of members of the Habsburgs by famous artists such as Lucas Cranach, Peter Paul Rubens and Diego Velázquez.

ANDREAS HOFER (1767–1810)

Andreas Hofer is regarded as Austria's national hero, widely extolled in its literature and poetry. In 1809, he led the Tyrolean uprising against the Bavarian rulers, who were allied with Napoleon's forces. He succeeded in beating the Bavarians, and forced the French army, led by Marshal Lefebvre, to retreat from Tyrol after their defeat on Bergisel, a hill just outside Innsbruck *(see p243)*. Hofer assumed civilian power in Tyrol, but was soon betrayed and captured, and subsequently executed by the French in the town square of Mantua.

Hofkirche

Hofkirche, the court church, was built by Ferdinand I to house the tomb of his grandfather, Emperor Maximilian I. The tomb was designed by Maximilian himself and although his plans were never fully realized, the ensuing structure, completed in 1587, is very impressive indeed and ranks as a masterpiece of Renaissance sculpture. At the centre of the church stands the sarcophagus with a kneeling figure of the emperor. Reliefs on the side panels depict scenes from the emperor's life; the tomb is guarded by larger-than-life cast-iron statues. The tomb is, in fact, empty – Maximilian was laid to rest in Wiener Neustadt, in Lower Austria.

Vaults
The vaults acquired their present form in the early 17th century, when the church was rebuilt in the Baroque style.

★ **Tomb of Maximilian I**
The cenotaph, at the centre of the church, is guarded by giant figures representing members of Maximilian I's family, including his daughter-in-law, Joanna the Mad, and his spiritual forefathers.

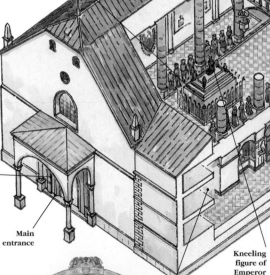

Main Portal
The grand Renaissance portal leading into the church was built in 1553–63 as a tribute to the House of Maximilian I.

Main entrance

Kneeling figure of Emperor Maximilian I

STAR FEATURES

★ Silberne Kapelle

★ Tomb of Maximilian I

★ **Silberne Kapelle**
The silver chapel holds the tombs of Archduke Ferdinand II and his beloved wife, Philippine Welser, by the Dutch artist, Alexander Colin.

An onion dome
crowns the octa-
gonal tower of
the church

Charles the Bold
*The statue of Charles the
Bold, Duke of Burgundy
and Maximilian's father-in-
law, stands to the right of the
tomb, closest to the high altar.*

Wilten

In the southeastern suburb of
Wilten stands a lovely Baroque
church, the Wilten Basilica,
built in 1751–6 on the
foundations of a former
chapel. The church was
intended to provide a worthy
setting for the picture of *Our
Lady at Four Columns*,
which miracles were
attributed to it. It was
designed by Franz de
Paula Penz and the
interior has been kept
in the Rococo style.
The main altarpiece,
with its gold, pink and
yellow colour scheme,
includes a 14th-century
painting of the Madon-
na. It is surrounded by
an intricate canopy
structure resting on
slender columns.
The ceiling paint-
ings are by an Augs-
burg artist, Matthäus Gündter,
and show in the presbytery
Saint Mary Our Advocate and
in the nave *Ester and Judith*.
The Romanesque abbey of
Wilten has a church built in
the 12th century, devoted to
St Lawrence. According to
legend, the abbey was built by
the giant Haymo, in atonement for the murder of
another giant, Thyrsus; both
are commemorated by statues.
Burned and destroyed several
times over, the abbey was
rebuilt in Baroque style in the
17th–18th centuries.

Bergisel

**Tiroler Kaiserjägermuseum
am Bergisel** Bergisel 3.
(0512) 582312. Apr–Oct:
9am–5pm daily.
**Riesenrundgemälde der Schlacht
am Bergisel** Rennweg 39.
(0512) 584434. Apr–Oct:
9am–5pm daily.
On 13 August 1809, Bergisel,
or Isel Mountain, in the south
of the city, was the scene of
a bloody battle fought by
Andreas Hofer *(see p241)* and
his army of insurgent highlanders, who defeated the
combined occupying forces
of Bavarians and French.
The hill is a popular place
for weekend walks among
Innsbruck residents.
A monument to Andreas
Hofer and the Imperial

**Statue of Andreas
Hofer on Bergisel**

Fusiliers' Museum (at No. 3
Bergisel) serves as a reminder
of the 1809 battle as well as
of later battles by this
famous regiment.
In Innsbruck's north, at
the foot of Hungerburg
Hill on the opposite side
of the Inn river, stands
a twelve-sided build-
ing which houses the
Riesenrundgemälde,
a giant panoramic
painting of the
Battle of Bergisel,
painted by Zeno
Diemer in 1896.
Measuring 10 x 100 m
(33 x 328 ft), the pano-
rama is a *trompe l'œil*
painting depicting an
abbreviated version of
the entire battle.
On Bergiselschanze,
one of the competi-
tions in the world-
famous Vierschan-
zentournee (four hills' ski-
jumping tournament) is held
every year on 4 January.

Alpenzoo

Weiherburggasse 37A. *(0512)
292323.* Apr–Sep: 9am–6pm;
Oct–Mar: 9am–5pm.
On the southern slopes of
Bergisel is a fascinating alpine
zoo, housing a comprehensive
collection of alpine fauna.
There are some 2,000 animals
here, representing more than
150 species typically found in
an alpine habitat, including
the alpine ibex and bear, and
many local birds, fish and reptiles. A cable car from Hunger-
berg Talstation takes you to
the zoo; the ride is free with
an entry ticket to the zoo.

**An otter in Alpenzoo, on Bergisel
south of Innsbruck**

The emblematic Mint Tower of Burg Hasegg in Hall in Tirol

Igls ❷

Road map B4. 🏠 *2,000*. 🚍
ℹ️ *Hilberstraße 15 (0512) 377101*.

THIS SMALL town south of Innsbruck, which had long been popular as a holiday centre and winter-sports resort, was given a new face for the 1976 Winter Olympic Games when modern toboggan and bobsleigh runs were built. The nearby Patscherkofel (2,247 m/7,372 ft high) is a popular destination for winter skiing expeditions and summer rambles. It is served by a funicular, a chair lift and five T-bars. An old salt track, Römerstraße, runs above the Sill Valley, providing views of the famous Europabrücke (Europe Bridge) *(see p252)*, which spans the alpine gorges and is part of the busiest motorway network connecting northern Europe with Italy.

The **Aegidiuskirche** in Igls, the church of St Giles, probably dates back to the 13th century but has been remodelled in the Baroque period. It has beautiful vault frescoes by Josef Michael Schmitzer.

Near Igls is the interesting pilgrimage chapel Heiligwasser (1662), with attractive stuccowork created in 1720 as well as a wooden statue of the Virgin Mary dating back to the early 15th century.

Coat of arms of Hall in Tirol

Hall in Tirol ❸

Road map B4. 🏠 *12,000*. 🚍 🚊
ℹ️ *Wallpachgasse 5 (05223) 56269*.
🇼 *www.tiscover.at/hall*

HALL RANKS mostly as a holiday resort, but the Old Town, with much of its original architecture intact, bears testimony to the town's former glory. The symbol of Hall is the twelve-sided tower, known as the Mint Tower, of **Burg Hasegg**. This castle, with its beautiful inner courtyard, once formed a corner section of the town's fortifications. It was the seat of the Tyrolean rulers and, in the 16th century, it became the mint. Today the castle houses the town museum.

In the Old Town, the **Town Hall** with its steep Gothic roof consists of two parts: the 1406 Königshaus (Royal House) with a beautiful debating hall with exposed-beam ceiling; and is a large building on the south side of Oberer Stadtplatz, with a Renaissance portal and a balcony from which the town fathers used to make their proclamations. The 14th-century **Nikolauskirche**, the church of St Nicholas, nearby, has a lovely portal featuring the Sorrowful Christ, the Virgin Mary and St Nicholas, and an attractive Baroque interior. Particularly worth

seeing is the Waldlaufkapelle, which is closed off from the rest of the church interior by a wrought-iron grille. It houses a collection of reliquaries.

Wattens ❹

Road map B4. 🏠 *7,700*. 🚍 🚊
ℹ️ *(05224) 52904*.

THE SWAROVSKI factory of decorative glass and glass jewellery and its museum in Wattens are a unique and fascinating experience. Here you can see the world's largest cut crystal (300,000 carats), and a crystal wall 11 m (36 ft) high, with several tons of glittering semi-precious stones.

🏛 Swarovski Kristallwelten
Kristallweltenstraße 1. 📞 *(05224) 51080*. 🕐 *9am–6pm*. 🅿️

ENVIRONS: Volders has an unusual church devoted to St Charles Borromeo, dating from 1620–54.

The entrance to Swarovski Kristallwelten in Wattens

Schwaz ❺

Road map C4. 🏠 *12,000*. 🚍 🚊
ℹ️ *Franz-Josef-Straße 2 (05242) 63240-0*.

DURING THE 16th century, this busy commercial town in the Inn river valley was the second largest in the Tyrol. Schwaz suffered extensive damage during the battle of 1809, but it has preserved some lovely historic sights.

The imposing Renaissance Schloss Tratzberg

The most impressive of these is the 15th-century **Pfarrkirche**, with its high copper-shingled tower and beautiful, crenellated gables. The most striking elements inside are the stone balustrade of the gallery with intricate lacework (c.1520) and an impressive Baroque organ enclosure. The figures of St Anne, St Ursula and St Elizabeth on the altarpiece are original Gothic decorations. The statues of St George and St Florian, the patron saints of Austria, were added at a later date. The double **cemetery chapel** (1504–7) has a lovely covered staircase leading to the upper chapel, which has a carved wooden altar. The lower chapel has original 16th-century frescoes depicting the Crucifixion and the Mount of Olives.

The late-Gothic **Franziskanerkirche**, the Franciscan church and monastery, has retained its original Gothic interior, clearly visible despite Baroque additions made in the 18th century. The cloister along the south wall of the church was built in 1509–12 by Christof Reichartinger; it shows a series of 16th-century paintings with Passion scenes.

Schwaz was once a major centre for the production of silver, and one of the mines, the **Silberbergwerk**, is now open to the public and can be explored by train and a guided tour on foot.

🏛 Silberbergwerk
Alte Landstraße 3a. **▐** (05242)
72372-0. **◯** May–Oct: 8:30am–5pm
daily, Nov–Apr: 9:30am–4pm daily.
W www.silberbergswerk.at

Tratzberg ❻

Road map C4. 🚌 🚉 **▐** (05242)
6356620. **◯** Apr–Oct: 10am–4pm.
W www. schloss-tratzberg.at 🗺 🐾
🔲 ♿

A SHORT WAY from Schwaz, in the Inn river valley, stands the impressive Renaissance Schloss Tratzberg. This castle was once a frontier fortress which guarded Andechs county against the Bavarians. It changed hands many times and is now the private property of the Enzenberg family, with a small museum.

The castle is entered from the west side through a Renaissance portal. The inner courtyard with its heavily decorated low arcades was built in two stages: the first around 1500 and the second in the late 16th century. The most interesting parts of the castle are the armoury, with its tremendous collection of early arms; the Royal Room, with its exposed beam ceiling, once used by Anna of Bohemia, the widow of Duke Henry of

Tyrol; and finally the Habsburg Hall, with the family tree of Emperor Maximilian I and 148 portraits. The room has a red marble column at its centre and is covered by a coffered ceiling. The emperor's room on the second floor retains its original intricately carved wooden ceiling, and the bedroom is decorated by a series of 16th-century paintings of a knightly tournament created by Hans Schäufelein. The Fugger family room still boasts its original Renaissance decor. Its best feature is the richly inlaid door dating from 1515.

Achensee ❼

Road map C4. 🚌 🚉

SITUATED between the Inn and the Isar river basins is Achensee, the largest lake in Tyrol, about 9 km (6 miles) long. On its northern shore the Karwendel mountain range extends up to Innsbruck. On its eastern shore are the Rofan Mountains, with their highest peak, the Rofanspitze, rising to 2,259 m (7,411 ft).

Achensee can be reached by cog-wheel steam train from **Jenbach**. Worth seeing in this village is the church of St. Wolfgang, a late-Gothic structure built in 1487–1500 by Gilg Mitterhofer from Schwaz; its Baroque tower is a later addition. Although repeatedly rebuilt, it still has its late-Gothic side portals and ogival windows; one of the side altars has a late-Gothic statue of the Madonna.

Sailing yachts on Achensee, Tyrol's largest lake

Charming flower displays outside the alpine houses in Alpbach

Alpbach ❽

Road map C4. 👥 2,500. ⓘ
(05336) 6000. 🅦 www.alpbach.at

IN A HIGH mountain valley on the Alpbach river lies the town of the same name that once a year becomes the intellectual capital of Europe. Every year since 1945, delegates representing the worlds of science, politics, economics and culture have gathered here to discuss the future of the world. Before the fall of communism in the Eastern bloc countries in 1989, Austria's central position in Europe made this the most appropriate place for people from East and West to meet. Today their discussions are rather more academic, yet Alpbach has retained its great importance on Europe's political and intellectual map.

The floral displays outside the alpine houses and chalets in Alpbach rank among the best in the country. The little town also has the interesting **Church of St Oswald**. Its earliest records date from 1369, although it was altered in 1500 and the Baroque interior dates from 1724. The naves have ceiling paintings by Christof Anton Mayr (1751); the sculptures in the presbytery (c.1779) are the work of Franz Xaver Nissel.

Wörgl ❾

Road map C4. 👥 11,000.
🚉 Bahnhofstraße 4 (05332) 76007.

THE INDUSTRIAL town of Wörgl, at the fork of Inn river and Brixentaler Ache (a stream), is an important road and rail hub. The earliest settlement on the site, revealed by archaeological finds on the northeastern outskirts of town, date from the Bronze Age. In later years this was the site of a Roman settlement, and in the 4th century a Christian community was founded in the area. In the 13th century Wörgl belonged to Bavaria; during the reign of Maximilian I it finally became incorporated into Tyrol. Wörgl and its environs were the scene of fierce fighting during the Napoleonic

Monument to the Battle of 1809 in Wörgl

wars, when the Tyrolean highlanders fought for their independence from the Bavarians and the French. A monument commemorating the battle now stands in front of **St Lawrence's church**. This church, built in 1748, is Baroque in style and has interesting stucco decorations, vault paintings, a main altar with Baroque sculptures and an attractive medieval statue of the Madonna.

Wörgl's location between the two tourist regions of Kaisergebirge and the Kitzbühel Alps makes it a convenient base for winter and summer expeditions.

Söll ❿

Road map C4. 👥 3,000.
ⓘ (05333) 5216.

SÖLL, A SMALL town in the foothills of the Hohe Salve, part of the Wilder Kaiser (Wild Emperor) massif, grew around the **Church of St Peter and St Paul**. Built in 1361 but completely altered in the Baroque style in 1768 by Franz Bock of Kufstein, it contains beautiful vault paintings by Anton Mayr and, by the same artist, a picture of the Madonna in the main altarpiece. The town has many attractive houses with picturesque façades.

The greatest attraction of Söll, however, is the **Hohe Salve** mountain, rising to 1,828 m (5,997 ft) and visible from every point in the town. Two gondolas provide transport to the summit. There is a small chapel here, and the view over Brixental, the Kitzbühel Alps and the High Tauern Mountains in the distance, is truly majestic. Söll lies at the centre of a large skiing region, **Ski-welt Wilder Kaiser-Brixental**, in the southern part of Kaisergebirge, which also includes several other attractive resorts, such as the picturesque town of **Scheffau** nearby.

Visitors sunbathing on Hohe Salve, near Söll

Kufstein ⓫

Road map C4. 🏔 *15,000.*
🚩 🚏 🔰 *(05372) 62207.*

THE REMAINS of a Stone Age
settlement have been
found in this health resort
and tourist centre on the
Bavarian border.

On a rocky hill to the north
of the town stands the Feste
Kufstein, a mighty fortress
with a small barbican and the
Emperor's Tower. Today it
houses a **Regional Museum**
and, on the ground floor of
the tower, the Heldenorgel
(Heroes' Organ), built to
commemorate all who were
killed in World War I. The
late-Gothic **Church of St
Vitus** was rebuilt in the 17th
century in the Baroque style,
but in the 20th century it was
partly returned to its original
Gothic appearance. Nearby
stands the Holy Trinity Chapel,
with a beautiful Baroque altar
dating from 1765.

ENVIRONS: Hechtsee and
Stimmersee, two small, scenic
lakes west of Kufstein, are
excellent for water sports
enthusiasts. About 30 km
(22 miles) northeast of
Kufstein, beyond the Kaisergebirge ridge known as Zahmer Kaiser (Tame Emperor),
is **Walchsee**, a beguiling town
and lake of the same name,
with many fine houses with
picturesque façades and a
good water sports centre.
The road from Kufstein along
the Sparchenbach river leads
to Stripsenkopf, at 1,807 m
(5,929 ft) the highest peak
in the Zahmer Kaiser
range, with great
views of the
Kaiser-
gebirge.

St. Johann in Tirol ⓬

Road map C4. 🏔 *8,000.*
🚩 🚏 🔰 *(05352) 63335-0.*

ST. JOHANN in Tirol is a
popular winter sports
resort, boasting good downhill
runs on the northern slopes
of the Kitzbüheler Horn and
splendid conditions for cross-
country skiing. The town has
several Baroque buildings
with picturesque elevations,
and the walls of the parish
house feature the original
frescoes from 1480. The first
large Baroque church in the
area was built in 1728 by
Abraham Milbauer, on the
site of an earlier Gothic structure. Inside **Mariä Himmelfahrtskirche** (church of
the Assumption of the Virgin
Mary) are magnificent vault
paintings by one of the great
masters of Baroque art, Simon
Benedikt Faistenberger.

Kitzbühel ⓭

Road map C4. 🏔 *8,500.* 🚩 🚏
🔰 *Hinterstadt 18 (05356) 777-0.*

ONCE THE undisputed win-
ter sports capital of the
country, Kitzbühel now has
to share its crown with other
resorts. The alpine town is
surrounded by several mountain massifs, with scores of
well-signposted trails. The
best conditions are offered by
the Hahnenkamm–Steinberg-
kogel–Pengelstein group to

**A picturesque snow-covered scene
in Kitzbühel**

the southwest, the Kitzbüheler
Horn to the north, the Stuck-
kogel and the Thurn Pass.
This is where the famous
Hahnenkammrennen, a down-
hill skiing race, takes place at
the end of January each year.

Kitzbühel is more than a
sporting resort; untouched by
wartime ravages, it has many
historic sights. The **Andreas-
kirche** was built in 1435 on
the site of a Romanesque
church. In 1785 it was rebuilt
in the Baroque style, and it
has recently been restored.
Inside are late-Gothic columns
and 15th-century traceries
and frescoes. There is also an
interesting main altarpiece, by
Simon Benedikt Faistenberger.

Adjacent to the parish
church is **Liebfrauenkirche**
(church of Our Lady), with a
square tower. The main altar
is also by Faistenberger. The
14th-century St Catherine's
church in the city centre is
now a monument to those
killed in the two world wars.

The mighty fortress with the Emperor's Tower in Kufstein

Zillertaler Alpen ⑭

The ZILLERTAL, the valley of the Ziller river, extends from Innau to the Austro-Italian border. Initially a wide upland, beyond Mayrhofen it splits into four narrower valleys that cut into the mountain ranges. Artificial lakes and large dams were built into most of the local rivers to provide a power supply for the entire region. The present popularity of winter sports has contributed to the rapid development of Zillertal. Especially popular with skiers are the Tuxer glacier runs, the Mayrhofen-Finkenberg trail and the town of Zell am Ziller. The well-marked trails in breathtakingly beautiful countryside lure ramblers here in the summer, and there are many attractive cycling routes.

Zillertaler Alpen
The Zillertaler Alps, a side range of the High Tauern, are steep crystalline mountains. Their highest peak is the Hochfeiler at 3,510 m/ 11,516 ft.

★ Tuxer Tal
The valley of the Tuxer Bach (Tuxer stream) is picturesque, with many attractive resorts. Tuxer Ferner, the local glacier, offers the best year-round skiing conditions in the entire area.

KEY

═══	Major road
═══	Minor road
- -	Cable car, chairlift
═══	River
☀	Viewpoint

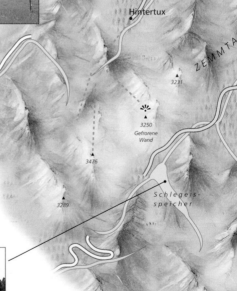

Lanersbach

TUXERTAL

Hintertux

ZEMMTALGRUND

Ginyl

2887

169

3231

☀

3250
Gefrorene
Wand

3476

3289

Schlegeis-speicher

3478

Schlegeisspeicher
The largest artificial lake in the area is scenically situated at the foot of the Hoch-feiler Massif and the Schlegeis glacier.

STAR SIGHTS

★ Tuxer Tal

★ Zell am Ziller

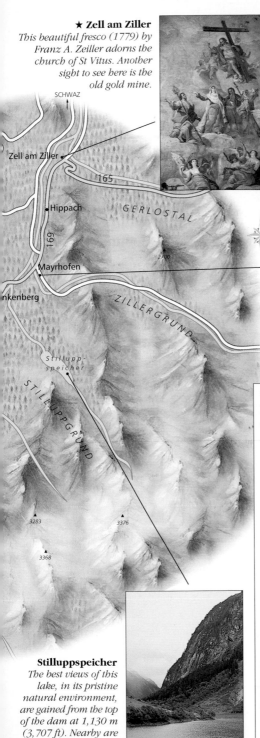

★ Zell am Ziller

*This beautiful fresco (1779) by
Franz A. Zeiller adorns the
church of St Vitus. Another
sight to see here is the
old gold mine.*

Mayrhofen

*In this picturesque resort, the
most popular tourist destination
in the Zillertal, the wide valley
narrows and divides into four
smaller alpine valleys.*

```
0 km                    5
0 miles                 5
```

TYROLEAN NATIONAL COSTUMES

The Tyrolean version of Austria's
national costume is not reserved
for special occasions – here many
people wear it every day. The man's
Tracht consists of leather shorts
(summer) or breeches (winter)
held in place by braces and tied
under the knees, thick socks and a
Loden jacket made of thick, woollen
cloth, with bone buttons. To this is
added a felt hat with a distinctive
tuft of coarse animal hair. The
woman's *Dirndl* comprises a puffed-
sleeve blouse with a bodice and a
pleated skirt with an apron.
Women also wear hats or scarves.

**A young couple dressed in typical
Tyrolean outfits**

Stilluppspeicher

*The best views of this
lake, in its pristine
natural environment,
are gained from the top
of the dam at 1,130 m
(3,707 ft). Nearby are
two waterfalls.*

Europabrücke, the highest road bridge in Europe

Brenner ⑮

Road map B5.

AT AN ALTITUDE of 1,374 m (4,508 ft), the Brenner Pass is the lowest passage across the Eastern Alps, and as such one of the most easily accessible routes connecting northern Europe with Italy. Separating the Stubai Alps from the Zillertal Alps, the pass was originally used by the Romans as a trade and military route. A highway suitable for carriage traffic was built in 1772, and the first trans-alpine railway line was opened here in 1867. Today the motorway leading across the wide saddle of the Brenner also boasts the highest and most impressive road bridge in Europe, the Europabrücke, 815 m (2,674 ft) long.

Stubaital ⑯

Road map B4. 🚌 ℹ️ *Fulpmes, Bahnstraße 17 (05225) 62235.* 🌐 *www.stubai.at*

TRAVELLING ON the Brenner motorway from Innsbruck towards Italy you will pass the Stubai Alps to your right,

a high ridge massif with few valleys. The lowest route into the centre of the massif runs along the Stubaital (Stubai Valley), with its busy tourist resorts of Fulpmes and Neustift. The highest peak of the Stubai Alps, Zuckerhütl (Little Sugar Loaf), rises to 3,507 m (11,506 ft). The Stubaital is a very quiet place, particularly when compared with the neighbouring Zillertal, winding its way above a busy motorway. The Stubai glacier provides excellent conditions for all-year skiing and walking.

Fulpmes, a popular tourist centre in the Stubaital

Ötztal ⑰

Road map B4. 🚌 🅿️ ℹ️ *Ötz, Hauptstraße 66 (05252) 6669.*

FOLLOWING THE course of the Ötztaler Ache, a tributary of the Inn river, is the long valley of Ötztal. At its southern end, near the border with Italy, rises the Ötztaler Alpen range, with many peaks above 3,500 m (11,500 ft): the Wildspitze at 3,774 m (12,381 ft) is Tyrol's highest summit.

Nestling within the Ötztaler Alps is also the highest parish in Austria, the ski resort of Obergurgl at 1,927 m (6,322 ft). The largest settlement in the lower part of Ötztal is **Ötz**, an old village with attractive, colourful houses. The paintings on the Star Inn date from 1573 and 1615. On a steep slope stands the church of St George and St Nicholas, which retains some original Gothic features, including a vault and portals.

The largest town at the upper end of the Ötz Valley is **Längenfeld**, where you find the church of St Catherine. It has a 74-m (243-ft) high Gothic tower, a decorative west portal and a Baroque interior.

Ötztal's administrative centre is the old Tyrolean village of **Sölden**. There is good skiing on Tiefenbachferner and superb views from Gaislacher Kogel and Wilder Mann.

In 1991, a frozen human body was discovered on the Italian side of the Ötztal Alps. Although over 5,000 years old, Ötzi, as he was named, was perfectly preserved by the ice, along with some 70 artifacts.

Seefeld ⑱

Road map B4. 🅿️ 🎿 *3,000.* ℹ️ *Klosterstraße 43 (05212) 2313.*

THIS SMALL town, occupying a large sunny plateau, is one of the most attractive places near Innsbruck. It is a smart resort, with elegant shops along a wide promenade, and boasts a variety of attractions. In the 1964 and 1976 Winter Olympics, Seefeld was the venue for all the Nordic skiing contests,

◁ A man-made lake at the foot of Zillertaler Alpen

enhancing the town's prosperity and reputation. The local cross-country skiing trails are the longest in the Alps, measuring some 250 km (155 miles).

At the centre of Seefeld stands the huge 15th-century church of St Oswald while at the western end of the town is a chapel built on the orders of Archduke Leopold V to house a crucifix dating from the early 16th century and said to have miraculous powers. The crucifix stands within the altarpiece of this small, circular building with a Renaissance portal and onion dome.

Visitors to Seefeld can also enjoy a trip to the casino, one of the largest in Austria.

View of Zugspitze from the Ehrwald side

Ehrwald ⑲

Road map B4. 🚌 🚉 🏔 *2,500.*
ℹ️ *Kirchplatz 1 (05673) 2395.*

NESTLING BELOW the western side of Zugspitze (2,965 m/ 9728 ft), the highest peak of the Bavarian Alps, is the resort village of Ehrwald. On the German side of the mountain is the resort of Garmisch-Partenkirchen, the most popular winter sports centre in that area. Several Austrian and German resorts, including Garmisch-Partenkirchen and Ehrwald, have joined up to form one vast skiing area.

The summit of Zugspitze can be reached from both the German and the Austrian sides. From Ehrwald, you take the cable car from the lower station of Ehrwald/ Obermoos. The upper station affords magnificent views. To the south, beyond the mountain ranges of Kaiser-

gebirge, Karwendelgebirge and Dachstein, you can see the snow-covered peaks of the High Tauern. To the east, there are the Arlberg mountains with Silvretta and Rätikon, with the peaks of the Appenzeller Alpen in between, and the Allgäu and Ammergau mountains in the distance. To the north, Bavaria can be seen.

Clemens Krauss, the founder of the famous Vienna New Year's Day Concerts, lived in Ehrwald and lies buried here.

Reutte ⑳

Road map B4. 🏔 *6,000.*
ℹ️ *Untermarkt 34 (05672) 62336.*

REUTTE IS THE largest town in the Außerfern district, a remote area that was cut off from the world for a considerable time: it is said that the first car arrived here only in 1947. Reutte can be reached from Innsbruck via the Fern Pass, a route first used in Roman times. In the valley of the Lech river, it is today the main town and trade centre of the region. In medieval times it grew rich on the salt trade, and to this day it has some lovely town houses with oriel windows, open staircases and painted façades. Many of the paintings are by Johann Jakob Zeiller,

the best-known member of an artistic family that settled in Reutte in the 17th and 18th centuries – they once lived at No. 1 Zeiller Platz.

The 15th-century convent church of St Anna features several interesting works of art. In the main altarpiece is a picture of the Madonna with Child and St Anna (c.1515) and two vast figures of St Magnus and St Afra dating from the early 18th century.

The **Heimatmuseum** (regional museum) has a fine collection of paintings by outstanding masters of the Baroque, mainly of the Zeiller family members, as well as exhibits associated with transport and salt mining.

Specimens representative of the local flora can be seen in the **Alpenblumengarten**, an alpine flower garden on top of the Hahnenkamm, at a height of about 1,700 m (5,577 ft) above sea level.

🏛 **Heimatmuseum**
Grünes Haus, Untermarkt 25.
📞 *(05672) 72304.* ⏱ *May–Oct: 10am–noon, 2–5pm Tue–Sun.*

ENVIRONS: A short distance east of Reutte is the beautiful, 5-km (3-mile) long **Plansee**, where one of the small pleasure boats can take you on a cruise on the tranquil waters. In winter the entire lake freezes over and becomes one giant ice-skating rink.

Plansee, a tranquil, picturesque lake near Reutte

Warth, a town situated within the most famous winter sports region

Elbigenalp ㉑

Road map A4. 850.
(05634) 5315.

THE LECH RIVER valley, which is parallel to the Inn river valley and snakes between mountain passes, cuts a deep ravine between the Allgäuer Alps and the Lechtal Alps. About half-way between the towns of Reutte and Warth lies Elbigenalp, a small village worth visiting for the local **Nikolauskirche** (church of St Nicholas). Built in the 14th century, the church's oldest surviving parts include the Gothic tower, presbytery and font. It was altered in the Baroque style, and the vault and wall paintings as well as the Stations of the Cross are the work of the artistic Zeiller family, who lived in Reutte.

St Martin's cemetery chapel in Elbigenalp has interesting original Gothic frescoes depicting scenes from the life of St Magdalene and the *Dance of Death* by Anton Falger.

Lech am Arlberg ㉒

Road map A4. 1,400.
(05583) 2161–0.
www.lech-zuers.at

THIS SMALL resort is situated on a large plateau at an altitude of 1,450 m (4,757 ft), not far from the source of the Lech river. Lech is regarded as one of Austria's most beautiful and most elegant mountain resorts. In order to protect the natural environment, some years ago the local authorities drastically limited the available accommodation, thus creating an exclusive resort. The fame of the resort spread around the world and many celebrities and royals began to spend their winter holidays in Lech, including the late Diana, Princess of Wales.

The town's development has been closely associated with the construction of the Arlberg and Flexen passes, which made Lech accessible in the winter months. Lifts and cable cars were built, and the vast snowy slopes of the Arlberg began to attract winter sports enthusiasts. Summer, too, can be very pleasant here, and there are many beautiful trails for walking or mountain cycling. Sights to see include the 15th-century Gothic **church of St Nicholas**, with an even older tower. In addition, there are swanky hotels, chic shops, smart cafés and restaurants, which combine to make Lech a tourist magnet for the wealthy.

Lech has joined Zürs, Stuben and St Anton to form a large single skiing region.

Zürs am Arlberg ㉓

Road map A4. 130.
(05583) 2245.

ZÜRS, A TINY resort some 6 km (4 miles) south of Lech, lies at an altitude of 1,716 m (5,630 ft). Along with

A fabulous scenery of snowy mountain peaks rising above Zürs am Arlberg

neighbouring Lech, Zürs places a great emphasis on the protection of the natural environment. As a rule, the few hotels and pensions accept only regular guests in their very limited number of rooms. The exclusive nature of the resort, its elegant cafés, restaurants and a famous discothèque provide truly world-class après-ski entertainment, while the expansive ski slopes and the fairly heavy snowfalls over many months attract dedicated winter sports enthusiasts. Austria's first chair lifts were built in Zürs in 1937 and the first skiing competitions were held here as early as 1906. Lifts and cable cars take you to a number of excellent viewing points.

Lünersee, a reservoir lake at the foot of Schesaplana

Arlberg **24**

See pp256–7.

Ischgl, one of Austria's most attractive skiing resorts

Ischgl **25**

Road map A5. **1,500.**
(05444) 52660.

I SCHGL, ON THE Trisanna river at the eastern end of the Silvrettastraße, is one of the loveliest Austrian resorts. An international ski centre, at an altitude of 1,377 m (4,518 ft), it provides access to 200 km (120 miles) of ski runs and 40 lifts within the Silvretta range on the Austrian–Swiss border. The town is also an ideal starting point for a drive along the Silvrettahochalpenstraße, a hairpin mountain road, often snow-covered – and therefore closed – from November until late May, which connects the Montafon Valley where Schruns is the best-known resort – and the Ill river with the Trisanna Valley. The road drops by 1,000 m (3,280 ft) over just 15 km (9 miles).

The area around the Silvretta-Stausee, a reservoir on the Bielerhöhe Pass at 2,036 m (6,680 ft), has been made a national park; the ski runs in the Silvretta massif start here. The most beautiful views are to be had from Hohes Rad, 2,934 m (9,626 ft). The high mountain section of Silvrettastraße ends in Galtür, a lovely village on the Ballunspitze.

Lünersee **26**

Road map A5.

L ÜNERSEE LIES at the foot of the Schesaplana peak (2,965 m/9,728 ft), at an altitude of 1,907 m (6,257 ft). Once this was the largest lake in Eastern Austria, surrounded by rugged mountains crisscrossed with ravines. The dam built here in 1958 raised the water level by 27 m (89 ft), creating an artificial reservoir that now powers Lünersee and Rodund power stations.

Bludenz **27**

Road map A4. **15,000.**
Werdenbergerstraße 42 (05552) 62170. **www.bludenz.at**
Chocolate Festival (early Jul).

B EAUTIFULLY situated at the confluence of five alpine valleys, the town of Bludenz is now a popular resort with excellent skiing areas in its environs. An 10th-century document survives in which Otto I gives the Bishop of Chur a church "in loco Plutenes". During the reign of Friedrich IV the Poor, the town became an administrative centre and power base for the region.

Despite several devastating fires, Bludenz still has some interesting historic sights. The oldest building is **Oberes Tor** (Upper Gate), which houses the local history museum. Inside St Lawrence church (1514) are two original altars made from black marble and two paintings (1510) showing the Marriage of the Virgin Mary and the Visitation. The seat of the regional authorities is Gayenhofen castle, a medieval building remodelled in Baroque style in 1643 by Franz Andrä von Sternbach.

Today, the town is permeated by chocolate smells from the Suchard factory, producers of the famous confectionery and organizers of an annual chocolate festival.

The octagonal tower of the Laurentiuskirche in Bludenz

Arlberg ㉔

THE ARLBERG Pass in the Eastern Alps is part of the European watershed between the catchment areas of the North Sea, the Black Sea, the tributaries of the Rhine and the Danube. Arlberg used to be completely cut off from the rest of the country, oriented more towards Germany and Switzerland, until the railway tunnel was built in 1880–84, connecting Vorarlberg with the rest of Austria. The tunnel, at an altitude of 1,310 m (4,298 ft), measures 10,238 m (33,589 ft) in length, and was for many years the longest in Austria. Today, the Arlberg region has some of the country's most exclusive ski resorts.

Valluga ⑦
The breathtaking view extending from the summit at 2,809 m (9,216 ft) embraces the Rätikon Mountains, the Montafon Valley as well as the Brenner, Ötztal and Stubai Alps.

Flexenpass ⑥
The pass is surrounded by the Rätikon mountain peaks, including Zimbaspitze and Schesaplana. Thanks to a system of avalanche defences, the road across remains passable in winter.

Feldkirch

Lech

Stuben ⑤
This quiet village at the foot of the Albonagrat (2,334 m/ 7,658 ft) has ski runs leading to St. Anton. The name ("cosy living room") refers to the cabins from where travellers set off on the mountain trails.

Arlbergtunnel ④
The new road tunnel underneath the Arlberg Pass, 14 km (9 miles) long, was the longest in the world when it opened in 1978.

Landeck ①

Schloss Landeck, built in about 1200 and rebuilt after a fire, has retained its original grand hall with a late-Gothic vault, and a chapel with early 16th-century frescoes. Today, the castle is the home of the local folk museum.

TIPS FOR VISITORS

Length of the route: *45 km (28 miles).*

Stopping-off points: *the hotel by the hospice in St. Christoph offers accommodation. There are many restaurants and excellent shops in St. Anton am Arlberg.*

KEY

▤	Motorway
▬	Suggested route
▭	Scenic route
═	Other road
∼	River, lake
▯ ▪	Tunnel
✹	Viewpoint

0 km   5

0 miles   5

Innsbruck

Davos

S16 E60

316 E60

188

171

315

① ② ③

St. Christoph ③

The town's small statue of St Christopher, from the old hospice in St. Christoph, was replaced with a new sculpture after fire damage in 1957. The hospice itself is today a luxury hotel. Austria's first regular ski-school was founded in this town in 1901.

St. Anton am Arlberg ②

The largest tourist resort in Arlberg, St. Anton is surrounded by numerous ski trails, and good snow conditions are guaranteed throughout the season.

Bregenzer Wald ㉘

THE BREGENZER WALD (Bregenz Forest)
occupies the northern part of Vorarlberg and
extends along the Bregenzer Ache valley. This
region has maintained much of its individual
character. Its inhabitants cherish their traditions,
and the architecture, the national costumes and
the dialect spoken here differ from those found
in the rest of the country. Bregenz Forest has
many picturesque resorts with excellent facilities
for visitors. Apart from Bregenz itself, two larger
urban centres have become established on its
borders – Dornbirn, and Feldkirch, the "gateway to Austria", with its beautifully preserved old town.

Lindau

Schwarzenberg ⑥
This was the home town
of Angelika Kauffmann, a
prominent artist of
the Neo-Classicist
period. Her paintings
depicting Christ's
apostles and
disciples can be
seen in the local
Holy Trinity
church.

Ammenegg ⑦
From the forecourt of the
Sonnblick Inn in Ammen-
egg visitors can enjoy
lovely views which, on a
clear day, extend as far as
Lake Constance and the
peaks of the Swiss Alps.

Feldkirch

Dornbirn ⑧
The largest town in Vor-
arlberg, this is a centre for
the textile industry. The
Museum *inatura* houses
modern displays on the
natural environment and
the history of the region.

ANGELIKA KAUFFMANN

Angelika Kauffmann, a Swiss painter
(1741–1807) of idealized portraits in
sentimental or Neo-Classical style, was
associated with German, English and
Italian artistic circles. She left many works
in Schwarzenberg, where she had
family links. The local church has an
altarpiece by her and also a small
bust. More works by this celebrated
artist can be seen in the Vorarlberger
Landesmuseum in Bregenz.

Rappenlochschlucht ⑨
The road to the Rappenloch
gorge runs steeply uphill along
the Dornbirner Ache stream,
and ends at a reservoir.

Bezau ⑤
This picturesque village set among orchards has a lovely church, dating from 1771, and a small but interesting museum devoted to the region's folk art.

Mellau ④
A quiet village on the Bregenzer Ache, Mellau is famous for its wooden houses with shingle-clad roofs, characteristically adorned with flowers.

Bregenzer Ache ③
The valley of Bregenzer Ache, running from Lechtaler Alpen, is the main axis of the Bregenzer Forest. The river flows between steep rock faces and gentle hills, past pleasant villages, down a long winding gorge, on its way to Bodensee (Lake Constance).

Schröcken ②
The church in Schröcken, at the foot of the Widderstein (2,533 m/8,310 ft), has a richly decorated interior and beautiful stained-glass windows.

Hochtannbergpass ①
The pass between Schröcken and Warth winds its scenic way along the upper Bregenzer Ache, and reaches its highest point near Schröcken at 1,679 m (5,508 ft).

KEY

▬	Suggested route
▬	Scenic route
=	Other road
=	River, lake
✳	Viewpoint

TIPS FOR VISITORS

Length of the route: *50 km (31 miles).*
Stopping-off points: *there are restaurants and accommodation in Dornbirn, the largest town.*
Further attractions: Heimat-museum Schwarzenberg, *Kleberhaus.* ☎ *(05512) 2967.* ◯ *May–Sep: 2–4pm Tue, Thu, Sat, Sun; Oct: 2–4pm Tue, Sat.* 🎨

0 km   3

0 miles   3

Au
Schoppernau
200

Bregenz ㉙

THE CAPITAL of Vorarlberg since 1923, Bregenz is strategically – and attractively – situated on the eastern shore of Bodensee (Lake Constance), at the edge of the Rhine valley and the foot of the Austrian and Swiss Alps. It is a meeting point of four countries: Austria, Germany, Switzerland and the Principality of Liechtenstein. The Romans established the settlement of Brigantium, and later it became the Alemanni town of Brancantia. In 1451 and 1523 Bregenz came under Habsburg rule, and during the Thirty Years' War, it was destroyed by the Swedes. Attractions in Bregenz include walks on the nearby Pfänder massif, and boat trips out on the lake.

View of Bregenz, on the shores of Lake Constance

Exploring Bregenz

Oberstadt (upper town) is the oldest part of Bregenz, with a number of well-preserved historic buildings and the remains of 13th-century fortifications. Innenstadt (inner city) is much newer. It has a theatre and an interesting regional museum. The promenades along Lake Constance, always shrouded in a gentle mist, are worth exploring, as are the grounds of the popular Bregenz summer festivals.

Vorarlberger Landesmuseum

Kornmarktplatz 1.
(05574) 46050. *9am–noon, 2–5pm Tue–Sun.*

The Vorarlberg Regional Museum holds collections of prehistoric relics, artifacts dating from the Roman time of the settlement of Brigantium and objects from the days of the Alemanni settlers, all found in Bregenz and its vicinity. A separate department is devoted to regional handicrafts and customs, old weaponry, coins and medals, as well as regional costumes. One particularly fascinating exhibit is the collection of portable organs. The museum also has an art gallery which holds many beautiful portraits by Angelika Kauffmann (1741–1807), whose family came from Bregenzer Wald *(see p258)*. Other interesting exhibits are early artifacts, Roman and Gothic sculptures and paintings, old altarpieces, and beautiful gold and silver ornaments. The jewels of this museum are the 9th-century stone tablet from Lauterach and the early 16th-century crucifix from the collegiate church in Mehrerau.

Rathaus

Rathausstraße 4.

The former granary built in 1686 became the town's chancellery in 1720 and, in 1810, the seat of the town's authorities. It remains the town hall to this day.

Renaissance altarpiece of 1610, in Seekapelle St. Georg

Seekapelle St. Georg

Rathausstraße.

The small chapel of St George, known as the Lakeside Chapel, stands close to the church of the same name. Its walls, once lapped by the lake, are now separated from the water by a street and a railway line. The chapel was built in 1445 and altered in the Baroque style in 1690–98, but it has preserved a Renaissance altarpiece, dating from 1615. Depicted at its centre is the Madonna at the foot of the Cross; the two small side niches contain scenes from the Passion.

Martinsturm

Martinsplatz. **Vorarlberger Militärmuseum Martinsturm** Martinsgasse 3B. *(05574) 46632.* *May–Oct.*

The rectangular St Martin's Tower, the symbol of Bregenz,

The Martinsturm, topped with a Baroque dome

was probably built in the 14th century on earlier Romanesque foundations. Its present look and its staircase date from 1599, while the Baroque cupola was added at a later date. With its Venetian windows and overall muted colour scheme the tower is reminiscent of Moorish architecture. It houses a small museum with displays of arms and weaponry.

In the adjacent St Martin's Chapel, recently discovered frescoes can be seen, dating from 1362 and depicting Christ in Mandorla with the symbols of the four evangelists and portraits of the chapel founders, members of the Monfort family

🏛 Altes Rathaus
Oberstadt.
The Old Town Hall, built in 1662 by Michael Kuen, was the seat of the Bregenz municipal authorities until the 19th century. This solid, half-timbered structure stands in the centre of Oberstadt, close to the former town gate, Unteres Tor (Lower Gate). A relief depicts Epona, the Celtic

The 17th-century, half-timbered Altes Rathaus

goddess of agriculture who is shown on horseback, holding a horn of plenty.

🏛 Zisterzienserkloster Mehrerau
Mehrerauerstraße 66. 📞 (05574) 71461. ⏰ 8:30–11am, 4–5pm Mon–Sat, 3–4pm Sun. ✎
To the west of the city centre stands the Zisterzienserkloster Mehrerau, the Cistercian monastery that has been a centre of spiritual and intellectual life since the 11th century.

VISITORS' CHECKLIST

Road map A4.
🚶 28,000. 🚉 🚌
ℹ Bahnhofstraße 14 (05574) 49590.
🌐 www.bregenz.at
🎭 Bregenzer Festspiele (mid-Jul–mid-Aug).

The church and monastery complex, originally built for the Benedictines and subsequently taken over by the Cistercians, was remodelled in 1740 in the Baroque style by Franz Anton Beer; the new tower was built using material from the previous Romanesque basilica. It was destroyed in the Napoleonic wars, rebuilt in 1855 and renovated in the 20th century. Inside, two pictures survive with the Stations of the Cross and two late-Gothic statues of the Madonna. The late-Gothic altar in the capitular room dates from 1582.

Adjacent to the reconstructed church and the Romanesque crypt there is now a secondary school, a monastery and a sanatorium.

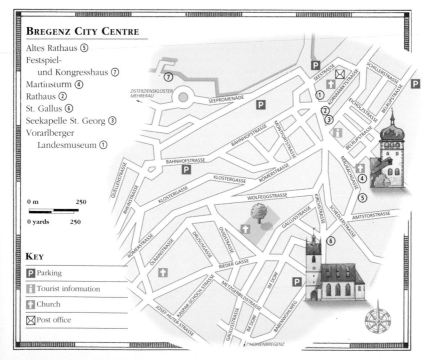

BREGENZ CITY CENTRE

Altes Rathaus ⑤
Festspiel- und Kongresshaus ⑦
Martinsturm ④
Rathaus ②
St. Gallus ⑥
Seekapelle St. Georg ③
Vorarlberger Landesmuseum ①

0 m   250
0 yards   250

KEY

🅿 Parking
ℹ Tourist information
✝ Church
✉ Post office

↟ St. Gallus
Kirchplatz 3.

Opposite the city centre, on the banks of the Thalbach stream, stands the Stadtpfarr-kirche St. Gallus (the parish church of St Gallus). According to legend, a previous church on this site had been consecrated by Gallus, an Irish missionary who arrived here in the 7th century. The present church was consecrated in 1318, and the sandstone gate tower in front of it was added in the 15th century. Another tower was added in 1672, and in 1738 the church was altered in the Baroque style, to plans by Anton Beer. At that time the nave was raised and a chapel was added in the transept.

The rather modest interior of the church is typical of Vorarlberg's ecclesiastical style and contrasts sharply with the styles of Tyrol and Bavaria, where Baroque opulence is much more in evidence. The main altarpiece includes statues of the saints Gallus, Peter, Paul and Ulrich, while the side chapel has figures of saints Magnus and Nicholas. St Magnus, an 8th-century Benedictine monk from St. Gallen, is the patron saint of the Allgäu, the region between the Tyrol and Vorarlberg; St Nicholas is said to keep a careful watch over the navigation on Bodensee. The beautiful stalls in the presbytery are made from walnut wood. They have deep inlays and the backrests are decorated on the outside with the effigies of saints.

Decorative detail on the wall of Stadt-pfarrkirche St. Gallus

⊞ Festspiel- und Kongresshaus
Platz der Wiener Symphoniker 1.
☎ (05574) 4130.

The Festspielgelände (festival grounds) consists of a complex of buildings created specifically for the Bregenz arts festival that has been held every year since 1946, from late July until late August. The festival events feature theatre and opera perform-ances, as well as symphony concerts and fine art exhib-itions. Since 1955, the shows have been staged at the Theater am Kornmarkt, a building in the city centre erected in 1838 as a gran-ary and converted into a theatre in 1955.

In 1980, a modern festival and con-gress complex was opened, including show and concert halls, exhibition rooms and a congress centre. The most spectacular of the festival venues, however, is the famous Seebühne, a floating stage extending far onto the lake. Shows and concerts are staged here and watched by the public on the shore. The summer programme includes opera, operetta, musical and ballet. Behind the festival grounds is the Spielcasino Bregenz.

Gateway of the ruined Hohen-bregenz fortress

♨ Hohenbregenz
The Hohenbregenz fortress, whose ruins stand to this day on Gebhardsberg, was built in the 10th century. In 1338, the recorded owner of the castle was Hugo de Montfort. In 1451, following the death of the last ruler of that line, the castle, together with the town and Bregenz province, was bought by Sigismund of Tyrol. In 1647, the castle was blown up by the Swedish troops of General Wrangel during the Thirty Years' War, leaving only ruins. The original parts still standing today are the gateway, walls, barbican and a single turret.

In 1723, a chapel devoted to the saints Gebhard and George was built on top of Gebhardsberg and it became a popular pilgrimage site. St Gebhard, a 10th-century Bishop of Constance, was the son of Ulrich of Bregenz, born in Hohenbregenz.

ENVIRONS: At the foot of the **Pfänder** (1,065 m/3,494 ft), southeast of the present town, stood the Roman settlement of Brigantium. Today, this area is a favourite destination for walkers; you can also reach the top of the hill by cable car. From this summit, there are magnificent views extending across Bodensee (Lake Constance) and all of Bregenz. Far to the south, the ranges of the Allgäuer Alps can be seen on a clear day, as well as the ice-covered Schesa-plana massif, the deep ravine of the Rhine and the Swiss peaks of Altmann and Säntis.

Seebühne, the floating stage on Lake Constance

Bodensee ③⓪

Road map A4. 🚊 🚌 🛈 *Boden-
see-Alpenrhein Tourismus, Bregenz,
Römerstraße 2 (05574) 43443.*
W *www.bodensee-alpenrhein.at*

BODENSEE, or Lake Constance
as it is also known, is one
of the largest and best-known
European lakes. It divides
its waters between the three
countries surrounding it:
Austria, Germany and Switzerland. Austria actually only
claims a very small part of it:
the total area of the lake is
538.5 sq km (208 sq miles),
of which only 38 sq km
(14.7 sq miles) is Austrian.
Bodensee is 74 km (44 miles)
long, and as such the largest
lake in the Alps. Once the
lake was much larger, but
with time deposits carried by
the Rhine have reduced its
size. The Rhine flows into the
lake in a broad delta, wholly
in Austrian territory. Having
passed through the entire
length of Bodensee, it emerges in a waterfall as a turbulent mountain river near
Schaffhausen, in Switzerland.
The countryside around the
lake benefits from a pleasant,
moderate climate. Even before
World War II, Bodensee was
considered to be one of
Europe's most polluted lakes,
just as the Rhine was one of
the dirtiest rivers. However,
for several years now it has
met all the standards set for
environmental protection.

Today, Bodensee forms not
so much a border as a link
between the countries that lie
on its shores. For Austria it is
a highly convenient transport
route to western Europe,
while for the inhabitants of
the surrounding towns and
villages, as well as for the
visitors that arrive here from
the neighbouring countries in
great numbers every summer,
it provides excellent facilities
for water sports and relaxation.

The mountains around the
town of Bregenz extend right
up to the water, creating a
picturesque setting for the
countless artistic events that
take place here, such as the
Bregenz Spring and the internationally acclaimed Bregenz
Festival. Many performances
take place on the famous
Seebühne or floating stage.

A number of interesting
towns line the shores of
Bodensee, including Lindau,
the flower island of Mainau,
and Friedrichshafen on the
German side, which can be
reached by ferry or pleasure
craft sailing from Bregenz.

**17th-century lace in the Stickerei-
museum in Lustenau**

Lustenau ③①

Road map A4. 🏘 20,000. 🚊 🚌
🛈 *Rathausstraße 1 (05577) 81810.*

AFAIRLY LARGE town, Lustenau
lies 5 km (3 miles) north
of the mouth of the Rhine as
it joins Bodensee, on the
border with Switzerland. It is
famous for its beautiful
embroidery and lace-making,
popular throughout Austria.

It was at Lustenau that the
Romans under the leadership
of Emperor Constantine II
defeated the Alemanni tribes
who had risen up against the
empire. The earliest historic
records date from 887, when
the settlement belonged to
the Carolingians. Until 1806,
it was a free territory within
the empire. In 1814, after the
Congress of Vienna, Lustenau
came under Austrian rule.

During the 19th century,
the town developed into one
of Austria's most important
centres for the textile industry, known primarily for its
linen products. One of the
most interesting sights in
Lustenau is the **Stickereimuseum** (Embroidery
Museum) at No. 20 Ponten-
straße, which exhibits both
early hand-made and modern
machine-made embroidery,
and some early embroidery
machines. Also worth visiting
is the Rhine Museum at No. 4
Höchsterstraße.

🏛 Stickereimuseum
Pontenstraße 20. ☎ *(05577) 83234.*
◯ *8am–noon, 2–5pm Mon–Thu,
8am–noon Fri.*

A picturesque sunset over the vast expanse of Bodensee

CARINTHIA & EAST TYROL

C ARINTHIA AND EAST TYROL, *Austria's two southernmost regions, are bordered by Slovenia and Italy in the south, and Styria and Salzburger Land to the east and north. Between them they have many attractions, including the Carinthian lakes and the Hohe Tauern National Park. East Tyrol is separate from the rest of Tyrol, and has closer transport and cultural links with Carinthia.*

The earliest inhabitants of what is now Kärnten (Carinthia) were the Celtic Carnuni. In the 1st century AD it was part of the Roman province of Noricum, and in the 6th century was overrun by the Slav tribe of the Carantani, from whom it probably took its name. Although Carinthia belonged to the Habsburgs from 1335, a Slav national minority has survived in the area to this day. After World War I the newly-formed state of Yugoslavia tried to annex part of Carinthia from the defeated Austro-Hungarian Empire, but a plebiscite kept the region with Austria. The beauty of its landscape and its pleasant, Mediterranean climate attract many foreign visitors to Carinthia, and numerous Austrians also have second homes here. The most scenic route in the Austrian Alps, the Großglockner Hochalpenstraße, separates Carinthia from the East Tyrol, passing through Salzburger Land. Carinthia's two main towns are its capital Klagenfurt, and Villach.

After World War I, the southern part of Tyrol (Südtirol) became an autonomous province of Italy. Thus, geographically isolated from other parts of the Tyrol, East Tyrol (Osttirol) grew closer to its Carinthian neighbour than it was to the Tyrolean administration in Innsbruck. The entire province is surrounded by high mountain ranges and much of it is home to the Hohe Tauern National Park. The administrative centre of East Tyrol is Lienz.

A giant relief model of the province of Carinthia in the Schillerpark pavilion in Villach *(see p274)*

◁ The hilltop fortress of Hochosterwitz, poised like an eagle's nest above the St. Veit valley

Exploring Carinthia and East Tyrol

HIGH MOUNTAIN peaks that descend right down to expansive lakes make these southernmost regions of Austria a paradise for visitors. Excellent on-shore facilities attract water sports enthusiasts, while the mountain glaciers enable committed skiers to enjoy the slopes even in summer. The loveliest parts of the region are the scenic route of Großglockner Hochalpenstraße and the Hohe Tauern National Park. While Carinthia is a lake district, East Tyrol is an inaccessible region of high mountains. In winter, cars need to be properly equipped, and not all roads are passable.

The Hohe Tauern National Park, one of the great attractions of the region

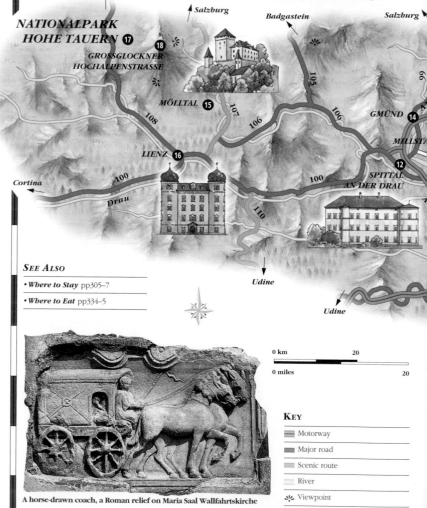

NATIONALPARK HOHE TAUERN ⑰

⑱

GROSSGLOCKNER HOCHALPENSTRASSE

Kitzbühel

Salzburg

Badgastein

Salzburg

MÖLLTAL ⑮

108   *107*

106

105

GMÜND ⑭

MILLST

LIENZ ⑯

100

100

⑫

SPITTAL AN DER DRAU

Cortina

Drau

110

Udine

Udine

SEE ALSO

- *Where to Stay* pp305–7
- *Where to Eat* pp334–5

0 km		20
0 miles		20

A horse-drawn coach, a Roman relief on Maria Saal Wallfahrtskirche

KEY

   Motorway

   Major road

   Scenic route

   River

   ⚜ Viewpoint

GETTING THERE

Villach, in Carinthia, is one of Austria's most important road transport hubs. The southern motorway which comes from Vienna passes through Villach and Klagenfurt, Carinthia's capital, which also has a small passenger airport. The easiest way to reach Lienz, in East Tyrol, is via Carinthia. Road and railway tunnels through the mountain ranges provide convenient transport links.

Church in Gratschach, at the foot of Landskron

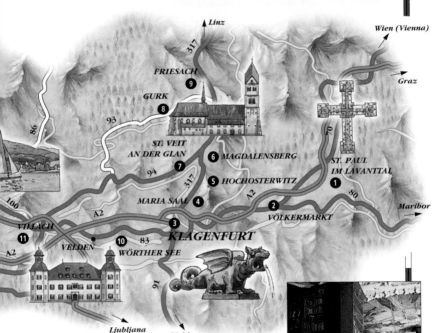

Linz

Wien (Vienna)

Graz

FRIESACH ❾

GURK ❽

ST. VEIT AN DER GLAN ❼

❻ **MAGDALENSBERG**

ST. PAUL IM LAVANTTAL ❶

❺ **HOCHOSTERWITZ**

MARIA SAAL ❹

❷

VÖLKERMARKT

Maribor

❸

KLAGENFURT

VILLACH ⓫

VELDEN

❿ **WÖRTHER SEE**

83

Ljubljana

Ljubljana

SIGHTS AT A GLANCE

Friesach ❾
Gmünd ⓮
Gurk ❽
Hochosterwitz ❺
Klagenfurt pp270–73 ❸
Lienz ⓰
Magdalensberg ❻
Maria Saal ❹
Millstatt ⓭
Mölltal ⓯
Hobe Tauern National Park (pp278–9) ⓱

St. Paul im Lavanttal ❶
St. Veit an der Glan ❼
Spittal an der Drau ⓬
Villach ⓫
Völkermarkt ❷

Excursions

Großglockner Hochalpenstraße ⓲
Around Wörther See ❿

The marvellous library in the abbey of St. Paul im Lavanttal

Late 15th-century fresco in the abbey church, St. Paul im Lavanttal

St. Paul im Lavanttal ❶

Road map E5. 🏛 *4,000.* 🚍 🚹
🚹 *Hauptstraße 10 (04357) 201722.*

On the banks of the Lavant river stands one of the largest churches in Austria, the **Benedictine Abbey of St Paul**. Within the abbey complex is a well-preserved Romanesque church. The apse is decorated with reliefs showing the Adoration of the Magi and the enthroned Christ. Frescoes behind the main altar depict the founders of the abbey and various saints. The abbey museum also houses many magnificent works of art, including early chasubles, an 11th-century cross-shape reliquary that once belonged to Queen Adelaide, and an art collection with paintings by Peter Paul Rubens and Martin Johann Schmidt, and superb woodcuts by Albrecht Dürer and Rembrandt.

Benedictine Abbey of St Paul
Hauptstraße 1. 📞 *(04357) 201922.*
⭘ *May–Oct: 9am–5pm.* 📷 🏛 🅿

Völkermarkt ❷

Road map E5. 🏛 *12,000.* 🚍
🚹 *Hauptplatz 1 (04232) 257147.*

This town lies on the banks of a reservoir created by damming the Drau river, 25 km (16 miles) east of the Carinthian capital, Klagenfurt. It grew up around the bridge across the Drau and the 12th-century church of St Rupert, whose Romanesque tower still rises above the town. The **Kirche St. Magdalena** (church of Mary Magdalene), built in 1240 and altered in the 15th century, has a lovely late-Romanesque west portal. Its interior is late-Gothic, with some earlier features, such as the 14th-century frescoes next to the entrance. In one of the side chapels and in the presbytery, details of late-Gothic frescoes can be seen.

In Völkermarkt's Hauptplatz stands a former ducal palace, now the seat of the local authorities, and an arcaded late-Gothic town hall.

The Romanesque portal of Kirche St. Magdalena in Völkermarkt

Klagenfurt ❸

See pp270–73.

Maria Saal ❹

Road map E5. 🏛 *4,200.* 🚍 🚹
🚹 *Am Platze 7 (04223) 2214.*

The first church was erected at Maria Saal in the 8th century, and a secondary Christianization was conducted from here, which is why it became known as the cradle of Carinthia. The pilgrimage church, built in 1430–56, has a stone statue of the Virgin Mary in the high altar from 1420. On the outer walls of the church are two remarkable Roman reliefs, one depicting the cart of Death, the other showing Achilles pulling the body of Hector behind the chariot. The relief on the south wall, showing the Coronation of the Virgin Mary, is the work of Hans Valkenauer.

Opposite the church is a late-Gothic octagonal mortuary and the cemetery chapel. It has beautiful 15th-century vault frescoes with the family tree of Jesus, as well as a late-Gothic altar with scenes from the life of St Mary and an altar of St George slaying the dragon. The Sachsen-Kapelle (Saxon Chapel) is devoted to St Modestus, who founded the church and whose tombstone has survived to this day.

Archaeological excavations near Maria Saal, at the site of the Roman town of Virunum, the capital of Noricum, have yielded relics including the Bronze-Age carved stone throne of the Princes of Carinthia *(see p38)*.

Hochosterwitz ❺

Road map E5. 📞 *(04213) 2020.*
⭘ *Apr, Oct: 9am–5pm; May–Sep: 8am–6pm.* 📷 📷 📷
🌐 *www.burg-hochosterwitz.or.at*

The fortress of Hochosterwitz, one of the symbols of Carinthia, perches on a rock 160 m (525 ft) high and is clearly visible from afar. Although the origins of the castle can be traced back to Roman times, it was built in the 16th century by Domenico dell'Allio. The present fortress is the result of Renaissance remodelling of earlier Roman-esque and Gothic structures. A fief from the mid-16th century, it later became the property of the Khevenhüller family, who own it to this day. Both fortress and fortifications are open to visitors; the access road runs in a loop between the old walls, passing through 14 gates. There is also a local museum.

The turreted fortress of Hochosterwitz is said to have inspired Walt Disney's animated version of *Snow White*.

The slopes of Magdalensberg, site of fascinating archaeological finds

Magdalensberg ❻

Road map E5. 👥 *2,200.* 🛈 *Deinsdorf 10, Pischeldorf (04224) 2213.*

On top of Magdalene Hill, rising 1,056 m (3,465 ft) from the Glan valley, are the remains of a town believed to be ancient Noricum, dating from the late-Celtic and early-Roman periods. Numerous finds, fragments of statues and the remains of old altars testify to the overlapping nature of Celtic and Roman cultures, with some later Christian additions.

Below the summit are the scant remains of a Roman temple and secular buildings dating from the 1st century AD. In spring and summer, the finds can be viewed in the open-air archaeological park and in the museum.

There is a small church on top of Magdalensberg, with a three-headed stone statue in the nave. This, as well as the hilltop location of the church, indicate the pagan, Celtic origins of the area.

St. Veit an der Glan ❼

Road map E5. 👥 *13,600.* 🚌 🚉 🛈 *Hauptplatz 1 (04212) 5555668.*

From 1174 to 1518, St. Veit an der Glan was the seat of the dukes of Spanheim, who ruled Carinthia during the Middle Ages; it then lost its position to Klagenfurt.

Many historic buildings are preserved in the old town around Hauptplatz, including the beautifully decorated **Rathaus** (town hall) of 1468, altered in the Baroque style. It has a lovely 16th-century arcaded courtyard. The 12th-century **Pfarrkirche St. Veit** (parish church of St Vitus) contains stone carvings from various periods; the altars are made in the Baroque style.

The most recent symbol of St. Veit is the unusual Kunsthotel Fuchs Palast, a modern hotel built in 1998 to designs by the outstanding artist, Ernst Fuchs. It is themed around

Baroque stuccowork on the Rathaus façade, St. Veit an der Glan

the signs of the zodiac. Also worth a visit is the Kärntner Eisenbahnmuseum (Carinthian Railway Museum), which has exhibits and documents on the history of the local railways.

Gurk ❽

Road map E5. 👥 *1,300.* 🚌 🛈 *Dr. Schnerichstraße 12 (04266) 812527.* **Cathedral** *(04266) 8236.*

Gurk, the former ecclesiastical capital of Carinthia, is dominated by a cathedral church, built in 1140–1200 by Bishop Roman and one of the most outstanding achievements of Austrian Romanesque architecture. The Gothic vestibule is adorned by stained-glass windows (1340) and Gothic frescoes. The original main portal and door have carved and painted Romanesque medallions. Inside it is a startling combination of pure Romanesque and Gothic, with net vaulting and a Baroque main altar. The striking crypt is supported by 100 columns.

The medieval fortress of Hochosterwitz, one of the symbols of Carinthia

Klagenfurt: Street-by-Street ❸

SITUATED AT THE eastern end of Wörther See, the warmest lake in Austria, Klagenfurt, the attractive provincial capital of Carinthia, is an important trade centre and transport hub founded in the 12th century. In 1544, it was almost entirely destroyed by fire and had to be rebuilt. Reconstruction was undertaken mainly by Italian architects and it is highly reminiscent of Italian towns in style. In the 16th century, Klagenfurt was the centre of the Counter-Reformation. During the Baroque period it was extended and partially rebuilt, although most of its historic buildings date from an earlier era. Its historic centre is the district around Alter Platz (Old Square).

Stadtpfarrkirche St. Egid
This Baroque church was built on the site of an earlier church destroyed by an earthquake in 1692. Its spire rises to 91 m (299 ft).

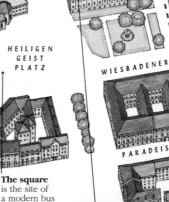

URSULINENGASSE

HERRENGASSE

HEILIGEN GEIST PLATZ

WIESBADENER STRASSE

PARADEISERGASSE

The square is the site of a modern bus station.

Heiligengeistkirche
The church of the Holy Spirit, built in 1355 and altered in 1660, features a beautiful altarpiece by Lorenzo Glaber and an interesting Baroque pulpit.

★ Landhaus
The 16th-century Landhaus boasts a lovely galleried inner courtyard and a magnificent heraldic hall with ceiling paintings by Josef Ferdinand Fromiller.

KEY

- - - Suggested route

Altes Rathaus
One of the most attractive sights is the galleried courtyard of the 17th-century former town hall. Once known as Weltzer Palace, now as Rosenberg Palace, it was the first seat of the Klagenfurt town authorities.

Dragon Fountain
In Neuer Platz (New Square) is a fountain with the mythical Lindwurm dragon, created by Ulrich Vogelsang in 1593; a town symbol, it has found its way into the Klagenfurt coat of arms.

0 m	75
0 yards	75

The Diözesanmuseum houses Austria's largest collection of church furnishings as well as many early sacred art objects. Its most famous exhibit is a 12th-century stained-glass panel of Mary Magdalene, which is believed to be the oldest artifact of its kind in Austria.

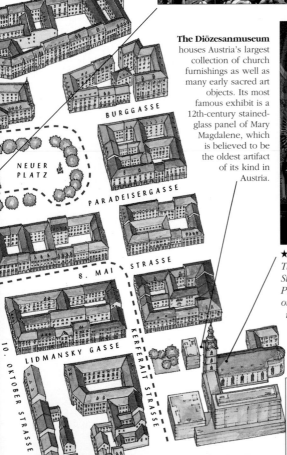

★ Dom St. Peter und Paul
The Cathedral of St Peter and St Paul, originally built as a Protestant church, was taken over and altered by the Jesuits in 1604, and in 1727 it was completely rebuilt after a major fire. The high altar (1752) is the work of Daniel Gran.

STAR SIGHTS

★ **Dom St. Peter und Paul**

★ **Landhaus**

Market in the historic Old Town of Klagenfurt

Exploring Klagenfurt

Klagenfurt lies south of the Glan river, 30 km (19 miles) from the Slovenian and 60 km (37 miles) from the Italian borders. Its Old Town, laid out on a rectangular grid, extends between Hauptplatz, Alter Platz and Neuer Platz, 4 km (2 miles) from Wörther See. The road to the lake runs through Europapark and the Minimundus exhibition.

🏛 Landhaus

Landhaushof. 📞 (0463) 57757.
🕐 Apr–Oct: 9am–1pm, 2–5pm daily.
▨ ✆ 🅿

The Landhaus, the present seat of the Carinthian provincial government, stands on the western side of Alter Platz. Commissioned by the Carinthian estates, it was built in

The attractive, galleried courtyard of the Landhaus

1574 on the site of a former ducal palace to designs by Antonio Verda of Lugano and Franz Freymann. The resulting structure is Klagenfurt's most important secular building and a Renaissance gem, with two symmetrically spaced spires, beyond which is an open two-storey, galleried courtyard. The domes crowning the two towers and the decorated elevation date from 1740. The most beautiful room in the Landhaus, the Wappensaal (heraldic hall), dates from the same period. It is almost entirely the work of Josef Ferdinand Fromiller, the foremost Carinthian artist of the day. The walls of the hall display hundreds of Carinthian coats of arms, while the ceiling painting shows the Carinthian nobles paying homage to Charles VI; the flat ceiling is made to look vaulted in this *trompe l'oeil*. The north wing of the Landhaus houses the remains of the armoury.

Many old buildings have survived in the town centre nearby, including the Town Hall with a galleried Renaissance courtyard. The Trinity Column in Alter Platz, heart of the shopping district, dates from 1680; the crescent and cross were added after the victory over the Turks (1683).

🏛 Neuer Platz

Neuer Platz.
The square is dominated by Lindwurmbrunnen (Dragon Fountain), whose winged beast has become the symbol and crest of the town. The dragon was carved from a single block of stone by Ulrich Vogelsang, in 1593, while the giant who eventually saved the town was added later by Michael Hönel. The unveiling of this monument in 1636 was a great public event.

The Town Hall, formerly the Palace of the Rosenberg family, has been the seat of the municipal authorities since 1918. Built in 1582 and altered in 1650, it has an interesting Renaissance stairway. Originally outside the town walls surrounding Spanheim Castle, it became the centre of the new Renaissance town. In 1764, Neuer Platz was the site of the first monument to be erected to Maria Theresa in Austria. The square is lined on all sides by many 16th- and 17th-century mansions with beautiful façades.

17th-century Old Town Hall in Alter Platz

🏛 Dom St. Peter und Paul

Domplatz. 📞 (0463) 54950.
🕐 7am–7pm daily.

Klagenfurt's cathedral was built in 1578 as a Protestant church by Klagenfurt's Mayor, Christoph Windisch. In 1604, the church was taken over by the Jesuits, and was elevated to the rank of cathedral in 1787, when the bishopric was transferred from Gurk to Klagenfurt. In 1723, following a fire, the late-Gothic interior was rebuilt in the Baroque style. The cathedral was badly damaged in World War II, during the 1944 bombing raids, but has been restored to its former splendour.

Rich stucco decoration on the walls and ceiling blend elements of various architectural styles into one successful composition. The vault frescoes were painted by Josef Ferdinand Fromiller, while the gallery stucco was the work of Kilian Pittner. Daniel Gran painted the main altarpiece in 1752. The vestry holds the last work by Johann Martin Schmidt.

🏛 Landesmuseum Kärnten

Museumgasse 2. 📞 (0463) 53630 552. 🕐 9am–4pm Tue–Sat, 10am–1pm Sun, public holidays. 📷 🚫 🎫

The collections of the Regional Museum, founded in 1844, illustrate several centuries of history in Carinthia as well as its art, rooted in Celtic and Roman cultures. The floor mosaic of a young Dionysus surrounded by hedonistic satyrs is a beautiful example of Roman art. One of the museum's curiosities is a "dragon's skull" (in fact a rhinoceros), found nearby, which served as a model for the fountain dragon in Neuer Platz. Its discovery gave credence to the legend that a dragon once tormented the town, demanding the sacrifice of animals and humans.

The museum also holds many works of art and handicraft. One of its most interesting exhibits is a carved altar from the St. Veit school. In the park in front is a small collection of stones, including some Roman stone statues.

🏛 Minimundus

Villacher Straße 241. 📞 (0463) 21194. 🕐 Apr, Oct: 9am–5pm; May–Jun, Sep: 9am–6pm; Jul–Aug: 9am–9pm. 📷 🚫 🎫 P 🚻 🍴

Europapark, a large green space west of Klagenfurt, is home to this theme park, with over 170 miniature models of the world's most famous buildings. They are crafted in minute detail to a scale of 1:25, and have been added to since 1959, when a children's charity, *Rettet das*

Statue on the side altar in the Dom

Kind, set up the first architectural miniatures near Wörther See. All the profits go to the foundation. Among the models from all continents are Rome's St Peter's Basilica, Paris's Eiffel Tower, London's Big Ben, Brussels's Atomium, Agra's Taj Mahal and New York's Statue of Liberty. Not surprisingly, Austria's own historic buildings, such as the Stephansdom in Vienna, are heavily represented. Many other achievements and inventions are also represented by miniature models, for example Austrian watermills, Mississippi paddle steamers and the earliest steam trains.

ENVIRONS: The town of Klagenfurt is surrounded by lakes and mountains; the closest is **Wörther See** (*see pp276–7*), which gave the Carinthian capital its byname, Rose of the Wörther See. **Viktring Abbey**, 6 km (4 miles) south-

Stained-glass window in the Cistercian Abbey in Viktring

west of Klagenfurt, belonged to the Cistercian monks who arrived in Viktring in 1142. The many castles and palaces in the vicinity testify to the region's prosperity. Sights worth visiting include the fortified castle of **Mageregg** (1590, altered in 1841), surrounded by a zoological park for local animals. The lovely 12th-century **Schloss Hallegg**, which has preserved its old turret, was remodelled in the 16th century and turned into a Renaissance residence with two inner courtyards.

Models of Salzburg Cathedral and Ort Castle, in Minimundus

Friesach ⑨

Road map E5. 🏛 *5,500.* 🚌 🚉
ℹ *Fürstenhofplatz 1 (04268) 4300.*

FRIESACH IS Carinthia's oldest
town, with a history going
back to 860, when the nearby
fortress of **Petersberg** was
founded. Traces of the town's
glorious past have survived to
this day, including a moated
town wall, 820 m (2,690 ft)
long, and several castle towers.
Of the fortress itself, only the
six-storey keep on Petersberg
survives. In the former chapel
room, on the fourth floor, the
remains of 12th-century frescoes can be seen.

Adjacent to the fortress is
Peterskirche (church of St
Peter), which has a Gothic
altar (1525) with a Romanesque statue of the Madonna
(c.1200). The **Dominikaner-
kloster** (Dominican abbey)
from 1217 holds a 14th-century
Madonna, a wooden crucifix
(1300) and other medieval
artifacts. The church of St
Blaise, built by the Teutonic
Knights in 1213 on the ruins
of an earlier church, has some
original 12th-century frescoes.

Around Wörther See ⑩

See pp276–7.

Villach ⑪

Road map E5. 🏛 *57,000.* 🚌 🚉
ℹ *Rathausplatz 1 (04242) 2052900.*

CARINTHIA'S second largest
town is an important
tourist centre, health resort
and transport hub. The
earliest archaeological finds
testifying to the region's
colonization date
from Celtic times. It
has a small old town.
**Stadtpfarrkirche St.
Jakob** (parish church
of St Jacob) was built
after a powerful earth-
quake in 1348, and
later rebuilt. Its most
notable features are
the Renaissance
chapels of the Görz-
Dietrichstein and the
Khevenhüller families
and the 95-m (312-ft)
high tower. The
Municipal Museum,
in a 16th-century
building at No. 38
Widmanngasse,
covers regional
history, archaeology
and art. In **Schiller-
park** you can see an astonishing 3D-map of Carinthia, at
a scale of 1:10,000.

ENVIRONS: Lovely 14th-century
frescoes and a late-Gothic altar
(c.1520) can be seen in the
church of **Maria Gail**, 3 km
(2 miles) southeast of Villach.

Spittal an der Drau ⑫

Road map D5. 🏛 *16,000.* 🚌 🚉
ℹ *Schloss Porcia, Burgplatz 1
(04762) 5650220.*

THE TOWN OF Spittal is dominated by the Goldeck
peak (2,142 m/7,028 ft). The
history of the town began in
the 12th century, when Count
Ortenburg founded a church
and a *Spittal* or hospice on
this site. The town owes its
Renaissance character to the
vast 16th-century **Schloss
Porcia**, which is also known
as Salamanca Palace
after its builder,

Schloss Porcia's galleries, Spittal an der Drau

the Spanish nobleman Gabriel
of Salamanca. The Porcia
family, who owned the palace
from 1662 until 1918, added
to its decor while preserving
the original architecture based
on Spanish Renaissance
palaces. Its most beautiful
aspect is the galleried inner
courtyard; be sure to have a
close look at the rich decorations of its individual storeys.
The well-preserved palace
now houses a museum of folk
art on the two top floors.

ENVIRONS: On a hill near the
village of St. Peter in Holz,
5 km (3 miles) northwest of
Spittal an der Drau, stand the
ruins of an Early Christian
church and the **Römer-
museum Teurnia**. The hill
was settled first by Celts, then
by Romans, and the museum
exhibits many small items,
scripts and coins.

Millstatt ⑬

Road map D5. 🏛 *3,400.* 🚌 ℹ
Rathaus, Marktplatz 8 (04766) 2022.

THE GREATEST attraction in
Millstatt, on the northern
shore of Millstätter See, is a
Benedictine Abbey dating
from 1070. From then until
1469 it was run by the Hirsau
Benedictines; later the monastery and church passed into
the hands of the Order of the
Knights of St George, and
from 1598 until 1773 it was
owned by the Jesuits.

The modern thermal bath complex in the spa town of Villach

The most beautiful part of the abbey is its Renaissance courtyard surrounded by two-storey arcades. This was built in the 16th century, when the abbey was run by the Order of St George. The monastery is linked with the church by a 12th-century cloister whose pillars, decorated by medieval carvers, display a grotesque world of animals, plants and faces. Even older, dating back to the Carolingian period, are the magical ornaments on the old buildings, possibly representing some pagan spells. An eye-catching feature inside the church is the Romanesque portal, made by master craftsman Rudger in 1170. In the side chapels are the red marble tombs of the Order's Grand Masters. Also worth seeing is a fresco from 1519, depicting the Last Judgement.

Courtyard of the Benedictine Abbey in Millstatt

Gmünd **⑭**

Road map D5. **🏠** *2,600.* **🚌**
ℹ️ *Hauptplatz 20 (04732) 221514.*

IN THE 12TH CENTURY, the Archbishops of Salzburg who ruled Gmünd began to encircle the town with mighty fortifications, many of which survive to this day, including old gate turrets and bastions. Two castles tower over the town: the older one, **Altes Schloss**, was destroyed by a fire in 1886, but has recently been restored and is now used as a cultural centre. It was commissioned in 1506 by Archbishop Leonhard. The **Neues Schloss** (New Castle) was built in 1651–4 by Count Christoph Lodron. Today the

An alley in Gmünd, famous for its former Porsche factory

former castle keep houses a school and a concert hall.

The Austrian-born designer Ferdinand Porsche worked in Gmünd in 1944–50, and 52 of the classic "365" models were hand-made locally. The most famous models and construction frames are displayed in the **Porsche Museum**.

🏛 Porsche Museum
Gmünd. **📞** *(04732) 2471.*
🕐 *15 May–15 Oct: 9am–6pm, 16 Oct–14 May: 10am–4pm.*
W *www.porschemuseum.at.*

Mölltal **⑮**

Road map D5. **🚌** **🚏**

THE MÖLL RIVER, a tributary of the Drau and overshadowed by Großes Reißeck peak, runs along the Mölltal, a valley whose upper reaches form a natural extension of the magnificent road known as Großglockner Hochalpenstraße. The river meanders scenically between the high mountain peaks. The road along the valley, starting in Winklern, is an important transit route between Carinthia at one end and Lienz and the Dolomites at the other, winding its way between old mills, waterfalls and huts.

The parish of **Großkirchheim** was once a major mining district, and the 16th-century **Schloss Großkirchheim** now houses an interesting mining museum.

In **Döllach** you can see the interesting late-Gothic church

of St Andrew, and in **Sagritz** the originally late-Gothic church of St George. **Schloss Falkenstein**, near Obervellach, has an unusual tower with a wooden top.

Lienz **⑯**

Road map D5. **🏠** *13,000.* **🚌** **🚏**
ℹ️ *Europaplatz 1 (04852) 65265.*

THE TOWN HAS been the capital of East Tyrol since 1919 but its origins date back to the Middle Ages. The **Stadtpfarrkirche St Andrä** (parish church of St Andrew), a triple-nave Gothic basilica, was built in the 15th century; western sections include parts of an earlier Romanesque church. Today, following many alterations, the church is predominantly Baroque in style. Inside are a fresco by J. A. Mölk and a high altar by Franz Engele. The **Franziskanerkirche** (Franciscan church), built around 1350, features original 15th-century frescoes and a Gothic Pietà standing by a side altar.

High above the town sits **Schloss Bruck**, the seat of the Görz Counts, built between the 13th and 16th centuries. The castle has a tall Romanesque turret; its main body contains a Romanesque chapel with 13th- and 15th-century frescoes. Today it also houses a regional museum with Gothic and Baroque artifacts and paintings by the local Tyrolean artist Albin Egger-Lienz (1868–1926).

The Romanesque tower of Schloss Bruck in Lienz

Around Wörther See ⑩

WÖRTHER SEE is the warmest lake in Austria; in summer, the temperature of its waters reaches 24–28°C. Numerous resorts are lined along its shores; the largest of these is the modern, brash town of Velden, with its casino. Krumpendorf and the exclusive resort of Pörtschach lie on the easily accessible northern shore; quiet Reifnitz is on the southern shore. Not far from Wörther See are other, smaller lakes, including Ossiacher See, in a scenic mountain setting. To the south, the Carinthian lake district extends along the Slovenian border, surrounded by the snowy peaks of the enchanting Karawanken Alps.

Ossiach ①
The former Benedictine Abbey in Ossiach and its church were built in the 11th-century and altered in the early-Baroque style. The oldest monastery in Carinthia, it was burned down by Turkish invaders and is now a hotel.

Schloss Landskron ②
Not much remains of the original medieval castle, but the ruins are nevertheless impressive. Today, the bird of prey show, held on the slopes of the castle hill, and "Monkey Mountain" are the greatest attractions nearby.

```
0 km        4
0 miles     4
```

Bodensdorf

Spittal am der Drau

Villach

Tarvisio *Faaker See*

A2 E66

83

Drava

A11 E61

94

83

Jesenice

Rosegg ③
This small village between Wörther See and Faaker See has a beautiful 200-year-old landscaped wildlife park, attempting to recreate a natural habitat for its resident animals and birds.

Schloss Velden ④
The well-known, swanky resort on the shores of Wörther See boasts an early-Baroque castle, originally built by the Khevenhüller family, which featured as setting for a popular Austrian TV series. It is now an elegant hotel.

TIPS FOR DRIVERS

Length of route: *45 km (28 miles).*
Stopping-off points: *there are several resorts around the lake offering restaurants and hotels; Velden is the largest resort.*
Further attractions: *Wildpark in Rosegg.* [(045271) 5257. ☐ *Apr–Nov.*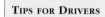

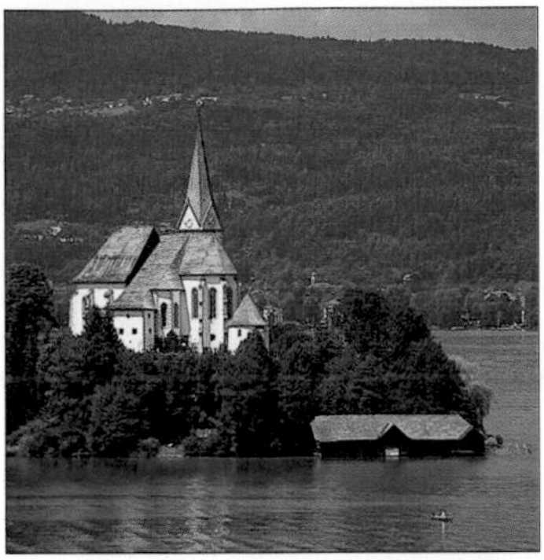

Maria Wörth ⑤
On a promontory that extends far into the lake, stands a 12th-century church built on earlier foundations and featuring original 11th-century Romanesque frescoes.

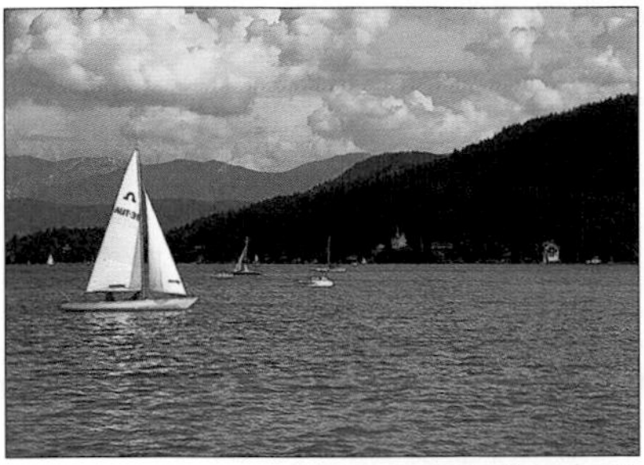

Wörther See ⑥
Wörther See is Austria's warmest lake and its shores have become known as the Austrian Riviera. Entertainment here ranges from relaxation to swimming and all sorts of water sports.

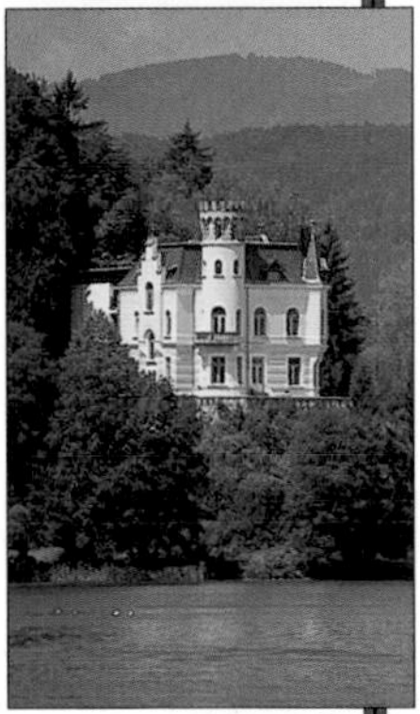

Reifnitz ⑦
Established as early as 1195, this was once one of the mightiest castles in Carinthia. All that remains today are the main body and the castle keep.

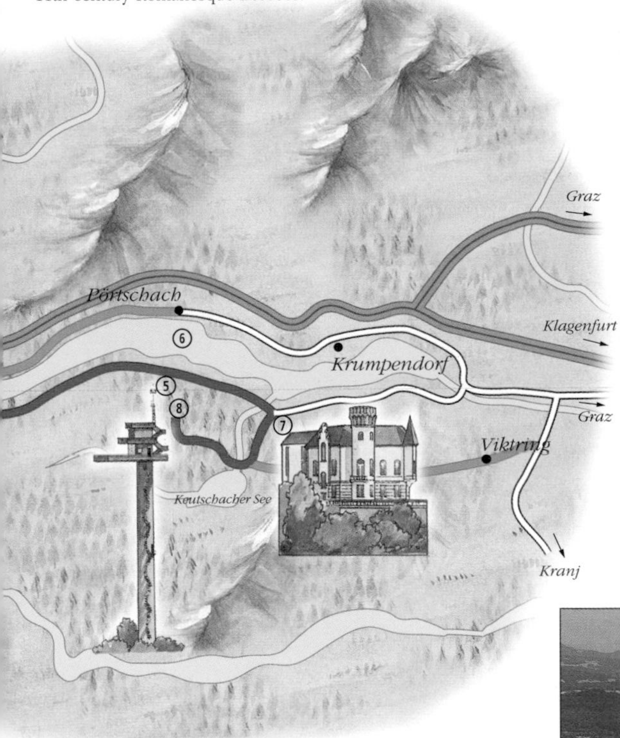
Graz
Pörtschach
⑥
Klagenfurt
Krumpendorf
⑤
⑧
⑦
Graz
Viktring
Keutschacher See
Kranj

Key

- Motorway
- Suggested route
- Scenic route
- Other road
- River, lake
- Viewpoint

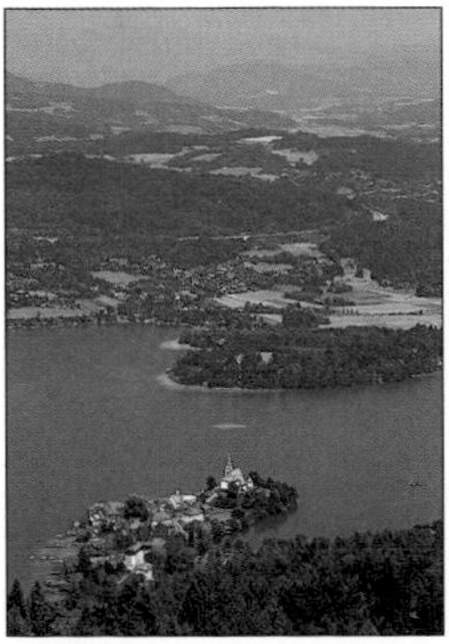

Pyramidenkogel ⑧
The wooded Pyramidenkogel, rising 850 m (2,789 ft) above the lake, has a tower at its top affording the most fantastic views over the entire area, including Wörther See itself, with the Karawanken Alps to the south, and several neighbouring lakes.

Hohe Tauern National Park ⑰

THE BEAUTIFUL area around Austria's highest peak, the Großglockner, is a national park. The unique landscape, flora and fauna of the region, the Hohe Tauern, is jointly protected by the provincial governments of Salzburger Land, Tyrol and Carinthia. The Hohe Tauern has more than 300 peaks rising above 3,000 m (9,850 ft) and several glaciers – the Pasterze is the longest and most spectacular. This whole national park area is protected by law and visitors are asked to keep to the marked trails. On its edges are many popular tourist resorts such as Badgastein, Kaprun, Zell am See and East Tyrol's capital, Lienz.

Artificial Lakes
One of the great attractions of the Hohe Tauern is its many pictur-esque reservoirs, gathering the crystal-clear meltwaters from the glaciers high above each spring.

★ Pasterze Glacier
The largest glacier in the Eastern Alps is 10 km (6 miles) long and covers an area of 19.5 sq km (7.6 sq miles). Its far end can be reached by stairs carved into the ice or by cable car.

★ Großglockner
Austria's highest peak (3,797 m/ 12,457 ft) towers at the border between Carinthia and East Tyrol, a crucifix marking the summit.

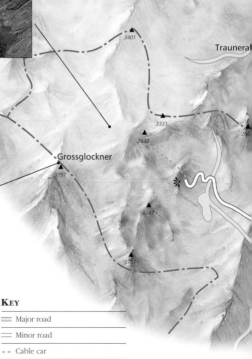

Traunera

Grossglockner
3797

3368
3564
3401
3331
2548
3247
3797

KEY

═══	Major road
═══	Minor road
- -	Cable car
▬ ▬	Provincial border
≈≈≈	River
☀	Viewpoint

0 km   2

0 miles   2

Edelweißspitze

Edelweißspitze, 2,572 m/8,438 ft high, is the central peak of the Fusch-Rauriser range. There are amazing views from the viewing tower at the summit.

VISITORS' CHECKLIST

Road map D4.
🛈 *Nationalparkrat Hohe Tauern, Matrei in Osttirol, Kirchplatz 2.*
(04875) 5112.
W *www.hohetauern.at.*

Alpine Flora

An impressive range of alpine plantlife, such as this aromatic alpine tansy (Tanacetum) can be seen in the park at different altitudes.

ZELL AM SEE

Ferleiten

Edelweissspitze
2577

▲ 2924

▲ 2588

▲ 3006

▲ 3103

Schareck
2604

Heiligenblut

107

LIENZ

Cable Car to Schareck

Schareck peak (2,606 m/ 8,550 ft) in the Goldberg-gruppe (Gold Mountains) can be reached by cable car, with one change en route. Schareck is an excellent starting point for excursions into the upper mountains.

Alpine Ibex

This protected species inhabits the upper regions of the Alps. It is easiest to see them in the Ferleiten Reserve (see p280).

STAR SIGHTS

★ **Großglockner**

★ **Pasterze Glacier**

Großglockner Hochalpenstraße ⑱

Tʀᴀᴠᴇʀsɪɴɢ ᴛʜᴇ Hohe Tauern National
Park is the Großglockner High Alpine
Road, regarded as one of the world's
most beautiful mountain routes.
Completed in 1935, the road was built
along the old mountain passes between
Bruck in Salzburger Land and Heiligenblut in Carinthia. Measuring 47.8 km
(29.7 miles) long, it forms part of a
north–south route from Bavaria to Italy.
Branching off the main road are two
trails leading to viewpoints. The highest
point of the route is Hochtor, at 2,505 m
(8,218 ft), the lowest is Bruck, at 755 m
(2,477 ft). With the 1.5 km (1 mile) rise
in altitude, the flora also changes.

Hochtor ⑤
The Hochtor (High Gate) is the highest
point along the Großglockner Hochalpenstraße. Here the road runs
through a tunnel measuring
2.3 km (1.5 miles) in length.

Fuscher Törl ⑥
The road winds its
way above steep
ravines, offering
splendid views
on both sides of
this ridge to the
Goldberggruppe
(Gold Mountains).

**Viewing Tower on
Edelweißspitze ⑦**
The tower built on
top of Edelweißspitze
(2,572 m/8,438 ft)
affords fantastic
views of the Groß-
glockner to the west
and the Goldberg-
gruppe to the east.

**Alpine Naturschau
Museum ⑧**
Situated at an altitude
of 2,260 m (7,415 ft)
is a small museum of
the local flora, fauna
and ecology, offering
free admission to
visitors. In Ferleiten, to
the north, is an alpine
animal reserve.

Kᴇʏ

▄▄	Suggested route
═	Other road
⁻ ⁻	Cable car
≈	River, lake
▪ ▪	Provincial border
✤	Viewpoint

Schareck ④
The Schareck peak, part of the Goldberg massif, was once mined for gold. From here visitors can see the Schildberg peak and the looming Großglockner massif to the west, as well as the superb high-altitude ski slopes.

Observatory ③
The Swarovski Tower, built in 1998 above Franz-Josefs-Höhe, enables visitors to view the magnificent alpine landscape using the latest optical equipment.

0 km   4

0 miles   4

Heiligenblut ①
The church in Heiligenblut was built in the 15th century by monks from Admont. Inside is a beautiful altar from the workshop of Michael Pacher, and a richly carved tabernacle said to house a phial of Christ's blood.

Franz-Josefs-Höhe ②
Along the Gletscherstraße (Glacier Road) is a viewing terrace at 2,369 m (7,772 ft), giving fabulous views of both Großglockner and the Pasterze Glacier.

TRAVELLERS' NEEDS

WHERE TO STAY

AUSTRIA HAS a highly developed infra-structure, and you should find it easy to locate the exact type of accommodation that you are looking for. There is a great number of hotels and pensions, offering different standards of accommodation and service at a range of prices. You can also find friendly private lodgings and good campsites. The rooms are mostly well furnished and comfortable, the staff kind and courteous. Away from towns, where transport is not always readily available, hotel staff may even offer to collect travellers without cars from railway or coach stations. Within the list of hotels on pages 288–307, there is a choice of around 170 hotels and pensions, which represent various price categories and a high standard of service. Information on other types of overnight accommodation can be found on pages 286–7.

A hotel complex in Kampl, in a typically scenic location

THE RANGE OF HOTELS

HOTELS AND pensions are awarded one to five stars, as in other countries, with the number of stars depending on the facilities offered by the hotel rather than the standard of service. Generally speaking, pensions have fewer facilities but they often offer a more homely atmosphere.

Your choice of hotel will be determined by what you are intending to do during your time in Austria. Visitors who are mainly interested in sightseeing and are likely to be constantly on the move, may prefer to stay in less costly private lodgings or pensions. Sports enthusiasts need to look for hotels that offer the appropriate facilities. Alternatively, you may be seeking peace and quiet, or you may wish to improve your overall health and wellbeing; in this case you'll want to seek out one of the numerous, well-equipped spa hotels. Whatever your plans, you should not be stuck for choice as the choice of hotels is truly vast.

HOW TO BOOK

AS IN OTHER countries, hotel accommodation can be booked directly by post, telephone, fax, email or through the internet. Reservations can be made directly with the hotel or through a local tourist office. The **Wiener Tourismusverband** (Vienna Tourism Association) or a local tourist centre may be able to assist if you are booking for small groups. They will mail out brochures and leaflets on request, including abroad, and provide detailed information on the accommodation.

It is generally advisable to book some time in advance, particularly for the summer months, Christmas and Easter.

INTERNATIONAL AND AUSTRIAN CHAIN HOTELS

IN ADDITION TO well-known and popular hotel chains, such as Mercure and **Hilton**, it is also worth considering are **50plus Hotels** which

A majestic hotel in the elegant ski resort of Badgastein

mostly offer spa facilities and access to various health treatments. The largest clusters of such hotels are to be found in the vicinity of Salzburg and in Vorarlberg province. Other hotel chains include Romantik-Hotels, Grand Hotel, Marriott, Bristol, **Austria Trend**, Hotel-Post, Renaissance and **Ibis**. All offer high standards and good service, but only a few have air-conditioned rooms.

The impressively grand lobby of the Imperial Hotel

◁ **Casino and Kurpark by night in Baden**

WHERE TO STAY

285

HOTELS IN HISTORIC BUILDINGS

VISITORS WHO are looking for something a bit special should consider a stay at one of the many medieval castles that have been converted into hotels. Often the name *Schlosshotel* is used to indicate that an establishment is a hotel within a palace. Some excellent examples of such converted fortresses or palaces are: Burg Oberranna; Hotel Schloss Dürnstein in the Wachau region; Burghotel Deutschlandsberg in Styria; or one of the various Renaissance or Baroque palaces or mansions such as Raffelsberger Hof in Weißenkirchen (in Lower Austria), Schlosshotel Oth in Baden near Vienna, Schloss Feyregg in Bad Hall (Upper Austria) and the Hotel Palais Schwarzenberg in Vienna. Each of these offers up-to-date accommodation facilities in luxurious surroundings, richly furnished but exuding the romantic atmosphere of a bygone age. Schloss Fuschl in Hof near Salzburg, for example, is now not only a palace but an entire resort, including a well-equipped health spa. Hunting lodges, usually based in the countryside, are also popular with visitors, and many guests return every year to take part in the hunt.

Prices at such historic hotels are often higher than those demanded by other well-known hotels; a single room at the Schwarzenberg Palace in Vienna, for example, will cost you about € 250–400 per night, while a similar room in one of the Inter-Continental hotels costs € 210–300.

Generally speaking, Vienna is an expensive city to stay in. In the provinces accommodation in palaces and mansions costs around € 100–250, with a select few, such as Herrenhaus Tennerhof in the top winter sports resort of Kitzbühel, charging as much as € 600–800. Information about

The cosy, candle-lit interior of the Weismayr Hotel in Badgastein

accommodation in converted palaces can be obtained from the local tourist offices, which also have all the relevant brochures, catalogues and booking details.

HOTEL PRICES

THE PRICE OF hotel accommodation is dictated not only by the category of the hotel, but also by its location and local events and traditions. Differences may be significant, even within the same category. Accommodation in Vienna, Salzburg and Graz is often expensive, and many hotels and pensions situated in prime locations are overpriced. You can cut costs by staying outside the main town centres; in Vienna, for example, you can expect to pay approximately a fifth

Sign of the Golden Eagle in Innsbruck

A charming rustic pension in the mountainous region of Lech

less for a room in an establishment just outside the Ringstraße, and less still further afield. Staying in provincial towns tends to be somewhat cheaper, but even here you will encounter a wide range of prices. You will find less costly accommodation if you time your visit to fall outside the main tourist season – if, for example, you visit a resort specializing in winter sports during the summer months. In the cities, you may also be able to negotiate discounted room rates for weekend visits or longer stays.

HIDDEN EXTRAS

WHEN BOOKING a room you should check in advance if any additional charges, such as *Kurtaxe* (health spa tax) or for cleaning on departure, will be levied. Generally, prices are inclusive of taxes such as *MWSt* (VAT), but occasionally these are separate. In all but the five-star hotels, breakfast is included. Other typical extra costs to watch out for are charges for off-road parking, especially in the larger cities, unfavourable rates of exchange and high costs for making phone calls.

If you have opted for full-board accommodation in a pension, you will need to take the additional cost for lunch and dinner drinks into account, and you should also allow for a small tip.

If you are renting an apartment, it is worth checking whether the cost of electricity is included in the rent or whether it is metered.

A concert at the elegant hotel Schwarzenberg Palace in Vienna

PENSIONS AND GASTHÖFE

Pensions are widespread and popular in Austria. Less formal than a hotel, they are typically run by a family and usually provide modest accommodation, breakfast and a pleasant family atmosphere – guests often meet the owners. Most rooms have *en suite* bathrooms and toilet, some have telephone, TV and a balcony. In smaller towns and villages, the owners often invite their guests to join in at social evenings with music, dancing or a barbecue.

A *Gasthof* is a traditional inn with a restaurant on the ground floor and rooms to rent above. A wide range of establishments is covered by this description, from small, inexpensive, family-run hotels with modestly equipped rooms, to the most luxurious accommodation in an exquisitely restored country inn.

INEXPENSIVE ACCOMMODATION

Relatively inexpensive accommodation can often be found in private homes. In attractive tourist areas, it is common for owners of larger villas and private houses to rent rooms to tourists. Vacancies are generally indicated by the sign *Fremdenzimmer* or *Zimmer frei*. The standard of furnishing varies; some rooms are *en suite*, for others the bathroom facilities are shared.

Breakfast may or may not be included in the room price.

Young people travelling in groups can stay at a *Jugendherberge* (Youth Hostel), the least expensive option for an overnight stay. Most are of a high standard, and some are located in old castles, beautiful villas or other historic buildings. Tourist offices can provide details.

AGROTOURISM

Families with children often enjoy holidays on a farm. There is a large network of such farms, fully adapted to put up guests. Some offer self-catering facilities, in others meals can be provided by the farmer, on a similar basis as in pensions, offering bed and breakfast *(Zimmer mit Frühstück)*, half-board *(Halbpension)* or full

board *(Vollpension)*. The number of rooms for let in a *Bauernhof*, and the prices that are charged, vary. Rooms are of a perfectly acceptable standard, and for children from towns and cities it is an ideal opportunity to observe the daily work on a farm and to have direct contact with farm animals. There may also be the opportunity to go horseriding, or hire a bike, boat or fishing tackle, so that a full programme of outdoor activities can be enjoyed by the whole family.

Information on *Bauernhof* (farm) holidays with pictures and detailed descriptions and price lists can be obtained from tourist offices. Tourist offices in many provinces also send out free brochures to interested holidaymakers.

MOUNTAIN HOSTELS AND SHELTERS

Mountain hostels and shelters can be found along all the major walking trails. They exist even in Vienna: on the banks of the Old Danube, no higher than 155 m (509 ft), stands a picturesque hut, although it is reserved exclusively for groups. Lower Austria has a large number of hostels, some at relatively low altitudes.

A stone statue outside a Salzburg hotel

In the High Alps travellers can find numerous huts or shelters. They usually have rooms for two, three or many more people to share, and sleeping is on simple

A caravan site on the shores of Ossiacher See in Carinthia

A mountain hostel near Schöpfl, in the Vienna Woods

mattresses. The higher in the mountains you climb and the more remote you are, the less luxurious the huts. Hostels can provide you with information on the local hiking trails, current climbing conditions and the weather forecasts.

Depending on the popularity of an area and the season, hostels will be open either all year round or only during the summer months, usually until the end of September or October. Some open only at the weekend, even in summer, or by appointment, or they may be closed one day in the week, on the *Ruhetag* (rest day). The Österreichischer Alpenverein (ÖAV) or the local tourist bureaux will be able to advise you.

CAMPING

TRAVELLING with a camping trailer, camper van or just a tent is popular in Austria, and there are dedicated campsites in all the larger towns and popular resorts. Generally of high standard, sites are equipped with washrooms and kitchens, and they allow caravan owners to exchange gas bottles and use washing machines, dishwashers and ironing rooms. Some sites have fixed caravans for hire, and almost all have a playground for children. A few are adapted for the needs of disabled people. Restaurants, bars and grocery stores can usually be found nearby.

The average price is typically € 7–23 per day for two people sharing; in addition a health resort tax *(Kurtaxe)* may be charged by some, and the use of showers and electricity will be extra.

TRAVELLING WITH CHILDREN

IN LARGER towns, most public squares have some form of playing equipment such as swings, slides or wooden climbing towers. Similar facilities are often provided by hotels and pensions, and even some restaurants may have allocated a separate corner or room for children to play in. In many hotels and pensions it is possible to book a child-minding service. In restaurants, there is usually a children's menu on offer.

Some pensions, particularly those aimed at families with children, organize special activities for young people; these might include all sorts of sport activities, ranging from skiing, skating and tobogganing to horse-riding, tennis, swimming and cycling. Some even offer beginners' rock-climbing lessons and canoeing. Children of all ages will also enjoy visiting Austria's numerous castles and fortresses.

Choosing a Hotel

	NUMBER OF ROOMS	RESTAURANT	GARDEN OR TERRACE	SWIMMING POOL	AIR CONDITIONING

T HE HOTELS IN THIS GUIDE have been chosen on the basis of attractive location, high standards, affordable prices and range of sports facilities offered. Entries are listed by region, starting with Vienna, with colour-coded thumb tabs in the margins to indicate the areas covered on each page. A map of Vienna can be found on pages 50–51; a road map is featured inside the back cover.

	NUMBER OF ROOMS	RESTAURANT	GARDEN OR TERRACE	SWIMMING POOL	AIR CONDITIONING
VIENNA					
INNER CITY: *Bajazzo* €€ Esslinggasse 7, 1010. **Map 2 B2.** ((01) 533 89 03. FAX 535 39 97. W www.hotelbajazzo.com This small, tastefully furnished, four-star hotel, situated in a quiet street in the centre of Vienna, was modernized in 2002. 1 🛏 TV 🔌 🖂	12				
INNER CITY: *Neuer Markt* €€ Seilergasse 9, 1010. **Map 2 B4.** ((01) 512 23 16. FAX 513 91 05. @ neuermarkt@hotelpension.at W www.hotelpension.at Fair-sized pension in an excellent location near Hofburg. Rooms have telephone, radio, cable and satellite TV. The less expensive rooms have showers but no WC. 1 🛏 TV	37				
INNER CITY: *Amadeus* €€€ Wildpretmarkt 5, 1010. **Map 2 C3.** ((01) 533 87 38. FAX 533 87 38 38. @ amadeus.vienna@aon.at W www.hotel-amadeus.at A small four-star hotel close to Stephansdom with decor appropriate for Mozart's era; the red carpets, upholstery and lampshades are complemented by chandeliers and murals depicting scenes from old Vienna. 1 🛏 TV 🔌 🧍 🖂	30				■
INNER CITY: *Arenberg* €€€ Stubenring 2, 1010. **Map 3 D4.** ((01) 512 52 91, 512 19 11. FAX 513 93 56. @ arenberg@ennet.at W www.arenberg.at A smart hotel occupying two floors of a house opposite Stadtpark, where the Strauss concerts are performed in the summer. Traditionally furnished rooms are decorated with beautiful antique wallpaper. There is an honesty bar, where guests can help themselves to drinks and mark them on their tab. TV 🔌 🧍 🔌 P 🖂	22				■
INNER CITY: *Capricorno* €€€ Schwedenplatz 3–4, 1010. **Map 3 D3.** ((01) 533 31 040. FAX 533 76 71 4. @ capricorno@schick-hotels.com W www.schick-hotels.com Modern plush hotel, winner of the Golden Tulip Award, in an excellent location right next to the Danube Canal. It offers the perfect setting for visitors wishing to enjoy a relaxing break or to experience the cultural life of the city. 1 🛏 TV P 🟨 🖂	46				■
INNER CITY: *Am Parkring* €€€€ Parkring 12, 1010. **Map 3 D5.** ((01) 514 80 0. FAX 514 80 40. @ parkring@schick-hotels.com W www.schick-hotels.com Hotel opposite the Stadtpark, where Strauss waltzes are performed in the summer. Tastefully furnished rooms are equipped with radio, satellite TV and minibar. The hotel has a conference room with a full range of technical facilities. Self-service breakfast bar. 🖂 🔌 🧍 P 🖂	64	●			■
INNER CITY: *Am Stephansplatz* €€€€ Stephansplatz 9, 1010. **Map 2 C4.** ((01) 534 05 0. FAX 534 05 711. @ office@hotelstephansplatz.at W www.hotelamstephansplatz.at Luxury hotel situated in the heart of the city, next to the Stephansdom. It has traditionally, tastefully furnished rooms and pleasant, helpful service. 1 🛏 TV 🖂 🧍 🔌 🟨 🖂	60	●			
INNER CITY: *Europa* €€€€ Neuer Markt 3 (entrance Kärntner Straße 18), 1010. **Map 2 B4.** ((01) 51 59 40. FAX 513 81 38. @ europa.wien@austria-trend.at W www.austria-trend.at The hotel, which has been awarded a badge for its environmentally sound policies, is situated in the very heart of the city. On one side, its rooms overlook a quiet square and on the other, they face the pedestrianized Kärntner Straße, ensuring an excellent rest. All rooms have modern furnishings and internet access. 1 🛏 TV 🟨 🖂 🔌	116	●			■

		Price categories & key	NUMBER OF ROOMS	RESTAURANT	GARDEN OR TERRACE	SWIMMING POOL	AIR CONDITIONING

Price categories for a twin room with bathroom or shower, and including breakfast, service and tax, in euros:
€ up to € 90
€€ € 91–140
€€€ € 141–180
€€€€ € 181–260
€€€€€ above € 260

RESTAURANT
The restaurant is open to non-residents and hotel guests.

GARDEN OR TERRACE
The hotel is set in a garden or has an outside terrace or courtyard with plants.

SWIMMING POOL
The hotel has a swimming pool.

AIR CONDITIONING
All rooms are air-conditioned.

Hotel		Rooms	Rest.	Garden	Pool	Air
NORTH OF MARIAHILFER STRASSE: *Admiral* €€		78				
NORTH OF MARIAHILFER STRASSE: *Hotel Atlanta* €€		59	●			
NORTH OF MARIAHILFER STRASSE: *Ibis Wien Mariahilf* €€		341	●			■
NORTH OF MARIAHILFER STRASSE: *Museum* €€		15				
SOUTH OF THE RING: *Am Schubertring* €€€		39				■
SOUTH OF THE RING: *Im Palais Schwarzenberg* €€€€€		44	●			■
FURTHER AFIELD: *Liechtenstein Appartements* €		6				
FURTHER AFIELD: *Residenz Johann Strauss* €		28				

NORTH OF MARIAHILFER STRASSE: *Admiral*   €€   78
Karl-Schweighofer-Gasse 7, 1070. Map 4 B1. ((01) 521 41-0. FAX 521 41-16.
@ hoteladmiralwien@aon.at W www.admiral.co.at
Excellently situated, swanky hotel, near the shops of Mariahilfer Straße as well as two of Vienna's largest museums. The hotel has a garage, a car park and a bicycle room.

NORTH OF MARIAHILFER STRASSE: *Hotel Atlanta*   €€   59
Währinger Straße 33, 1090. Map 2 A2. ((01) 405 12. FAX 405 53 75.
@ hotel.atlanta@aon.at W www.icnet.at/hotelatlanta
A traditional hotel, situated outside the Ring but still within easy reach of the city centre. The rooms are tastefully furnished and comfortable. Internet access available.

NORTH OF MARIAHILFER STRASSE: *Ibis Wien Mariahilf*   €€   341
Mariahilfer Gürtel 22-24, 1060. ((01) 599 98. FAX 597 90 90.
@ H0796@accor-hotels.com W www.ibishotel.com
A modern, high-rise building situated in a busy part of town, near Mariahilfer Straße *(see p83)* and Westbahnhof, a bustling shopping street with many department stores, smart shops and elegant restaurants.

NORTH OF MARIAHILFER STRASSE: *Museum*   €€   15
Museumstraße 3, 1070. Map 1 C5. ((01) 523 44 26-0. FAX 523 44 26-30.
@ hotel.museum@surfeu.at
A classic Viennese pension, right on the doorstep of the main museums and also close to the shops of Mariahilfer Straße. The façade is coated with *putti* and wrought-iron balconies. The owners personally see to the comfort of their guests. Cosy rooms have quite standard furnishings.

SOUTH OF THE RING: *Am Schubertring*   €€€   39
Schubertring 11. Map 2 C5. ((01) 71 70 20. FAX 713 99 66.
@ hotel.amschubertring@chello.at W www.schubertring.at
An elegant hotel situated in an historic building with beautifully furnished rooms (all with minibar). The bar is decorated with wall frescoes and art-deco–style drawings. Very attentive service.

SOUTH OF THE RING: *Im Palais Schwarzenberg*   €€€€€   44
Schwarzenbergplatz 9, A-1030. Map 5 E1. ((01) 79 84 51 50. FAX 789 47 14.
@ hotel@palais-schwarzenberg.com W www.palais-schwarzenberg.at
Occupying a portion of the huge Baroque Schwarzenberg Palace in its 7.5-ha (18-acre) landscaped park, this hotel has an undeniably breathtaking setting. Each of its imaginative, vaulted public rooms, including its conservatory dining room, are also cosy and relaxing. The main building has the larger, better bedrooms, which are decorated with antiques and fine paintings. The adjacent stable block has smaller, more modern rooms.

FURTHER AFIELD: *Liechtenstein Appartements*   €   6
Große Schiffgasse 19, 1020. Map 2 C2. ((01) 216 84 99, 216 84 98.
FAX 214 76 90. @ pensionliechtenstein@chello.at W www.pension.liechtenstein.at
Modest apartments equipped with basic cooking facilities, close to the Danube Canal. A generous traditional breakfast is served, and there is a comfortable, homely atmosphere.

FURTHER AFIELD: *Residenz Johann Strauss*   €   28
Einsiedlergasse 19, 1050. Map 4 A5. (Tel/Fax: (01) 544 13 51.
@ office@appartements-wien.com W www.appartements-wien.com
A hotel of apartment-suites with kitchen facilities, telephone, radio, cable and satellite TV. There is a homely atmosphere and while no breakfast is served, the suites have facilities for preparing light meals. Guests with musical instruments are especially welcome. Cash payment preferred.

Price categories for a twin room with bathroom or shower, and including breakfast, service and tax, in euros: € up to € 90 €€ € 91–140 €€€ € 141–180 €€€€ € 181–260 €€€€€ above € 260	**RESTAURANT** The restaurant is open to non-residents and hotel guests. **GARDEN OR TERRACE** The hotel is set in a garden or has an outside terrace or courtyard with plants. **SWIMMING POOL** The hotel has a swimming pool. **AIR CONDITIONING** All rooms are air-conditioned.			

	NUMBER OF ROOMS	RESTAURANT	GARDEN OR TERRACE	SWIMMING POOL	AIR CONDITIONING
FURTHER AFIELD: *Ibis Wien Messe* €€ Lassallestraße 7a, 1020. █ *(01) 217 70 0.* FAX *217 70-555.* @ H2736@accor-hotels.com W www.ibishotel.com A large, very modern hotel, with a garage, near the famous Prater funfair and good transport connections at Praterstern. The rooms are pleasantly decorated, mainly in light wood. ① 🛏 TV & 🛏 🖿 Y ▮▮	166	●			▪
FURTHER AFIELD: *Capri* €€ Praterstraße 44 46, 1020. Map 3 E2. █ *(01) 214 84 04.* FAX *214 27 85.* @ office@hotelcapri.at W www.hotelcapri.at A modern hotel situated next to an underground station, close to the town centre and to the Prater, Vienna's famous park and funfair. Large, pleasant rooms; internet access. The owner takes care of his guests personally. ① 🛏 TV 🖿 🖿 P 🖿 Y 🖿	68				
FURTHER AFIELD: *Excellence* €€ Alser Straße 21, 1080. Map 1 B2. █ *(01) 407 96 20.* FAX *407 96 20-11.* @ info@pension-excellence.com A luxury pension, two tram stops from the Ring and Vienna University. Stylish rooms with minibar, satellite TV; two computers with Internet access in the lobby; friendly staff. ① 🛏 TV Y 🖿 P	27				
FURTHER AFIELD: *Vienna* €€ Große Stadtgutgasse 31, 1020. Map 3 E1. █ *(01) 214 33 17.* FAX *216 10 79.* @ hotel.vienna@aon.at W www.hotelvienna.at A small, modern hotel close to Karmelitermarkt and to the Prater. Rooms are well equipped, with radio, cable TV and a minibar. ① 🛏 TV 🖿 & P 🖿	39	●			
FURTHER AFIELD: *City Central* €€€ Taborstraße 8, 1020. Map 3 D3. █ *(01) 21 10 50.* FAX *211 05 140.* @ city.central@schick-hotels.com A long-established hotel situated in a stylish building, completely restored in 1990. Smart rooms, equipped with minibars and hairdryers. The conservatory is a popular place for people to meet over a cup of coffee, and the breakfast buffet is renowned for its opulence. ① 🛏 TV 🖿 🖿 & Y 🖿 🖿	58		▪		▪
FURTHER AFIELD: *Mercure Wien City* €€€ Hollandstraße 3–5, 1020. Map 2 C2. █ *(01) 21 31 30.* FAX *213 13 230.* @ h1568@accor-hotels.com W www.mercure.at Part of the international Mercure chain. The Mercure stands just a few steps away from the Danube Canal and is about 10 minutes' walk from Stephansplatz. In the summer, breakfast is served on the terrace. TV & P 🖿 🖿	123	●	▪		▪
FURTHER AFIELD: *Stefanie* €€€€ Taborstraße 12, 1020. Map 3 D3. █ *(01) 21 15 00.* FAX *211 50 160.* @ stefanie@schick-hotels.com An elegant and stylish traditional hotel, one of five belonging to the Schick family. The hotel, which is situated very close to the Danube Canal, has its own parking garage and bicycle storage. ① 🛏 TV & Y P 🖿	130	●	▪		▪

LOWER AUSTRIA AND BURGENLAND

BAD TATZMANNSDORF: *Landhaus Pannonia* €€ Parkstraße 20, 7431. **Road map** G4. █ *(03353) 82 48.* FAX *82 48-30.* @ info@hotel-landhaus-pannonia.at A cosy and very well equipped hotel, which is part of a Hungarian chain, with decor typical of Lower Austria. The hotel has a sauna and a solarium, and offers bicycles for hire. It also has a children's room, a conservatory, and a restaurant that serves good traditional food and excellent wines. ① 🛏 TV Y 🖿 🖿	27	●	▪	●	

BAD TATZMANNSDORF: *Steigenberger Golf- & Thermalhotel* €€€€ 177
Am Golfplatz 1, 7431. **Road map** G4. **(** *(03353) 88 41 607.* **FAX** *88 41-138.*
@ hotel@steigenberger.at **W** www.burgenlandresort.at
Luxury hotel in the health resort famous for its hot springs. In addition to the
bathing facilities, it also offers a sauna, solarium and massages as well as golf,
tennis, squash, horse-riding and angling. The rooms have balconies. Child-
minding services are available, at a separate charge. 🔟 🛏 📺 🏃 🍴 🛏 🎿 ✉

BADEN: *Hotel Admiral am Kurpark* €€€ 21
Renngasse 8, 2500. **Road map** G3.
(*(02252) 867 99-0.* **FAX** *867 99-8.* **@** office@hotel-admiral.at **W** www.hotel-admiral.at
The hotel is situated near the Kurpark and casino. Tastefully furnished, smart
rooms offer an excellent, relaxing environment. The hotel has its own beauty
parlour and a modern, well-equipped business centre.
🔟 🛏 📺 🌊 🍹 🏃 🍴 🛏 P

BADEN: *Grand Hotel Sauerhof* €€€€ 88
Weilburgstraße 11–13, 2500. **Road map** G3.
(*(02252) 412 51-0.* **FAX** *43 626.* **@** sauerhof@sauerhof.at **W** www.sauerhof.at
A luxury hotel within a palace dating back to 1820, surrounded by well-
maintained parkland. The rooms, recently modernized in the old Viennese
style, have excellent facilities. Award-winning restaurants, an elegant lounge
and conference rooms all ensure a comfortable stay for guests.
🔟 🛏 📺 🌊 🍹 🏃 🍴 ♿ 🍴 🛏 P 🎿 ✉

DEUTSCH SCHÜTZEN-EISENBERG: *Privatzimmer Reiger* € 5
Untere Kellergasse 182, 7474 Eisenberg. **Road map** G4.
(*(03365) 23 46-0.* **FAX** *23 46-9.* **@** reiger@eisenberg.at **W** www.reiger.com
A charming country house standing on a hill amid vineyards, in the southern
part of Burgenland. Guests are invited to taste the local house wines, served
with a cold snack, or to visit the adjacent wine cellars. 📺 🛏 ✉

EGGENBURG: *Stadthotel Eggenburg* € 30
Kremser Straße 8, 3730. **Road map** F2. **(** *(02984) 35 31.* **FAX** *35 31-101.*
@ stadthotel.eggenburg@aon.at
Stylishly furnished hotel, situated in a small medieval town near the Czech
border and Schloss Rosenburg. The restaurant will satisfy gourmet tastes, and
wine lovers will discover it has a large selection of regional wines. 📺 🌊 🍹
🍴 🛏 ✉

EISENSTADT: *Gasthof Ohr* € 29
Ruster Straße 51, 7000. **Road map** G3.
(*(02682) 624 60.* **FAX** *64 26 09.* **@** hotel.ohr@burgenland.org
A family hotel, standing some distance from the town centre. The elegant
rooms are functionally equipped. The kitchen specializes in typical Austrian
dishes and regional cuisine. Horse-riding is on offer. 📺 🍹 P ✉

EISENSTADT: *Hotel Burgenland* €€ 87
Schubertplatz 1, 7000. **Road map** G3. **(** *(02682) 696.* **FAX** *65531.*
@ burgenland@austria-hotels.co.at
An imposing, modern building belonging to the Austria Hotels International
Group. The rooms are light and spacious. Features sauna, solarium and
bicycle hire. 🏃 🛏 P ✉ 🍴 🎿 ✉

FEUERSBRUNN: *Mörwald Hotel Villa Katharina* €€ 10
Feuersbrunn, 3483. **Road map** F3. **(** *(02738) 22 98.* **FAX** *22 98-60.*
@ zur_traube@moerwald.at **W** www.moerwald.at
An elegant hotel near Krems and the terraced vineyards of the Wachau region.
It has a sauna. The restaurant "Zur Traube" nearby serves excellent cuisine
and a large choice of regional and international wines. 🏃 ♿ 🛏 ✉

ILLMITZ: *Gasthof Post* €€ 40
Apetloner Straße 2, 7142. **Road map** G3. **(** *(02175) 23 21.* **FAX** *232 14.*
@ posthotel@netway.at
A modest but comfortable pension set on the eastern shores of Neusiedler See,
which is known for its good food. Cash payment is preferred. 🔟 🛏 📺 🍹 🛏 P

JENNERSDORF: *Pension Krainz* € 15
Henndorf-Therme 2, 8282 Loipersdorf. **Road map** G5.
(*(03329) 466 11.* **FAX** *466 11-30.* **W** www.tennis-loipersdorf.at
A pension based in an interesting building with a bright red roof, set amid
green hills, near the border with Styria. Guests can play golf or tennis, or relax
in the cosy restaurant with its own fireplace. 🔟 🛏 ✉

Price categories for a twin room with bathroom or shower, and including breakfast, service and tax, in euros:
€ up to € 90
€€ € 91–140
€€€ € 141–180
€€€€ € 181–260
€€€€€ above € 260

RESTAURANT
The restaurant is open to non-residents and hotel guests.

GARDEN OR TERRACE
The hotel is set in a garden or has an outside terrace or courtyard with plants.

SWIMMING POOL
The hotel has a swimming pool.

AIR CONDITIONING
All rooms are air-conditioned.

	NUMBER OF ROOMS	RESTAURANT	GARDEN OR TERRACE	SWIMMING POOL	AIR CONDITIONING
KREMS: *Am Förthof* € Förthofer Donaulände 8, 3504. **Road map** F3. ☎ *(02732) 833 45.* **FAX** *833 45-40.* @ hotel.foerthof@netway.at This modern hotel offers well-equipped, comfortable rooms with balconies. Those at the front of the building afford beautiful views over the Danube river and Göttweig Abbey. In good weather, lunch is served in the garden, under chestnut trees, while dinner is held on the terrace. Offers a wide selection of wines. 1 🛏 TV 🏊 🛐 P 🖥	20	●	■	●	
KRONBERG: *Landgut Kronberghof* €€ Am Russbach 3, 2123. **Road map** G3. ☎ *(02245) 43 04.* **FAX** *430 44.* @ info@kronberghof.at W www.kronberghof.at The Kronberg estate, once an old mill, lies 15 km (9 miles) north of Vienna. The hotel, decorated in a simple but attractive folk style, offers an idyllic atmosphere with a golf course, bicycles and horse-riding. 1 🛏 TV 🛐 🍴 🛐 P 🖥	15	●	■	●	
LAADEN: *Gasthof Zur Linde* € Hauptplatz 28, 3053. **Road map** F3. ☎ *(02774) 83 78-0.* **FAX** *83 78-20.* A charming family inn offering modest but well-equipped rooms decorated in a rustic style. Its popular restaurant serves regional and international dishes; you should also try some of the seasonal specialities. 🛏 TV 🛐	10	●			
MAUERBACH: *Berghotel Tulbingerkogel* €€ Tulbingerkogel 1, 3001. **Road map** F3. ☎ *(02273) 73 91.* **FAX** *73 91 73.* @ hotel@tulbingerkogel.at W www.tulbingerkogel.at From the terrace of this hotel, guests can enjoy magnificent views over the Vienna Woods and the Danube valley. There is a conservatory and a small, cosy lounge with fireplace. The chef uses vegetables from the hotel's own garden, mushrooms that have been collected in the local woods and meat from traditionally reared animals. The hotel also has a wellness area, which includes a swimming pool, sauna and steam bath. 1 🛏 TV 🏊 🛐 🛐 🛐 🛐 🍴 🛐 P 🖥	46	●	■	●	
MÖLLERSDORF: *Hotel-Restaurant Holzinger* € Teichgasse 2, 2513. **Road map** G3. ☎ *(02252) 524 55.* **FAX** *52 45 54.* @ holzinger@home.at W www.tiscover.at/hotel-holzinger The hotel, situated in the Vienna Woods, 17 km (11 miles) from Vienna, enjoys a great reputation for the exceptional hospitality extended by the landlady, who sees to the comfort of her guests, while the chef spoils them with national and international delicacies. 1 TV 🛐 🛐 🛐 🛐 P 🖥	40	●	■		
MÖRBISCH AM SEE: *Privathotel "Das Schmidt"* €€€ Raiffeisenstraße 8, 7072. **Road map** G3. ☎ *(02685) 82 94.* **FAX** *84 48 13.* @ das.schmidt@aon.at W www.tiscover.at/das.schmidt A romantic building with arcades, to the west of Neusiedler See, surrounded by a large garden. It has a sauna, solarium, indoor pool, fitness room and bicycle hire. Open from April until October. 1 🛏 🏊 🛐 🛐 🛐	29	●	■	●	
NEUHOFEN AN DER YBBS: *Hotel Kothmühle* €€ 3364. **Road map** E3. ☎ *(07475) 521 12.* **FAX** *52 11 28.* @ office@kothmuehle.at A romantic mill-house, blending the modern and the traditional, with arched vaults in the porch and a small fountain in the garden. The wellness area includes pools, a sauna and a steam room. In the restaurant, all dishes are prepared using local produce. 1 TV 🛐 🛐 🛐 🛐 P 🖥	95	●	■	●	
NEUSIEDL AM SEE: *Hotel Wende* €€€ Seestraße 42. **Road map** G3. ☎ *(02167) 81 11–0.* **FAX** *8111-649.* @ anfrage@hotel-wende.at W www.hotel-wende.at A hotel complex close to the lake, although not in a particularly attractive location. Spacious, well-equipped rooms with balconies and a good restaurant. Bicycle hire and a sauna are available on site. 1 🛏 🛐	105	●		●	

OBERPULLENDORF: *Sport-Hotel Kurz* €€ 35
Stadiongasse 16, 7350. **Road map** G4. **(** *(02612) 432 33.* **FAX** *432 33-60.*
@ oberpullendorf@sport-hotel-kurz.at
A modern hotel with a large swimming pool. Outdoor and indoor tennis
courts and bicycle hire. Cash payment is preferred. 1 ☎ TV 🛉

PAMHAGEN: *Vila Vita Hotel und Feriendorf Pannonia* €€€ 160
Storchengasse 1, 7152. **Road map** G3. **(** *(02175) 218 00.* **FAX** *2180-444.*
@ info@vilavitapannonia.at W www.vilavitahotels.com
The Hungarian-style hotel occupies a single-storey building on the shores of
Neusiedler See. Arcades and red mansard roofs with small windows add to its
romantic atmosphere. The hotel has a private beach, outdoor and indoor
swimming pools, sauna, solarium, fitness room and indoor tennis court, horse
stables, beauty parlour and bicycle hire. 1 ☎ 🛉 🛏 🛉

PERSENBEUG-METZLING: *Fischrestaurant-Motel Donaurast* € 8
Wachaustraße 28, 3680. **Road map** F3. **(** *(07412) 524 38.* **FAX** *524 38 22.*
@ donaurast@wvnet.at
A hotel with a private jetty, in the Wachau wine-growing region, right on the
banks of the Danube river. The Danube bicycle trail passes next to the house.
The restaurant is famous for its fish dishes and desserts. 1 ☎ TV 🛉 🛏 🗐

RASTENFELD: *Hotel-Restaurant Ottenstein* € 77
EVN Platz, 2344. **Road map** F2.
(*(02826) 251.* **FAX** *251-26.* @ rezeption@hotelottenstein.at
Situated near an 11th-century castle, the hotel is renowned for its gourmet
restaurant. Here you can spend an enchanting weekend enjoying regional
food and tasting local and international wines. 1 ☎ TV 🛉 🛏 P 🗐

RUST: *Hotel Sifkovits* €€ 34
Am Seekanal 8, 7071, **Road map** G3. **(** *(02685) 276 or 360.* **FAX** *360 12.*
@ hotel@sifkovits.at W www.tiscover.at/hotel.sifkovits
A modest but cosy hotel on the eastern shore of Neusiedler See. It offers a
fitness room and a sauna for guests who enjoy working out and a large
meadow with deckchairs for sun-worshippers. The menu includes dishes for
guests with special dietary needs. Open Apr–Oct. 1 ☎ 🛏 P 🗐

RUST: *Seehotel Rust* €€€ 110
Am Seekanal 2-4, 7071. **Road map** G3. **(** *(02685) 38 10.* **FAX** *381-419.*
@ seehotel.rust@austria-trend.at
This large, swanky hotel in an historic villa, part of the Austria Trend Group,
stands amid greenery on the eastern shore of Neusiedler See, where it has a
private beach. Comfortable rooms, indoor and outdoor tennis courts, sauna
and steam bath. Famous for its excellent cuisine. 1 ☎ TV 🛏 🛉 🗐

ST. AEGYD AM NEUWALDE: *Landgasthof Zum Blumentritt* € 10
Markt 20, 3193. **Road map** F3. **(** *(02768) 22 77.* **FAX** *22 77-1.*
@ zumblumentritt@aon.at W www.come.to/zumblumentritt
A combination of restaurant and pension, this is an old-fashioned inn
where you can enjoy good food and excellent wine, and then lose excess
weight in the sauna, or refresh your tan in the solarium. 1 TV 🛉 🗐

ST. PÖLTEN: *Austria Trend Hotel Metropol* € 87
Schillerplatz 1, 3100. **Road map** F3. **(** *(02742) 70 700.* **FAX** *70 700 133.*
@ metropol@austria-trend.at
This hotel, in a quiet part of the city centre, offers modern business facilities and
traditional Austrian hospitality. Sauna and steam bath. 1 ☎ TV 🏊 🛉 🛉 🗐

SEMMERING: *Belvedere* €€ 17
Hochstraße 60, 2680. **Road map** F4. **(** *(02664) 22 70.* **FAX** *22 67 42.*
@ hotel.belvedere@telecom.at
Built in the style of alpine inns, this small hotel is famous for its excellent
Austrian cuisine. Although situated right in the centre of town, it has a
magnificent garden where, weather permitting, guests can enjoy outstanding
fish dishes and other regional specialities. 1 ☎ TV 🔛 🔖 🛏 P 🗐

SEMMERING: *Hotel "Panhans"* €€€ 113
Hochstraße 32, 2680. **Road map** F4. **(** *(02664) 81 81.* **FAX** *81 81-513.*
@ hotel@panhans.at W www.panhans.at
Situated in a mountainous region, this distinctive, white, grand hotel, with
arcades built in 1888, was modernized and extended in 1993. It now has a
"Vitalclub" with a whirlpool, sauna and fitness room. Its smart restaurant has
been awarded two chef's hats. 1 ☎ TV 🔛 🛏 🗐

Price categories for a twin room with bathroom or shower, and including breakfast, service and tax, in euros:
€ up to € 90
€€ € 91–140
€€€ € 141–180
€€€€ € 181–260
€€€€€ above € 260

RESTAURANT
The restaurant is open to non-residents and hotel guests.

GARDEN OR TERRACE
The hotel is set in a garden or has an outside terrace or courtyard with plants.

SWIMMING POOL
The hotel has a swimming pool.

AIR CONDITIONING
All rooms are air-conditioned.

	NUMBER OF ROOMS	RESTAURANT	GARDEN OR TERRACE	SWIMMING POOL	AIR CONDITIONING
STEGERSBACH: *Hotel Birdie Therme Stegersbach* €€€	86	●	■	●	
WEISSENKIRCHEN/WACHAU: *Hotel-Weingasthof Donauwirt* €€	11	●	■		
WILHELMSBURG: *Landgasthof Reinberger* €	15	●	■		
ZWETTL: *Hotel Schwarz-Alm* €€	38	●	■		
BAD AUSSEE: *Hotel Erzherzog Johann* €€€	62	●	■	●	
BAD BLUMAU: *Rogner-Bad Blumau* €€€	243	●	■		
BAD GLEICHENBERG: *Hotel Stenitzer* €	30	●	■		
BAD RADKERSBURG: *Das Kurhotel im Park* €€	160	●	■	●	■

STEGERSBACH: *Hotel Birdie Therme Stegersbach* €€€
Golfstraße 1, 7551. **Road map** G4. **(** *(03326) 500-0.* **FAX** *500-800.*
@ info@golfschaukel.at **W** www.dietherme.com
A large complex of blue and white buildings, this fanciful spa hotel was designed by the Austrian artist Gottfried Kumpf. On offer for guests are golf, thermal baths and various other health treatments. Comfortable, superbly equipped rooms. 1 ⌂ TV ☑

WEISSENKIRCHEN/WACHAU: *Hotel-Weingasthof Donauwirt* €€
Wachaustraße 47, 3610. **Road map** F3. **(** *(02715) 22 47.* **FAX** *22 47-47.*
@ donauwirt@pgv.at **W** www.donauwirt.at
The 16th-century granary, which has belonged to the Rosenberg family for the past 130 years, has now been turned into a hotel with a unique interior. Its thick walls, arched vaults and exposed brickwork transport visitors back to a bygone age. The hotel restaurant serves delicious seasonal food, including lamb, asparagus and game, and new-vintage wine. Due to flood damage, the hotel was closed for reconstruction until March 2003. 1 ⌂ TV ✦ ⌂ ☑

WILHELMSBURG: *Landgasthof Reinberger* €
Kreisbacher Straße 11, 3150. **Road map** F3. **(** *(02746) 23 64.* **FAX** *23 64-35.*
@ reinberger@synops.at
A traditional inn, on the edge of the historic region of Mostviertel. The rustic style of its interior combines well with the modern facilities. An excellent place for those who enjoy good wine. 1 ⌂ TV ✦ ⌂ ☑

ZWETTL: *Hotel Schwarz-Alm* €€
Gschwendt 43, 3910. **Road map** F2. **(** *(02822) 531 73.* **FAX** *531 73-11.*
@ hotel.schwarzalm@wvnet.at
The only hotel in Waldviertel, the Schwarz-Alm stands in the middle of a meadow surrounded by forests. It is a beer-lover's paradise – the famous Austrian *Zwettler* beer is brewed in this region. 1 ⌂ TV ↻ ⌘ ⌂ P ☑

STYRIA

BAD AUSSEE: *Hotel Erzherzog Johann* €€€
Kurhausplatz 62, 8990. **Road map** D4. **(** *(03622) 525 07.* **FAX** *525 07-680.*
@ info@erzherzogjohann.at **W** www.erzherzogjohann.at
Situated in a central but quiet part of the town, this hotel with a golden façade has stylish, well-equipped rooms. There is an underground walkway to the city's wellness area, with a swimming pool, sauna, steam bath and fitness room. The restaurant serves innovative dishes. 1 ⌂ TV ⌂ ☑

BAD BLUMAU: *Rogner-Bad Blumau* €€€
Blumau 100, 8283. **Road map** F4. **(** *(03383) 51 00–94 49.* **FAX** *51 00–808.*
@ spa.blumau@rogner.com **W** www.blumau.com
This stunning hotel complex, built in 1997, was designed by the artist Friedensreich Hundertwasser. Its guests can enjoy hot-water pools, thermal spas, a vast sunbathing island, Turkish, Roman and Swedish baths plus numerous restaurants. 1 ⌂ TV ✦ ⌂ P ☑

BAD GLEICHENBERG: *Hotel Stenitzer* €
Stefanie-Stenitzer-Schulstraße 51, 8344. **Road map** F5.
(*(03159) 22 50.* **FAX** *22 50-60.* @ hotel.stenitzer@aon.at **W** www.hotel-stenitzer.com
A small, very elegant hotel with a sauna, solarium, gym, bicycle hire and a sunbathing meadow where guests can relax in deckchairs. Open Mar–Oct.
1 ⌂ TV ↻ ⌂ P

BAD RADKERSBURG: *Das Kurhotel im Park* €€
Kurhausstraße 5, 8490. **Road map** F5. **(** *(03476) 257 10.* **FAX** *20 85 45.*
@ res@kip.or.at **W** www.kurhotel-im-park.at
The spa hotel, in the middle of a park, has thermal baths, a sauna, solarium, gym, a beauty parlour and a sunbathing area. It also offers health consultations and bicycle hire. 1 ⌂ TV ✦ ↻ ⌂ Y ⌂ P ☑

BAD RADKERSBURG: *Thermenhotel Radkersburger Hof* €€ | 121
Thermenstraße 11, 8490. **Road map** F5. **☎** *(03476) 356 00.* **FAX** *(03476) 35 80.*
@ info@radkersburgerhof.at **W** www.radkersburgerhof.at
Several buildings at the edge of a forest and close to sunny fields make up
this spa hotel complex, offering thermal bath treatments. It also has a sauna,
solarium, gym and tennis courts, and offers bicycle hire for guests who wish
to explore the area. **TV 🛁 ⚡ Y 🛏 P 🌊**

BAD WALTERSDORF: *Hotel & Spa der Steirerhof Bad Waltersdorf* €€€€ | 169
Wagerberg 125, 8271. **Road map** F4. **☎** *(03333) 32 11-0.* **FAX** *32 11-444.*
@ reservierung@dersteirerhof.at **W** www.dersteirerhof.at
A large building with a swimming pool complex, sauna, solarium, gym, ladies'
spa with steam bath and beauty parlour. Besides taking thermal baths, guests
can also play tennis and cycle. The rooms are decorated in relaxing pastel
shades. **1 🛁 TV ⚡ 🛁 🔒 & Y 🛏 P 🌊**

BRUCK AN DER MUR: *Arcotel Landskron* €€€ | 45
Am Schiffertor 3, 8600. **Road map** F4. **☎** *(03862) 584 58-0.* **FAX** *584 58-6.*
@ landskron@arcotel.at **W** www.arcotel.at
This modern hotel in the town centre, right next to the Mur river, was
opened in 1993. Past the hotel is a picturesque bicycle track that runs along
the riverbank between Salzburg and Graz, over a distance of 300 km (190
miles). The Arcotel Landskron has a sauna and a steam bath.
1 🛁 TV Y 🛏 🌊

FELDBACH: *Familienhotel Etmisslerhof* €€ | 26
8622 Etmissl. **Road map** F5. **☎** *(03861) 84 44.* **FAX** *84 44-40.*
@ etmisslerhof@kom.at
This comfortable family hotel in the alpine Hochschwab region offers a daily
programme for children. It has indoor and outdoor pools, a sauna, steam
bath, tennis courts and an excellent restaurant. **1 🛁 TV 🔒 🛏 P 🌊**

FOHNSDORF: *Hotel Schloss Gabelhofen* €€€ | 57
Schlossgasse 54, 8753. **Road map** F4 **☎** *(03573) 555 50.* **FAX** *55 55-6.*
@ hotel-schloss@gabelhofen.at **W** www.gabelhofen.at
The hotel, which is in a converted 16th-century castle, is surrounded by a
large garden on the edge of a forest. Besides soaking in the atmosphere of a
bygone age, facilities are on tap for guests to enjoy playing tennis and golf,
horse-riding, rock climbing and fishing, and ice skating and skiing in winter.
You can even try your luck panning for gold in the so-called "Puszta Forest".
1 🛁 TV 🛁 Y 🛏 P 🌊

FROHNLEITEN: *Hotel Frohnleitnerhof* € | 29
Hauptplatz 14a, 8130. **Road map** F4. **☎** *(03126) 41 50.* **FAX** *41 50-555.*
@ info@frohnleitnerhof.at **W** www.frohnleitnerhof.at
A small hotel situated in the centre of town. The facilities include sauna
and golf. A courtesy bus shuttles between hotel and railway station. Open
Feb–Dec. **1 🛁 TV 🛁 🛏 🌊**

GRAZ: *Best Western Hotel Daniel* €€ | 110
Europaplatz 1, 8021. **Road map** F4. **☎** *(0316) 71 10 80.* **FAX** *71 10 85.*
@ daniel@weitzer.com **W** www.hoteldaniel.com
Hotel situated in the commercial district of Graz, ten minutes' walk from the
Old Town, part of the Best Western Group. All standard rooms are equipped
with radio, minibar, satellite TV and telephone, and have soundproof
windows. Executive rooms also have large desks and balconies with good
views over the town. **1 🛁 TV & Y P 🌊**

GRAZ: *Austria Trend Hotel Europa Graz* €€€ | 114
Bahnhofgürtel 89, 8020. **Road map** F4. **☎** *(0316) 707 60.* **FAX** *707 66 06.*
@ europa.graz@austria-trend.at **W** www.austria-trend.at/eug
A large, modern hotel situated only a few minutes walk from the town centre,
right opposite the main railway station. It has cosy, functionally furnished
rooms, and meeting room facilities for up to 250 people. The *Vier Jahreszeiten*
(Four Seasons) Restaurant serves seasonal delicacies and excellent Styrian
wines. **1 🛁 TV 🛁 🔒 & Y 🛏 P 🌊**

GRAZ: *Erzherzog Johann* €€€ | 62
Sackstraße 3–5, 8010. **Road map** F4. **☎** *(0316) 81 16 16.* **FAX** *81 15 15.*
@ office@erzherzog-johann.com **W** www.erzherzog-johann.com
This is Graz's most historic hotel, overlooking the main square in town.
Originally built as a palace, it was converted into a hotel in 1852. It is famous
for its glass-roofed courtyard and excellent service.
1 🛁 TV ⚡ 🛁 🔒 & Y 🛏 P 🌊

Price categories for a twin room with bathroom or shower, and including breakfast, service and tax, in euros:
€ up to € 90
€€ € 91–140
€€€ € 141–180
€€€€ € 181–260
€€€€€ above € 260

RESTAURANT
The restaurant is open to non-residents and hotel guests.

GARDEN OR TERRACE
The hotel is set in a garden or has an outside terrace or courtyard with plants.

SWIMMING POOL
The hotel has a swimming pool.

AIR CONDITIONING
All rooms are air-conditioned.

	Number of Rooms	Restaurant	Garden or Terrace	Swimming Pool	Air Conditioning
GRAZ: *Grand Hotel Wiesler* €€€€	97	●			■
KAPFENBERG: *Hotel Böhlerstern* €	37	●	■		
KNITTELFELD: *Hotel Verde* €€	40	●	■		
LEOBEN/NIKLASDORF: *Brücklwirt* €	70	●	■	●	
MARIAZELL: *Hotel Drei Hasen* €€	50	●	■		
MARIAZELL: *Hotel Schwarzer Adler* €€	32	●	■		
RAMSAU: *Peter Rosegger* €€	13	●	■		
SCHLADMING: *Alte Post* €	40	●			

GRAZ: *Grand Hotel Wiesler*
Grieskai 4–8, 8020. **Road map** F4. **(** *(0316) 706 60.* **FAX** *70 66 76.*
@ wiesler@weitzer.com **W** www.hotelwiesler.com
The only five-star hotel in Graz, with views over the historic Old Town, the Wiesler stands on the banks of the Mur river. Tradition blends harmoniously with modern comfort. The hotel café is decorated with beautiful mosaics from 1910, designed by Leopold Forstner, pupil of Gustav Klimt.

KAPFENBERG: *Hotel Böhlerstern*
Friedrich-Böhler-Straße 13, 8605. **Road map** F4. **(** *(03862) 25 55 96 375.*
FAX *25 55 96-165.* @ reception@boehlerstern.at **W** www.boehlerstern.at
This small, stylish hotel on the Vienna–Klagenfurt route features attractive wooden panelling and graceful balustrades on the stairs. The rooms are well equipped and tastefully furnished, with predominantly light-coloured wood.

KNITTELFELD: *Hotel Verde*
Gaalerstraße 4, 8720. **Road map** E4. **(** *(03512) 725 93.* **FAX** *72 59 39.*
@ hotel@verde.at **W** www.verde.at
A modern, four-star hotel, belonging to the Best Western chain, with a sauna and solarium in the vicinity. Guests can enjoy horse-riding, cycling, golf and fishing.

LEOBEN/NIKLASDORF: *Brücklwirt*
Leobener Straße 90, 8712. **Road map** F4. **(** *(03842) 817 27.* **FAX** *817 27-5.*
@ reception@bruecklwirt.co.at **W** www.bruecklwirt.co.at
A modern hotel next to the motorway to Leoben. The rooms, although not large, are comfortable, and the tiled bathrooms are light and spotlessly clean. There is a sauna, solarium and steam bath. The restaurant serves excellent local cuisine and a candle-lit dinner on the terrace is a truly unforgettable experience.

MARIAZELL: *Hotel Drei Hasen*
Wiener Straße 11, 8630. **Road map** F4. **(** *(03882) 24 10.* **FAX** *24 10-800.*
@ dreihasen@aon.at
A traditional, family-run hotel situated near the famous basilica and opposite the cable-car station, the Drei Hasen (Three Hares) has garage parking, a sauna, gym and an attractive first-floor terrace. Bicycle hire is available nearby.

MARIAZELL: *Hotel Schwarzer Adler*
Hauptplatz 1, 8630. **Road map** F4. **(** *(03882) 286 30.* **FAX** *28 63 50.*
@ adler-mz@kom.at **W** www.tiscover.at/adler-mz
The four-star Schwarzer Adler (Black Eagle) complex in the centre of town consists of two buildings: the main hotel and the restaurant with pension. The terrace has a magnificent view of the mountains. There is also a day bar and a café.

RAMSAU: *Peter Rosegger*
Ramsau 233, 8972. **Road map** D4. **(** *(03687) 81 223-0.* **FAX** *81 223-8.*
@ peter.rosegger@netway.at **W** www.tiscover.at/peter.rosegger
A Swiss chalet-style country hotel, on the edge of a forest, in a quiet, secluded area. It is an excellent base for rock-climbing. It can boast plush rooms and the best restaurant of the region, which serves a range of local specialities; the smoked trout is particularly worth trying.

SCHLADMING: *Alte Post*
Hauptplatz 10, 8970. **Road map** D4. **(** *(03687) 225 71.* **FAX** *225 71-8.*
@ office@alte-post.at **W** www.alte-post.at
The hotel, in an historic building dating from 1618, is famous for its attractive *Stube* (reception room) and vaulted rooms. Its two restaurants serve good regional and Austrian food in an authentic setting.

SCHLADMING: *Gasthof Kirchenwirt* € | 16
Salzburgerstraße 27, 8970. **Road map** D4. 📞 *(03687) 224 35.* 📠 *224 35-16.*
@ info@kirchenwirt-schladming.com W www.kirchenwirt-schladming.com
This hotel, in the centre of an old mountain village near Planai, is an excellent base for active holidays. It has a cosy, old-fashioned bar and a stylish restaurant serving regional specialities. Very friendly service. 1 🛏 TV 🛌 P 🏊

UPPER AUSTRIA

AIGEN-VOGLHUB: *Gasthof Grabnerwirt* € | 7
Lindau 5, 5351. **Road map** D4. 📞 *(06132) 245 52.* 📠 *245 52-4.*
A small, sunny village pension near Bad Ischl. The landlady personally attends to her guests and strives to create a pleasant home atmosphere. Television can be watched in the TV room, while the lounge is intended for pleasant chats over a beer or two. Payment by cash only. 🛗

ALTMÜNSTER: *Gasthof Pension "Urzn"* € | 19
Gmundnerberg 91, 4813. **Road map** D3. 📞 *(07612) 872 14.* 📠 *899 27.*
@ gasthaus@urzn.at
A picturesque *Bauernhof* (farm) with views over the mountains and the picturesque Traunsee. Some rooms have balconies. TV 🛗 🛌 P

BAD ISCHL: *Austria Classic Hotel Goldenes Schiff* €€ | 56
Adalbert Stifter-Kai 3, 4820. **Road map** D4. 📞 *(06132) 242 41.* 📠 *242 41-58.*
@ office@goldenes-schiff.at W www.goldenes-schiff.at
This traditional, family-run hotel stands on the banks of the Traun river, in a health resort famous for the hunting lodge where Franz Joseph I got engaged to the Bavarian Princess Elisabeth. Traditional furnishings; sauna and solarium, tennis and fishing. 1 🛏 TV 🛌 Y 🛌 P 🏊

BAD LEONFELDEN: *Kurhotel Bad Leonfelden* €€€ | 88
Spielau 8, 4190. **Road map** E3. 📞 *(07213) 63 63.* 📠 *63 63-292.*
@ office@kurhaus.at W www.kurhaus.at
Part of the 50plus Hotels chain, this hotel situated at the edge of a forest offers various treatments – poultices, exercise and massage for example – for a range of ailments. It also has a slimming centre, and offers diets. The smart rooms have functional furnishings. 1 TV 🏊 🛌 🛗 & P 🏊 *V, MC, EC*

GMUNDEN: *Austria am See* € | 6
Sparkassegasse 1, 4810. **Road map** D3. 📞 *(0676) 35 06 231 or (07673) 3591.*
Private accommodation in a good location on Traunsee, in superbly kept buildings. All rooms have radios and desks. A small kitchen and refrigerator is available for the use of guests, and there is also a reading room. TV Y

GMUNDEN: *Seehotel Schwan* €€ | 35
Rathausplatz 8, 4810. **Road map** D3. 📞 *(07612) 633 91.* 📠 *633 91-8.*
@ noestlingerschwan@direkt.at W www.seehotel-schwan.at
This hotel, part of the Best Western chain, stands on a boulevard along Traunsee. Plush rooms offer views over the lake, some with balconies. The restaurant specializes in fish and *Hausmannskost* (home cooking). Garage parking. 1 TV 🛌 🛗 & P 🏊

GMUNDEN: *Schlosshotel "Freisitz Roith"* €€€ | 19
Traunsteinstraße 87, 4810. **Road map** D3.
📞 *(07612) 64 905.* 📠 *64 905-17.* @ info@schlosshotel.at W www.schlosshotel.at
Hotel in a converted 16th-century castle, open during the summer and over Christmas and New Year, catering mainly for families and conferences. Features a sauna, solarium and fitness room. 1 TV 🛌 🛗 & P 🏊

HALLSTATT: *Seehotel Grüner Baum* €€€ | 20
Marktplatz 104, 4830. **Road map** D4. 📞 *(06134) 82 63.* 📠 *84 20.*
@ gruener.baum@magnet.at
Hotel in a small fairy-tale town, on a mountain slope above Hallstätter See, in a traditional yellow building dating from 1760. Rooms with balconies overlook a charming square or the lake. Facilities include a sauna, solarium, bicycles and a laundry room. 1 TV 🛌 🛗 & P 🏊

LINZ: *Courtyard by Marriott Hotels Linz* €€ | 236
Europaplatz 2, 4020. **Road map** E3. 📞 *(0732) 6959-0.* 📠 *60 60 90.*
@ cy.lnzcy.room.reservation@marriott.com W www.marriott.at/lnzcy
This modern, classy hotel is in a rather unprepossessing building in the town centre, next door to the Linz Design Centre. Among other facilities on offer are a solarium, a beauty salon, a fitness room with sauna and massage, and a business centre. 1 🛏 TV & Y 🛌 P 🏊

For key to symbols *see back flap*

Price categories for a twin room with bathroom or shower, and including breakfast, service and tax, in euros:
€ up to € 90
€€ € 91–140
€€€ € 141–180
€€€€ € 181–260
€€€€€ above € 260

RESTAURANT
The restaurant is open to non-residents and hotel guests.

GARDEN OR TERRACE
The hotel is set in a garden or has an outside terrace or courtyard with plants.

SWIMMING POOL
The hotel has a swimming pool.

AIR CONDITIONING
All rooms are air-conditioned.

		NUMBER OF ROOMS	RESTAURANT	GARDEN OR TERRACE	SWIMMING POOL	AIR CONDITIONING
LINZ: *Hotel Ibis Linz* Kärntner Straße 18–20, 4020. **Road map** E3. (*(0732) 694 01.* FAX *69 40 19.* @ H1722-GM@Accor-Hotels.com New, elegant hotel in the town centre, close to the main railway station *(Hauptbahnhof).* Buffet breakfast. 1 ⛪ TV ≈ ⚡ ⛪ ⛪ ⛪	€	146	●			■
LINZ: *Arcotel Nike* Untere Donaulände 9, 4020. **Road map** E3. (*(0732) 762 60.* FAX *762 62.* @ nike@arcotel.at W www.arcotel.at Large, modern and elegant hotel on the banks of the Danube. The tastefully furnished rooms are very well equipped. Hotel facilities include garage parking, sauna, solarium and fitness room. 1 ⛪ ⚡ TV ≈ ≋ ⛪ ⛪ ⛪	€€	176	●	■	●	■
LINZ: *Austria Trend Hotel Schillerpark* Rainerstraße 2–4, 4020. **Road map** E3. (*(0732) 6950-0.* FAX *6950-9.* @ schillerpark@austria-trend.at W www.austria-trend.at Having undergone a thorough refurbishment in 1999, the hotel now has comfortable rooms and studios arranged in accordance with the principles of Feng Shui. It also houses a casino, three restaurants, three bars and a coffee shop. 1 ⛪ TV ≈ ⚡ ⛪ ⛪ ⛪	€€€	111	●			■
MONDSEE: *Seegasthof Weiße Taube* St. Lorenz 116, 5310. **Road map** D3. (*(06232) 22 77.* FAX *39 01.* Traditional alpine pension on the shores of Mondsee, in the Salzkammergut region. Alongside its standard rooms, it also offers some less expensive ones with a shared shower and WC along the corridor. Guests are always guaranteed a place on the hotel lakeside beach, and you can also play table tennis, go fishing, hire a bicycle, or hike up the mountain trails. 1 ⛪ P	€	45	●	■		
MONDSEE: *Restop Mondsee Panoramahotel* Loibichl, 5311. **Road map** D3. (*(06232) 28 76-0.* FAX *28 76-5.* @ panoramahotel.mondsee@eurest.at W www.eurest.at/panoramahotel This modern hotel, visible from afar, has a large terrace providing magnificent views over Mondsee and the surrounding mountains. It is situated a mere 30 km (19 miles) from Salzburg. Room furnishings are standard, although pleasant and well equipped. 1 ⛪ TV ⛪ ⛪ ⛪ P ⛪	€€	40	●	■		
ST. GEORGEN IM ATTERGAU: *Söllinger's Attergauhof* Attergaustraße 41, 4880. **Road map** D3. (*(07667) 64 06.* FAX *64 06-15.* @ hotel.attergauhof@netway.at W www.attergauhof.at A charming little hotel near Attersee. It has a private car park and garage, a sauna, solarium, bicycle hire, and a meadow on which to relax in a deck chair. The high terrace affords a lovely view over the region. There is a free courtesy bus for visitors arriving by train. 1 TV ⛪ P ⛪	€	28	●	■		
ST. WOLFGANG: *Hotel Weißes Rössl* Markt 74, 5360. **Road map** D4. (*(6138) 23 06-66.* FAX *23 06-41.* @ office@weissesroessl.at W www.weissesroessl.at This modernized hotel in a golden-yellow building has featured in many films. The luxurious rooms, terraces resting on pillars above the lake waters, combined with delicious fish dishes served to the tunes of the zither, make for a special experience. Famous for its unusual furnishings and excellent service, it attracts guests come from all over the world. Book well in advance. 1 ⛪ TV ⛪ P ⛪	€€€	72	●	■	●	
ST. WOLFGANG: *Appesbach Das Herrenhaus am See* Aupromenade 18, 5360. **Road map** D4. (*(06138) 22 09.* FAX *22 09-14.* @ office@appesbach.com W www.appesbach.com Exclusive four-star hotel situated in a former private mansion on the shores of Wolfgangsee. It offers peace and quiet, first-class service, numerous sports facilities, a sauna and a fitness room. Most rooms have a lake view, some with a balcony or deck. It has an excellent restaurant, although this is open to residents only. 1 TV ⛪ ⛪ ⛪ ⛪ ⛪ ⛪ ⛪ P ⛪	€€€€€	26		■		

SCHÄRDING: *Hotel zur Stiege* € 26
Schlossgasse 2-6, 4780. **Road map** D3. **[** (07712) 30 70-0. **FAX** 30 70-84.
@ hotel.stiege@aon.at W www.members.aon.at/hotel.stiege
A small hotel in a stylish house, with functional room furnishings. Offers
bicycles for hire, and special meals for those on diets. **1 TV & ☂ P ≋**

SCHÄRDING: *Schärdinger Hof* € 42
Innbruckstraße 6-8, 4780. **Road map** D3. **[** (07712) 44 04-0. **FAX** 44 08.
@ info@schaerdingerhof.at
The hotel is situated in a small town, 100 km (62 miles) northwest of Linz
near the Bavarian border. Tastefully furnished rooms and a good restaurant
serving vegetarian and local dishes. **1 ☂ TV ☂ P ≋**

TRAUNKIRCHEN: *Hotel Post Austria Classic* €€ 54
Ortsplatz 5, 4801. **Road map** D3. **[** (07617) 230 70. **FAX** 28 09.
@ post@traunseehotels.at W www.traunseehotels.at/post
A charming hotel on the shores of Traunsee in the Salzkammergut. It has a
private beach, sauna, solarium and bicycle hire. All rooms have cable TV,
telephone and a safe. Traditional Austrian cuisine and dishes for those with
special dietary needs. **1 ☂ TV ☂ Y ≋**

WEISSENBACH AM ATTERSEE: *Hotel Post* €€ 37
Ischlerstraße 1, 4854. **Road map** D3. **[** (07663) 81 41. **FAX** 81 42 45.
@ office@hpw.at W www.hpw.at/attersee
Hotel right on the edge of Attersee. There is a private beach next to the hotel,
open for residents only. Facilities for tennis, miniature golf, bowling and
fishing. Open May–Sep. **1 ☂ TV Y P**

WINDISCHGARSTEN: *Berggasthof Zottensberg* € 24
Edelbach 55, 4580. **Road map** E4. **[** (07566) 309. **FAX** 309-31.
@ berggasthof@zottensberg.at
Typical alpine hotel at an altitude of 900 m (2,953 ft). Facilities include garage
parking, a sauna, solarium, table tennis and kitchen. It is situated only 10 km
(6 miles) from a skiing centre. The large, rustic dining room is subdivided into
many cosy corners and niches affording excellent privacy. There is also an
alpine hut to rent, a game reserve to explore and horses. **1 TV P**

WINDISCHGARSTEN: *Windischgarstenhof* € 48
Edelbach 17, 4580 Windischgarsten. **Road map** E4. **[** (07562) 73 31. **FAX** 73 31-55.
@ info@windischgarstenhof.at
Hotel near the beautiful Kalkalpen National Park, based in a typically alpine
building in a quiet, secluded spot, surrounded by greenery. Offers massage,
poultices and therapeutic exercises. No credit cards. **1 ☂ TV & P**

SALZBURGER LAND

BADGASTEIN: *Hotel Weismayr* €€ 77
Kaiser-Franz-Joseph-Straße 6, 5640. **Road map** D4. **[** (06434) 25 94-0. **FAX** 25 94-14.
@ info@weismayr.com W www.weismayr.com
Since 1832, this hotel has ranked as one of the best in the region. It boasts an
excellent breakfast bar and superb four-course dinners as well as fitness room
and sauna. **1 ☂ TV ☂ Y ☂ ≋**

BADGASTEIN: *Arcotel Elisabethpark* €€€ 120
Kaiser-Franz-Joseph-Straße 5, 5640. **Road map** D4. **[** (06434) 255 10. **FAX** 25 51-10.
@ elisabethpark@arcotel.at
Situated in the town centre, opposite the casino, this hotel has a large garden,
restaurant, café and bar. Other facilities include a sauna, fitness room and
bicycle hire. **1 ☂ TV ☂ ☂ ☂ Y ☂ P ≋**

EUGENDORF: *Landgasthof Holznerwirt* €€ 57
Dorfstraße 4, 5301. **Road map** D3. **[** (06225) 82 05. **FAX** 82 05-19.
@ hotel@holznerwirt.at W www.holznerwirt.at
This country hotel, standing next to the church in Eugendorf, has comfortable
rooms, some with balconies, furnished in a rustic style. The atmosphere is
pleasant and homely. A tennis centre and horse stud are nearby. **☂ TV P ≋**

FILZMOOS: *Haus Geierberg II* € 7
Neuberg 196, 5532. **Road map** D4. **[** (06453) 87880. **FAX** 788831.
@ info@geierberg.at W www.geierberg.at
This pension is a complex of three buildings, standing at the edge of a forest,
right next to a ski lift. Facilities include a sauna, solarium and a separate
playroom for children. All rooms have telephones and satellite TV. **TV ☂ ≋**

<table>
<tr><td>

Price categories for a twin room with bathroom or shower, and including breakfast, service and tax, in euros:
€ up to € 90
€€ € 91–140
€€€ € 141–180
€€€€ € 181–260
€€€€€ above € 260

</td><td>

RESTAURANT
The restaurant is open to non-residents and hotel guests.

GARDEN OR TERRACE
The hotel is set in a garden or has an outside terrace or courtyard with plants.

SWIMMING POOL
The hotel has a swimming pool.

AIR CONDITIONING
All rooms are air-conditioned.

</td></tr>
</table>

	NUMBER OF ROOMS	RESTAURANT	GARDEN OR TERRACE	SWIMMING POOL	AIR CONDITIONING
FILZMOOS: *Tannenhof* € Filzmoos 84, 5332. **Road map** D4. (*(06453) 82 02.* FAX *84 60.* @ info@sieberer.at Inexpensive pension with its own bakery and a tiny cake shop, in the central area of Filzmoos. Some rooms have balconies. [1] 🖼 TV 🏃 🏠	13		■		
FILZMOOS: *Hubertus* €€€ Am Dorfplatz 1, 5532. **Road map** D4. (*(06453) 8204.* FAX *820 46.* @ info@hotelhubertus.at W www.hotelhubertus.at Every detail is perfect in this centrally located hotel. Anglers have the use of a 20-km (12-mile) stretch of mountain stream and two lakes. The restaurant is regarded as the best in the area; the owner, Johanna Maier, is the only female chef to have been awarded four chef's hats. [1] 🖼 TV 🏃 P 🗐	14	●	■		
FUSCHL AM SEE: *Hotel Seewinkel* €€ Fuschl am See, 5330. **Road map** D4. (*(06226) 83 44.* FAX *83 44-18.* @ hotel@seewinkel.com This alpine-style house, its balconies decorated with an abundance of flowers, stands right at the edge of the lake and only a few minutes walk from the town centre. The facilities include a sauna, solarium, bicycles and a rowing boat. [1] 🖼 TV 🏃 P 🗐	27	●	■		
FUSCHL AM SEE: *Hotel Schloss Fuschl* €€€€ Hof bei Salzburg, 5322. **Road map** D4. (*(06229) 22 53-0.* FAX *22 53-531.* @ reservation@schlossfuschl.at W www.arabellasheraton.at This large hotel, on the shores of the lake, is one of the Leading Hotels of the World group. It occupies a late-15th century building that once belonged to the Bishop of Salzburg who used it as a hunting lodge. Modernized in the 19th century, it now caters for a very discerning clientele. The hotel restaurant, with a lovely view over the lake, is regarded as one of the best in Austria. [1] 🖼 TV 🏃 🗐	84	●	■	●	
GROSSARL: *Alte Post* €€ Marktplatz 24, 5611. **Road map** D4. (*(06414) 207.* FAX *207-115.* @ altepost@ping.at This traditional family hotel offers many attractions for children and grown-ups alike. The interior is very tastefully decorated. During the winter months, a free bus service takes guests up to the ski lifts. All rooms have radio and satellite TV, many have balconies. There is also a sauna, solarium and fitness room. [1] 🖼 TV 🏃 P 🗐	40	●	■	●	
KLEINARL: *Pension Viehhof* € Kleinarl 190, 5603. **Road map** D4. (*(06418) 240.* FAX *240-31.* @ pension.viehhof@aon.at W www.algo.at/viehhof This small pension stands right next to the cable-car station and a skiing-school assembly point. In winter, you can participate in a weekly sledge ride accompanied by a local band, or try other snow-based activities, then relax in the sauna or sunbathe in the solarium. TV 🖼	15		■		
KLEINARL: *Gästehaus Keil* €€ Kleinarl 173, 5603. **Road map** D4. (*(06418) 618.* FAX *618-40.* @ info@keil.at A comfortable pension, entirely renovated and remodelled in 1999. The decor is smart, particularly in the dining room, which features an exposed-beam wooden ceiling. The rooms have balconies. [1] 🖼 TV 🏃	18		■	●	
SALZBURG: *Centro-hotel* € Auerspergstraße 24, 5020. **Road map** D3. (*(0662) 88 22 21.* FAX *88 22 21-55.* @ reception@centro-hotel.at A modern hotel situated in the town centre, near Mirabell Park and Palace. All rooms have telephone and cable TV, most have balconies. There is also an Internet corner. Large groups may negotiate prices. [1] 🖼 TV 🔽 🏃 🏠 🗐	42		■		

SALZBURG: *Parkhotel Billroth* € | 250
Billrothstraße 10–18, 5020. **Road map** D3. ☎ *(0662) 930 30-70.* **FAX** *930 30-77.*
@ office@billllroth-hotels.at
Large, inexpensive, tastefully furnished hotel, catering especially for young
people and students. Open Jul–Aug, plus three weeks in Sep. 1 🛏 🍴 P 🖳

SALZBURG: *Bergland* €€ | 18
Rupertgasse 15, 5020. **Road map** D3. ☎ *(0662) 87 23 18-0.* **FAX** *872318-8.*
@ pkuhn@berglandhotel.at
This newly refurbished small hotel has been in the hands of the same family
for three generations. It stands at the foot of Kapuzinerberg, in the centre of
town. The facilities include bicycle hire, a library and an Internet corner.
Rooms (all non-smoking) are comfortable and tastefully furnished.
🛏 TV 🖳 🔲 P

SALZBURG: *NH Salzburg City* €€€€ | 140
Franz-Josef-Straße 26, 5020. **Road map** D3. ☎ *(0662) 88 20 41.* **FAX** *87 42 40.*
@ nhsalzburg@nh-hotels.com
A large hotel, occupying a historic building in the town centre, near Mirabell
Park. The facilities include a sauna, solarium, gym and bicycle hire. Spacious
rooms with a modern, tasteful decor. 1 🛏 TV 🖳 🔲 ♿ 🍽 🍴 P 🖳

SALZBURG: *Hotel Sacher Salzburg* €€€€€€ | 118
Schwarzstraße 5–7, 5020. **Road map** D3. ☎ *(0662) 889 77.* **FAX** *889 77-14.*
@ salzburg@sacher.com W www.sacher.com
A magnificent hotel on the banks of the Salzach river. Among its past guests
feature famous names such as The Beatles, The Rolling Stones and Hillary
Clinton. It belongs to the Gürtler family, who also own the Sacher Hotel in
Vienna. Each room has a different decor, all created with the utmost care and
attention. Friendly and discreet service. On sunny days, guests can enjoy lunch
on the terrace, with views of the Hohensalzburg fortress. 1 🛏 TV 🔲 🖳

ST. GILGEN: *Pension Seeblick* € | 14
Pöllach 29, 5340. **Road map** D4. ☎ *(06227) 26 82.* **FAX** *26 82.*
@ pension.seeblick@aon.at
This small, pleasant, typically alpine pension on the shores of Wolfgangsee in
the Salzkammergut region, has been run by the same family for three
generations. Rooms have balconies and lake views. 1 🛏 TV 🍴 P

ST. GILGEN: *Parkhotel Billroth* €€€ | 45
Billrothstraße 2, 5340. **Road map** D4. ☎ *(06227) 22 17.* **FAX** *22 18 25.*
@ office@billroth.at W www.billroth.at
A smart villa, decorated in late-19th-century style, surrounded by a large
park and close to a lake but only ten minutes' walk from the town centre.
It has spacious rooms, which are tastefully and lavishly decorated.
1 🛏 TV 🔲 P 🖳

ZELL AM SEE: *Sporthotel Alpenblick* €€ | 70
Alte Landesstraße 6, 5700. **Road map** D4. ☎ *(06542) 54 33.* **FAX** *54 33-1.*
@ hotel@alpenblick.at W www.alpenblick.at
A charming hotel that has beautiful views over the lake and the surrounding
mountains. Apart from its superb location and great comfort, its attractions are
its sports facilities, including a swimming pool, sauna and gym, cycling, golf
and sailing, as well as skiing in the winter season. Open Jan–Mar, May–Nov.
1 🛏 TV 🏃 ♿ 🖳

TYROL AND VORARLBERG

AU IM BREGENZER WALD: *Hotel Rössle* €€ | 32
Lisse 90, 6883. **Road map** A4. ☎ *(05515) 22 16.* **FAX** *2216-6.*
@ hotel@roessle-am.at
A light-coloured wooden house, against a backdrop of majestic rocks. The
tastefully decorated rooms, with a restaurant serving good food and a great
selection of wines all combine to make for a pleasant stay. In addition, it
offers a sauna, solarium, fitness room and bicycle hire. Open May–Oct,
Dec–mid-Apr. 🛏 🏃 ♿ 🍴 🖳

AU IM BREGENZER WALD: *Krone in Au* €€€ | 68
Jaghausen 4, 6883. **Road map** A4. ☎ *(05515) 220 10.* **FAX** *22 01-201.*
@ krone-au@vol.at W www.krone-au.at
A typical timber-framed alpine building, with flower-bedecked balconies and a
large terrace. It has a sauna, solarium, indoor swimming pool, gym and
bicycle hire. Anglers can enjoy fishing here, too. 1 🛏 🏃 🖳

For key to symbols *see back flap*

Price categories for a twin room with bathroom or shower, and including breakfast, service and tax, in euros:
€ up to € 90
€€ € 91–140
€€€ € 141–180
€€€€ € 181–260
€€€€€ above € 260

RESTAURANT
The restaurant is open to non-residents and hotel guests.

GARDEN OR TERRACE
The hotel is set in a garden or has an outside terrace or courtyard with plants.

SWIMMING POOL
The hotel has a swimming pool.

AIR CONDITIONING
All rooms are air-conditioned.

	NUMBER OF ROOMS	RESTAURANT	GARDEN OR TERRACE	SWIMMING POOL	AIR CONDITIONING
BEZAU: *Gasthof Sonne* €	30	●	■		
BLUDENZ: *Schlosshotel Dörflinger* €€	45	●	■		
BREGENZ: *Messmer Hotel* €€	80	●	■		
BREGENZ: *Hotel Germania* €€€	40	●	■		
BREGENZ: *Weißes Kreuz* €€€	44	●			
FELDKIRCH: *Hotel-Gasthof Löwen* €	68	●	■		
FELDKIRCH: *Central Hotel Löwen* €€	68	●			
FINKENBERG: *Sport- und Wellnesshotel Stock* €€	75	●	■	●	

BEZAU: *Gasthof Sonne* €
Kriechere, 6870. **Road map** A4. ☎ (05514) 22 62. FAX 29 12. @ info@gasthof-sonne.at
W www.gasthof-sonne.at
A pension surrounded by green spaces, with windows facing a sunny meadow where you can relax after exhausting excursions or sporting activities. Guests can also make use of the hotel's sauna, solarium, fitness room and bicycles.

BLUDENZ: *Schlosshotel Dörflinger* €€
Schlossplatz 5, 6700. **Road map** A4. ☎ (05552) 630 16. FAX 63 01 68.
@ info@schlosshotel.cc W www.schlosshotel.cc
The hotel stands on a rocky outcrop, and its windows provide views over the centre of Bludenz. There is a former palace nearby, and a golf course and ski lifts are just a few steps from the hotel. Rooms are tastefully furnished and the hotel restaurant offers regional cuisine.

BREGENZ: *Messmer Hotel* €€
Kornmarktstraße 16, 6900. **Road map** A4. ☎ (05574) 423 56. FAX 42 35 66.
@ hotel.messmer@bregenznet.at
Although this hotel is in a rather modest, unprepossessing building, it has a smart interior. The comfortable rooms are well equipped. Extra facilities on offer include a sauna, a fitness room and bicycle hire.

BREGENZ: *Hotel Germania* €€€
Am Steinenbach 9, 6900. **Road map** A4. ☎ (05574) 427 66. FAX 42 76 64.
@ office@hotel-germania.at W www.hotel-germania.at
A simple, white building, with a tastefully furnished and comfortable interior. The rooms are fitted with desks for business travellers. The hotel organizes cycling trips, and its facilities include a sauna, solarium and fitness room. Garage parking is available.

BREGENZ: *Weißes Kreuz* €€€
Römerstraße 5, 6900. **Road map** A4. ☎ (05574) 498 80. FAX 49 88 67.
@ hotelweisseskreuz@kinz.at W www.bestwestern-ce.com/weisseskreuz
The hotel belongs to the Best Western Hotel chain. The furniture reflects regional traditions, with typically alpine furnishings. There is a sauna and the hotel offers bicycles for hire. The restaurant features local and Austrian dishes.

FELDKIRCH: *Hotel-Gasthof Löwen* €
Feldkirch-Nofels, Kohlgasse 1, 6800. **Road map** A4. ☎ (05522) 3583. FAX 35 83 55.
@ office@hotel-loewen.at
A large pension in a country house that provides a homely, family atmosphere. There is a sauna and it also offers bicycles for hire.

FELDKIRCH: *Central Hotel Löwen* €€
Schlossgraben 13, 6800. **Road map** A4. ☎ (05522) 720 70. FAX 720 70-5.
@ info@central-hotel-loewen.at
An imposing, solid building, with a façade painted in imperial yellow. It has tastefully furnished rooms and a private sauna. There is a buffet breakfast and special diets are catered for on request. The hotel is reopening in Dec 2003.

FINKENBERG: *Sport- und Wellnesshotel Stock* €€
Dorf 142, 6292. **Road map** C4. ☎ (05285) 67 75. FAX 67 75-421.
@ sporthotel@stock.at W www.sporthotel-stock.com
A typically Tyrolean hotel, located in a beautiful setting at the foot of the Zillertal Alps. In winter, after skiing you can enjoy the indoor swimming pool or the beauty salon, and in the summer you can go cycling or fishing.

FONTANELLA/FASCHINA: *Hotel Faschina* €€€ 39
Faschina 55. **Road map** A4. (*(05510) 224.* FAX *224 26.*
@ hotel@faschina.at W www.hotel-faschina.at
The hotel occupies a flat-roof building, departing from alpine architectural traditions. It has indoor and outdoor swimming pools, a sauna, solarium, fitness room, beauty parlour, tennis courts and bicycles. Anglers may try their luck in the local fish pond, and the chef will prepare their catch as requested.

FONTANELLA/FASCHINA: *Hotel Walserhof* €€€ 39
Faschina 66, 6733. **Road map** A4. (*(05510) 217.* FAX *217-13.*
@ hotel.walserhof.faschina@aon.at W www.walserhof.at
A typical alpine hotel situated at an altitude of 1,500 m (4,921 ft), featuring an unusual, attractive garden on the garage roof. The hotel is particularly suited to families with children. It has indoor and outdoor swimming pools, a sauna, solarium, fitness room, tennis courts, hairdresser and bicycle hire. Anglers may also enjoy fishing.

FULPMES: *Waldhof* €€€ 26
Gröbenweg 19, 6166. **Road map** B4. (*(05225) 621 75.* FAX *642 83.*
@ waldhof@fulpmes.at W www.bergwelthotel.at
This small hotel surrounded by greenery is set in a typical white-plastered, timber-framed alpine house. It has a pleasant family atmosphere. All guests can make use of the sauna and solarium, exercise in the gym or ride bicycles.

HALL IN TIROL: *Austria Classic Hotel Heiligkreuz* €€ 35
Reimmichlstraße 18, 6060. **Road map** B4. (*(05223) 571 14.* FAX *57 11 45.*
@ info@heiligkreuz.at W www.heiligkreuz.at
A hotel with a genuine family atmosphere. Boasts a beautiful interior, with dark wood panelling and comfortable furniture in elegant rooms. The restaurant serves traditional classics.

IMST: *Romantik-Hotel Post* €€ 30
Eduard-Wallhöfer-Platz 3, 6460. **Road map** B4. (*(05412) 665 54.* FAX *665 19 55.*
@ romantikhotel.post@netway.at
A hotel set in the 15th-century Sprengenstein Castle, in a village nestling at the foot of the eastern Lechtal Alps. Combines the traditional with the modern to create a romantic ambience. In addition, there are weekly golf tournaments in spring and autumn, plus other "events of the week" and organized group excursions.

INNSBRUCK: *Alt-Pradl* €€ 33
Pradler Straße 8, 6020. **Road map** B4. (*(0512) 34 51 56.* FAX *34 51 56-8.*
@ altpradl-hotel@tirol.com
The hotel stands at a junction, and all the rooms therefore have a sunny aspect and offer town views. The facilities include private garage parking, sauna, solarium and gym.

INNSBRUCK: *Goldener Adler* €€€ 34
Herzog-Friedrich-Straße 6, 6020. **Road map** B4. (*(0512) 57 11 11.* FAX *58 44 09.*
@ office@goldeneradler.com W www.goldeneradler.com
The hotel occupies a historic building adorned with paintings. Its illustrious former guests have included Goethe, Mozart and Emperor Joseph II. Its great advantage is its central location – in the very heart of the Old Town. The stylishly furnished rooms have a modern charm. The restaurant is famous for its excellent regional cuisine.

INNSBRUCK: *Parkhotel Leipzigerhof* €€€ 55
Defreggerstraße 13, 6020. **Road map** B4. (*(0512) 34 35 25.* FAX *39 43 57.*
@ reception@parkhotel-leipzigerhof.at
Newly refurbished hotel, opened in the spring of 2002. It stands in a quiet, secluded spot, near Innsbruck's Stadtpark, a short distance from the railway station. The facilities include a sauna and solarium. The *Deffreggerstube* Restaurant and beer garden are highly recommended.

INNSBRUCK: *Weißes Rössl* €€€ 15
Kiebachgasse 8 in der Altstadt, 6020. **Road map** B4.
(*(0512) 58 30 57.* FAX *58 30 575.* @ weisses@roessl.at
This hotel is set in a townhouse in central Innsbruck, featuring the heavy walls and raftered ceilings typical of this area. With a history of guests spanning 600 years, this establishment is popular with the locals and visitors alike for its well-priced restaurant.

	NUMBER OF ROOMS	RESTAURANT	GARDEN OR TERRACE	SWIMMING POOL	AIR CONDITIONING

Price categories for a twin room with bathroom or shower, and including breakfast, service and tax, in euros:
€ up to € 90
€€ € 91–140
€€€ € 141–180
€€€€ € 181–260
€€€€€ above € 260

RESTAURANT
The restaurant is open to non-residents and hotel guests.

GARDEN OR TERRACE
The hotel is set in a garden or has an outside terrace or courtyard with plants.

SWIMMING POOL
The hotel has a swimming pool.

AIR CONDITIONING
All rooms are air-conditioned.

KIRCHBERG IN TIROL: *Hotel Sportalm*   €€€€ | 27 | ● | ■ | ● |
Brandseitweg 26-28, 6365. **Road map** C4.
((05357) 277 80. **FAX** 33 47 30. @ info@hotel-sportalm.at W www.hotel-sportalm.at
Typical alpine hotel with distinctive dark-wood balconies. Apart from standard rooms it also has six suites and six holiday apartments. Facilities include table tennis and a swimming pool, open summer and winter. The restaurant serves regional and vegetarian dishes. 1 🔳 📺 🔳 ✉

KIRCHBERG IN TIROL: *Tyroler Hof*   €€€€ | 25 | ● | ■ | |
Möselgasse 11, 6365. **Road map** C4.
((05357) 26 66. **FAX** 26 65 65. @ info@tyrolerhof.at
A newly refurbished hotel with a lovely garden, near the centre of this small town. The facilities include a sauna, solarium and bicycle hire. Its rooms are huge: 25–28 sq m (269–301 sq ft); the family suite 72 sq m (775 sq ft). Rooms are half price in summer. Open mid-Dec–April, end May–mid Oct. 🔳 ✉

KITZBÜHEL: *Astron Sporthotel*   €€€€ | 132 | ● | ■ | |
Schwarzseestraße 8–10, 6370. **Road map** C4.
((05356) 632 11-0. **FAX** 632 11-15.
@ kitzbuehel@astron-hotels.de W www.astron-hotels.com/kitzbuehel
Ideal for sports enthusiasts, this hotel stands in the middle of a vast ski centre. It has a large restaurant, *Tiroler Stuben*, typically Tyrolean in style, as well as nine conference rooms of different sizes. The facilities include sauna, solarium, fitness room, hairdresser, bicycle hire and mini-golf. 1 🔳 🔳 🔳 P 🔳

KITZBÜHEL: *Goldener Greif*   €€€€€ | 47 | ● | | ● |
Hinterstadt 24, 6370. **Road map** C4. ((05356) 643 11. **FAX** 650 01.
@ info@hotel-goldener-greif.at W www.hotel-goldener-greif.at
This lovely 13th-century building, decorated with typical Tyrolean paintwork, was converted into a hotel between 1954 and 1969. Although modernized, it has preserved its historic Tyrolean charm, especially in its inviting lobby with fireplace. 1 🔳 📺 🔳 🔳 🔳 🔳 🔳 🔳 P 🔳

KITZBÜHEL: *Schloss Lebenberg*   €€€€€ | 109 | ● | ■ | ● |
Lebenbergstraße 17, 6370. **Road map** C4.
((05356) 690 10. **FAX** 64405.
@ schloss.lebenberg@austria-trend.at W www.tiscover.com/schloss-lebenberg.at
A hotel in the majestic Schloss Lebenberg, with lovely views of the mountains. As early as 1885, the palace was converted into an exclusive pension for hunters, and it still caters for them today. Apart from standard rooms it also features 42 suites. The Tapestry Room, with its interesting wooden ceiling and crystal chandeliers is an excellent venue for receptions. 1 🔳 📺 🔳 🔳 ✉

KLEINWALSERTAL/RIEZLER: *Hotel-Pension Widdersteinblick*   €€ | 15 | | ■ | |
Eggstraße 24, 6991. **Road map** A4. ((05517) 56 01. **FAX** 34 58.
@ hotel.widdersteinblick@aon.at
A small, family-run pension. Typical alpine house with flower-bedecked balconies. Here you can play golf, go horse-riding or cycling. 1 🔳 🔳 ✉

MAYRHOFEN: *Hotel Berghof*   €€ | 100 | ● | ■ | ● |
Sternplatz 220, 6290. **Road map** C4. ((05285) 62254. **FAX** 622 54-90.
@ info@hotelberghof.at
The hotel, in the centre of Mayrhofen, occupies a large traditional country-style building. The facilities include a sauna, solarium, outdoor and indoor tennis courts, squash and bicycle hire. 1 📺 🔳 🔳 🔳 🔳 🔳 🔳 P 🔳

MAYRHOFEN: *Elisabeth*   €€€€ | 32 | ● | ■ | ● |
Einfahrt Mitte 432, 6290. **Road map** C4.
((05285) 67670. **FAX** 67 67-67. @ thalerfamilie@elisabethhotel.com
Hotel in an elegant new Tyrolean-style building, beautifully decorated, with luxurious, beautifully panelled bedrooms. All rooms have balconies and views of the mountains. The excellent *Gute Stube*, decorated with paintings, serves local and international specialities. Booking is necessary. 1 🔳 📺 🔳

OETZ: *Posthotel Kassl* €€€ | 50 ● ■ ●

Hauptstraße 70, 6433. **Road map** B4. *(05252) 63 03.* FAX *21 76.*
@ posthotel.kassl@oetz.at
Hotel in a typically Tyrolean house, with wooden balconies and a mansard roof with a small tower. It has an indoor swimming pool, sauna, solarium, gym and bicycle hire, and facilities for squash and fishing.
1

PERTISAU: *Hotel Post am See* €€ | 63 ● ■ ●

Pertisau 82, 6213. **Road map** C4.
(05243) 52 07. FAX *52 11-80.* @ kobinger.hotelpost@tirol.com
A spacious Tyrolean house on the southwestern shore of Achensee, at an altitude of 950 m (3,117 ft). It has an indoor swimming pool, lakeside beach, sauna, solarium and fitness room; it also offers facilities for sailing, fishing and saline baths. 1 TV P

CARINTHIA AND EAST TYROL

BAD BLEIBERG: *Der Bleibergerhof* €€€ | 80 ● ■ ●

Drei Lärchen 150, 9530. **Road map** E5.
(04244) 22 05. FAX *22 05-70.*
@ office@bleibergerhof.at W www.bleibergerhof.at
Modern hotel, with numerous terraces, situated only 40 km (25 miles) from Klagenfurt. Its speciality is its thermal and saline baths.
TV P

BAD KLEINKIRCHHEIM: *Hotel Kapeller* € | 20

Schartenweg 8, 9546. **Road map** E5.
(04240) 48 20. FAX *482 40.*
@ kapeller@bkk.at W www.tiscover.com/kapeller
A small hotel with garage parking, standing on a sunny meadow near the forest, some 50 km (31 miles) from Klagenfurt. The facilities include a sauna, solarium, bicycle hire and golf course. Rooms are furnished in a rustic style.
1 TV

BAD KLEINKIRCHHEIM: *Hotel Die Post* €€€€ | 99 ● ■ ●

Familie Ronacher-Rippstein, 9546. **Road map** E5.
(04240) 212. FAX *650.*
@ ronacher@diepost.com W www.diepost.com
Plush, beautifully located, modern hotel offering thermal and saline baths and other therapies for respiratory and rheumatic conditions. The facilities include a sauna, solarium, fitness room and beauty parlour with hairdressing. Each room has a south-facing balcony. 1 TV P

BODENSDORF: *Stofflwirt* € | 8 ● ■

Deutschberg 6, 9551. **Road map** E5.
(04243) 69 20. FAX *69 25.* @ stofflwirt.mitterer@aon.at
Pension at an altitude of 750 m (2,460 ft), with numerous terraces and a lovely view of Ossiacher See, about 2 km (1 mile) away. Typical alpine-style interior.
1 TV P

FAAK AM SEE: *Pensionen–Ferienwohnungen Waldruh-Tannenheim* € | 16 ■

Halbinselstraße 1–3, 9583. **Road map** E5.
(04254) 22 95. FAX *2295-4.* @ pension.waldruh@aon.at
Complex of buildings at the edge of a forest, on a promontory in Faaker See, with views over the surrounding mountains. Rooms have telephones and safes. Facilities offered include horse-riding, fishing, bicycle hire, table tennis and summer barbecues in the garden. Cash payment only.
1 TV P

FELD AM SEE: *Hotel Lindenhof* €€ | 24 ● ■

Dorfstraße 8, 9544. **Road map** E5.
(04246) 22 74. FAX *22 74-50.* @ urlaub@landhotel-lindenhof.at
A small hotel with terraces, near Milstätter See, decorated in a rustic style. It has a sauna, solarium, fitness room, bicycle hire and a private lakeside beach. Also on offer are facilities for tennis and fishing. Tastefully furnished rooms.
1 TV P

FELDKIRCHEN: *Hotel Rainer* € | 19 ● ■

Eppensteinerstraße 1, 9560. **Road map** E5.
(04276) 20 97. FAX *20 97-22.* @ hotel-rainer@happynet.at
A modest but comfortable small hotel situated between Klagenfurt and Villach, with garage parking. Tastefully furnished rooms, and a delicious buffet breakfast. TV

For key to symbols *see back flap*

Price categories for a twin
room with bathroom or shower,
and including breakfast, service
and tax, in euros:
€ up to € 90
€€ € 91–140
€€€ € 141–180
€€€€ € 181–260
€€€€€ above € 260

RESTAURANT
The restaurant is open to non-residents and hotel guests.

GARDEN OR TERRACE
The hotel is set in a garden or has an outside terrace
or courtyard with plants.

SWIMMING POOL
The hotel has a swimming pool.

AIR CONDITIONING
All rooms are air-conditioned.

	NUMBER OF ROOMS	RESTAURANT	GARDEN OR TERRACE	SWIMMING POOL	AIR CONDITIONING
GROSSKIRCHHEIM: *Hotel Post* €€ Großkirchheim, 9843. **Road map** E5. [((04825) 205. FAX 205-19. @ hotel.sauper@peak.at Typical Austrian hotel aiming mainly at tourists who enjoy active holidays and wish to spend their time rambling, cycling and fishing. Features a sauna and solarium, to relax after a sporty day. ▯ ▯	40	●	■		
HEILIGENBLUT: *Hotel Post* €€ Hof 1, 9844. **Road map** D4. [((04824) 22 45. FAX 22 45-81. @ hotel.post-heiligenblut@netway.at �W www.hotelpost-heiligenblut.at Typical alpine hotel, situated between the Schober mountain range and the Großglockner Glacier. All rooms have balconies. There is also a small meadow where you can relax in a deckchair, a sauna and a solarium. Suites are also available. ▯ ▯ ▯ ▯	50	●	■	●	
KATSCHBERG: *Alpen-Sport-Hotel Bogensperger* €€ Katschberg 1, 9863. **Road map** D4. [((04734) 220. FAX 35 31 51. @ info@hotel-bogensperger.at �W www.hotel-bogensperger.at A well-equipped alpine hotel, set amidst greenery. Facilities include an indoor swimming pool, sauna, solarium and gym. Sports enthusiasts can play tennis and anglers can enjoy a spot of fishing. ▯ ▯ ▯ ▯	70	●	■	●	
KLAGENFURT: *Trigon* €€ Kinoplatz 6, 9020. **Road map** E5. [((0463) 351 95. FAX 351 95-20. @ hotel.trigon@net4you.co.at �W www.hotels.or.at/trigon A pleasant hotel with garage parking, occupying a modern building with an interesting design. The comfortable rooms are well-kept and clean. In-house facilities on offer to guests include a sauna and a solarium. ▯ ▯ ▯ ▯ ▯ ▯ ▯ ▯ ▯	39				■
KLAGENFURT: *Arcotel Moser Verdino* €€€ Domgasse 2, 9020. **Road map** E5. [((0463) 578 78. FAX 516 76-5. @ moserverdino@arcotel.at �W www.arcotel.at The hotel occupies an imposing corner building, one of the most beautiful Art Nouveau structures in this small city. Its sunny rooms are comfortable and tastefully furnished. A sauna is available for the use of guests. ▯ ▯ ▯ ▯ ▯ ▯	71				
LIENZ: *Parkhotel Tristacher See* €€ 9900 Lienz. **Road map** D5. [((04852) 676 66. FAX 67699. @ tristachersee@osttirol.com �W www.parkhotel-tristachersee.com An hotel with a beautiful location on the shores of Tristacher See, in the Dolomite mountain range. There is a large roofed terrace right next to the lake. In its unusual rooms, dark panelling complements the sumptuousness of the soft furnishings. It also boasts an excellent restaurant, famous for its fish dishes. Closed in Oct. ▯ ▯ ▯ ▯	45	●	■	●	
LIENZ: *Traube* €€€ Hauptplatz 14, 9900. **Road map** D5. [((04852) 644 44. FAX 641 84. @ hotel.traube@tirol.com Old-fashioned furniture and antiques create a comfortable interior. In front of the historic building is a swimming pool with great views of the mountains. There is also a restaurant, serving Italian specialities. ▯ ▯ ▯ ▯	51	●		●	
MARIA WÖRTH: *Hotel Wörth* €€€ Seepromenade 12, 9082. **Road map** E5. [((04273) 22 76-0. FAX 22 76-57. @ info@hotelwoerth.com �W www.hotelwoerth.com Elegant hotel with typically alpine exterior and a large terrace, on the shores of Wörther See in one of the most beautiful parts of Austria. The large restaurant windows allow guests to enjoy the spectacular scenery from inside whatever the weather. On offer are a sauna, solarium, gym, bicycles, as well as horse riding, tennis, sailing and fishing. Open May–Oct. ▯ ▯ ▯ ▯ ▯	35	●	■		

OSSIACH: *Gasthof Ossiacherhof* € 5
Alt-Ossiach 12, 9570. **Road map** E5. **[** and **FAX** *(04243) 22 09.*
@ ossiacherhof@gmx.at W www.tiscover.at/ossiacherhof
A tiny, inexpensive pension on the shores of Ossiacher See, between Klagen-
furt and Villach. Private beach with cabins next to the house. Table tennis.
There are also self-catering apartments for two to five persons. 🛠

OSSIACH: *Strandgasthof Seewirt* €€ 12
Josefine Köllich, 9570. **Road map** E5. **[** *(04243) 22 68.* **FAX** *31 68.*
@ koellich.seewirt@net4you.co.at
A pleasant pension on the shores of Ossiacher See, next to the church where
concerts are held as part of the "Carinthian Summer" festival in summer. In the
summer, the restaurant tables are placed outdoors and guests may take their
meals in the shade of the trees. The pension owns 8 hectares (20 acres) of the
lake, where guests can fish. Tennis courts, a golf course and a water-skiing
school are all nearby. Open May–Oct. 1 TV ≈ 📶 🛠 Y 🏠 P 🔗

PÖRTSCHACH: *Schloss Leonstein* €€ 35
Hauptstraße 228, 9210. **Road map** E5.
[*(04272) 28 16-0.* **FAX** *28 23.* @ info@leonstein.at
A 500-year old palace with antique furniture, situated – alas – between a
motorway and a main road. Its restaurant ranks among the best in town; in
the summer the tables are placed outside, in the courtyard. Features a sauna,
golf course and tennis court. 1 🔗 TV 🔗

PÖRTSCHACH: *Schloss Seefels* €€€ 73
Pörtschach/Töschling, 9210. **Road map** E5. **[** *(04272) 23 77.* **FAX** *37 04.*
@ office@seefels.at W www.seefels.at
A hotel with cosmopolitan clientele. Its buildings are set within a large
park, on the shores of the lake. The elegant rooms mirror the grandeur
expected of a large hotel. Efficient and friendly service. Guests may enjoy
boat rides on the lake or play golf on the adjacent course.
1 🔗 TV 🔗 🔗

SATTENDORF: *Gasthof "Zum Wasserfall"* € 15
Sattendorf 28, 9520. **Road map** E5.
[*(04248) 23 15.* **FAX** *23 15-15.*
Pension situated only a few minutes walk from Ossiacher See. The owner
personally supervises the preparation of tasty, traditional meals, takes care to
create a pleasant atmosphere and attends to the individual needs of the
guests. The pension facilities include a sauna, solarium and fitness room.
1 TV ≈ 📶 🛠 🔗 Y 🏠 P 🔗

SEEBODEN: *Hotel Bellevue* €€ 53
Am Waldrand 24, 9871. **Road map** D5.
[*(04762) 813 46 0.* **FAX** *813 46-68.* @ hotel-bellevue@aon.at
A fair-sized hotel on the western shore of Millstätter See. Typically alpine
architecture, all rooms have balconies. Facilities include an indoor swimming
pool, sauna, solarium and fitness room. Guests may enjoy golf and fishing.
1 🔗 TV 🛠 🏠 🔗

VELDEN: *Hotel Samonig* €€ 33
Mozartstraße 1, 9220. **Road map** E5. **[** *(04274) 25 72.* **FAX** *41 97.*
@ hotel@samonig.cc W www.samonig.cc
An inexpensive hotel, in a quiet part of Velden, near the casino. Tastefully
furnished interior and family atmosphere. Sauna, heated swimming pool and
18-hole golf course. 1 🔗 TV 📶 🔗 Y P 🔗

VELDEN: *Casinohotel Mösslacher* €€€ 38
Am Corso 10, 9220. **Road map** E5. **[** *(04274) 512 33.* **FAX** *512 30.*
@ casino-hotel.velden@aon.at W www.casino-hotel-velden.at
The hotel offers not only comfortable rooms and suites, but also an authentic
Viennese atmosphere in Le Café. In the summer the American Bar and the
Schinakl are Velden's most popular meeting places.
1 🔗 TV 📶 🔗 Y 🏠 P 🔗

VILLACH: *Hotel Carinthia* €€ 96
Ossiacher Zeile 39, 9500. **Road map** E5. **[** *(04242) 20 02.* **FAX** *20 02-390.*
@ carinthia@austria-trend.at W www.austria-trend.at
This fair-sized hotel, with garage parking, situated only five minutes walk from
the town centre offers modern, comfortably furnished rooms. It has a solarium
and a fitness studio. The Venice Restaurant serves Austrian and international
cuisine. 1 🔗 TV ≈ Y 🏠 P 🔗

WHERE TO EAT

Austrian cuisine, although not known as one of the top-ranking in the world, nevertheless produces delicious country foods, innovative modern dishes, and a wonderful array of cakes and desserts. Shaped by the culinary traditions of many nationalities, it includes elements of Italian, Polish, Hungarian and Czech cuisines. In the larger cities, as well as the local cuisine, you are also likely to find Italian, Greek, Turkish and Chinese

Mozartkugeln, decorated with a portrait of Mozart

restaurants – eating out is a popular pastime here. Nearly all Austrian eateries – whether restaurant, café, *Gasthaus* or *Heuriger* – serve a version of the world-famous *Schnitzel*.

The restaurants listed on pages 316–31 have been selected from the best on offer, across all price ranges. They are organized by region and price. The phrasebook *(p384)* will help you order a meal; some restaurants will have English menus.

A beautifully illuminated restaurant on the shores of Bindsee

WHAT TO EAT AND WHEN

For breakfast Austrians tend to eat a roll or two with butter and jam, accompanied by coffee. Most hotels have a self-service breakfast bar. Breakfast is generally served throughout the day, and even small bakeries usually have a few tables where you can quietly enjoy your pastries.

Most restaurants serve lunch from noon to 2 or 3pm. Many offer a *Tagesmenü* (fixed-price menu of the day), or a *Tages-teller* (dish of the day), as one of the best-priced options.

In Austrian homes, dinner is eaten early, at about 6pm. In restaurants, however, food is generally served throughout the evening. Wine, fruit juice or water are normally drunk

with the meal, and stronger drinks, such as one of the locally produced fruit brandies, may be served as a *digestif.* Some establishments serve food throughout the day.

OPENING HOURS

A few small grocery stores, bakeries and coffee houses open as early as 7am in the morning; most open between 8am and 10am.

Restaurants serve as meeting points for socializing with family and friends as much as for eating, and many places will stay open as late as 2am, sometimes later. If the atmosphere is particularly friendly, often in smaller restaurants, guests may even stay until dawn the following day.

Many places close for one day a week (the Ruhetag), and may also be closed on public holidays. At a country inn it may be difficult to order a meal after 9pm. Your hotel or pension will advise you of their serving times.

TYPES OF RESTAURANTS AND SNACK BARS

A wide range of restaurants, bars and snack bars offer modest or grand meals any time of day. There is a large number of luxurious restaurants, often based within the luxury hotels, which serve first-class international menus prepared by top chefs.

A *Wirtshaus* is a country inn, a *Gasthaus* a slightly more sophisticated restaurant, both typically concentrating on local cuisine. The best-known and best-liked of all

Tables set in front of a typical *Wirtshaus* inn, in Lech

Interior of a *Gasthaus* in St. Christoph

Austrian restaurants is the *Heuriger*, a simple, often seasonal wine bar in the wine-growing villages, with light meals at low prices. Here, wine is served at your table in a glass mug, and you fetch your food from a buffet. If fir branches are displayed outside it means the *Heuriger* is open and serving the home-pressed vintage.

In cities you can get basic fare at a *Beisl* (snack bar) or a *Würstelstand*, a street kiosk serving a variety of sausages with bread and mustard, with quality varying from simple and dull to innovative and stylish. At an *Imbiss-Stube* you can get a light snack such as a bowl of soup, or order the daily set menu. This is usually displayed on a blackboard outside. Many cafés also serve good food, but you should watch the prices, as they can be higher than in restaurants.

DRESS CODE

THE OLDER generation of Austrians tend to dress formally when going out to eat at a good restaurant, but more casual clothes are also acceptable. In luxury or hotel restaurants it is wise to err on the side of conservatism. In the grander restaurants in the cities, smarter clothes (jacket and tie for men, or evening wear) are invariably expected. At a *Heuriger*, the locals let their hair down, and you can wear what you feel comfortable in. Swimwear is acceptable only in lakeside beach bars.

RESERVATIONS

IN GENERAL it is wise to make a reservation if you wish to eat in a particular restaurant, especially if any kind of entertainment is on offer, if the restaurant is in a popular spot or if its cuisine is highly recommended. During the high season and in busy tourist areas it is often essential to book. Even a simple snack bar such as a *Beisl* may have a faithful local clientele and you may wander in and expect to find a free table. If you are going to a *Heuriger* in a group you will need to book a table.

PRICES AND TIPS

IT IS DIFFICULT to generalize about prices. Lunch at an average restaurant should cost about 7–10 per person. For an evening meal you need to allow two or three times that price, or more if drinks are included. Self-service establishments usually charge by the size of the plate.

In the more expensive restaurants, the bill may include *Gedeck,* the cover

charge, or a cover charge may be made for the bread served at the table.

Although a service charge is almost always included in the bill, you are expected to leave an additional sum of up to 10 per cent for service.

Credit cards are accepted in most luxury and hotel restaurants, but the majority of snack bars accept only cash.

CHILDREN AND VEGETARIANS

SOME RESTAURANTS offer smaller servings for children and light eaters, but these may be only marginally less expensive than the regular portions. Many do not have a special children's menu with favourites such as french fries and hamburgers – except at the fast-food chains, children are generally expected to eat the same as their elders.

Austrians are avid meat-eaters, but most popular restaurants in the main tourist areas do offer vegetarian dishes. Pasta, mixed vegetables or a *Salatplatte* (mixed salad) with bread or *Salzstangerl* are popular. Many places, such as the *Heurigen*, offer buffets with a selection of vegetarian dishes to choose from.

A *Heuriger* awaiting its guests, in the vicinity of Mörbisch

What to Eat: Savoury Foods

Vollkorn-Bauernbrot

Salzstangerl

Siebenkorn-brot

A USTRIAN COOKING is surprisingly varied, a reflection of imperial days when culinary traditions from many parts of Europe influenced the country's cooks. Best-known outside Austria is *Wiener Schnitzel*, which may have originated in Milan. Soups are rich in flavour and often include *Knödel* (dumplings). In winter, roast goose and duck appear on the menus as well as game dishes such as *Rehrücken* (saddle of venison). *Bauernschmaus* is a popular mixed meat platter. Vegetarians can enjoy the many noodle dishes, *Eierschwammerl* (chanterelle mushrooms) and *Spargel* (asparagus).

Semmel

Hausbrot

Frankfurter mit Senf
Frankfurters and other types of sausage are sold at street kiosks, often with mustard.

Leberknödelsuppe
This clear beef broth includes small dumplings made from beef liver, seasoned with marjoram and parsley.

Frittatensuppe
Thin strips of lightly seasoned fried egg pancake are added to a clear beef or chicken soup, sprinkled with parsley.

Eierspeise
Thick scrambled egg omelette is served in the pan, often sprinkled with fresh chives.

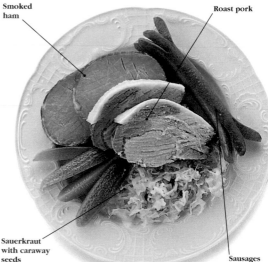

Smoked ham

Roast pork

Sauerkraut with caraway seeds

Sausages

Eierschwammerl
Chanterelle mushrooms are served fresh in autumn or preserved, in a salad.

Bauernschmaus
This simple country platter of hot meats can be found in many Austrian restaurants and is often served with dumplings. The meats include frankfurters, a selection of ham, smoked pork, and roast pork or pork cutlet.

Rindsgulasch
Originally from Hungary, this paprika-seasoned beef stew often comes with dumplings.

Gefüllte Kalbsbrust
Breast of veal is filled with a variety of meat or vegetable stuffings, then roasted.

Erdäpfelgulasch
This hot potato goulash often includes Frankfurter sausages or smoked meats.

Wiener Schnitzel
The breaded veal or pork escalope is fried until golden.

Slices of beef

G'röste Erdäpfel (fried potatoes)

Horse-radish and apple sauce

Tafelspitz mit g'röste Erdäpfel
A lean cut of beef is simmered gently with vegetables in stock, then thickly sliced and served with g'röste Erdäpfel (fried grated potatoes) and an apple and horseradish sauce. It is a typical lunchtime dish and was allegedly eaten every day by the Emperor Franz Joseph I.

Gemischter Salat
Mixed salad ingredients are often arranged side by side.

Heringssalat
A typical salad, based on pickled herring and potatoes.

Beef and rice stuffing

Tomato sauce

Gefüllte Paprika
Green peppers are stuffed with minced beef and rice and cooked in a tomato sauce.

What to Eat: Sweet Foods

Few countries in the world can rival Austria's devotion to all things sweet. Austrians enjoy cakes mid-morning, lunchtime and afternoon, and set aside time, known as *Jause*, for coffee and cake. The finest *Torten* (gâteaux), pastries and cakes are sold by *Konditoreien* (confectioners), where they can often be consumed on the premises, together with a steaming cup of hot coffee, while perusing the local paper. Often the cakes are topped with *Schlagobers*, a generous dollop of whipped cream. Traditional Austrian desserts can be found in all good restaurants and are typically rich. Sweet desserts also tend to be accompanied by a cup of coffee.

Tempting cakes and gâteaux in a shop window

DESSERTS AND COFFEE

Desserts are always accom-panied by a cup of coffee in Austria, never anything else. In its most basic form, the small, strong, black coffee is simply called *Mokka*. But there are many variations: *Melange* (Viennese coffee) is made of half coffee, half milk, rather like the Italian capuccino; *Einspänner* is coffee topped with whipped cream; *Brauner* is coffee with a little milk; *Maria Theresa* is enlivened with a dash of orange liqueur; *Mazagran* contains vanilla ice cream, a dash of Maraschino liqueur and rum; and finally, *Türkischer Kaffee* is strong, dark Turkish coffee.

Apfelstrudel
Apple and raisins are encased in a light strudel pastry dusted with icing sugar. The strudel may be served hot or cold, with whipped cream. Other fillings are raspberry or blackberry.

Palatschinken
Thicker than a French crêpe, this Austrian pancake is filled with curd jam, cheese, fruit or chocolate sauce and dusted with icing sugar. Palatschin-ken are delicious hot or cold.

Reisauflauf mit Äpfeln
Reisauflauf *is a rich rice soufflé. It can be cooked in a creamy and light style or as a heartier dessert. Here it includes apple and is served with raspberry syrup.*

Mohr im Hemd
This rich chocolate pudding is steamed and served with hot chocolate sauce. Chilled whipped cream, usually scented with vanilla sugar is added just before serving.

Topfenknödel
Light curd cheese dumplings are coated with breadcrumbs (or ground walnuts) which have been fried crisply in butter, and served hot with a fruit compote or purée.

CAKES AND PASTRIES

E VERY VISITOR to Vienna should try a *Sachertorte* at the famous Hotel Sacher, but there are dozens of others. *Linzertorte*, introduced to Austrian tables in 1827 by the confectioner Johann Konrad Vogel from Linz, is a classic almond and jam pastry, while *Guglhupf* is traditionally made with yeast, in many variations. Or try a *Dobostorte*, a sponge cake sandwiched together with chocolate butter cream. *Mozartkugeln* are a famous Salzburg creation – delicious chocolate balls, filled with chocolate, marzipan and pistachio cream, and sold wrapped in silver foil with a portrait of Mozart.

Dobostorte
Invented by pâtissier Josef Dobos in Hungary in 1887, this rich cake alternates equal layers of sponge and chocolate butter cream and is glazed with caramel. Dobosschnitten, made of the same mixture, are sold in individual rectangles.

Linzertorte
A sweet almond pastry case is filled with raspberry, apricot or redcurrant jam and decorated with lattice pastry.

Sachertorte
The famous Sachertorte chocolate cake has a thin layer of apricot or plum jam beneath its thick, smooth icing.

Mohnstrudel
A sweet, moist, yeast-based dough spread with ground poppy seeds and raisins and folded over into a roulade.

Guglhupf
Baked in a fluted ring mould, variations on Guglhupf include this marbelized chocolate version, Marmorguglhupf.

Rehrücken
Shaped like the saddle of venison after which it is named, this rich chocolate cake is studded with almonds.

Esterházytorte
Available as a round cake or in rectangular slices, this sweetest of gâteaux is coated with feathered icing.

ORIGINAL SACHERTORTE

This celebrated chocolate gâteau was invented in 1832 by Prince Metternich's pastry chef, Franz Sacher. Its uniqueness lies in the combination of sweet chocolate and the lightly acid taste of plum or apricot jam, encased in chocolate icing. It has always been available from the Hotel Sacher shop in Kärntner Straße, which sells it in a variety of sizes. When the nearby Demel Konditorei claimed that they had been sold the secret recipe and their *Sachertorte* was authentic, a lengthy court case ensued. Sacher won the right to the term "Original Sachertorte" but was unable to stop imitations being sold.

What to Drink in Austria

Austria is a source of excellent wine and good rich beers. Austrian wine is mainly white, though there are excellent local red wines. The wine is drunk before it has finished maturing: *Most*, available from late summer, is the product of the first fermentation of the grapes. In early autumn, this is followed by *Sturm*, a gently fizzing, low-alcohol drink produced by the next stage of grape fermentation. Finally, the *Heuriger*, new-vintage wine, is served. Sweet *Eiswein* is made from grapes left on the vines until the first frosts. Some first-class brandies are also produced – fruit brandies and *Schnaps* are typical drinks.

Vineyards beyond the villages north and west of Vienna, producing *Heuriger* wines

Chardonnay from Styria and sparkling wine from Lower Austria

AUSTRIAN WINES

The most popular wine in Austria is Grüner Veltliner *(see below)*, a grape variety that also makes an excellent *Eiswein*. Other varietal wines include superb dry Rieslings, especially from the Wachau, and rich Weißburgunders (Pinot Blanc), Chardonnays and Traminers. Red wines tend to be soft and lush – robust reds come from the Blaufränkisch and Zweigelt grapes.

Riesling from the Wachau can be light or full-bodied in style.

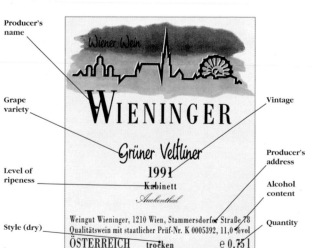

Producer's name
Grape variety
Level of ripeness
Style (dry)
Vintage
Producer's address
Alcohol content
Quantity

Grüner Veltliner is a fresh, fruity white grape. It makes a dry wine that is widely available.

St Laurent is a soft red wine from the Neusiedler See region; it is rich and stylish.

Blaufränkisch is a quality red wine – the best is produced in Burgenland.

**Krügel or 0.5-litre
tankard**

Seidl **or standard
0.3 litre measure**

Krügel **or 0.5-litre
of pale beer**

Pfiff, **the smallest
measure of beer, a
0.2-litre glass**

Kaiser **is a
light beer**

Weizengold
wheat beer

Gösser Spezial,
a rich beer

AUSTRIAN BEERS

GOOD MALTY BEERS have been produced in Austria for more than 150 years. The most popular beers are made by the Gösser brewery in Styria – light *Gösser Gold*, stronger *Gösser Spezial* and dark, sweet *Gösser Stiftsbräu*. One of the oldest breweries, based in Schwechat, Lower Austria, produces a variety of pale beers and a slimming beer (so it is claimed) – *Adam Schlank & Rank*. In Vienna, beer from the local brewery in the Ottakring district, the pale sweet *Gold Fassl*, is popular although Bavarian-style wheat beers such as *Weizengold* are also available. The most popular alcohol-free beer in Austria is *Null Komma Josef*.

Bierhof beer mat advertising a pub in the Haarhof.

Null Komma Josef, (Nought Point Joseph), an alcohol-free beer.

OTHER AUSTRIAN DRINKS

Austria offers a good range of non-alcoholic fruit juices such as *Himbeersaft* (raspberry juice) or *Johannisbeersaft* (blackcurrant juice). *Almdudler* (alpine pasture yodler), a herbal lemonade, is also a speciality. Fruit is the basis of many types of schnaps (sometimes called *Brand*). This powerful eau-de-vie is distilled from berries such as juniper or fruits such as apricots *(Marillen)* and quince *(Quitten)*. It is worth paying the extra to sample the schnaps from specialists. Mixer drinks are popular: they include *Radler* (cyclist), a beer with lemonade. An innkeeper is said to have invented this drink on a hot day when, almost out of beer, he served it to thirsty cyclists.

**Apricot
schnaps**

Wiener Rathauskeller, a popular beer-drinkers' haunt

Choosing a Restaurant

THE RESTAURANTS in this book have been chosen for their good food and interesting location. Venues are listed province by province, starting with Vienna. The colour-coded thumb tabs in the margin correspond to the relevant pages in the book. Maps of Vienna can be found on pages 117–21, and the road map for Austria is at the back of the book.

	CREDIT CARDS	GARDEN OR TERRACE	AUSTRIAN WINES	WHEELCHAIR ACCESS

VIENNA

INNER CITY: *Art of Life*   €   ■ ● ■ ●
Stubenring 14. **Map 2 D4.** ((01) 512 55 53. FAX 512 55 53. w www.artoflife.at
New, elegant yet inexpensive restaurant, situated opposite the museum of applied arts, specializing in vegetarian and fish dishes, and organic wine; has an area allocated for non-smokers. ● Sun.

INNER CITY: *Palatschinkenkuchl*   €
Köllnerhofgasse 4. **Map 2 C4.** ((01) 512 31 05.
A pleasant milk bar, considered a curiosity in Vienna. Specializes mainly in *Palatschinken*, stuffed pancakes. ○ 10am–midnight daily.

INNER CITY: *Weibel 3*   €   ■ ● ■ ●
Riemergasse 1–3. **Map 2 C4.** ((01) 513 31 10. FAX 513 31 10. w www.weibel.at
A small restaurant near the Ring and Stadtpark. Good European food, plus a large selection of vegetable dishes. ● Sat after 5pm, Sun, public holidays.

INNER CITY: *Enoteca Frizzante*   €€   ■ ● ■ ●
Kumpfgasse 3. **Map 2 C4.** ((01) 513 07 47. FAX 513 31 09.
A pleasant restaurant serving Austro-Italian cuisine. There is a private room for larger parties. Booking is recommended. ● Sun, public holidays, 24–30 Dec.

INNER CITY: *Expedit*   €€   ■
Wiesingerstraße 6. **Map 3 D4.** ((01) 512 33 13. w www.expedit.net
Traditional Ligurian cuisine and pasta dishes in an unpretentious, modern restaurant. The food served here is also sold in the affiliated shop.

INNER CITY: *Hansen*   €€   ■ ● ■ ●
Wipplingerstraße 34 (Börse). **Map 2 B3.** ((01) 532 05 42. FAX 532 05 42–10.
w www.hansen.co.at
An interesting restaurant in the basement of the former Stock Exchange, in a section known as the Roman Hall, next to an exclusive garden shop. Excellent Austrian and European cuisine. Booking is recommended.

INNER CITY: *Harry's Time*   €€   ■ ● ■ ●
An der Hülben 1. **Map 3 D4.** ((01) 512 45 56. FAX 512 31 02. w www.harrys-time.at
A restaurant and wine bar full of surprises, including themed evenings. *Harry's Abendmahl* (Harry's supper) is a good-value dinner where for € 36 you will be served a never-ending selection of starters and main courses, until you've had enough. ○ 11am–1am Mon–Fri, 6pm–1am Sat. ● Sun, public holidays.

INNER CITY: *Kanzleramt*   €€   ■ ● ■ ●
Schauflergasse 6. **Map 2 B4.** ((01) 533 13 09. FAX 535 39 45.
A discreetly elegant restaurant, frequented by Austrian politicians, including the Chancellor. Serves good, traditional Austrian food. ○ 11am–midnight.
● Sun, public holidays.

INNER CITY: *Laurel*   €€   ● ■ ●
Salzgries 15. **Map 2 C3.** ((01) 532 57 04. FAX 532 57 04.
Italian restaurant with Mediterranean-style decor, situated near the Danube Canal. The restaurant occupies several rooms. Booking is recommended.

INNER CITY: *Plachutta*   €€   ■ ● ■ ●
Wollzeile 38. **Map 3 D4.** ((01) 512 15 77. FAX 512 15 77–20. w www.plachutta.at
Famous restaurant, serving good Austrian cuisine. Beef dishes, including *Tafelspitz*, are a speciality. Booking is recommended.

INNER CITY: *Rosenberger Markt*   €€   ■ ● ■ ●
Maysedergasse 2. **Map 2 B5.** ((01) 512 34 58.
Smart complex, near the Opera House and opposite the Sacher Hotel, with a cosy coffee house, *Heuriger*, bistro, and a market restaurant on several floors; varied selection of fresh salads and fruit juices. ○ 11am–11pm daily.

		CREDIT CARDS	GARDEN OR TERRACE	AUSTRIAN WINES	WHEELCHAIR ACCESS

Prices of a three-course meal without drinks, including cover charge, tax and service, in euros:
€ up to € 20
€€ € 20–35
€€€ € 35–45
€€€€ € 45–55
€€€€€ over € 55.

CREDIT CARDS
Credit cards are accepted.

GARDEN OR TERRACE
Weather permitting, it is possible to eat *al fresco*.

AUSTRIAN WINES
A good selection of Austrian wines.

WHEELCHAIR ACCESS
Easy access and facilities for the disabled.

INNER CITY: *Schimanszky*	€€	■	●	■	●

Biberstraße 2. **Map** 3 D4. 🍴 **FAX** *(01) 513 45 43.*
Decorated in white and green, with contemporary art on the walls, this restaurant serves modern takes on traditional Austrian fare. ● *Sun.*

| **INNER CITY:** *Bauer* | €€€ | ■ | ● | ■ | ● |

Sonnenfelsgasse 17. **Map** 2 C4. 🍴 *(01) 512 98 71.* **FAX** *512 98 71.*
A small, popular restaurant serving interesting new dishes. Starters include *pâté de foie gras* with marinated raisins and white radish in vinegar. Booking recommended. ○ *6pm–midnight Mon, 12–3pm, 6pm–midnight Tue–Fri.* ● *Sat, Sun.*

| **INNER CITY:** *Castillo Grill Room* | €€€ | ■ | ● | ■ | ● |

Biberstraße 8. **Map** 3 D4. 🍴 *(01) 512 71 23.* **FAX** *(01) 513 94 04.*
The most original of the handful of French restaurants in Vienna. Although it has an American-style buffet bar, the cuisine is 100 per cent French. Its specialities include goat dishes, lobster sauces, and frogs and snails baked in pastry. Booking is recommended.

| **INNER CITY:** *La Ninfea* | €€€ | ■ | ● | ■ | ● |

Schauflergasse 6. **Map** 2 B4. 🍴 *(01) 532 91 26.*
A stylish Italian restaurant, patronized by famous politicians and journalists. Quality Mediterranean-style cuisine. ● *Sun, public holidays.*

| **INNER CITY:** *Lebenbauer Vollwert* | €€€ | ■ | ● | ■ | ● |

Teinfaltstraße 3. **Map** 2 A3.
🍴 *(01) 533 55 56.* **FAX** *533 55 56–11.*
A restaurant offering a good selection of meat and vegetarian dishes.
○ *11am–2:30pm, 5:30–10pm Mon–Fri.* ● *Sat, Sun.*

| **INNER CITY:** *Martinelli* | €€€ | ■ | ● | ■ | ● |

Freyung 3. **Map** 2 B3.
🍴 *(01) 533 67 21.* **FAX** *533 67 21–20.*
A smart Italian restaurant situated in Schloss Harrach. Serves Mediterranean food and a good selection of vegetarian dishes. ○ *noon–3pm, 6pm–midnight daily.*

| **INNER CITY:** *Zum weißen Rauchfangkehrer* | €€€ | ■ | ● | ■ | ● |

Weihburggasse 4. **Map** 2 C4.
🍴 *(01) 512 34 71.* **FAX** *512 34 71–28.* **W** *www.weisser-rauchfangkehrer.at*
An attractive, classic country-style restaurant, serving traditional Austrian cuisine, with a strong emphasis on seasonal produce. ○ *5pm–midnight Tue–Sat (groups by special arrangement).*

| **INNER CITY:** *Cantinetta Antinori* | €€€€ | ■ | ● | ■ | ● |

Jasomirgottstraße 3/5. **Map** 2 C4.
🍴 *(01) 533 77 22.* **FAX** *533 77 22–11.* **W** *www.antinori.at*
An elegant restaurant specializing in the delicious cuisine of Tuscany. Its highlights include *carpaccio* with Parmesan, mozzarella with sautéed vegetables in truffle oil, and, of course, many variations on pasta. A large selection of Italian wines. ○ *11am–11pm daily.*

| **INNER CITY:** *Le Siècle* | €€€€ | ■ | ● | ■ | ● |

Parkring 16/Weihburggasse 32. **Map** 3 D5.
🍴 *(01) 515 17–3440.* **FAX** *512 22 15.*
An elegant restaurant on the Ring, inside the converted Schloss Henckel-Donnersmarck. Offers a wide choice of excellent fish and vegetable dishes. Conference rooms available. ○ *noon–2:30pm, 7–10pm Mon–Fri.* ● *Sat, Sun.*

| **INNER CITY:** *Do & Co Stephansplatz* | €€€€€ | ■ | ● | ■ | ● |

Stephansplatz 12 (Haashaus). **Map** 3 C4.
🍴 *(01) 535 39 69.* **FAX** *535 39 59.* **W** *www.doco.com*
An exclusive restaurant on the 7th floor of the famous Haashaus, opposite Stephansdom, with splendid views over the square and the neighbouring streets. Exquisite European and Asian cuisine. Booking is recommended.

<table>
<tr><td>

Prices of a three-course meal without drinks, including cover charge, tax and service, in euros:
€ up to € 20
€€ € 20–35
€€€ € 35–45
€€€€ € 45–55
€€€€€ over € 55.

</td><td>

CREDIT CARDS
Credit cards are accepted.
GARDEN OR TERRACE
Weather permitting, it is possible to eat *al fresco*.
AUSTRIAN WINES
A good selection of Austrian wines.
WHEELCHAIR ACCESS
Easy access and facilities for the disabled.

</td></tr>
</table>

	CREDIT CARDS	GARDEN OR TERRACE	AUSTRIAN WINES	WHEELCHAIR ACCESS
INNER CITY: *Meinl am Graben* €€€€€ Graben 19. **Map 2** B4. ☎ *(01) 532 33 34-35.* FAX *532 33 34–23.* W *www.meinl.com* An elegant, traditional restaurant in the famous Meinl's delicatessen and coffee shop. Crayfish, wild mushrooms, *Tafelspitz* (boiled beef) and chicken breast all feature on the menu. There are also several bars, a coffee house and a wine bar. ◻ *8am–midnight Mon–Fri, 8:30am–midnight Sat.* ● *Sun.*	▪	●	▪	●
NORTH OF MARIAHILFER STRASSE: *Arnes* € Westbahnstraße 10. **Map 1** C3. ☎ *(01) 523 27 68.* Small restaurant with Mediterranean flair, specializing in Greek and Kurdish cuisine. The menu includes favourites such as Arnes kebabs, souvlaki, fresh Greek salads, stuffed vine leaves and sheep's cheese, and there is also a good selection of vegetarian dishes. ◻ *10:30am–midnight Mon–Sat.*		●	▪	
NORTH OF MARIAHILFER STRASSE: *Naschmarkt II* € Schottengasse 1. **Map 2** A3. ☎ *(01) 533 51 86.* A very pleasant self-service cafeteria, right in the heart of town. Specializes in oriental dishes, which are prepared in front of guests. ◻ *10:30am–7:30pm Mon–Fri, 10:30am–3pm Sat, Sun, public holidays.*	▪		▪	●
SOUTH OF THE RING: *Demi Tass* € Prinz-Eugen-Straße 28. **Map 5** E2. ☎ *(01) 504 31 19.* FAX *606 75 72.* A pleasant Hindu restaurant where the chef prepares North Indian dishes, which have been slightly modified to accommodate European preferences. The menu includes curries made from chicken and lamb as well as vegetarian dishes. ◻ *11:30am–2:30pm, 6–11:30pm Mon–Sat.* ● *Sun.*	▪	●	▪	●
SOUTH OF THE RING: *Royal Shere Punjab* € Paulanergasse 8. **Map 4** C2. ☎ FAX *(01) 952 84 16.* One of few Indian restaurants in Vienna, dominated by that country's hot chilli and coriander spices. The menu is limited, but includes some interesting and unusual dishes from the Punjab region, including food cooked on the charcoal grill and in the clay oven. ◻ *11:30am–3pm, 6–11:30pm Mon–Sat, 6–11:30pm Sun.*	▪		▪	
SOUTH OF THE RING: *Wok* € Operngasse 20. **Map 4** C1. ☎ *(01) 585 21 02.* The only Indonesian restaurant in the city, with an interior decorated in 1960s style. Recommended dishes include the peanut sauce and seafood dishes with coconut. The menu also includes Thai and Chinese specialities.	▪	●	▪	●
SOUTH OF THE RING: *Da Pablo* €€ Rennweg 11. **Map 5** E2. ☎ *(01) 714 60 03.* An Italian restaurant offering simple, tasty food, with a good selection of fish dishes, often cooked by the owner himself. Excellent wines. Visitors to the nearby theatres and concert halls often enjoy a meal here after their evening entertainment. ◻ *11am–3pm, 6pm–midnight Mon–Fri.* ● *Sun, public holidays.*	▪	●	▪	●
SOUTH OF THE RING: *Pan e Wien* €€ Salesianergasse 25. **Map 5** E1. ☎ *(01) 710 38 70.* FAX *(01) 718 89 71.* A small, typical Italian trattoria, offering basic yet appetizing food. The chef attaches particular importance to the freshness of the produce he uses. The highlights on the menu include: ravioli stuffed with veal, fried chicken breast and knuckle of lamb, all accompanied by a selection of fresh vegetables. ● *Sat, Sun.*	▪		▪	
SOUTH OF THE RING: *Rioja Club* €€ Paulanergasse 7. **Map 4** C2. ☎ *(0676) 534 90 50.* W *www.rioja.at* A Spanish restaurant, probably the longest and narrowest in Vienna, with glass cases displaying typical produce from the Iberian Peninsula. Here you can indulge in an authentic selection of tasty *tapas* dishes, and wash everything down with an excellent wine. ◻ *5pm–11pm Mon, 11am–11pm Tue, 11am–9pm Wed–Fri, 11am–5pm Sat.* ● *Sun.*		●	▪	●

SOUTH OF THE RING: *Gussbaus* €€€
Gusshausstraße 23. **Map 5 D2.** (*(01) 504 47 50.* FAX *504 94 64.*
A restaurant with interesting food at good-value prices, including, for
example, chicken with lentils and risotto. Set menu; prices vary between € 7
and € 43. There is also a fair selection of wines. ● *Sun.*

SOUTH OF THE RING: *Maestro* €€€
Heumarkt 8 / Lothringerstraße 20. **Map 5 E1.** (*(01) 714 89 11.* FAX *242 00–721.*
A stylish restaurant in Vienna's Konzerthaus. Before and after concerts, you
can enjoy elaborate snacks, grilled fish and the ever-popular Viennese
Tafelspitz (boiled beef). Has an area allocated for non-smokers. Booking is
recommended. ● *Jul to mid-Aug.*

SOUTH OF THE RING: *Vestibül im Burgtheater* €€€
Dr. Karl-Lueger-Ring 2 3. **Map 2 A3.** (*(01) 532 49 99.* W *www.vestibuel.at*
One of Vienna's trendiest restaurants, this luxury brasserie is based inside
the former imperial entrance wing of the Burgtheater, and has the finest
terrace in Vienna. The food is contemporary Austrian with French
influences. ○ *11am–11pm Mon–Fri, 6–11pm Sat.* ● *Sun, public holidays.*

FURTHER AFIELD: *Altes Pressbaus* €
Cobenzlgasse 15. (*(01) 320 02 03.* FAX *320 02 03–23.*
The oldest wine bar in the popular Grinzing district (formerly Weindorf),
located within a genuine old grape-press house. Like any *Heuriger*, it serves
only new-vintage wine. Booking is recommended during the high season,
in November and December. ○ *from 4pm daily.* ● *Jan, Feb.*

FURTHER AFIELD: *Göbel* €
Stammersdorfer Kellergasse 151. (*(01) 294 84 20.* FAX *290 60 59.*
A *Heuriger* wine bar in a very old street, lined with wine cellars, in the
northeastern part of Vienna. Traditional new-vintage wine and light snacks.
○ *May–Oct: from 11am Sat, Sun; from 3pm Mon.* ● *Winter.*

FURTHER AFIELD: *Kiang* €
Landstraßer Hauptstraße 50. **Map 3 F5.** (*(01) 715 34 70.*
A modern Chinese restaurant, offering simple yet tasty Asian starters and
main courses in pleasant surroundings.

FURTHER AFIELD: *Pancho* €
Blumauergasse 1a. **Map 3 E1.** (*(01) 212 58 69.* FAX *212 58 48.*
A small Mexican restaurant based in a former garage. Typical Mexican food,
spicy dishes, Mexican beer and wine. Happy hour: 6–8pm.

FURTHER AFIELD: *Seidl* €
Ungargasse 63. **Map 3 E5.** (*(01) 713 17 81.* FAX *713 17 81.*
A small, pleasant restaurant where you can sample genuine Viennese
schnitzel, roasted *Blunz'n* (a type of black pudding without barley) and
cheese ravioli, which can be followed by a layered cream cake for dessert.
The lunchtime set menu is particularly good value at € 6. ✦ ● *Sat, Sun, 24
Dec–6 Jan.*

FURTHER AFIELD: *Wieninger* €
Stammersdorfer Straße 78. (*(01) 292 41 06.* FAX *292 86 71.* W *www.wieninger.at*
A romantic wine bar on the northeastern outskirts of Vienna, not far from
the surrounding vineyards. Serves rich and varied buffet food, including
Blunzn (black pudding). ○ *From 15 Mar.* ● *Mon, Tue, Wed in winter.*

FURTHER AFIELD: *Bayou* €€
Leopoldsgasse 51 / Karmelitermarkt. **Map 3 D2.** (*(01) 214 77 52.*
A Creole restaurant, its interior decorated to resemble a bazaar. Try spicy
Louisiana sausages and enjoy the accompanying sounds of Cajun-style
music. ♫ ○ *6pm–midnight Mon–Sun; hot food served until 11pm.*

FURTHER AFIELD: *Chang* €€
Waaggasse 1. **Map 4 C2.** (*(01) 961 92 12.*
A modern Chinese restaurant specializing in a large variety of soups,
including Miso, and noodle dishes; the menu cheanges weekly. ● *Sun.*

FURTHER AFIELD: *Jumbo Cook* €€
Keilgasse 6. (*(01) 966 19 91.*
A Chinese restaurant serving traditional Hong Kong cuisine. Specialities
include a variety of Chinese soups, beef in black bean sauce, and lamb
cutlets in honey. ● *Mon morning.*

Prices of a three-course meal without drinks, including cover charge, tax and service, in euros:
€ up to € 20
€€ € 20–35
€€€ € 35–45
€€€€ € 45–55
€€€€€ over € 55.

CREDIT CARDS
Credit cards are accepted.

GARDEN OR TERRACE
Weather permitting, it is possible to eat *al fresco.*

AUSTRIAN WINES
A good selection of Austrian wines.

WHEELCHAIR ACCESS
Easy access and facilities for the disabled.

	CREDIT CARDS	GARDEN OR TERRACE	AUSTRIAN WINES	WHEELCHAIR ACCESS

FURTHER AFIELD: *Piccolo* — €
Gredlerstraße 10. **Map** 3 D3. 🎨 *(01) 216 12 83.*
A restaurant-café set in a narrow street connecting Taborstraße with Lilienbrunngasse, close to the Danube Canal and Marienbrücke, only 10 minutes' walk from Stephansdom. Tasty, traditional Viennese cuisine at moderate prices. ⬤ *6am–midnight daily, 11am–midnight Sun.*

| | ■ | ● | ■ | |

FURTHER AFIELD: *Sooser Weinhaus* — €
Karmelitergasse 11. **Map** 3 D2. 🎨 *(01) 214 48 70.*
A pleasant inn serving typical Viennese dishes. Thursdays are *Wiener Schnitzel*-days, when the favourite Viennese dish is served at very moderate prices. Set menu. ⬤ *8am–midnight Mon–Sat.* ⬤ *Sun.*

| | ■ | ● | ■ | ● |

FURTHER AFIELD: *Benkei* — €
Ungargasse 6. **Map** 3 E5. 🎨 *(01) 718 18 88.*
A Japanese restaurant with grand ambitions; its sushi bar is certainly one of the most appetizing in the region. Apart from the standard dishes, it also serves its own specialities. ⬤ *noon–3pm, 6–11:30pm daily.*

| | | ● | ■ | ● |

FURTHER AFIELD: *Hietzinger Bräu* — €€
Auhofstraße 1. 🎨 *(01) 877 70 87.* **FAX** *877 70 87–22.*
Part of the Plachutta chain, this formal restaurant is close to Schönbrunn Park. Traditional beef dishes are typically washed down with beer or one of the excellent wines. *Tafelspitz* (boiled beef) is the house speciality, served in a number of different guises. Booking is recommended.

| | ■ | ● | ■ | |

FURTHER AFIELD: *Lusthaus* — €€
Freudenau 254/Prater Hauptallee. 🎨 *(01) 728 95 65.* Ⓦ www.lusthaus-wien.at
A traditional restaurant, enjoying a beautiful location in a round building at one end of the vast Prater funfair, near the horseracing track. The food is modern Austrian, including pasta dishes and venison, depending on the season. Desserts are a speciality. On weekends and public holidays it is a popular destination with families. ⬤ *Summer noon–11pm Mon–Fri; noon–6pm Sat, Sun and public holidays; winter noon–6pm Sat, Sun, public holidays.* ⬤ *Wed.*

| | ■ | ● | ■ | ● |

FURTHER AFIELD: *Schuppich–Cucina Triestina* — €€
Rotensterngasse 18. **Map** 3 E2. 🎨 *(01) 212 43 40.*
Austro-Italian dishes and well worth investigating. The wooden interior with vaulted ceilings creates a cosy atmosphere – there are toys available for children. 👶 ⬤ *6pm–1am Wed–Sat, 11am–midnight Sun.*

| | ■ | | ■ | |

FURTHER AFIELD: *Stadtwirt* — €€
Untere Viaduktgasse 45. **Map** 3 E4. 🎨 *(01) 713 38 28.*
An old-fashioned, country-style inn, serving sausages, roast bacon, fish dishes and Hungarian-style cabbage. Desserts include strudel, pancakes, cheese dumplings and *Kaiserschmarrn* (Emperor's "nothing" pudding with raisins). ⬤ *9am–midnight Mon–Fri, 4pm–1am Sat.* ⬤ *Sun from 5pm.*

| | ■ | ● | ■ | ● |

FURTHER AFIELD: *Stradina* — €€
Praterstraße 40. **Map** 3 E2. 🎨 *(01) 212 18 12.* Ⓦ www.stradina.at
An authentic Italian restaurant where you can experience the taste of stuffed sweetcorn manna, pumpkin risotto and genuine spaghetti carbonara. Even the coffee served here comes from the Trentino, and the adjacent ice cream parlour belongs to the same chef. ⬤ *Sun.*

| | ■ | ● | ■ | |

FURTHER AFIELD: *Niky's Kuchlmasterei* — €€
Obere Weißgerberstraße 6. **Map** 3 E3. 🎨 *(01) 712 90 00.* **FAX** *712 90 00–16.*
Ⓦ www.kuchlmasterei.at
A restaurant with an unusual Baroque interior, offering creative, modern Viennese cooking. Specialities include *Schnitzel* made with French pastry, roast asparagus, lobster in lemon and garlic and veal knuckle. It also has an excellent wine list. Booking is recommended. ⬤ *Sun, public holidays.*

| | ■ | ● | ■ | ● |

FURTHER AFIELD: *Taverna Lefteris* €€
Hörnesgasse 17. **[** *(01) 713 74 51.* **FAX** *710 70 30.*
A small, Greek restaurant serving traditional food from Crete. The menu is
dominated by vegetables in yoghurt sauce, moussaka and spit-roasted meat.
There is a good selection of wines, and from Oct–May you can enjoy live
music every Tuesday. **♫ ○** *6pm–midnight.* **●** *Sun, public holidays.*

FURTHER AFIELD: *Tempel* €€
Praterstraße 56, Innenhof. **Map 3 E2.** **[** *(01) 214 01 79.* **FAX** *214 01 79.*
A restaurant with a unique atmosphere, elegant decor and outdoor seating.
It offers a wide choice of dishes, ranging from seafood to beef and veal.
The good value set menu, sophisticated desserts and excellent French wines
make this a favourite eating place. **●** *Sat L, Sun, Mon.*

FURTHER AFIELD: *Vincent* €€€
Große Pfarrgasse 7. **Map 3 D1.** **[** *(01) 214 15 16.* **FAX** *214 14 14.*
A restaurant with ambitions; its flower-bedecked interior evokes a tropical
sea paradise, and the candlelight creates a romantic atmosphere. The
original cuisine offers a great selection of fish and seasonal dishes. There is
a good selection of Austrian and top international wines. A separate area is
allocated to non-smokers. **○** *6pm–midnight Mon–Sat.* **●** *Sun.*

LOWER AUSTRIA AND BURGENLAND

ALLAND: *Zur Grube* €€
Groisbach 24, 2534a. **Road map F3.** **[** *(02258) 2361.* **FAX** *2361.*
A genuine country inn, situated a mere 3 km (2 miles) from Alland. Here, you
can enjoy homemade pork trotters in jelly, *Wiener Schnitzel* of truly
gargantuan proportions or medallions of game, depending on the season.
Booking is recommended. **●** *Mon, Tue.*

AMSTETTEN: *Stadtbrauhof* €€€
Hauptplatz 14, 3300. **Road map E3.** **[** *(07472) 628 00.*
The Stadtbrauhof is one of the most traditional restaurants in the region.
Having started with the exquisite beef *carpaccio* marinated in olive oil and
lemon juice, you can order the equally superb English roast beef, accompanied
by a tasty seasonal salad using fresh ingredients; alternatively, fill up on a
traditional thick soup with liver dumplings, followed by roast pork with
onions. Booking is recommended. The inn also holds folkloristic events as
well as wine tastings.

BAD SCHONAU: *Kurhotel* €€
Am Kurpark 1, 2853. **Road map G4.** **[** *(02646) 82 51-728.* **FAX** *82 51-394.*
Many of the elegant spa hotels have good restaurants; the chef at this one
has been awarded two chef's hats by the Gault-Millau restaurant guide.
Guests are offered seafood *pot au feu*, roast duck in orange sauce and
Asian-style vegetables; in addition, of course, to a wide variety of regional
dishes from Lower Austria.

BADEN: *Grand Hotel Sauerhof (Rauhenstein)* €€€€
Weilburgstraße 11–13, 2500. **Road map G3.**
[*(02252) 412 51.* **FAX** *480 47.* **[W]** *www.sauerhof.at*
An exclusive restaurant, located in a unique Biedermeier palace dating
from 1820, in the heart of this spa city. Traditional Austrian food is served,
in winter in front of a crackling fire in a real fireplace, and in summer
outside, on a large terrace. There is also a good choice of wines. Booking
is recommended.

BADEN: *Do & Co Casino* €€€€€
Kaiser-Franz-Ring 1, 2500. **Road map G3.**
[*(02252) 435 02.* **FAX** *435 02-430.*
A menu capable of satisfying even the most discerning palate; specialities
include such unusual creations as *foie gras* served with fried apple in ginger
and tamarillo sauce, asparagus with prawns in basil sauce, Asian caviar *torbico*
and venison with almond noodles. **[&]**

BADEN: *Mercure Parkhotel* €€€€
Kaiser-Franz-Ring 5, 2500. **Road map G3.**
[*(02252) 443 86.* **FAX** *805 78.*
A bright and elegant restaurant decorated with flowers and pictures.
Regional and international cuisine, offering a three-course lunch at midday,
and a four-course dinner in the evening. You can also buy a pass and
chips for the adjacent casino.

		CREDIT CARDS	GARDEN OR TERRACE	AUSTRIAN WINES	WHEELCHAIR ACCESS

Prices of a three-course meal without drinks, including cover charge, tax and service, in euros:
€ up to € 20
€€ € 20–35
€€€ € 35–45
€€€€ € 45–55
€€€€€ over € 55.

CREDIT CARDS
Credit cards are accepted.
GARDEN OR TERRACE
Weather permitting, it is possible to eat *al fresco*.
AUSTRIAN WINES
A good selection of Austrian wines.
WHEELCHAIR ACCESS
Easy access and facilities for the disabled.

BADEN: *Primavera*   €€€€€
Weilburgstraße 3, 2500. **Road map** G3.
((02252) 855 51. **FAX** 855 51.
This is an exclusive but comfortable restaurant offering outstanding cuisine, with the main focus on French-Mediterranean dishes. It has a "Kaffeehaus" atmosphere and there are only a few tables, so you are advised to book early. The well-known, somewhat eccentric chef, who has been awarded two chef's hats by Gault-Millau, is happy to give excellent advice on his wines. ● *Sun, Mon.* ✖

BERNDORF/ÖDLITZ: *Waldgasthof Schimanszky*   €€
Rosenstraße 18, 2560. **Road map** F3. **(** (02672) 823 20. **FAX** 841 40.
The road sign describes this as a roast-chicken snack bar, but in reality it is an interesting restaurant, belonging to the owner of a famous Viennese restaurant in Biberstraße. Besides chicken, it also sells home-made jams and pickles to take away. ● *Mon, Tue.*

BROMBERG: *Jeitler – Landgasthaus*   €€
Oberschlatten 1, 2833. **Road map** G4. **(** (02629) 8267. **FAX** 8267-4.
Three cosy, newly decorated and upholstered rooms make this a very pleasant restaurant and it is also well run. A range of starters and tidbits are served on a platter. Sorrel soup served with salmon-stuffed ravioli is also popular with guests. Entrées are traditional and include pork, beef and poultry. ● *Tue, Wed, Thu before noon.*

DÜRNSTEIN: *Loibnerhof*   €€€
Unterloiben 7, 3601. **Road map** F3. **(** (02732) 828 90. **FAX** 82 8 90-3.
Sitting in an orchard under apricot trees, drinking wine from a jug, you truly feel as if you are in the countryside at this village inn near Dürnstein. Dishes include spit-roasted chicken, *Schnitzel* fried in butter and roast duck, and outstanding regional dishes. Prices vary, but there are set menus ranging in price from € 7 to € 40. Booking is strongly recommended.
● *Mon, Tue.*

DÜRNSTEIN: *Schloss Dürnstein*   €€€€
Dürnstein, 3601. **Road map** F3.
((02711) 212. **FAX** 212–30. **W** www.schloss.at
This elegant restaurant is based in a new castle built by the Thiery family, descendants of the French Huguenots. There is a lovely terrace overlooking the mountains and the Danube river can be seen flowing below. The award-winning restaurant combines regional and international specialities, featuring fish, saddle of lamb, *Tafelspitz* (boiled beef), roast chicken and the ubiquitous *Schnitzel*. A wide selection of wines is also available.
◯ *19 Mar–6 Nov.* ● *in winter, till Mar.*

GRAFENEGG: *Schloss Grafenegg*   €€€€€
Grafenegg 12, 3485. **Road map** F3.
((02735) 2616–0. **FAX** 2616–60. **W** www.grafenegg.at
Grafenegg Castle has an award-winning international restaurant, which serves seasonal dishes in elegant surroundings. Decorated in light colours, it has a welcoming and modern atmosphere. The castle also hosts exhibition previews, culinary seminars, receptions and weddings. Once a month there is a jazz-brunch. ◯ *Wed–Sun 10am–10pm.*
● *Mon, Tue, Jan.*

HAAG-STADT: *Mitter*   €€€€€
Linzer Straße, 3350. **Road map** E3. **(** (07434) 424 26. **FAX** 424 26-42.
A small, town inn, 17 km (11 miles) from Enns, which features regional and international food, including specialities from the "Mostviertel", the cider-producing region. Favourites include brown bread soup, home-made *Sulz* (brawn) and apple dumplings, all of which are made with the locally produced cider. ● *Thu.*

HINTERBRÜHL BEI MÖDLING: *Hexensitz*   €€€
Johannesstraße 35, 2371. **Road map** G3. 〖 *(02236) 229 37.* **FAX** *89 31 84.*
W www.hexensitz.at
If you are travelling from Vienna to Mödling (25 km/16 miles), you will
pass the inviting *Hexensitz* (witches' seat), where you can enjoy dinner in
the gentle shade of chestnut trees. Guests are offered a choice of several
dining rooms, each with an intimate atmosphere, good wines, and, above
all, superlative Austrian cooking. Prices vary. ◯ *11:30am–2pm, 6pm–10pm
Wed–Sat, 6pm–10pm Tue, 11:30am–2pm Sun.* ● *Mon.*

HOHENBERG: *Zwei Linden*   €
Markt 8, 3192. **Road map** F3. 〖 *(02767) 8377.*
The "Two Linden Trees" is a beautifully located village inn in the
breathtaking scenery of Lower Austria, 16 km (10 miles) from the small
town of Lilienfeld. Classic Austrian cuisine, including cream of garlic soup,
roast pork with onions, *Schnitzel* fried in lard and another classic,
Kartoffelsalat (potato salad).

KALTENBACH/VITIS: *Zum Topf*   €€
Kaltenbach 26, 3902. **Road map** F2. 〖 *(02841) 8329.* **FAX** *805 90.*
Amid the romantic, gentle hills of northeastern Lower Austria, some
12 km (7 miles) from the small town of Thaya, near the Czech border,
stands the "To the Pot" restaurant. Serves regional food, such as garlic soup,
potato dumplings and trout in a wine sauce, and offers a large selection of
good wines. Busy at weekends and on public holidays. ● *Mon, Tue.*

KASTEN: *Pedro's Landhaus*   €€€
Dörfl 19, 3072. **Road map** D3. 〖 *(02744) 7387.* **FAX** *7389.*
This exclusive restaurant, based in a converted castle in the southwestern
part of Lower Austria, some 30 minutes' drive from Vienna, serves Viennese
and international food. It is famous for its cold starter buffet and its dessert
dishes, and waiters prepare the salads at the guests' table. Every Friday, a
six-course gala dinner with overnight accommodation is hosted here,
sometimes with dancing. Booking is recommended. ● *Sun.*

KREMS: *Zum Kaiser von Österreich*   €€
Körnermarkt 9, 3500. **Road map** F3. 〖 *(02732) 860 01.* **FAX** *860 01-4.*
An elegant restaurant in a stylish, pink house with a Baroque façade
located in the town centre, near the pedestrianized zone. The menu
includes a wide selection of Italian dishes.

KRITZENDORF: *Preisecker*   €€
Hauptstraße 40, 3420. **Road map** G3. 〖 *(02243) 24138.* **FAX** *251 02.*
Regulars like to meet over a tankard of beer in the bar of this village inn
with a century-long tradition. The adjacent salon caters for more demanding tastes. Regional cooking is complemented by imaginative dishes from
around the world. Occasionally the inn organizes themed menus, for
example, "South Indian Impressions", which are entirely devoted to the
culinary traditions of one particular region. Booking is recommended.
◯ *from 11:30am; from 11am Fri, Sat, Sun.* ● *Wed.*

LANGENLEBARN: *Floh*   €€€
Tullner Straße 1, 3425. **Road map** F3.
〖 *(02272) 628 09.* **FAX** *628 09-4.* W www.derfloh.at
An attractive village restaurant, 35 km (22 miles) from Vienna, 5 km
(3 miles) from Tulln. The menu at "Flea" is dominated by fresh vegetables,
fish and game dishes. ◯ *9am–11pm Thu–Mon.* ● *Tue, Wed.*

LANGENLOIS: *Heurigenhof Bründlmayer*   €
Walterstraße 14, 3550. **Road map** F3. 〖 *(02734) 2883.* **FAX** *2883-4.*
A romantic wine bar with an inner courtyard garden, right at the heart of
this small town. Apart from trying the new-vintage wine, you can also order
an inexpensive and tasty meal, including small snacks to accompany the
Heurigen, called *Heurigenschmankerl.* ◯ *Mar–end Nov.* ● *Mon–Wed.*

LAXENBURG: *Kaiserbahnhof*   €€
Kaiser-Franz-Joseph-Platz 3, 2361. **Road map** G3.
〖 *(02236) 710 420.* **FAX** *710 420-5.* W www.kaiserbahnhof.at
A former railway station with a new glass-fronted extension now accommodates the "Emperor's Station". Situated in an attractive small, imperial
town close to Vienna, it is a popular day-trip destination. Although it
particularly aims to attract a younger clientele, the classical Austrian dishes
with a modern touch are popular with diners of all ages. ● *Mon.*

For key to symbols *see back flap*

Prices of a three-course meal without drinks, including cover charge, tax and service, in euros:
€ up to € 20
€€ € 20–35
€€€ € 35–45
€€€€ € 45–55
€€€€€ over € 55.

CREDIT CARDS
Credit cards are accepted.

GARDEN OR TERRACE
Weather permitting, it is possible to eat *al fresco*.

AUSTRIAN WINES
A good selection of Austrian wines.

WHEELCHAIR ACCESS
Easy access and facilities for the disabled.

	CREDIT CARDS	GARDEN OR TERRACE	AUSTRIAN WINES	WHEELCHAIR ACCESS

MAISSAU: *Naderer* €€
Am Berg 44, 3712. **Road map** F3. ☎ (02958) 823 34-0. FAX 823 34-4.
Splendid views from the terrace make a meal at this traditional inn near Vienna doubly enjoyable. The building is painted in a traditional yellow colour and situated on a hill at an altitude of 400 m (1,312 ft), where the forests end and the vineyards begin. The menu features the inevitable *Schnitzel* and roast pork. There is also a set menu. ⚑

Credit Cards · Garden or Terrace · Austrian Wines

MARIA TAFERL: *Krone – Kaiserbof* €€€
Maria Taferl 24, 3672. **Road map** F3. ☎ (07413) 63 55. FAX 63 55-83.
A hotel restaurant in the village centre, 13 km (8 miles) from Melk, in a region of gentle, terraced hills and expansive valleys, with a magnificent view over the Danube and the entire region. Serves traditional Austrian cuisine at a wide range of prices. ● *Jan, Feb, Nov, Dec.*

Credit Cards · Garden or Terrace · Austrian Wines

MAUTERN: *Nikolaihof Wachau Weinstube* €
Nikolaigasse 3, 3512. **Road map** F3. ☎ (02732) 829 01. FAX 764 40.
W www.nikolaihof.at
A wine bar in the Wachau region, 4 km (2 miles) from Krems. The buffet, a platter with a good selection of regional and vegetarian starters, is particularly good. In the wine bar guests may enjoy a choice of 18 of the Nikolaihof's own organic wines, served in the courtyard or in torch-lit rooms. Receptions are held in the Baroque halls. ○ *May–mid-Nov: 5–11pm Wed–Sat.*
● *Sun–Tue.*

Austrian Wines · Wheelchair Access

MAYERLING: *Kronprinz* €€€€€
Mayerling 1, 2534. **Road map** G3. ☎ (02258) 23 78. FAX 23 78-41.
Visitors retracing the footsteps of Archduke Rudolf in Mayerling can enjoy a princely meal. River crayfish, lobster, quail's eggs, wild mushrooms, fish, pigeon and champagne sauce all feature on this truly magnificent menu. Booking is recommended. ○ *noon–3pm, 6:30–midnight daily.*

Credit Cards · Garden or Terrace · Austrian Wines · Wheelchair Access

MICHELBACH: *Schwarzwallner* €
Untergoin 6, 3074. **Road map** F3. ☎ (02744) 82 41. FAX 84 94.
An old bar, a room with a tiled stove, and behind it a conservatory and a terrace combine to make this restaurant special. The cuisine matches the homely setting: bread with dripping, *Blunzl* (fried black pudding) with sauerkraut, roast lamb and game. ● *Tue, Wed.*

Credit Cards · Garden or Terrace · Austrian Wines

MITTERBACH/ST. SEBASTIAN: *Filzwieser* €
Bundesstraße 78, 3224a. **Road map** F3. ☎ (03882) 25 04. FAX 25 04-31.
Filzweiser lies on the border between Lower Austria and Styria, 5 km (3 miles) beyond the famous Mariazell church. You can enjoy a tasty and inexpensive meal at this restaurant with a menu featuring the cuisines of both regions. There is also a set menu and a fair selection of local wines.

Credit Cards · Garden or Terrace · Austrian Wines

MÖDLING: *Babenbergerbof* €€€
Babenbergergasse 6, 2340. **Road map** G3. ☎ (02236) 222 46. FAX 222 46-6.
An elegant restaurant in a hotel catering mainly for short-stay guests. A mere 30 km (19 miles) from Vienna and 13 km (8 miles) from Baden, the building stands at the edge of a pedestrianized zone of the village. Offers tasty Viennese and Mediterranean food, including *Tafelspitz* and fish dishes, and a large selection of wines. ● *2 weeks in Jan.*

Credit Cards · Garden or Terrace · Austrian Wines · Wheelchair Access

PAMHAGEN: *Vila Vita (Pannonia)* €€€
Storchengasse 1, 7152. **Road map** G4. ☎ (02175) 21 80-0. FAX 21 80-444.
W www.vilavitahotels.com
A well-known, country-style restaurant near Neusiedler See, part of a hotel and holiday village. Austrian regional dishes are gradually being replaced by more international cuisine, with a strong presence of Asian dishes. Smoked and poached trout are particular house specialties.
○ *7am–11pm daily.*

Credit Cards · Garden or Terrace · Austrian Wines · Wheelchair Access

POTTCHING: *Der Reisinger* €€
Hauptstraße 83, 7033. **Road map** G3. ☎ *(02631) 22 12.* FAX *20 90.*
W www.der-reisinger.at
An attractive country-style village inn offering venison steak, game pâté, mushroom ragoût and tasty dumplings. Excellent selection of Austrian and international wines, especially from Burgenland. ● *Mon–Wed, Sun evening.*

PURBACH: *Kloster am Spitz* €€€
Storchengasse 1, 7152. **Road map** G3. ☎ *(02683) 55 19.* FAX *55 10-20.*
A cloistered restaurant with great views of the lake. Famous for its wide selection of vegetarian and Pannonian dishes, including *Backhendl* (fried chicken). A popular Sunday destination. ● *Mon–Wed, mid-Dec–mid-Mar.*

RITZING: *Horvath* €€€
Lange Zeile 92, 7323. **Road map** G4. ☎ *(02619) 672 29.* FAX *672 29.*
A cluster of blue buildings, 22 km (14 miles) west of Deutschkreutz in the midst of the gentle Odenburg hills. A favourite place for Sunday outings, not only for its renowned *Wiener Schnitzel*, but also for its tasty jugged rabbit, courgettes, roast lamb and roast duck. ● *Mon.*

RUST: *Inamera* €€
Oggauer Straße 29, 7071. **Road map** G3. ☎ *(02685) 64 73.* FAX *64 73-18.*
W www.inamera.at
This small town, much visited by nesting storks, boasts an elegant restaurant with innovative cooking, including new takes on popular local dishes and international favourites, such as stuffed cabbage accompanied by celery purée, roast duck and *pâté de foie gras*. Advance booking is recommended. ● *Mon, Tue.*

RUST: *Rusterhof* €€€
Rathausplatz 18, 7071. **Road map** G3. ☎ *(02685) 64 16.* FAX *64 16-11.*
W www.rusterhof.at
The best season to visit this small town is early summer, when the storks can be seen in numerous nests built on the chimneys and roofs of the houses along Rathausplatz. The Rusterhof, right at the centre of the town, has a comfortable beer salon and a scenic patio. The regional cuisine on offer includes asparagus soup, duck liver, veal fillet, as well as many cheeses and desserts. The wines are from the Spitz monastery. Booking is recommended. ● *Mon.*

ST. MARGARETHEN: *Eselmühl* €€€
Margarethen, 7062. **Road map** G3. ☎ *(02680) 28 00.* FAX *28 00-2.*
The "Donkey Mill", in an ancient building 5 km (3 miles) from Rust and 9 km (6 miles) from Eisenstadt, attracts families with children. The menu includes creative dishes incorporating regional products of the highest quality, such as *carpaccio* of lamb with goat's cheese, pork fillet with roast ham, pancakes with Italian soft cheese ricotta, roasted mushrooms and many other delicacies. ● *Mon, Tue.*

SCHUTZEN/GEB.: *Eselböck Taubenkobel* €€€€€
Hauptstraße 33, 7081. **Road map** G3. ☎ *(02684) 22 97.* FAX *22 97-18.*
W www.taubenkobel.at
The restaurant, situated 6 km (4 miles) from Eisenstadt, serves tasty regional cuisine. Occasional themed evenings, fetauring the cuisines of Russia, Peru, Bolivia, Turkey or Indonesia. Evelyne Eselböck, known as one of the Austria's best sommeliers, serves regional wines from Burgenland as well as French and Italian wines. ● *Mon, Tue.*

WEIDEN/SEE: *Zur Blauen Gans* €€
Seepark. **Road map** G3. ☎ *(02167) 75 10.* FAX *78 40.* W www.blaue-gans.at
An attractive restaurant on the shores of a lake, 4 km (2 miles) from Neusiedl am See, specializing in modern French cuisine. Here you can sample such unusual delights as roast lotus shoots with salmon tartare, a spicy fish soup, and roast fowl with wild mushrooms. ● *Tue, Wed.* ♿

STYRIA

BAD RADKERSBURG: *Kurhotel im Park* €€
Im Kurpark, 8490. **Road map** F5. ☎ *(03476) 25 71-55.* FAX *20 85-45.*
An elegant restaurant, based in a luxury hotel with thermal baths. Even during the summer it is a pleasure to eat in the winter garden. The regional specialities include lamb chops, leg of lamb and fish. Try also a refreshing glass of champagne with elderberry flowers. ● *Jan.*

Prices of a three-course meal without drinks, including cover charge, tax and service, in euros:
€ up to € 20
€€ € 20–35
€€€ € 35–45
€€€€ € 45–55
€€€€€ over € 55.

CREDIT CARDS
Credit cards are accepted.
GARDEN OR TERRACE
Weather permitting, it is possible to eat *al fresco.*
AUSTRIAN WINES
A good selection of Austrian wines.
WHEELCHAIR ACCESS
Easy access and facilities for the disabled.

		CREDIT CARDS	GARDEN OR TERRACE	AUSTRIAN WINES	WHEELCHAIR ACCESS
BAD WALTERSDORF: *Thermenhof* Wagerberg 120, 8271. **Road map** F4. ☎ *(03333) 28 01-0.* FAX *28 01-40.* W www.thermenhof.at Despite its location in a spa resort, the prices at this establishment are fairly modest; for as little as € 13 you can enjoy a first-class dinner. The short but imaginative menu includes chef's specials such as cream of asparagus soup, roast duck and boiled beef.	€€	■	●	■	●
BAD WALTERSDORF: *Safenhof* Bad Waltersdorf 78, 8271. **Road map** F4. ☎ *(03333) 22 39.* FAX *22 39-15.* In the afternoon, this country-style restaurant, based at an inn, turns into a village wine bar. It continues to serve food, including cold marinated veal brisket, calf-foot jelly with pumpkin oil, fried scampi and several asparagus dishes during the season. Large selection of Austrian wines. ● *Mon.*	€€	■	●	■	
ETMISSL: *Hubinger (Vital-Gasthof)* Etmissl Nr. 25, 8622. **Road map** F4. ☎ *(03861) 81 14.* FAX *81 14-23.* An attractive inn, typical of the region, in a small village with a cosy *Gaststube* (restaurant). The menu is dominated by roast pork, chicken and cheesecake, although it does include some more unusual dishes, such as roast goat, lamb cutlet and trout. ● *Mon.*	€€€	■	●	■	●
FISCHBACH: *Forsthaus* 8654 Fischbach, 8654. **Road map** F4. ☎ *(03170) 201.* FAX *201.* This restaurant is based in an interesting, 400-year-old forester's hut, belonging to the local manor house and typical of the region. Veal, lamb and fish dishes are particularly good; set menu also available. ● *Wed.*	€€	■	●		
FROHNLEITEN: *Frohnleitnerhof* Hauptplatz 14a, 8130. **Road map** E4. ☎ *(03126) 41 50-0.* FAX *41 50-555.* W www.frohnleitnerhof.at This brewery, owned by a hotel, is possibly the only restaurant in Austria where you can order beetroot borsch served with shrimps. The roast lamb is also popular. ● *Sun.*	€€	■	●	■	●
GAMLITZ: *Jaglhof (Gastwirtschaft Wohnen & Wein)* Sernau 25, 8462. **Road map** F5. ☎ *(03454) 66 75.* FAX *66 75-12.* An attractive inn set in greenery, a five-minute drive from the "Wine Route" of southern Styria. Has a light, airy interior and a pleasant view from the terrace. The chef's specials include trout, pumpkin dishes and lamb cutlets. Good wines are available directly from the producers. ● *Mon.*	€€€		●	■	●
GAMLITZ: *Sattlerhof* Sernau 2a, 8462. **Road map** F5. ☎ *(03453) 44 54-0.* FAX *44 54-44.* W www.sattlerhof.at A restaurant for gourmets, in a small, comfortable and beautifully situated hotel. Serves home-made sparkling wine. Other house specialities include roast duck and goat. ○ *6pm–10pm.* ● *Sun, Mon.*	€€€	■	●	■	
GRAZ: *Mayers* Sackstraße 29, 8010. **Road map** F4. ☎ *(0316) 81 33 91.* An interesting, modern building made of steel, stone and glass. The third-floor restaurant affords magnificent views over the city. Excellent food, mainly European, Mediterranean and Far Eastern dishes, with an extensive menu, including a set menu. ● *Sat, Sun.* ♿	€€	■	●	■	●
GRAZ: *Ohnime – Di Gallo* Purbergstraße 56, 8010. **Road map** F4. ☎ *(0316) 39 11 43.* FAX *39 11 43-19.* W www.ohnime.at This hotel-restaurant serves international favourites and regional specialities, including home-made pasta. A large selection of wines (also for sale) and very good coffee. ● *Sun.*	€€	■	●	■	

GRAZ: *Hirschenwirt*   €€€
Rupertistraße 115, 8075. **Road map** F4. [(0316) 46 56 00.
Although the chef is known for his traditional tastes, this attractive
restaurant has managed to attract a fairly large number of regulars, coming
to enjoy the delicious roast duck or fish. A set menu and a large selection
of wines and personable service. ● *Sun, Mon.*

GRAZ: *Iohan*   €€€
Landhausgasse 1, 8010. **Road map** F4. [(0316) 82 13 12. FAX 81 54 10.
A chic restaurant with subdued lighting and a romantic atmosphere,
frequented by young people. The international menu tends towards Asian
and Italian dishes. ● *Sun, Mon, public holidays.* ✕

GRAZ: *Mod (Hotel zum Dom)*   €€€€€
Bindergasse 1, 8010. **Road map** F4. [(0316) 82 48 00 41. FAX 82 48 00 41.
Elegant restaurant in the town centre, within the historic Old Town district.
Dishes particularly worth recommending include the *carpaccio* of
mountain beef with fried mushrooms and the Corsican fish soup. Good
wines. ● *Sun, Mon.*

GRÖBMING: *Landhaus St. Georg*   €€€€
Gröbming 555, 8962. **Road map** E4. [(03685) 22 7 40. FAX 22 7 40-60.
W www.st-georg.at
From the outside, this hotel-restaurant, part of the Silencehotel group, is a
large village house, typical of the region. The restaurant caters primarily for
the hotel guests, and you will need to book for lunch. Prices are high, but
the set menus comprise several courses. The restaurant serves innovative
dishes based on regional produce, such as pumpkin soup and asparagus.

HARTBERG: *Schloss Hartberg*   €€
Herrengasse 1, 8230. **Road map** F4. [(03332) 618 50.
Based in an old castle, this ambitious restaurant offers modern cuisine,
incorporating fashionable dishes from around the world and catering for
the latest dietary trends. The specials include: smoked duck breast served
with marinated vegetables, artichokes and lamb fillet. ⬜ *6pm–2am Mon–Sat.*

HOHENTAUERN: *Passhöhe*   €€
Hohentauern 110, 8785. **Road map** E4. [(03618) 219. FAX 219-4.
A small, well-equipped and beautifully furnished inn on the Hohentauern
Pass. A true haven for hikers and skiers who appreciate the warm family
atmosphere and the good set menu – the house speciality is breast of
Barbary duck with dumplings and red cabbage. ● *Wed, Nov.* ✚

IRDNING: *Hirsch'n Wirt*   €€€
Aigner Straße 22, 8952. **Road map** F4. [(03682) 224 45. FAX 224 45 -5.
W www.hirschenwirt.at
This restaurant opens in the evenings; lunch is served by appointment
only. Booking is also recommended for evening meals. There are three
unpretentious, tastefully decorated dining rooms serving fairly down-to-
earth, traditional food. Choice of vegetarian dishes, depending on seasonal
availability of ingredients. ● *Tue.*

KNITTELFELD: *Forellenhof Gursch*   €€
Flatschach 6, 8720. **Road map** E4. [(03577) 22 0 10. FAX 220 09.
This restaurant, some 10 km (6 miles) from Judenburg, and 35 km (22
miles) from Leoben, has its own trout farm. Its interior decorations are from
the 1970s, but the cuisine is thoroughly modern. The menu is dominated
by fish and vegetable dishes, but there is also a wide choice of delicious
meat dishes. ⬜ *By appointment.* ● *Sun from 3pm, Mon, Tue.* ✕

LASSNITZHÖHE: *Kotzian*   €
Hauptstraße 25, 8301. **Road map** F4. [(03133) 22 47. FAX 22 47-99.
An *Imbiss* (snack bar) by the bakery, at the centre of the village, where you
can get a good, inexpensive meal. The menu features fillet of beef, veal,
and wild mushrooms when in season. ● *Wed, Thu.*

REIN: *Landgasthof Schaupp*   €€€
Eisbach/Tallak 53, 8103. **Road map** F4.
[(03124) 517 32. FAX 517 32-7.
A mere 10 km (6 miles) from Graz, set amid green hills, this inn is a family
favourite. Sunday visitors are offered country-style beef consommé with
strips of meat, chicken fillet sprinkled with pumpkin seed, and regional
delicacies. A fair selection of local wines. ● *Tue, Wed.*

<table>
<tr><td colspan="2">

Prices of a three-course meal without drinks, including cover charge, tax and service, in euros:
€ up to € 20
€€ € 20–35
€€€ € 35–45
€€€€ € 45–55
€€€€€ over € 55.

</td><td colspan="4">

CREDIT CARDS
Credit cards are accepted.
GARDEN OR TERRACE
Weather permitting, it is possible to eat al fresco.
AUSTRIAN WINES
A good selection of Austrian wines.
WHEELCHAIR ACCESS
Easy access and facilities for the disabled.

</td></tr>
</table>

	CREDIT CARDS	GARDEN OR TERRACE	AUSTRIAN WINES	WHEELCHAIR ACCESS
ST. SEBASTIAN/MARIAZELL: *Lurgbauer* €€€ Lurg 1, 3224 **Road map** F4. (03882) 37 18. FAX 37 18. This restaurant, situated only 5 km (3 miles) from the famous Mariazell pilgrimage site, is known for its beef dishes, especially *Tafelspitz* and beef tenderloin. In the summer months meals are served on the terrace. Booking is recommended. ○ Dec–Apr: Fri–Sun only; May–Oct: Wed–Sun. ● Mon, Tue, Oct.		●	■	
TURNAU: *Wirtshaus Steirereck* €€€€ Pogusch 21, 8625. **Road map** F4. (03863) 2000 or 5151. FAX 51 51 51. w www.steirereck.at The "Styrian Corner" inn is deservedly popular – regarded as one of the best restaurants in the region, it also enjoys a reputation as a venue for romantic get-togethers. The cuisine combines traditional and modern elements, with a good selection of vegetarian dishes. ● Mon–Wed.		●	■	●

UPPER AUSTRIA				
ATTNANG-PUCHHEIM: *Christian's* €€€ Gmundner Straße, 4800. **Road map** D3. (07674) 646 33. A modern establishment with a restaurant, hotel and lovely garden, near the basilica, 4 km (2 miles) from Vöcklabruck. The set menu is dominated by fish dishes. A wide range of prices, from around € 7 to € 40. ● Sun, Mon.	■	●	■	
BAD ISCHL: *Villa Schratt* €€€€ Steinbruch 43, 4820. **Road map** D4. (06132) 276 47. FAX 276 47-4. w www.villaschratt.at Mrs Schratt was the "secret" love of Emperor Franz Joseph I – so secret that the whole world knew about it. The restaurant offers tasty, traditional dishes such as fillet of venison, *foie gras* mousse in Cumberland sauce, cream of mushroom soup made from local chanterelles and duck with red cabbage, followed by the famous Schratt *Guglhupf* for dessert. Booking is recommended. ● Tue, Wed.	■	●	■	
GMUNDEN: *Schloss Freisitz Roith* €€€ Traunsteinstraße 87, 4810. **Road map** D3. (07612) 649 05. FAX 649 05-17. w www.schlosshotel.at A charming restaurant with a conservatory offering great views over the town, the lake (Traunsee) and the castle. The gastronomic delights include potato soup served with mushroom-stuffed ravioli, fresh-water fish and pumpkin in a cream sauce and ravioli stuffed with chanterelles. Booking is recommended. Set menu available. ● Feb.	■	●	■	●
GRIESKIRCHEN: *Waldschänke* €€€ Grieskirchen, 4710. **Road map** E3. (07248) 623 08. FAX 666 44. An attractive restaurant, where guests are well looked after. The set lunch menu consists of four courses; *foie gras* is served in endless variations, while the celery soup is enhanced by truffles. Booking is recommended. ● Mon, last week Jul, first week in Aug.	■	●	■	
LINZ: *Chizuru (Japan)* €€€ Johann-Konrad-Vogel-Straße 11, 4020. **Road map** E3. (0732) 77 27 79. FAX 77 27 79. A Japanese restaurant, renowned for its set menu. The menu doesn't change, so you can always eat the same favourite dishes. Prices vary considerably; a full meal costs anything from € 5 to over € 40. ● Sun, first week in Aug.		●		●
LINZ: *Der Neue Vogelkäfig* €€€ Holzstraße 8, 4020. **Road map** E3. (0732) 77 01 93. FAX 77 01 93-2. Although located in an industrial part of Linz, and not the cheapest, this small restaurant with a homely ambience is popular and enjoys a great reputation. The "New Bird Cage" serves international food, with a focus on beef dishes. There is a delicious five-course dinner at € 32. ● Sat, Sun.	■	●	■	

MONDSEE: *Restaurant im Königshof* €€€
Am See 28, 5310. **Road map** D3. ☎ *(06232) 56 27.* **FAX** *56 27-55.*
A restaurant based in a former castle, at the centre of a charming little
town, with lovely views of the lake from the terrace and conservatory. The
menu is dominated by fresh-water fish, although it also offers venison,
lamb and chicken. The restaurant is famous for its desserts. Booking is
recommended. ● *Sun (except in summer), Jan, Feb.*

MONDSEE: *Seegasthof Lackner* €€€€
Mondseestraße 1, 5310. **Road map** D3. ☎ *(06232) 23 59.* **FAX** *23 59-50.*
W www.seehotel-lackner.at
A very nice restaurant, with views over the lake and of the surrounding
mountains, situated in a charming small town 27 km (16 miles) from
Salzburg. Guests are offered fresh-water fish, beef and many delicacies
traditional to Upper Austria. Prices vary from around € 14 to over
€ 40 per person. ● *Winter till Apr, closed one day a week on varying days.*

NUSSDORF/ATTERSEE: *Bräugasthof Aichinger* €€
Am Anger 1, 4865. **Road map** D3. ☎ *(07666) 80 07.* **FAX** *80 07-50,*
Set far away from the main roads, in a beautiful landscape of lakes in the
Salzkammergut mountains, this brewery inn serves seasonal delicacies in a
quiet, peaceful garden. The menu includes asparagus (when in season),
green salad, potatoes, fresh-water fish and thousands of other regional
delicacies. The restaurant is renowned for its vegetarian dishes. Good food
is accompanied by a wide selection of wines. ● *Mon, Feb.*

ST. WOLFGANG: *Lachsen* €€€€
Ried 5, 5360. **Road map** D4. ☎ *(06138) 24 32.* **FAX** *24 32-4.*
A popular village inn enjoying a great location amid meadows, with a ter-
race overlooking the lake (Wolfgangsee). The menu concentrates on fresh-
water fish and there's a wide selection of regional dishes. Booking is essential.
Payment is by cash only. ○ *Nov–Mar: Thu–Sun; closing day varies*

SCHNEEGATTERN: *Pühringer* €€
Kobernausserwaldstraße 21, 5212. **Road map** D3. ☎ *(07746) 32 14.* **FAX** *32 14-4.*
A relaxing setting in a garden, by a fountain. The easy atmosphere is
helped by good regional cuisine with a solid menu featuring pork chops,
rabbit jelly, rice with vegetables and poppy-seed dumplings. Booking is
recommended. ● *Tue, Wed.* 🔆

TRAUNKIRCHEN: *Post (Austria Classic Hotel)* €€
Ortsplatz 5, 4801. **Road map** D3. ☎ *(07617) 230 70.* **FAX** *28 09.*
A traditional restaurant and hotel that specializes in fish from the Salzkammergut lake and roast chicken while offering a wide selection of
salads, as well as fresh produce from local farms. Booking is
recommended.

TRAUNKIRCHEN: *Traunsee Landhotel* €€
Klosterplatz 4, 4801. **Road map** D3. ☎ *(07617) 22 16.* **FAX** *31 96.*
A romantic restaurant in the town centre, on the shores of Traunsee with a
view of the Traunstein Mountains. Traditional Austrian cuisine is dominated
by fish from the waters of the Salzkammergut lakes, *Tafelspitz* (boiled
beef), lamb chops, scampi with seasonal asparagus, good vegetarian dishes
and, of course, dumplings. ○ *Apr–late Sep.* 🔆

SALZBURGER LAND

ANIF: *Schlosswirt zu Anif* €€
Salzachtalstraße 7, 5081. **Road map** D4. ☎ *(06246) 721 75.* **FAX** *721 75-80.*
W www.schlosswirt-anif.com
A stylish restaurant set in a romantic castle, popular for Sunday outings. In
the summer you can eat in the garden. Great emphasis is placed on
beautiful table arrangements and presentation. The ducks from the castle
pond reappear on the restaurant menu, which also features roast chicken,
crayfish and beef. Booking is recommended.

BERGHEIM: *Gmachl* €€€
Dorfstraße 35, 5101. **Road map** D3. ☎ *(0662) 45 21 24.* **FAX** *45 21 24-68.*
W www.gmachl. at
A mere 3 km (2 miles) from Salzburg, next to the church and the town
hall, is this hotel-restaurant frequently used as a venue for seminars. The
Austrian cuisine is excellent and the restaurant is always full. It is advisable
to book a table well in advance.

For key to symbols *see back flap*

Prices of a three-course meal without drinks, including cover charge, tax and service, in euros:
€ up to € 20
€€ € 20–35
€€€ € 35–45
€€€€ € 45–55
€€€€€ over € 55.

CREDIT CARDS
Credit cards are accepted.

GARDEN OR TERRACE
Weather permitting, it is possible to eat *al fresco*.

AUSTRIAN WINES
A good selection of Austrian wines.

WHEELCHAIR ACCESS
Easy access and facilities for the disabled.

	CREDIT CARDS	GARDEN OR TERRACE	AUSTRIAN WINES	WHEELCHAIR ACCESS

BRUCK/GLOCKNERSTRASSE: *Taxhof*   €€€
Bruck/Glocknerstraße, 5671. **Road map** D4. ((06545) 62 61. FAX 62 61-6.
A pleasant restaurant in a refurbished farmhouse. The terrace affords magnificent views of the mountains. Regional cuisine from the Pinzgau district, including beef jelly sprinkled with Styrian pumpkin oil, and spinach dumplings. ● Mon, Nov, three weeks after Easter. ○ From 4pm.

BRUCK/GLOCKNERSTRASSE: *Zacherlbräu*   €€€
Glocknerstraße 14, 5671, **Road map** D4. ((06545) 72 42. FAX 72 42.
W www.zacherlbraeu.at
A traditional restaurant, much frequented by lovers of the local food. The owners also have a cattle farm, so their home-reared beef is a speciality of the house; plus pork, home-made cheeses and fresh herbs. The restaurant has been awarded a chef's hat by Gault-Millau. Good wines, excellent beer and schnaps are also served. It is advisable to book in advance. ● Mon.

ELIXHAUSEN: *Gmachl*   €€
Dorfstraße 14, 5161. **Road map** D3. ((0662) 48 02 12-0. FAX 48 02 12-72.
W www.gmachl.com
A smart restaurant in a hotel, often hosting conferences and seminars. The restaurant is also popular with individual guests. Austrian cuisine with international accents dominates the menu. Gmachl also has its own butcher's shop. ● Sun evening, Christmas, three weeks in Jul.

EUGENDORF BEI SALZBURG: *Don Carlos*   €
Golfplatz, 5301. **Road map** D3. ((06225) 871 11. FAX 871 00.
Despite its Spanish name this restaurant serves Austro-Italian food, with seafood and *Schnitzel* a speciality. Booking is recommended. ● Jan, Feb.

FILZMOOS: *Hubertus (Genießerhotel)*   €€€€€
Am Dorfplatz 1, 5532. **Road map** D4. ((06453) 82 04. FAX 82 0 66.
W www.hubertus-filzmoos.at
Known as a gourmet restaurant, the Hubertus offers modern food with Mediterranean and Asian influences. The chef, Johanna Mayer, is the only woman in the world to have been awarded four chef's hats. Fish features prominently on the menu. Booking is recommended. ● Mon.

FUSCHL AM SEE: *Ebner's Waldhof (Silencehotel)*   €€€
Seestraße 30, 5330. **Road map** D3. ((06226) 82 64. FAX 86 44.
W www.ebners-waldhof.at
A hotel-restaurant beautifully situated on the promenade along the shores of the lake, 20 km (12 miles) from Salzburg. The wood-panelled interior confirms its regional character, as does the cuisine. Dishes are made from local produce, including fish from the lake. 🏃

GOLDEGG/SEE: *Zum Auerhahn*   €€
March 35, 5622. **Road map** D4. ((06415) 82 73. FAX 82 73-4.
Despite its modest appearance, this restaurant, hidden on an estate behind the Goldegg mountain, serves excellent food. The menu features roast lamb, fillet of beef, veal and of course fish. ● Wed.

GOLDEGG/SEE: *Zum Bierführer*   €€€
Hofmark 19, 5622. **Road map** D4. ((06415) 81 02. FAX 81 02.
The interior of the "Beer Guide", an ancient horse station where beer was stored, is decorated with horseracing trophies. It also has a well-kept garden and terrace with views. Traditional Austrian cuisine. ● Mon.

GOLLING: *Bürgerstube*   €
Am Marktplatz 56, 5440. **Road map** D4. ((06244) 422 00. FAX 69 12 42.
An unpretentious restaurant, with a good family atmosphere and excellent seasonal food. Goulash, roast chicken or duck, and *Schnitzel* are always available. ● Sun, Mon morning, 2 weeks in Jan, 1 week in Oct.

HALLEIN/TAXACH: *Hohlwegwirt* €€€€
Salzachtal-Bundesstraße Nord 62, 5400. **Road map** D4. ¶ *(06245) 824 15.*
FAX *82 4 15-72.*
A pleasant restaurant on the road between Hallein and Anif. Serves good
Austrian cuisine. The menu includes asparagus, game, wild mushrooms
and lamb dishes; and there is also a rich selection of wines and cheeses.
Prices vary widely. ● *Mon, Sun evening.*

SALZBURG: *Alt Salzburg* €€€€
Bürgerspitalgasse 2, 5020. **Road map** G5. ¶ *(0662) 84 14 76.* **FAX** *84 14 76-4.*
W www.altsalzburg.at
A country-style restaurant in the centre of town, with very friendly service.
Traditional Austrian fare prepared to a high standard. Booking is
recommended. ● *Sun, Mon before noon.*

TYROL AND VORARLBERG

AU/BREGENZERWALD: *Krone in Au* €€€€€
Jaghausen 4, 6883. **Road map** A4. ¶ *(05515) 22 01-0.* **FAX** *22 01-201.*
W www.krone-au.at
A nostalgic, colonnaded restaurant near the church, on the road from Hoch-
tannberg to Eheintal, 42 km (26 miles) from Dorbim. Traditional cuisine
with a modern, light touch, including vegetarian dishes and a large salad
buffet. ● *Mon, Sun evening.*

AURACH: *Giggling-Stube* €€€€€
Aurach/Kitzbühel, 6370a. **Road map** C4. ¶ *(05356) 648 88.* **FAX** *732 05.*
Prices here are high, but the menu and service are truly superb. The chef
has been awarded a chef's hat by Gault-Millau a staggering 16 times. Tyrolean-
Italian delicacies are served in quiet surroundings, yet only 3 km (2 miles)
from Kitzbühel. Booking is advised. ◯ *Evenings only.* ● *Mon, Apr, May, Jun.*

BEZAU: *Gams* €€€
Platz 44, 6870. **Road map** A4. ¶ *(05514) 22 20.* **FAX** *22 20-24.*
W www.hotel-gams.at
The menu at this pleasant restaurant, 28 km (17 miles) from Dornbirn, is
dictated by seasonal, fresh, local produce. Its speciality is duck in orange
sauce; there is also a wide choice of vegetarian dishes. ● *Mon, Tue.*

BEZAU: *Post* €€€
Brugg 35, 6870. **Road map** A4. ¶ *(05514) 22 07.* **FAX** *22 07-22.*
W www.hotelpostbezau.at
A pleasant establishment with friendly service. Mainly regional food, but
with international influences. Offers a large selection of fish and vegetarian
dishes. There is a wide range of prices. ● *Sun evenings, Mon.*

BRAZ/BLUDENZ: *Rössle* €€
Arlbergstraße 67, 6751. **Road map** A4. ¶ *(05552) 28 10 50.* **FAX** *281056.*
www.roesslebraz.at
An interesting inn, near Bludenz, traditionally decorated in red wood,
serving equally traditional food, including *Schnitzel*, goulash, roast meat or
fish. A large selection of wines and cheeses. ● *Mon, Tue until 5pm.*

BRAZ/BLUDENZ: *Traube* €€€€
Klostertaler Straße 12, 6751. **Road map** A4. ¶ *(05552) 281 03-0.* **FAX** *28 1 03-40.*
A traditional restaurant, with a family atmosphere. The award-winning
regional and international cuisine tends towards simple, rich dishes;
Tafelspitz is a speciality. A wide selection of wines. ● *Nov.*

BREGENZ: *Casino-Restaurant "Falstaff"* €€€€€
Symphonikerplatz 3, 6900. **Road map** A4. ¶ *(05574) 444 33.* **FAX** *444 33.*
W www.falstaff-bregenz.at
An elegant restaurant based in the Bregenz Casino. The menu includes such
highlights as fish from Bodensee (Lake Constance), served with tortellini
stuffed with fish; fish fillet served on Italian dill; or roast rabbit.

BREGENZ: *Deuring-Schlössle* €€€€€
Ehre-Guta-Platz 4, 6900. **Road map** A4. ¶ *(05574) 478 00.* **FAX** *478 00-80.*
W www.deuring-schloessle.com
An exclusive restaurant in an old castle, near the theatre stage on Boden-
see. Despite its high prices, it is very popular, particularly during the Bregenz
Festival. The short menu features Viennese, Austrian and international
dishes. Booking is recommended. ● *Mon am.*

Prices of a three-course meal without drinks, including cover charge, tax and service, in euros:
€ up to € 20
€€ € 20–35
€€€ € 35–45
€€€€ € 45–55
€€€€€ over € 55.

CREDIT CARDS
Credit cards are accepted.
GARDEN OR TERRACE
Weather permitting, it is possible to eat *al fresco.*
AUSTRIAN WINES
A good selection of Austrian wines.
WHEELCHAIR ACCESS
Easy access and facilities for the disabled.

	CREDIT CARDS	GARDEN OR TERRACE	AUSTRIAN WINES	WHEELCHAIR ACCESS

BREGENZ: *Germania*   €€€€
Am Steinenbach 9, 6900. **Road map** A4. **C** *(05574) 427 66.* **FAX** *427 66-4.*
W www.hotel-germania.at
An elegant and long-established hotel-restaurant. The cuisine is based on seasonal regional produce, with a menu dominated by veal and fresh-water fish from Bodensee; Italian and Asian dishes are also on offer. The table settings are particularly attractive. ○ *4–11:30pm Mon–Sat.* ● *Sun.*

| | ■ | ● | ■ | |

BRIXLEGG: *Sigwart's Tiroler Weinstuben*   €€€
Marktstraße 40, 6230. **Road map** C4. **C** *(05337) 633 90.* **FAX** *633 90-15.*
In this more than 200-year-old building TV stars and other celebrities can be spied enjoying the excellent wine as well as the rustic cuisine, which features freshly baked country bread with dripping, pig trotters in jelly, and tomato soup with cheese dumplings. For more refined palates, there are dishes such as veal *carpaccio* with truffles or lasagne with mussels in caviar sauce. Whatever you choose, you can expect to eat well here for around € 35. ● *Mon, Tue.*

| | ■ | ● | ■ | |

DORNBIRN: *Rickatschwende*   €€€
Bödelestraße, 6850. **Road map** A4. **C** *(05572) 253 50-0.* **FAX** *253 50-70.*
W www.rickatschwende.com
The specialities at this attractive restaurant with a cosy atmosphere, 11 km (7 miles) from Bregenz, include goat's cheese, asparagus and ragoût made with wild mushrooms. There is also a choice of dietary and light meals as well as vegetarian dishes. ● *Sun, Mon am.* ✗

| | ■ | ● | ■ | |

EICHENBERG: *Schönblick*   €€€€
Dorf 6, 6941a. **Road map** A4. **C** *(05574) 459 65.* **FAX** *459 65-7.*
W www.schoenblick.at
Mountaintop views are always thrilling, and the one from Eichenberg is unforgettable. Both the terrace and the windows of the restaurant overlook Bodensee, a good part of Switzerland and the Allgäu region in Germany. Try the house special: *Eichenberger Töpfle*, a combination of pork fillet and *Spätzle* (the local pasta) in mushroom sauce. ● *Mon, Tue until 5pm.* ✗

| | | ● | ■ | |

ELLMAU: *Der Bär*   €€€€
Kirchbichl 9, 6452. **Road map** C4. **C** *(05358) 23 95.* **FAX** *23 95-56.*
Any visitor who falls into the hands of the proprietary Windisch brothers does not have time to reach for the menu. Before you know what is happening, you will find yourself at the bar enjoying the starters, then moving on to the recommended Tyrolean-Italian dishes, including *Tafelspitz, Kaiserschmarrn*, bacon dumpling, *vitello tonnato* and *carpaccio*, washed down with good wine. ● *Oct–mid-Dec, Apr–Jun.*

| | ■ | ● | ■ | ● |

ELLMAU: *Kaiserhof*   €€€€
Harmstätt 8, 6452. **Road map** C4. **C** *(05358) 20 22.* **FAX** *20 22-600.*
A beautifully located restaurant, between St. Johann (17 km/11 miles) and Kufstein (16 km/10 miles). The set menus consist of four or six courses; among the chef's specials are potato ravioli, roast chicken and veal tongue.
● *Mon–Wed, mid-Nov–mid-Dec, mid-Apr to mid-May.*

| | ■ | ● | ■ | |

ERL: *Beim Dresch*   €€
Oberweidau 2, 6343. **Road map** C4. **C** *(05373) 81 29.* **FAX** *81 29-3.*
W www.dresch.at
The restaurant formerly known as Tiroler Stuben (Tyrolean Living Room) is a modest inn situated 15 km (9 miles) from Kufstein, in Erl's main street, near a theatre that stages Passion plays in late July and early August. It serves good, traditional Austrian cuisine, including *Kaiserschmarrn, Käsespätzle* (cheese noodles), and at good-value prices: a good meal will set you back as little as € 11. Occasionally there is an Italian or Thai buffet.
● *Wed, Thu until 5pm.* ✗

| | ■ | ● | ■ | |

FELDKIRCH: *Alpenrose* €€
Rosengasse 4–6, 680. **Road map** A4. ☎ *(05522) 721 75.* ₣ₐₓ *721 75-5.*
A small, very pleasant restaurant with a homely atmosphere. Here, you can eat fish from Bodensee (Lake Constance), served on a bed of spinach with lobster or crayfish sauce, as well as homemade ravioli and pasta, veal fillet or *Tafelspitz* (boiled beef). A good selection of cheeses. ● *Sun.*

FISS: *Schlosshotel Fiss* €€€€
Fiss, 6533. **Road map** C4. ☎ *(05476) 63 97.* ₣ₐₓ *63 97.*
A tastefully furnished restaurant in an old castle with a particularly pleasant atmosphere. The chef's specials include beef consommé with spinach-stuffed ravioli, scampi fried in garlic mousse and mountain lamb roasted with olives. Although prices are generally high, the set menu costs as little as € 20. ● *mid-Oct–Dec, mid-Apr to mid-Jun.*

HIPPACH: *Sieghard* €€
Schwendau 83, 6283. **Road map** C4. ☎ *(05282) 33 09.* ₣ₐₓ *37 32.*
When you've been here once, you will want to come back again and again. Among the main draws are the ravioli, filled with Italian ricotta cheese and potatoes and served in a rich, buttery cream of chestnut soup, as well as the almond bread. Prices vary from € 10 to € 50. Booking is recommended. ● *Mon, late Oct–early Dec.*

HOPFGARTEN: *Fuchswirt* €€
Kelchsau 11, 6361. **Road map** C4. ☎ *(05335) 71 71.* ₣ₐₓ *71 71-4.*
A traditional village inn, 23 km (14 miles) from Kitzbühel. The chef's specials include tuna *carpaccio*, goat goulash and cheese dumplings, served with tipsy strawberries. ● *Tue, Jun, Nov.*

INNSBRUCK: *Koreth* €€
Hauptplatz 1, 6020. **Road map** B4. ☎ *(0512) 26 34 59.* ₣ₐₓ *27 55 89.*
In good weather you can eat in the garden of this long-standing, country-style restaurant. Especially worth trying are the Riesling and cream soup, spring onion soup, veal goulash, and the Tuscan wines. Set menu. ● *Wed.*

INNSBRUCK: *Schwarzer Adler* €€
Kaiserjägerstraße 2, 6020. **Road map** B4. ☎ *(0512) 58 71 09.* ₣ₐₓ *56 16 97.*
ⓦ www.deradler.com
Part of the Romantikhotel chain, this restaurant has several cosy rooms. The chef generally recommends fish, crayfish or game. Booking is advisable. ● *Sun, public holidays.*

INNSBRUCK: *Thai Li* €€
Marktgraben 3, 6020. **Road map** B4. ☎ *(0512) 56 28 13.*
An attractive and inexpensive Thai restaurant right in the centre of town. Although there are some dishes costing more than € 20, you can eat a good lunch here for as little as € 7–8. Booking is recommended. ● *Mon, Sun evening.*

INNSBRUCK: *Goldener Adler* €€€
Altstadt, 6020. **Road map** B4.
☎ *(0512) 57 11 11.* ₣ₐₓ *58 44 09.* ⓦ www.goldeneradler.com
A long-established restaurant, one of the oldest inns in Europe, which has counted many famous people as its guests, including at one time Mozart and Goethe. These days, you can order ostrich fillet and ravioli with *foie gras*, veal *carpaccio* or mozzarella with farmed salmon.

INNSBRUCK: *Kapeller* €€€
Ambras, Philippine-Welser-Straße 96, 6020. **Road map** B4. ☎ *(0512) 34 31 06.*
₣ₐₓ *34 31 06-68.* ⓦ www.kapeller.at
Situated near Schloss Ambras, this restaurant is proud of its traditions going back to the 16th century. It is a regular haunt of business people who appreciate its location and good atmosphere. There is also an attractive terrace and a garden for outdoor dining. The menu offers traditional Austrian fare, based on seasonal produce. Good wines. Booking is recommended. ● *Sun, Mon am, public holidays.*

INNSBRUCK: *Europa-Stüberl* €€€
Brixner Straße 6, 6020. **Road map** B4. ☎ *(0512) 59 31.* ₣ₐₓ *58 78 00.*
ⓦ www.europatyrol.at
One of Innsbruck's finest restaurants, not only because of its decor. The menu is dominated by game, lamb, fish and poultry dishes; and a special section is devoted to Tyrolean-Austrian specialities. Dishes start at around € 14. Booking is recommended.

For key to symbols *see back flap*

		CREDIT CARDS	GARDEN OR TERRACE	AUSTRIAN WINES	WHEELCHAIR ACCESS

Prices of a three-course meal without drinks, including cover charge, tax and service, in euros:
€ up to € 20
€€ € 20–35
€€€ € 35–45
€€€€ € 45–55
€€€€€ over € 55.

CREDIT CARDS
Credit cards are accepted.
GARDEN OR TERRACE
Weather permitting, it is possible to eat *al fresco*.
AUSTRIAN WINES
A good selection of Austrian wines.
WHEELCHAIR ACCESS
Easy access and facilities for the disabled.

KITZBÜHEL: *Tennerhof*   €€€€€   ■ ● ■ ●
Griesenauweg 26, 6370. **Road map** C4.
((05356) 631 81. **FAX** 631 81-70.
A fairly exclusive restaurant in this famous winter resort. The menu features dishes such as quail's eggs, salmon, caviar and asparagus (when in season). Despite the elevated prices, the restaurant is popular and it is advisable to book a table. ● *Tue, Oct–mid-Dec, Apr–May.*

KUFSTEIN: *Tiroler Fliegerstube*   €€   ● ■
Au 326 (am Segelssugplatz), 6330. **Road map** C4.
((05372) 64 1 70. **FAX** 64170-5.
A good restaurant in a charming little town dominated by a medieval fortress. Traditional Tyrolean cuisine, including cheese and spinach dumplings, and ravioli with ceps. Set menu. ● *Mon, Tue.* ♿

SEEFELD: *Habhof*   €€€   ■ ● ■
Landstraße 1, 6100. **Road map** B4.
((05212) 47 11. **FAX** 47 11-5. W www.habhof.at
A hotel-restaurant, 21 km (13 miles) west of Innsbruck, on the road from Seefeld to Telfs. From the terrace you can enjoy fabulous views over the Inn river. The menu includes unusual dishes such as calf's foot jelly, potato spaghetti, fish and lamb cutlets. There is also Tyrolean music on Sundays. Booking is recommended. ● *Thu in summer.*

STUMM/ZILLERTAL: *Landgasthof Linde*   €€   ■
Dorf 2, 6272. **Road map** C4.
((05283) 22 77-0. **FAX** 22 77-50.
The exterior of this restaurant, named after the spreading lime tree growing in front of the house, perfectly matches its sunny interior, and is typical of the region. The set menu includes roast duck, lamb and dumplings. ● *Mon, Tue.*

VOLDERS/WATTENS: *Ross-Stall-Taverne*   €€€   ■ ● ■
Bundesstraße 5, 6111. **Road map** B4.
((05224) 552 60. **FAX** 552 60.
From the outside, this restaurant looks more like a stable, but inside a top restaurant awaits you, with very friendly service. The cuisine specializes in fish dishes, including tuna *carpaccio* and octopus in a lemon-olive sauce, all of a very high standard. Booking is recommended. ● *Sun.*

ZELL/ZILLER: *Alpenhotel Zellerhof*   €€   ● ■
Bahnhofstraße 3, 6280. **Road map** C4.
((05282) 2612. **FAX** 26 12-65.
A small, typically Tyrolean restaurant. The menu offers mainly regional food, although there are some more modern additions. Booking is recommended. ● *1 Oct–20 Dec, 1 Apr–30 Jun.* ♿

CARINTHIA AND EAST TYROL

BAD BLEIBERG OB VILLACH: *Der Bleibergerhof*   €€€€€   ■ ●
Drei Lärchen 150, 9530. **Road map** D5.
((04244) 22 05. **FAX** 22 05-70. W www.bleibergerhof.at
An exclusive restaurant, with a menu featuring light, healthy meals, using organic produce. Soups and salads are available from a self-service buffet. Booking is recommended. ● *Sun evening–Wed noon.*

BODENSDORF: *Urbani-Wirt*   €€€   ■ ● ■
Bundesstraße 50, 9551. **Road map** E5.
((04243) 22 86-64. **FAX** 22 86-60.
An attractive restaurant where you can cut your own slice of bread from an enormous, home-baked loaf, or select a bottle of wine in the wine cellar. Good traditional Carinthian cuisine (set menu). There is also a children's playground in the garden. ● *Mon, Tue, mid-Jun–mid-Sep.* ♿

FAAKERSEE: *Tschebull* €
Egg am Faakersee, 9580. **Road map** E5. **(** *(04254) 21 91.* **FAX** *21 91-37.*
An attractive restaurant on the shores of Faakersee, serving alpine-Adriatic
cuisine, featuring Carinthian, Slovenian and Italian influences, for example
knuckle of lamb with polenta. ● *Mon, Tue in winter.*

FELD AM SEE: *Landhotel Lindenhof (Vinum)* €€
Dorfstraße 8, 9544. **Road map** D5. **(** *(04246) 22 74.* **FAX** *22 74-50.*
W www.landhotel-lindenhof.at
It is a real pleasure to drop in at this cosy establishment for a meal or, at
least for a drink. The restaurant is known for its summer barbecues and its
wine tasting sessions. One of the specialities is *Schilcher-Rahmsuppe*, a
cream soup made with the local Schilcher wine. The wine list features
more than 140 wines, and excellent wines are served from morning until
late. ○ *Winter: Wed–Sun evenings only; summer: Tue–Sun lunchtime and evening.*
● *Winter: Mon, Tue; summer: Mon.*

FERLACH: *Antonitsch Glainach* €
Glainach 12, 9170. **Road map** E5. **(** *(04227) 22 26.* **FAX** *42 36.*
A traditional Carinthian village inn that is over 500 years old. The stars of
the menu are roast pork, roast chicken and Carinthian dumplings. You can
eat well here for as little as € 9 from the set menu, so it is worth reserving
a table in advance. ○ *Winter: Wed–Sun evenings only; summer: Tue–Sun lunchtime
and evening.* ● *Winter: Mon, Tue; summer: Mon.*

KLAGENFURT: *St. Petersburg* €€
Waagplatz 3, 9020. **Road map** E5. **(** *(0463) 59 12 18.*
A taste of Russia in Klagenfurt. Russian food is particularly popular for an
early afternoon meal, and the menu features such unusual delights as
sauerkraut soup. There is a terrace which overlooks the garden; booking is
recommended. ● *Sat, Sun.*

KRUMPENDORF: *Hudelist* €€€€
Wieningerallee 12, 9201. **Road map** E5. **(** *(04229) 2681.* **FAX** *2681-20.*
This attractive establishment, situated 6 km (4 miles) from Klagenfurt,
specializes in game. The menu also features a wide range of other dishes,
with prices starting as low as € 8.50. ● *Sat.*

LIENZ: *Parkhotel Tristachersee* €€€€
Tristachersee 1, 9900. **Road map** D5. **(** *(04852) 676 66.* **FAX** *676 99.*
W www.parkhotel-tristachersee.at
The terrace of this hotel-restaurant, beautifully situated on the lakeshore,
affords a magnificent view of the dark-green lake and the surrounding
mountains. The interior is typically Tyrolean, with a number of separate
rooms called *Stuben* (living rooms). Tasty regional food, including fish
dishes such as carp and trout. Prices vary. ● *Apr, mid-Oct to mid-Dec.*

MATREI: *Rauter* €€€€
Matrei/Osttirol, 9971. **Road map** C5.
(*(04875) 66 11.* **FAX** *66 13.*
A charming establishment, popular with climbers, at the centre of a small
village in the Hohe Tauern National Park. Its interior is typical of East Tyrol
province, and the cuisine features regional culinary highlights; its specialities are *Schlutzkrapfen* (cheese ravioli) and poppy seed noodles. Besides
wines from all over Europe, you can also choose from three types of local
spring water. Booking is recommended. ⚡

PÖRTSCHACH: *Schloss Leonstain* €
Pörtschach, 9210. **Road map** E5.
(*(04272) 28 16-81.* **FAX** *28 23.* W www.leonstain.at
An established restaurant awarded one chef's hat by Gault-Millau, located
in a converted castle, the Leonstain serves good yet inexpensive food. Its
unusual menu combines Carinthian favourites with Asian specialities; you
can order a local dish of roast partridge as easily as an exotic Thai coconut
soup. The castle also has a beautiful courtyard. ● *Oct–Apr.*

PÖRTSCHACH: *Schloss Seefels* €€€€
Töschling 1, 9210. **Road map** E5.
(*(04272) 23 77.* **FAX** *37 04.* W www.seefels.at
An exclusive restaurant in an old castle, 14 km (9 miles) from Klagenfurt.
From the winter garden you can enjoy excellent views of Wörther See and
the surrounding mountains. Offers regional dishes prepared to a high
standard. Specialities include fish from the lake. ● *Early Nov–20 Dec.*

For key to symbols *see back flap*

SHOPPING IN AUSTRIA

UNTIL QUITE recently, shops in Austria kept to strict opening and even stricter closing hours. Around lunchtime or after 6 pm for example, no self-respecting Austrian would dream of doing any shopping, even in Vienna. The *Wochenende* (weekend) was even more sacrosanct – at many shops it started on Friday evening. Today though, opening hours have become liberalized, and now it is much more common for shops to stay open at lunchtime and for longer in the evenings.

Markets, ranging from international fairs to street and flea markets, are widely popular with visitors, and there is an excellent range of goods to buy. Check out traditional crafts and clothes, speciality foods and drinks, as well as exquisite ceramics and glassware.

Bust of Emperor Franz Joseph I

OPENING HOURS

SHOPS USUALLY open at 8:30 or 9am and close at 6pm or later. Supermarkets open from 8am to 7pm, and until 5pm on Saturdays. The Mercur and Billa supermarkets are open late on Fridays, until 7:30pm, and Billa branches at Vienna's Nordbahnhof railway station and at the airport open seven days a week.

Smaller shops still close at lunchtime for an hour or so. In provincial towns opening hours may vary from those in Vienna and be more suited to the local needs.

MARKETS AND FAIRS

MARKETS AND FAIRS are a firm part of tradition in Austria. The country hosts many international fairs, where anything from household items and construction machinery to modern jewellery or Austrian folk art, wines and spirits are exhibited.

Shop window, displaying typical souvenirs in Innsbruck

For holiday-makers there are countless charming street markets, which are often held in the main square of small villages. On Friday and Saturday mornings, some streets close to traffic and fill with market stalls offering produce straight from the farm, including fruit, vegetables, flowers, meat products and freshly baked goods. The market is often surrounded by historic buildings, allowing you to combine shopping and sightseeing.

The Naschmarkt near Karlsplatz in Vienna is the biggest street market in Austria, and besides food and clothes, there is also a flea market on Saturdays. The dates and venues for other flea markets or antiques fairs are published in the daily papers.

VAT REFUNDS

EXCEPT FOR citizens of other EU countries, visitors to Austria are entitled to reclaim *Mehrwertsteuer* (abbreviated as MwSt), the equivalent of VAT, on their purchases. The rate is 20% on industrial goods and 10% on food products. You need to tell the vendor that you are buying the goods for export. Larger department stores will be able to provide you with the appropriate form; alternatively, you can get it from customs. Fill in the form and present it together with the receipt when you leave Austria. You may be asked to show the goods, which must still be in their original packaging, unopened and unused. If the money is not refunded at the border, you can apply for it by writing to Global Refund Austria, A-1030 Vienna, Trubelgasse 19 (tel 01–79 84 4 00, fax 79 840-44) and have it sent by post or transferred to your bank account.

Wine shop in a private vineyard in Mörbisch

A typical market selling a wide range of goods in Deutschlandsberg

END-OF-SEASON SALES

T WICE A YEAR, the shopping scene is enlivened by seasonal price reductions; the *Winterschlussverkauf* (winter sales) start in the last week of January, and the *Sommer-schlussverkauf* (summer sales) at the end of July. This is a good time to buy clothes, sports equipment and shoes. Look for much reduced skis, an anorak or a warm coat; or you could find a lovely dress or a lightweight suit at half its original price or less. Occasionally a shop will sell all its stock at the same price in order to make room for new collections.

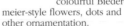

Billa supermarket logo

Different rules apply to electronic goods, for which price reductions are governed by supply and demand. Large department stores tend to reduce some prices in late autumn, particularly on electrical goods, but this depends on individual establishments.

There is no fixed season for food price reductions, which may occur at any time. If you are looking for a bargain, keep an eye out for the promotional leaflets issued by most supermarkets.

CERAMICS AND CRYSTAL GLASS

A USTRIA IS FAMOUS for its beautiful porcelain from the Augarten factory, based in the Viennese park, where Johann Strauss once played his waltzes. The decorations on vases, jugs, boxes and tableware reflect the artistic trends of past centuries, from Baroque through Neo-Classical and Biedermeier right up to the present day. Porcelain goods can be purchased in the shop in Graben or from the factory, which is open to visitors. Also worth buying is the attractive hand-painted pottery from Gmunden, with colourful Bieder-meier-style flowers, dots and other ornamentation.

Glassware – including superb chandeliers and delicate tableware – tends to be highly original, although expensive. Many people also collect imaginative crystal ornaments such as dogs and cats made by Swarovski.

CRAFTS AND FOLK ART

H AND-EMBROIDERED items, such as tablecloths, are also in great demand. The true works of art in this field are ladies' evening purses, miniature pictures and even jewellery, embroidered in *petit point* with 300 to 2,500 stitches per sq cm (2,000 to 16,000 stitches per sq inch). This work, carried out with the aid of a magnifying glass, is so exhausting that it can be done only for a maximum of three hours a day.

Folk costumes are another popular purchase. They vary in the detail, but the woman's *Dirndl* always consists of a skirt with an apron, a waist-coat and a white, often embroidered blouse, while the man's *Tracht* includes short or calf-length leather trousers and a distinctively cut felt jacket. All this is topped by a jaunty hat adorned with feathers or goats' beard.

ALCOHOLIC DRINKS

M OST SUPERMARKETS stock a good selection of Austrian wines, but if you head to one of the vineyards you can try before you buy. Visit one of the many vineyards in the Wachau Valley or among the hills of Burgenland, and you can sample the wine, and even buy direct. One of the stronger drinks would also be a good souvenir – try *Weinbrand* (cognac), *Slivovitz* (plum brandy), *Obstler* (fruit brandy) or *Marillenbrand* (apricot liqueur).

SPECIALITY FOODS

T HE MOST POPULAR purchases from the food counter are Austrian chocolates in their many guises. You can buy good-quality confectionery at most supermarkets; popular chains include Billa, Merkur, Inter-Spar, Eurospar, Zielpunkt and Hofer, with the latter charging the lowest prices. There are also smaller food stores, especially in the large cities, but these are generally more expensive.

Sweets and confectionery in front of a shop in Salzburg

What to Buy in Austria

HE RANGE OF SOUVENIRS worth buying in Austria is vast, ranging from the unashamedly kitsch to the exquisite and delicate. The most typical purchases are chocolates and all kinds of alcoholic drinks which are often attractively packaged. Quality purchases include Tyrolean costumes and warm winter coats made of loden as well as attractive porcelain or glassware made in Austria, including the stunning Swarovski crystal chandeliers.

Ad for folk fashion shop

Sissi Figurines
The Austrian people's love for "Sissi", Emperor Franz Joseph's unhappy wife, knows no bounds. It is evident to this day from the many statuettes of the Empress Elisabeth, on sale all over the country.

SOUVENIRS
In a country as reliant on tourism as Austria, the souvenir industry naturally plays an important role, with market stalls, shops and motorway service stations all offering an enormous selection of *Andenken* (souvenirs) designed to help you remember your stay in one of Austria's provinces – and hopefully make you come back for more.

Glass Snow-storms
Glass snow-storms with swirling snow-flakes may be considered as kitsch by some, yet they remain very popular with tourists, and children are particularly keen on them. Inside, you can see any number of famous Austrian landmarks such as the Big Wheel in the Prater, a symbol of Vienna.

Wanderhut
The Tyrolean "walker's hat" is popular with mountain walkers. In winter it protects against the cold; in summer it provides shade from the sun, which can be surprisingly fierce in the mountains.

Augarten Figurines
An attractive souvenir from the Augarten porcelain makers are the delicate, hand-finished porcelain figurines of the famous white Lipizzaner stallions and riders from the Spanish Riding School in Vienna.

Bells
In the autumn, the cattle of Tyrol and Vorarlberg are driven down from the Alm, the summer mountain pastures, and the bells around their necks have always fascinated visitors. The bells come in all shapes and sizes, often highly decorated. They make, of course, a great souvenir.

Handicrafts and Folk Art
Austria is deservedly proud of its local crafts traditions. In specialist shops or markets you can find delicate embroidery and lacework or great wood carvings, such as this mask.

Saddles
One of the more unusual gifts you can find are intricately made miniature horses with tack and saddles, often copies of items seen in the collections of armouries and arsenals.

CERAMICS

Austria is famous for its traditional and modern ceramics. Whether you choose a fine porcelain figure from Augarten or a hand-painted, ornamental faience from Gmunden, they will add elegance to your home. Many factories also produce less costly items, such as busts of the famous.

Modern Ceramics
This curiously shaped tea service, produced at the Provincial College for Ceramics at Stoob, would make a great addition to any tea-time table.

Bust of Mozart
Mozart memorabilia such as this bust are sold all over Salzburg, a city devoted to marketing the memory of Wolfgang Amadeus Mozart.

Dinner Service
Attractive ceramic tableware, such as this colourful dinner service from Klagenfurt, would make a welcome present to bring home or a useful and practical addition to your own household collection.

CONFECTIONERY

Austrian confectioners, of whom many were suppliers to the Imperial Court, look back with pride on centuries of tradition. The *Sachertorte* has a particularly distinguished history, but there are numerous other specialities worth bringing back for friends and family – if you can bear to share!

Mozartkugeln
This speciality chocolate from Salzburg, produced in various shapes and wrapped in silver foil, always bears the portrait of the famous composer.

Gingerbread
Gingerbread hearts are decorated with a variety of mostly romantic messages and intricate patterns in coloured icing. This one says "Because I love you".

Christmas decorations in a confectionery shop window

ALCOHOLIC DRINKS

Many Austrian wines have come a long way and are now highly regarded by connoisseurs. The country produces some excellent white dry and dessert wines, as well as the heavier Rieslings. Among the reds, Styrian Schilcher and Blaufränkisch from Burgenland can both compete with Italian and Spanish wines. Austria also produces other alcoholic beverages, including fruit brandies and liqueurs.

Glass tankards, an excellent present for beer lovers

Beer
Although they are little known abroad, Austria produces some very fine beers. Try some of the local brands and take home a few bottles – you won't easily find them elsewhere.

Wine
Specially sealed and bottled at the vineyard where it is produced, a bottle of Austrian wine makes an unusual but welcome present.

OUTDOOR ACTIVITIES

Austria is an ideal country for sports enthusiasts all year round. For winter sports you can find some 22,000 perfect pistes for downhill skiing and 16,000 km (10,000 miles) of dedicated trails for cross-country skiing in the Alps as well as some 14,000 km (9,000 miles) of walking trails, which are cleared of snow so that you can admire the stunning mountain scenery unimpeded.

Downhill run on a snowboard

The countless lakes are perfectly suited for water skiing, sailing and wind surfing, and of course for swimming in summer, while the Tyrolean Alps are a paradise for rock climbers and mountaineers.

Throughout Austria there are also superb facilities for more unusual sports, such as glacier climbing, snowshoe walking, rafting, canoeing, bungee jumping or paragliding.

SKIING

THE MAIN SPORT in the Alps is, of course, skiing. Visitors have a choice from skiing on the gentlest family slopes to braving rough runs down the steep slopes of the high Alps, from staying in the deep, fresh snow of the nursery slopes to venturing onto extremely difficult "black" downhill runs. Even nighttime skiing is possible, since some of the runs are illuminated at night.

The best areas for skiing are in Upper and Lower Austria and in Styria. Around Innsbruck, one of Austria's largest winter sports areas, year-round skiing is possible, for example in the Stubaital, Glungezer, Axamer Lizum and Mutterer Alm.

The Salzburg region has some 860 km (530 miles) of ski trails and 270 ski lifts, and resorts such as Filzmoos and Kleinarl regularly host many famous skiing contests. The permanent glaciers, such as those in the Ötztal Alps, welcome skiers all year round.

Most Austrian winter sports centres sell passes which give access to all the local ski facilities. If you wish to experience the thrill of skiing down the route that has been used in the World Cup since 1972, go to the Planai slopes in the Styrian resort of Schladming.

The Baroque monastery in Stams in Tyrol has a skiing college whose graduates include several international champions. Those who are more interested in the high life among Europe's aristocracy and in the pleasures of *après-ski*, should make for the pistes in Lech and Zürs am Arlberg, in Voralberg, and in Kitzbühel, in Tyrol.

Langlauf, nordic or cross-country skiing, is also well catered for in Austria, with numerous attractive routes, called *Loipe.* Almost all cross-country routes also have sprint sections, where you can try out your steps.

A skier studying an information board in the mountains

SNOWBOARDING

SNOWBOARDING, one of the recent Olympic disciplines to have arrived in Europe from the United States, is fast becoming one of the most popular sports in Austria. Once no more than a teenage craze, it has long since turned serious – Austria was one of the first countries to hold contests in the discipline, and the annual event in Seefeld, Tyrol, has become a meeting ground for the world's snowboarding elite. Austrians won many medals in the last two Olympic Winter Games, both in the parallel slalom and the half pipe (something between a ski piste and a bobsleigh run), and one of the first snowboarding champions, Stefan Gimpl, enjoys great popularity in his country.

Tyrol is the snowboarder's paradise and home of the International Snowboarding Federation. Young people from all over the world come here to participate in the Powder Turns, in Kaprun or Saalbach-Hinterglemm.

Downhill skiing – Austria's most popular sport

SLEIGHS AND TOBOGGANS

As well as skiing, almost all Austrian winter sports centres have facilities for bobsleigh and toboggan rides. Resorts such as Ischgl, in western Tyrol, are famous for their excellent tobogganing facilities. There are also several summer sleigh runs, for example in northern Tyrol. Sleigh hire costs between € 3 and € 5 per day. In some places it is possible to carry your sleigh up the hill on the mountain lift, but you cannot carry it down again – you have to ride it along the track.

If you're not too keen on racing down the mountain, you can enjoy the romantic and more leisurely pursuit of admiring the countryside while being transported in a horse-drawn sleigh, for € 12 to € 15 per person. The hire of a whole carriage costs between € 40 and € 70.

MOUNTAINEERING

Wherever there are mountains you will always find rock climbers and mountaineers. In Austria, the largest organization for climbers is the **Österreichischer Alpenverein**. It has more than 190 regional divisions all over Austria, with its headquarters in Vienna. Besides selling maps, books and guides, the association also runs a library and hires out equipment, it maintains mountain hostels and walking trails, organizes skiing courses and runs a

Mountaineering – a sport for the brave and determined

Ramblers on one of the many mountain trails in summer

school of mountaineering. Members of the Alpenverein enjoy many discounts, for example on accommodation in mountain huts. There is also a meteorological phone-line, giving information about current and expected weather conditions, including any avalanche warnings, which allows rock climbers to make the appropriate arrangements for their expedition.

WALKING

Rambles on the mountain trails are a popular activity, enjoyed by Austrians and visitors alike. The Rosengartenschlucht, a ravine northwest of Imst whose sides reach 100 m (328 ft) in height, is a particularly attractive walk; you walk along the valley of the Ötz River and get to see the Stuibenfall, Tyrol's tallest waterfall, created by a fallen rock. Many rambling trails can also be found in the region of Eben im Pongau. In Kleinarl, one of the attractions is the *Fackelwanderungen*, nighttime walk with torches. In the Salzkammergut, a lift takes visitors to the top of the Grünberg or Feuerkogel mountains, where many long tourist trails grant walkers views of the fairy-tale landscape of the alpine lakes.

There are walking trails all over the country, and they are all clearly signposted and marked on tree trunks by black-and-white signs. As with the ski runs, the level of difficulty is indicated by a colour. Local tourist offices have detailed maps of the

area. And, if you don't trust your map-reading skills, you can always hire a mountain guide or join a rambling group.

CYCLING

On the flat, bicycles are an ideal and inexpensive way of getting around. In the mountains, cycling becomes more of an endurance test. Nonetheless, mountain-biking is popular and every holiday resort and most hotels offer bikes for hire. St. Johann, in the highest part of the Alps, plays host to various international cycling races. In June and September, cyclists meet in East Tyrol to compete in an arduous race around the Lienz Dolomites. Less ambitious cyclists choose the scenic *Radwege* along rivers such as the Danube or Drau. In Vienna, despite heavy car traffic, cyclists can be seen everywhere. In towns and suburbs, many cycle routes have been marked; you can see them on maps available in any bookshop.

Visitors on a winter mountain biking expedition

Yachting marina in Mörbisch

WATER SPORTS

SNOW IS NOT the only element attracting sports enthusiasts to Austria – an abundance of rivers and lakes offer much to the summer visitor, whether it's in the form of relaxation or active holidays. The lovely lakes in the Salzkammergut, especially, are worth exploring.

Austrian lakes come in all shapes and sizes, but most are suitable for swimming and sailing. The largest and most famous are Bodensee (Lake Constance) and Neusiedler See. The latter, easily accessible from Vienna, is a 40-km (25-mile) long lake on the Hungarian border, and the venue every weekend for an Olympic-standard regatta. There are sailing and windsurfing schools on many Austrian lakes, and on the larger ones waterskiing and paraskiing are also on offer.

Scuba-diving is also possible at certain times of the year and in designated areas of some lakes, particularly in the Salzkammergut.

Many mountain rivers, particularly those in the western part of Austria, flow through narrow ravines and tumble down in numerous waterfalls – thus creating endless thrills for canoeists and competitors in the annual white-water rafting contests. An especially popular rafting event takes place along a gorge, the Imsterschlucht.

Even in Vienna you can enjoy watersports – along the Old Danube many places hire out water skis, rowing or sailing boats, without the need to prove any special expertise.

Lastly, the lakes and rivers are perfect for fishing. Local tourist offices will be able to advise you on where the best spots are, and sell you a licence.

HORSE RIDING

HORSE RIDING, while not as popular as skiing, also has many followers. Lower Austria has a number of studs which offer a variety of riding holidays. Some hotels, too, own their own horses or have an arrangement with a local riding centre which allows guests to use its facilities. In many resorts, riding lessons can also be booked in indoor arenas, which is especially useful during bad weather or in the winter months.

Even if your visit only takes you to Vienna, you still don't have to forego the pleasures of horse riding – the Prater funfair, once the favourite riding course of the Empress Elisabeth, is open to this day to lovers of the sport.

Horse riding is one of the more costly activities, but it is not exorbitant; in the Tyrol, for example, one hour's riding in winter costs about € 15 per person – about the same as you would have to pay for hiring a tennis court.

TENNIS

INDOOR TENNIS courts, which are also open in winter, can be found in any of the larger resorts and in many hotels; outdoor courts are available in most cities. They are less common in the mountain resorts which specialize in other sports. Prices vary; in Styria the cost of hiring a court for one hour is around € 13–17 during the day, or € 18–19 in the evening.

Hang-gliding – a spectacular sport, enjoyed in Stubaital

EXTREME SPORTS

SO-CALLED extreme sports, such as rafting, canyoning, speed-boat racing, paragliding, hang-gliding, bungee jumping or free climbing, are all well represented in Austria. New companies open every day, offering equipment hire and organized events to tempt the adventurous who are seeking an adrenaline kick.

Horse riding along the shores of Neusiedler See

DIRECTORY

SKIING, SNOWBOARDING, TOBOGGANING

Dachstein Gletscherbahn
8972 Ramsau am Dachstein.
[(03687) 812 41.
w www.planai.at

Zell am See/ Kaprun Information
5700 Zell am See.
[(06542) 770.

Österreichischer Bob- und Skeletonverband
Haus des Sports,
Stadionstraße 1,
6020 Innsbruck.
[(0512) 20 02 50.
w www.bobskeleton.at

Tourismus- gemeinschaft Mölltaler Gletscher
9831 Flattach.
[(04785) 615.

Tourismusverband Neustift im Stubaital
6167 Neustift.
[(05226) 2228.

Tourismusverband Ötztal Arena
6450 Sölden.
[(05254) 5100.

Tourismusverband Pitztal
6473 Wennz.
[(05414) 869 99.

Tourismusverband Tux
Lanersbach 472.
6293 Tux.
[(05287) 8506.

ROCK CLIMBING, MOUNTAINEERING

Österreichischer Alpenverein
Wilhelm-Greil-Straße 15,
6010 Innsbruck.
[(0512) 595 47.
w www.alpenverein.at

Österreichischer Touristenklub
Bäckerstraße 16,
1010 Vienna.
[(01) 51 23 844.
w www.touristenklub.at

Verband Alpiner Vereine Österreichs
Bäckerstraße 16,
1010 Vienna.
[(01) 512 54 88.
w www.vavoe.at

WALKING, RAMBLING

Europa- Wanderhotels
9773 Irschen 10.
[(04710) 2780.
w www.wanderhotels.com

CYCLING

Mountain Bike Holidays
Glemmerstraße 21,
5751 Maishofen.
[(06542) 80 480–28.

Radtouren in Österreich
Postfach 1,
5300 Hallwang bei Salzburg.
[(0662) 6688.

WATERSKIING, SAILING

Austrian Water Ski Federation
Veitingergasse 23,
1130 Vienna.
[(0664) 33 55 602..
w www.oewsv.at

Österreichischer Segelverband
7100 Neusiedl am See.
[(02167) 40243-0.

HORSE RIDING

Reiten in Österreich Reitarena Austria
4121 Altenfelden.
[(07282) 5992.
w www.tiscover.at/reiten
w www.reitarena.at

Urlaub am Reiterbauernhof
Gabelsbergerstraße 19,
5020 Salzburg.
[(0662) 88 02 02.

TENNIS

Multi Tennis Austria
Fleischmarkt 1,
9020 Klagenfurt.
[(0463) 59 09 50–50.
w www.tennisinfo.at

EXTREME SPORTS

Absolute Outdoor
8940 Liezen.
[(03612) 253 43.
w www.rafting.at

Action Club Zillertal
6290 Mayrhofen.
[(05285) 62 977.
w www.action-club- zillertal.com

Adventure Club Tuxertal
6293 Tux.
[(05287) 87 287.
w www.natursport.at

Aktiv-Zentrum
6874 Bizau.
[(05514) 31 48.
w www.aktiv-zentrum.at

Austria-Adventure Sportagentur
Simonystraße 21, 4030 Linz.
[(0732) 300 507.

Austria-Adventure Sportagentur Klappacher
Hofzeile 7–9/3/16,
1190 Vienna.
[(01) 368 76 17 or
(0664) 460 75 83
w www.outdoor- experts.at.

Austria-Adventure Sportagentur Raab
Camp Salza, Ulrichstraße 21, 4400 St. Ulrich.
[(7252) 46 706.

Club Aktiv Mölltal
9832 Stall/Mölltal 13.
[(04823) 81 04.
w www.cam.at

Club Montée Adventure Center
Schlossbad,
Wiespach,
5400 Hallein.
[(0664) 41 23 623.
w www.montee.com

Dachstein Tauern Balloons
8967 Haus im Ennstal.
[(03686) 2781.
w www.dachstein- tauern-balloons.at

Feelfree
Dr. Alois Amprosi,
Platzlweg 5,
6430 Ötz.
[(05252) 60350.
w www.feelfree.at

Flugschule Salzkammergut
Flachbergweg 46,
4810 Gmunden.
[(07612) 730 33.
w www.paragleiten.net

Freelife
Parzer Weg 65,
4203 Altenberg.
[(07230) 79160.

Gesäuse Sportagentur Floßmeisterei
8933 St. Gallen 210.
[(03632) 7345.
w www.sport.xeis.at

Jauntal Bungy & Event GmbH
9113 Ruden.
[(04234) 222.
w www.bungy.at

Kormoran (Canyoning)
Bahnhofstraße 6–8,
2000 Stockerau.
[(02266) 647 63.

Outdoor Leadership
Steinach 3,
4822 Bad Goisern.
[(06135) 6058.
w www.outdoor- leadership.com

Österreichischer Aero Club
Prinz Eugen-Straße 12,
1040 Vienna.
[(01) 505 10 28.
w www.oe.aeroclub.at

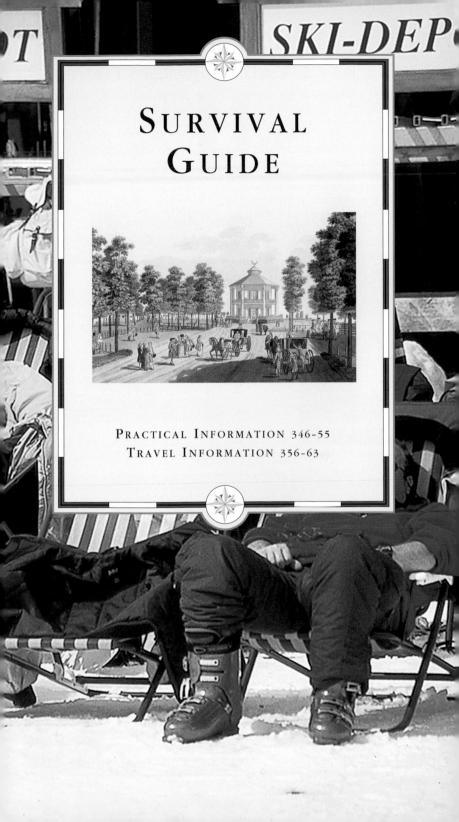

SURVIVAL
GUIDE

PRACTICAL INFORMATION

AUSTRIA is a fantastic holiday destination, for both winter and summer. It features numerous attractions, from well-equipped alpine skiing centres to quaint and charming villages, from fascinating historic sights in the towns to the superb collections of its museums – there is something on offer for every taste and budget. Visitors will have no problems

Sign for tourist information

finding suitable accommodation, interesting restaurants or enjoyable cultural events, and the tourist offices in most towns and villages will be only too pleased to furnish you with all the information you require. Alternatively, you can find useful details on the Internet. Many larger towns and all major sights post helpful hints and fascinating facts on their own websites.

Visitors crowding around a cable car station in Ischgl

WHEN TO VISIT

THERE IS NO such thing as a low season in Austria – the tourist season continues virtually all year round. Most hotels divide the year into two main parts: spring–summer (1 May–30 Sep) and autumn–winter (1 Oct–30 Apr). The winter season peaks at Christmas and again from the end of January to the beginning of March. Only small hotels and pensions far from winter sports facilities close for the winter. Ski enthusiasts can enjoy the Alps from Christmas until Easter, while walkers are best advised to visit in the spring, when there is a breeze in the air and the mountain slopes display a rich tapestry of colourful flowers.

The peak of the summer season is between June and August, and this period coincides with the greatest number of cultural events, festivals

and village fairs all over the country. At any time of year you will be able to discover and explore new sides of this multi-faceted country.

IMMIGRATION AND VISA FORMALITIES

NATIONALS FROM most European and many overseas countries do not need a visa to enter Austria. You will need a national identity card or, in the case of Britain which does not have an identity card, a valid passport. Citizens of EU countries can stay as long as they like. Visitors from the US, Canada, Australia or New Zealand are welcome for up to three months, or longer with a visa obtained from the Austrian Embassy or Consulate in their home country before the first date of entry.

Dogs and cats require a current rabies vaccination certificate; motorists need a green card as proof of third-party insurance.

CUSTOMS REGULATIONS

NATIONALS OF EU countries, including Britain and Ireland, may take home unlimited quantities of duty-paid alcoholic drinks and tobacco goods as long as these are intended for their own consumption, and it can be proven that the goods are not intended for resale.

Citizens of the US and Canada are limited to a maximum of 200 cigarettes (or 50 cigars) and one litre of spirits (or $2\frac{1}{4}$ litres of wine or 3 litres of beer). Regulations for residents of Australia and New Zealand vary slightly from these guidelines.

If you are in doubt, consult the customs offices in your own country before you travel to Austria.

Up-to-date information on what may be brought into Austria can be found on the Internet at www.bmf.gv.at and in the *Zollinfo* brochure, available at the border.

A useful orientation board and map of the local area in Zell am See

◁ Tourists relaxing in an alpine ski resort

EMBASSIES AND CONSULATES

THE EMBASSIES for all countries, including the UK, are based in Vienna. Some larger cities have consulates where you can turn for help *(see p349)*.

TOURIST INFORMATION

THERE ARE MANY local tourist offices all over Austria, offering useful advice to visitors on accommodation, restaurants, excursions and cultural events *(see p287)*. Offices are sign-posted with the white letter "i" against a green background *(see opposite)*. Every province also has its own tourist information centre, where you can turn for help. Most of the local tourist offices offer their services free and hand out free leaflets, maps and information booklets.

You can plan your trip in advance by getting in touch with travel agencies or the representatives of **Österreich Werbung** (the Austrian National Tourist Office) directly. For cheaper accommodation and information about youth hostels or pop concerts, the multilingual team at **Jugendinformation Wien** will provide assistance.

OPENING HOURS

THIS GUIDE provides the opening times for each individual sight you may want to visit. Most businesses start work at around 8am and close at about 4pm. On Fridays, many close early and, even if they do not, it may be hard to get anything done. Most shops are open from Monday to Friday, 8am to 6pm (sometimes 7.30pm) and on Saturdays from 8am mostly until 5pm (in larger cities), with a one- or two-hour break at midday. Shops also close on Sundays and public holidays, and in the countryside some close on Wednesday afternoons.

On the first Saturday in the month shops stay open late.

Banks in many towns are open from 8am until 4pm (5:30pm on Thursdays); smaller branches close at lunchtime. All banks remain closed on Saturdays, but you can change money at the airport, the main railway stations or in bureaux de change, or use an automatic teller machine.

MUSEUMS AND HISTORIC MONUMENTS

THE NATIONAL list of palaces, castles and ruins comprises a staggering 2,000 sights, and this does not even include Austria's countless churches, monasteries or abbeys. Vienna alone has more than 60 museums, and Styria over 200; of these only 58 are state-owned; the remainder belong to associations, churches, companies or private individuals. Opening hours vary and depend on the local tourist seasons. Generally speaking, museums are open from 10am until 4pm or 7pm. Once a week they stay open longer, some until 9pm or even midnight. Some museums

Sign of a pension in Lofer

A group of sightseers admiring historic buildings in Innsbruck

close for one day in the week, usually on a Monday.

Check times, special events and arrangements for guided tours locally. For groups of 10 people or more it is often possible to arrange the time of their visit in advance – and you may be eligible for a group discount. At the end of a guided tour it is customary to leave a small tip.

ADMISSION PRICES

MUSEUM ENTRANCE fees can vary from €2 to €7. Admission to historic houses costs about €10–15. Children up to the age of 6 (in some museums, up to the age of 7) are admitted free, and 6–15 year-olds pay half price, as do senior citizens (60 and over). There are also reductions for students. Some museums offer family tickets (admitting for example two adults and three children); a few allow free admission on a particular day in the week.

An adult cinema ticket costs around €7–10. Some cinemas sell tickets at lower prices at the beginning of the week. For theatre tickets you will need to set aside €30–40 or more; musicals cost upwards of €40. Concert tickets start at around €14. The three-day *Wien-Karte* entitles you to unlimited use of all public transport facilities for 72 hours as well as reduced admission to some museums, and discounts in selected shops and restaurants.

Signposts help visitors find the way to the alpine huts

A range of foreign-language newspapers and magazines on street stands

INFORMATION FOR DISABLED VISITORS

AUSTRIA IS BETTER prepared to receive disabled visitors than many other countries, but many trams and buses cannot accommodate wheelchairs. At train stations, you need to ask about lifts when you get your ticket. Facilities vary at underground stations, so it is best to check first. In some regions the facilities are fairly basic, but concessions on tickets are available for disabled visitors.

Special parking spaces are set aside for disabled drivers and are clearly marked as such; if your car displays the appropriate sticker, parking is also free of charge.

All public toilets have special cubicles for the wheelchair-bound. Information about facilities for the disabled can be obtained from the local tourist information offices.

Most of the main sights have access ramps. Contact the museums in advance so they can organize help with wheelchairs if needed.

Some of the larger 5-star hotels have special facilities for disabled guests, such as rooms where the beds are equipped with handgrips and similar aids exist in bathroom and toilet. Some also have extra-wide showers that allow easy wheelchair access. Some few restaurants have access ramps for wheelchairs.

TRAVELLING WITH CHILDREN

MANY HOTELS offer a free stay or reduced rates for children under the age of 12 who share a room with their parents. Children up to the age of 15 pay half fare on public transport; on Sundays, public holidays and during the summer vacations they travel for free. They are also entitled to reduced admission when visiting museums and historic sights. Many restaurants offer smaller portions for children. The large supermarkets and also chemists have a department with essential items for babies.

INFORMATION FOR YOUNG PEOPLE

STUDENTS holding an international student card and a valid college ID are entitled to discounts on railways and municipal public transport, as well as reduced admission to cinemas, museums and sports events. They will also be offered accommodation in a *Jugendherberge* (youth hostel) at a lower price. Up-to-date information on accommodation in student dormitories and youth hostels can be obtained from any tourist office.

RELIGION

AUSTRIA IS a predominantly Catholic country – as is apparent from the large number of Catholic churches; Protestants make up just 5 per cent of the population. There is also a fair-sized immigrant population from various national backgrounds and following various religious faiths; probably the largest group among them are the Muslims. In Vienna, there is a sizeable Jewish community, which has its own synagogues, while the cemeteries are communal.

LANGUAGE

ALTHOUGH ALL Austrians officially speak German, in reality they speak "Austrian". While this variety of Low German does not differ from High German as markedly as Swiss German, its pronunciation and even some rules of grammar and vocabulary may make it seem like a different language.

Added to this are several Austrian dialects, which differ from province to province. Austrians are the first to admit that it would be impossible to learn them all in their countless regional varieties. For instance, visitors who know a little German find *Tirolerisch,* the dialect spoken in Tyrol, completely incomprehensible.

You will have few problems making yourself understood in English, especially in the larger cities and main tourist centres. English is also spoken by most young people who learn it at elementary school.

Information board on a building in Innsbruck

EVERYDAY CUSTOMS

PEACE AND QUIET are highly valued by Austrians who live outside the cities. They are friendly and easy-going people who tend to keep up their traditions, especially in the mountainous regions. Austrians, especially the older generation, tend to be very courteous, and they expect the same from visitors. When asked for directions, an Austrians will always do their best to help. On foot, if they hear someone approaching from behind, they will step aside to allow them to pass, and you should thank them. If an Austrian pushes you inadvertently, they will quite probably apologize.

It is worth knowing a few phrases, too, such as, when meeting someone, *Wie geht es Ihnen?*, to enquire after their health. In the morning, *Guten Morgen* is the standard greeting, at lunchtime *Mahlzeit*, later in the day *Guten Tag*. Everywhere and at any time *Grüß Gott* is used, literally "greet the Lord".

NEWSPAPERS AND RADIO

THE MOST POPULAR dailies, the *Kurier* or the *Kronen Zeitung* give detailed TV, radio, cinema and theatre listings, information on concerts, lectures, meetings, flea markets, as well as weekend excursions. *Die Presse* and *Der Standard* provide serious political commentaries. The most popular weekly magazine is the *News*, and the leading monthly *Profil*. There are also countless illustrated women's magazines. German magazines and newspapers are available everywhere.

Foreign-language papers, such as *The Times, Financial Times, Guardian International, The Herald Tribune* or *Le Monde* are available from central kiosks in the larger towns. In Vienna, foreign newspapers can be bought at

Tourist information for students and young travellers

the Südbahnhof and Nordbahnhof railway stations or at the Morava bookshop at No. 11 Wollzeile.

Austria has two main radio stations. Ö1 plays classical music and transmits the news in English, French and German on weekdays at 8am. Ö3 plays popular music and transmits regular traffic bulletins. Radio FM4 broadcasts in English from 1am to 2pm daily on 103.8 MHz. It covers regional and international news as well as cultural events. There are also several private radio stations playing mainly pop music. Cable stations carry the BBC World Service around the clock.

ELECTRICAL ADAPTORS

THE VOLTAGE in Austria is 220V AC. Plugs have two small round pins. It is a good idea to buy a multi-adaptor before coming to Austria, as they are not easy to find here. Some of the more expensive hotels may offer guest adaptors, but usually only for use with electric shavers.

TIME

AUSTRIA uses Central European Time (GMT plus one hour). Clocks move forward one hour on the last Sunday in March and back on the last Sunday in October.

Personal Security and Health

Austria is one of Europe's safest countries. Tourists are unlikely to encounter any violence (though there is an increase in petty crimes such as pick-pocketing in busy tourist areas) and the police and emergency services are easy to contact. Pharmacists are respected and their advice is often sought by locals. A visit to the pharmacy, unless the problem is serious, is probably the easiest choice if you are feeling unwell. Above all, this is a peaceful country, a land of historic sights, works of art, and beautiful, stunning scenery.

SOS sign on a U-Bahn platform

POLICE

In Vienna, in the provincial capitals, and in all the larger towns, public order is maintained by the *Polizei*. The police also run lost property departments (*Fundbüro*), which can be found in any district police station. In the provinces, policing is carried out by the *Gendarmerie*.

PERSONAL SECURITY AND PROPERTY

There are few places in Austria to steer clear of, even at night. However, it is as well to be careful. Avoid areas around stations at night and pay extra attention at funfairs or large gatherings. Don't become an easy target for thieves: never leave items visible in a car; carry money and documents safely. Women should avoid placing bags on the floor in cafés and restaurants.

In case of a theft, report it without delay to the nearest *Polizeiwache* (police station). If you lose traveller's cheques, seek help at the nearest bank, which will stop them. Credit and debit card thefts should be reported immediately to your credit card company or bank. Contact your consulate if you lose your passport, or if it is stolen.

LOST PROPERTY

Go to the nearest police station in the first instance. If they do not succeed in restoring your property within seven days, then try the lost property bureau (*Fundbüro*). For property lost on railways or the Schnellbahn, go to the Westbahnhof in Vienna and enquire in person.

ACCIDENTS AND EMERGENCIES

Britain has a reciprocal arrangement with Austria whereby emergency hospital treatment is free if you have a British passport. Visits to doctors, dentists or outpatient departments are also free of charge, but getting free treatment can involve a lot of bureaucracy. Britons should be sure to get the form E111, available from post offices, before travelling. It is also a good idea to take out full health insurance. Visitors from other countries should establish what is required to cover their medical treatment either with their home embassy or with their medical insurance company.

If you are ill, it is best to go to a clinic at a state hospital. In Vienna, the main hospital (and the largest in Europe) is the **Allgemeines Kranken-haus** (General Hospital) in the ninth district. People without insurance or money to pay for medical services are cared for at the **Krankenhaus der Barmher-**

Police motorcycle   **Policeman**

Fire engine

Police car

Ambulance

DIRECTORY

HOSPITALS

Allgemeines Krankenhaus
Währinger Gürtel 18–20,
1090 Vienna.
 (01) 404 00-0.

Krankenhaus der Barmherzigen Brüder
(Brothers of Mercy Hospital),
Große Mohrengasse 9,
1020 Vienna.
 (01) 211 210.

IMPORTANT TELEPHONE NUMBERS

Dental Emergency Service
(at night, weekends, public holidays) Vienna.
 (01) 51 22 078.

International Pharmacy
Kärntner Ring 17, Vienna.
 (01) 512 28 25.

Lost Property Office
Bastiengasse 36, 1180 Vienna.
 (01) 4000-8091.

Pharmacy Information Line
Vienna. *(01) 15 50.*

zigen Brüder (Brothers of Mercy Hospital), which also runs a free emergency dental clinic. In a medical emergency, call an ambulance (*Rettungsdienst*).

Policewoman

Fireman

HEALTH PRECAUTIONS

Tick-borne encephalitis is a possible danger wherever there are deciduous trees in Austria. Only a tiny proportion of ticks carry the disease, which may cause brain damage and in some cases lead to death. Most Austrians and foreign residents are inoculated against it. Inoculation is done in several stages, but is not usually recommended for holidaymakers. The risk of infection is minimal, but to be on the safe side, if you are bitten, do not remove the tick but go to an outpatients department.

PHARMACIES

If it is not an emergency, it is best to go to an *Apotheke* (pharmacy) for advice on medicines and treatment. Pharmacies

Façade of a typical *Apotheke* (pharmacy) in Vienna

display a red "A" sign and operate a night rota system. Any closed pharmacies will display the address of the nearest one open, and the **Pharmacy Information Line** also has details of some which are open.

Apart from medicines, pharmacies also sell some herbal remedies. *Reformhäuser* specialize in such products and natural healthcare.

Banking and Currency

Bank Austria Creditanstalt

Bank Austria logo

IN RECENT YEARS, Austrian banking services have become more accessible. There are now several money-changing machines (*see directory*), and many shops, hotels and restaurants accept credit cards, although some still only take cash. You can take any amount of money into Austria, in euros or other currencies. The largest Austrian banks, including Bank Austria Creditanstalt, BAWAG and Raiffeisenbank, have branches in most of the provincial cities.

MONEY EXCHANGE

THE BEST PLACE to change money is at a bank; there is a minimum handling fee of about € 3.60 per transaction. Although you can use travel agents and hotels, the banks give you a better rate and charge less commission. Railway station *Wechselstuben* (bureaux de change) charge 4 per cent on the exchanged sum. Exchanging a larger amount of money at one time can save on commission. You can also exchange pounds sterling for euros at an automatic money-changing machine.

Logo of a bank in Zell am See

Most banks are open from 8:30am to 12:30pm and from 1:30pm to 4pm Monday to Friday (to 5:30pm on Thursdays). A few, such as the main Creditanstalt bank in Vienna, some banks in the provincial capitals as well as those in the busier tourist resorts or close to railway stations and airports, have extended opening hours.

CREDIT CARDS

THE BANKS operate a large network of ATMs, many of which take foreign credit cards with PIN codes. This facility will be clearly stated on the front of the machine – just look for the logo of your card. Instructions are often given in English and other languages.

At most hotels, shops and restaurants you can pay by credit card, although some do not take all cards. It is best to always carry some cash on you. Some establishments also set a minimum sum that can be paid for by credit card. Make sure you report lost or stolen cards to your own or the nearest Austrian bank without delay.

TRAVELLER'S CHEQUES

TRAVELLER'S CHEQUES are the safest way to carry large sums of money. Choose a well-known name such as American Express, Visa, Thomas Cook or cheques issued through a bank.

Cheques can be cashed at any bank or bureau de change, and some larger shops and hotels will also accept payment by traveller's cheque.

A Bankomat automatic money-dispensing machine

Currency conversion machine that accepts foreign banknotes

THE EURO

Austria, in common with several other countries in the European Union, introduced a new currency, the euro, in January 2002. After an initial transitional period when both old and new currencies were used side by side, the old currency (the Austrian Schilling) was withdrawn. The process of transition from the Austrian Schilling to the euro officially ended on 28 February 2002.

Anyone still holding bank notes in Austrian Schillings may exchange these only at the National Bank in Austria.

The euro notes are the same in all the euro-zone countries; the coins bear different national motifs but they can be used freely throughout the twelve countries in the euro-zone.

Bank Notes

Euro bank notes have seven denominations. The grey 5-euro note is the smallest, followed by the pink 10-euro note, blue 20-euro note, orange 50-euro note, green 100-euro note, yellow 200-euro note and purple 500-euro note. All notes show the stars of the European Union and architectural motifs.

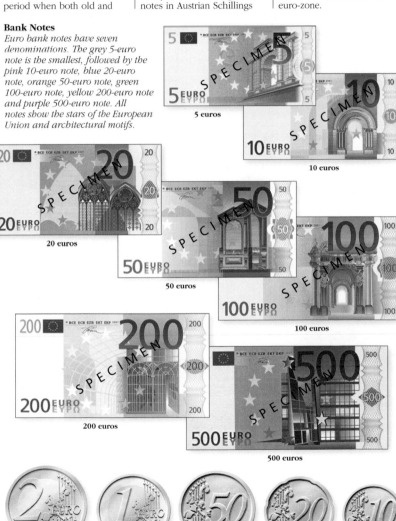

5 euros

10 euros

20 euros

50 euros

100 euros

200 euros

500 euros

2 euros

1 euro

50 cents

20 cents

10 cents

Coins

The euro has eight coin denominations: 1 euro and 2 euros; 50 cents, 20 cents, 10 cents, 5 cents, 2 cents and 1 cent. The 2- and 1-euro coins are both silver and gold in colour. The 50-, 20- and 10-cent coins are gold. The 5-, 2- and 1-cent coins are bronze.

5 cents

2 cents

1 cent

Using the Telephone

THE AUSTRIAN telephone system has recently undergone a process of modernization – the privatized company Telekom Austria has lost its monopoly, and other companies have entered the market, including Tele2 and Priority. Prices have been modified, and there are now four different time tariffs for domestic and international calls. To phone outside Austria, try using a telephone booth at a post office, as you will be able to pay at the counter rather than using coins.

Emergency phone sign

TYPES OF TELEPHONES

THERE ARE two types of payphones in Austria, card- or coin-operated phones. Most phones carry instructions in English and other languages. Coin-operated telephones accept 10-, 20- and 50-cent as well as 1- and 2-euro coins. In card phones you can use a magnetic phonecard known as *Telefon-Wertkarte*, which may be purchased at newsagents and post offices for €3.64 or €7.28. Austria has one of the most expensive telephone systems in Europe, so make sure you have plenty

of change. On some older phones, a red or black button needs to be pushed once the coins have been accepted and the call has been answered – otherwise the recipient will not be able to hear you.

USING THE TELEPHONE

INTERNATIONAL and domestic dialling codes can be found in the first volume of the telephone directory. Directories are usually available in telephone boxes, but may be too tatty to use. Post offices have directories in good condition, or contact directory enquiries

Coin-operated phone   **Sign for cardphone**

(see Reaching the Right Number below).

You can phone from hotels, pensions, restaurants, post offices, and booths in the street or at railway stations. For international calls it is best to avoid hotels as they tend to charge a hefty premium rate for calls.

Cheap-rate calling times for international calls from Austria is between 6pm and 8am at weekends; for domestic calls it is between 8pm and 6am, and weekends.

USING A CARD PHONE

1 Lift the receiver and wait for the dialling tone.

2 Insert the credit card as shown by the arrow, or use a phone card *(below)*.

3 Wait for the value of available credit to be displayed.

4 Key in the phone number required.

5 Replace the receiver at the end of the call and withdraw the card.

2 Instead of a credit card, you can use a phone card in this slot.

USING A COIN-OPERATED PHONE

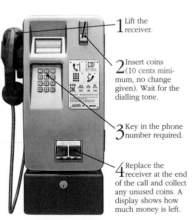

1 Lift the receiver.

2 Insert coins (10 cents minimum, no change given). Wait for the dialling tone.

3 Key in the phone number required.

4 Replace the receiver at the end of the call and collect any unused coins. A display shows how much money is left.

REACHING THE RIGHT NUMBER

- International dialling code for Austria is +43.
- For Austrian directory enquiries, dial 11811. For international directory enquiries, dial 0900 118877 (EU and neighbouring countries 118877).
- Railway timetable information: 05 17 17.
- Road conditions and snowfall: 15 84.
- Central Post Office Information (Zentrale Postauskunft): (0810) 010 100.

- To ring home from Austria, dial the appropriate country code, followed by the number. Omit the 0 from the local area code.
- For the **UK** dial 0044.
- For the **Irish Republic** dial 00353.
- For the **USA** dial 001.
- For **Australia** dial 0061.
- For **New Zealand** dial 0064.
- For international or national telegrams, dial 0800 100 190.

Mail and Postal Services

Decorative stamp

BESIDES BUYING postage stamps *(Briefmarken)* and arranging for the delivery of letters, parcels and telegrams, you can also make telephone calls, send moneygrams and send or receive fax messages at a post office. You can collect correspondence marked *Postlagernd (poste restante)* but you will need proof of identity. In addition, the post office sells phonecards and collectors' stamps and cashes traveller's cheques; some also exchange currency.

Post office sign

OPENING HOURS

THE OPENING hours for post offices vary. In Vienna, the main post offices open 8am–6pm Monday to Friday, 8am–10am on Saturdays. Sub-post offices open 8am–noon and 2–6pm Monday to Friday.

In other provinces, opening hours are adapted to the local needs – in smaller resorts the post office is only open in the morning. The addresses of post offices can be found in local telephone directories, or ask at your hotel.

SENDING A LETTER

YOU CAN BUY postage stamps at post offices, which also have stamp-vending machines. Letters for Europe weighing

Yellow post- or mailbox

Vienna's Districts
Vienna is divided into 23 Bezirke *(urban districts) as shown here. The district number is part of the Vienna postcode. For example, the 23rd district is written as A-1230. The inset shows the area covered by our Street Finder maps 1–5 (see pp117–21).*

up to 20 g cost 55 cents, as do postcards. A registered letter costs €2.03. In the address, add the standard country code, as used on car number plates, before the town or post code, for example GB for Britain, F for France.

Postboxes are yellow. Those with a red band are emptied at night, weekends and on public holidays, as well as on weekdays.

In order to send a parcel, registered letter or express package, you need to fill in a form which is available at the post office. A parcel weighing less then 2 kg may be sent more cheaply as a letter. The post office also sells suitable cardboard boxes for posting parcels.

MAIN POST OFFICES

IN ALL LARGE towns, the main post offices and those in the railway stations open for longer hours in the evening, as well as on Saturdays, Sundays and bank holidays; they may, however, only offer a

limited range of postal services after their normal opening hours.

In Vienna, the following post offices remain open all week: Fleischmarkt 19, Westbahnhof, Südbahnhof, Franz-Josefs-Bahnhof and Schwechat Airport. In Innsbruck, the main post offices are at No. 2 Maximilianstraße and at the Hauptbahnhof railway station. The post office at the Hauptbahnhof railway station at No. 17 Südtiroler Platz in Salzburg stays open from 6am to 11pm every day of the week.

INTERNET AND E-MAIL

MORE AND MORE Internet services are becoming available at post offices, and there is an increasing number of Internet cafés, called Speednet-Café or Internet-Café. Here you can sit in comfort at a computer terminal while enjoying a cup of coffee, and surf the Internet or send and receive e-mails. Charges are generally reasonable, about €3 per hour, depending on the number of users.

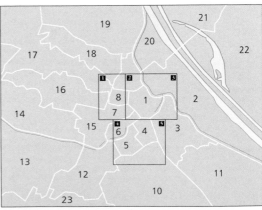

GETTING TO AUSTRIA

As a POPULAR tourist destination, Austria is well served by both air and rail. The major cities – Vienna, Linz, Graz, Innsbruck, Salzburg and Klagenfurt – have international airports and there are direct flights from all main European cities as well as from the USA, Canada, Japan and Australia. Vienna is a key transit point between West and East, and

An Austrian Airlines aircraft

about eight million passengers a year pass through its Schwechat airport.

There are good rail and coach links, too, but from Britain this involves a long journey, often overnight, and is not significantly cheaper than air travel. The motorway network linking Austria and the rest of Europe is extensive, and the roads are clearly signposted and well maintained.

The transit area at Schwechat International Airport in Vienna

AIR TRAVEL

THERE ARE several flights a day between London's Heathrow and Vienna's Schwechat Airport operated by British Airways and by Austria's national airline Austrian Airways. Austrian also serves Innsbruck from London Gatwick and Vienna from Manchester. Of the "low-cost" airlines Ryanair flies from London Stansted to Graz, Klagenfurt, Linz and Salzburg, with connections from Glasgow and Dublin; and british european flies from Birmingham and London Gatwick to Salzburg.

If you wish to fly from the United States, there are direct flights with Delta from New York and Orlando. Lauda Air runs flights from Los Angeles, and Austrian Airlines from Chicago. There are also direct flights from Sydney and Toronto.

Thanks to its central location Vienna's Schwechat Airport is a major European transit

airport. All the major airlines have offices here. The airport is 19 km (12 miles) from the city centre, easily accessible by train or bus. A modern airport, it is very easy and quick to use. Its supermarket is often used by the Viennese because of its longer shopping times – it opens from 7:20am to 7pm, seven days a week and on holidays.

Busse nach: / Busses to:

City Air Terminal	11:10
Süd-/Westbahnhof	11:40
Vienna Int. Centre	12:50
Bratislava	13:20

Bus transfer information board

DOMESTIC FLIGHTS

DOMESTIC FLIGHTS within Austria are operated by Tyrolean Airways, part of the Austrian Airlines Group. There are daily flights from Vienna to Graz, Klagenfurt, Innsbruck, Salzburg and Linz. Air travel in Austria is expensive and, with extra time needed

for checking in, the journey to and from the airport and for retrieving your luggage, it is not always the fastest and best way of getting to another destination in Austria.

SPECIAL DEALS

IT IS NOT NECESSARY to pay full price for a scheduled ticket. There are good deals if you shop around the discount agencies and the Internet. You can usually get APEX tickets if you book at least two weeks in advance and if you can travel at days other than the weekend. Charters are available at very competitive rates. Weekend package offers, including the price of two nights at a good hotel, can be excellent value, sometimes costing less than the economy-ticket price. In addition, budget airlines often have special extra-low deals.

Frequent travellers with British Airways or Austrian Airlines enjoy many privileges if they join the respective frequent fliers' programmes. including priority on standby lists and upgrades to business class. Such programmes also often award points for car hire from major companies such as Avis, Europcar, Hertz or Sixt, as well as overnight stays at major hotel chains such as the Hilton, Holiday Inn or Marriot.

Travellers with special needs, for example wheelchair users, should notify the airlines of their requirements. On scheduled flights, children up to the age of two travel free (or

The modern building of Schwechat International Airport near Vienna

at 10 per cent of the price); children aged 2–12 years pay half price. On budget airlines they pay the full fare.

AUSTRIAN AIRPORTS AND TRANSFERS

Many business travellers to Vienna never leave the airport: opposite the terminal building is the five-star luxury hotel Astron, and next to it the vast World Trade Centre, where many companies have their head offices.

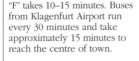

Logo of Austrian Airlines

Vienna's airport has all the facilities that a traveller might need: information desks, service desks, shops, automatic money-exchange machines, bureaux de change and banks (though the rates for exchanging money at the airport are less favourable than elsewhere).

The taxi journey from the airport to the centre of Vienna costs around €25; you can buy a ticket in advance inside the airport building. Flughafen-taxi Neudeck also has vans available in its fleet. Alternatively, you can hire a car at the airport, from companies such as Avis, Budget, Europcar, Hertz or Thrifty. All you need when hiring a vehicle is a driver's licence, a passport and a credit card for the deposit.

The CAT (City Airport Train: www.cityairporttrain.com) leaves every half hour and takes you to Wien Mittestation. The journey time is 16 minutes and the fare (one way) is €9. Buses go to Südbahnhof and Westbahnhof. They depart every 25 minutes and the 30-minute journey costs €8 one way.

The cheapest means of transport into the city is the suburban railway line, the *Schnellbahn*, which operates an hourly service.

Salzburg Airport, which is at No. 95 Innsbrucker Bundesstraße, is situated extremely close to the town centre, a mere 4 km (2 miles) to the west. It can be reached by bus or taxi. Innsbruck Airport is also located near the town centre (4 km/2 miles) and the transfer by taxi or bus "F" takes 10–15 minutes. Buses from Klagenfurt Airport run every 30 minutes and take approximately 15 minutes to reach the centre of town.

DIRECTORY

AUSTRIAN AIRLINES

Offices in the UK
5th & 6th Floor, 10 Wardour Street, London W1D 6BQ.
☎ (020) 7434 7350.

Reservations
Kärntnerring 18, 1010 Vienna.
☎ (0) 51 789.
ⓦ www.aua.com.

Airport Information
☎ (01) 7007-2231 or 2232.

OTHER AIRLINES

British Airways
☎ (0845) 7733377.
ⓦ www.britishairways.com

british european
Reservations for UK passengers:
☎ (0871) 7000535.
ⓦ www.flybe.com

Ryanair
☎ From Ireland: (0818) 303030.
From the UK: (0871) 246 0000.
ⓦ www.ryanair.com

Tyrolean Airways
☎ 051789.
ⓦ www.tyrolean.at

KLM
☎ (01) 795 67 232
ⓦ www.klm.com/at-ge

CAR HIRE

Avis
☎ 3602 77 15 43.
ⓦ www.avis.at

Hertz City
☎ 700 73 26 61 or 79532.
ⓦ www.hertz.at

Shopping centre inside Vienna's Schwechat International Airport

Travelling by Train

Sᴵᴛᴜᴀᴛᴇᴅ ɪɴ ᴛʜᴇ heart of Europe, with Vienna as its main railway hub, Austria has excellent rail links with every important centre on the Continent, and there is a good network of lines within the country itself. The trains are comfortable, clean and safe; they run frequently and regularly. Punctuality is one of the main benefits – the old adage that you can set your watch by an Austrian train is largely true, although a few minutes' delay can occur. Unfortunately railway tickets are expensive. The largest railway line is the ÖBB – Österreichische Bundesbahnen, the Austrian Federal Railway Lines, and there are also 12 smaller, private railway lines.

Vienna's Franz-Josefs-Bahnhof, the terminal for trains from the north

Trains

Öꜱᴛᴇʀʀᴇɪᴄʜɪꜱᴄʜᴇ Bundesbahnen – ÖBB – runs several types of services. The modern EuroCity trains (marked with the letters EC) cover long-distance routes in record time. Night passengers travel on the EuroNight (EN) or CityNight-Line, with sleeping cars and couchettes. Comfortable InterCity (IC) and SuperCity trains connect major towns and tourist resorts. Every seat on the InterCity Express has a radio with headphones installed, and the first-class carriages are equipped with videos as well as power points for laptop computers. Domestic lines are also served by the D-Züge (D), long-distance trains running every day, at greater or lesser speed. More recently, the local routes have acquired modern, double-decker City Shuttle trains.

Bundesbahn logo

Motorists can also travel by rail with their cars between Mallnitz in Carinthia and the Gastein Valley. The cost of transport is about € 10.

Seat Reservations

Iɴ ᴀᴜꜱᴛʀɪᴀ, it is not compulsory to reserve a seat, even on express or international routes. It is entirely up to you, though trains can become busy, particularly during the peak tourist season in summer or when there is snow.

Reservations can be made at the ticket offices of any of the larger stations, at the ÖBB Reiseservicecenter or online at www.oebb.at The computerized system allows staff to check which seats are still available on any given train. Reserved seats are marked on the door of each compartment; you should take note of your carriage number when

you are boarding, and again at the compartment door. Seat reservations are included in the price of first-class tickets.

Railway Stations

Tʜᴇ ɢᴇʀᴍᴀɴ word for a railway station is *Bahnhof*, and the main railway station is *Hauptbahnhof*. The capital city of each province has a *Hauptbahnhof*, Vienna has two. Railway stations are sometimes sited away from the city centre. They have bureaux de change, luggage deposits and information desks, with English-speaking staff. If there is no ticket office, you can buy a ticket from the platform machine or on the train.

Arriving from Britain

Iꜰ ʏᴏᴜ ᴀʀᴇ ᴛʀᴀᴠᴇʟʟɪɴɢ from Britain to Vienna by train, you will probably arrive at the Westbahnhof. This station has interchanges with the U3 and U6 underground lines, the Schnellbahn and several tram and bus routes. The travel agency (Reisebüro) at Westbahnhof is open from 8am to 7pm on weekdays and 8am to 1pm on Saturdays; staff here will be able to provide information as well as help with the booking of hotel rooms or other accommodation.

The Südbahnhof handles trains from southern and eastern areas, and is linked to the Schnellbahn and several tram and bus lines. Trains from the north arrive at Franz-Josefs-Bahnhof; this is served

Railway line passing right by the stunning Melk Abbey

by the Schnellbahn and the cross-city tram "D", which takes you directly to the Ringstraße in the centre.

TICKETS

RAILWAY TICKETS are expensive. A second-class ticket from Vienna to Salzburg, 300 km (190 miles) away, costs €39.80 and this price is not influenced by the speed of the train. Prices are not calculated by the time it takes to reach your destination but according to the class of travel. Up to two children under six years, accompanied by an adult, travel for free. Each additional child, and children aged 6–15 years, pay half price.

Ticket offices can be found in all larger railway stations. They also sell tickets for international routes. You can book a ticket on the phone with ÖBB Reiseservicecenter

The Schnellbahn, Vienna's suburban train line

Railway viaduct near Mattersburg

(05 17 17) or online. International tickets, with only a few exceptions, are valid for two months; domestic tickets, for journeys over 100 km (62 miles), are valid for one month.

There are many types of tickets, such as group, family and tourist travel, with or without concessions. When buying a ticket, seek advice at the ticket office of the Reiseservicecenter as to which is best for you.

Young people up to the age of 26 years may travel at a lower cost at certain times and on some types of trains. Further information may be obtained from a ticket office, the ÖBB Reiseservicecenter or via the Internet (www.oebb.at). If you are in possession of a credit card or *Vorteilscard Master Card* (advantage card) you may have your ticket printed straight away. It is then valid in conjunction with proof of age and identity.

A large number of different *Vorteilscards* are available at low prices, giving reductions on rail travel – Classic, at €99.90, gives 45 per cent reduction on all Austrian ÖBB trains and the majority of private lines, for one year; senior citizens can buy the cards at €26.90. There is a family version *(Vorteilscard Familie)* for € 19.90; one for young people up to the age of 26 *(Vorteilscard<26)*; for the disabled *(Vorteilscard Spezial)*, and for the blind *(Vorteilscard Blind)*. When buying these cards, you will need to have with you proof of identity and a recent photograph. Alternatively, holders of a *Vorteilscard Master Card* can buy tickets on the phone, by SMS and via the Internet.

LUGGAGE

IT IS POSSIBLE to have your luggage collected from your home and delivered directly to your hotel, or vice versa. Within Austria, the charges are: €14.90 for one item of luggage, €19.90 for two items, €24.90 for three items. Holders of a *Vorteilscard* pay €9.90 for one item, €14.90 for two items and €18.90 for three items respectively.

RAILWAY NETWORK MAP

KEY

━━━ Main railway routes

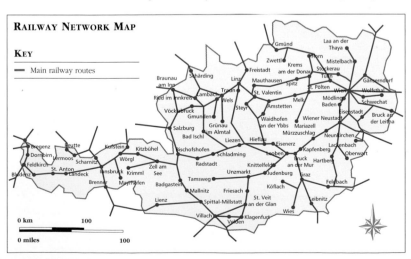

0 km   100

0 miles   100

Travelling by Car

T RAVELLING BY car on Austrian roads can be a real pleasure. The road surfaces are in good condition and Austrians tend to comply with the traffic laws. Even in crowded cities, the traffic is relatively calm – you are forbidden to sound your horn other than to warn others of a danger. Routes are generally well signposted, but even so the motorists should carry an accurate map of the area. Motorways are marked with the letter A (for *Autobahn*) or E (for European motorway route); in addition, there are fast-traffic roads and a network of secondary roads that often pass through very scenic regions.

The spectacular Großglockner Hochalpenstraße *(see pp280–81)*

DRIVING IN AUSTRIA

V ISITORS ARRIVING by car can make use of any of a number of border crossings. Those with nothing to declare are directed toward the green channel; when importing goods on which duty is to be paid, you will have to pass through the red channel.

A toll is charged on the motorways and some other fast-traffic roads (in urban areas as well as the country-side). It is collected via a pre-paid disc, known as *Auto-bahnpickerl*, which can be bought at border crossing points, and from kiosks and petrol stations in Austria. The discs, valid for 10 days, two months or one year, currently cost €7.63, €21.80 or €72.60 respectively. A 10-day disc is valid from 9am on the day of issue until midnight of the ninth day thereafter. Stick the disc to the top left corner of your car windscreen. The disc does not entitle the driver to use any private pay-roads, of which fortunately there are very few; usually such roads

are situated at high altitudes. You will also be asked to pay a separate charge for going across alpine passes and through tunnels.

WHAT TO TAKE

V ISITORS TRAVELLING by car in Austria need to carry a valid passport and driver's licence as well as their vehicle's registration document and green card (insurance policy). The vehicle must have a plaque showing the country of registration, and it must also be equipped with a first-aid box and a red warning triangle. In

winter, it is obligatory to have winter tyres and snow chains, which are essential for driving on the mountain roads.

ROADS AND SIGNPOSTS

M OTORWAYS *(Autobahnen)* and the slip roads leading to them are signposted with white lettering on blue boards; on maps, motorways are shown as yellow lines between two thinner lines. An inn near a turning is indicated by a short sign with black lettering on white background.

Fernstraßen (long-distance roads) or *Bundesstraßen* (federal roads) are marked in red, and *Landstraßen* (country roads) in yellow. On the road, traffic signs are black-and-white. The written ones you may need to know are: *Stau* – traffic jam, *Schnee* – snow, *Umleitung* – diversion, and *Baustelle* – road works. All the remaining road signs follow the European standard.

ROAD TRAFFIC REGULATIONS

I N AUSTRIA, motorists drive on the right-hand side of the road. The speed limit on motorways is 130 km/h (81 mph), and on other roads 100 km/h (62 mph). In towns and built-up areas the limit is 50 km/h (31 mph), but only 30 km/h (19 mph) in Graz. Lorries, caravans and cars with trailers are restricted to 100 km/h (62 mph) on motorways. While not everyone follows the prescribed speed limits, Austrian police carry out checks with infra-red guns and can fine you on the spot. Drivers and passengers are obliged to wear seatbelts

A toll station at the entrance to a pay-road in the mountains

at all times. Children up to the age of 15, or until they reach a height of 1.5 m (5 ft), are not allowed to travel in the front seat, unless the car is equipped with a special child restraint.

DRIVING IN TOWNS

FINDING A PLACE in which to park is not easy, especially in the centre of the larger towns; it is often best to use a multi-storey car park which is indicated by the word *Parkhaus. Frei* means that parking spaces are available.

Cars left in a controlled parking zone, indicated by blue lines on the road, must display a parking ticket or be parked validly near a meter (see below for how to buy a parking ticket from a meter). In most parts of Vienna parking is restricted to resident permit holders. Visitors may park for up to 2 hours, if they display a parking card (from newsagents).

It is never worth leaving your car in a prohibited area – a traffic warden will arrive immediately, impose a fine and arrange for your car to be towed away. Retrieving an impounded car is a lengthy, costly and difficult procedure.

A road hugging the edge of the Seidewinktal valley

CAR HIRE

MAJOR CAR HIRE firms, such as Autohansa, Avis, Denzel, Europcar, Hartl, Hertz and Trendcar, all have offices in Austria. Car hire is more expensive at the airport,

Schneekettenpflicht
Angertal
in 500 m

Sign informing motorists of the need to fit wheel-chains

but it is the only place where you will be able to hire a car late at night or at weekends.

To hire a car you must be 19 or over, and for some car companies the age limit is 25; you must also hold a valid passport and a driver's licence as well as a credit card or charge card from an approved company. (A charge card can sometimes be obtained from selected tourist offices, inside or outside Austria.)

A car may be hired for any duration and dropped off at any agreed point, to be collected by the hire company Not all destinations, however, have suitable drop off points. Cars may be taken outside Austria to approved EU countries. You may also take hired cars to some, but not to all Eastern Europe countries, only with special permission from the hiring company.

ARRIVING BY COACH

EUROLINES runs coaches from London Victoria to Wien Mitte. This is also the terminal station for routes to Eastern European cities like Bratislava and Budapest, and domestic routes from eastern Austria. The Südbahnhof coach station handles routes from southern and southwestern Austria.

Coaches are equipped to the European standard and tickets may be cheaper than rail travel, but the journey from the UK is long and fares are not particularly cheap. Often, budget airlines offer a more convenient way to travel at a comparable cost.

TRAVELLING BY COACH

THE ENTIRE country is served by an excellent coach network, allowing you to reach almost any destination including some remote places not connected to the rail network. Prices are similar to those charged for rail travel.

HITCHHIKING

IT IS NOT ALWAYS easy to get a lift in Austria; few drivers are willing to take hitchhikers. If you decide to thumb a lift, the best point to wait is by the exit road from a town. Young people waiting there often carry cardboard notices stating their desired destination. As anywhere, women travelling alone should take extra care. In some provinces, children below the age of 16 are forbidden to hitchhike.

Parking meters
In many towns you will have to obtain a ticket from a parking meter to park your car. Display it on the windscreen.

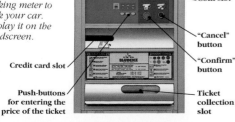

Date and time display

Coin slot

"Cancel" button

"Confirm" button

Credit card slot

Push-buttons for entering the price of the ticket

Ticket collection slot

Getting Around Towns

Finding your way around an unfamiliar town, even with a map, is often difficult. One-way traffic systems, pedestrianized areas and parking restrictions are all designed to keep car traffic out. Walking is the easiest and most enjoyable way to get around the compact city centres, where most of the historic sights are to be found. Austrian towns generally have a well-developed public transport system, including buses and, in most cities, trams. Vienna also has an underground network (metro) – the quickest way to reach any destination. In some cities, travel cards give you unlimited travel on all local transport facilities for a specified number of days.

WALKING

Pedestrians have priority, even on roads – but you should never rely on this. Try to use subways or crossings where there are signals, especially when crossing wide roads with fast-moving traffic. Visitors from the UK and Australia need to remember that motorists drive on the right. Do not cross a road when the red signal shows even if there is no traffic – you may be spot-fined for jay walking. Watch out also for cyclists who share the pavement with pedestrians.

In larger cities, guided walking tours are available during the summer months, which will take you past all the sights. Exploring themes such as the Baroque, or Vienna 1900, they are available in English and other languages. For information contact the local tourist offices.

Tourists strolling through a mountain village

BICYCLES

Cycle routes usually run on the pavement and are clearly marked with lines and arrows. Pedestrians need to take extra care not to stray into the cycling area. Where there is no cycle route, cyclists join the road traffic and are obliged to adhere to all normal traffic rules. There are special posts on pavements and in public squares for parking and securing bicycles. In Vienna, bike paths take you around the Ringstraße and past many of the sights. Bikes may also be hired from some stations, at a discount if you have a train ticket.

One of the most scenic long-distance cycling routes is the *Radweg* (cycle track) along the Danube river.

TAXIS

You can recognize a taxi by the TAXI sign on the roof. They are usually saloon cars, often Mercedes. If a taxi is for hire, the sign will be illuminated. In the centre of a city it is easier to get a taxi at one of the taxi ranks, rather than hailing it in the street. Taxi ranks can be found near railway stations and large hotels. Alternatively, you can book a taxi by phone. In the rush hour it may be faster to travel by underground or by tram. All taxis have meters and charges are calculated per kilometre travelled. A short journey costs from €5–10; additional charges are made for more than one passenger, luggage, late night and weekend journeys. In Vienna, a taxi to the airport will cost about €30. It is usual to tip 10 per cent of the fare, rounding up the fare to the nearest euro.

BUSES

Many city centres are served by hopper buses, while larger buses take visitors to the inner suburbs. Municipal bus lines are often extensions of tram lines. This is signalled by a letter in the number of the bus, thus bus No. 46A extends the route of tram No. 46, making it easy to find the correct line.

TRAMS

Along with buses and the underground, trams are the most convenient form of transport in the cities. It is easy to track your progress as

Horse-drawn carriage trip in Salzburg

each stop is announced by a pre-recorded voice and all carriages display the route map, indicating the stops.

The doors are released by pressing a button. Make sure you press the button to signal your intention to get out – trams or buses may continue without stopping if no one is waiting at the station.

TICKETS

TICKETS can be bought at newsagents, in blocks of five or ten, or in suburban railway stations where blocks of two or four are also available. You should always buy a ticket before travelling, since it is not always possible to buy one from the driver or the ticket machine inside the vehicle. Having boarded the

bus, tram or train you need to stamp your ticket at the start of your journey; you will not need to stamp it again if you change to a different line or different mode of transport.

The tickets are valid for travel on all forms of transport within a town, within varying time limits. For a *Kurzstrecke* or short distance, which is clearly marked on the route maps, you need a half-price *Kurzstreckenfahrschein*, which will entitle you to travel only within a stated zone. Besides single tickets, you may also buy a 24-hour pass, a *Streifenkarte* (strip of tickets) valid for three or eight days, a *Wochenkarte* valid for one week, a *Monatskarte*, valid for one month, or a *Jahreskarte*, which permits you to travel for one year.

A typical red-and-white tram in one of Vienna's busy streets

The rules of public transport vary between the provinces in Austria. Tourist offices and hotels will be able to advise you on local regulations.

MAKING A JOURNEY BY UNDERGROUND

1 To determine which line to take, travellers should look for their destination on a U-Bahn map. The five lines are distinguished by colour and number (U1, U2, U3, U4 & U5). Simply trace the line to your destination, making a note of where you need to change lines. Connections to other forms of transport are also shown.

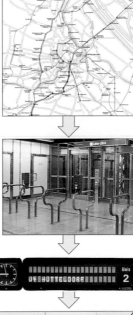

Pull handle to open door

2 Tickets can be bought from a newsagent, ticket vending machines or ticket offices. To get to the trains, insert your ticket into the ticket-stamping machine in the direction of the arrow. Wait for the ping indicating that it is validated, and pass through the barrier. Follow the signs (with the number and colour of the line) to your platform.

The door opens out to the side

3 Once you are on the platform, check the direction and destination of the train on an electronic destination indicator.

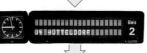

Sign showing stops on line 3 of the U-Bahn, including the connecting stops

4 Stops along the line are shown on a plan. A red arrow in the corner shows the direction in which the train enters the station.

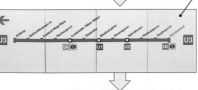

5 At your destination follow the *Ausgang* signs to reach street level.

← Ausgang

6 At stations with more than one exit, use the map of the city to check which street or square you will come out at.

General Index

Acknowledgments

DORLING KINDERSLEY would like to thank the following people whose contributions and assistance have made the preparation of this book possible.

CONSULTANT
Gerhard Bruschke

READER
Judith Meddick

FACT-CHECKERS
Martina Bauer, Melanie Nicholson-Hartzell

PROOFREADER
Emily Hatchwell

INDEXER
Helen Peters

DESIGN AND EDITORIAL ASSISTANCE
Jo Cowen, Sam Merrell, Marianne Petrou, Sadie Smith

SENIOR EDITOR
Jacky Jackson/Wordwise Associates Ltd.

MANAGING ART EDITOR
Kate Poole/Ian Midson

PUBLISHING MANAGER
Helen Townsend

SPECIAL ASSISTANCE
WIEDZA I ŻYCIE would like to thank the following people for their help in the preparation of this guide:

Mr. Roman Skrzypczak of the Austrian Tourist Information Centre for his help in obtaining materials and for facilitating contacts with other Austrian institutions.

ADDITIONAL PHOTOGRAPHY
Maciej Bronarski, Dip. Ing. Walter Hildebrand, Renata and Marek Kosińscy, Piotr Kiedrowski, Peter Wilson, Paweł Wroński

MAPS
An Bundesamt Eich- und Vermessungwesen, Lundesaufnahme (BEV).

The publisher would also like to thank all the people and institutions who allowed photographs belonging to them to be reproduced, as well as granting permission to use photographs from their archives:

Agencja Forum (Krzysztof Wójcik)
Artothek (Susanne Vierthaler and Holger Gehrmann)

Basilika Mariazell, Benediktiner-Superiorat
(P. Karl Schauer OSB, Superior)
Brahms Museum, Mürzzuschlag
Burgenländisches Landesmuseum, Eisenstadt
(Julia Raab and Gerard Schlag)
Corbis (Gabriela Ściborska)
Chorherrenstift Klosterneuburg-Stiftsmuseum
(Mag. Wolfgang Huber)
Die Österreich Werbung, Bildarchiv (Dr. Dietmar Jungreithmair)
DK Library
FIS Wintersportmuseum, Mürzzuschlag (Mag. Hannes Nothnagl)
Festung Hochensalzburg
Heeresgeschichtliches Museum in Arsenal
(Peter Enne)
Kunsthistorisches Museum, Wien (Elisabeth Reicher)
Lurgrotte Peggau
Museum Schloss Greillenstein (Elisabeth Kuefstein)
Museumsverein Schloss Rosenau, Österreichisches Freimaurermuseum
Naturpark Grebenzen Büro St. Lambrecht (Frater Gerwig Romirer)
Österreichischen Freilichtmuseum, Stübing bei Graz (Egbert Pöttler)
Rathaus w St. Pölten (Andrea Jäger)
Salzburger Burgen und Schlösser, Betriebsführung
Stadtmarketing Eisenstadt, Schloss Estarházy
(Guenter Schumich)
Stift Melk, Kultur and Tourismus
(Maria Prüller)
Wien-Tourismus (Waltraud Wolf)
Zefa (Ewa Kozłowska)

PICTURE CREDITS

Key: t = top; tr = top right; tra = top right above; tl = top left; tlb = top left below; cla = centre left above; ca = centre above; cra = centre right above; cl = centre left; c = centre; cr = centre right; clb = centre left below; cb = centre below; crb = centre right below; bl = bottom left; bla = bottom left above b = bottom; br = bottom right; bra = bottom right above; brb = bottom right below.

ARTOTHEK Chr. Brandstätter 27c; Photobusiness 27t; Ernst Reinhold 26b
AV MEDIENSTELLE DER ERZDIÖZESE WIEN 36b

BASILIKA MARIAZELL 184-185
BENEDIKTINERSTIFT ST. LAMBRECHT 174t
BRAHMS MUSEUM (Mürzzuschlag) 168c
BRONARSKI, MACIEJ 337b
BURGENLÄNDISCHES LANDESMUSEUM (Eisenstadt) 22bl, 154tr

CORBIS: 46cr; Ali Meyer 27b, 41t; Archivo Iconografico, SA 28t, 29t, 40b, 43c, 45t; Jonathan Blair 31t; Corbis Sygma 31b; Bettmann 43t, 46br; Leonard de Selva 46t; AFP 47c, 47t, 47b; Massimo Listri 142t, 242t; Wolfgang Kaehler 143c; James A. Sugar 160cla; Bob Krist 221bl, 221br

FESTUNG HOHENSALZBURG (Salzburg) 223cra
FREILICHTMUSEUM STÜBING 167t, 167br
HEERESGESCHICHTLICHES MUSEUM, WIEN 39c, 44b, 46bl; Österreichische Galerie 44t

KIEDROWSKI, PIOTR 339brb
KOSIŃSCY, RENATA AND MAREK 15b, 20tl, 20bl, 21t, 21cla, 21cl, 21cr, 21cb, 21bl, 21dc, 21br
KUNSTHISTORISCHES MUSEUM, WIEN 40t, 40cra, 40cb, 42c, 84–87

LURGROTTE, PEGGAU 168t

MUSEUM SCHLOSS GREILLENSTEIN 141tl
MUSEUMSVEREIN SCHLOSS ROSENAU, ÖSTERREICHISCHES FREIMAURERMUSEUM 141br

ÖSTERREICH WERBUNG: 14b; Ascher 17t; Bald 15c; Bartl 3, 51c, 92t, 115t, 132t, 338clb; Bohnacker 162b, 197b, 206t; Carniel 208t; W. Daemon 81b; Diejun 1, 38c, 182tlb, 183bla, 338tl, 338br; Fankhauser 34t, 249br 341br; Gottfried 263b; H. Graf 67t; Gruenert 200t, 233b, 253b; Haider 23b, 44cl, 76b; Haller 45cra; Herzberger 114t, 221tr, 339clb, 359t; Hinterndorfer Ch. 146b; Imprima 134b; Jalain 35b; Jellasitz 155t; Jezierzański 140t, 175t, 179c; Kalmar 29b, 77t, 77b, 108t, 338cla, 338bl; Kneidinger 17c, 181b, 193t; Lamm 175b, 178c, 178b, 179b; Landova 199t; R. Liebing 16b, 286b; Mallaun 212t, 233t, 252t, 256t, 257t, 340b, 341bl; Markowitsch 32t, 33b, 104t, 127t, 179t,

181t, 221tr, 241c, 247t, 339tl; Mayer 59b, 246t; Nechansky 259tl; A. Niederstrasser 2–3, 246b; OEW-Bildarchiv 146t, 338cra; Robert Pfeifer 74b; Pigneter 190t, 191b, 207t; G. Popp 148-149, 182br, 342b; Porizka 193b, 207b, 209b; Ramstorfer 42bl; Salzburger Burgen/S/B 217ca; Schmeja 339tr; Simoner 22t, 147b, 156; Storto 42br 205t, 253t; Trumler 22cla, 23t, 23cl, 23crb, 36, 37br, 37bl, 39t, 40cla, 42t, 43b, 65cb, 111b, 134c, 140bl 141bl, 145tra. 145cl, 145cr, 145b, 183t, 192b, 194bla, 195b, 196, 197tlb, 199bl, 206b, 239c, 240t, 270brb, 273tra. 338tr; W. Weinhaeupl 207c, 213t, 225b, 272t; H. Wiesenhofer 17b, 32c, 32b, 33t, 35t, 41crb, 138t, 145glw, 154b, 161t, 162t, 162c, 163b, 169t, 183brb, 201t, 254b, 270bla; Winderer 34b

RATHAUS (St. Pölten) 132b
REUTERS 30b, 30t, 30c

STIFT MELK 142cla, 142clb, 142br 143t, 143bl, 143br

WROŃSKI, PAWEŁ 230t, 285t, 285c, 308t, 336c, 339bl, 339bra
WINTERSPORTMUSEUM (Mürzzuschlag) 168c
WIEN-TOURISMUS 48–49, 58tr, 59t, 64tlb, 64b

ZEFA: Damm 176-177, 234; Kalt 12; Mathis 235b; K. Meier 210; Raga 214c; Rose 20-21c, 181t; Spichtinger 180t; Weir 178t

JACKET: Front: POWERSTOCK: main image: DK PICTURE LIBRARY: Wojciech Mędrzak c; Back: AUSTRIAN NATIONAL TOURIST OFFICE: A. Niederstrasser b; DK PICTURE LIBRARY: Peter Wilson t; Spine: POWERSTOCK

**All other images © Dorling Kindersley
For further information see:
www.dkimages.com**

Phrase Book

IN EMERGENCY

Help!	Hilfe!	hilf-er
Stop!	Halt!	hult
Call	Holen Sie	hole'n zee
.....a doctor	...einen Arzt	...ine'n artst
.....an ambulance	...einen	...ine'n
	Krankenwagen	krank'nvarg'n
.....the police	...die Polizei	...dee pol-its-eye
.....the fire brigade	...die Feuerwehr	...dee foy-er-vair
Where is	Wo finde ich ein	voh fin-der ish ine
a telephone?	Telefon?	tel-e-fone?
Where is the	Wo ist das	voh ist duss
hospital?	Krankenhaus?	krunk'n-hows?

COMMUNICATION ESSENTIALS

Yes	Ja	yah
No	Nein	nine
Please	Bitte	bitt-er
Thank you	Danke vielmals	dunk-er feel-malse
Excuse me	Gestatten	g'shtatt'n
Hello	Grüss Gott	groos got
Goodbye	Auf Wiedersehen	owf veed-er-zay-ern
morning	Vormittag	for-mit-targ
afternoon	Nachmittag	nakh-mit-targ
evening	Abend	ahb'nt
yesterday	Gestern	gest'n
today	Heute	hoyt-er
tomorrow	Morgen	morg'n
here	hier	hear
there	dort	dort
What?	Was?	vuss?
When?	Wann?	vunn?
Where?	Wo/Wohin?	voh/vo-hin?

USEFUL PHRASES & WORDS

Where is...?	Wo befindet sich...?	voe b'find't zish...?
Where are...?	Wo befinden sich...?	voe b'find'n zish...?
How far is it to...?	Wie weit ist...?	vee vite ist...?
Do you speak	Sprechen Sie	shpresh'n zee
English?	englisch?	eng-glish?
I don't understand	Ich verstehe nicht	ish fair-shtay-er nisht
I'm sorry	Es tut mir leid	es toot meer lyte
big	gross	grohss
small	klein	kline
open	auf/offen	owf/off'n
closed	zu/geschlossen	tsoo/g's hloss'n
left	links	links
right	rechts	reshts
near	in der Nähe	in dair nay-er
far	weit	vyte
up	auf, oben	owf, obe'n
down	ab, unten	up, oont'n
early	früh	froo
late	spät	shpate
entrance	Eingang/Einfahrt	ine-gung/ine-fart
exit	Ausgang/Ausfahrt	ows-gung/ows-fart
toilet	WC/Toilette	vay-say/toy-lett-er

MAKING A TELEPHONE CALL

I'd like to place a	Ich möchte ein	ish mer-shter ine
long-distance	Ferngespräch	fairn-g'shpresh
call	machen	mukh'n
I'd like to call	Ich möchte ein	ish mer-shter ine
collect	Rückgespräch	rook-g'shpresh
	machen	mukh'n
local call	Ortsgespräch	orts-g'shpresh
Can I leave a	Kann ich etwas	kunn ish ett-vuss
message?	ausrichten?	ows-rikht'n

STAYING IN A HOTEL

Do you have a	Haben Sie ein	harb'n zee ine
vacant room?	Zimmer frei?	tsimm-er fry?
double room	ein Doppelzimmer	ine dopp'l-tsimm-er
twin room	ein Doppelzimmer	ine dopp'l-tsimm-er
single room	ein Einzelzimmer	ine-ts'l-tsimm-er
with a bath/shower	mit Bad/Dusche	mitt bart/doosh-er
key	Schlüssel	shlooss'l
I have a	Ich habe ein	ish harb-er ine
reservation	Zimmer reserviert	tsimm-er
		rezz-er-veert

SIGHTSEEING

bus	der Bus	dair booss
tram	die Strassenbahn	dee stra-sen-barn
train	der Zug	dair tsoog
art gallery	Galerie	gall-er-ee
bus station	Busbahnhof	booss-barn-hofe
bus (tram) stop	die Haltestelle	dee hal-te-shtel-er
castle	Schloss, Burg	shloss, boorg
palace	Schloss, Palais	shloss, pall-ay
post office	das Postamt	dee pohs-taamt
cathedral	Dom	dome
church	Kirche	keersh'er
garden	Garten, Park	gart'n, park
museum	Museum	moo-zay-oom
information (office)	Information	in-for-mut-see-on

SHOPPING

How much does	Wieviel	vee-feel kost't
this cost?	kostet das?	duss?
I would like...	Ich hätte gern...	ish hett-er gairn...
Do you have...?	Haben Sie...?	harb'n zee...?
expensive	teuer	toy-er
cheap	billig	bill-igg
bank	Bank	bunk
book shop	Buchladen	bookh-lard'n
chemist/pharmacy	Apotheke	App-o-tay-ker
hairdresser	Friseur/Frisör	freezz-er/freezz-er
market	Markt	markt
newsagent	Tabak Trafik	tab-ack tra-feek
travel agent	Reisebüro	rye-zer-boo-roe

EATING OUT

Have you got a	Haben Sie einen	harb'n zee ine'n
table for...	Tisch für...	tish foor...
people?	Personen?	pair-sohn'n?
The bill please	Zahlen, bitte	tsarl'n bitt-er
I am a vegetarian	Ich bin Vegetarier	ish bin vegg-er-tah-ree-er
Waitress/waiter	Fräulein/Herr Ober	froy-line/hair oh-bare
menu	die Speisekarte	dee shpize-er-kart-er
wine list	Weinkarte	vine-kart-er
breakfast	Frühstück	froo-shtook
lunch	Mittagessen	mit-targ-ess'n
dinner	Abendessen	arb'nt-ess'n

MENU DECODER

Ei	eye	egg
Eis	ice	ice cream
Fisch	fish	fish
Fleisch	flysh	meat
Garnelen	gar-nayl'n	prawns
gebacken	g'buck'n	baked/fried
gebraten	g'brart'n	roast
gekocht	g'kokht	boiled
Gemüse	g' mooz-er	vegetables
vom Grill	fom grill	grilled
Hendl/Hahn/Huhn	hend'l/harn/hoon	chicken
Kaffee	kaf-fay	coffee
Kartoffel/Erdäpfel	kar-toff'l/air-dupf'l	potatoes
Käse	kayz-er	cheese
Knödel	k'nerd'l	dumpling
Lamm	lumm	lamb
Meeresfrüchte	mair-erz-froosh-ter	seafood
Milch	milhk	milk
Mineralwasser	minn-er-arl-vuss-er	mineral water
Obst	ohbst	fresh fruit
Pfeffer	pfeff-er	pepper
Pommes frites	pomm-fritt	chips
Reis	rice	rice
Rind	rint	beef
Rostbraten	rohst-brart'n	steak
Rotwein	roht-vine	red wine
Salz	zults	salt
Schinken/Speck	shink'n/shpeck	ham
Schlag	shlahgg	cream
Schokolade	shock-o-lard-er	chocolate
Schwein	shvine	pork
Tee	tay	tea
Wasser	vuss-er	water
Weisswein	vyce-vine	white wine
Wurst	voorst	sausage (fresh)
Zucker	tsook-er	sugar

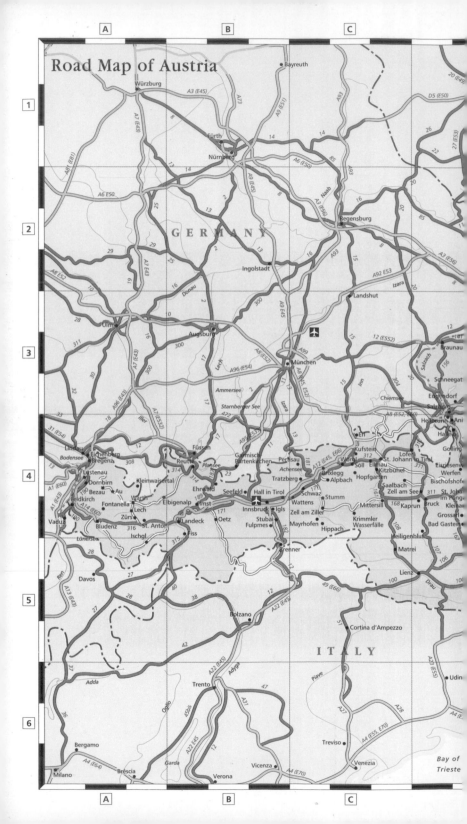